Discovering Computers Fundamentals

With SAM 2.0 Student Getting Started Guide

Gary B. Shelly | Misty E. Vermaat

CENGAGE
Learning·

Australia • Brazil • Japan • Korea • Mexico • Singapore • Spain • United Kingdom • United States

Discovering Computers Fundamentals: With SAM 2.0 Student Getting Started Guide

Gary B. Shelly | Misty E. Vermaat

Executive Editors:
Maureen Staudt
Michael Stranz

Senior Project Development Manager:
Linda deStefano

Marketing Specialist:
Courtney Sheldon

Senior Production/Manufacturing Manager:
Donna M. Brown

Production Editorial Manager:
Kim Fry

Sr. Rights Acquisition Account Manager:
Todd Osborne

Enhanced Discovering Computers, Fundamental: Your Interactive Guide to the Digital World, 2013 Edition, 1st Edition
Gary B. Shelly | Misty E. Vermaat

© 2013 Cengage Learning. All rights reserved.

For product information and technology assistance, contact us at
Cengage Learning Customer & Sales Support, 1-800-354-9706

For permission to use material from this text or product,
submit all requests online at **cengage.com/permissions**
Further permissions questions can be emailed to
permissionrequest@cengage.com

This book contains select works from existing Cengage Learning resources and was produced by Cengage Learning Custom Solutions for collegiate use. As such, those adopting and/or contributing to this work are responsible for editorial content accuracy, continuity and completeness.

Compilation © 2012 Cengage Learning
ISBN-13: 978-1-285-11952-6

ISBN-10: 1-285-11952-5

Cengage Learning
5191 Natorp Boulevard
Mason, Ohio 45040
USA
Cengage Learning is a leading provider of customized learning solutions with office locations around the globe, including Singapore, the United Kingdom, Australia, Mexico, Brazil, and Japan. Locate your local office at:
international.cengage.com/region.

Cengage Learning products are represented in Canada by Nelson Education, Ltd.
For your lifelong learning solutions, visit **www.cengage.com/custom.**
Visit our corporate website at **www.cengage.com.**

Printed in the United States of America

Discovering Computers — Fundamentals
Your Interactive Guide to the Digital World

Table of Contents at a Glance

Discovering Computers — Fundamentals
Your Interactive Guide to the Digital World

Table of Contents

CHAPTER **3**

Application Software 107

Special Feature

Digital Communications 141 – 154

CHAPTER **4**

The Components of the System Unit 155

CHAPTER **5**

Input and Output 187

Special Feature

Buyer's Guide: How To Purchase Computers and Mobile Devices

CHAPTER **8**

Communications and Networks   313

CHAPTER **9**

Database Management   351

CHAPTER **10**

Computer Security and Safety, Ethics, and Privacy   381

CHAPTER **11**

Information System Development and Programming Languages   417

CHAPTER **12**

Enterprise Computing

463

Special Feature

Living Digitally

↗ LOOKING AHEAD

Preface

The Shelly Cashman Series® offers the finest textbooks in computer education. This book is our answer to the many requests we have received from instructors and students for a textbook that provides a succinct, yet thorough, introduction to computers.

In *Discovering Computers — Fundamentals* you will find an educationally sound, highly visual, and easy-to-follow pedagogy that presents a complete, yet to the point, treatment of introductory computer subjects. With this edition we are introducing an interactive, multi-media e-book and CourseMate Web site that include animated figures, relevant video, and interactive activities in the e-book, making the learning experience engaging and interesting. Students will finish the course with a solid understanding of computers, how to use computers, and how to access information on the Web.

Objectives of this Text, e-Book, and CourseMate Web Site

Discovering Computers — Fundamentals: Your Interactive Guide to the Digital World is intended for use as a stand-alone solution or in combination with an applications, Internet, or programming textbook in a full-semester introductory computer course. No experience with computers is assumed. The objectives of this offering are to:

- Provide a concise, yet comprehensive introduction to computers
- Present the most-up-to-date technology in an ever-changing discipline
- Give students an understanding of why computers are essential components in business and society
- Teach the fundamentals of computers and computer nomenclature, particularly with respect to personal computer hardware and software, the Web, and enterprise computing

Hallmarks of Discovering Computers — Fundamentals

To date, more than six million students have learned about computers using a *Discovering Computers* textbook. With the Web integration and interactivity, streaming up-to-date audio and video, extraordinary step-by-step visual drawings and photographs, unparalleled currency, and the Shelly and Cashman touch, this offering will make your computer concepts course exciting and dynamic. Hallmarks of Shelly Cashman Series *Discovering Computers* include:

A Proven Pedagogy

Careful explanations of complex concepts, educationally-sound elements, and reinforcement highlight this proven method of presentation.

Essential Computer Concepts Coverage

This book offers the same breadth of topics as our well-known *Discovering Computers: Your Interactive Guide to the Digital World*, but the depth of coverage focuses on the basic knowledge required to be computer literate in today's digital world.

A Visually Appealing Book that Maintains Student Interest

The latest technology, pictures, drawings, and text are combined artfully to produce a visually appealing and easy-to-understand book. Many of the figures include a step-by-step presentation (see page 111), which simplifies the more complex computer concepts. Pictures and drawings reflect the latest trends in computer technology.

- Present the material in a visually appealing, interactive, and exciting manner that motivates students to learn
- Present strategies for purchasing a desktop computer, notebook computer, a Tablet PC, and personal mobile devices
- Offer alternative learning techniques and reinforcement via the Web
- Offer distance-education providers a textbook with a meaningful and exercise-rich digital learning experience

Distinguishing Features

Discovering Computers — Fundamentals includes a variety of compelling features, certain to engage and challenge students, making learning with *Discovering Computers — Fundamentals* an enriched experience. These compelling features include:

- Multi-media rich and interactive e-book and CourseMate Web site that engage students in learning about computer concepts.

- Animations, relevant and timely video, interactive in-chapter activities and Quiz Yourself reinforcement exercises embedded in the e-book, combined with the integration of interactive activities, videos, and end-of-chapter student assignments on the CourseMate Web site offer students an exceptional learning solution.
- Digital Communications special feature provides students with practical examples of collaborative and productive uses of digital communications.
- Exploring Computer Careers and Green Computing end-of-chapter student assignments challenge students to apply the concepts learned in the chapter.
- CNET At the Movies videos highlight current technology events of interest to students, involving them in the constant evolution of the computing world.
- Ethics and Issues, Looking Ahead, FAQ, Web Links, Companies on the Cutting Edge, and Technology Trailblazers include the most relevant and interesting examples to students.

Latest Technologies and Terms

The technologies and terms your students see in this book are those they will encounter when they start using computers. Only the latest application software packages are shown throughout the book.

Web Integrated

This book uses the Web as a major learning tool. The purpose of integrating the Web into the book is to (1) offer students additional information and currency on important topics; (2) use its interactive capabilities to offer creative reinforcement and online quizzes; (3) make available alternative learning techniques with Web-based learning games, practice tests, and interactive labs; (4) underscore the relevance of the Web as a basic information tool that

can be used in all facets of society; (5) introduce students to doing research on the Web; and (6) offer instructors the opportunity to organize and administer their traditional campus-based or distance-education-based courses on the Web using various learning management systems.

Extensive End-of-Chapter Student Assignments

A notable strength of *Discovering Computers — Fundamentals* is the extensive student assignments and activities at the end of each chapter. Well-structured student assignments can make the difference between students merely participating in a class and students retaining the information they learn. The end-of-chapter student assignments include: Chapter Review, Key Terms, Checkpoint, Problem Solving, Learn How To, Learn It Online, and Web Research.

Instructor Resources

The Instructor Resources include both teaching and testing aids.

Instructor's Manual Includes lecture notes summarizing the chapter sections, figures and boxed elements found in every chapter, teacher tips, classroom activities, lab activities, and quick quizzes in Microsoft Word files.

Syllabus Easily customizable sample syllabi that cover policies, assignments, exams, and other course information.

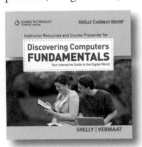

Figure Files Illustrations for every figure in the textbook in electronic form. Figures are provided both with and without callouts.

Solutions to Exercises Includes solutions for all end-of-chapter student assignments. Also includes Tip Sheets, which are suggested starting points for the Problem Solving exercises.

PowerPoint Presentations — Course Presenter A one-click-per-slide presentation system that provides PowerPoint slides for every subject in each chapter. Several computer-related video clips are available for optional presentation. Course Presenter provides consistent coverage for multiple lecturers.

Test Bank & Test Engine Test Banks include 112 questions for every chapter, featuring objective-based and critical thinking question types, and including page number references and figure references, when appropriate. Also included is the test engine, ExamView, the ultimate tool for your objective-based testing needs.

Printed Test Bank A Rich Text Format (.rtf) version of the test bank you can print.

NEW! Computer Concepts CourseMate

The new Computer Concepts CourseMate for *Discovering Computers — Fundamentals* is the most expansive digital site for any computer concepts text in the market today! The content in the CourseMate solution is integrated into each page of the text, giving students easy access to current information on important topics, reinforcement activities, and alternative learning techniques. Integrating the Computer Concepts CourseMate into the classroom keeps today's students engaged and involved in the learning experience.

The Computer Concepts CourseMate includes an integrated, multi-media rich and interactive digital book, and a variety of interactive Quizzes and Learning Games, Exercises, Web Links, Videos, and other features that specifically reinforce and build on the concepts presented in the chapter. These interactive activities are tracked within the CourseMate Engagement Tracker, making it easy to assess students' retention of concepts. This digital solution encourages students to take learning into their own hands and explore related content on their own to learn even more about subjects in which they are especially interested.

All of these resources on the Computer Concepts CourseMate for *Discovering Computers — Fundamentals* enable students to get more comfortable using technology and help prepare students to use the Internet as a tool to enrich their lives.

Contact Us

Colleges, Universities, Continuing Education Departments, Post-Secondary Vocational Schools, Career Colleges, Business, Industry, Government, Trade, Retailer, Wholesaler, Library, and Resellers
Call Cengage Learning at 800-354-9706

K-12 Schools, Secondary Vocational Schools, Adult Education, and School Districts
Call Cengage Learning at 800-354-9706

In Canada
Call Nelson Cengage Learning at 800-268-2222

Anywhere
www.cengage.com/coursetechnology

Visual Walkthrough of the Book

Practical. Hands-on. Interactive.
A Proven Pedagogy for Today's Students.

Chapter Opener
Before reading the chapter, carefully read through the Objectives to familiarize yourself with the material in each chapter.

Initial Chapter Figure
Carefully study the first figure in each chapter because it provides an easy-to-follow overview of the major purpose of the chapter.

Interactive e-Book Activity Icon
Several elements in each chapter are interactive learning activities in the e-book and are identified by this icon.

CourseMate Icon
Visit the Computer Concepts CourseMate Web site for access to many of the interactive chapter elements.

Web Links
Obtain current information and a different perspective about key terms and concepts by visiting the Web Links found in the margins throughout the book.

Step Figures
Each chapter includes numerous step figures that present the more complex computer concepts using a step-by-step pedagogy.

FAQs
FAQ (frequently asked questions) boxes offer common questions and answers about subjects related to the topic at hand.

Ethics & Issues
Ethics & Issues boxes raise controversial, computer-related topics of the day, challenging readers to consider closely general concerns of computers in society.

Looking Ahead
The Looking Ahead boxes offer a glimpse of the latest advances in computer technology that will be available, usually within five years.

Innovative Computing
Discover different and innovative ways of using various technologies and learn how computing is applied creatively to solve problems.

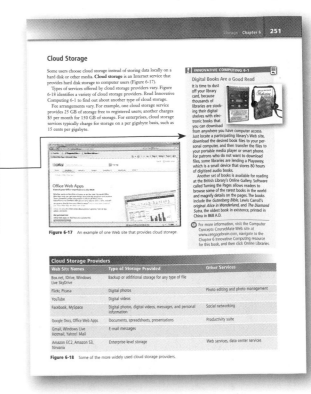

Quiz Yourself

Three Quiz Yourself boxes per chapter help ensure retention by reinforcing sections of the chapter material, rather than waiting for the end of chapter to test. Use Appendix A for a quick check of the answers, and access additional Quiz Yourself quizzes via the Computer Concepts CourseMate Web site for interactivity and easy use.

Computer Usage @ Work

Learn about how computers are used in 12 different professional industries, including transportation, municipal services, education, sports, and construction.

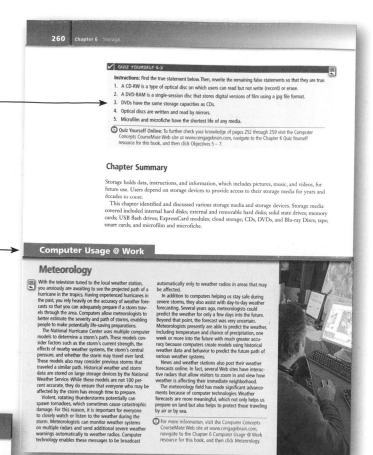

✔ QUIZ YOURSELF 6-3

Instructions: Find the true statement below. Then, rewrite the remaining false statements so that they are true.

1. A CD-RW is a type of optical disc on which users can read but not write (record) or erase.
2. A DVD-RAM is a single-session disc that stores digital versions of film using a jpg file format.
3. DVDs have the same storage capacities as CDs.
4. Optical discs are written and read by mirrors.
5. Microfilm and microfiche have the shortest life of any media.

Quiz Yourself Online: To further check your knowledge of pages 252 through 259 visit the Computer Concepts CourseMate Web site at www.cengagebrain.com, navigate to the Chapter 6 Quiz Yourself resource for this book, and then click Objectives 5 – 7.

Chapter Summary

Storage holds data, instructions, and information, which includes pictures, music, and videos, for future use. Users depend on storage devices to provide access to their storage media for years and decades to come.

This chapter identified and discussed various storage media and storage devices. Storage media covered included internal hard disks; external and removable hard disks; solid state drives; memory cards; USB flash drives; ExpressCard modules; cloud storage; CDs, DVDs, and Blu-ray Discs; tape; smart cards; and microfilm and microfiche.

Computer Usage @ Work

Meteorology

With the television tuned to the local weather station, you anxiously are awaiting to see the projected path of a hurricane in the tropics. Having experienced hurricanes in the past, you rely heavily on the accuracy of weather forecasts so that you can adequately prepare if a storm travels through the area. Computers allow meteorologists to better estimate the severity and path of storms, enabling people to make potentially life-saving preparations.

The National Hurricane Center uses multiple computer models to determine a storm's path. These models consider factors such as the storm's current strength, the effects of nearby weather systems, the storm's central pressure, and whether the storm may travel over land. These models also may consider previous storms that traveled a similar path. Historical weather and storm data are stored on large storage devices by the National Weather Service. While these models are not 100 percent accurate, they do ensure that everyone who may be affected by the storm has enough time to prepare.

Violent, rotating thunderstorms potentially can spawn tornadoes, which sometimes cause catastrophic damage. For this reason, it is important for everyone to closely watch or listen to the weather during the storm. Meteorologists can monitor weather systems on multiple radars and send additional severe weather warnings automatically to weather radios. Computer technology enables these messages to be broadcast automatically only to weather radios in areas that may be affected.

In addition to computers helping us stay safe during severe storms, they also assist with day-to-day weather forecasting. Several years ago, meteorologists could predict the weather for only a few days into the future. Beyond that point, the forecast was very uncertain. Meteorologists presently are able to predict the weather, including temperature and chance of precipitation, one week or more into the future with much greater accuracy because computers create models using historical weather data and behavior to predict the future path of various weather systems.

News and weather stations also post their weather forecasts online. In fact, several Web sites have interactive radars that allow visitors to zoom in and view how weather is affecting their immediate neighborhood.

The meteorology field has made significant advancements because of computer technologies. Weather forecasts are more meaningful, which not only helps us prepare on land but also helps to protect those traveling by air or by sea.

For more information, visit the Computer Concepts CourseMate Web site at www.cengagebrain.com, navigate to the Chapter 6 Computer Usage @ Work resource for this book, and then click Meteorology.

Companies on the Cutting Edge

SEAGATE TECHNOLOGY Storage Solutions Supplier

The average household with a broadband Internet connection will need nearly 1 TB of storage for its personal media collections, and Seagate has the storage solutions for practically every digital need. The company offers more than 40 products for the personal computing, consumer electronics, and enterprise computing fields.

Seagate has been at the forefront of the digital storage world since it developed the first 5.25-inch hard disk for the personal computer in 1980. In 2008 it shipped its one billionth hard disk, making the company's production for the past 30 years a total of 79 million terabytes. Seagate expects to ship its two billionth hard disk by 2013.

Seagate recently introduced the FreeAgent DockStar network adapter. This device allows users to access their digital media from anywhere in the world and share these files with anyone. The FreeAgent DockStar network adapter also enables users to link their digital content to online social networks such as Facebook, Twitter, and MySpace.

SANDISK CORPORATION Flash Memory Storage Supplier

The number of flash memory card formats is growing, and only one company has the rights to design, develop, manufacture, and market every one of them: SanDisk. The company is the world's largest supplier of flash memory storage products and also has lines of portable media players.

The company was founded in 1988, and one of its earliest flash drives was used on a U.S. space shuttle three years later. Today SanDisk is developing rewritable 3-D memory products that will store data vertically, and company executives believe this technology will replace flash products in the next decade.

SanDisk recently introduced the world's fastest 32 GB SDHC card. The 32 GB SanDisk Extreme SDHC card boasts read and write speeds of 30 megabytes per second. The increased speeds enable photographers to take pictures quickly without having to wait long for the card to record the images. In addition, computer users also are able to transfer data to and from the card quickly.

For more information, visit the Computer Concepts CourseMate Web site at www.cengagebrain.com and then navigate to the Chapter 6 Companies on the Cutting Edge resource for this book.

Technology Trailblazers

AL SHUGART Storage Expert

Al Shugart said that his real goal in life was to have fun, and he spent his life doing the things that gave him the most pleasure. The day after receiving his bachelor's degree in engineering physics in 1951, he landed a job at IBM doing what he loved to do: fixing broken items and developing new technology. He was promoted to supervisor of the product development team that developed the first removable hard disk drive.

Shugart then left IBM, became vice president of Memorex, and then started Shugart Associates and began developing floppy disks. In 1979 he founded Seagate Technology with a friend. As his company grew to become the world's largest hard disk manufacturer, he had fun placing his dog, Ernest, on the ballot for a Congressional seat.

Shugart served as president and CEO of Al Shugart International, a venture capital firm in California, until his death in 2006.

MARK DEAN IBM Inventor

Web 2.0 applications demand large, inexpensive storage, and Mark Dean is hard at work helping to meet this need. As vice president of IBM's Almaden Research Center lab in California, Dean is responsible for developing innovative products.

Dean joined IBM after graduating from Stanford University with a degree in electrical engineering. He led a team that developed the first CMOS microprocessor to operate at one gigahertz and has more than 40 patents or patents pending that are used in more than 40 million personal computers manufactured each year. Three of his patents are among the nine registered for the architecture of the original personal computer.

Dean is the first African-American to be appointed to IBM Fellow, the company's highest level of technical merit. He also was inducted in the National Inventors Hall of Fame.

For more information, visit the Computer Concepts CourseMate Web site at www.cengagebrain.com and then navigate to the Chapter 6 Technology Trailblazers resource for this book.

Companies on the Cutting Edge and Technology Trailblazers

Everyone who interacts with computers should be aware of the key computer-related companies and of the more famous leaders of the computer industry.

End-of-Chapter Student Assignments

Chapter Review
Use the Chapter Review before taking an examination to ensure familiarity with the computer concepts presented. This section includes each objective, followed by a one- or two-paragraph summary.

Key Terms
Before taking a test, use the Key Terms page as a checklist of terms to know. Visit the Computer Concepts CourseMate Web site for additional information on the Key Terms.

Checkpoint
Use these multiple choice, true/false, matching, and short answer exercises to reinforce understanding of the topics presented in the chapter.

Learn How To

Apply the concepts in the chapter to every day life with these hands-on activities. Learn how the Learn How To activities fit into your life with relevant scenarios, visual demonstrations, and practice questions via the Computer Concepts CourseMate Web site.

266 Chapter 6 Storage

Learn How To

The Learn How To activities step you through fundamental technology skills when using a computer. The Learn How To exercises enable you to become more proficient with these skills.

Premium Activity: To relate this Learn How To activity to your everyday life, see a visual demonstration of the activity, and complete a short assessment, visit the Computer Concepts CourseMate Web site at www.cengagebrain.com and then navigate to the Chapter 6 Learn How To resource for this book.

Learn How To 1: Maintain a Hard Disk

A computer's hard disk is used for the majority of storage requirements. It is important, therefore, to ensure that each hard disk on a computer is operating at peak efficiency, both to use the available storage space effectively and to make disk operations as fast as possible.

Two tasks that maximize disk operations are removing unused or unnecessary files and folders by using the Disk Cleanup utility program and consolidating files and folders into contiguous storage areas using the Disk Defragmenter utility program. Defragmenting allows your system to access stored files and folders more efficiently.

A. Cleanup Disk

To clean up the disk by removing any programs and data that are not required for the computer, complete the following steps:

1. Click the Start button on the Windows taskbar and then click Computer on the Start menu.
2. When the Computer window opens, right-click the hard disk icon for drive C (or any other hard disk you want to select) and then click Properties on the shortcut menu.
3. If necessary, click the General tab in the disk drive Properties dialog box to display the General sheet.
4. Click the Disk Cleanup button in the General sheet to display the Disk Cleanup Options dialog box.
5. The Disk Cleanup dialog box is displayed and contains a message that indicates the amount of space that can be freed up is being calculated.
6. After the calculation is complete, the Disk Cleanup dialog box specifies the amount of space that can be freed up and the files to delete, some of which are selected automatically (Figure 6-31). Select those items from which you wish to delete files.
7. Click the OK button in the Disk Cleanup dialog box.
8. A dialog box asks if you are sure you want to perform these actions. Click the Delete Files button. The Disk Cleanup dialog box illustrates the progress of the cleanup. When the cleanup is complete, the dialog box closes.

B. Defragment Disk

After removing all the unnecessary files from the hard disk, the next step in disk maintenance is to defragment all the files on the disk. When a file is stored on disk, the data in the file sometimes is stored contiguously, and other times is stored in a noncontiguous manner. The greater the amount of data on a disk, the more likely files will be stored noncontiguously. When a file is stored in a noncontiguous manner, it can take significantly longer to find and retrieve data from the file. One of the more useful utilities to speed up disk operations, therefore, is the defragmentation program, which combines all files so that no files are stored in a noncontiguous manner. To use the defragmentation program, complete the following steps:

1. If necessary, click the Tools tab in the Properties dialog box for the hard disk to be defragmented.
2. Click the Defragment now button in the Tools sheet to open the Disk Defragmenter window (Figure 6-32). This window displays the Disk Defragmenter schedule, when Disk Defragmenter was run last, and when Disk Defragmenter is scheduled to run next.
3. Click the Defragment disk button. The defragmentation process begins. During the defragmentation process, the Stop operation button replaces the Defragment disk button. The defragmentation process can consume more than one hour in some cases, depending on the size of the hard disk and the amount of processing that must occur. You can cancel the operation at any time by clicking the Stop operation button in the Disk Defragmenter window.
4. When the process is complete, the Defragment disk button will replace the Stop operation button.
5. Click the Close button to close the Disk Defragmenter window.

Proper disk maintenance is critically important so that disk operation is as efficient as possible.

Disk Cleanup dialog box
amount of space to be freed up
Files to delete area
OK button
Figure 6-31

Storage Chapter 6 267

Learn How To

Exercises

Caution: The exercises for this chapter that require actual disk maintenance are optional. If you are performing these exercises on a computer that is not your own, obtain explicit permission to complete these exercises. Keep in mind that these exercises can require significant computer time and the computer may be unusable during this time.

1. Display the Properties dialog box for a hard disk found on the computer. Display the General sheet. What is the capacity of the hard disk? How much space is used? How much free space is available? Click the Disk Cleanup button. How much space can be freed up if you use the Disk Cleanup program? Click the OK button to clean up the disk. How long did it take to perform the disk cleanup? Submit your answers to your instructor.

2. Display the Properties dialog box for a hard disk found on the computer. Display the Tools sheet. Click the Defragment now button. In the Disk Defragmenter window, click the Defragment disk button. How could you tell when the defragmentation process was completed? How long did defragmentation require? Submit your answers to your instructor.

Disk Defragmenter window
Defragment disk button
Close button
Figure 6-32

Learn It Online

The Learn It Online exercises are interactive Web exercises designed to reinforce and expand your understanding of the chapter concepts. The descriptions below briefly summarize each exercise.

To complete the Learn It Online exercises, visit the Computer Concepts CourseMate Web site at www.cengagebrain.com, navigate to the Chapter 6 resources for this book, click the link for the exercise you want to complete, and then read the instructions.

1 At the Movies — Thumb-drive (USB Flash Drive) Encryption
Watch a movie to learn how people who store personal and confidential information on USB flash drives can use third-party programs to password-protect the files so that others cannot access them and then answer questions about the movie.

2 Student Edition Labs — Maintaining a Hard Drive (Hard Disk) and Managing Files and Folders
Enhance your understanding and knowledge about maintaining a hard disk and managing files and folders by completing the Maintaining a Hard Drive and Managing Files and Folders Labs.

3 Practice Test
Take a multiple choice test that checks your knowledge of the chapter concepts and review the resulting study guide.

4 Who Wants To Be a Computer Genius²?
Play the Shelly Cashman Series version of this popular game by answering questions to find out if you are a computer genius. Panic buttons are available to provide assistance during game play.

5 Crossword Puzzle Challenge
Complete an interactive crossword puzzle to reinforce concepts presented in this chapter.

6 Windows Exercises
Step through the Windows 7 exercises to learn about the Recycle Bin, working with files, the hard disk, and Disk Cleanup.

7 Exploring Computer Careers
Read about a career as a computer technician, search for related employment advertisements, and then answer related questions.

8 Web Apps — TurboTax Online
Learn how to use TurboTax Online to create an account, start a new tax return from scratch, review your tax return, and then print and file your tax return.

Learn It Online

The Learn It Online exercises, which include At the Movies online CNET videos, practice tests, interactive labs, learning games, and Web-based activities, offer a wealth of online reinforcement.

Storage   **Chapter 6**   **265**

Problem Solving

The Problem Solving exercises extend your knowledge of the chapter concepts by seeking solutions to practical computer problems that you may encounter at home, school, or work. The Collaboration exercise should be completed with a team.

In the real world, practical problems often can be solved in multiple ways. Provide one solution to each of the following problems using available resources, such as articles on the Web or in print, blogs, podcasts, videos, television, user guides, other individuals, and electronics and computer stores. You may need to use multiple resources to obtain an answer. Present your solutions in the form requested by your instructor (brief report, presentation, discussion, or other means).

@ Home

1. **Old Movies**   During the past two decades, you have been recording home movies on VHS tapes. It is becoming more difficult to locate blank VHS tapes, and you are worried that if your current VCR breaks, it will be hard to find a store that sells them new. A friend suggests that you copy these movies to an optical disc. What steps will you take to convert these movies?

2. **Possible Head Crash**   When you turn on your computer, you hear a clicking sound coming from inside the computer. Furthermore, you realize that Windows is not starting automatically. You talk to a friend who said that your hard disk might have experienced a head crash. What might have caused this?

3. **Missing Cable**   You are attempting to install a new 1 TB hard disk in your computer. You have found the empty bay for the new hard disk, but you cannot locate the cable that connects it to the computer. What are your next steps?

4. **Memory Card Problems**   For the past two years, you have been using the same Secure Digital (SD) memory card to take pictures with your digital camera. When you insert the SD memory card in your computer's card reader to transfer the pictures, your computer does not display the contents of the card. When you put the card back into your digital camera, you can see that the pictures still are stored on the card. What might be wrong?

@ Work

5. **Disk Not Recognized**   The information technology manager at your company has purchased external hard disks for employees to use to back up their files. When you connect the external hard disk to the USB port on your computer, the computer displays a message stating that it cannot recognize the device. What might you do to correct this problem?

6. **File Will Not Open**   Your computer is unable to open a file on an optical disc that you just inserted into the optical disc drive. You have been able to access other files on the same disc, but one file in particular is not opening. What might be causing this?

7. **Backing Up Data**   It has been several years since your office computer was upgraded, and you just received an e-mail message stating that you finally will receive a new computer next week. The e-mail message also stated that all employees will be responsible for backing up their data. What files will you back up?

8. **Optical Disc Problem**   Your colleague gives you an optical disc containing some video files. When you insert the disc in your computer, the disc burning software asks if you would like to finalize the disc. How will you respond?

Collaboration

9. **Computers in Meteorology**   Your environmental sciences instructor is teaching a lesson about how computers advanced the meteorology field. Form a team of three people to prepare a brief report about how computers and meteorology are connected. One team member should research how meteorologists predicted weather patterns computer use became mainstream. Another team member should create a timeline illustrating when and how co were introduced to the meteorology field, and the third team member should research the types of computer ha and software required for a typical news station to forecast and present the weather.

Problem Solving and Collaboration

Tackle everyday computer problems and put the information presented in each chapter to practical use with the Problem Solving @ Home and Problem Solving @ Work exercises. Work as a team to solve the Collaboration exercise.

Web Research

The Web Research exercises broaden your understanding of chapter concepts by presenting questions that require you to search the Web for answers.

1 **Search Sleuth**
Use one of the search engines listed in Figure 2-8 in Chapter 2 on page 65 or your own favorite search engine to find the answers to the following questions. Copy and paste the Web address from the Web page where you found the answer. Some questions may have more than one answer. If required, submit your answers to your instructor. (1) What album did Hillsong United release in 2008 on a flash drive embedded in a rubber wristband? (2) What country uses the MyKad smart card for national identification? (3) What product did HP develop in 2004 based on the efforts of engineer Daryl Anderson? (4) What products are available for sale at the SanDisk Plaza? (5) For what storage medium are phase change alloys used? (6) What company introduced using a hard disk for accounting projects in 1956?

2 **Green Computing**
Data storage is doubling every 18 months according to some computer industry experts, and consumers and businesses are turning to environmentally sound methods of backing up and storing files. Accessing hard disks consumes 80 percent of a storage system's electrical consumption, so companies have developed products that reduce a system's energy usage. Businesses invest in cooling systems that dissipate the heat generated when servers and storage hardware operate. Locate Web sites that describe these products and how they operate efficiently to conserve energy. How much energy savings do they claim to make in one year? To what extent are carbon dioxide and other greenhouse gases reduced? How do they maximize the use of power and cooling resources? Review your search results and then write a 50-word summary of your findings.

3 **Social Networking**
Privacy on social networking Web sites such as MySpace and Facebook is an international concern, and the Electronic Privacy Information Center (epic.org/privacy/socialnet) features news, policies, and resources discussing safeguarding and controlling personal information. At least one-fourth of hiring managers admit to researching job applicants' "digital dirt" by searching social networks and blogs, and some employers search social networking Web sites for profiles of current employees. Visit the Reputation Defender (reputationdefender.com) and Defend My Name (defendmyname .com) Web sites and read about the services offered. Then view the standards posted on the MySpace and Facebook Web sites regarding privacy and allowable content. Summarize the information you read and viewed.

4 **Blogs**
Exercise and nutrition advice is available from experts who post firsthand experiences in their blogs. These authorities may be people who share a particular experience, such as losing weight or training for a marathon, or who have specialized training in the fitness field. For example, noted author Lou Schuler discusses nutrition, weight training, and issues of particular interest to men (malepatternfitness.com). Other popular fitness blogs are featured by The Families .com (fitness.families.com/blog) and Diet-Blog (diet-blog.com). Athlete Blog Central (yardbarker.com/athletes) lists blogs that professional and amateur athletes and their fans write. Visit these sites and read the posts. Which stories received more than 25 comments? Which food, exercises, and programs are featured?

5 **Ethics in Action**
The United States Federal Bureau of Investigation used a controversial program until January 2005 to monitor and store the e-mail and Internet activity of suspected criminals. Originally called Carnivore, the surveillance program was renamed DCS1000. The program was designed to track the activities of potential terrorists, spies, drug traffickers, and organized crime ring members. FBI agents needed to obtain a court order to monitor an individual, but privacy advocates claim the software tracked people not covered under the court order. View online sites that provide information about DCS1000 or Carnivore, including HowStuffWorks (howstuffworks.com/carnivore.htm). What commercial software has replaced Carnivore? Write a report summarizing your findings, and include a table of links to Web sites that provide additional details.

Web Research

Each Web Research exercise requires follow-up research on the Web and suggests writing a short article or presenting the findings of the research to the class.

Special Features

Six special features following Chapters 1, 2, 3, 5, 7, and 12 encompass topics from the history of computers, to hot topics on the Web 2.0, to a buyer's guide, to the latest in new technology and digital communications.

Special Feature

Timeline
Milestones in Computer History

Visit the Computer Concepts CourseMate Web site at www.cengagebrain.com and then navigate to the Timeline feature resource for this book.

1937 Dr. John V. Atanasoff and Clifford Berry design and build the first electronic digital computer. Their machine, the Atanasoff-Berry-Computer, or ABC, provides the foundation for advances in electronic digital computers.

1945 John von Neumann poses in front of the electronic computer built at the Institute for Advanced Study. This computer and its von Neumann architecture served as the prototype for subsequent stored program computers worldwide.

1947 William Shockley, John Bardeen, and Walter Brattain invent the transfer resistance device, eventually called the transistor. The transistor would revolutionize computers, proving much more reliable than vacuum tubes.

1946 Dr. John W. Mauchly and J. Presper Eckert, Jr. complete work on the first large-scale electronic, general-purpose digital computer.

Special Feature

Digital Video Technology

Everywhere you look, people are capturing moments they want to remember. They shoot movies of their vacations, birthday parties, activities, accomplishments, sporting events, weddings, and more. Because of the popularity of digital video cameras and mobile devices with built-in digital cameras, increasingly more people desire to capture their memories digitally, instead of on film. As shown in Figure 1, people have the ability to modify and share the digital videos they create. When you use special hardware and/or software, you can copy, manipulate, and distribute digital videos using your personal computer and the Internet. Amateurs can achieve professional quality r... cated hardware and software. select a video camera, record videos, edit a video, and distri Digital recordings deliver s based movie making. With di reside on storage media such

or memory card. Unlike film, storage media can be reused, which reduces costs, saves time, and provides immediate results. Digital technology allows greater control over the creative process, both while recording video and in the editing process. You can check results immediately after capturing a video to determine whether it meets your expectations. If you are dissatisfied with a video, you can erase it and recapture it, again and again. Today, many mobile devices, such as smart phones and PDAs, allow you to capture video.

As shown in Figure 1, digital video cameras, and mobile

digital video camera

Special Feature

Making Use of the Web

INFORMATION LITERACY IS DEFINED as having the practical skills needed to evaluate information critically from print and electronic resources and to use this information accurately in daily life. Locating Web sites may be profitable for your educational and professional careers, as the resources may help you research class assignments and make your life more fulfilling and manageable.

Because the Web does not have an organizational structure to assist you in locating reliable material, you may need additional resources to guide you in searching. To help you find useful Web sites, this Special Feature describes specific ... of Web addresses ... areas of interest. ... terial and help you ... e to your life.

Special Feature

Living Digitally

OUR DIGITAL LIVES are filled with a variety of products. We listen to portable media players to audio files we create or download. We record and view video content that matches our viewing interests. We play recorded files wherever and whenever we desire. We play games solo or with multiple friends across the globe. Our home networks link security, energy monitoring, and leisure activities throughout the house. Wherever we go in our lives, technology is a pervasive part of our daily existence.

Microsoft Xbox 360
PSPgo
3-D video display
avatar
Slingbox
Sony PlayStation 3
head-mounted display
Rock Band

Digital products in our lives often include features that overlap in various entertainment and home automation categories.

- Audio
- Video
- Recording
- Gaming
- Digital Home

Nintendo DSi
video camera
smart phone
Studio Instruments software
Nero optical disc burning software
combination drive

Special Feature

Digital Communications

DIGITAL COMMUNICATIONS, which factor largely in many people's personal and business lives, include any transmission of information from one computer or mobile device to another (Figure 1). This feature covers many forms of digital communications: e-mail; text messaging, instant messaging, and picture/video messaging; digital voice communications; blogs and wikis; online social networks, chat rooms, and Web conferences; and content sharing.

... lives to engage in digital communications.

Special Feature

Buyer's Guide:
How to Purchase Computers and Mobile Devices

AT SOME POINT, perhaps while you are taking this course, you may decide to buy a computer or mobile device (Figure 1). The decision is an important one and will require an investment of both time and money. Like many buyers, you may have little experience with technology and find yourself unsure of how to proceed. You can start by talking to your friends, coworkers, and instructors about their computers and mobile devices. What type of computers and mobile devices did they buy? Why? For what purposes do they use their computers and mobile devices?

desktop computer
notebook computer
portable media player
smart phone
digital camera

Figure 1 Computers and mobile devices.

Visual Walkthrough of the Computer Concepts CourseMate for Discovering Computers — Fundamentals

Interactive. Current. Engaging.
Your Interactive Guide to the Digital World!

Introduce the most current technology into the classroom with the Computer Concepts CourseMate for Discovering Computers — Fundamentals. An integrated ebook and a wide range of online learning games, quizzes, practice tests, videos, and Web links expand on the topics covered in the text with hands-on reinforcement. The Pointer Icon integrated into each page of the text illustrates when to access the CourseMate Web site and quickly shows students the connection between the text and the digital solution.

Who Wants to Be a Computer Genius?[2]

The Who Wants to Be a Computer Genius?[2] learning game allows students to quiz themselves on chapter content within a dynamic and entertaining game scenario. Question results are provided instantly so that students quickly see which concepts they understand and which concepts they need to study. Page remediation is included with question results so students know exactly where in the text to find the information they need.

EngagementTracker
EngagementTracker makes assessing students easy by tracking student progress on the interactive activities. Clear and visual reports illustrate the class progress as a whole.

Wheel of Terms
Wheel of Terms is an interactive study tool for learning the Key Terms in each chapter. This learning game presents students with a short definition of one of the chapter's Key Terms and prompts them to type the correct term as the answer.

Introduction to Computers

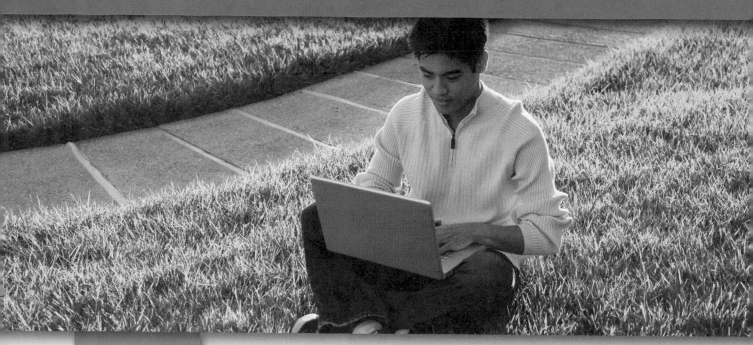

Objectives

After completing this chapter, you will be able to:

1 Explain why computer literacy is vital to success in today's world

2 Describe the five components of a computer: input devices, output devices, system unit, storage devices, and communications devices

3 Discuss the advantages and disadvantages that users experience when working with computers

4 Discuss the uses of the Internet and World Wide Web

5 Distinguish between system software and application software

6 Differentiate among types, sizes, and functions of computers in each of these categories: personal computers (desktop), mobile computers and mobile devices, game consoles, servers, mainframes, supercomputers, and embedded computers

7 Explain how home users, small office/home office users, mobile users, power users, and enterprise users each interact with computers

8 Discuss how society uses computers in education, finance, government, health care, science, publishing, travel, and manufacturing

A World of Computers

Computers are everywhere: at work, at school, and at home (Figure 1-1). Mobile devices, such as many cell phones, often are classified as computers. Computers are a primary means of local and global communication for billions of people. Employees correspond with clients, students with classmates and teachers, and family with friends and other family members.

Through computers, society has instant access to information from around the globe. Local and national news, weather reports, sports scores, airline schedules, telephone directories, maps and directions, job listings, credit reports, and countless forms of educational material always are accessible. From the computer, you can make a telephone call, meet new friends, share photos and videos, share opinions, shop, book flights, file taxes, take a course, receive alerts, and automate your home.

In the workplace, employees use computers to create correspondence such as e-mail messages, memos, and letters; manage calendars; calculate payroll; track inventory; and generate invoices. At school, teachers use computers to assist with classroom instruction. Students use computers to complete assignments and research. Instead of attending class on campus, some students take entire classes directly from their computer.

Figure 1-1 People use all types and sizes of computers in their daily activities.

People also spend hours of leisure time using a computer. They play games, listen to music or radio broadcasts, watch or compose videos and movies, read books and magazines, share stories, research genealogy, retouch photos, and plan vacations.

Many people believe that computer literacy is vital to success. **Computer literacy**, also known as **digital literacy**, involves having a current knowledge and understanding of computers and their uses. Because the requirements that determine computer literacy change as technology changes, you must keep up with these changes to remain computer literate.

This book presents the knowledge you need to be computer literate today. As you read this first chapter, keep in mind it is an overview. Many of the terms and concepts introduced in this chapter will be discussed in more depth later in the book.

What Is a Computer?

A **computer** is an electronic device, operating under the control of instructions stored in its own memory, that can accept data, process the data according to specified rules, produce results, and store the results for future use.

Data and Information

Computers process data into information. **Data** is a collection of unprocessed items, which can include text, numbers, images, audio, and video. **Information** conveys meaning and is useful to people.

As shown in Figure 1-2, for example, computers process several data items to print information in the form of a cash register receipt.

DATA

2 Medium Sodas	$1.49 each
1 Small Turkey Sub	$3.49 each
1 Caesar Salad	$4.49 each
1 Bag of Chips	$0.99 each
3 Cookies	$0.39 each
Amount Received	$20.00

PROCESSES

- Computes each item's total price by multiplying the quantity ordered by the item price (i.e., 2 * 1.49 = 2.98).
- Organizes data.
- Sums all item total prices to determine order total due from customer (13.12).
- Calculates change due to customer by subtracting the order total from amount received (20.00 - 13.12 = 6.88).

INFORMATION

Arrow Deli
10 Park Street
Maple River, DE 20393
(734) 555-2939

QTY	ITEM	TOTAL
2	Medium Sodas	2.98
1	Small Turkey Sub	3.49
1	Caesar Salad	4.49
1	Bag of Chips	0.99
3	Cookies	1.17
	Total Due	13.12
	Amount Received	20.00
	Change	6.88

Thank You!

Figure 1-2   A computer processes data into information. In this simplified example, the item ordered, item price, quantity ordered, and amount received all represent data. The computer processes the data to produce the cash register receipt (information).

Information Processing Cycle

Computers process data (input) into information (output). Computers carry out processes using instructions, which are the steps that tell the computer how to perform a particular task. A collection of related instructions organized for a common purpose is referred to as software. A computer often holds data, information, and instructions in storage for future use. Some people refer to the series of input, process, output, and storage activities as the **information processing cycle**. Recently, communications also has become an essential element of the information processing cycle.

The Components of a Computer

A computer contains many electric, electronic, and mechanical components known as **hardware**. These components include input devices, output devices, a system unit, storage devices, and communications devices. Figure 1-3 shows some common computer hardware components.

Input Devices

An **input device** is any hardware component that allows you to enter data and instructions into a computer. Five widely used input devices are the keyboard, mouse, microphone, scanner, and Web cam (Figure 1-3).

A computer keyboard contains keys you press to enter data into the computer. A mouse is a small handheld device. With the mouse, you control movement of a small symbol on the screen, called the pointer, and you make selections from the screen.

A microphone allows a user to speak into the computer. A scanner converts printed material (such as text and pictures) into a form the computer can use.

A Web cam is a digital video camera that allows users to create movies or take pictures and store them on the computer instead of on tape or film.

Output Devices

An **output device** is any hardware component that conveys information to one or more people. Three commonly used output devices are a printer, a monitor, and speakers (Figure 1-3).

A printer produces text and graphics on a physical medium such as paper. A monitor displays text, graphics, and videos on a screen. Speakers allow you to hear music, voice, and other audio (sounds).

Figure 1-3 Common computer hardware components include the keyboard, mouse, microphone, scanner, Web cam, printer, monitor, speakers, system unit, hard disk drive, external hard disk, optical disc drive(s), USB flash drive, card reader/writer, memory cards, and modem.

System Unit

The **system unit** is a case that contains electronic components of the computer that are used to process data (Figure 1-3 on the previous page). The circuitry of the system unit usually is part of or is connected to a circuit board called the motherboard.

Two main components on the motherboard are the processor and memory. The **processor**, also called the **CPU** (**central processing unit**), is the electronic component that interprets and carries out the basic instructions that operate the computer. **Memory** consists of electronic components that store instructions waiting to be executed and data needed by those instructions. Most memory keeps data and instructions temporarily, which means its contents are erased when the computer is shut off.

Storage Devices

Storage holds data, instructions, and information for future use. For example, computers can store hundreds or millions of customer names and addresses. Storage holds these items permanently.

A computer keeps data, instructions, and information on **storage media**. Examples of storage media are USB flash drives, hard disks, optical discs, and memory cards. A **storage device** records (writes) and/or retrieves (reads) items to and from storage media. Storage devices often function as a source of input because they transfer items from storage to memory.

A USB flash drive is a portable storage device that is small and lightweight enough to be transported on a keychain or in a pocket (Figure 1-3). The average USB flash drive can hold about 4 billion characters.

A hard disk provides much greater storage capacity than a USB flash drive. The average hard disk can hold more than 320 billion characters. Hard disks are enclosed in an airtight, sealed case. Although some are portable, most are housed inside the system unit (Figure 1-4). Portable hard disks are either external or removable. An external hard disk is a separate, freestanding unit, whereas you insert and remove a removable hard disk from the computer or a device connected to the computer.

An optical disc is a flat, round, portable metal disc with a plastic coating. CDs, DVDs, and Blu-ray Discs are three types of optical discs. A CD can hold from 650 million to 1 billion characters. Some DVDs can store two full-length movies or 17 billion characters (Figure 1-5). Blu-ray Discs can store about 46 hours of standard video, or 100 billion characters.

Some mobile devices, such as digital cameras, use memory cards as the storage media. You can use a card reader/writer (Figure 1-3) to transfer stored items, such as digital photos, from the memory card to a computer or printer.

Figure 1-4   Most hard disks are housed inside the system unit.

Figure 1-5   A DVD in a DVD drive.

Communications Devices

A **communications device** is a hardware component that enables a computer to send (transmit) and receive data, instructions, and information to and from one or more computers or mobile devices. A widely used communications device is a modem (Figure 1-3).

Communications occur over cables, telephone lines, cellular radio networks, satellites, and other transmission media. Some transmission media, such as satellites and cellular radio networks, are wireless, which means they have no physical lines or wires.

Advantages and Disadvantages of Using Computers

Society has reaped many benefits from using computers. A **user** is anyone who communicates with a computer or utilizes the information it generates. Both business and home users can make well-informed decisions because they have instant access to information from anywhere in the world. Students, another type of user, have more tools to assist them in the learning process.

Advantages of Using Computers

The benefits from using computers are possible because computers have the advantages of speed, reliability, consistency, storage, and communications.
- **Speed:** When data, instructions, and information flow along electronic circuits in a computer, they travel at incredibly fast speeds. Many computers process billions or trillions of operations in a single second.
- **Reliability:** The electronic components in modern computers are dependable and reliable because they rarely break or fail.
- **Consistency:** Given the same input and processes, a computer will produce the same results — consistently. Computers generate error-free results, provided the input is correct and the instructions work.
- **Storage:** Computers store enormous amounts of data and make this data available for processing anytime it is needed.
- **Communications:** Most computers today can communicate with other computers, often wirelessly. Computers allow users to communicate with one another.

Disadvantages of Using Computers

Some disadvantages of computers relate to the violation of privacy, public safety, the impact on the labor force, health risks, and the impact on the environment.
- **Violation of Privacy:** In many instances, where personal and confidential records stored on computers were not protected properly, individuals have found their privacy violated and identities stolen.
- **Public Safety:** Adults, teens, and children around the world are using computers to share publicly their photos, videos, journals, music, and other personal information. Some of these unsuspecting, innocent computer users have fallen victim to crimes committed by dangerous strangers.
- **Impact on Labor Force:** Although computers have improved productivity and created an entire industry with hundreds of thousands of new jobs, the skills of millions of employees have been replaced by computers. Thus, it is crucial that workers keep their education up-to-date. A separate impact on the labor force is that some companies are outsourcing jobs to foreign countries instead of keeping their homeland labor force employed.
- **Health Risks:** Prolonged or improper computer use can lead to health injuries or disorders. Computer users can protect themselves from health risks through proper workplace design, good posture while at the computer, and appropriately spaced work breaks. Two behavioral health risks are computer addiction and technology overload. Computer addiction occurs when someone becomes obsessed with using a computer. Individuals suffering from technology overload feel distressed when deprived of computers and mobile devices.
- **Impact on Environment:** Computer manufacturing processes and computer waste are depleting natural resources and polluting the environment. **Green computing** involves reducing the electricity consumed and environmental waste generated when using a computer. Strategies that support green computing include recycling, regulating manufacturing processes, extending the life of computers, and immediately donating or properly disposing of replaced computers.

Green Computing
For more information, visit the Computer Concepts CourseMate Web site at www.cengagebrain.com, navigate to the Chapter 1 Web Link resource for this book, and then click Green Computing.

Instructions: Find the true statement below. Then, rewrite the remaining false statements so that they are true.

1. A computer is a motorized device that processes output into input.

2. A storage device records (reads) and/or retrieves (writes) items to and from storage media.

3. An output device is any hardware component that allows you to enter data and instructions into a computer.

4. Computer literacy involves having a current knowledge and understanding of computers and their uses.

5. Three commonly used input devices are a printer, a monitor, and speakers.

Quiz Yourself Online: To further check your knowledge of pages 2 through 7, visit the Computer Concepts CourseMate Web site at www.cengagebrain.com, navigate to the Chapter 1 Quiz Yourself resource for this book, and then click Objectives 1 – 3.

Networks and the Internet

A **network** is a collection of computers and devices connected together, often wirelessly, via communications devices and transmission media. When a computer connects to a network, it is **online**. Networks allow computers to share **resources**, such as hardware, software, data, and information. Sharing resources saves time and money.

The **Internet** is a worldwide collection of networks that connects millions of businesses, government agencies, educational institutions, and individuals (Figure 1-6). More than one billion people around the world use the Internet daily for a variety of reasons, including the following: to communicate with and meet other people; to conduct research and access a wealth of information and news; to shop for goods and services; to bank and invest; to participate in online training; to engage in entertaining activities, such as planning vacations, playing online games, listening to music, watching or editing videos, and books and magazines; to share information, photos, and videos; to download music and videos; and to access and interact with Web applications. Figure 1-7 shows examples in each of these areas.

The Internet

For more information, visit the Computer Concepts CourseMate Web site at www.cengagebrain.com, navigate to the Chapter 1 Web Link resource for this book, and then click The Internet.

Figure 1-6   The Internet is the largest computer network, connecting millions of computers and devices around the world.

Figure 1-7 Home and business users access the Internet for a variety of reasons.

People connect to the Internet to exchange information with others around the world. E-mail allows you to send and receive messages to and from other users (read Ethics & Issues 1-1 for a related discussion). With instant messaging, you can have a live conversation with another connected user. In a chat room, you can communicate with multiple users at the same time — much like a group discussion. You also can use the Internet to make a telephone call.

Businesses, called access providers, offer access to the Internet free or for a fee. By subscribing to an access provider, you can use your computer and a modem to connect to the many services of the Internet.

The **Web**, short for World Wide Web, is one of the more popular services on the Internet. The Web contains billions of documents called Web pages. A **Web page** can contain text, graphics, animation, audio, and video. The nine screens shown in Figure 1-7 on the previous page are examples of Web pages.

Web pages often have built-in connections, or links, to other documents, graphics, other Web pages, or Web sites. A **Web site** is a collection of related Web pages. Some Web sites allow users to access music and videos that can be downloaded, or transferred to storage media in a computer or portable media player. Once downloaded, you can listen to the music through speakers, headphones, or earbuds, or view the videos on a display device.

Anyone can create a Web page and then make it available, or publish it, on the Internet for others to see. Millions of people worldwide join online communities, each called a **social networking Web site** or **online social network**, that encourage members to share their interests, ideas, stories, photos, music, and videos with other registered users. Hundreds of thousands of people today also use blogs to publish their thoughts on the Web. A **blog** is an informal Web site consisting of time-stamped articles in a diary or journal format, usually listed in reverse chronological order. As others read the articles in a blog, they reply with their own thoughts (to learn more about creating and using blogs, complete the Learn How To 1 activity on page 34). Podcasts are a popular way people verbally share information on the Web. A **microblog**, such as Twitter, allows users to publish short messages, usually between 100 and 200 characters, for others to read. A **podcast** is recorded audio stored on a Web site that can be downloaded to a computer or a portable media player such as an iPod.

A **Web application** is a Web site that allows users to access and interact with software from any computer or device that is connected to the Internet. Examples of software available as Web applications include those that allow you to send and receive e-mail messages, prepare your taxes, organize digital photos, create documents, and play games.

Web sites such as social networking Web sites, blogs, and Web applications are categorized as Web 2.0 sites. The term **Web 2.0** refers to Web sites that provide a means for users to share personal information (such as social networking Web sites), allow users to modify the Web site contents (such as some blogs), and/or have software built into the site for users to access (such as Web applications).

Ethics & Issues

 For the complete text of the Ethics & Issues boxes found in this chapter, visit the Computer Concepts CourseMate Web site at www.cengagebrain.com and then navigate to the Chapter 1 Ethics & Issues resource for this book.

ETHICS & ISSUES 1-1

What Should Be Done about Identity Theft?

Using e-mail and other techniques on the Internet, scam artists are employing a technique known as phishing to try to steal your personal information, such as credit card numbers, banking information, and passwords. For example, an e-mail message may appear to be a request from your bank to verify your Social Security number and online banking password. Instead, the information you submit ends up in the hands of the scammer, who then uses the information for a variety of unethical and illegal acts. Sadly, the result often is identity theft. You can help to deter identity theft in several ways: 1) shred your financial documents before discarding them, 2) do not click links in unsolicited e-mail messages, and 3) enroll in a credit monitoring service. Consumer advocates often blame credit card companies and credit bureaus for lax security standards. Meanwhile, the companies blame consumers for being too gullible and forthcoming with private information. Both sides blame the government for poor privacy laws and light punishments for identity thieves. But while the arguments go on, law enforcement agencies bear the brunt of the problem by spending hundreds of millions of dollars responding to complaints and finding and processing the criminals.

Who should be responsible for protecting the public from online identity theft? Why? Should laws be changed to stop it, or should consumers change behavior? What is an appropriate punishment for identity thieves? Given the international nature of the Internet, how should foreign identity thieves be handled? Why?

? FAQ 1-1

What U.S. Web sites are visited most frequently?

A recent survey found that Google's Web site is visited most frequently, with Microsoft and Yahoo! not far behind. The chart to the right shows the five most frequently visited Web sites, as well as the approximate number of unique visitors per month.

For more information, visit the Computer Concepts CourseMate Web site at www.cengagebrain.com, navigate to the Chapter 1 FAQ resource for this book, and then click Top Web Sites.

An **FAQ** (frequently asked question) helps you find answers to commonly asked questions. Web sites often post an FAQ section, and each chapter in this book includes FAQ boxes related to topics in the text.

Top U.S. Web Sites

Source: ClickZ

Computer Software

Software, also called a **program**, is a series of related instructions, organized for a common purpose, that tells the computer what task(s) to perform and how to perform them. You interact with a program through its user interface. Software today often has a graphical user interface. With a **graphical user interface** (**GUI** pronounced gooey), you interact with the software using text, graphics, and visual images such as icons. An icon is a miniature image that represents a program, an instruction, or some other object. You can use the mouse to select icons that perform operations such as starting a program.

The two categories of software are system software and application software. Figure 1-8 shows an example of each of these categories of software, which are explained in the following sections.

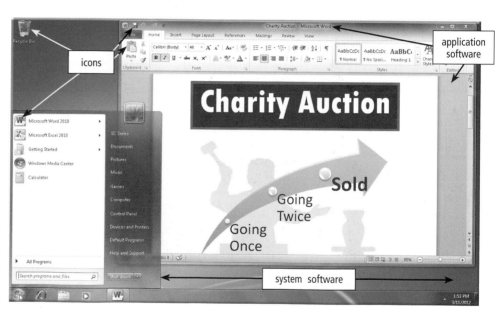

Figure 1-8 Today's system software and application software usually have a graphical user interface.

System Software

System software consists of the programs that control or maintain the operations of the computer and its devices. System software serves as the interface between the user, the application software, and the computer's hardware. Two types of system software are the operating system and utility programs.

Operating System An **operating system** is a set of programs that coordinates all the activities among computer hardware devices. It provides a means for users to communicate with the computer and other software. Many of today's computers use Microsoft's Windows, the latest version of which is shown in Figure 1-8, or Mac OS, Apple's operating system.

When a user starts a computer, portions of the operating system are copied into memory from the computer's hard disk. These parts of the operating system remain in memory while the computer is on.

Windows

For more information, visit the Computer Concepts CourseMate Web site at www.cengagebrain.com, navigate to the Chapter 1 Web Link resource for this book, and then click Windows.

Utility Program   A **utility program** allows a user to perform maintenance-type tasks usually related to managing a computer, its devices, or its programs. For example, you can use a utility program to transfer digital photos to an optical disc. Most operating systems include several utility programs for managing disk drives, printers, and other devices and media. You also can buy utility programs that allow you to perform additional computer management functions.

Application Software

Application software consists of programs designed to make users more productive and/or assist them with personal tasks. A widely used type of application software related to communications is a Web browser, which allows users with an Internet connection to access and view Web pages or access programs. Other popular application software includes word processing software, spreadsheet software, database software, and presentation software.

Many other types of application software exist that enable users to perform a variety of tasks. These include personal information management, note taking, project management, accounting, document management, computer-aided design, desktop publishing, paint/image editing, audio and video editing, multimedia authoring, Web page authoring, personal finance, legal, tax preparation, home design/landscaping, travel and mapping, education, reference, and entertainment (e.g., games or simulations).

Software is available at stores that sell computer products (Figure 1-9) and also online at many Web sites.

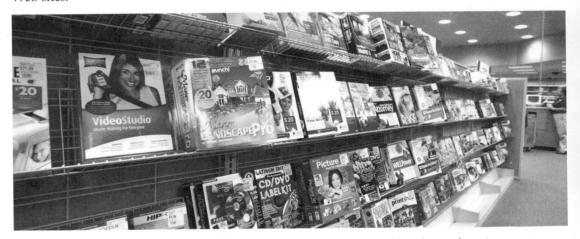

Figure 1-9   Stores that sell computer products have shelves stocked with software for sale.

Installing and Running Programs

When purchasing software from a retailer, you typically receive a box that includes an optical disc(s) that contains the program. If you acquire software from a Web site on the Internet, you may be able to download the program; that is, the program transfers from the Web site to the hard disk in your computer.

The instructions in software are placed on storage media, either locally or online. To use software that is stored locally, such as on a hard disk or optical disc, you usually need to install the software. Web applications that are stored online, by contrast, usually do not need to be installed.

Installing is the process of setting up software to work with the computer, printer, and other hardware. When you buy a computer, it usually has some software preinstalled on its hard disk. This enables you to use the computer the first time you turn it on. To begin installing additional software from an optical disc, insert the program disc in an optical disc drive. To install downloaded software, the Web site typically provides instructions for how to install the program on your hard disk.

Once installed, you can run the program. When you instruct the computer to **run** an installed program, the computer loads it, which means the program is copied from storage to memory. Once in memory, the computer can carry out, or **execute**, the instructions in the program so that you can use the program. Figure 1-10 illustrates the steps that occur when a user installs and runs a program.

Installing and Running a Computer Program

Step 1: INSTALL

When you insert a program disc, such as a photo editing program, in the optical disc drive for the first time, the computer begins the procedure of installing the program on the hard disk.

Step 2: RUN

Once installed, you can instruct the computer to run the program. The computer transfers instructions from the hard disk to memory.

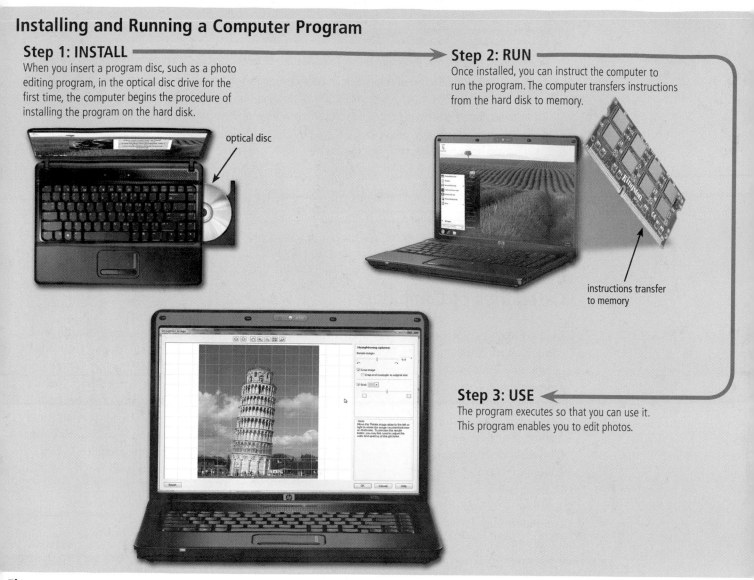

optical disc

instructions transfer to memory

Step 3: USE

The program executes so that you can use it. This program enables you to edit photos.

Figure 1-10 This figure shows how to install and run a computer program.

Software Development

A **programmer**, sometimes called a **developer**, is someone who develops software or writes the instructions that direct the computer to process data into information. Complex programs can require thousands to millions of instructions.

Programmers use a programming language or program development tool to create computer programs. Popular programming languages include C++, Visual C#, Visual Basic, JavaScript, and Java. Figure 1-11 shows a simple Visual Basic program.

```
Public Class frmPayrollInformation

    Private Sub btnCalculatePay_Click(ByVal sender As System.Object, ByVal e As System.
    EventArgs) Handles btnCalculatePay.Click
        'This procedure executes when the user clicks the
        'Calculate Pay button. It calculates regular
        'and overtime pay and displays it in the window.

        ' Declare variables
        Dim strHoursWorked As String
        Dim strHourlyRate As String
        Dim decHoursWorked As Decimal
        Dim decHourlyRate As Decimal
        Dim decRegularPay As Decimal
        Dim decOvertimeHours As Decimal
        Dim decOvertimePay As Decimal
        Dim decTotalPay As Decimal

        ' Calculate and display payroll information
        strHoursWorked = Me.txtHoursWorked.Text
        strHourlyRate = Me.txtHourlyRate.Text
        decHoursWorked = Convert.ToDecimal(strHoursWorked)
        decHourlyRate = Convert.ToDecimal(strHourlyRate)

        If decHoursWorked > 40 Then
            decRegularPay = 40 * decHourlyRate
            Me.txtRegularPay.Text = decRegularPay.ToString("C")
            decOvertimeHours = decHoursWorked - 40
            decOvertimePay = (1.5 * decOvertimeHours) * decHourlyRate
            Me.txtOvertimePay.Text = decOvertimePay.ToString("C")
            decTotalPay = decRegularPay + decOvertimePay
            Me.txtTotalPay.Text = decTotalPay.ToString("C")
        Else
            decRegularPay = decHoursWorked * decHourlyRate
            Me.txtRegularPay.Text = decRegularPay.ToString("C")
            Me.txtOvertimePay.Text = "$0.00"
            Me.txtTotalPay.Text = decRegularPay.ToString("C")
        End If
    End Sub
End Class
```

Figure 1-11 Some of the instructions in a program.

Categories of Computers

Industry experts typically classify computers in seven categories: personal computers (desktop), mobile computers and mobile devices, game consoles, servers, mainframes, supercomputers, and embedded computers. A computer's size, speed, processing power, and price determine the category it best fits. Due to rapidly changing technology, however, the distinction among categories is not always clear-cut. This trend of computers and devices with technologies that overlap, called **convergence**, leads to computer manufacturers continually releasing newer models that include similar functionality and features. For example, newer cell phones often include media player, camera, and Web browsing capabilities. As devices converge, users need fewer devices for the functionality that they require. When consumers replace outdated computers and devices, they should dispose of them properly (read Ethics & Issues 1-2 for a related discussion).

Figure 1-12 summarizes the seven categories of computers. The following pages discuss computers and devices that fall in each category.

⚡ **ETHICS & ISSUES 1-2**

Should Recycling of Electronics Be Made Easier?

Experts estimate that about one billion computers have been discarded to date. The discarded items often are known as e-waste. As technology advances and prices fall, many people think of computers, cell phones, and portable media players as disposable items. These items often contain several toxic elements, including lead, mercury, and barium. Computers and mobile devices thrown into landfills or burned in incinerators can pollute the ground and the air. A vast amount of e-waste ends up polluting third world countries. One solution is to recycle old electronic equipment, but the recycling effort has made little progress especially when compared to recycling programs for paper, glass, and plastic.

Some lawmakers prefer an aggressive approach, such as setting up a recycling program that would be paid for by adding a $10 fee to the purchase price of computers and computer equipment, or forcing computer manufacturers to be responsible for collecting and recycling their products. California already requires a recycling fee for any products sold that include certain electronic equipment. Manufacturers have taken steps, such as offering to recycle old computers and using energy efficient and environmentally friendly manufacturing techniques, but some claim that consumers should bear the responsibility of disposing of their old computer parts. While some companies have

set up recycling programs, many claim that forcing them to bear the cost of recycling programs puts the company at a competitive disadvantage when compared to foreign companies that may not be forced to maintain a recycling program.

Why is electronics recycling not as popular as other types of recycling? How can companies make it easier to recycle electronics while being compensated fairly for the cost of recycling? Should the government, manufacturers, or users be responsible for recycling of obsolete equipment? Why? Should the government mandate a recycling program for electronics? Why or why not?

Categories of Computers

Category	Physical Size	Number of Simultaneously Connected Users	General Price Range
Personal computers (desktop)	Fits on a desk	Usually one (can be more if networked)	Several hundred to several thousand dollars
Mobile computers and mobile devices	Fits on your lap or in your hand	Usually one	Less than a hundred dollars to several thousand dollars
Game consoles	Small box or handheld device	One to several	Several hundred dollars or less
Servers	Small cabinet	Two to thousands	Several hundred to a million dollars
Mainframes	Partial room to a full room of equipment	Hundreds to thousands	$300,000 to several million dollars
Supercomputers	Full room of equipment	Hundreds to thousands	$500,000 to several billion dollars
Embedded computers	Miniature	Usually one	Embedded in the price of the product

Figure 1-12   This table summarizes some of the differences among the categories of computers. These should be considered general guidelines only because of rapid changes in technology.

Personal Computers

A **personal computer** is a computer that can perform all of its input, processing, output, and storage activities by itself. A personal computer contains a processor, memory, and one or more input, output, and storage devices. Personal computers also often contain a communications device.

Two popular architectures of personal computers are the PC (Figure 1-13) and the Apple (Figure 1-14). The term, PC-compatible, refers to any personal computer based on the original IBM personal computer design. Companies such as Dell and Toshiba sell PC-compatible computers. PC and PC-compatible computers usually use a Windows operating system. Apple computers usually use a Macintosh operating system (Mac OS).

Two types of personal computers are desktop computers and notebook computers.

Figure 1-13   PC and PC-compatible computers usually use a Windows operating system.

Figure 1-14   Apple computers, such as the iMac, usually use a Macintosh operating system.

Desktop Computers

A **desktop computer** is designed so that the system unit, input devices, output devices, and any other devices fit entirely on or under a desk or table. In some models, the monitor sits on top of the system unit, which is placed on the desk. The more popular style of system unit is the tall and narrow tower, which can sit on the floor vertically.

Mobile Computers and Mobile Devices

A **mobile computer** is a personal computer you can carry from place to place. Similarly, a **mobile device** is a computing device small enough to hold in your hand. The most popular type of mobile computer is the notebook computer.

display

keyboard

hinge

optical
disc drive

Figure 1-15
On a typical notebook computer, the keyboard is on top of the system unit, and the display attaches to the system unit with hinges.

Notebook Computers

A **notebook computer**, also called a **laptop computer**, is a portable, personal computer often designed to fit on your lap. Notebook computers are thin and lightweight, yet can be as powerful as the average desktop computer. A **netbook**, which is a type of notebook computer, is smaller, lighter, and often not as powerful as a traditional notebook computer. Most netbooks cost less than traditional notebook computers, usually only a few hundred dollars. Some notebook computers have touch screens, allowing you to interact with the device by touching the screen, usually with the tip of a finger.

On a typical notebook computer, the keyboard is on top of the system unit, and the display attaches to the system unit with hinges (Figure 1-15). These computers weigh on average from 2.5 to more than 10 pounds (depending on configuration), which allows users easily to transport the computers from place to place. Most notebook computers can operate on batteries or a power supply or both.

Tablet PCs   Resembling a letter-sized slate, the **Tablet PC**, or tablet computer, is a special type of notebook computer you can interact with by touching the screen with your finger or a digital pen. One design of Tablet PC, called a convertible tablet, has an attached keyboard. Another design, which does not include a keyboard, is called a slate tablet (Figure 1-16) and provides other means for typing. Tablet PCs are useful especially for taking notes in locations where the standard notebook computer is not practical.

Mobile Devices

Mobile devices, which are small enough to carry in a pocket, usually store programs and data permanently on memory inside the system unit or on small storage media such as memory cards. You often can connect a mobile device to a personal computer to exchange information. Some mobile devices are **Internet-enabled**, meaning they can connect to the Internet wirelessly. Because of their reduced size, the screens on handheld computers are small.

Figure 1-16
The iPad is a widely used slate tablet.

Popular types of mobile devices are smart phones and PDAs, e-book readers, handheld computers, portable media players, and digital cameras.

Smart Phones and PDAs   Offering the convenience of one-handed operation, a **smart phone** (Figure 1-17) is an Internet-enabled phone that usually also provides personal information management functions such as a calendar, an appointment book, an address book, a calculator, and a note-pad. In addition to basic phone capabilities, a smart phone allows you to send and receive e-mail messages and access the Web — usually for an additional fee. Many models also function as a portable media player and include built-in digital cameras so that you can share photos or videos. Many smart phones also offer a variety of application software such as word processing, spreadsheet, and games.

Figure 1-17   Some smart phones have touch screens; others have mini keyboards.

Many smart phones have keypads that contain both numbers and letters so that you can use the same keypad to dial phone numbers and enter messages. Others have a built-in mini keyboard. Some have touch screens, and some include a stylus. Instead of calling someone's smart phone or cell phone, users often send messages to others by pressing buttons on their phone's keypad, keys on the mini keyboard, or images on an on-screen keyboard. Types of messages users send with smart phones include text messages, instant messages, picture messages, and video messages.

- A **text message** is a short note, typically fewer than 300 characters, sent to or from a smart phone or other mobile device.
- An **instant message** is a real-time Internet communication, where you exchange messages with other connected users.
- A **picture message** is a photo or other image, sometimes along with sound and text, sent to or from a smart phone or other mobile device. A phone that can send picture messages often is called a **camera phone**.
- A **video message** is a short video clip, usually about 30 seconds, sent to or from a smart phone or other mobile device. A phone that can send video messages often is called a **video phone**.

A **PDA** (personal digital assistant), which often looks like a smart phone, provides personal information management functions such as a calendar, an appointment book, an address book, a calculator, and a notepad. A PDA differs from a smart phone in that it usually does not provide phone capabilities and may not be Internet-enabled, support voice input, have a built-in camera, or function as a portable media player.

E-Book Readers   An **e-book reader** (short for electronic book reader), or e-reader, is a handheld device that is used primarily for reading e-books (Figure 1-18). An **e-book,** or digital book, is an electronic version of a printed book, readable on computers and other digital devices. Most e-book readers have a touch screen and are Internet-enabled.

Figure 1-18
An e-book reader.

Handheld Computers   A **handheld computer**, sometimes referred to as an **Ultra-Mobile PC** (**UMPC**), is a computer small enough to fit in one hand. Industry-specific handheld computers serve mobile employees, such as parcel delivery people, whose jobs require them to move from place to place.

Portable Media Players   A **portable media player** is a mobile device on which you can store, organize, and play digital media (Figure 1-19). For example, you can listen to music; watch videos, movies, and television shows; and view photos on the device's screen. With most, you download the digital media from a computer to the portable media player or to media that you insert in the device.

Figure 1-19   The iPod, shown here, is a popular portable media player.

earbuds

Portable media players usually include a set of earbuds, which are small speakers that rest inside each ear canal. Some portable media players have a touch screen; others have a touch-sensitive pad that you operate with a thumb or finger, to navigate through digital media, adjust volume, and customize settings.

Digital Cameras   A **digital camera** is a device that allows users to take pictures and store the photographed images digitally, instead of on traditional film (Figure 1-20). Although digital cameras usually have some amount of internal storage to hold images, most users store images on small storage media such as memory cards. Digital cameras typically allow users to review, and sometimes modify, images while they are in the camera.

Often users prefer to download images from the digital camera to the computer. Or, you can remove the storage media such as a memory card from the digital camera and insert it in a card reader in or attached to the computer.

Digital Cameras

For more information, visit the Computer Concepts CourseMate Web site at www.cengagebrain.com, navigate to the Chapter 1 Web Link resource for this book, and then click Digital Cameras.

Figure 1-20   With a digital camera, users can view photographed images immediately through a small screen on the camera to see if the picture is worth keeping.

! INNOVATIVE COMPUTING 1-1

Wii a Welcome Medical Skill Builder

A patient awaiting laparoscopic procedures may be less tense knowing that the surgeons have honed their dexterity and coordination using a Nintendo Wii. Preliminary studies have found that doctors can improve their fine motor control by playing video games that emphasize subtle hand movements used in minimally invasive surgeries. Researchers are developing Wii surgery simulators that will allow doctors to practice their skills at home or in break rooms at hospitals.

The Wii game system is finding a medical home in other nontraditional places. Physical therapists urge arthritic patients to use Wiihabilitation to build endurance and increase their range of motion. Therapeutic recreation with the Wii's sports games may help patients recovering from strokes, fractures, and combat injuries.

Researchers in a testing lab in California are experimenting with using the Wii's motion-activated controls in non-gaming applications, such as allowing doctors to explain X-ray images to patients.

For more information, visit the Computer Concepts CourseMate Web site at www.cengagebrain.com, navigate to the Chapter 1 Innovative Computing resource for this book, and then click Medical Wii.

Game Consoles

A **game console** is a mobile computing device designed for single-player or multiplayer video games (Figure 1-21). Standard game consoles use a handheld controller(s) as an input device(s); a television screen as an output device; and hard disks, optical discs, and/or memory cards for storage. The compact size and light weight of game consoles make them easy to use at home, in the car, in a hotel, or any location that has an electrical outlet. Three popular models are Microsoft's Xbox 360, Nintendo's Wii (pronounced wee), and Sony's PlayStation 3. Read Innovative Computing 1-1 for a look at how Nintendo Wii applications are being used in the medical field.

A handheld game console is small enough to fit in one hand. With the handheld game console, the controls, screen, and speakers are built into the device. Some models use cartridges to store games; others use a memory card or a miniature optical disc. Many handheld game consoles can communicate wirelessly with other similar consoles for multiplayer gaming. Two popular models are Nintendo DS Lite and Sony's PlayStation Portable (PSP).

In addition to gaming, many game console models allow users to listen to music, watch movies, keep fit, and connect to the Internet.

handheld game console

game console

Figure 1-21   Game consoles provide hours of video game entertainment.

Servers

A **server** controls access to the hardware, software, and other resources on a network and provides a centralized storage area for programs, data, and information (Figure 1-22). Servers support from two to several thousand connected computers at the same time.

People use personal computers or terminals to access data, information, and programs on a server. A terminal is a device with a monitor, keyboard, and memory.

Figure 1-22   A server controls access to resources on a network.

Mainframes

A **mainframe** is a large, expensive, powerful computer that can handle hundreds or thousands of connected users simultaneously (Figure 1-23). Mainframes store huge amounts of data, instructions, and information. Most major corporations use mainframes for business activities. With mainframes, enterprises are able to bill millions of customers, prepare payroll for thousands of employees, and manage thousands of items in inventory. One study reported that mainframes process more than 83 percent of transactions around the world.

Servers and other mainframes can access data and information from a mainframe. People also can access programs on the mainframe using terminals or personal computers.

Figure 1-23   Mainframe computers can handle thousands of connected computers and process millions of instructions per second.

Supercomputers

A **supercomputer** is the fastest, most powerful computer — and the most expensive (Figure 1-24). The fastest supercomputers are capable of processing more than one quadrillion instructions in a single second.

Applications requiring complex, sophisticated mathematical calculations use supercomputers. Large-scale simulations and applications in medicine, aerospace, automotive design, online banking, weather forecasting, nuclear energy research, and petroleum exploration use a supercomputer.

Figure 1-24   This supercomputer, IBM's Roadrunner, can process more than one quadrillion instructions in a single second.

Embedded Computers

An **embedded computer** is a special-purpose computer that functions as a component in a larger product. A variety of everyday products contain embedded computers:

• Consumer electronics
• Home automation devices
• Automobiles
• Process controllers and robotics
• Computer devices and office machines

Because embedded computers are components in larger products, they usually are small and have limited hardware. Embedded computers perform various functions, depending on the requirements of the product in which they reside. Embedded computers in printers, for example, monitor the amount of paper in the tray, check the ink or toner level, signal if a paper jam has occurred, and so on. Figure 1-25 shows some of the many embedded computers in cars.

Adaptive cruise control systems detect if cars in front of you are too close and, if necessary, adjust the vehicle's throttle, may apply brakes, and/or sound an alarm.

Advanced airbag systems have crash-severity sensors that determine the appropriate level to inflate the airbag, reducing the chance of airbag injury in low-speed accidents.

Tire pressure monitoring systems send warning signals if tire pressure is insufficient.

Cars equipped with wireless communications capabilities, called telematics, include such features as navigation systems, remote diagnos and alerts, and Internet access.

Drive-by-wire systems sense pressure on the gas pedal and communicate electronically to the engine how much and how fast to accelerate.

Figure 1-25   Some of the embedded computers designed to improve your safety, security, and performance in today's automobiles.

Examples of Computer Usage

Every day, people around the world rely on different types of computers for a variety of applications. To illustrate the range of uses for computers, this section takes you on a visual and narrative tour of five categories of users: a home user, a small office/home office (SOHO) user, a mobile user, a power user, and an enterprise user.

Home User

In an increasing number of homes, the computer is a basic necessity. Each family member, or **home user**, spends time on the computer for different reasons. These include personal financial management, Web access, communications, and entertainment (Figure 1-26).

On the Internet, home users access a huge amount of information, conduct research, take college classes, pay bills, manage investments, shop, listen to the radio, watch movies, read books, file taxes, book airline reservations, make telephone calls, and play games. They also communicate with others around the world through e-mail, blogs, instant messages, and chat rooms. Home users share ideas, interests, photos, music, and videos on social networking Web sites.

With a digital camera, home users take photos and then send the electronic images to others. Many home users have a portable media player, so that they can listen to downloaded music and/or podcasts at a later time through earbuds attached to the player. They also usually have one or more game consoles to play video games.

Today's homes typically have one or more desktop computers. Some home users network multiple desktop computers throughout the house, often wirelessly. These small networks allow family members to share an Internet connection and a printer.

Home users have a variety of software. They type letters, homework assignments, and other documents with word processing software. Personal finance software helps the home user with personal finances, investments, and family budgets. Other software assists with preparing taxes, keeping a household inventory, setting up maintenance schedules, and protecting computers against threats and unauthorized intrusions.

Reference software, such as encyclopedias, medical dictionaries, or a road atlas, provides valuable information for everyone in the family. With entertainment software, the home user can play games, compose music, research genealogy, or create greeting cards. Educational software helps adults learn to speak a foreign language and youngsters to read, write, count, and spell.

? FAQ 1-3

How many households do not use the Internet or related technologies?

A recent survey estimates that 18 percent of U.S. households have no Internet access. Furthermore, about 20 percent of U.S. heads of households have never sent an e-mail message. The chart to the right illustrates the lack of experience with computer and Internet technology.

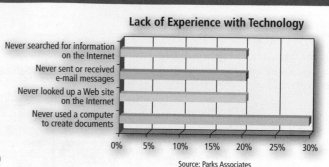

Lack of Experience with Technology

Never searched for information on the Internet
Never sent or received e-mail messages
Never looked up a Web site on the Internet
Never used a computer to create documents

0% 5% 10% 15% 20% 25% 30%

Source: Parks Associates

For more information, visit the Computer Concepts CourseMate Web site at www.cengagebrain.com, navigate to the Chapter 1 FAQ resource for this book, and then click Experience with Technology.

Figure 1-26 The home user spends time on a computer for a variety of reasons.

Small Office/Home Office User

Computers assist small business and home office users in managing their resources effectively. A **small office/home office** (**SOHO**) includes any company with fewer than 50 employees, as well as the self-employed who work from home. Small offices include local law practices, accounting firms, travel agencies, and florists. SOHO users typically use a desktop computer. Many also use smart phones.

SOHO users access the Internet — often wirelessly — to look up information such as addresses, directions, postal codes, flights (Figure 1-27a), and package shipping rates or to send and receive e-mail messages, or make telephone calls. Many have entered the e-commerce arena and conduct business on the Web. Their Web sites advertise products and services and may provide a means for taking orders.

To save money on hardware and software, small offices often network their computers. For example, the small office connects one printer to a network for all employees to share.

SOHO users often work with basic business software such as word processing and spreadsheet programs that assist with document preparation and finances (Figure 1-27b). They are likely to use other industry-specific types of software. An auto parts store, for example, will have software that allows for looking up parts, taking orders and payments, and updating inventory.

Mobile User

Today, businesses and schools are expanding to serve people across the country and around the world. Thus, increasingly more employees and students are **mobile users**, who work on a mobile computer or device while away from a main office, home office, or school (Figure 1-28). Some examples of mobile users are sales representatives, real estate agents, insurance agents, meter readers, package delivery people, journalists, and students.

Figure 1-27a   (Web access)

Figure 1-27b   (spreadsheet program)

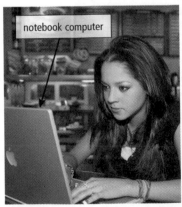

Figure 1-27   People with a home office and employees in small offices typically use a personal computer for some or all of their duties.

Figure 1-28   Mobile users have a variety of computers and devices so that they can work, do homework, send messages, connect to the Internet, or play games while away from a wired connection.

Mobile users often have a mobile computer and/or mobile device. With these computers and devices, the mobile user can connect to other computers on a network or the Internet, often wirelessly accessing services such as e-mail and the Web. Mobile users can transfer information between their mobile devices and another computer. For entertainment, the mobile user plays video games on a handheld game console and listens to music or watches movies on a portable media player.

The mobile user works with basic business software such as word processing and spreadsheet software. With presentation software, the mobile user can create and deliver presentations to a large audience by connecting a mobile computer or device to a video projector that displays the presentation on a full screen.

Power User

Another category of user, called a **power user**, requires the capabilities of a powerful desktop computer, called a workstation. Examples of power users include engineers, scientists, architects, desktop publishers, and graphic artists (Figure 1-29). Power users typically work with multimedia, combining text, graphics, audio, and video into one application. These users need computers with extremely fast processors because of the nature of their work.

The power user's workstation contains industry-specific software. For example, engineers and architects use software to draft and design floor plans, mechanical assemblies, or vehicles. A desktop publisher uses software to prepare marketing literature. A graphic artist uses software to create sophisticated drawings. This software usually is expensive because of its specialized design.

Power users exist in all types of businesses. Some also work at home. Their computers typically have network connections and Internet access.

Figure 1-29   This graphic artist uses a powerful computer to develop computer games.

Enterprise User

An enterprise has hundreds or thousands of employees or customers that work in or do business with offices across a region, the country, or the world. Each employee or customer who uses a computer in the enterprise is an **enterprise user** (Figure 1-30).

Many large companies use the words, **enterprise computing**, to refer to the huge network of computers that meets their diverse computing needs. The network facilitates communications among employees at all locations. Users access the network through desktop computers, mobile computers, and mobile devices.

Enterprises use computers and the computer network to process high volumes of transactions in a single day. Although they may differ in size and in the products or services offered, all generally use computers for basic business activities. For example, they bill millions of customers or prepare payroll for thousands of employees. Some enterprises use blogs to open communications among employees and/or customers.

Enterprises typically have e-commerce Web sites, allowing customers and vendors to conduct business online. The Web site showcases products, services, and other company information. Customers, vendors, and other interested parties can access this information on the Web.

The marketing department in an enterprise uses desktop publishing software to prepare marketing literature. The accounting department uses software for accounts receivable, accounts payable, billing, general ledger, and payroll activities.

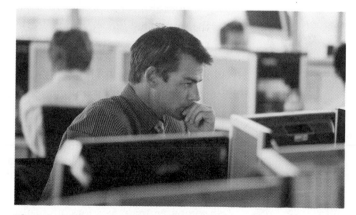

Figure 1-30   An enterprise can have hundreds or thousands of users in offices across a region, the country, or the world.

Enterprise Computing
For more information, visit the Computer Concepts CourseMate Web site at www.cengagebrain.com, navigate to the Chapter 1 Web Link resource for this book, and then click Enterprise Computing.

Enterprise users work with word processing, spreadsheet, database, and presentation software. They also may use calendar programs to post their schedules on the network. And, they might use smart phones or other mobile devices to maintain contact information. E-mail programs and Web browsers enable communications among employees, vendors, and customers.

Many employees of enterprises today telecommute. **Telecommuting** is a work arrangement in which employees work away from a company's standard workplace and often communicate with the office through the computer. Employees who telecommute have flexible work schedules so that they can combine work and personal responsibilities, such as child care.

Computer Applications in Society

The computer has changed society today as much as the industrial revolution changed society in the eighteenth and nineteenth centuries.

People interact directly with computers in fields such as education, finance, government, health care, science, publishing, travel, and manufacturing. In addition, they can reap the benefits from breakthroughs and advances in these fields. The following pages describe how computers have made a difference in people's interactions with these disciplines. Read Looking Ahead 1-1 for a look at how embedded computers may improve the quality of life.

↗ LOOKING AHEAD 1-1

Embedded Computers May Improve Quality of Life

The weather forecast may be as close as your fingertips if plans to integrate embedded computers in everyday objects become a reality. Researchers are envisioning an umbrella with an embedded cell phone in the handle that will dial and then download the local forecast. The handle will glow green for good weather and flash red for imminent storms.

Dancers can pin a small flower with an embedded motion-detecting computer to their clothes. When they move, the embedded computer senses action and then synchronizes the tempo of music to this movement. Other embedded computers woven into clothing can monitor heart and breathing rates.

Wearing hidden embedded computers can help the elderly and people recovering from accidents and surgeries monitor their walking stride and pace. When their steps are uneven, the embedded computer can sound a warning and perhaps prevent a fall. Other embedded computers can give subtle feedback on the quality of physical activity.

For more information, visit the Computer Concepts CourseMate Web site at www.cengagebrain.com, navigate to the Chapter 1 Looking Ahead resource for this book, and then click Embedded Computers.

Education

Education is the process of acquiring knowledge. In the traditional model, people learn from other people such as parents, teachers, and employers. Many forms of printed material such as books and manuals are used as learning tools. Today, educators also are turning to computers to assist with education (Figure 1-31).

Many schools and companies equip labs and classrooms with computers. Some schools require students to have a mobile computer or mobile device to access the school's network or Internet wirelessly.

Students use software to assist with learning or to complete assignments. To promote education by computer, many vendors offer substantial student discounts on software.

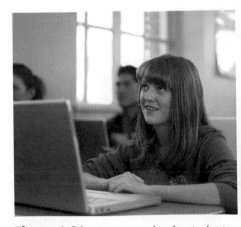

Figure 1-31 In some schools, students have mobile computers on their desks during classroom lectures.

Sometimes, the delivery of education occurs at one place while the learning occurs at other locations. For example, students can take a class on the Web. More than 70 percent of colleges offer distance learning classes. A few even offer entire degrees online.

Finance

Many people and companies use computers to help manage their finances. Some use finance software to balance checkbooks, pay bills, track personal income and expenses, manage investments, and evaluate financial plans. This software usually includes a variety of online services. For example, computer users can track investments and do online banking. With **online banking**, users access account balances, pay bills, and copy monthly transactions from the bank's computer right into their computers (Figure 1-32).

Investors often use **online investing** to buy and sell stocks and bonds — without using a broker. With online investing, the transaction fee for each trade usually is much less than when trading through a broker.

Figure 1-32 An online banking Web site.

Government

A government provides society with direction by making and administering policies. To provide citizens with up-to-date information, most government offices have Web sites. People access government Web sites to file taxes, apply for permits and licenses, pay parking tickets, buy stamps, report crimes, apply for financial aid, and renew vehicle registrations and driver's licenses.

Employees of government agencies use computers as part of their daily routine. Military and other agency officials use the U.S. Department of Homeland Security's network of information about domestic security threats to help protect our nation. Law enforcement officers have online access to the FBI's National Crime Information Center (NCIC) through in-vehicle computers, fingerprint readers, and mobile devices (Figure 1-33). The NCIC contains more than 52 million missing persons and criminal records, including names, fingerprints, parole/probation records, mug shots, and other information.

Figure 1-33 Law enforcement officials have in-vehicle computers and mobile devices to access emergency, missing person, and criminal records in computer networks in local, state, and federal agencies.

Health Care

Nearly every area of health care uses computers. Whether you are visiting a family doctor for a regular checkup, having lab work or an outpatient test, or being rushed in for emergency surgery, the medical staff around you will be using computers for various purposes:

- Doctors use the Web and medical software to assist with researching and diagnosing health conditions.
- Doctors use e-mail to correspond with patients.
- Pharmacists use computers to file insurance claims.
- Robots deliver medication to nurse stations in hospitals.
- Hospitals and doctors use computers and mobile devices to maintain and access patient records.

- Computers and computerized devices assist doctors, nurses, and technicians with medical tests (Figure 1-34).
- Computers monitor patients' vital signs in hospital rooms and at home.
- Surgeons implant computerized devices, such as pacemakers, that allow patients to live longer.
- Surgeons use computer-controlled devices to provide them with greater precision during operations, such as for laser eye surgery and robot-assisted heart surgery.

Figure 1-34   Doctors, nurses, technicians, and other medical staff use computers and computerized devices to assist with medical tests.

Two forms of long-distance health care are telemedicine and telesurgery. Through **telemedicine**, health-care professionals in separate locations conduct live conferences on the computer. For example, a doctor at one location can have a conference with a doctor at another location to discuss a bone X-ray. Live images of each doctor, along with the X-ray, are displayed on each doctor's computer.

With **telesurgery**, a surgeon performs an operation on a patient who is not located in the same physical room as the surgeon. Telesurgery enables surgeons to direct robots to perform an operation via computers connected to a high-speed network.

Science

All branches of science, from biology to astronomy to meteorology, use computers to assist them with collecting, analyzing, and modeling data. Scientists also use the Internet to communicate with colleagues around the world.

Breakthroughs in surgery, medicine, and treatments often result from scientists' use of computers. Tiny computers now imitate functions of the central nervous system, retina of the eye, and cochlea of the ear. A cochlear implant allows a deaf person to listen. Electrodes implanted in the brain stop tremors associated with Parkinson's disease. Cameras small enough to swallow — sometimes called a camera pill — take pictures inside your body to detect polyps, cancer, and other abnormalities (Figure 1-35).

How a Camera Pill Works

Step 1
A patient swallows a tiny capsule that contains a miniature disposable camera, lights, a transmitter, and batteries. The camera is positioned at the clear end of the capsule.

Step 2
As the capsule moves through the inside of the patient's body, the camera snaps about 50,000 pictures, which are transmitted to a recording device worn as a belt on the patient's waist.

Step 3
The doctor transfers the data on the recording device to a computer so that it can be processed and analyzed.

 Figure 1-35   This figure shows how a camera pill works.

Publishing

Publishing is the process of making works available to the public. These works include books, magazines, newspapers, music, film, and video. Special software assists graphic designers in developing pages that include text, graphics, and photos; artists in composing and enhancing songs; filmmakers in creating and editing film; and journalists and mobile users in capturing and modifying video clips.

Many publishers make their works available online (Figure 1-36). Some Web sites allow you to copy the work, such as a book or music, to your desktop computer, mobile computer, smart phone, or other mobile device.

Figure 1-36   Many magazine and newspaper publishers make the content of their publications available online.

Travel

Many vehicles manufactured today include some type of onboard navigation system. Some mobile users prefer to carry specialized handheld navigation devices (Figure 1-37).

In preparing for a trip, you may need to reserve a car, hotel, or flight. Many Web sites offer these services to the public. For example, you can order airline tickets on the Web. If you plan to drive somewhere and are unsure of the road to take to your destination, you can print directions and a map from the Web.

Figure 1-37   This handheld navigation device gives users turn-by-turn voice-prompted directions to a destination.

Manufacturing

Computer-aided manufacturing (CAM) refers to the use of computers to assist with manufacturing processes such as fabrication and assembly. Often, robots carry out processes in a CAM environment. CAM is used by a variety of industries, including oil drilling, power generation, food production, and automobile manufacturing. Automobile plants, for example, have an entire line of industrial robots that assemble a car (Figure 1-38).

Figure 1-38   Automotive factories use industrial robots to weld car bodies.

Instructions: Find the true statement below. Then, rewrite the remaining false statements so that they are true.

1. A desktop computer is a portable, personal computer designed to fit on your lap.
2. A personal computer contains a processor, memory, and one or more input, output, and storage devices.
3. Each enterprise user spends time on the computer for different reasons that include personal financial management, Web access, communications, and entertainment.
4. A home user requires the capabilities of a workstation or other powerful computer.
5. Mainframes are the fastest, most powerful computers — and the most expensive.
6. With embedded computers, users access account balances, pay bills, and copy monthly transactions from the bank's computer right into their personal computers.

Quiz Yourself Online: To further check your knowledge of pages 14 through 27, visit the Computer Concepts CourseMate Web site at www.cengagebrain.com, navigate to the Chapter 1 Quiz Yourself resource for this book, and then click Objectives 6 – 8.

Chapter Summary

Chapter 1 introduced you to basic computer concepts. You learned about the components of a computer. Next, the chapter discussed networks, the Internet, and computer software. The many different categories of computers, computer users, and computer applications in society also were presented.

This chapter is an overview. Many of the terms and concepts introduced will be discussed further in later chapters. For a history of hardware and software developments, read the Timeline feature that follows this chapter.

Computer Usage @ Work

Transportation

What is transportation like without computers? Delivery drivers use clipboards to hold their records. Human navigators use paper maps to track routes for pilots. Ship captains rely solely on experience to navigate through shallow waters. Today, the transportation industry relies heavily on computer usage.

As presented in this chapter, many vehicles include onboard navigation systems to help you navigate from one location to another. These systems also usually provide other services such as dispatching roadside assistance, unlocking the driver's side door if you lock the keys in your vehicle, and tracking the vehicle if it is stolen.

The shipping and travel industries identify items during transport using bar codes, which are identification codes that consist of lines and spaces of different lengths. When you ship a package, the shipping company, such as UPS or FedEx, places a bar code on the package to indicate its destination to a computer. Because a package might travel to its destination by way of several trucks, trains, and airplanes, computers automatically route the package as efficiently as possible.

When you travel by airplane, baggage handling systems ensure that your luggage reaches its destination on time. When you check in your baggage at the airport, a bar code identifies the airplane on which the bags should be placed. If you change planes, automated baggage handling systems route your bags to connecting flights with very little, if any, human intervention. When the bags reach their destination, they are routed automatically to the baggage carousel in the airport's terminal building.

Pilots of high-technology commercial, military, and space aircraft today work in a glass cockpit, which features computerized instrumentation, navigation, communication, weather reports, and an autopilot. The electronic flight information shown on high-resolution displays is designed to reduce pilot workload, decrease fatigue, and enable pilots to concentrate on flying safely.

Boats and ships also are equipped with computers that include detailed electronic maps, help the captain navigate, as well as calculate the water depth and provide a layout of the underwater surface so that the captain can avoid obstructions.

As you travel the roadways, airways, and waterways, bear in mind that computers often are responsible for helping you to reach your destination as quickly and safely as possible.

For more information, visit the Computer Concepts CourseMate Web site at www.cengagebrain.com, navigate to the Chapter 1 Computer Usage @ Work resource for this book, and then click Transportation.

Companies on the Cutting Edge

APPLE Innovative Industry Products

Apple recently sold a record 5.2 million of its latest iPhone models in one quarter, establishing the company's appeal to both consumer and corporate cell phone users. Apple is noted for introducing innovative products, starting with the Apple II, which was the first mass-marketed personal computer, in 1977 and the Macintosh, which featured a graphical user interface, in 1984.

Steve Jobs and Steve Wozniak founded Apple in 1976 when they marketed the Apple I, a circuit board they had developed in Jobs's garage. Under Jobs's direction as CEO, Apple developed the OS X operating system; iLife for working with photos, music, videos, and Web sites; and iWork, a collection of business programs. Apple also is leading the digital media revolution with its iPod portable media players, iPad tablet computer, and iTunes online store, which is the most popular Web site selling music. More than 10 million downloads occur each day from Apple's App Store, for a total download count exceeding 7 billion.

AMAZON Retailer Focused on Consumers

Online shoppers can find practically any product they desire on Amazon.com. Billing itself as the "Earth's most customer-centric company," it offers books, movies, electronics, clothing, toys, and many other items.

Jeff Bezos founded Amazon in 1995 knowing that book lovers would gravitate toward a Web site offering the convenience of browsing through millions of book titles in one sitting. He fulfilled orders for customers in every U.S. state and 45 additional countries during the first 30 days of business, all shipped from his Seattle-area garage.

The company has grown to permit third parties to sell products on its Web site. Its Kindle portable reader wirelessly downloads more than 450,000 books along with blogs, magazines, and newspapers to a high-resolution electronic paper display. Recently, it launched Kindle Singles, which are Kindle books with up to 30,000 words, the equivalent of two chapters of a typical book.

For more information, visit the Computer Concepts CourseMate Web site at www.cengagebrain.com and then navigate to the Chapter 1 Companies on the Cutting Edge resource for this book.

Technology Trailblazers

BILL GATES Microsoft Founder

When Bill Gates stepped down from his day-to-day activities at Microsoft in 2008, his action marked the end of an era that shaped the computer world. He remains the company's chairman and advisor, but he now devotes much of his time directing the Bill & Melinda Gates Foundation, a philanthropic organization working to help people worldwide lead healthy, productive lives. His foundation currently is awarding $3 billion in grants to improve education and graduation rates via technology, with an emphasis on online learning.

Gates learned to program computers when he was 13 years old. Early in his career, he developed the BASIC programming language for the MITS Altair, one of the first microcomputers. He founded Microsoft in 1975 with Paul Allen, and five years later they licensed the first operating system, called PC-DOS, to IBM for $80,000. This decision to license, rather than sell, the software is considered one of the wisest business decisions Gates ever made. Today, Microsoft's Windows and Office products dominate the software market.

TOM ANDERSON MySpace Cofounder and President

Having more than 11 million friends is all in a day's work for Tom Anderson, the current president and one of the founders of MySpace, one of the world's largest online social networks. Every MySpace account includes Anderson as a default first friend who is invited to view each personal network.

When Anderson's own rock group failed, he needed a place to post his songs. He started MySpace in 2003 with his friend, Chris DeWolfe, as a free tool to help musicians promote their songs and allow music lovers to create their own Web pages devoted to sharing their favorite music with like-minded admirers. Two years later they sold the business to Rupert Murdoch's News Corporation for $580 million. Anderson graduated from the University of California – Los Angeles in 2001 with a master's degree in film and from the University of California – Berkeley in 1998 with a bachelor's degree in English and rhetoric.

For more information, visit the Computer Concepts CourseMate Web site at www.cengagebrain.com and then navigate to the Chapter 1 Technology Trailblazers resource for this book.

Chapter Review

The Chapter Review reinforces the main concepts presented in this chapter.

To listen to an audio version of this Chapter Review, visit the Computer Concepts CourseMate Web site at www.cengagebrain.com and then navigate to the Chapter 1 Chapter Review resource for this book.

1. **Why Is Computer Literacy Vital to Success in Today's World?** **Computer literacy**, also called digital literacy, involves having current knowledge and understanding of computers and their uses. As computers become an increasingly important part of daily living, many people believe that computer literacy is vital to success. Because the requirements that determine computer literacy change as technology changes, you must keep up with these changes to remain computer literate.

2. **List and Describe the Five Components of a Computer.** A **computer** is an electronic device, operating under the control of instructions stored in its own memory, that can accept data, process the data according to specified rules, produce results, and store the results for future use. The electric, electronic, and mechanical components of a computer, or **hardware**, include input devices, output devices, a system unit, storage devices, and communications devices. An **input device** allows you to enter data or instructions into a computer. An **output device** conveys information to one or more people. The **system unit** is a case that contains the electronic components of a computer that are used to process data. A **storage device** records and/or retrieves items to and from **storage media**. A **communications device** enables a computer to send and receive data, instructions, and information to and from one or more computers.

3. **What Are the Advantages and Disadvantages That Users Experience When Working with Computers?** A **user** is anyone who communicates with a computer or utilizes the information it generates. Advantages of using a computer include speed, reliability, consistency, storage, and communications. The disadvantages include violation of privacy, public safety, impact on the labor force, health risks, and impact on the environment.

Visit the Computer Concepts CourseMate Web site at www.cengagebrain.com, navigate to the Chapter 1 Quiz Yourself resource for this book, and then click Objectives 1 – 3.

4. **How Are the Internet and World Wide Web Used?** The Internet is a worldwide collection of networks that connects millions of businesses, government agencies, educational institutions, and individuals. People use the Internet to communicate with and meet other people; conduct research and access information and news; shop for goods and services; bank and invest; participate in online training; engage in entertaining activities; download music and videos; share information, photos, and videos; and to access and interact with Web applications. The **Web**, short for World Wide Web, contains billions of documents called Web pages.

5. **What Are the Differences between System Software and Application Software?** **Software**, also called a **program**, is a series of related instructions, organized for a common purpose, that tells the computer what tasks to perform and how to perform them. The two categories of software are system software and application software. **System software** consists of the programs that control or maintain the operations of a computer and its devices. Two types of system software are the **operating system**, which coordinates activities among computer hardware devices, and **utility programs**, which perform maintenance-type tasks usually related to managing a computer, its devices, or its programs. **Application software** consists of programs designed to make users more productive and/or assist them with personal tasks. Popular application software includes a Web browser, word processing software, spreadsheet software, database software, and presentation software.

Visit the Computer Concepts CourseMate Web site at www.cengagebrain.com, navigate to the Chapter 1 Quiz Yourself resource for this book, and then click Objectives 4 – 5.

6. **What Are the Differences among the Types, Sizes, and Functions in the Following Categories: Personal Computers (Desktop), Mobile Computers and Mobile Devices, Game Consoles, Servers, Mainframes, Supercomputers, and Embedded Computers?** A **personal computer** is a computer that can perform all of its input, processing, output, and storage activities by itself. A **mobile computer** is a personal computer that you can carry from place to place, and a **mobile device** is a computing device small enough to hold in your hand. A game console is a mobile computing device designed for single-player or multiplayer video games. A **server** controls access to the hardware, software, and other resources on a network and provides a centralized storage area for programs, data, and information. A **mainframe** is a large, expensive, powerful computer that can handle hundreds or thousands of connected users simultaneously and can store huge amounts of data, instructions, and information. A **supercomputer** is the fastest, most powerful, and most expensive computer and is used for applications requiring complex, sophisticated mathematical calculations. An **embedded computer** is a special-purpose computer that functions as a component in a larger product.

7. How Do the Various Types of Computer Users Interact with Computers?   Computer users can be separated into five categories: home user, small office/home office user, mobile user, power user, and enterprise user. A **home user** is a family member who uses a computer for a variety of reasons, such as personal financial management, Web access, communications, and entertainment. A **small office/home office** (**SOHO**) includes any company with fewer than 50 employees or a self-employed individual who works from home and uses basic business software and sometimes industry-specific software. **Mobile users** are employees and students who work on a computer while away from a main office, home office, or school. A **power user** can exist in all types of businesses and uses powerful computers to work with industry-specific software. An **enterprise user** works in or interacts with a company with many employees and uses a computer and computer network that processes high volumes of transactions in a single day.

8. How Does Society Use Computers in Education, Finance, Government, Health Care, Science, Publishing, Travel, and Manufacturing?   In education, students use computers and software to assist with learning or take distance learning classes. In finance, people use computers for **online banking** to access information and **online investing** to buy and sell stocks and bonds. Government offices have Web sites to provide citizens with up-to-date information, and government employees use computers as part of their daily routines. In health care, computers are used to maintain patient records, assist doctors with medical tests and research, file insurance claims, provide greater precision during operations, and as implants. All branches of science use computers to assist with collecting, analyzing, and modeling data and to communicate with scientists around the world. Publishers use computers to assist in developing pages and make their works available online. Many vehicles use some type of online navigation system to help people travel more quickly and safely. Manufacturers use **computer-aided manufacturing** (**CAM**) to assist with manufacturing processes.

Visit the Computer Concepts CourseMate Web site at www.cengagebrain.com, navigate to the Chapter 1 Quiz Yourself resource for this book, and then click Objectives 6 – 8.

Key Terms

You should know the Key Terms. The list below helps focus your study.

To see an example of and a definition for each term, and to access current and additional information from the Web, visit the Computer Concepts CourseMate Web site at www.cengagebrain.com and then navigate to the Chapter 1 Key Terms resource for this book.

application software (12)
blog (10)
camera phone (17)
communications device (6)
computer (3)
computer literacy (3)
computer-aided
  manufacturing (CAM)
  (27)
convergence (14)
CPU (central processing
  unit) (6)
data (4)
desktop computer (16)
developer (13)
digital camera (18)
digital literacy (3)
e-book (17)
e-book reader (17)
embedded computer (19)
enterprise computing
  (23)
enterprise user (23)
execute (12)

FAQ (11)
game console (18)
graphical user interface
  (GUI) (11)
green computing (7)
handheld computer (17)
hardware (4)
home user (20)
information (4)
information processing
  cycle (4)
input device (4)
installing (12)
instant message (17)
Internet (8)
Internet-enabled (16)
laptop computer (16)
mainframe (19)
memory (6)
microblog (10)
mobile computer (16)
mobile device (16)
mobile users (22)
netbook (16)

network (8)
notebook computer (16)
online (8)
online banking (25)
online investing (25)
online social network (10)
operating system (11)
output device (5)
PDA (17)
personal computer (15)
picture message (17)
podcast (10)
portable media
  player (17)
power user (23)
processor (6)
program (11)
programmer (13)
resources (8)
run (12)
server (19)
small office/home office
  (SOHO) (22)
smart phone (17)

social networking
  Web site (10)
software (11)
storage device (6)
storage media (6)
supercomputer (19)
system software (11)
system unit (6)
Tablet PC (16)
telecommuting (24)
telemedicine (26)
telesurgery (26)
text message (17)
Ultra-Mobile PC (UMPC)
  (17)
user (7)
utility program (12)
video message (17)
video phone (17)
Web (10)
Web 2.0 (10)
Web application (10)
Web page (10)
Web site (10)

Checkpoint

The Checkpoint exercises test your knowledge of the chapter concepts. The page number containing the answer appears in parentheses after each exercise.

To complete the Checkpoint exercises interactively, visit the Computer Concepts CourseMate Web site at www.cengagebrain.com and then navigate to the Chapter 1 Checkpoint resource for this book.

Multiple Choice Select the best answer.

1. Computer literacy, also known as digital literacy, involves having a current knowledge and understanding of _____. (3)
   a. computer programming
   b. computers and their uses
   c. computer repair
   d. all of the above

2. _____ is/are a collection of unprocessed items, which can include text, numbers, images, audio, and video. (4)
   a. Data   b. Instructions
   c. Programs   d. Information

3. Millions of people worldwide join online communities, each called _____, that encourage members to share their interests, ideas, stories, photos, music, and videos with other registered users. (10)
   a. a podcast
   b. enterprise computing
   c. a social networking Web site or online social network
   d. a blog

4. _____ consists of the programs that control or maintain the operations of the computer and its devices. (11)
   a. A graphical user interface (GUI)
   b. A communications device
   c. System software
   d. Application software

5. Two types of _____ are desktop computers and notebook computers. (15)
   a. servers
   b. supercomputers
   c. mainframe computers
   d. personal computers

6. Five popular types of _____ are smart phones, PDAs, handheld computers, portable media players, and digital cameras. (17)
   a. mobile devices
   b. notebook computers
   c. desktop computers
   d. tower computers

7. A(n) _____ message is a real-time Internet communication, where you exchange messages with other connected users. (17)
   a. text   b. instant
   c. picture   d. video

8. Many large companies use the word(s), _____, to refer to the huge network of computers that meets their diverse computing needs. (23)
   a. information technology
   b. telecommuting
   c. enterprise computing
   d. multimedia

Matching Match the terms with their definitions.

_____ 1. information processing cycle (4)

_____ 2. processor (6)

_____ 3. storage device (6)

_____ 4. portable media player (17)

_____ 5. digital camera (18)

a. records (writes) and/or retrieves (reads) items to and from storage media

b. mobile device on which you can store, organize, and play digital media

c. fastest, most powerful computer — and the most expensive

d. electronic component that interprets and carries out the basic instructions for a computer

e. series of input, process, output, and storage activities

f. device that allows users to take pictures and store the photographed images digitally, instead of on traditional film

Short Answer Write a brief answer to each of the following questions.

1. What does it mean to be computer literate? _____ What is a computer? _____

2. Describe two health risks posed by computers. _____ How might computers have a negative effect on the environment? _____

3. What are five common storage devices? _____ How are they different? _____

4. What is a Web application? _____ What are some features of a Web 2.0 site? _____

5. How is hardware different from software? _____ What are two types of system software and how are they used? _____

6. How do computers benefit individuals' health care? _____ How does telesurgery differ from telemedicine? _____

Problem Solving

The Problem Solving exercises extend your knowledge of the chapter concepts by seeking solutions to practical computer problems that you may encounter at home, school, or work. The Collaboration exercise should be completed with a team.

In the real world, practical problems often can be solved in multiple ways. Provide one solution to each of the following problems using available resources, such as articles on the Web or in print, blogs, podcasts, videos, television, user guides, other individuals, and electronics and computer stores. You may need to use multiple resources to obtain an answer. Present your solutions in the form requested by your instructor (brief report, presentation, discussion, or other means).

@ Home

1. **Incorrect Grade Report**   Your grade report came in the mail today. On the grade report, your grade point average (GPA) is not what you expect. After computing it manually, you discover that the GPA on your grade report is incorrect. What might be causing the error?

2. **Suspicious Charges**   Your credit card company called to inform you that your account has a suspicious charge. Upon further investigation, you realize the charge does not belong to you. What steps will you take to correct the problem?

3. **Problematic Player**   After charging your portable media player overnight, you turn it on only to find that it is reporting a low battery. Seconds later, it shuts off automatically. What might be wrong?

4. **Inaccessible Media**   You insert an optical disc with digital photos from your most recent family vacation and discover that your computer will not read the optical disc. What might be wrong?

@ Work

5. **Insufficient Disk Space**   Recently, you purchased a USB flash drive that you plan to use to store work-related files. When you attempt to store a file on the USB flash drive, the computer displays an error message indicating that the file will not fit. How could a brand new USB flash drive not have enough room to store the first file you attempted to store on it?

6. **Power Outage**   The power in your office has been out for the last two hours and has just come back on. When you attempt to start your computer by pressing the power button, nothing happens. What is your next step before calling technical support?

7. **Incorrect Login Credentials**   Upon returning to the office from a well-deserved two-week vacation, you turn on your computer. Upon entering your user name and password, an error message appears stating that your password is incorrect. What are your next steps?

8. **Software Installation**   You are attempting to install a program on your office computer. After inserting the installation disc and specifying that you would like to begin the installation, your computer appears to begin installing the software. Halfway through the installation process, an error message appears stating that you must have administrative privileges to perform the installation. Why were you not informed immediately upon beginning the installation? What are your next steps?

Collaboration

9. **Computers in Transportation**   Your project team has been accepted to present a business proposal to a group of potential investors. Because the presentation will take place in San Francisco, CA, you will need to transport people and ship some materials to that location. Form a team of three people and determine how to use technology to ship materials and how to make travel arrangements. One team member should research the steps required to use a Web site to make flight reservations, one team member should determine the steps necessary to print a UPS shipping label from their computer and track the package while it is en route, and another team member should find directions from San Francisco International Airport to a nearby hotel.

Learn How To

The Learn How To activities step you through fundamental technology skills when using a computer. The Learn How To exercises enable you to become more proficient with these skills.

Premium Activity: To relate this Learn How To activity to your everyday life, see a visual demonstration of the activity, and complete a short assessment, visit the Computer Concepts CourseMate Web site at www.cengagebrain.com and then navigate to the Chapter 1 Learn How To resource for this book.

Learn How To 1: Create and Use Your Own Blog

A blog can contain any information you wish to place in it. Originally, blogs consisted of Web addresses, so that an individual or group with a specific interest could direct others to useful places on the Web. Today, blogs contain addresses, thoughts, diaries, and anything else a person or group wants to share.

CREATE A BLOG button

Take a quick tour link

Once you have created a blog, you can update it. A variety of services available on the Web can help you create and maintain your blog. One widely used service is called Blogger. To create a blog using Blogger, complete the following steps:

1. Start your Web browser, type blogger.com in the Address bar, and then press the ENTER key to display the Blogger home page (Figure 1-39).
2. Click the CREATE A BLOG button on the Blogger home page.
3. Enter the data required on the 'Create Blogger Account' page. Your e-mail address and password will allow you to change and manage your

Figure 1-39

blog. Your Display name is the name that will be shown on the blog as the author of the material on the blog. Many people use their own names, but others use pseudonyms as their "pen names" so that they are not readily identifiable.
4. Click the Continue arrow and then enter your Blog title and Blog address. These are the names and addresses everyone will use to view your blog.
5. Click the Continue arrow to display the 'Choose a template' screen.
6. Choose a template for your blog and then click the Continue arrow.
7. Your blog will be created for you. When you see the 'Your blog has been created!' screen, click the START BLOGGING arrow.
8. From the screen that is displayed, you can post items for your blog, specify settings, change the layout, and view your blog.
9. When you have posted all your information, click the Sign out link at the top right of the screen. You will be logged out.
10. To edit your blog and add or change information on it, visit the Blogger home page and sign in by entering your user name and password. You will be able to post to your blog.
11. Others can view your blog by entering its address in the browser's Address bar and then pressing the ENTER key.

Exercises

1. Start your Web browser and visit blogger.com. Click the 'Take a quick tour' link and go through all the screens that explain about a blog. What did you learn that you did not know? What type of blog do you find most compelling — a group or an individual blog? Why? Submit your answers to your instructor.

2. Optional: Create your own blog. Carefully name it and begin your posts at this time. What is your blog name and address? What is its primary purpose? Is it an individual or group blog? Write a paragraph containing the answers to these questions and any other information you feel is pertinent. Submit this paragraph to your instructor.

Learn How To 2: Use the Computer Concepts CourseMate Web Site for Discovering Computers Fundamentals

The Computer Concepts CourseMate Web site for Discovering Computers Fundamentals provides a variety of activities, exercises, and other resources. To use the site, you first establish a user name and password for your student account and then register this book. Perform the following steps to create a student account and register this book:

1. Start the Web browser.
2. Type www.cengagebrain.com in the Address bar of the Web browser and then press the ENTER key to display the CengageBrain home page.

3. If you do not have an account, follow the on-screen instructions to sign up for a new student account. If you already have an account, log in with your user name and password.

4. Register this book by entering its Access Code in the appropriate text box and then clicking the corresponding button.

5. To open the resources for this book, click the button corresponding to Computer Concepts CourseMate Web site for Discovering Computers.

Exercise

1a. After creating a student account and registering this book as described in the steps above, start your Web browser, type www.cengagebrain.com in the Address bar of the browser, and then press the ENTER key to display the CengageBrain home page.

1b. Log in to your student account with your user name and password.

1c. Open the resources for this book by clicking the button corresponding to Computer Concepts CourseMate Web site for Discovering Computers.

1d. Select Chapter 1 and then click each resource listed below the chapter title to display the content associated with the selected resource.

1e. Write a report that describes the use of each of the Chapter 1 resources for this book. Which resources do you think will prove the most valuable to you when using the book and the Web site? Why? Submit your report to your instructor.

Learn It Online

The Learn It Online exercises are interactive Web exercises designed to reinforce and expand your understanding of the chapter concepts. The descriptions below briefly summarize each exercise.

To complete the Learn It Online exercises, visit the Computer Concepts CourseMate Web site at www.cengagebrain.com, navigate to the Chapter 1 resources for this book, click the link for the exercise you want to complete, and then read the instructions.

1 At the Movies — Computer History in a Barn

Watch a movie to tour the Digibarn Computer Museum and then answer questions about the movie.

2 Student Edition Labs — Using Input Devices and Using Windows

Enhance your understanding and knowledge about input devices and the Windows operating system by completing the Using Input Devices and Using Windows Labs.

3 Practice Test

Take a multiple choice test that checks your knowledge of the chapter concepts and review the resulting study guide.

4 Who Wants To Be a Computer Genius²?

Play the Shelly Cashman Series version of this popular game by answering questions to find out if you are a computer genius. Panic buttons are available to provide assistance during game play.

5 Crossword Puzzle Challenge

Complete an interactive crossword puzzle to reinforce concepts presented in this chapter.

6 Windows Exercises

Step through the Windows 7 exercises to learn how to use help, improve mouse skills, and identify computer information.

7 Exploring Computer Careers

Read about a career as a computer salesperson, search for relevant employment advertisements, and then answer related questions.

8 Web Apps — Google Maps

Learn how to locate businesses in your area, view a location's surroundings via satellite, and find directions from one location to another using Google Maps.

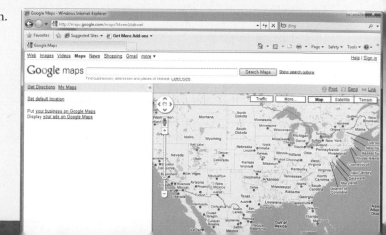

Web Research

The Web Research exercises broaden your understanding of the chapter concepts by presenting questions that require you to search the Web for answers.

1 Search Sleuth

Use one of the search engines listed in Figure 2-8 in Chapter 2 on page 65 or your own favorite search engine to find the answers to the following questions. Copy and paste the Web address from the Web page where you found the answer. Some questions may have more than one answer. If required, submit your answers to your instructor. (1) What company was the first to sell a USB flash drive? (2) What is the significance of the Universal symbol on Apple's Mac application programs? (3) Which retailers offer to dispose of old computers and other electronic products properly to help protect the environment? (4) What are three Illustrative Grant Commitments the Bill & Melinda Gates Foundation has made? (5) According to *Fortune*, at what company do MBA students most want to work when they graduate? (6) Who created the first set of icons for the Macintosh computer? What sound does her Clarus the Dogcow make? (7) What company manufactured the first notebook computer, the UltraLite, in 1989?

2 Green Computing

Computer usage requires electricity, whether to power the system unit and monitor, recharge batteries, or print. In addition, the computer manufacturing process depletes natural resources and often uses toxic chemicals. As you learned in this chapter, many environmentally conscious people practice green computing by attempting to reduce electricity and environmental waste. Examine your computing practices, and determine 10 ways that you can use less power on your computing equipment at home, work, and school. Consider how often you use the printer and the types of documents you print. Examine your monitor, system unit, and printer. Do you see any notation indicating they are environmentally sound? Do they hibernate or go into a power save mode when not being used? Write a 50-word summary of the green computing practices in your life.

3 Social Networking

One of the more popular social networking Web sites is Facebook. This quickly growing service differentiates itself from other online social networks by having widespread privacy controls. In addition, its development platform, called f8, allows developers to create programs (called applications) that users can add to a Web page. Hostels, for example, lets world travelers research and rate hostels and includes photos and descriptions. Visit the Facebook site (facebook.com), click the About link at the bottom of the page, and then read about Facebook's features. What are three of Facebook's top features? What information is given in the recent Facebook blog posts? Visit the AppRate Web site (apprate.com) and then summarize three Facebook application reviews and ratings.

4 Blogs

Blogs profiling the music industry discuss new technologies, legal issues, podcasts, and business news. Visit the CNET blog (blogs.cnet.com) and then read and summarize at least three of the articles in the Most Recent Posts section. Locate the Crave, Gaming and Culture, and Green Tech features and then read and summarize at least one story from each blog. Then visit the iLounge (ilounge.com) Web site and read reviews of at least three new products for the iPhone. Would you purchase any of the products discussed? What books and buyer's guides are available to download from the Library? Which iPod cases and speakers received favorable reviews? Read and summarize at least three stories and associated comments in the News section.

5 Ethics in Action

The Internet has increased the ease with which students can plagiarize material for research paper assignments. Teachers are using online services, such as Turnitin and PlagiarismDetect.com, to help detect plagiarized papers and to help students understand how to cite sources correctly. Visit the Turnitin Web site (turnitin.com) and then write a summary of how this service is used. How does this service attempt to prevent plagiarism through the Turnitin Write Cycle? How prevalent is plagiarism on your campus? What is your school's official policy on disciplining students who submit plagiarized papers? Does your school have an honor code? If required, submit your summary to your instructor.

Special Feature

Timeline

Milestones in Computer History

Visit the Computer Concepts CourseMate Web site at www.cengagebrain.com and then navigate to the Timeline Feature resource for this book.

1937 Dr. John V. Atanasoff and Clifford Berry design and build the first electronic digital computer. Their machine, the Atanasoff-Berry-Computer, or ABC, provides the foundation for advances in electronic digital computers.

1945 John von Neumann poses in front of the electronic computer built at the Institute for Advanced Study. This computer and its von Neumann architecture served as the prototype for subsequent stored program computers worldwide.

1947 William Shockley, John Bardeen, and Walter Brattain invent the transfer resistance device, eventually called the transistor. The transistor would revolutionize computers, proving much more reliable than vacuum tubes.

1951 · **1947** · **1946** · **1945** · **1943** · **1937**

1943 During World War II, British scientist Alan Turing designs the Colossus, an electronic computer created for the military to break German codes. The computer's existence is kept secret until the 1970s.

1946 Dr. John W. Mauchly and J. Presper Eckert, Jr. complete work on the first large-scale electronic, general-purpose digital computer. The ENIAC (Electronic Numerical Integrator And Computer) weighs 30 tons, contains 18,000 vacuum tubes, occupies a 30 × 50 foot space, and consumes 160 kilowatts of power.

1951 The first commercially available electronic digital computer, the UNIVAC I (UNIVersal Automatic Computer), is introduced by Remington Rand. Public awareness of computers increases when the UNIVAC correctly predicts that Dwight D. Eisenhower will win the presidential election.

1952 Dr. Grace Hopper considers the concept of reusable software in her paper, "The Education of a Computer." The paper describes how to program a computer with symbolic notation instead of detailed machine language.

1957 The IBM 305 RAMAC computer is the first to use magnetic disk for external storage. The computer provides storage capacity similar to magnetic tape that previously was used but offers the advantage of semi-random access capability.

1959 More than 200 programming languages have been created.

1959 IBM introduces two smaller, desk-sized computers: the IBM 1401 for business and the IBM 1620 for scientists.

1957 FORTRAN (FORmula TRANslation), an efficient, easy-to-use programming language, is introduced by John Backus.

1952 **1953** **1957** **1958** **1959** **1960**

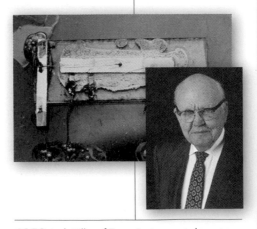

1953 Core memory, developed in the early 1950s, provides much larger storage capacity than vacuum tube memory.

1953 The IBM model 650 is one of the first widely used computers. The computer is so successful that IBM manufactures more than 1,000. IBM will dominate the mainframe market for the next decade.

1958 Jack Kilby of Texas Instruments invents the integrated circuit, which lays the foundation for high-speed computers and large-capacity memory. Computers built with transistors mark the beginning of the second generation of computer hardware.

1960 COBOL, a high-level business application language, is developed by a committee headed by Dr. Grace Hopper.

1965 Dr. John Kemeny of Dartmouth leads the development of the BASIC programming language.

1968 In a letter to the editor titled, "GO TO Statements Considered Harmful," Dr. Edsger Dijkstra introduces the concept of structured programming, developing standards for constructing computer programs.

1969 Under pressure from the industry, IBM announces that some of its software will be priced separately from the computer hardware, allowing software firms to emerge in the industry.

1968 Computer Science Corporation (CSC) becomes the first software company listed on the New York Stock Exchange.

IBM

1965 Digital Equipment Corporation (DEC) introduces the first minicomputer, the PDP-8. The machine is used extensively as an interface for time-sharing systems.

CSC STOCK PRICE NYSE/COMPOSITE Corrected Data for Dividends		
DATE	PRICE	HIGH	LO
01/02/68	2.83	2.97	2
01/03/68	2.60	2.81	2
01/04/68	2	2	
01/05/68	5		
01/08/68	5	2.60	
01/09/68	5	2.60	
01/10/68			
	2.51		
	2.51	13,500	
	2.48	23,400	
	2.49	7.800	

1969 The ARPANET network is established, which eventually grows to become the Internet.

ARPANET

1964 **1965** **1968** **1969** **1970**

1964 The number of computers has grown to 18,000. Third-generation computers, with their controlling circuitry stored on chips, are introduced. The IBM System/360 computer is the first family of compatible machines, merging science and business lines.

1968 Alan Shugart at IBM demonstrates the first regular use of an 8-inch floppy disk.

1964 IBM introduces the term word processing for the first time with its Magnetic Tape/Selectric Typewriter (MT/ST). The MT/ST was the first reusable storage medium that allowed typed material to be edited without having to retype the document.

1970 Fourth-generation computers, built with chips that use LSI (large-scale integration) arrive. While the chips used in 1965 contained up to 1,000 circuits, the LSI chip contains as many as 15,000.

1975 MITS, Inc. advertises one of the first microcomputers, the Altair. The Altair is sold in kits for less than $400 and within the first three months 4,000 orders are taken.

1979 The first public online information services, CompuServe and the Source, are founded.

1979 VisiCalc, a spreadsheet program written by Bob Frankston and Dan Bricklin, is introduced.

1981 The IBM PC is introduced, signaling IBM's entrance into the personal computer marketplace. The IBM PC quickly garners the largest share of the personal computer market and becomes the personal computer of choice in business.

1975 Ethernet, the first local area network (LAN), is developed at Xerox PARC (Palo Alto Research Center) by Robert Metcalfe.

Bob Metcalfe's 1972 sketch of his original "ethernet" vision
Image provided courtesy of Palo Alto Research Center Inc., a Xerox Company

1971 **1975** **1976** **1979** **1980** **1981**

1980 IBM offers Microsoft Corporation cofounder, Bill Gates, the opportunity to develop the operating system for the soon-to-be announced IBM personal computer. With the development of MS-DOS, Microsoft achieves tremendous growth and success.

1981 The first computer virus, Elk Cloner, is spread via Apple II floppy disks, which contained the operating system. A short rhyme would appear on the screen when the user pressed Reset after the 50th boot of an infected disk.

1971 Dr. Ted Hoff of Intel Corporation develops a microprocessor, or microprogrammable computer chip, the Intel 4004.

1976 Steve Jobs and Steve Wozniak build the first Apple computer. A subsequent version, the Apple II, is an immediate success. Adopted by elementary schools, high schools, and colleges, for many students, the Apple II is their first contact with the world of computers.

1980 Alan Shugart presents the Winchester hard disk, revolutionizing storage for personal computers.

1982 3,275,000 personal computers are sold, almost 3,000,000 more than in 1981.

Apple

3.275 Million

1982 Compaq, Inc. is founded to develop and market IBM-compatible PCs.

COMPAQ

1984 Apple introduces the Macintosh computer, which incorporates a unique, easy-to-learn, graphical user interface.

1982 Hayes introduces the 300 bps smart modem. The modem is an immediate success.

1984 Hewlett-Packard announces the first LaserJet printer for personal computers.

1982   **1983**   **1984**   **1986**

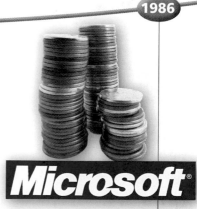

Microsoft

1986 Microsoft has public stock offering and raises approximately $61 million.

1983 Instead of choosing a person for its annual award, *TIME* magazine names the computer Machine of the Year for 1982, acknowledging the impact of computers on society.

1983 Lotus Development Corporation is founded. Its spreadsheet software, Lotus 1-2-3, which combines spreadsheet, graphics, and database programs in one package, becomes the best-selling program for IBM personal computers.

WWW

1989 While working at CERN, Switzerland, Tim Berners-Lee invents the World Wide Web.

1991 Kodak announces the first digital SLR (single-lens reflex) camera. The Kodak DCS 100 is developed mostly for photojournalism purposes and stores the photos and batteries in a separate unit.

1989 Nintendo introduces the Game Boy, its first handheld game console.

1991 World Wide Web Consortium releases standards that describe a framework for linking documents on different computers.

1991

1992

1989

1988

1989 The Intel 486 becomes the world's first 1,000,000 transistor microprocessor. It executes 15,000,000 instructions per second — four times as fast as its predecessor, the 80386 chip.

1992 Microsoft releases Windows 3.1, the latest version of its Windows operating system. Windows 3.1 offers improvements such as TrueType fonts, multimedia capability, and object linking and embedding (OLE). In two months, 3,000,000 copies of Windows 3.1 are sold.

1988 Microsoft surpasses Lotus Development Corporation to become the world's top software vendor.

1993 Several companies introduce computers using the Pentium processor from Intel. The Pentium chip contains 3.1 million transistors and is capable of performing 112,000,000 instructions per second.

1994 Jim Clark and Marc Andreessen found Netscape and launch Netscape Navigator 1.0, a Web browser.

1994 Linus Torvalds creates the Linux kernel, a UNIX-like operating system that he releases free across the Internet for further enhancement by other programmers.

1993 The U.S. Air Force completes the Global Positioning System by launching its 24th Navstar satellite into orbit. Today, GPS receivers can be found in cars, notebook computers, and smart phones.

1994 Apple introduces the first digital camera intended for consumers. The Apple QuickTake 100 is connected to home computers using a serial cable.

1993

1994

1993 Microsoft releases Microsoft Office 3 Professional, the first version of Microsoft Office for the Windows operating system.

1994 Yahoo!, a popular search engine and portal, is founded by two Stanford Ph.D. students as a way to keep track of their personal interests on the Internet. Currently, Yahoo! has approximately 12,000 employees and more than 500 million unique visitors to its Web site.

1994 Amazon is founded and later begins business as an online bookstore. Amazon eventually expands to sell products of all types and facilitates the buying and selling of new and used goods. Today, Amazon has approximately 17,000 employees.

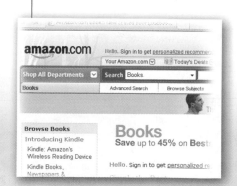

1993 The White House launches its Web site, which includes an interactive citizens' handbook and White House history and tours.

1996 U.S. Robotics introduces the PalmPilot, an inexpensive user-friendly personal digital assistant (PDA).

1995 Sun Microsystems launches Java, an object-oriented programming language that allows users to write one program for a variety of computer platforms.

1996 Microsoft releases Windows NT 4.0, an operating system for client-server networks.

1997

1995

1996

1997 Intel introduces the Pentium II processor with 7.5 million transistors. The new processor, which incorporates MMX technology, processes video, audio, and graphics data more efficiently and supports programs such as movie editing, gaming, and more.

1995 Microsoft releases Windows 95, a major upgrade to its Windows operating system. Windows 95 consists of more than 10,000,000 lines of computer instructions developed by 300 person-years of effort.

1995 eBay, an online auction Web site, is founded. Providing an online venue for people to buy and sell goods, it quickly becomes the world's largest online marketplace as it approaches 100 million active users worldwide.

1997 Microsoft releases Internet Explorer 4.0 and seizes a key place in the Internet arena.

1998 Google files for incorporation and is now the most used search engine, capturing more than 60 percent of the market over other search engines.

1998 Apple Computer introduces the iMac, the next version of its popular Macintosh computer. The iMac wins customers with its futuristic design, see-through case, and easy setup.

1999 Microsoft introduces Office 2000, its premier productivity suite, offering new tools for users to create content and save it directly to a Web site without any file conversion or special steps.

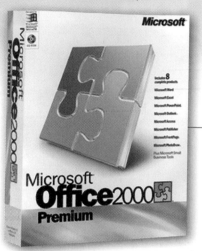

1999 Open source software, such as the Linux operating system and the Apache Web server created by unpaid volunteers, begin to gain wide acceptance among computer users.

1999 Intel introduces the Pentium III processor. This processor succeeds the Pentium II and can process 3-D graphics more quickly. The Pentium III processor contains between 9.5 and 44 million transistors.

1998

1999

1998 E-commerce booms. Companies such as Amazon.com, Dell, and E*TRADE spur online shopping, allowing buyers to obtain a variety of goods and services.

1998 Microsoft ships Windows 98, an upgrade to Windows 95. Windows 98 offers improved Internet access, better system performance, and support for a new generation of hardware and software.

1999 Governments and businesses frantically work to make their computers Y2K (Year 2000) compliant, spending more than $500 billion worldwide.

2000 Shawn Fanning, 19, and his company, Napster, turn the music industry upside down by developing software that allows computer users to swap music files with one another without going through a centralized file server.

2001 Microsoft releases major operating system updates with Windows XP for personal computers and servers. Windows XP is significantly more reliable than previous versions, features a 32-bit computing architecture, and offers a new look and feel.

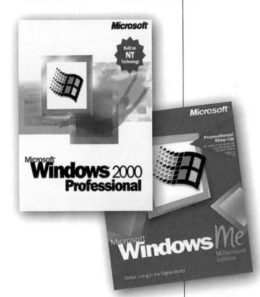

2000 Microsoft ships Windows 2000 and Windows Me. Windows 2000 offers improved behind-the-scenes security and reliability.

2001 Intel unveils its Pentium 4 chip with clock speeds starting at 1.4 GHz. The Pentium 4 includes 42 million transistors.

2000

2001

2001 Microsoft introduces Office XP, the next version of the world's leading suite of productivity software. Features include speech and handwriting recognition, smart tags, and task panes.

2000 E-commerce achieves mainstream acceptance. Annual e-commerce sales exceed $100 billion, and Internet advertising expenditures reach more than $5 billion.

2000 Telemedicine uses satellite technology and video conferencing to broadcast consultations and to perform distant surgeries. Robots are used for complex and precise tasks.

2001 Wikipedia, a free online encyclopedia, is introduced. Additional wikis begin to appear on the Internet, enabling people to share information in their areas of expertise. Although some might rely on wikis for research purposes, the content is not always verified for accuracy.

2000 Dot-com companies (Internet based) go out of business at a record pace — nearly one per day — as financial investors withhold funding due to the companies' unprofitability.

2002 After several years of negligible sales, the Tablet PC is reintroduced to meet the needs of a more targeted audience.

2003 Wireless computers and devices, such as keyboards, mouse devices, home networks, and wireless Internet access points become commonplace.

2002 Digital video cameras, DVD burners, easy-to-use video editing software, and improvements in storage capabilities allow the average computer user to create Hollywood-like videos with introductions, conclusions, rearranged scenes, music, and voice-over.

2003 Microsoft ships Office 2003, the latest version of its flagship Office suite. More than 400 million people in 175 nations and 70 languages are using a version of Office.

2002

2003

2002 Microsoft launches its .NET strategy, which is a new environment for developing and running software applications featuring ease of development of Web-based services.

2003 In an attempt to maintain their current business model of selling songs, the Recording Industry Association of America (RIAA) files more than 250 lawsuits against individual computer users who offer copyrighted music over peer-to-peer networks.

2002 DVD burners begin to replace CD burners (CD-RW). DVDs can store up to eight times as much data as CDs. Uses include storing home movies, music, photos, and backups.

myspace.com
a place for friends™

2002 Intel ships its revamped Pentium 4 chip with the 0.13 micron processor and Hyper-Threading (HT) Technology, operating at speeds of 3.06 GHz. This new development eventually will enable processors with a billion transistors to operate at 20 GHz.

2003 MySpace, an online social network, is founded. MySpace allows users to share information, photos, and videos, as well as stay in touch with their friends and make new friends. MySpace eventually grows to nearly 200 million users, making it one of the more popular and successful online social networks.

SPECIAL FEATURE

2004 Companies such as RealNetworks, Microsoft, Sony, and Walmart stake out turf in the online music store business started by Apple Computer.

2004 USB flash drives become a cost-effective way to transport data and information from one computer to another.

USB flash drive

2004 Flat-panel LCD monitors overtake bulky CRT monitors as the popular choice of computer users.

2004 106 million, or 53 percent, of the 200 million online population in America accesses the Internet via broadband.

2004 The smart phone overtakes the PDA as the mobile device of choice.

2004 Major retailers begin requiring suppliers to include radio frequency identification (RFID) tags or microchips with antennas, which can be as small as one-third of a millimeter across, in the goods they sell.

2004 Facebook, an online social network originally available only to college students, is founded. Facebook eventually opens registration to all people and immediately grows to more than 110 million users with more than 10 billion photos, 30 million of which are uploaded daily.

2004

2004 Linux, the open source operating system, makes major inroads into the server market as a viable alternative to Microsoft Windows Server 2003, Sun's Solaris, and the UNIX operating systems.

2004 Sony unveils its PlayStation Portable (PSP). This handheld game console is the first to use optical discs.

2004 Mozilla releases its first version of the Firefox Web browser. Firefox provides innovative features that enhance the Web browsing experience for users, including tabbed browsing and a Search box. Firefox quickly gains popularity and takes market share away from Microsoft's Internet Explorer.

2004 Apple Computer introduces the sleek iMac G5. The new computer's display device contains the system unit.

Video iPod

2005 Apple releases the latest version of its popular pocket-sized iPod portable media player. First it played songs, then photos, then podcasts, and now, in addition, up to 150 hours of music videos and television shows on a 2.5" color display.

2005 YouTube, an online community for video sharing, is founded. YouTube includes content such as home videos, movie previews, and clips from television shows. In November 2006, Google acquires YouTube.

2005 Microsoft introduces Visual Studio 2005. The product includes Visual Basic, Visual C#, Visual J#, Visual C++, and SQL Server.

Spyware
Pharming
Spam Phishing
Spim Spit

2005 Spam, spyware, phishing, pharming, spim, and spit take center stage, along with viruses, as major nuisances to the 801 million computer users worldwide.

2005

2005 Microsoft unveils Windows XP Media Center Edition 2005. This operating system focuses on delivering media content such as music, digital photos, movies, and television.

2005 Microsoft releases the Xbox 360, its latest game console. Features include the capability to play music, display photos, and network with computers and other Xbox gamers.

2005 Blogging and podcasting become mainstream methods for distributing information via the Web.

Blogging
Podcasting

2006 Sony launches its PlayStation 3. New features include a Blu-ray Disc player, high-definition capabilities, and always-on online connectivity.

2006 Microsoft and Mozilla release new versions of their respective Web browsers. Microsoft's Internet Explorer 7 and Mozilla's Firefox 2 offer easier browsing through the use of tabs and allow search capabilities directly from the toolbar.

2006 Web 2.0, a term coined in 2004, becomes a household term with the increase in popularity of online social networks, wikis, and Web applications.

2006 Text, picture, and video messaging continue to increase as popular communications methods. In addition to people sending informal messages to each other, businesses and other institutions use messaging to allow people to vote in polls, receive targeted advertisements, and view news updates.

2006 Nintendo Wii is introduced and immediately becomes a leader in game consoles. The Wii is being used in revolutionary ways, such as training surgeons.

2006 Intel introduces its Core 2 Duo processor family. Boasting record-breaking performance while using less power, the family consists of five desktop computer processors and five mobile computer processors. The desktop processor includes 291 million transistors, yet uses 40 percent less power than the Pentium processor.

2006

2006 IBM produces the fastest supercomputer, Blue Gene/L. It can perform approximately 28 trillion calculations in the time it takes you to blink your eye, or about one-tenth of a second.

2006 Nintendo releases the Nintendo DS Lite, a handheld game console with new features such as dual screens and improved graphics and sound.

2006 Apple begins selling Macintosh computers with Intel microprocessors.

2007 Intel introduces Core 2 Quad, a four-core processor made for dual-processor servers and desktop computers. The larger number of cores allows for more energy-efficient performance and optimizes battery performance in notebook computers.

2007 Video blogs, or vlogs, grow in popularity along with YouTube. Vlogs allow users to video their message instead of entering text via a regular blog. The growth in the popularity of vlogs is attributed to several factors, including the use of video portable media players. Podcasting also increases in popularity for the same reasons. A podcast is distinguished from other digital audio formats by its capability to be downloaded automatically.

2007 Apple introduces the iPhone and sells 270,000 phones in the first 2 days. iPhone uses iTouch technology that allows you to make a call simply by tapping a name or number in your address book. In addition, it stores and plays music like an iPod. Also, Apple sells its one billionth song on iTunes.

2007 VoIP (Voice over Internet Protocol) providers expand usage to include Wi-Fi phones. The phones enable high-quality service through a Wireless-G network and high-speed Internet connection.

2007 Apple releases its Mac OS X version 10.5 "Leopard" operating system, available in a desktop version and server version. The system includes a significantly revised desktop, with a semitransparent menu bar and an updated search tool that incorporates the same visual navigation interface as iTunes.

2007

2007 Wi-Fi hotspots are popular in a variety of locations. People bring their computers to coffeehouses, fast food restaurants, or bookstores to access the Internet wirelessly, either free or for a small fee.

2007 Blu-ray Discs increase in popularity, overcoming and replacing HD DVD in less than one year. A Blu-ray Disc can store approximately 9 hours of high-definition (HD) video on a 50 GB disc or approximately 23 hours of standard-definition (SD) video.

2007 Half of the world's population uses cell phones. More and more people are using a cell phone in lieu of a landline in their home.

2007 Microsoft releases Office 2007. New features include the most significant update to the user interface in more than a decade, including the introduction of the Ribbon, which replaces the toolbars in most of the programs, and the capability to save documents in XML and PDF formats.

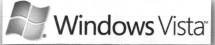

2007 Microsoft ships the latest version of its widely used operating system, Windows Vista. Vista offers the Basic interface and the Aero interface, which offers several graphical features, including transparent windows. Internet Explorer 7 is included with Windows Vista.

2008 Microsoft introduces Windows Server 2008, the successor to Windows Server 2003.

2008 Bill Gates retires from Microsoft. He continues as chairman and advisor on key development projects.

2008 Dell offers a hybrid computer. Smaller than a desktop computer but larger than a notebook computer, these hybrid computers contain features comparable to their larger counterparts and can work more easily in a home entertainment environment.

2008 Netflix, an online movie rental company, and TiVo, a company manufacturing digital video recorders (DVRs), make Netflix movies and television episodes available on TiVo (DVRs).

2008

2008 WiMAX goes live! The advantage of this technology is the capability to access video, music, voice, and video calls wherever and whenever desired. Average download speeds are between 2 Mbps and 4 Mbps. By year's end, Sprint has approximately 100 million users on its network.

2008 Smart phones become smarter. Smart phones introduced this year include enhanced features such as touch screens with multi-touch technology, mobile TV, tactile feedback, improved graphics, GPS receivers, and better cameras.

2008 Computer manufacturers begin to offer solid state drives (SSDs) instead of hard disks, mostly in notebook computers. Although SSDs have a lower storage capacity, are more expensive, and slightly more susceptible to failure, they are significantly faster.

2008 Google releases its new Web browser. Google Chrome uses an entirely unique interface and offers other features such as dynamic tabs, crash control, and application shortcuts.

2008 Mozilla releases Firefox 3, the latest version of its Web browser. Firefox 3 offers greater security, a more user-friendly interface, and other improvements to enhance the Web browsing experience.

Firefox 3

2009 Web applications continue to increase in popularity. Web applications make it easier to perform tasks such as word processing, photo editing, and tax preparation without installing software on your computer.

2009 In June 2009, federal law requires that all full-power television stations broadcast only in digital format. Analog television owners are required to purchase a converter box to view over-the-air digital programming.

2010 Kinect for Xbox 360 changes the way people play video games. Game players now can interact with the game with a series of sensors, as well as a camera, tracking their movements in 3-D.

2009 Microsoft releases Internet Explorer 8, also known as IE8. IE8 offers new features such as InPrivate Browsing, Accelerators, and support for WebSlices.

2009 Microsoft releases the newest version of its Windows operating system, Windows 7. This version provides greater stability and security; a more flexible, user-friendly interface; and requires fewer computing resources to operate.

2009

2010

2009 Intel releases the Core i5 and Core i7 line of processors. These processors offer increased performance for some of the more demanding tasks. Intel also enhances its Core processor family by releasing multi-core processors, designed to increase the number of instructions that can be processed at a given time.

2010 AMD develops a 12-core processor, which contains two 6-core processors, each on an individual chip. Power consumption is similar to that of a 6-core processor but offers reduced clock speed.

2009 Computers and mobile devices promote fitness by offering games and programs to help users exercise and track their progress. These games and programs also are used to assist with physical rehabilitation.

2010 Microsoft releases Office 2010, the latest version of its Office suite. This version is available in multiple editions and continues to help people work more efficiently. Office Web apps, available free to Windows Live users, offer online access to scaled-down versions of Word, PowerPoint, Excel, and OneNote.

2009 Social networking revolutionizes communications. Schools, radio stations, and other organizations develop pages on popular online social networks, such as Facebook, creating closer connections with their stakeholders.

2010 Adobe releases the latest version of its design suite, Adobe CS5. This new suite has many performance and interface enhancements over previous versions and takes advantage of new technologies such as multi-touch.

2011 Individuals and enterprises increase their focus on green computing. Computer manufacturers not only sell more energy-efficient hardware, they also provide easy ways in which customers can recycle their old computers and devices.

2010 Apple releases the iPad, a revolutionary mobile device with a 9.7-inch multi-touch screen. The iPad boasts up to 10 hours of battery life, connects wirelessly to the Internet, and is capable of running thousands of apps.

2010 Hard disk capacity continues to increase at an exponential rate, with the largest hard disks storing more than 2.5 TB of data and information. Solid state storage also is becoming more popular, with storage capacities increasing and prices decreasing.

2011 Netbooks prove to be an attractive alternative to traditional notebook computers. Netbooks are smaller and lighter than traditional notebook computers, while providing nearly the same functionality.

2011

2010

2011 E-books and e-book readers explode in popularity. Many novels, textbooks, and other publications now are available digitally and can be read on an e-book reader, computer, or mobile device.

2011 Decreases in storage costs and increases in Internet connection speeds persuade more users to use cloud storage for their data. Cloud storage also provides users with the convenience of accessing their files from almost anywhere.

2011 A new generation of Web browsers is released to support HTML5, enabling Web pages to contain more vivid, dynamic content.

2011 More than 200 types of mobile devices are using Google Android, an operating system originally designed for mobile devices.

Chapter Two

The Internet and World Wide Web

Objectives

After completing this chapter, you will be able to:

1 Identify and briefly describe various broadband Internet connections

2 Describe the types of Internet access providers: Internet service providers, online service providers, and wireless Internet service providers

3 Explain the purpose of a Web browser and identify the components of a Web address

4 Describe how to use a search engine to search for information on the Web

5 Describe the types of Web sites: portal, news, informational, business/marketing, blog, wiki, online social network, educational, entertainment, advocacy, Web application, content aggregator, and personal

6 Recognize how Web pages use graphics, animation, audio, video, virtual reality, and plug-ins

7 Identify the steps required for Web publishing

8 Explain how e-mail, mailing lists, instant messaging, chat rooms, VoIP, FTP, and newsgroups and message boards work

9 Identify the rules of netiquette

The Internet

One of the major reasons business, home, and other users purchase computers is for Internet access. The **Internet**, also called the **Net**, is a worldwide collection of networks that links millions of businesses, government agencies, educational institutions, and individuals. The Internet is a widely used research tool, providing society with access to global information and instant communications.

Today, more than one billion home and business users around the world access a variety of services on the Internet, some of which are shown in Figure 2-1. The World Wide Web, or simply the Web, and e-mail are two of the more widely used Internet services. Other services include chat rooms, instant messaging, and VoIP (Voice over Internet Protocol).

The Internet has its roots in a networking project started by an agency of the U.S. Department of Defense. The goal was to build a network that (1) allowed scientists at different locations to share information and work together on military and scientific projects and (2) could function even if part of the network were disabled or destroyed by a disaster such as a nuclear attack. That network, called ARPANET, became functional in September 1969, linking scientific and academic researchers across the United States.

The original ARPANET consisted of four main computers, one each located at the University of California at Los Angeles, the University of California at Santa Barbara, the Stanford Research Institute, and the University of Utah. Each of these computers served as a host on the network. A host or server is any computer that provides services and connections to other computers on a network. By 1984, ARPANET had more than 1,000 individual computers linked as hosts. Today, more than 550 million hosts connect to this network, which is known now as the Internet.

Figure 2-1   People around the world use a variety of Internet services in daily activities. Internet services allow home and business users to access the Web for activities such as conducting research, reading blogs, or sharing videos; to send e-mail messages; or to converse with others using chat rooms, instant messaging, or VoIP.

The Internet consists of many local, regional, national, and international networks. Both public and private organizations own networks on the Internet. These networks, along with telephone companies, cable and satellite companies, and the government, all contribute toward the internal structure of the Internet.

Each organization on the Internet is responsible only for maintaining its own network. No single person, company, institution, or government agency controls or owns the Internet. The World Wide Web Consortium (W3C), however, oversees research and sets standards and guidelines for many areas of the Internet. More than 350 organizations from around the world are members of the W3C.

Connecting to the Internet

Many home and small business users connect to the Internet via high-speed **broadband** Internet service. With broadband Internet service, your computer or mobile device usually is connected to the Internet the entire time it is powered on. Examples of broadband Internet service include the following:

- **Cable Internet service** provides high-speed Internet access through the cable television network via a cable modem.
- **DSL** (digital subscriber line) provides high-speed Internet connections using regular telephone lines.
- **Fiber to the Premises (FTTP)** uses fiber-optic cable to provide high-speed Internet access to home and business users.
- **Fixed wireless** provides high-speed Internet connections using a dish-shaped antenna on your house or business to communicate with a tower location via radio signals.
- A **Wi-Fi** (wireless fidelity) network uses radio signals to provide high-speed Internet connections to wireless computers and devices.

- A **cellular radio network** offers high-speed Internet connections to devices with built-in compatible technology or computers with wireless modems.
- **Satellite Internet service** provides high-speed Internet connections via satellite to a satellite dish that communicates with a satellite modem.

Employees and students typically connect their computers to the Internet through a business or school network. The business or school network connects to a high-speed broadband Internet service.

Mobile users access the Internet using a variety of services. Most hotels and airports provide wired or wireless Internet connections. Wireless Internet services such as Wi-Fi networks, allow mobile users to connect easily to the Internet with notebook computers, smart phones, and other mobile devices while away from a telephone, cable, or other wired connection. Many public locations, such as airports, hotels, schools, and coffee shops, are **hot spots** that provide Wi-Fi Internet connections to users with mobile computers or devices.

Many home users set up a Wi-Fi network, which sends signals to a communications device that is connected to a high-speed Internet service such as cable or DSL. Instead of using broadband Internet service, however, some home users connect to the Internet via dial-up access, which is a slower-speed technology. **Dial-up access** takes place when the modem in your computer connects to the Internet via a standard telephone line that transmits data and information using an analog (continuous wave pattern) signal. Users may opt for dial-up access because of its lower price or because broadband access is not available in their area.

? FAQ 2-1

How popular is broadband?

According to a study performed by Pew Internet & American Life Project, 63 percent of American adults have broadband Internet connections at home. Adoption of broadband connections increases during good economic times, while some may hesitate to make the switch during an economic downturn. It is believed that once the price of a broadband connection decreases, and broadband is available in more rural areas, its popularity will increase further.

 For more information, visit the Computer Concepts CourseMate Web site at www.cengagebrain.com, navigate to the Chapter 2 FAQ resource for this book, and then click Broadband.

Access Providers

An **access provider** is a business that provides individuals and organizations access to the Internet free or for a fee. For example, some Wi-Fi networks provide free access while others charge a per use fee. Other access providers often charge a fixed amount for an Internet connection, usually about $5 to $24 per month for dial-up access and $13 to $120 for higher-speed access. Many Internet access providers offer services such as news, weather, financial data, games, travel guides, e-mail, photo communities, and online storage to hold digital photos and other files. (A file is a named unit of storage.)

Access providers are categorized as ISPs, online service providers, and wireless Internet service providers. An **ISP (Internet service provider)** is a regional or national access provider. A regional ISP usually provides Internet access to a specific geographic area. A national ISP is a business that provides Internet access in cities and towns nationwide. National ISPs usually offer more services and have a larger technical support staff than regional ISPs. Examples of national ISPs are AT&T and EarthLink.

In addition to providing Internet access, an **online service provider (OSP)** also has many members-only features such as instant messaging or their own customized version of a Web browser. The two more popular OSPs are AOL (America Online) and MSN (Microsoft Network). AOL also provides free access to its services to any user with a high-speed Internet connection.

A **wireless Internet service provider**, sometimes called a wireless data provider, is a company that provides wireless Internet access to computers and mobile devices, such as smart phones and portable media players with built-in wireless capability (such as Wi-Fi) or to computers using wireless modems or wireless access devices. Wireless modems usually are in the form of a USB flash drive or a card that inserts in a slot in a computer or mobile device. Examples of wireless Internet service providers include AT&T, Boingo Wireless, Sprint Broadband Direct, T-Mobile, and Verizon Wireless.

Wireless Modems

For more information, visit the Computer Concepts CourseMate Web site at www.cengagebrain.com, navigate to the Chapter 2 Web Link resource for this book, and then click Wireless Modems.

How Data and Information Travel the Internet

Computers connected to the Internet work together to transfer data and information around the world using various wired and wireless transmission media. Several main transmission media carry the heaviest amount of traffic on the Internet. These major carriers of network traffic are known collectively as the **Internet backbone.**

In the United States, the transmission media that make up the Internet backbone exchange data and information at several different major cities across the country. That is, they transfer data and information from one network to another until reaching the final destination (Figure 2-2).

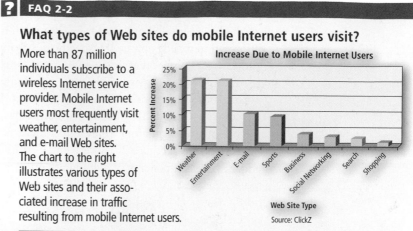

❓ FAQ 2-2

What types of Web sites do mobile Internet users visit?

More than 87 million individuals subscribe to a wireless Internet service provider. Mobile Internet users most frequently visit weather, entertainment, and e-mail Web sites. The chart to the right illustrates various types of Web sites and their associated increase in traffic resulting from mobile Internet users.

Increase Due to Mobile Internet Users

Web Site Type

Source: ClickZ

🖥 For more information, visit the Computer Concepts CourseMate Web site at www.cengagebrain.com, navigate to the Chapter 2 FAQ resource for this book, and then click Mobile Internet.

How a Home User's Data and Information Might Travel the Internet Using a Cable Modem Connection

Step 1
You initiate an action to request data or information from the Internet. For example, you request to display a Web page on your computer screen.

Step 2
A cable modem transfers the computer's digital signals to the cable television line in your house.

Step 3
Your request (digital signals) travels through cable television lines to a central cable system, which is shared by up to 500 homes in a neighborhood.

Step 4
The central cable system sends your request over high-speed fiber-optic lines to the cable operator, who often also is the ISP.

Step 5
The ISP routes your request through the Internet backbone to the destination server (in this example, the server that contains the requested Web site).

Step 6
The server retrieves the requested Web page and sends it back through the Internet backbone to your computer.

Figure 2-2 This figure shows how a home user's data and information might travel the Internet using a cable modem connection.

Internet Addresses

The Internet relies on an addressing system much like the postal service to send data and information to a computer at a specific destination. An **IP address**, short for Internet Protocol address, is a number that uniquely identifies each computer or device connected to the Internet. The IP address usually consists of four groups of numbers, each separated by a period. In general, the first portion of each IP address identifies the network and the last portion identifies the specific computer.

These all-numeric IP addresses are difficult to remember and use. Thus, the Internet supports the use of a text name that represents one or more IP addresses. A **domain name** is the text version of an IP address. Figure 2-3 shows an IP address and its associated domain name. As with an IP address, the components of a domain name are separated by periods.

Figure 2-3   The IP address and domain name for the Google Web site.

The text in the domain name up to the first period identifies the type of Internet server. In Figure 2-3, for example, the www indicates a Web server. The Internet server portion of a domain name often is not required.

Every domain name contains a **top-level domain** (**TLD**), which is the last section of the domain name. A generic TLD (gTLD), such as the com in Figure 2-3, identifies the type of organization associated with the domain. Figure 2-4 lists some gTLDs. For international Web sites outside the United States, the domain name also includes a country code TLD (ccTLD), which is a two-letter country code, such as au for Australia or fr for France.

When you specify a domain name, a server translates the domain name to its associated IP address so that data and information can be routed to the correct computer. This server is an Internet server that usually is associated with an Internet access provider.

Examples of Generic Top-Level Domains

Generic TLD	Intended Purpose	Generic TLD	Intended Purpose
aero	Aviation community members	mil	Military organizations
biz	Businesses of all sizes	mobi	Delivery and management of mobile Internet services
cat	Catalan cultural community	museum	Accredited museums
com	Commercial organizations, businesses, and companies	name	Individuals or families
coop	Business cooperatives such as credit unions and rural electric co-ops	net	Network providers or commercial companies
edu	Educational institutions	org	Nonprofit organizations
gov	Government agencies	pro	Certified professionals such as doctors, lawyers, and accountants
info	Business organizations or individuals providing general information	tel	Internet communications
jobs	Employment or human resource businesses	travel	Travel industry

Figure 2-4   In addition to the generic TLDs listed in this table, proposals for newer TLDs continually are evaluated.

Instructions: Find the true statement below. Then, rewrite the remaining false statements so that they are true.

1. An access provider is a business that provides individuals and organizations access to the Internet free or for a fee.
2. A wireless Internet service provider is a number that uniquely identifies each computer or device connected to the Internet.
3. An IP address, such as www.google.com, is the text version of a domain name.
4. Satellite Internet service provides high-speed Internet access through the cable television network via a cable modem.

🖥 **Quiz Yourself Online:** To further check your knowledge of pages 56 through 60, visit the Computer Concepts CourseMate Web site at www.cengagebrain.com, navigate to the Chapter 2 Quiz Yourself resource for this book, and then click Objectives 1 – 2.

The World Wide Web

The **World Wide Web** (**WWW**), or **Web**, a widely used service on the Internet, consists of a worldwide collection of electronic documents. Each electronic document on the Web, called a **Web page**, can contain text, graphics, animation, audio, and video. Additionally, Web pages usually have built-in connections to other documents. A **Web site** is a collection of related Web pages and associated items, such as documents and pictures, stored on a Web server. A **Web server** is a computer that delivers requested Web pages to your computer. Some industry experts use the term **Web 2.0** to refer to Web sites that provide a means for users to share personal information (such as social networking Web sites), allow users to modify Web site content (such as wikis, which are discussed later in this chapter), and have application software built into the site for visitors to use (such as e-mail and word processing programs). Read Looking Ahead 2-1 for a look at Web 3.0.

Browsing the Web

A **Web browser**, or **browser**, is application software that allows users to access and view Web pages or access Web 2.0 programs. To browse the Web, you need a computer or mobile device that is connected to the Internet and that has a Web browser. The more widely used Web browsers for personal computers are Internet Explorer, Firefox, Opera, Safari, and Google Chrome.

Web 3.0 to Reinvent the Virtual World

When Tim Berners-Lee developed the World Wide Web 20 years ago, he envisioned a service that allowed users to exchange information seamlessly. The Web has evolved through versions 1.0 and 2.0, and work is underway to develop Web 3.0, also known as the Semantic Web.

This next generation of the Web is predicted to perform practically any imaginable task, according to some researchers. For example, your computer will be able to scan a Web page much as you do to look for specific useful information. If you need the location of the nearest eye doctor and the time when your brother's flight from Chicago actually will land, Web 3.0 will provide those facts and then search your calendar to see if you can fit the doctor's appointment in your schedule in time to pick up your brother at the airport. In essence, the Web will become one huge searchable database, and automated agents of every type will retrieve the data we need to live productive lives.

🖥 For more information, visit the Computer Concepts CourseMate Web site at www.cengagebrain.com, navigate to the Chapter 2 Looking Ahead resource for this book, and then click Web 3.0.

Which Web browser currently has the highest market share?

Windows Internet Explorer (IE) currently is the most popular browser, with approximately 68 percent of the market share. The chart to the right illustrates the market share of the more popular Web browsers.

Market Share

4%
6%
22%
68%

☐ Internet Explorer ☐ Firefox ■ Safari ☐ Other

Source: Market Share by Net Applications

🖥 For more information, visit the Computer Concepts CourseMate Web site at www.cengagebrain.com, navigate to the Chapter 2 FAQ resource for this book, and then click Browser Market Share.

With an Internet connection established, you start a Web browser. The browser retrieves and displays a starting Web page, sometimes called the browser's home page. Figure 2-5 shows how a Web browser displays a home page.

Another use of the term, **home page**, refers to the first page that a Web site displays. Similar to a book cover or a table of contents for a Web site, the home page provides information about the Web site's purpose and content. Often it provides connections to other documents, Web pages, or Web sites, which can be downloaded to a computer or mobile device. **Downloading** is the process of a computer or device receiving information, such as a Web page, from a server on the Internet.

How a Web Browser Displays a Home Page

Step 1
Start the Web browser software by clicking the Web browser icon on the taskbar or typing the Web browser name in the search box on the Start menu.

Internet Explorer Web browser name in search results on Start menu

search box

Internet Explorer Web browser icon on taskbar

Step 2
Behind the scenes, the Web browser looks up its home page setting. For illustration purposes only, the screen below shows the home page setting is msn.com.

msn.com

msn.com

Step 3
The Web browser communicates with a server maintained by your Internet access provider. The server translates the domain name of the home page to an IP address and then sends the IP address to your computer.

207.68.172.234

Step 4
The Web browser uses the IP address to contact the Web server associated with the home page and then requests the home page from the server. The Web server sends the home page to the Web browser, which formats the page for display on your screen.

Figure 2-5 This figure shows how a Web browser displays a home page.

Web Addresses

A Web page has a unique address, which is called a **URL** (Uniform Resource Locator) or **Web address**. For example, the home page for the United States National Park Service Web site has a Web address of http://www.nps.gov. A Web browser retrieves a Web page using its Web address.

If you know the Web address of a Web page, you can type it in the Address bar at the top of the browser window. If you type http://www.nps.gov/grsm/planyourvisit/wildlifeviewing.htm as the Web address in the Address bar and then press the ENTER key, the browser downloads and displays the Web page shown in Figure 2-6.

A Web address consists of a protocol, domain name, and sometimes the path to a specific Web page or location on a Web page. Many Web page addresses begin with http://. The http, which stands for Hypertext Transfer Protocol, is a set of rules that defines how pages transfer on the Internet. To help minimize errors, many browsers and Web sites do not require you enter the http:// and www portions of the Web address.

When you enter the Web address, http://www.nps.gov/grsm/planyourvisit/wildlifeviewing.htm in the Web browser, it sends a request to the Web server that contains the nps.com Web site. The server then retrieves the Web page that is named wildlifeviewing.htm in the grsm/planyourvisit path and delivers it to your browser, which then displays the Web page on the screen.

To save time, many users create bookmarks for their frequently visited Web pages. A **bookmark**, or **favorite**, is a saved Web address that you access by clicking the bookmark name in a list. That is, instead of entering a Web address to display a Web page, you can click a previously saved bookmark.

For information about useful Web sites and their associated Web addresses, read the Making Use of the Web feature that follows this chapter.

Figure 2-6   After entering http://www.nps.gov/grsm/planyourvisit/wildlifeviewing.htm as the Web address in the Address bar, this Web page at the United States National Park Service Web site is displayed.

Navigating Web Pages

Most Web pages contain links. A **link**, short for **hyperlink**, is a built-in connection to another related Web page or part of a Web page. Links allow you to obtain information in a nonlinear way. That is, instead of accessing topics in a specified order, you move directly to a topic of interest.

Branching from one related topic to another in a nonlinear fashion is what makes links so powerful. Some people use the phrase, **surfing the Web**, to refer to the activity of using links to explore the Web.

A link can be text or an image. Text links may be underlined and/or displayed in a color different from other text on the Web page. Pointing to, or positioning the pointer on, a link on the screen typically changes the shape of the pointer to a small hand with a pointing index finger. Pointing to a link also sometimes causes the link to change in appearance or play a sound. The Web page shown in Figure 2-7 contains a variety of link types, with the pointer on one of the links.

Each link on a Web page corresponds to a Web address or document. To activate a link, you **click** it, that is, point to the link and then press the left mouse button. Clicking a link causes the Web page or document associated with the link to be displayed on the screen. The linked object might be on the same Web page, a different Web page at the same Web site, or a separate Web page at a different Web site in another city or country.

Most current Web browsers support **tabbed browsing**, where the top of the browser displays a tab (similar to a file folder tab) for each Web page you open. To move from one open Web page to another, you click the tab in the Web browser.

Because some Web sites attempt to track your browsing habits or gather personal information, some current Web browsers include a feature that allows you to disable and/or more tightly control the dissemination of your browsing habits and personal information. Read Ethics & Issues 2-1 for a related discussion.

Tabbed Browsing

For more information, visit the Computer Concepts CourseMate Web site at www.cengagebrain.com, navigate to the Chapter 2 Web Link resource for this book, and then click Tabbed Browsing.

Figure 2-7   This browser window has several open tabs. The current tab shows a Web page that has various types of links.

Should the Government Allow You to Sign Up for a Do-Not-Track List?

When you visit a Web site that includes an advertisement, someone probably is recording the fact that you visited that Web site and viewed the advertisement with your browser. Over time, companies that specialize in tracking who views which online advertisements can amass an enormous amount of information about your online Web surfing habits. Through tracking the Web sites a user visits, the products they buy, and the articles they read, a company may attempt to profile the visitor's beliefs, associations, and habits. Although a user may think he or she is anonymous while navigating the Web, the company can attempt through various means to link the user's true identity with the user's online profile. The company can sell online profiles, with or without the user's true identity, to other advertisers or organizations. Some privacy groups have called for the government to allow consumers to sign up for a do-not-track list modeled after the popular do-not-call list.

Should organizations be allowed to track your Web surfing habits? Why or why not? Should organizations be allowed to associate your real identity with your online identity and profit from the information? Should the government force companies to give you the option of not being tracked? Why or why not? What are the benefits and dangers of online tracking?

Searching the Web

The Web is a worldwide resource of information. A primary reason that people use the Web is to search for specific information, including text, pictures, music, and video. The first step in successful searching is to identify the main idea or concept in the topic about which you are seeking information. Determine any synonyms, alternate spellings, or variant word forms for the topic. Then, use a search tool to locate the information.

Two types of search tools are search engines and subject directories. A **search engine** is a program that finds Web sites, Web pages, images, videos, news, maps, and other information related to a specific topic. A **subject directory** classifies Web pages in an organized set of categories or groups, such as sports or shopping, and related subcategories.

Some Web sites offer the functionality of both a search engine and a subject directory. Google and Yahoo!, for example, are widely used search engines that also provide a subject directory. To use Google or Yahoo!, you enter the Web address (google.com or yahoo.com) in the Address bar in a browser window. The table in Figure 2-8 lists the Web addresses of several popular general-purpose search engines and subject directories.

Ethics & Issues

For the complete text of the Ethics & Issues boxes found in this chapter, visit the Computer Concepts CourseMate Web site at www.cengagebrain.com and then navigate to the Chapter 2 Ethics & Issues resource for this book.

Widely Used Search Tools

Search Tool	Web Address	Search Engine	Subject Directory
A9	a9.com	X	
AlltheWeb	alltheweb.com	X	
AltaVista	altavista.com	X	
AOL Search	search.aol.com	X	
Ask	ask.com	X	
Bing	bing.com	X	
Cuil (pronounced cool)	cuil.com	X	
Dogpile	dogpile.com	X	
Excite	excite.com	X	X
Gigablast	gigablast.com	X	X
Google	google.com	X	X
Lycos	lycos.com	X	
MSN	msn.com	X	X
Open Directory Project	dmoz.org	X	X
WebCrawler	webcrawler.com	X	
Yahoo!	yahoo.com	X	X

Figure 2-8
Popular search engines and subject directories.

Search Engines A search engine is helpful in locating information for which you do not know an exact Web address or are not seeking a particular Web site. Some search engines look through Web pages for all types of information. Others can restrict their searches to a specific type of information, such as images, videos, audio, news, maps, people or businesses, and blogs.

Search engines require that you enter a word or phrase, called **search text**, that describes the item you want to find. Your search text can be broad, such as spring break destinations, or more specific, such as Walt Disney World. Figure 2-9 shows one way to use the Google search engine to search for the phrase, Aspen Colorado ski resorts. The results shown in Step 3 include nearly 150,000 links to Web pages, called hits, that reference Aspen Colorado ski resorts. Each hit in the list has a link that, when clicked, displays an associated Web site or Web page. Most search engines sequence the hits based on how close the words in the search text are to one another in the titles and descriptions of the hits. Thus, the first few links probably contain more relevant information.

How to Use a Search Engine

Step 1
Type the search engine's Web address (in this case, google.com) in the Address bar in the Web browser.

Step 2
Press the ENTER key. When the Google home page is displayed, type **Aspen Colorado ski resorts** as the search text and then point to the Google Search button.

Step 4
Click the Aspen Snowmass link to display a Web page with a description and links to skiing in Aspen.

Step 3
Click the Google Search button. When the results of the search are displayed, scroll through the links and read the descriptions. Point the Aspen Snowmass link.

Figure 2-9 This figure shows how to use a search engine.

Some Web browsers contain an Instant Search box that, when filled in, uses a predefined or default search engine to perform searches. Using the Instant Search box eliminates the steps of displaying the search engine's Web page prior to entering the search text.

If you enter a phrase with spaces between the words in the search text, most search engines display results (hits) that include all of the words. The following list identifies techniques you can use to improve your searches. To learn more about searching for information, complete the Learn How To 2 activity on pages 88 and 89.

- Use specific nouns.
- Put the most important terms first in the search text.
- Use the asterisk (*) to substitute characters in words. For example, retriev* displays hits containing retrieves, retrieval, retriever, and any other variation.
- Use quotation marks to create phrases so that the search engine finds an exact sequence of words.
- List all possible spellings, for example, email, e-mail.
- Before using a search engine, read its Help information.
- If the search is unsuccessful with one search engine, try another.

Subject Directories   A subject directory provides categorized lists of links arranged by subject (Figure 2-10). Using this search tool, you locate a particular topic by clicking links through different levels, moving from the general to the specific.

Types of Web Sites

Thirteen types of Web sites are portal, news, informational, business/marketing, blog, wiki, online social network, educational, entertainment, advocacy, Web application, content aggregator, and personal. Many Web sites fall into more than one of these categories.

Portal   A **portal** is a Web site that offers a variety of Internet services from a single, convenient location (Figure 2-11a). Most portals offer these free services: search engine; news; sports and weather; Web publishing; reference tools such as yellow pages, stock quotes, and maps; shopping; and e-mail communications services. Popular portals include AltaVista, AOL, Excite, GO.com, iGoogle, Lycos, MSN, and Yahoo!.

News   A news Web site contains newsworthy material including stories and articles relating to current events, life, money, sports, and the weather (Figure 2-11b). Newspapers and television and radio stations are some of the media that maintain news Web sites.

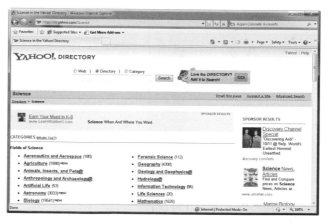

Figure 2-10
A subject directory provides categorized lists of links.

Figure 2-11a
(portal)

Figure 2-11b
(news)

Figure 2-11   Types of Web sites. *(continued on next page)*

Figure 2-11c (informational)

Figure 2-11d (business/marketing)

Figure 2-11e (blog)

Figure 2-11f (wiki)

Wiki

For more information, visit the Computer Concepts CourseMate Web site at www.cengagebrain.com, navigate to the Chapter 2 Web Link resource for this book, and then click Wiki.

Figure 2-11 Types of Web sites. *(continued)*

Informational An informational Web site contains factual information (Figure 2-11c). Many United States government agencies have informational Web sites providing information such as census data, tax codes, and the congressional budget. Other organizations provide information such as public transportation schedules and published research findings.

Business/Marketing A business/marketing Web site contains content that promotes or sells products or services (Figure 2-11d). Nearly every enterprise has a business/marketing Web site. Many companies also allow you to purchase their products or services online.

Blog A **blog**, short for Weblog, is an informal Web site consisting of time-stamped articles, or posts, in a diary or journal format, usually listed in reverse chronological order (Figure 2-11e). A blog that contains video clips is called a **video blog** or **vlog**. A **microblog** allows users to publish short messages, usually between 100 and 200 characters, for others to read. Twitter is a popular microblog. The term **blogosphere** refers to the worldwide collection of blogs, and the **vlogosphere** refers to all vlogs worldwide. Blogs reflect the interests, opinions, and personalities of the author and sometimes site visitors. Blogs have become an important means of worldwide communications.

Wiki A **wiki** is a collaborative Web site that allows users to create, add to, modify, or delete the Web site content via their Web browser. Most wikis are open to modification by the general public. Wikis usually collect recent edits on a Web page so that someone can review them for accuracy. The difference between a wiki and a blog is that users cannot modify original posts made by the blogger. A popular wiki is Wikipedia, a free Web encyclopedia (Figure 2-11f). Read Ethics & Issues 2-2 for a related discussion.

ETHICS & ISSUES 2-2

Should You Trust a Wiki for Academic Research?

As wikis have grown in number, size, and popularity, some educators and librarians have shunned the sites as valid sources of research. While many wikis are tightly controlled with a limited number of contributors and expert editors, these usually focus on narrowly-defined, specialized topics. Most large wikis, such as Wikipedia, often involve thousands of editors, many of whom remain anonymous. Recently, television station reporters purposely vandalized entries on Wikipedia for John Lennon and Elvis Presley in an attempt

either to discredit Wikipedia or to test how quickly corrections are made. Editors quickly corrected the information. In other situations, rival political factions falsified or embellished wiki entries in an attempt to give their candidate an advantage. Some wiki supporters argue that most wikis provide adequate controls to correct false or misleading content quickly and to punish those who submit it. One popular wiki now requires an experienced editor to verify changes made to certain types of articles. Some propose that wikis should be used

as a starting point for researching a fact, but that the fact should be verified using traditional sources.

Should wikis be allowed as valid sources for academic research? Why or why not? Would you submit a paper to your instructor that cites a wiki as a source? An encyclopedia? Why or why not? What policies could wikis enforce that could garner more confidence from the public? If a wiki provided verification of the credentials of the author, would you trust the wiki more? Why or why not?

Online Social Networks   An **online social network**, also called a **social networking Web site**, is a Web site that encourages members in its online community to share their interests, ideas, stories, photos, music, and videos with other registered users (Figure 2-11g). Popular social networking Web sites include MySpace and Facebook, with Facebook alone boasting more than 300 million active users. A **media sharing Web site** is a specific type of online social network that enables members to share media such as photos, music, and videos. Flickr, Fotki, and Webshots are popular photo sharing communities; PixelFish and YouTube are popular video sharing communities.

Educational   An educational Web site offers exciting, challenging avenues for formal and informal teaching and learning (Figure 2-11h). For a more structured learning experience, companies provide online training to employees; and colleges offer online classes and degrees. Instructors often use the Web to enhance classroom teaching by publishing course materials, grades, and other pertinent class information.

Entertainment   An entertainment Web site offers an interactive and engaging environment (Figure 2-11i). Popular entertainment Web sites offer music, videos, sports, games, ongoing Web episodes, sweepstakes, chat rooms, and more.

Advocacy   An advocacy Web site contains content that describes a cause, opinion, or idea (Figure 2-11j). These Web sites usually present views of a particular group or association.

Web Application   A **Web application**, or **Web app**, is a Web site that allows users to access and interact with software through a Web browser on any computer or device that is connected to the Internet. Some Web applications provide free access to their software (Figure 2-11k). Others offer part of their software free and charge for access to more comprehensive features or when a particular action is requested. Examples of Web applications include Google Docs (word processing, spreadsheets, presentations), TurboTax Online (tax preparation), and Windows Live Hotmail (e-mail).

Figure 2-11g
(online social network)

Figure 2-11h
(educational)

Figure 2-11i
(entertainment)

Figure 2-11j
(advocacy)

Figure 2-11k
(Web application)

Figure 2-11   Types of Web sites. *(continued on next page)*

Figure 2-11l (content aggregator)

Figure 2-11m (personal)

Figure 2-11 Types of Web sites. *(continued)*

Criteria for Evaluating a Web Site's Content

Evaluation Criteria	Reliable Web Sites
Affiliation	A reputable institution should support the Web site without bias in the information.
Audience	The Web site should be written at an appropriate level.
Authority	The Web site should list the author and the appropriate credentials.
Content	The Web site should be well organized and the links should work.
Currency	The information on the Web page should be current.
Design	The pages at the Web site should download quickly, be visually pleasing, and easy to navigate.
Objectivity	The Web site should contain little advertising and be free of preconceptions.

Figure 2-12 Criteria for evaluating a Web site's content.

Content Aggregator A **content aggregator** is a business that gathers and organizes Web content and then distributes, or feeds, the content to subscribers for free or a fee (Figure 2-11l). Examples of distributed content include news, music, video, and pictures. Subscribers select content in which they are interested. Whenever this content changes, it is downloaded automatically (pushed) to the subscriber's computer or mobile device. **RSS 2.0**, which stands for Really Simple Syndication, is a specification that content aggregators use to distribute content to subscribers.

Personal A private individual or family not usually associated with any organization may maintain a personal Web site (Figure 2-11m). People publish personal Web pages for a variety of reasons. Some are job hunting. Others simply want to share life experiences with the world.

Evaluating a Web Site

Do not assume that information presented on the Web is correct or accurate. Any person, company, or organization can publish a Web page on the Internet. No one oversees the content of these Web pages. Figure 2-12 lists guidelines for assessing the value of a Web site or Web page before relying on its content.

Multimedia on the Web

Most Web pages include more than just formatted text and links. The more exciting Web pages use multimedia. **Multimedia** refers to any application that combines text with graphics, animation, audio, video, and/or virtual reality. Multimedia Web pages often require specific hardware and software and take more time to download because they contain large graphics files or video or audio clips. The sections that follow discuss how the Web uses graphics, animation, audio, video, and virtual reality.

Graphics A **graphic**, or graphical image, is a digital representation of nontext information such as a drawing, chart, or photo. Many Web pages use colorful graphical designs and images to convey messages (Figure 2-13). Read Innovative Computing 2-1 to find out how astronomers share graphics of the universe.

Figure 2-13 This Web page uses colorful graphical designs and images to convey its messages.

Of the graphics formats that exist on the Web, the two more common are JPEG and GIF formats. JPEG (pronounced JAY-peg) is a format that compresses graphics to reduce their file size, which means the file takes up less storage space. The goal with JPEG graphics is to reach a balance between image quality and file size. Digital photos often use the JPEG format. GIF (pronounced jiff) graphics also use compression techniques to reduce file sizes. The GIF format works best for images that have only a few distinct colors, such as company logos.

Some Web sites use thumbnails on their pages because graphics can be time-consuming to display. A **thumbnail** is a small version of a larger graphic. You usually can click a thumbnail to display a larger image.

Animation   Many Web pages use **animation**, which is the appearance of motion created by displaying a series of still images in sequence. Animation can make Web pages more visually interesting or draw attention to important information or links.

Audio On the Web, you can listen to audio clips and live audio. **Audio** includes music, speech, or any other sound. Simple applications on the Web consist of individual audio files available for download to a computer or device. Once downloaded, you can play (listen to) the contents of these files. Audio files are compressed to reduce their file sizes. For example, the **MP3** format reduces an audio file to about one-tenth its original size while preserving much of the original quality of the sound.

Some music publishers have Web sites that allow users to download sample tracks free to persuade them to buy all the songs contained on the CD. Others allow a user to purchase and download an entire CD (Figure 2-14). It is legal to download copyrighted music only if the song's copyright holder has granted permission for users to download and play the song.

To listen to an audio file on your computer, you need special software called a **player**. Most current operating systems contain a player, for example, Windows Media Player. Some audio files, however, might require you to download a player. Players available for download include iTunes and RealPlayer.

Some applications on the Web use streaming audio. **Streaming** is the process of transferring data in a continuous and even flow. Streaming allows users to access and use a file while it is transmitting. For example, streaming audio enables you to listen to music as it downloads to your computer.

Podcasting is another popular method of distributing audio. A **podcast** is recorded audio, usually an MP3 file, stored on a Web site that can be downloaded to a computer or a portable media player such as an iPod. Examples of podcasts include music, radio shows, news stories, classroom lectures, political messages, and television commentaries. Podcasters register their podcasts with content aggregators. Subscribers select podcast feeds they want to be downloaded automatically whenever they connect. Most smart phone users who subscribe to a wireless Internet service provider can listen to streaming audio and podcasts.

How to Purchase and Download Music Using iTunes

Step 1
Display the iTunes program on the screen. Search for, select, and pay for the music you want to purchase from the iTunes Music Store, which is integrated in the iTunes program.

Step 2
Download the music from the iTunes Music Store server to your computer's hard disk.

Step 3a
Listen to the music from your computer's hard disk.

Step 3b
Download music from your computer's hard disk to a portable media player. Listen to the music through earbuds attached to the portable media player.

Figure 2-14 This figure shows how to purchase and download music using iTunes.

Video On the Web, you can view video clips or watch live video. **Video** consists of images displayed in motion. Most video also has accompanying audio. You can use the Internet to watch live and prerecorded coverage of your favorite television programs or enjoy a live performance of your favorite vocalist. You can upload, share, or view video clips at a video sharing Web site such as YouTube. Educators, politicians, and businesses are using video blogs and video podcasts to engage students, voters, and consumers.

Video files often are compressed because they are quite large in size. These clips also are quite short in length, usually less than 10 minutes, because they can take a long time to download. The Moving Pictures Experts Group (MPEG) defines a popular video compression standard, a widely used one called MPEG-4 or **MP4**. Another popular video format is Adobe Flash. As with streaming audio, streaming video allows you to view longer or live video images as they download to your computer.

Virtual Reality **Virtual reality (VR)** is the use of computers to simulate a real or imagined environment that appears as a three-dimensional (3-D) space. VR involves the display of 3-D images that users explore and manipulate interactively. A VR Web site, for example, might show a house for sale. Potential buyers walk through rooms in the VR house by moving an input device forward, backward, or to the side.

Plug-ins Most Web browsers have the capability of displaying basic multimedia elements on a Web page. Sometimes, a browser might need an additional program, called a plug-in. A **plug-in**, or **add-on**, is a program that extends the capability of a browser. You can download many plug-ins at no cost from various Web sites (Figure 2-15).

? FAQ 2-4

How are social networking Web sites and Internet video affecting Internet traffic?

A report from Cisco Systems states that Internet traffic will double every two years until 2012. The volume of Internet traffic is increasing mostly because of Internet videos and social networking. In addition, the increased use of video conferencing by business users accounts for the increase in traffic.

For more information, visit the Computer Concepts CourseMate Web site at www.cengagebrain.com, navigate to the Chapter 2 FAQ resource for this book, and then click Internet Traffic.

Popular Plug-Ins

Plug-In Application		Description	Web Address
Acrobat Reader	Get ADOBE® READER®	View, navigate, and print Portable Document Format (PDF) files — documents formatted to look just as they look in print	adobe.com
Flash Player	Get ADOBE® FLASH® PLAYER	View dazzling graphics and animation, hear outstanding sound and music, display Web pages across an entire screen	adobe.com
Java	Java » Get it Now	Enable Web browser to run programs written in Java, which add interactivity to Web pages	java.com
QuickTime	Get QuickTime Free Download	View animation, music, audio, video, and VR panoramas and objects directly on a Web page	apple.com
RealPlayer	real RealPlayer DOWNLOAD	Listen to live and on-demand near-CD-quality audio and newscast-quality video, stream audio and video content for faster viewing, play MP3 files, create music CDs	real.com
Shockwave Player	Get ADOBE® SHOCKWAVE® PLAYER	Experience dynamic interactive multimedia, 3-D graphics, and streaming audio	adobe.com
Silverlight	Install Microsoft® Silverlight	Experience high-definition video, high-resolution interactive multimedia, and streaming audio and video	microsoft.com
Windows Media Player	Windows Media Player	Listen to live and on-demand audio, play or edit WMA and MP3 files, burn CDs, and watch DVD movies	microsoft.com

Figure 2-15 Most plug-ins can be downloaded free from the Web.

Web Publishing

Before the World Wide Web, the means to share opinions and ideas with others easily and inexpensively was limited to the media, classroom, work, or social environments. Today, businesses and individuals convey information to millions of people by creating their own Web pages.

Web publishing is the development and maintenance of Web pages. To develop a Web page, you do not have to be a computer programmer. For the small business or home user, Web publishing is fairly easy as long as you have the proper tools.

The five major steps to Web publishing are as follows:

1. Plan a Web site: Think about issues that could affect the design of the Web site.
2. Analyze and design a Web site: Design the layout of elements of the Web site such as links, text, graphics, animation, audio, video, and virtual reality.
3. Create a Web site: Use a word processing program to create basic Web pages or Web page authoring software to create more sophisticated Web sites.
4. Deploy a Web site: Transfer the Web pages from your computer to a Web server.
5. Maintain a Web site: Ensure the Web site contents remain current and all links work properly.

Web Page Authoring Software
For more information, visit the Computer Concepts CourseMate Web site at www.cengagebrain.com, navigate to the Chapter 2 Web Link resource for this book, and then click Web Page Authoring Software.

E-Commerce

E-commerce, short for electronic commerce, is a business transaction that occurs over an electronic network such as the Internet. Anyone with access to a computer or mobile device, an Internet connection, and a means to pay for purchased goods or services can participate in e-commerce.

Three types of e-commerce are business-to-consumer, consumer-to-consumer, and business-to-business. Business-to-consumer (B2C) e-commerce consists of the sale of goods and services to the general public. For example, Apple has a B2C Web site. Instead of visiting a retail store to purchase an iPod, for example, customers can order one directly from Apple's Web site.

E-retail, short for electronic retail, occurs when businesses use the Web to sell products (Figure 2-16). A customer (consumer) visits an online business through an **electronic storefront**, which contains product

An Example of E-Retail

Step 1
The customer displays the e-retailer's electronic storefront.

Step 2
The customer collects purchases in an electronic shopping cart.

Step 3
The customer enters payment information on a secure Web site. The e-retailer sends financial information to a bank.

Step 4
The bank performs security checks and sends authorization back to the e-retailer.

Step 5
The e-retailer's Web server sends confirmation to the customer, processes the order, and then sends it to the fulfillment center.

Step 6
The fulfillment center packages the order, prepares it for shipment, and then sends a report to the server where records are updated.

Step 7
While the order travels to the customer, shipping information is posted on the Web.

Step 8
The order is delivered to the customer, who may be required to sign a handheld computer or document to acknowledge receipt.

Figure 2-16   This figure shows an example of e-retail.

descriptions, images, and a shopping cart. The **shopping cart** allows the customer to collect purchases. When ready to complete the sale, the customer enters personal data and the method of payment, which should be through a secure Internet connection.

Consumer-to-consumer (C2C) e-commerce occurs when one consumer sells directly to another, such as in an online auction. With an **online auction**, users bid on an item being sold by someone else. The highest bidder at the end of the bidding period purchases the item. eBay is one of the more popular online auction Web sites.

As an alternative to entering credit card, bank account, or other financial information online, some shopping and auction Web sites allow consumers to use an online payment service such as PayPal or Google Checkout. To use an online payment service, you create an account that is linked to your credit card or funds at a financial institution. When you make a purchase, you use your online payment service account, which transfers money for you without revealing your financial information.

Most e-commerce, though, actually takes place between businesses, which is called business-to-business (B2B) e-commerce. Many businesses provide goods and services to other businesses, such as online advertising, recruiting, credit, sales, market research, technical support, and training.

Google Checkout
For more information, visit the Computer Concepts CourseMate Web site at www.cengagebrain.com, navigate to the Chapter 2 Web Link resource for this book, and then click Google Checkout.

✔ **QUIZ YOURSELF 2-2**

Instructions: Find the true statement below. Then, rewrite the remaining false statements so that they are true.

1. A blog is a Web site that uses a regularly updated journal format to reflect the interests, opinions, and personalities of the author and sometimes site visitors.

2. A Web browser classifies Web pages in an organized set of categories and related subcategories.

3. Business-to-consumer e-commerce occurs when one consumer sells directly to another, such as in an online auction.

4. The more widely used search engines for personal computers are Internet Explorer, Firefox, Opera, Safari, and Google Chrome.

5. To develop a Web page, you have to be a computer programmer.

Quiz Yourself Online: To further check your knowledge of pages 61 through 75, visit the Computer Concepts CourseMate Web site at www.cengagebrain.com, navigate to the Chapter 2 Quiz Yourself resource for this book, and then click Objectives 3 – 7.

Other Internet Services

The Web is only one of the many services on the Internet. The Web and other Internet services have changed the way we communicate. We use computers and mobile devices to send e-mail messages to the president, have a discussion with experts about the stock market, chat with someone in another country about genealogy, and talk about homework assignments with classmates via instant messages. Many times, these communications take place completely in writing — without the parties ever meeting each other.

The following pages discuss these Internet services: e-mail, mailing lists, instant messaging, chat rooms, VoIP (Voice over IP), FTP (File Transfer Protocol), and newsgroups and message boards.

E-Mail

E-mail (short for electronic mail) is the transmission of messages and files via a computer network. Today, e-mail is a primary communications method for both personal and business use.

You use an **e-mail program** to create, send, receive, forward, store, print, and delete e-mail messages. Outlook and Windows Live Mail are two popular desktop e-mail programs.

The steps in Figure 2-17 illustrate how to send an e-mail message using Outlook; Gmail and Windows Live Hotmail are two popular free e-mail Web applications. The message can be simple text or can include an attachment such as a word processing document, a graphic, an audio clip, or a video clip. To learn more about how to attach a file to an e-mail message, complete the Learn How To 1 activity on page 88.

Just as you address a letter when using the postal system, you address an e-mail message with the e-mail address of your intended recipient. Likewise, when someone sends you a message, he or she must have your e-mail address. An **e-mail address** is a combination of a user name and a domain name that

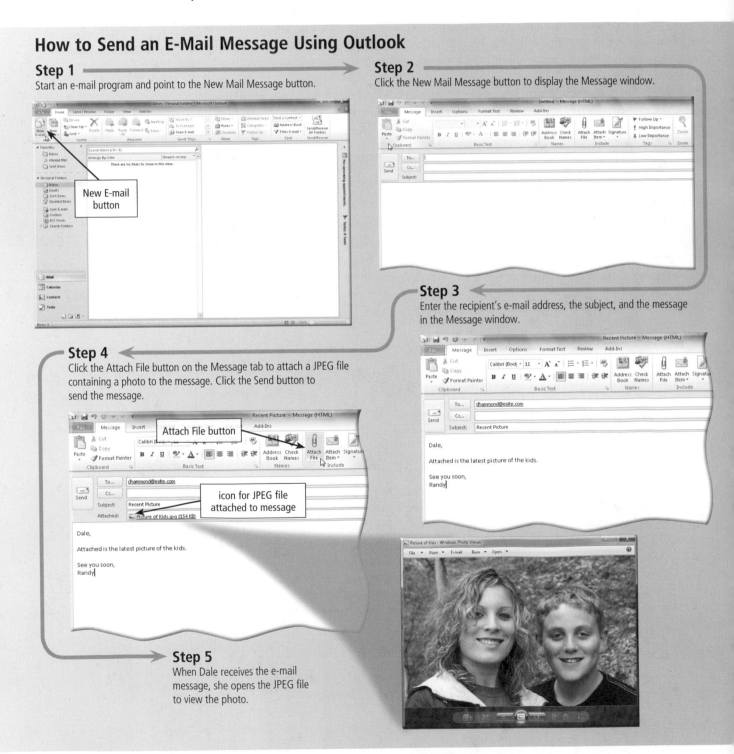

How to Send an E-Mail Message Using Outlook

Step 1
Start an e-mail program and point to the New Mail Message button.

New E-mail button

Step 2
Click the New Mail Message button to display the Message window.

Step 3
Enter the recipient's e-mail address, the subject, and the message in the Message window.

Step 4
Click the Attach File button on the Message tab to attach a JPEG file containing a photo to the message. Click the Send button to send the message.

Attach File button

icon for JPEG file attached to message

Step 5
When Dale receives the e-mail message, she opens the JPEG file to view the photo.

Figure 2-17 This figure shows how to send an e-mail message using Outlook.

identifies a user so that he or she can receive Internet e-mail. A **user name** is a unique combination of characters, such as letters of the alphabet and/or numbers, that identifies a specific user.

In an Internet e-mail address, an @ (pronounced at) symbol separates the user name from the domain name. Your service provider supplies the domain name. A possible e-mail address for Kiley Barnhill would be kbarnhill@esite.com, which would be read as follows: K Barnhill at e site dot com. Most e-mail programs allow you to create an **address book**, or contacts folder, which contains a list of names and e-mail addresses.

When you send an e-mail message, an outgoing mail server that is operated by your Internet access provider determines how to route the message through the Internet and then sends the message. As you receive e-mail messages, an incoming mail server — also operated by your Internet access provider — holds the messages in your mailbox until you use your e-mail program to retrieve them. Most e-mail programs have a mail notification alert that informs you via a message and/or sound when you receive new mail. Figure 2-18 illustrates how an e-mail message may travel from a sender to a receiver using a desktop e-mail program.

E-Mail
For more information, visit the Computer Concepts CourseMate Web site at www.cengagebrain.com, navigate to the Chapter 2 Web Link resource for this book, and then click E-Mail.

? | **FAQ 2-5**

Can my computer get a virus through e-mail?

Yes. A virus is a computer program that can damage files and the operating system. One way that virus authors attempt to spread a virus is by sending virus-infected e-mail attachments. If you receive an e-mail attachment, you should use an antivirus program to verify that it is virus free.

For more information, read the section about viruses and antivirus programs in Chapter 7, and visit the Computer Concepts CourseMate Web site at www.cengagebrain.com, navigate to the Chapter 2 FAQ resource for this book, and then click Viruses.

How an E-Mail Message May Travel from a Sender to a Receiver

Step 1
Using an e-mail program, you create and send a message.

Step 2
Your e-mail program contacts software on your service provider's outgoing mail server.

Step 3
Software on the outgoing mail server determines the best route for the data and sends the message, which travels along Internet routers to the recipient's incoming mail server.

Internet router

Step 4
When the recipient uses an e-mail program to check for e-mail messages, the message transfers from the incoming mail server to the recipient's computer.

Internet service provider's incoming mail server

Internet router

Figure 2-18 This figure shows how an e-mail message may travel from a sender to a receiver.

Mailing Lists

A **mailing list**, also called an e-mail list or distribution list, is a group of e-mail names and addresses given a single name. When a message is sent to a mailing list, every person on the list receives a copy of the message in his or her mailbox. For example, your credit card company may add you to its mailing list in order to send you special offers. To add your e-mail name and address to a mailing list, you **subscribe** to it. To remove your name, you **unsubscribe** from the mailing list.

Thousands of mailing lists exist about a variety of topics in areas of entertainment, business, computers, society, culture, health, recreation, and education.

Instant Messaging

Instant messaging (**IM**) is a real-time Internet communications service that notifies you when one or more people are online and then allows you to exchange messages or files or join a private chat room with them (Figure 2-19). **Real time** means that you and the people with whom you are conversing are online at the same time. Some IM services support voice and video conversations. For IM to work, both parties must be online at the same time. Also, the receiver of a message must be willing to accept messages.

An Example of Instant Messaging

Step 1
Log in to the IM server.

Step 2
The server determines if any of your established friends, family, or coworkers, called buddies, are online.

IM server

Step 3
You send instant messages, voice, and/or video communications to an online buddy.

Step 5
Your online buddy replies.

Step 4
Your instant message, voice, and/or video travels through a messaging server and then to the online buddy's computer.

messaging server

Figure 2-19   This figure shows an example of instant messaging.

To use IM, you may have to install instant messenger software on the computer or device, such as a smart phone, you plan to use. Some operating systems, such as Windows, include an instant messenger. Few IM programs follow IM standards. To ensure successful communications, all individuals on the contact list need to use the same or a compatible instant messenger.

Chat Rooms

A **chat** is a real-time typed conversation that takes place on a computer. A **chat room** is a location on an Internet server that permits users to chat with each other. Anyone in the chat room can participate in the conversation, which usually is specific to a particular topic.

As you type on your keyboard, a line of characters and symbols is displayed on the computer screen. Others connected to the same chat room server also see what you type (Figure 2-20). Some chat rooms support voice chats and video chats, in which people hear or see each other as they chat.

To start a chat session, you connect to a chat server through a program called a chat client. Today's browsers usually include a chat client. If yours does not, you can download a chat client from the Web. Once you have installed a chat client, you can create or join a conversation on the chat server to which you are connected.

Chat Rooms

For more information, visit the Computer Concepts CourseMate Web site at www.cengagebrain.com, navigate to the Chapter 2 Web Link resource for this book, and then click Chat Rooms.

Figure 2-20 As you type, the words and symbols you enter are displayed on the computer screens of other people in the same chat room. To save time many chat and IM users type abbreviations and acronyms for phrases, such as 'r u there?', which stands for 'Are You There?'.

VoIP

VoIP (Voice over IP, or Internet Protocol), also called Internet telephony, enables users to speak to other users over the Internet (instead of the public switched telephone network).

To place an Internet telephone call, you need a high-speed Internet connection (e.g., via cable or DSL modem); Internet telephone service; a microphone or telephone, depending on the Internet telephone service; and Internet telephone software or VoIP router, or a telephone adapter, depending on the Internet telephone service (Figure 2-21). VoIP services also are available on some mobile devices that have wireless Internet service. Calls to other parties with the same Internet telephone service often are free, while calls that connect to the telephone network typically cost about $15 to $35 per month.

Figure 2-21 One type of equipment configuration for a user making a call via VoIP.

FTP

FTP (File Transfer Protocol) is an Internet standard that permits the process of file uploading and downloading with other computers on the Internet. Uploading is the opposite of downloading; that is, **uploading** is the process of transferring documents, graphics, and other objects from your computer to a server on the Internet.

Many operating systems include FTP capabilities. An FTP site is a collection of files including text, graphics, audio clips, video clips, and program files that reside on an FTP server. Many FTP sites have anonymous FTP, whereby anyone can transfer some, if not all, available files. Some FTP sites restrict file transfers to those who have authorized accounts (user names and passwords) on the FTP server.

Newsgroups and Message Boards

A **newsgroup** is an online area in which users have written discussions about a particular subject (Figure 2-22). To participate in a discussion, a user sends a message to the newsgroup, and other users in the newsgroup read and reply to the message.

Some newsgroups require you to enter a user name and password to participate in the discussion. For example, a newsgroup for students taking a college course may require a user name

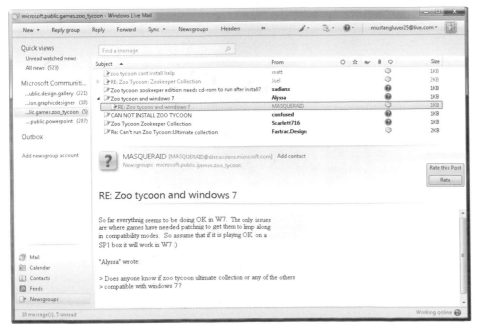

Figure 2-22 Users in a newsgroup read and reply to other users' messages.

and password to access the newsgroup. This ensures that only students in the course participate in the discussion. To participate in a newsgroup, typically you use a program called a newsreader.

A popular Web-based type of discussion group that does not require a newsreader is a **message board**. Many Web sites use message boards instead of newsgroups because they are easier to use.

Netiquette

Netiquette, which is short for Internet etiquette, is the code of acceptable behaviors users should follow while on the Internet; that is, it is the conduct expected of individuals while online. Netiquette includes rules for all aspects of the Internet, including the World Wide Web, e-mail, instant messaging, chat rooms, FTP, and newsgroups and message boards. Figure 2-23 outlines some of the rules of netiquette. Read Ethics & Issues 2-3 for a related discussion.

NETIQUETTE — Golden Rule: Treat others as you would like them to treat you.

1. In e-mail, chat rooms, and newsgroups:
   - Keep messages brief. Use proper grammar, spelling, and punctuation.
   - Be careful when using sarcasm and humor, as it might be misinterpreted.
   - Be polite. Avoid offensive language.
   - Read the message before you send it.
   - Use meaningful subject lines.
   - Avoid sending or posting flames, which are abusive or insulting messages. Do not participate in flame wars, which are exchanges of flames.
   - Avoid sending spam, which is the Internet's version of junk mail. Spam is an unsolicited e-mail message or newsgroup posting sent to many recipients or newsgroups at once.
   - Do not use all capital letters, which is the equivalent of SHOUTING!

   - Use **emoticons** to express emotion. Popular emoticons include

:)	Smile	:|	Indifference	:o	Surprised
:(	Frown	:\	Undecided		

   - Use abbreviations and acronyms for phrases:
     btw   by the way
     imho   in my humble opinion
     fyi   for your information
     ttfn   ta ta for now
     fwiw   for what it's worth
     tyvm   thank you very much
   - Clearly identify a spoiler, which is a message that reveals a solution to a game or ending to a movie or program.
2. Read the FAQ (frequently asked questions), if one exists. Many newsgroups and Web pages have an FAQ.
3. Do not assume material is accurate or up-to-date. Be forgiving of other's mistakes.
4. Never read someone's private e-mail.

Figure 2-23 Some of the rules of netiquette.

ETHICS & ISSUES 2-3

Would Banning Anonymous Comments Reduce Cyberbullying?

Recently, several high-profile cases highlighted the issue of cyberbullying. Cyberbullying is the harassment of computer users, often teens and preteens, through various forms of Internet communications. The behavior typically occurs via e-mail, instant messaging, and chat rooms, and can result in a traumatic experience for the recipient. The bullying may be in the form of threats, spreading of rumors, or humiliation. Usually, the perpetrators of cyberbullying remain anonymous. Many people believe that the anonymous nature of the Internet directly leads to this unscrupulous behavior. Some government officials and advocacy groups have asked for laws that would ban anonymous comments in chat rooms and require that Internet access providers verify and record the true identity of all users. Others have proposed that it be illegal to sign up for an e-mail account or instant messaging account with a fake screen name. Opponents of such plans claim that anonymity and privacy are too important to give up. They state, for example, that the right to be critical of the government in an anonymous forum is a basic right. The rights of everyone should not be infringed upon due to bad behavior of a small group of people.

Would banning anonymous comments reduce cyberbullying? Why or why not? What are the positive and negative aspects of the freedom to remain anonymous on the Internet? What other measures can be taken to reduce cyberbullying? What role can parents play in reducing cyberbullying?

✔ **QUIZ YOURSELF 2-3**

Instructions: Find the true statement below. Then, rewrite the remaining false statements so that they are true.

1. A chat room is a location on an Internet server that permits users to chat with each other.

2. An e-mail address is a combination of a user name and an e-mail program that identifies a user so that he or she can receive Internet e-mail.

3. FTP uses the Internet (instead of the public switched telephone network) to connect a calling party to one or more called parties.

4. Netiquette is the code of unacceptable behaviors while on the Internet.

5. VoIP enables users to subscribe to other users over the Internet.

Quiz Yourself Online: To further check your knowledge of pages 75 through 81, visit the Computer Concepts CourseMate Web site at www.cengagebrain.com, navigate to the Chapter 2 Quiz Yourself resource for this book, and then click Objectives 8 – 9.

Chapter Summary

This chapter presented the history and structure of the Internet. It discussed the World Wide Web at length, including topics such as browsing, navigating, searching, Web publishing, and e-commerce. It also introduced other services available on the Internet, such as e-mail, mailing lists, instant messaging, chat rooms, VoIP, FTP, and newsgroups and message boards. Finally, the chapter listed rules of netiquette.

Computer Usage @ Work

Entertainment

Do you wonder how music on the radio sounds so perfectly in tune, how animated motion pictures are created, or how one controls lighting during a concert? Not only does the entertainment industry rely on computers to advertise and sell their services on the Internet, computers also assist in other aspects, including audio and video composition, lighting control, computerized animation, and computer gaming.

As mentioned in this chapter, entertainment Web sites provide music and movies you can purchase and download to your computer or mobile device; live news broadcasts, performances, and sporting events; games you can play with other online users; and much more.

As early as 1951, computers were used to record and play music. Today, computers play a much larger role in the music industry. For example, if you are listening to a song on the radio and notice that not one note is out of tune, it is possible that software was used to change individual notes without altering the rest of the song.

Many years ago, creating cartoons or animated motion pictures was an extremely time-consuming task because artists were responsible for sketching thousands of drawings by hand. Currently, artists use computers to create these drawings in a fraction of the

time, which significantly can reduce the time and cost of development.

Computers also are used in the game industry. While some game developers create games from scratch, others might use game engines that simplify the development process. For example, LucasArts created the GrimE game engine, which is designed to create adventure games.

During a concert, lighting technicians use computer programs to turn lights off and on, change color, or change location at specified intervals. In fact, once a performance begins, the technicians often merely are standing by, monitoring the computer as it performs most of the work. A significant amount of time and effort, however, is required to program the computer to perform its required tasks during a live show.

The next time you listen to a song, watch a movie, play a game, or attend a concert, think about the role computers play in contributing to your entertainment.

For more information, visit the Computer Concepts CourseMate Web site at www.cengagebrain.com, navigate to the Chapter 2 Computer Usage @ Work resource for this book, and then click Entertainment.

Companies on the Cutting Edge

GOOGLE Popular Search Engine and Services

Google founders Sergey Brin and Larry Page have done very little advertising, but their Web site has become a household word, largely on favorable word-of-mouth reviews. They launched the Web site in 1998 in a friend's garage with the goal of providing the best possible experience for their loyal users who are looking for information presented clearly and quickly.

Google regularly scans more than one trillion Web pages in search of unique phrases and terms. Its thousands of connected computers deliver organized search results for the hundreds of millions of queries users input daily. Recently, the company updated its Google Earth product to allow users to explore the Moon, and also updated its popular advertising product, AdWords. Among its other services are Google Docs and YouTube.

eBAY World's Largest Online Marketplace

Millions of products are traded daily on eBay auctions, whether it is across town or across the globe. The more than 88 million registered worldwide shoppers generate at least $1.8 billion in annual revenue through purchases on the main Web site, eBay, along with items on Shopping.com, tickets on StubHub, classifieds on Kijiji, and other e-commerce venues.

The shoppers likely pay for their merchandise using PayPal, another eBay service. This merchant service allows buyers to transfer money from savings accounts or use their credit card without having to expose the account number to the seller. Other eBay companies are Rent.com, which offers listings for apartments and houses, and Shopping.com, which allows consumers to find and compare products. Recently, eBay introduced a program to more easily identify its top-rated sellers. It also invited buyers and sellers to become members of the eBay Green Team, which encourages and promotes environmentally friendly business practices.

 For more information, visit the Computer Concepts CourseMate Web site at www.cengagebrain.com and then navigate to the Chapter 2 Companies on the Cutting Edge resource for this book.

Technology Trailblazers

TIM BERNERS-LEE Creator of the World Wide Web

Being the creator of the World Wide Web is an impressive item on any resume, and it certainly helped Tim Berners-Lee become the 3Com Founders Professor of Engineering at the Massachusetts Institute of Technology in 2008. As a professor in the electrical engineering and computer science departments, he researches social and technical collaboration on the Internet.

Berners-Lee's interest in sharing information via Web servers, browsers, and Web addresses developed in 1989 while working at CERN, the European Organization for Nuclear Research, in Geneva, Switzerland. He continued to improve his design of a program that tracked random associations for several years and then became the director of the World Wide Web Consortium (W3C), a forum to develop Web standards, in 1994.

Recently, Queen Elizabeth bestowed the Order of Merit – the highest civilian honor – upon the British-born Berners-Lee.

MARK ZUCKERBERG Facebook Founder and CEO

As one of the youngest self-made billionaires in history, Mark Zuckerberg could have his choice of the finest things in life. Instead, he lives very modestly and walks to Facebook's Palo Alto headquarters.

Both Microsoft and AOL had recruited Zuckerberg during his senior year in high school in New Hampshire. He declined their job offers and decided to attend Harvard. In college, he and some friends developed several projects, laying the foundation that led to Facebook's eventual start. Harvard administrators claimed these Web sites violated students' privacy. He, however, had instant success launching Facebook from his dorm room, and the Web site's popularity quickly spread to other Ivy League and Boston-area colleges and then worldwide. He left his studies at Harvard University in 2004 and moved to California.

Today, Zuckerberg says he spends the majority of his time running the $15 billion company on very little sleep.

 For more information, visit the Computer Concepts CourseMate Web site at www.cengagebrain.com and then navigate to the Chapter 2 Technology Trailblazers resource for this book.

Chapter Review

The Chapter Review reinforces the main concepts presented in this chapter.

To listen to an audio version of this Chapter Review, visit the Computer Concepts CourseMate Web site at www.cengagebrain.com and then navigate to the Chapter 2 Chapter Review resource for this book.

1. **What Are the Various Broadband Internet Connections?** The **Internet** is a worldwide collection of networks that links millions of businesses, government agencies, educational institutions, and individuals. Many home and small business users connect to the Internet via high-speed **broadband** Internet service. **Cable Internet service** provides high-speed Internet access through the cable television network via a cable modem. **DSL** (digital subscriber line) provides high-speed Internet connections using regular telephone lines. **Fiber to the Premises (FTTP)** uses fiber-optic cable to provide high-speed Internet access. **Fixed wireless** high-speed Internet connections use a dish-shaped antenna to communicate via radio signals. A **Wi-Fi** network uses radio signals to provide Internet connections to wireless computers and devices. A **cellular radio network** offers high-speed Internet connections to devices with built-in compatible technology or computers with wireless modems. **Satellite Internet service** communicates with a satellite dish to provide high-speed Internet connections. Some home and small businesses connect to the Internet with **dial-up access**, which uses a modem in the computer and a standard telephone line.

2. **What Are the Types of Internet Access Providers?** An **access provider** is a business that provides access to the Internet free or for a fee. An **ISP** (**Internet service provider**) is a regional or national access provider. An **online service provider** (**OSP**) provides Internet access in addition to members-only features, such as instant messaging or customized Web browsers. A **wireless Internet service provider** provides wireless Internet access to computers and mobile devices with built-in wireless capability (such as Wi-Fi) or to computers using wireless modems or wireless access devices.

Visit the Computer Concepts CourseMate Web site at www.cengagebrain.com, navigate to the Chapter 2 Quiz Yourself resource for this book, and then click Objectives 1 – 2.

3. **What Is the Purpose of a Web Browser, and What Are the Components of a Web Address?** A **Web browser**, or **browser**, is application software that allows users to access and view Web pages or access Web 2.0 programs. A **Web address** is the unique address for each **Web page** and consists of a protocol, a domain name, and sometimes the path to a specific Web page or location on a Web page.

4. **How Do You Use a Search Engine to Search for Information on the Web?** A **search engine** is a program that finds Web sites, Web pages, images, videos, news, maps, and other information related to a specific topic. A search engine is helpful in locating information for which you do not know an exact Web address or are not seeking a particular Web site. Search engines require **search text** that describes the item you want to find. After performing the search, the search engine returns a list of hits, each one a **link** to an associated Web page.

5. **What Are the Types of Web Sites?** A **portal** is a Web site that offers a variety of Internet services from a single location. A news Web site contains newsworthy material. An informational Web site contains factual information. A business/marketing Web site promotes or sells products or services. A **blog** is an informal Web site consisting of time-stamped articles, or posts, in a diary or journal format, usually listed in reverse chronological order. A **wiki** is a collaborative Web site that allows users to create, add to, modify, or delete the Web site content via their Web browser. An **online social network**, or **social networking Web site**, encourages members to share their interests, ideas, stories, photos, music, and videos with other registered users. An educational Web site offers avenues for teaching and learning. An entertainment Web site offers an interactive and engaging environment. An advocacy Web site describes a cause, opinion, or idea. A **Web application**, or **Web app**, is a Web site that allows users to access and interact with software through a Web browser on any computer connected to the Internet. A **content aggregator** is a business that gathers and organizes Web content and then distributes, or feeds, the content to subscribers for free or a fee. A personal Web site is maintained by a private individual or family.

6. **How Do Web Pages Use Graphics, Animation, Audio, Video, Virtual Reality, and Plug-Ins?** More exciting Web sites use **multimedia**, which refers to any application that combines text with graphics, animation, video, and/or virtual reality. A **graphic**, or graphical image, is a digital representation of nontext information such as a drawing, chart, or photo. **Animation** is the appearance of motion created by displaying a series of still images in sequence. **Audio** includes music, speech, or any other sound. **Video** consists of full-motion images that are played back at various speeds. **Virtual reality** (**VR**) is the use of computers to simulate a real or imagined environment as a 3-D space. A **plug-in** is a program that extends the capability of a browser.

7. What Are the Steps Required for Web Publishing? **Web publishing** is the development and maintenance of Web pages. The five major steps to Web publishing are: (1) plan a Web site, (2) analyze and design a Web site, (3) create a Web site, (4) deploy a Web site, and (5) maintain a Web site.

Visit the Computer Concepts CourseMate Web site at www.cengagebrain.com, navigate to the Chapter 2 Quiz Yourself resource for this book, and then click Objectives 3 – 7.

8. How Do E-Mail, Mailing Lists, Instant Messaging, Chat Rooms, VoIP, FTP, and Newsgroups and Message Boards Work? E-mail (short for electronic mail) is the transmission of messages and files via a computer network. A **mailing list** is a group of e-mail names and addresses given a single name, so that everyone on the list receives a message sent to the list. **Instant messaging** (**IM**) is a **real-time** Internet communications service that notifies you when one or more people are online. A **chat room** is a location on an Internet server that permits users to **chat**, or conduct real-time typed conversations. **VoIP** (Voice over IP, or Internet Protocol) enables users to speak to other users over the Internet instead of the public switched telephone network. **FTP** (File Transfer Protocol) is an Internet standard that permits file **uploading** and **downloading** with other computers on the Internet. A **newsgroup** is an online area in which users have written discussions about a particular subject. A **message board** is a popular Web-based type of discussion group that is easier to use than a newsgroup.

9. What Are the Rules of Netiquette? **Netiquette**, which is short for Internet etiquette, is the code of acceptable behaviors users should follow while on the Internet. Keep messages short. Be polite. Use **emoticons**. Read the FAQ if one exists. Do not assume material is accurate or up-to-date, and never read someone's private e-mail.

Visit the Computer Concepts CourseMate Web site at www.cengagebrain.com, navigate to the Chapter 2 Quiz Yourself resource for this book, and then click Objectives 8 – 9.

Key Terms

You should know the Key Terms. The list below helps focus your study.

To see an example of and a definition for each term, and to access current and additional information from the Web, visit the Computer Concepts CourseMate Web site at www.cengagebrain.com and then navigate to the Chapter 2 Key Terms resource for this book.

access provider (58)
add-on (73)
address book (77)
animation (71)
audio (72)
blog (68)
blogosphere (68)
bookmark (63)
broadband (57)
browser (61)
cable Internet service (57)
cellular radio network (58)
chat (79)
chat room (79)
click (64)
content aggregator (70)
dial-up access (58)
domain name (60)
downloading (62)
DSL (57)
e-commerce (74)
electronic storefront (74)
e-mail address (76)
e-mail program (75)
emoticons (81)

favorite (63)
Fiber to the Premises (FTTP) (57)
fixed wireless (57)
FTP (80)
graphic (70)
home page (62)
hot spots (58)
hyperlink (64)
instant messaging (IM) (78)
Internet (56)
Internet backbone (59)
IP address (60)
ISP (Internet service provider) (58)
link (64)
mailing list (78)
media sharing Web site (69)
message board (81)
microblog (68)
MP3 (72)
MP4 (73)
multimedia (70)
Net (56)
netiquette (81)

newsgroup (80)
online auction (75)
online service provider (OSP) (58)
online social network (69)
player (72)
plug-in (73)
podcast (72)
portal (67)
real time (78)
RSS 2.0 (70)
satellite Internet service (58)
search engine (65)
search text (66)
shopping cart (75)
social networking Web site (69)
streaming (72)
subject directory (65)
subscribe (78)
surfing the Web (64)
tabbed browsing (64)
thumbnail (71)
top-level domain (TLD) (60)
unsubscribe (78)

uploading (80)
URL (63)
user name (77)
video (73)
video blog (68)
virtual reality (VR) (73)
vlog (68)
vlogosphere (68)
VoIP (80)
Web (61)
Web 2.0 (61)
Web address (63)
Web app (69)
Web application (69)
Web browser (61)
Web page (61)
Web publishing (74)
Web server (61)
Web site (61)
Wi-Fi (57)
wiki (68)
wireless Internet service provider (58)
World Wide Web (WWW) (61)

Checkpoint

The Checkpoint exercises test your knowledge of the chapter concepts. The page number containing the answer appears in parentheses after each exercise.

To complete the Checkpoint exercises interactively, visit the Computer Concepts CourseMate Web site at www.cengagebrain.com and then navigate to the Chapter 2 Checkpoint resource for this book.

Multiple Choice   Select the best answer.

1. _____ offers high-speed Internet connections to devices with built-in compatible technology or computers with wireless modems. (58)
   a. Cable Internet service
   b. A digital subscriber line
   c. A cellular radio network
   d. Fiber to the Premises (FTTP)

2. Instead of using broadband Internet service some home users connect to the Internet via _____, which is a slower-speed technology. (58)
   a. satellite Internet service
   b. cable Internet service
   c. DSL
   d. dial-up access

3. _____ is the process of a computer or device receiving information, such as a Web page, from a server on the Internet. (62)
   a. Uploading   b. Social networking
   c. Downloading   d. Blogging

4. A _____ is a Web site that allows users to post short text updates, usually between 100 and 200 characters. (68)
   a. podcast
   b. wiki
   c. microblog
   d. portal

5. A _____ is a specific type of online social network that enables members to share photos, music, and videos. (69)
   a. blog
   b. wiki
   c. podcast
   d. media sharing Web site

6. A(n) _____ is a small version of a larger graphic. (71)
   a. thumbnail
   b. wiki
   c. MP3
   d. portal

7. In _____ e-commerce, one consumer sells directly to another. (75)
   a. consumer-to-business
   b. business-to-business
   c. consumer-to-consumer
   d. business-to-consumer

8. The _____ standard permits uploading and downloading of files on the Internet. (80)
   a. FTP
   b. newsgroup
   c. message board
   d. mailing list

Matching   Match the terms with their definitions.

_____ 1. home page (62)

_____ 2. search engine (65)

_____ 3. MP3 (72)

_____ 4. e-mail address (76)

_____ 5. emoticons (81)

a. used to express emotions in e-mail, chat rooms, and newsgroups

b. the first page that a Web site displays

c. combination of a user name and a domain name that identifies an Internet user

d. program that finds Web sites, Web pages, images, videos, news, maps, and other information related to a specific topic

e. built-in connection to a related Web page or part of a Web page

f. format that reduces an audio file to about one-tenth its original size

Short Answer   Write a brief answer to each of the following questions.

1. Describe three different types of broadband Internet services. _____ What is the difference between a regional ISP and a national ISP? _____

2. How is a Web page different from a Web site? _____ How can you use a Web address to display a Web page? _____

3. What are the differences between blogs, wikis, and podcasts? _____ When might you use each? _____

4. What is a Web application? _____ What are some features and examples of Web applications? _____

5. What is one specification used by content aggregators to distribute content? _____ How might you evaluate the accuracy of a Web site? _____

Problem Solving

The Problem Solving exercises extend your knowledge of the chapter concepts by seeking solutions to practical computer problems that you may encounter at home, school, or work. The Collaboration exercise should be completed with a team.

In the real world, practical problems often can be solved in multiple ways. Provide one solution to each of the following problems using available resources, such as articles on the Web or in print, blogs, podcasts, videos, television, user guides, other individuals, and electronics and computer stores. You may need to use multiple resources to obtain an answer. Present your solutions in the form requested by your instructor (brief report, presentation, discussion, or other means).

@ Home

1. **Slow Internet Connection**   You just installed VoIP telephone service in your house. Each time you are on the telephone, however, you notice that your Internet connection slows down significantly. What could be causing this?

2. **No Wireless Connection**   When you return home to visit your parents and turn on your new notebook computer, it does not connect automatically to their wireless network. What is your next step?

3. **Incorrect Search Engine**   A class project requires that you conduct research on the Web. After typing the Web address for Google's home page and pressing the ENTER key, your Web browser redirects you to a different search engine. What could be wrong?

4. **New Browser Windows**   While browsing the Web, each time you click a link, the link's destination opens in a new browser window. You prefer to have each link open in a new tab so that your taskbar does not become cluttered. How will you resolve this?

@ Work

5. **Access Denied**   During your lunch hour, you decide to search the Web for possible vacation destinations. After visiting several airline and hotel Web sites, you attempt to visit the Web site for a Caribbean resort. Much to your surprise, the Web browser informs you that the Web site has been blocked. Why might this happen?

6. **Sporadic E-Mail Message Delivery**   The e-mail program on your computer has been delivering new messages only every hour, on the hour. Historically, new e-mail messages would arrive and be displayed immediately upon being sent by the sender. Furthermore, your coworkers claim that they sometimes do not receive your e-mail messages until hours after they are sent. What might be the problem?

7. **E-Mail Message Formatting**   A friend sent an e-mail message containing a photo to your e-mail account at work. Upon receiving the e-mail message, the photo does not display. You also notice that e-mail messages never display any formatting, such as different fonts, font sizes, and font colors. What might be causing this?

8. **Automatic Response**   When you return from vacation, a colleague informs you that when she sent e-mail messages to your e-mail address, she would not always receive your automatic response stating that you were out of the office. Why might your e-mail program not respond automatically to every e-mail message received?

Collaboration

9. **Computers in Entertainment**   The drama department at a local high school is considering developing a movie and has asked for your help. The drama teacher would like to incorporate technology wherever possible, in hopes that it would decrease the costs of the movie's production. Form a team of three people to help determine what technology can be used to assist in the movie's production. One team member should research the type of technology that can be used during the filming process. Another team member should research the types of hardware and software available for editing footage, and the third team member should research the hardware and software requirements for creating the media to distribute the finished product.

Learn How To

The Learn How To activities step you through fundamental technology skills when using a computer. The Learn How To exercises enable you to become more proficient with these skills.

Premium Activity: To relate this Learn How To activity to your everyday life, see a visual demonstration of the activity, and complete a short assessment, visit the Computer Concepts CourseMate Web site at www.cengagebrain.com and then navigate to the Chapter 2 Learn How To resource for this book.

Learn How To 1: Attach a File to an E-Mail Message

When you send an e-mail message, it sometimes is necessary to attach a file to supplement the body of the e-mail message. Most e-mail programs allow you to attach a file to your e-mail messages easily, but many do not allow you to attach files exceeding a specified size limit (which varies by your e-mail service). You can attach a file to an e-mail message by completing the following steps:

1. Start your e-mail program and compose a new e-mail message to your recipient. Make sure that you have a descriptive subject and that you explain in the e-mail message that you are attaching a file.
2. To attach a file, locate and click the Attach File button or link. If you are unable to locate this button, you may find an icon with a picture of a paperclip or a menu command to attach a file. Some e-mail programs also may have a text box in the new message window with an adjacent Browse button. In this case, click the Browse button.
3. Locate and click the file you wish to attach and then click the Open (or Insert or Select) button (Figure 2-24).
4. Verify that your e-mail message contains the attachment and then click the Send button.

Figure 2-24

When the recipient opens the e-mail message, he or she also will be able to open the attachment.

Exercises

1. Start your e-mail program. Compose a new e-mail message to your instructor, and attach a file containing your current course schedule. Verify that your message has been received and then close your e-mail program.

2. Locate three free e-mail Web applications. How many file attachments do these e-mail programs allow you to attach to one e-mail message? Is a maximum file size specified for an e-mail attachment? Can you pay to upgrade your e-mail account so that these restrictions are lifted? Submit these answers to your instructor.

Learn How To 2: Search the Web for Driving Directions, Addresses, and Telephone Numbers

In addition to searching the Web for information using search engines such as Google and Yahoo!, some Web sites are designed specifically to search for other information such as driving directions, addresses, and telephone numbers.

Search for Driving Directions

1. Start your Web browser, type mapquest.com in the Address bar, press the ENTER key to display the MapQuest home page, and then click the Directions tab.
2. Type the starting address (or intersection), city, state, and ZIP code (if you know it) in the appropriate text boxes in the Starting Location area of the Directions page.
3. Type the ending address (or intersection), city, state, and ZIP code (if you know it) in the appropriate text boxes in the Ending Location area of the Directions page.
4. Click the Get Directions button to display the driving directions.

Search for the Address and Telephone Number of a Business

1. If necessary, start your Web browser. Type yellowpages.com in the Address bar, and then press the ENTER key to display the Yellow Pages Local Directory home page.

2. Type the name of the business in the Find text box, and type the city, state, and ZIP (if you know it) in the Location text box.
3. Click the FIND button to display the search results.
4. Close your Web browser.

Exercises

1. If necessary, start Internet Explorer by clicking the Start button, and then click Internet Explorer on the Start menu. Type `mapquest.com` in the Address bar, and then press the ENTER key. Search for driving directions between your address and the address of a friend or family member. How many miles are between the two addresses? How long would it take you to drive from your address to the other address? Write a paragraph explaining whether you would or would not use MapQuest to retrieve driving directions. Submit this paragraph to your instructor.

2. Use the Web to search for another Web site that provides driving directions. Use the Web site to search for directions between the same two locations from Exercise 1. Are the driving directions the same as the ones that MapQuest provided? If not, why might they be different? Which Web site did you use? Do you prefer this Web site to MapQuest? Why or why not? Write a paragraph with your answers and submit it to your instructor.

3. Think about a company for which you would like to work. In your Web browser, display the Yellow Pages Web page (yellowpages.com) and then search for the address and telephone number of this company. If Yellow Pages does not display the desired information, what other Web sites might you be able to use to search for the address and telephone number for a company?

Learn It Online

The Learn It Online exercises are interactive Web exercises designed to reinforce and expand your understanding of the chapter concepts. The descriptions below briefly summarize each exercise.

To complete the Learn It Online exercises, visit the Computer Concepts CourseMate Web site at www.cengagebrain.com, navigate to the Chapter 2 resources for this book, click the link for the exercise you want to complete, and then read the instructions.

1 At the Movies — Tell Your Stories via Vlog
Watch a movie to learn about how to post your thoughts to a vlog and then answer questions about the movie.

2 Student Edition Labs — Connecting to the Internet, Getting the Most out of the Internet, and E-mail
Enhance your understanding and knowledge about the Internet and e-mail by completing the Connecting to the Internet, Getting the Most out of the Internet, and E-mail Labs.

3 Practice Test
Take a multiple choice test that checks your knowledge of the chapter concepts and review the resulting study guide.

4 Who Wants To Be a Computer Genius²?
Play the Shelly Cashman Series version of this popular game by answering questions to find out if you are a computer genius. Panic buttons are available to provide assistance during game play.

5 Crossword Puzzle Challenge
Complete an interactive crossword puzzle to reinforce concepts presented in this chapter.

6 Windows Exercises
Step through the Windows 7 exercises to learn about Internet properties, dial-up networking connections, and using Help to understand the Internet.

7 Exploring Computer Careers
Read about a career as a Web developer, search for related employment advertisements, and then answer related questions.

8 Web Apps — Windows Live Hotmail
Learn how to sign up for a free e-mail account, add a contact to your address book, and send an e-mail message.

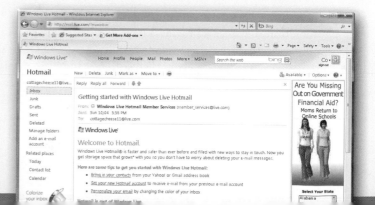

Web Research

The Web Research exercises broaden your understanding of the chapter concepts by presenting questions that require you to search the Web for answers.

1 Search Sleuth

Use one of the search engines listed in Figure 2-8 in Chapter 2 on page 65 or your own favorite search engine to find the answers to the following questions. Copy and paste the Web address from the Web page where you found the answer. Some questions may have more than one answer. If required, submit your answers to your instructor. (1) What were the title, date of publication, and purpose of the Internet Engineering Task Force's RFC 1 document? (2) What is the mission of the World Wide Web Consortium (W3C)? (3) What topic does the film *Adina's Deck* address? (4) What are the current figures on the Reporters Without Borders' Press Freedom Barometer? (5) What was eBay's original name, and what was the first item offered for auction? (6) Why did ConnectU sue Facebook in 2008 and 2004? (7) What is the cost to use Google's 411 service?

2 Green Computing

EcoSearch is a search engine dedicated to supporting the Earth's natural resources. Visit this Web site (ecosearch.org), use your word processing program to answer the following questions, and then, if required, submit your answers to your instructor. (1) From what company do the search results come? (2) Click the Learn More link on the page. What charities does EcoSearch support? (3) How can you get involved to help EcoSearch? (4) Click the EcoSearch Home link at the bottom of the page to return to the EcoSearch home page. In the text box, type `ecosearch donate profits` and then click the Search button. Click several of the resulting links and review the information. Write a 50-word summary of the information, including what percent of EcoSearch proceeds is donated to charities and how much money EcoSearch expects to donate each year.

3 Social Networking

MySpace is considered one of the pioneering Web sites that helped popularize the online social networking phenomenon. Calling itself "a place for friends," it allows the millions of registered members to create profiles for free and then invite friends to join their networks. The growth of this Web site has helped it emerge as one of the more popular search engines. Visit the MySpace site (myspace.com), type the name of your favorite musical artist or group in the search text box, and then click the Search button. How many search results were found? Visit some of these profiles. Which music videos, playlists, and ringtones are featured? How do you create and edit your own playlists and add a song to your profile? Then click the Safety Tips link at the bottom of the page and read the guidelines for posting information and reporting inappropriate content. Summarize the music profiles you viewed and the guidelines. If required, submit your summary to your instructor.

4 Blogs

Many of the best blogs in the blogosphere have received awards for their content and design. For example, loyal blogging fans nominate and vote for their favorite blogs by visiting the Blogger's Choice Awards Web site (bloggerschoiceawards.com). Visit this Web site, click the Best Blog Design, Best Blog About Blogging, and Best Education Blog links, and view some of the blogs receiving the largest number of votes. Then visit other award sites, including the Interactive Media Awards (interactivemediaawards.com), Bloggies (bloggies.com), and the Best of Blogs (thebestofblogs.com). Which blogs, if any, received multiple awards on the different Web sites? Who casts the votes? What criteria are used to judge these blogs?

5 Ethics in Action

Some Internet access providers have admitted they monitored their users' Web surfing activities without giving notice of this eavesdropping practice. Embarq and Charter Communications secretly tested advertising technology to gather data about specific Web searches and then display advertisements relating to these searches. Privacy experts claim these Internet access providers' practices violate federal privacy laws, including the wiretapping statute. Locate news articles discussing the Internet access providers' Web eavesdropping. Then locate Web sites that oppose this practice. Summarize the views of the advertisers and the privacy proponents. If required, submit your summary to your instructor.

Making Use of the Web

INFORMATION LITERACY IS DEFINED as having the practical skills needed to evaluate information critically from print and electronic resources and to use this information accurately in daily life. Locating Web sites may be profitable for your educational and professional careers, as the resources may help you research class assignments and make your life more fulfilling and manageable.

Because the Web does not have an organizational structure to assist you in locating reliable material, you may need additional resources to guide you in searching. To help you find useful Web sites, this Special Feature describes specific information about a variety of Web pages, and it includes tables of Web addresses so that you can get started. The material is organized in several areas of interest.

Web Exercises at the end of each area will reinforce the material and help you discover Web sites that may add a treasure trove of knowledge to your life.

Areas of Interest	
Fun and Entertainment	Shopping and Auctions
Research	Weather, Sports, and News
Blogs	Learning
Online Social Networks and Media Sharing	Science
Travel	Health
Environment	Careers
Finance	Literature and Arts
Government	

Fun and Entertainment
That's Entertainment

Rock 'n' Roll on the Web

Consumers place great significance on buying entertainment products for fun and recreation. Nearly 10 percent of the United States's economy is spent on attending concerts and buying optical discs, reading materials, sporting goods, and toys.

Many Web sites supplement our cravings for fun and entertainment. For example, you can see and hear the musicians inducted into the Rock and Roll Hall of Fame and Museum. If you need an update on your favorite reality-based television program or a preview of an upcoming movie, E! Online and Entertainment Weekly provide the latest features about actors and actresses. The Internet Movie Database contains reviews of more than one million titles (Figure 1).

Watch the surfers riding the waves and romp with pandas at the San Diego Zoo. Web cams can display live video on Web pages, taking armchair travelers across the world for views of natural attractions, monuments, and cities. Many Web sites featuring Web cams are listed in the table in Figure 2.

Figure 1   Visitors exploring the Internet Movie Database will find the latest news about their favorite television programs and movies.

Fun and Entertainment Web Sites

Entertainment	Web Address
allmusic	allmusic.com
E! Online	eonline.com
Entertainment Weekly's EW	ew.com/ew
Games.com	games.com
Internet Movie Database	imdb.com
Old Time Radio (OTR) — Radio Days: A Radio History	otr.com
Rock and Roll Hall of Fame and Museum	rockhall.com
World Radio Network	wrn.org
Yahoo! Entertainment	entertainment.yahoo.com

Web Cams	Web Address
Camvista	camvista.com
Discovery Kids — Live Cams	kids.discovery.com/cams/cams.html
EarthCam — Webcam Network	earthcam.com
ESRL/GMD Mauna Loa Live Camera	esrl.noaa.gov/gmd/obop/mlo/livecam/index.html
Gatorland	gatorland.com/gatorcam.php
Geocaching — The Official Global GPS Cache Hunt Site	geocaching.com
Panda Cam San Diego Zoo	sandiegozoo.org/zoo/ex_panda_station.html
WebCam Central	camcentral.com
Wild Birds Unlimited Bird FeederCam	wbu.com/feedercam_home.html

📺 For more information about fun and entertainment Web sites, visit the Computer Concepts CourseMate Web site at www.cengagebrain.com and then navigate to the Making Use of the Web Feature resource for this book.

Figure 2   When you visit Web sites offering fun and entertainment resources, you can be both amused and informed.

Fun and Entertainment Web Exercises

1 Visit the Geocaching site listed in Figure 2. Find the geocaches within five miles of your home or school and then print a map showing their locations. Then, visit the Discovery Kids — Live Cams Web site and view one of the animal cams in the Live Cams. What do you observe? Visit another Web site listed in Figure 2 and describe the view. What are the benefits of having Web cams at these locations throughout the world?

2 What are your favorite movies? Use the Internet Movie Database Web site listed in Figure 2 to search for information about two films, and write a brief description of the biographies of the major stars and director for each movie. Then, visit one of the entertainment Web sites and describe three of the featured stories. At the Rock and Roll Hall of Fame and Museum Web site, view the information about The Beatles and one of your favorite musicians. Write a paragraph describing the information available about these rock stars.

Research
Search and Ye Shall Find

Information on the Web

A recent Web Usability survey conducted by the Nielsen Norman Group found that 88 percent of people who connect to the Internet use a search engine as their first online action. Search engines require users to type words and phrases that characterize the information being sought. Bing (Figure 3), Google, and AltaVista are some of the more popular search engines. The key to effective searching on the Web is composing search queries that narrow the search results and place the more relevant Web sites at the top of the results list.

Keep up with the latest computer and related product developments by viewing online dictionaries and encyclopedias that add to their collections on a regular basis. Shopping for a new computer can be a daunting experience, but many online guides can help you select the components that best fit your needs and budget. If you are not confident in your ability to solve a problem alone, turn to online technical support. Hardware and software reviews, price comparisons, shareware, technical questions and answers, and breaking technology news are found on comprehensive portals. Figure 4 lists popular research Web sites.

Figure 3   The Bing Web site provides a search engine for images, videos, shopping, news, maps, and travel.

Research Web Sites

Research	Web Address
A9.com	a9.com
AccessMyLibrary	accessmylibrary.com
AltaVista	altavista.com
Answers.com	answers.com
Ask	ask.com
Bing	bing.com
ChaCha	chacha.com
CNET	cnet.com
eHow	ehow.com
Google	google.com
HotBot	hotbot.com
Librarians' Internet Index	lii.org
PC911	pcnineoneone.com
Switchboard	switchboard.com
Webopedia	webopedia.com
ZDNet	zdnet.com

For more information about research Web sites, visit the Computer Concepts CourseMate Web site at www.cengagebrain.com and then navigate to the Making Use of the Web Feature resource for this book.

Figure 4   Web users can find information by using research Web sites.

Research Web Exercises

1 Visit two of the research Web sites listed in Figure 4 to find three Web sites that review the latest digital cameras from Kodak and Canon. Make a table listing the research Web sites, the located Web site names, and the cameras' model numbers, suggested retail price, and features.

2 Visit the Webopedia Web site. Search this site for five terms of your choice. Create a table with two columns: one for the term and one for the Web definition. Then, create a second table listing five recently added or updated words and their definitions on this Web site. Next, visit the CNET Web site to choose the components you would buy if you were building a customized desktop computer and notebook computer. Create a table for both computers, listing the computer manufacturer, processor model name or number and manufacturer, clock speed, RAM, cache, number of expansion slots, and number of bays.

Blogs
Express Yourself

Blogosphere Growing Swiftly

Internet users are feeling the need to publish their views, and they are finding Weblogs, or blogs for short, the ideal vehicle. The blogosphere began as an easy way for individuals to express their opinions on the Web. Today, this communications vehicle has become a powerful tool, for individuals, groups, and corporations are using blogs to promote their ideas and advertise their products. It is not necessary to have a background in Web design to be able to post to a blog.

Bloggers generally update their Web sites frequently to reflect their views. Their posts range from a paragraph to an entire essay and often contain links to other Web sites. The more popular blogs discuss politics, lifestyles, and technology.

Individuals easily may set up a blog free or for a fee, using Web sites such as Blogger, Bloglines (Figure 5), and TypePad. In addition, online social networks may have a built-in blogging feature. Be cautious of the information you post on your blog, especially if it is accessible to everyone online.

Figure 5   Bloglines keeps readers abreast of the latest technology, entertainment, and political news in the blogosphere.

Corporate blogs, such as The GM FastLane Blog, discuss all aspects of the company's products, whereas all-encompassing blogs, such as the MetaFilter Community Weblog and others in Figure 6, are designed to keep general readers entertained and informed.

Blogs are affecting the manner in which people communicate, and some experts predict they will one day become our primary method of sharing information.

Blogs Web Sites

Blog	Web Address
A List Apart	alistapart.com
Blog.com	blog.com
Blog Flux	topsites.blogflux.com
Blogger	blogger.com
Bloglines	bloglines.com
Blogstream	blogstream.com
Davenetics*Remote Control Revolutionary	davenetics.com
Geek News Central	geeknewscentral.com
GM FastLane Blog	fastlane.gmblogs.com
kottke.org	kottke.org
MetaFilter Community Weblog	metafilter.com
Rocketboom	rocketboom.com
TreeHugger	treehuggertv.com
Twitter	twitter.com
TypePad	typepad.com

For more information about blogs Web sites, visit the Computer Concepts CourseMate Web site at www.cengagebrain.com and then navigate to the Making Use of the Web Feature resource for this book.

Figure 6   These blogs offer information about technology, news, politics, and entertainment.

Blogs Web Exercises

1 Visit three of the blog Web sites listed in Figure 6. Make a table listing the blog name, its purpose, the author, its audience, and advertisers, if any, who sponsor the blog. Then, write a paragraph that describes the information you found on each of these blogs.

2 Many Internet users read the technology blogs to keep abreast of the latest developments. Visit the Geek News Central and Bloglines blogs listed in Figure 6 and write a paragraph describing the top story in each blog. Read the posted comments, if any. Then, write another paragraph describing two other stories found on these blogs that cover material you have discussed in this course. Write a third paragraph discussing which one is more interesting to you. Would you add reading blogs to your list of Internet activities? Why or why not?

Online Social Networks and Media Sharing
Check Out My New Photos

Online Social Networks and Media Sharing Web Sites Gain Popularity

Do you ever wonder what your friends are doing? What about your friends' friends? The popularity of online social networks has increased dramatically in recent years. Online social networks, such as those listed in Figure 7, allow you to create a personalized profile that others are able to view online. These profiles may include information about you such as your hometown, your age, your hobbies, and pictures. You also may create links to your friends' pages, post messages for individual friends, or bulletins for all of your friends to see. Online social networks are great places to keep in touch with your friends and to network with professionals for business purposes.

If you would like to post pictures and videos and do not require the full functionality of an online social network, you might consider a media sharing Web site, which is a type of online social network. Media sharing Web sites such as YouTube and Phanfare (Figure 8) allow you to post media, including photos and videos, for others to view, print, and/or download. Media sharing Web sites, which may be free or charge a fee, provide a quick, efficient way to share photos of your last vacation or videos of your family reunion.

Online Social Networks and Media Sharing	
Online Social Networks	**Web Address**
Club Penguin	clubpenguin.com
Facebook	facebook.com
LinkedIn	linkedin.com
MySpace — a place for friends	myspace.com
orkut	orkut.com
Windows Live Spaces	spaces.live.com
Media Sharing	**Web Address**
flickr	flickr.com
Phanfare	phanfare.com
Photobucket	photobucket.com
Picasa	picasa.com
Shutterfly	shutterfly.com
Yahoo! Video	video.yahoo.com
YouTube	youtube.com

For more information about online social networks and media sharing Web sites, visit the Computer Concepts CourseMate Web site at www.cengagebrain.com and then navigate to the Making Use of the Web Feature resource for this book.

Figure 7   Online social networks and media sharing Web sites are popular ways to keep in touch with friends, meet new people, and share media.

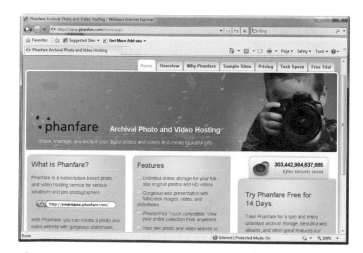

Figure 8   The Phanfare Web site allows users to share their photo and video files with people throughout the world.

Online Social Networks and Media Sharing Web Exercises

1 Many individuals now use online social networks. Visit two online social networks listed in Figure 7. (If you are attempting to access an online social network from your classroom and are unable to do so, your school may have restricted use of social networking Web sites.) Compare and contrast these two sites by performing the following actions and recording your findings. First, create a profile on each of these sites. If you find a Web site that charges a fee to sign up, choose another Web site. How easy is the sign-up process? Does either Web site ask for any personal information you are uncomfortable sharing? If so, what information? Once you sign up, make a list of five of your closest friends, and search for their profiles on each of these two sites. Which site contains more of your friends? Browse each site and make a list of its features. In your opinion, which site is better? Explain why.

2 Media sharing Web sites make it easy to share photos and videos with friends, family, and colleagues. Before choosing a media sharing Web site to use, do some research. Visit two media sharing Web sites in Figure 7. Is there a fee to post media to these Web sites? If so, how much? Are these Web sites supported by advertisements? Locate the instructions for posting media to these Web sites. Are the instructions straightforward? Do these Web sites impose a limit on the number and/or size of media files you can post? Summarize your responses to these questions in two or three paragraphs.

Travel
Get Packing!

Explore the World without Leaving Home

When you are ready to arrange your next travel adventure or just want to explore destination possibilities, the Internet provides ample resources to set your plans in motion.

To discover exactly where your destination is on this planet, cartography Web sites, including MapQuest and Yahoo! Maps, allow you to pinpoint your destination. View your exact destination using satellite imagery with Google Maps and Bing Maps (Figure 9).

Some excellent starting places are general travel Web sites such as Expedia Travel, Cheap Tickets, Orbitz, and Travelocity. Many airline Web sites allow you to reserve hotel rooms, activities, and rental cars while booking a flight. These all-encompassing Web sites, including those in Figure 10, have tools to help you find the lowest prices and details about flights, car rentals, cruises, and hotels. Comprehensive online guidebooks can provide useful details about maximizing your vacation time while saving money.

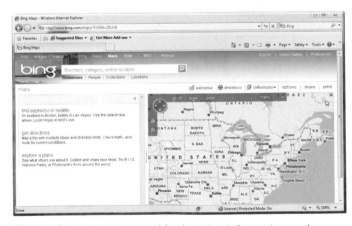

Figure 9   Bing Maps provides location information and satellite imagery for many regions on this planet.

Travel Web Sites

General Travel	Web Address
CheapTickets	cheaptickets.com
Expedia Travel	expedia.com
Kayak	kayak.com
Orbitz	orbitz.com
SideStep	sidestep.com
Travelocity	travelocity.com
Cartography	**Web Address**
Bing Maps	bing.com/maps
Google Maps	maps.google.com
MapQuest	mapquest.com
Maps.com	maps.com
Yahoo! Maps	maps.yahoo.com
Travel and City Guides	**Web Address**
Frommer's Travel Guides	frommers.com
GoPlanit	goplanit.com
U.S.-Parks US National Parks Travel Guide	www.us-parks.com
Virtual Tourist	virtualtourist.com

For more information about travel Web sites, visit the Computer Concepts CourseMate Web site at www.cengagebrain.com and then navigate to the Making Use of the Web Feature resource for this book.

Figure 10   These travel resources Web sites offer travel information to exciting destinations throughout the world.

Travel Web Exercises

1 Visit one of the cartography Web sites listed in Figure 10 and obtain the directions from your campus to one of these destinations: the Washington Monument in Washington, D.C.; the Statue of Liberty on Ellis Island in New York; Disneyland in Anaheim, California; or the Grand Old Opry in Nashville, Tennessee. How many miles is it to your destination? What is the estimated driving time? Use the Google Maps Web site to obtain an overhead image of this destination. Then, visit one of the general travel Web sites listed in the table and plan a flight from the nearest major airport to one of the four destinations for the week after finals and a return trip one week later. Which airline, flight numbers, and departure and arrival times did you select?

2 Visit one of the travel and city guides Web sites listed in Figure 10, and choose a destination for a getaway this coming weekend. Write a one-page paper giving details about this location, such as popular hotels and lodging, expected weather, population, local colleges and universities, parks and recreation, ancient and modern history, and tours. Include a map or satellite photo of this place. Why did you select this destination? How would you travel there and back? What is the breakdown of expected costs for this weekend, including travel expenditures, meals, lodging, and tickets to events and activities? Which Web addresses did you use to complete this exercise?

Environment
The Future of the Planet

Making a Difference for Earth

From the rain forests of Africa to the marine life in the Pacific Ocean, the fragile ecosystem is under extreme stress. Many environmental groups have developed informative Web sites, including those listed in Figure 11, in attempts to educate

Environment Web Sites	
Name	**Web Address**
Central African Regional Program for the Environment (CARPE)	carpe.umd.edu
Earthjustice	earthjustice.org
EarthTrends: Environmental Information	earthtrends.wri.org
Environmental Defense Fund	edf.org
Environmental Sites on the Internet	www.ima.kth.se/im/envsite/envsite.htm
EPA AirData — Access to Air Pollution Data	epa.gov/air/data
Global Warming	globalwarming.org
Green Computing Impact Organization	gcio.org
GreenNet	gn.apc.org
New American Dream	newdream.org
University of Wisconsin — Milwaukee Environmental Health and Safety Resources	uwm.edu/Dept/EHSRM/EHSLINKS
USGS Branch of Quality Systems	bqs.usgs.gov/acidrain

For more information about environment Web sites, visit the Computer Concepts CourseMate Web site at www.cengagebrain.com and then navigate to the Making Use of the Web Feature resource for this book.

Figure 11   Environment Web sites provide vast resources for ecological data and action groups.

worldwide populations and to increase resource conservation. The Environmental Defense Fund Web site (Figure 12) contains information for people who would like to help safeguard the environment.

On an international scale, the Environmental Sites on the Internet Web page developed by the Royal Institute of Technology in Stockholm, Sweden, has been rated as one of the better ecological Web sites. Its comprehensive listing of environmental concerns range from aquatic ecology to wetlands.

The U.S. federal government has a number of Web sites devoted to specific environmental concerns. For example, the U.S. Environmental Protection Agency (EPA) provides pollution data, including ozone levels and air pollutants, for specific areas. Its AirData Web site displays air pollution emissions and monitoring data from the entire United States and is the world's most extensive collection of air pollution data.

Figure 12   A visit to the Environmental Defense Fund Web site provides practical advice about protecting the environment.

Environment Web Exercises

1 The New American Dream Web site encourages consumers to reduce the amount of junk mail sent to their homes. Using the table in Figure 11, visit the Web site to learn how many trees are leveled each year to provide paper for these mailings and how many garbage trucks are needed to haul this waste. Read the letters used to eliminate names from bulk mail lists. To whom would you mail these letters? How long does it take to stop these unsolicited letters?

2 Visit the EPA AirData Web site. What is the highest ozone level recorded in your state this past year? Where are the nearest air pollution monitoring Web sites, and what are their levels? Where are the nearest sources of air pollution? Read two reports about two different topics, such as acid rain and air quality, and summarize their findings. Include information about who sponsored the research, who conducted the studies, when the data was collected, and the impact of this pollution on the atmosphere, water, forests, and human health. Whom would you contact for further information regarding the data and studies?

Finance
Money Matters

Cashing In on Financial Advice

You can manage your money with advice from financial Web sites that offer online banking, tax help, personal finance, and small business and commercial services.

If you do not have a personal banker or a financial planner, consider a Web adviser to guide your investment decisions. The MSN Money Web site (Figure 13) provides financial news and investment information.

If you are ready to ride the ups and downs of the Dow and the NASDAQ, an abundance of Web sites listed in Figure 14, including Reuters and Morningstar, can help you select companies that fit your interests and financial needs.

Claiming to be the fastest, easiest tax publication on the planet, the Internal Revenue Service Web site contains procedures for filing tax appeals and contains IRS forms, publications, and legal regulations.

Figure 13   The MSN Money Web site contains features and information related to college and family finances.

Finance Web Sites	
Advice and Education	**Web Address**
Bankrate	bankrate.com
ING Direct	ingdirect.com
LendingTree	lendingtree.com
Loan.com	loan.com
The Motley Fool	fool.com
MSN Money	moneycentral.msn.com
Wells Fargo	wellsfargo.com
Yahoo! Finance	finance.yahoo.com
Stock Market	**Web Address**
E*TRADE	us.etrade.com
Financial Engines	financialengines.com
Merrill Lynch	ml.com
Morningstar	morningstar.com
Reuters	reuters.com/investing
Valic	valic.com
Vanguard	vanguard.com
Taxes	**Web Address**
H&R Block	hrblock.com
Internal Revenue Service	www.irs.gov
Jackson Hewitt	jacksonhewitt.com
Liberty Tax Service	libertytax.com

For more information about finance Web sites, visit the Computer Concepts CourseMate Web site at www.cengagebrain.com and then navigate to the Making Use of the Web Feature resource for this book.

Figure 14   Financial resources Web sites offer general information, stock market analyses, and tax advice, as well as guidance and money-saving tips.

Finance Web Exercises

1 Visit three advice and education Web sites listed in Figure 14 and read their top business world reports. Write a paragraph about each, summarizing these stories. Which stocks or mutual funds do these Web sites predict as being sound investments today? What are the current market indexes for the DJIA (Dow Jones Industrial Average), S&P 500, and NASDAQ, and how do these figures compare with the previous day's numbers?

2 Using two of the stock market Web sites listed in Figure 14, search for information about Microsoft, Apple, and one other software vendor. Write a paragraph about each of these stocks describing the revenues, net incomes, total assets for the previous year, current stock price per share, highest and lowest prices of each stock during the past year, and other relevant investment information.

Government
Stamp of Approval

Making a Federal Case for Useful Information

When it is time to buy stamps to mail your correspondence, you no longer need to wait in long lines at your local post office. The U.S. Postal Service has authorized several organizations to sell stamps online.

You can recognize U.S. Government Web sites on the Internet by their gov top-level domain. For example, the Library of Congress Web site is loc.gov (Figure 15). Government and military Web sites offer a wide range of information. The Time Service Department Web site will provide you with the correct time. If you are looking for a federal document, FedWorld lists thousands of documents distributed by the government on its Web site. For access to the names of your congressional representatives, visit the extensive HG.org Web site. Figure 16 shows some of the more popular U.S. Government Web sites.

Figure 15   The Library of Congress Web site has resources about American history, world culture, and digital preservation.

Government Resources Web Sites

Postage	Web Address
Endicia	endicia.com
Pitney Bowes	pb.com
Stamps.com	stamps.com

Government	Web Address
FedWorld	www.fedworld.gov
HG.org — Worldwide Legal Directories	hg.org
Library of Congress	loc.gov
National Agricultural Library	nal.usda.gov
Smithsonian Institution	smithsonian.org
THOMAS (Library of Congress)	thomas.loc.gov
Time Service Department	tycho.usno.navy.mil
U.S. Department of Education	ed.gov
United States Department of the Treasury	treas.gov
U.S. Government Printing Office	www.access.gpo.gov
United States National Library of Medicine	nlm.nih.gov
United States Patent and Trademark Office	uspto.gov
USAJOBS	usajobs.opm.gov
The White House	whitehouse.gov

For more information about government Web sites, visit the Computer Concepts CourseMate Web site at www.cengagebrain.com and then navigate to the Making Use of the Web Feature resource for this book.

Figure 16   These Web sites offer information about buying U.S.-approved postage online and researching federal agencies.

Government Web Exercises

1 View the three postage Web sites listed in Figure 16. Compare and contrast the available services on each one. Consider postage cost, necessary equipment, shipping services, security techniques, and tracking capability. Explain why you would or would not like to use this service.

2 Visit the HG.org Web site listed in Figure 16. What are the names, addresses, and phone numbers of your two state senators and your local congressional representative? On what committees do they serve? Who is the chief justice of the Supreme Court, and what has been this justice's opinion on two recently decided cases? Who are the members of the president's cabinet? Then, visit two other Web sites listed in Figure 16. Write a paragraph about each Web site describing its content and features.

Shopping and Auctions
Bargains Galore

Let Your Mouse Do Your Shopping

From groceries to clothing to computers, you can buy just about everything you need with just a few clicks of your mouse. More than one-half of Internet users will make at least one online purchase this year. Books, computer software and hardware, and music are the hottest commodities.

The two categories of Internet shopping Web sites are those with physical counterparts, such as Walmart and Fry's Electronics (Figure 17), and those with only a Web presence, such as Amazon and Buy. Popular Web shopping sites are listed in Figure 18.

Another method of shopping for the items you need, and maybe some you really do not need, is to visit auction Web sites, including those listed in Figure 18. Categories include antiques and collectibles, automotive, computers, electronics, music, sports, sports cards and memorabilia, and toys. Online auction Web sites can offer unusual items, including *Star Wars* memorabilia or a round of golf with Jack Nicklaus. eBay is one of thousands of Internet auction Web sites and is the world's largest personal online trading community. In addition, craigslist is a free online equivalent of classified advertisements.

Figure 17   Fry's is a popular electronic retailer that sells a variety of products.

Shopping and Auctions Web Sites

Auctions	Web Address
craigslist	craigslist.org
eBay	ebay.com
Sotheby's	sothebys.com
uBid	ubid.com
U.S. Treasury — Seized Property Auctions	ustreas.gov/auctions
Books and Music	**Web Address**
Amazon	amazon.com
Barnes & Noble	bn.com
BookFinder	bookfinder.com
Computers and Electronics	**Web Address**
BestBuy	bestbuy.com
Buy	buy.com
Fry's Electronics	frys.com
Miscellaneous	**Web Address**
drugstore	drugstore.com
Google Product Search	google.com/products
SmashBuys	smashbuys.com
Walmart	walmart.com

For more information about shopping and auctions Web sites, visit the Computer Concepts CourseMate Web site at www.cengagebrain.com and then navigate to the Making Use of the Web Feature resource for this book.

Figure 18   Making online purchases can help ease the burden of driving to and fighting the crowds in local malls.

Shopping and Auctions Web Exercises

1 Visit two of the computers and electronics and two of the miscellaneous Web sites listed in Figure 18. Write a paragraph describing the features these Web sites offer compared with the same offerings from stores. In another paragraph, describe any disadvantages of shopping at these Web sites instead of actually visiting a store. Then, describe their policies for returning unwanted merchandise and for handling complaints.

2 Using one of the auction Web sites listed in Figure 18, search for two objects pertaining to your hobbies. For example, if you are a sports fan, you can search for a complete set of Upper Deck cards. If you are a car buff, search for your dream car. Describe these two items. How many people have bid on these items? Who are the sellers? What are the opening and current bids?

Weather, Sports, and News
What's News?

Weather, Sports, and News Web Sites Score Big Hits

Rain or sun? Hot or cold? Weather is the leading online news item, with at least 10,000 Web sites devoted to this field. Millions of people view The Weather Channel Web site (Figure 19) each month.

Baseball may be the national pastime, but sports aficionados yearn for everything from auto racing to cricket. The Internet has millions of pages of multimedia sports news, entertainment, and merchandise.

The Internet has emerged as a major source for news, with more than one-third of Americans going online at least once a week and 15 percent going online daily for reports of major news events. Many of these viewers are using RSS (Really Simple Syndication) technology to be notified when new stories about their favorite topics are available on the Internet. Popular weather, sports, and news Web sites are listed in Figure 20.

Figure 19   Local, national, and international weather conditions and details about breaking weather stories are available on The Weather Channel Web site.

Weather, Sports, and News Web Sites

Weather	Web Address
AccuWeather	accuweather.com
Infoplease Weather	infoplease.com/weather.html
Intellicast	www.intellicast.com
National Weather Service	www.crh.noaa.gov
The Weather Channel	weather.com
Sports	**Web Address**
CBS Sports	cbssports.com
ESPN	espn.com
NASCAR	nascar.com
International Olympic Committee	www.olympic.org
Sporting News Radio	radio.sportingnews.com
Yahoo! Sports	sports.yahoo.com
News	**Web Address**
FactCheck	factcheck.org
Geek.com	geek.com
Google News	news.google.com
MSNBC	msnbc.com
Onlinenewspapers	onlinenewspapers.com
privacy.org	privacy.org
SiliconValley	siliconvalley.com
starting page	startingpage.com/html/news.html
USA TODAY	usatoday.com
Washington Post	washingtonpost.com

For more information about weather, sports, and news Web sites, visit the Computer Concepts CourseMate Web site at www.cengagebrain.com and then navigate to the Making Use of the Web Feature resource for this book.

Figure 20   Keep informed about the latest weather, sports, and news events with these Web sites.

Weather, Sports, and News Web Exercises

1 Visit two of the sports Web sites in Figure 20 and write a paragraph describing the content these Web sites provide concerning your favorite sport. Visit Google News and then search for stories about this sports team or athlete. Then, create a customized news page with stories about your sports interests. Include RSS feeds to get regularly updated summaries on this subject.

2 Visit the Onlinenewspapers and starting page Web sites listed in Figure 20 and select two newspapers from each site. Write a paragraph describing the top national news story featured in each of these four Web pages. Then, write another paragraph describing the top international news story displayed at each Web site. In the third paragraph, discuss which of the four Web sites is the most interesting in terms of story selection, photos, and Web page design.

Learning
Yearn to Learn

Discover New Worlds Online

While you may believe your education ends when you finally graduate from college, learning is a lifelong process. You can increase your technological knowledge by visiting several Web sites (Figure 21) with tutorials about building your own Web sites, the latest news about the Internet, and resources for visually impaired users.

Learning Web Sites	
Learning How To's	**Web Address**
Bartleby: Great Books Online	bartleby.com
AT&T Knowledge Network Explorer	www.kn.pacbell.com/wired
BBC Learning	bbc.co.uk/learning
CBT Nuggets	cbtnuggets.com
HowStuffWorks	howstuffworks.com
Internet Public Library	ipl.org
Learn the Net	learnthenet.com
ScienceMaster	sciencemaster.com
Search Engine Watch	searchenginewatch.com
Wiredguide	wiredguide.com
Cooking	**Web Address**
Betty Crocker	bettycrocker.com
Chef2Chef	chef2chef.net
Food Network	foodnetwork.com

For more information about learning Web sites, visit the Computer Concepts CourseMate Web site at www.cengagebrain.com and then navigate to the Making Use of the Web Feature resource for this book.

Figure 21   The information gleaned from these Web sites can help you learn about many aspects of our existence.

The HowStuffWorks Web site has won numerous awards for its clear, comprehensive articles that demystify aspects of our everyday life. It includes ratings and reviews of products written by *Consumer Guide* editors.

A consortium of colleges maintains the Internet Public Library, which includes subject collections, reference materials, and a reading room filled with magazines and books. Volunteer librarians will answer your personal questions asked in its Ask an IPL Librarian form.

Enhancing your culinary skills can be a rewarding endeavor. No matter if you are a gourmet chef or a weekend cook, you will be cooking in style with the help of online resources, including those listed in Figure 21.

Have you ever wondered how to make a key lime pie? How about learning how to cook some easy, low-calorie dishes? Are you seeking advice from expert chefs? The Food Network Web site (Figure 22) is filled with information related to cooking, grilling, and healthy eating.

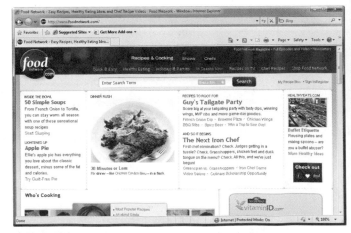

Figure 22   The Food Network Web site provides access to healthy recipes, grilling tips, and cookware.

Learning Web Exercises

1 Using one of the Learning How To's Web sites listed in Figure 21, search for information about installing memory in a computer. Write a paragraph about your findings. Then, review the material in the HowStuffWorks Web site listed in Figure 21, and write a paragraph describing articles on this Web site that are pertinent to your major.

2 Visit one of the cooking Web sites listed in Figure 21 and find two recipes or cooking tips that you can use when preparing your next meal. Write a paragraph about each one, summarizing your discoveries. Which Web sites allow you to create your own online recipe book? What are the advantages and disadvantages of accessing these Web sites on the new appliances and gadgets that might someday be in your kitchen?

Science

$$E = mc^2$$

Rocket Science on the Web

For some people, space exploration is a hobby. Building and launching model rockets allow these at-home scientists to participate in exploring the great frontier of space. For others, space exploration is their life. Numerous Web sites, including those in Figure 23, provide in-depth information about the universe.

Science Web Sites	
Periodicals	**Web Address**
Archaeology Magazine	archaeology.org
Astronomy Magazine	astronomy.com
New Scientist	newscientist.com
OceanLink	oceanlink.info
Science Magazine	sciencemag.org
Scientific American	sciam.com
Resources	**Web Address**
National Science Foundation (NSF)	nsf.gov
Science.gov: USA.gov for Science	science.gov
Thomson Reuters	scientific.thomson.com/free/
Science Community	**Web Address**
American Scientist	amsci.org
Federation of American Scientists	fas.org
NASA	www.nasa.gov
Sigma Xi, The Scientific Research Society	sigmaxi.org

For more information about science Web sites, visit the Computer Concepts CourseMate Web site at www.cengagebrain.com and then navigate to the Making Use of the Web Feature resource for this book.

Figure 23 Resources available on the Internet offer a wide range of subjects for enthusiasts who want to delve into familiar and unknown territories in the world of science.

NASA's Web site contains information about rockets, space exploration, the International Space Station, space transportation, and communications. Other science resources explore space-related questions about astronomy, physics, the earth sciences, microgravity, and robotics.

Rockets and space are not the only areas to explore in the world of science. Where can you find the latest pictures taken with the Hubble Space Telescope? Do you know how climate change is affecting the human body? You can find the answers to these questions and many others through the New Scientist Web site (newscientist.com) shown in Figure 24.

The National Science Foundation's Web site features overviews of current topics and an extensive Multimedia Gallery with audio and video files, photos, and paintings.

Science.gov is an outstanding resource for scientific databases and thousands of authoritative science Web sites. The U.S. government science information provided offers 200 million pages of research, with search results ranked by relevance and sorted by topic and year.

Figure 24 The New Scientist Web site covers news about space exploration, the environment, and technology.

Science Web Exercises

1 Visit the National Science Foundation Web site listed in the table in Figure 23. What are the topics of the latest science news and special reports? Which speeches and lectures are featured? What are the titles of image, video, and audio files in the Multimedia Gallery?

2 Visit the NASA Web site listed in the table in Figure 23. Click the Missions link and then click the Mission Calendar link. When are the next two launches scheduled? What are the purposes of these missions? Click the Careers @ NASA topic and then write a paragraph describing the internships, cooperative programs, and summer employment opportunities. Then, view two of the science community Web sites listed in Figure 23 and write a paragraph about each of these Web sites describing the information each contains.

Health
No Pain, All Gain

Store Personal Health Records Online

More than 75 million consumers use the Internet yearly to search for health information, so using the Web to store personal medical data is a natural extension of the Internet's capabilities. Internet health services and portals are available to store your personal health history, including prescriptions, lab test results, doctor visits, allergies, and immunizations.

Google Health allows users to create a health profile, import medical records, and locate medical services and doctors. Web sites such as healthfinder.gov (Figure 25) provide free wellness information to consumers. Wise consumers, however, verify the online information they read with their personal physician.

In minutes, you can register with a health Web site by choosing a user name and password. Then, you create a record to enter your medical history. You also can store data for your emergency contacts, primary care physicians, specialists, blood type, cholesterol levels, blood pressure, and insurance plan. No matter where you are in the world, you and medical personnel can obtain records via the Internet or fax machine. Some popular online health databases are shown in Figure 26.

Health Web Sites

Medical History	Web Address
Google Health	google.com/health
Lifestar	mylifestarphr.com
Medem	medem.com
PersonalMD	personalmd.com
Practice Solutions	practicesolutions.ca
Records for Living, Inc — Personal Health and Living Management	recordsforliving.com
WebMD	webmd.com

General Health	Web Address
Consumer and Patient Health Information Section (CAPHIS)	caphis.mlanet.org/consumer
Centers for Disease Control and Prevention	cdc.gov
familydoctor	familydoctor.org
healthfinder	healthfinder.gov
KidsHealth	kidshealth.org
LIVESTRONG.COM	livestrong.com
MedlinePlus	medlineplus.gov
PE Central: Health and Nutrition Web Sites	pecentral.org/websites/healthsites.html
Physical Activity Guidelines	health.gov/paguidelines

For more information about health Web sites, visit the Computer Concepts CourseMate Web site at www.cengagebrain.com and then navigate to the Making Use of the Web Feature resource for this book.

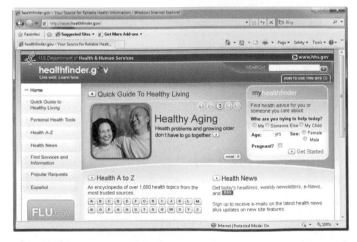

Figure 25   The healthfinder.gov Web site provides advice and tools to prevent illnesses and check drug interactions.

Figure 26   These health Web sites allow you to organize your medical information and store it in an online database and also obtain information about a variety of medical conditions and treatments.

Health Web Exercises

1. **Access one of the health Web sites listed in Figure 26.** Register yourself or a family member and then enter the full health history. Create an emergency medical card if the Web site provides the card option. Submit this record and emergency card to your instructor. If you feel uncomfortable disclosing medical information for yourself or a family member, you may enter fictitious information.

2. **Visit three of the health Web sites listed in Figure 26.** Describe the features of each. Which of the three is the most user-friendly? Why? Describe the privacy policies of these three Web sites. Submit your analysis of these Web sites to your instructor.

Careers
In Search of the Perfect Job

Web Helps Career Hunt

While your teachers give you valuable training to prepare you for a career, they rarely teach you how to begin that career. You can broaden your horizons by searching the Internet for career information and job openings.

First, examine some of the job search Web sites. These resources list thousands of openings in hundreds of fields, companies, and locations. For example, the USAJOBS Web site, shown in Figure 27, allows you to find information for Federal jobs. This information may include the training and education required, salary data, working conditions, job descriptions, and more. In addition, many companies advertise careers on their Web sites.

When a company contacts you for an interview, learn as much about it and the industry as possible before the interview. Many of the Web sites listed in Figure 28 include detailed company profiles and links to their corporate Web sites.

Figure 27 The USAJOBS Web site is the official location for federal jobs and information for job seekers.

Career Web Sites	
Job Search	**Web Address**
BestJobsUSA	bestjobsusa.com
CareerBuilder	careerbuilder.com
Careerjet	careerjet.com
CareerNET	careernet.com
CAREERXCHANGE	careerxchange.com
CollegeGrad.com	collegegrad.com
EmploymentGuide.com	employmentguide.com
Job.com	job.com
Job Bank USA	jobbankusa.com
JobWeb	jobweb.com
Monster	monster.com
USAJOBS	www.usajobs.gov
VolunteerMatch	volunteermatch.org
Yahoo! HotJobs	hotjobs.yahoo.com
Company/Industry Information	**Web Address**
Careers.org	careers.org
Forbes	forbes.com/leadership/careers
Fortune	fortune.com
Hoover's	hoovers.com
Occupational Outlook Handbook	stats.bls.gov/oco

For more information about career Web sites, visit the Computer Concepts CourseMate Web site at www.cengagebrain.com and then navigate to the Making Use of the Web Feature resource for this book.

Figure 28 Career Web sites provide a variety of job openings and information about major companies worldwide.

Careers Web Exercises

1 Use two of the job search Web sites listed in Figure 28 to find three companies with job openings in your field. Make a table listing the Web site name, position available, description, salary, location, desired education, and desired experience.

2 It is a good idea to acquire information before graduation about the industry in which you would like to work. Are you interested in the automotive manufacturing industry, the restaurant service industry, or the financial industry? Use two of the company/industry information Web sites listed in Figure 28 to research a particular career related to your major. Write a paragraph naming the Web sites and the specific information you found, such as the nature of the work, recommended training and qualifications, employment outlook, and earnings. Then, use two other Web sites to profile three companies with positions available in this field. Write a paragraph about each of these companies, describing the headquarters' location, sales and earnings for the previous year, total number of employees, working conditions, benefits, and competitors.

Literature and Arts
Find Some Culture

Get Ready to Read, Paint, and Dance

Brush up your knowledge of Shakespeare, grab a canvas, and put on your dancing shoes. Literature and arts Web sites, including those in Figure 29, are about to sweep you off your cyberfeet.

Literature and Arts Web Sites	
Literature	**Web Address**
Bartleby	bartleby.com
Bibliomania	bibliomania.com
The Complete Review	www.complete-review.com
eNotes	enotes.com
Fantastic Fiction	fantasticfiction.co.uk
Literary History	literaryhistory.com
Nobel Prize in Literature	nobelprize.org/nobel_ prizes/literature/laureates/ 1909/press.html
Project Gutenberg	gutenberg.org
Project MUSE	muse.jhu.edu
Arts	**Web Address**
absolutearts	absolutearts.com
The Children's Museum of Indianapolis	childrensmuseum.org
ARTINFO Gallery Guide	artinfo.com/galleryguide/
The Getty	getty.edu
Louvre Museum	louvre.fr
Montreal Museum of Fine Arts	mmfa.qc.ca
Museumstuff.com	museumstuff.com
The Museum of Online Museums	coudal.com/moom
National Gallery of Art	nga.gov

For more information about literature and arts Web sites, visit the Computer Concepts CourseMate Web site at www.cengagebrain.com and then navigate to the Making Use of the Web Feature resource for this book.

Figure 29   Discover culture throughout the world by visiting these literature and arts Web sites.

The full text of hundreds of books is available online from the Bibliomania and Project Gutenberg Web sites. The Complete Review provides summaries, reviews, and Web links about a variety of books and their authors. The Bartleby Web site features biographies, definitions, quotations, dictionaries, and indexes.

When you are ready to absorb more culture, you can turn to various art Web sites. Many museums have images of their collections online. Among them are the Getty Museum in Los Angeles, the Montreal Museum of Fine Arts, and the Louvre Museum in Paris (Figure 30).

The absolutearts Web site focuses on contemporary art and includes video interviews with artists, art history research, and artists' blogs.

The Museum of Online Museums Web site provides links to museum and gallery Web sites, such as the Museum of Modern Art, The Bauhaus Archive, and The Art Institute of Chicago.

Figure 30   Permanent and temporary exhibitions, educational activities, and a bookstore are featured on the Louvre Museum Web site.

Literature and Arts Web Exercises

1 Visit the Literary History Web site listed in Figure 29 and view one author in the Twentieth Century Literature, Nineteenth Century Literature, British Poets, and African American Literature sections. Read two literary criticism articles about each of the four authors and write a paragraph describing which of these authors is the most interesting to you. What are the advantages and disadvantages of reading literary criticism electronically?

2 Using the arts Web sites listed in Figure 29, search for three temporary exhibitions in galleries throughout the world. Describe the venues, the artists, and the works. Which permanent collections are found in these museums? Some people shop for gifts in the museums' stores. View and describe three items for sale.

Chapter Three

Application Software

Objectives

After completing this chapter, you will be able to:

1 Identify the four categories of application software

2 Describe characteristics of a user interface

3 Identify the key features of widely used business programs: word processing, spreadsheet, database, presentation, note taking, personal information manager, business software for phones, business software suite, project management, accounting, document management, and enterprise computing

4 Identify the key features of widely used graphics and multimedia programs: computer-aided design, professional desktop publishing, professional paint/image editing, professional photo editing, professional video and audio editing, multimedia authoring, and Web page authoring

5 Identify the key features of widely used home, personal, and educational programs: personal finance, legal, tax preparation, personal desktop publishing, personal paint/image editing, personal photo editing and photo management, clip art/image gallery, personal video and audio editing, travel and mapping, reference and educational, and entertainment

6 Discuss Web applications

7 Identify the types of application software used in communications

8 Describe the learning aids available for application software

Application Software

With the proper software, a computer is a valuable tool. Software allows users to create letters, reports, and other documents; develop multimedia presentations; design Web pages and diagrams; draw images; enhance audio and video clips; prepare taxes; play games; compose e-mail messages and instant messages; and much more. To accomplish these and many other tasks, users work with application software. **Application software** consists of programs designed to make users more productive and/or assist them with personal tasks. Application software has a variety of uses:

1. To make business activities more efficient
2. To assist with graphics and multimedia projects
3. To support home, personal, and educational tasks
4. To facilitate communications

The table in Figure 3-1 categorizes popular types of application software by their general use. Although many types of communications software exist, the ones listed in Figure 3-1 are application software oriented.

Application software is available in a variety of forms: packaged, custom, Web application, open source, shareware, freeware, and public domain.

- **Packaged software** is mass-produced, copyrighted retail software that meets the needs of a wide variety of users, not just a single user or company. Packaged software is available in retail stores or on the Web. Figure 3-1 shows some images of packaged software.
- **Custom software** performs functions specific to a business or industry. Sometimes a company cannot find packaged software that meets its unique requirements. In this case, the company may use programmers to develop tailor-made custom software.
- A **Web application** is a Web site that allows users to access and interact with software from any computer or device that is connected to the Internet. Types of Web applications include e-mail, word processing, and game programs.

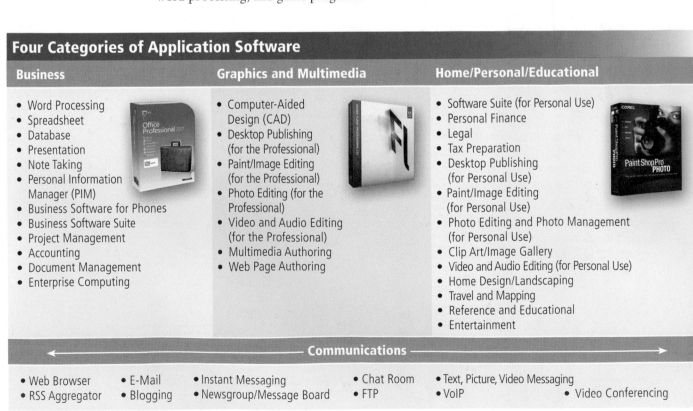

Four Categories of Application Software

Business	Graphics and Multimedia	Home/Personal/Educational
• Word Processing • Spreadsheet • Database • Presentation • Note Taking • Personal Information Manager (PIM) • Business Software for Phones • Business Software Suite • Project Management • Accounting • Document Management • Enterprise Computing	• Computer-Aided Design (CAD) • Desktop Publishing (for the Professional) • Paint/Image Editing (for the Professional) • Photo Editing (for the Professional) • Video and Audio Editing (for the Professional) • Multimedia Authoring • Web Page Authoring	• Software Suite (for Personal Use) • Personal Finance • Legal • Tax Preparation • Desktop Publishing (for Personal Use) • Paint/Image Editing (for Personal Use) • Photo Editing and Photo Management (for Personal Use) • Clip Art/Image Gallery • Video and Audio Editing (for Personal Use) • Home Design/Landscaping • Travel and Mapping • Reference and Educational • Entertainment

Communications

• Web Browser • RSS Aggregator	• E-Mail • Blogging	• Instant Messaging • Newsgroup/Message Board	• Chat Room • FTP	• Text, Picture, Video Messaging • VoIP • Video Conferencing

Figure 3-1 The four major categories of popular application software are outlined in this table. Communications software often is bundled with other application or system software.

- **Open source software** is software provided for use, modification, and redistribution. This software has no restrictions from the copyright holder regarding modification of the software's internal instructions and its redistribution. Open source software usually can be downloaded from the Internet, often at no cost.
- **Shareware** is copyrighted software that is distributed at no cost for a trial period. To use a shareware program beyond that period, you send payment to the program developer.
- **Freeware** is copyrighted software provided at no cost to a user by an individual or a company that retains all rights to the software.
- **Public-domain software** has been donated for public use and has no copyright restrictions. Anyone can copy or distribute public-domain software to others at no cost.

Thousands of shareware, freeware, and public-domain programs are available on the Internet for users to download. Examples include communications, graphics, and game programs.

The Role of System Software

System software serves as the interface between the user, the application software, and the computer's hardware (Figure 3-2). To use application software, such as a word processing program, your computer must be running system software — specifically, an operating system. Three popular personal computer operating systems are Windows, Mac OS, and Linux.

Each time you start a computer, the operating system is loaded (copied) from the computer's hard disk into memory. Once the operating system is loaded, it coordinates all the activities of the computer. This includes starting application software and transferring data among input and output devices and memory. While the computer is running, the operating system remains in memory.

Figure 3-2   A user does not communicate directly with the computer hardware. Instead, system software is the interface between the user, the application software, and the hardware. For example, when a user instructs the application software to print a document, the application software sends the print instruction to the system software, which in turn sends the print instruction to the hardware.

Antivirus Programs

For more information, visit the Computer Concepts CourseMate Web site at www.cengagebrain.com, navigate to the Chapter 3 Web Link resource for this book, and then click Antivirus Programs.

Utility Programs   A utility program is a type of system software that assists users with controlling or maintaining the operation of a computer, its devices, or its software. Utility programs typically offer features that provide an environment conducive to successful use of application software. For example, utility programs protect a computer against malicious software and unauthorized intrusions, manage files and disks, compress files, play media files, and burn optical discs. (To learn more about how to compress files, complete the Learn How To 2 activity on pages 138 and 139.)

One of the more important utility programs protects a computer against malicious software, or **malware**, which is a program that acts without a user's knowledge and deliberately alters the computer's operations. A computer virus is a type of malicious software. Chapter 7 discusses system software and utility programs in more depth.

?   FAQ 3-1

How many viruses exist on the Internet?

More than one million viruses exist on the Internet. This statistic stresses the importance of protecting your computer from various threats on the Internet, as well as practicing safe Web browsing habits. Not only is it possible to get a computer virus from downloading and opening an infected file or by opening an infected e-mail message, you also can fall victim to a computer virus simply by visiting a malicious Web site.

For more information, visit the Computer Concepts CourseMate Web site at www.cengagebrain.com, navigate to the Chapter 3 FAQ resource for this book, and then click Computer Viruses.

Working with Application Software

To use application software, you must instruct the operating system to start the program. The steps in Figure 3-3 illustrate one way to start and interact with the Paint program, which is included with the Windows operating system. The following paragraphs explain the steps in Figure 3-3.

Personal computer operating systems often use the concept of a desktop to make the computer easier to use. The **desktop** is an on-screen work area that has a graphical user interface. Step 1 of Figure 3-3 shows icons, a button, a pointer, and a menu on the Windows desktop. An **icon** is a small image displayed on the screen that represents a program, a document, or some other object. A **button** is a graphical element that you activate to cause a specific action to occur. One way to activate a button is to click it. To **click** a button on the screen requires moving the pointer to the button and then pressing and releasing a button on the mouse (usually the left mouse button). The **pointer** is a small symbol displayed on the screen that moves as you interact with the mouse or other pointing device. Common pointer shapes are an I-beam (I), a block arrow (↖), and a pointing hand (☝).

The Windows desktop contains a Start button on the lower-left corner of the taskbar. When you click the Start button, the Start menu is displayed on the desktop. A **menu** contains a list of commands from which you make selections. A **command** is an instruction that causes a program to perform a specific action.

As illustrated in Steps 1 and 2 of Figure 3-3, when you click the Start button and then click the All Programs command on the Start menu, the All Programs list is displayed on the Start menu. Clicking the Accessories folder in the All Programs list displays the Accessories list.

To start a program, you can click its program name on a menu or in a list. This action instructs the operating system to start the program, which means the program's instructions load from a storage medium (such as a hard disk) into memory. For example, when you click Paint in the Accessories list, Windows loads the Paint program instructions from the computer's hard disk into memory.

Once loaded into memory, the program appears in a window on the desktop (Step 3 of Figure 3-3). A **window** is a rectangular area of the screen that displays data and information. The top of a window has a **title bar**, which is a horizontal space that contains the window's name.

With the program loaded, you can create a new file or open an existing one. A **file** is a named collection of stored data, instructions, or information. A file can contain text, images, audio, and video. To distinguish among various files, each file has a file name. The title bar of the document window usually displays a document's file name. Step 4 of Figure 3-3 shows the contents of the file, Baby Buffalo, displaying in the Paint window.

In some cases, when you instruct a program to perform an activity such as print, the program displays a dialog box. A dialog box is a window that provides information, presents available options, or requests a response. Dialog boxes, such as the one shown in Step 5 of Figure 3-3, often contain option buttons, text boxes, check boxes, and command buttons.

One Way to Start and Interact with a Program from Windows

Step 1
When you turn on a PC-compatible computer, Windows loads into memory and displays the desktop on the screen. Click the Start button on the Windows taskbar to display the Start menu.

Step 2
Click All Programs on the Start menu to display the All Programs list. Click Accessories in the All Programs list and then point to Paint in the Accessories list.

Step 3
Click Paint. The Paint window opens on the desktop.

Step 5
Instruct the Paint program to print the photo. When the Print dialog box appears, click its Print button.

Step 4
Instruct the Paint program to open a file that is stored on the hard disk.

Figure 3-3 This figure shows one way to start and interact with a program from Windows.

Instructions: Find the true statement below. Then, rewrite the remaining false statements so that they are true.

1. Application software is used to make business activities more efficient; assist with graphics and multimedia projects; support home, personal, and educational tasks; and facilitate communications.
2. Public-domain software is mass-produced, copyrighted retail software that meets the needs of a wide variety of users, not just a single user or company.
3. To use system software, your computer must be running application software.
4. When a program is started, its instructions load from memory into a storage medium.

Quiz Yourself Online: To further check your knowledge of pages 108 through 111, visit the Computer Concepts CourseMate Web site at www.cengagebrain.com, navigate to the Chapter 3 Quiz Yourself resource for this book, and then click Objectives 1 – 2.

Business Software

Business software is application software that assists people in becoming more effective and efficient while performing their daily business activities. Business software includes programs such as word processing, spreadsheet, database, presentation, note taking, personal information manager, business software for phones, business software suites, project management, accounting, document management, and enterprise computing software. Figure 3-4 lists popular programs for each of these categories.

Popular Business Programs

Application Software	Manufacturer	Program Name
Word Processing	Microsoft	Word
	Apple	Pages
	Corel	WordPerfect
Spreadsheet	Microsoft	Excel
	Apple	Numbers
	Corel	Quattro Pro
Database	Microsoft	Access
	Corel	Paradox
	Oracle	Oracle Database
	Sun	MySQL
Presentation	Microsoft	PowerPoint
	Apple	Keynote
	Corel	Presentations
Note Taking	Microsoft	OneNote
	Agilix	GoBinder
	Corel	Grafigo
	SnapFiles	KeyNote
Personal Information Manager (PIM)	Microsoft	Outlook
	Google	Calendar
	IBM	Lotus Organizer
	Palm	Desktop
	Mozilla	Thunderbird
Business Software for Phones	CNetX	Pocket SlideShow
	DataViz	Documents To Go
	Microsoft	Word Mobile Excel Mobile PowerPoint Mobile Outlook Mobile
	Mobile Systems	MobiSystems Office Suite
	Ultrasoft	Money

Application Software	Manufacturer	Program Name
Business Software Suite (for the Professional)	Microsoft	Office Office for Mac
	Apple	iWork
	Google	Google Docs
	Sun	OpenOffice.org StarOffice
	Corel	WordPerfect Office
	IBM	Lotus SmartSuite
Project Management	CS Odessa	ConceptDraw PROJECT
	Microsoft	Project
	Oracle	Primavera SureTrak Project Manager
Accounting	Intuit	QuickBooks
	Microsoft	Accounting
	Sage Software	Peachtree
Document Management	Adobe	Acrobat
	Enfocus	PitStop
	Nuance	PDF Converter
Enterprise Computing	Oracle	PeopleSoft Enterprise Human Capital Management
	Sage Software	Sage MAS 500
	MSC Software	MSC.SimManager
	Oracle	Oracle Manufacturing
	SAP	mySAP Customer Relationship Management
	NetSuite	NetERP
	Syntellect	Syntellect Interaction Management Suite

Figure 3-4 Popular business software.

Word Processing Software

Word processing software, sometimes called a word processor, allows users to create and manipulate documents containing mostly text and sometimes graphics (Figure 3-5). Millions of people use word processing software every day to develop documents such as letters, memos, reports, mailing labels, newsletters, and Web pages.

A major advantage of using word processing software is that users easily can change what they have written. Word processing software also has many features to make documents look professional and visually appealing. For example, you can change the shape, size, and color of characters; apply special effects such as three-dimensional shadows; and organize text in newspaper-style columns.

Most word processing software allows users to incorporate graphical images, such as digital photos and clip art, in documents. **Clip art** is a collection of drawings, photos, and other images. In Figure 3-5, a user inserted an image of a baseball player in the document. With word processing software, you easily can modify the appearance of an image after inserting it in the document.

You can use word processing software to define the size of the paper on which to print and specify the margins. A feature, called wordwrap, allows users to type words in a paragraph continually without pressing the ENTER key at the end of each line. As you type more lines of text than can be displayed on the screen, the top portion of the document moves upward, or scrolls, off the screen. Read Ethics & Issues 3-1 for a related discussion.

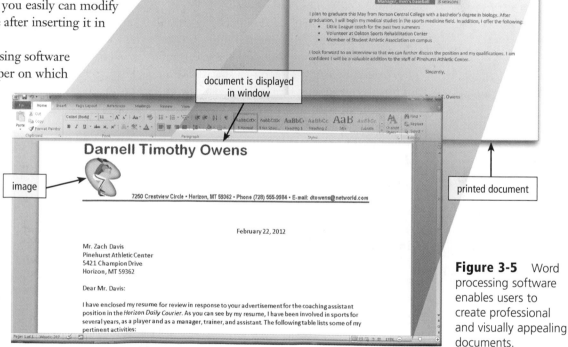

document is displayed in window

image

printed document

Figure 3-5 Word processing software enables users to create professional and visually appealing documents.

Are Word Processing Programs Making Students Lazy?

Today, word processing programs fix spelling and grammar mistakes, automatically format documents with templates, help correctly reference works cited in a document, and seem to do everything short of generating an idea for a document. Some educators believe that the proliferation of word processing automation is cheating students of the fundamental ability to perform these tasks on their own. Research shows that as word processing programs became more popular over the past years, the quality of written work done without the aid of this software has dropped dramatically. Opponents of using word processing software for assignments point out the quality of e-mail and instant messages is markedly worse than works written with the aid of modern word processing programs.

Proponents of the use of word processing programs for educational use point out that automation is the way writing should be done now and in the future. The higher quality of works produced using the software is well worth not sacrificing time toward teaching students less modern tactics. Students are more productive and able to focus on the topics at hand, rather than worry about spelling errors.

Are word processing programs making students lazy? Why or why not? Should educators have the ability to turn off time-saving features, such as the AutoCorrect and grammar checker features, in their student's word processing programs? Why? Do students need the ability manually to check spelling and grammar, format a document, and reference cited works in a document, in the same way that students still learn multiplication and long division? Why or why not?

Word Processing Software

For more information, visit the Computer Concepts CourseMate Web site at www.cengagebrain.com, navigate to the Chapter 3 Web Link resource for this book, and then click Word Processing Software.

Ethics & Issues

For the complete text of the Ethics & Issues boxes found in this chapter, visit the Computer Concepts CourseMate Web site at www.cengagebrain.com and then navigate to the Chapter 3 Ethics & Issues resource for this book.

Word processing software typically includes a spelling checker, which reviews the spelling of individual words, sections of a document, or the entire document. The spelling checker compares the words in the document with an electronic dictionary that is part of the word processing software. Some word processing programs also check for contextual spelling errors, such as a misuse of homophones (words pronounced the same but have different spellings or meanings, such as one and won).

Developing a Document

With application software, such as a word processing program, users create, edit, format, save, and print documents. When you **create** a document, you enter text or numbers, insert images, and perform other tasks using an input device such as a keyboard, mouse, or digital pen. If you are using Microsoft Word to design a flyer, for example, you are creating a document.

To **edit** a document means to make changes to its existing content. Common editing tasks include inserting, deleting, cutting, copying, and pasting. Inserting text involves adding text to a document. Deleting text means that you are removing text or other content. Cutting is the process of removing a portion of the document and storing it in a temporary storage location, sometimes called a clipboard. Pasting is the process of transferring an item from a clipboard to a specific location in a document.

When users **format** a document, they change its appearance. Formatting is important because the overall look of a document significantly can affect its ability to communicate clearly. Examples of formatting tasks are changing the font, font size, and font style.

A **font** is a name assigned to a specific design of characters. Cambria and Calibri are examples of fonts. **Font size** indicates the size of the characters in a particular font. Font size is gauged by a measurement system called points. A single point is about 1/72 of an inch in height. The text you are reading in this book is about 10 point. Thus, each character is about 5/36 (10/72) of an inch in height. A **font style** adds emphasis to a font. Bold, italic, underline, and color are examples of font styles. Figure 3-6 illustrates fonts, font sizes, and font styles.

During the process of creating, editing, and formatting a document, the computer holds it in memory. To keep the document for future use requires that you save it. When you **save** a document, the computer transfers the document from memory to a storage medium such as a USB flash drive or hard disk. Once saved, a document is stored permanently as a file on the storage medium. To learn more about how to save a file, complete the Learn How To 1 activity on page 138.

When you **print** a document, the computer places the contents of the document on paper or some other medium. Instead of printing a document and physically distributing it, some users e-mail the document to others on a network such as the Internet.

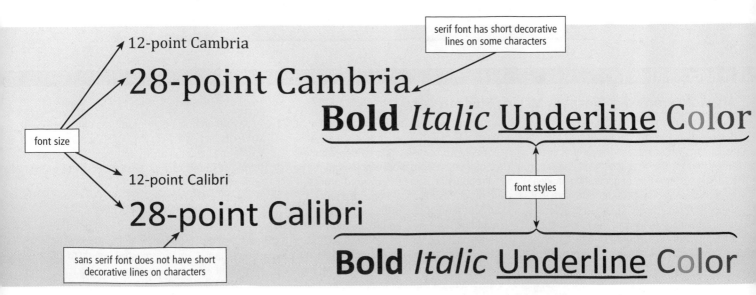

Figure 3-6 The Cambria and Calibri fonts are shown in two font sizes and a variety of font styles.

Spreadsheet Software

Spreadsheet software allows users to organize data in rows and columns and perform calculations on the data. These rows and columns collectively are called a **worksheet** (Figure 3-7). Most spreadsheet software has basic features to help users create, edit, and format worksheets. The following sections describe the features of most spreadsheet programs.

Spreadsheet Organization   A spreadsheet file is similar to a notebook that can contain more than 1,000 related individual worksheets. Data is organized vertically in columns and horizontally in rows on each worksheet (Figure 3-7). Each worksheet usually can have more than 16,000 columns and 1 million rows. One or more letters identify each column, and a number identifies each row. Only a small fraction of these columns and rows are visible on the screen at one time. Scrolling through the worksheet displays different parts of it on the screen.

A cell is the intersection of a column and row. The spreadsheet software identifies cells by the column and row in which they are located. For example, the intersection of column B and row 4 is referred to as cell B4. As shown in Figure 3-7, cell B4 contains the number, $3,383,909.82, which represents the sales for January.

Cells may contain three types of data: labels, values, and formulas. The text, or label, entered in a cell identifies the worksheet data and helps organize the worksheet. Using descriptive labels, such as Gross Margin and Total Expenses, helps make a worksheet more meaningful.

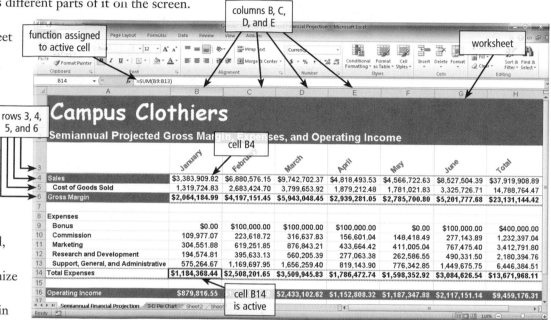

Figure 3-7   With spreadsheet software, you create worksheets that contain data arranged in rows and columns, and you can perform calculations on the data in the worksheets.

Calculations   Many of the worksheet cells shown in Figure 3-7 contain a number, called a value, that can be used in a calculation. Other cells, however, contain formulas that generate values. A formula performs calculations on the data in the worksheet and displays the resulting value in a cell, usually the cell containing the formula. When creating a worksheet, you can enter your own formulas. In Figure 3-7, for example, cell B14 could contain the formula B9+B10+B11+B12+B13, which would add together (sum) the contents of cells B9, B10, B11, B12, and B13. That is, this formula calculates the total expenses for January.

A function is a predefined formula that performs common calculations such as adding the values in a group of cells or generating a value such as the time or date. For example, the function =SUM(B9:B13) instructs the spreadsheet program to add all of the numbers in cells B9 through B13.

Recalculation   One of the more powerful features of spreadsheet software is its capability of recalculating the rest of the worksheet when data in a worksheet changes. Spreadsheet software's capability of recalculating data also makes it a valuable budgeting, forecasting, and decision making tool.

Spreadsheet Software
For more information, visit the Computer Concepts CourseMate Web site at www.cengagebrain.com, navigate to the Chapter 3 Web Link resource for this book, and then click Spreadsheet Software.

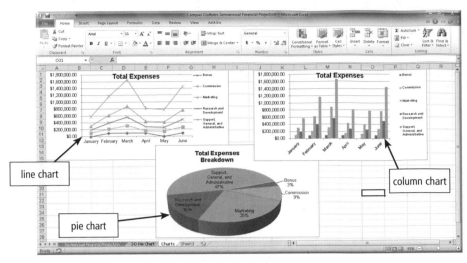

Figure 3-8 Three basic types of charts provided with spreadsheet software are line charts, column charts, and pie charts. The charts shown here were created using the data in the worksheet in Figure 3-7.

Charting Another standard feature of spreadsheet software is charting, which depicts the data in graphical form. A visual representation of data through charts often makes it easier for users to see at a glance the relationship among the numbers. Three popular chart types are line charts, column charts, and pie charts. Figure 3-8 shows examples of these charts that were plotted using the five types of expenses for each of the months shown in the worksheet in Figure 3-7 on the previous page. A line chart shows a trend during a period of time, as indicated by a rising or falling line. A column chart, also called a bar chart, displays bars of various lengths to show the relationship of data. The bars can be horizontal, vertical, or stacked on top of one another. A pie chart, which has the shape of a round pie cut into slices, shows the relationship of parts to a whole.

Database Software

A **database** is a collection of data organized in a manner that allows access, retrieval, and use of that data. In a manual database, you might record data on paper and store it in a filing cabinet. With a computerized database, such as the one shown in Figure 3-9, the computer stores the data in an electronic format on a storage medium such as a hard disk.

Database software is application software that allows users to create, access, and manage a database. Using database software, you can add, change, and delete data in a database; sort and retrieve data from the database; and create forms and reports using the data in the database.

With most personal computer database programs, a database consists of a collection of tables, organized in rows and columns. Each row, called a record, contains data about a given person, product, object, or event. Each column, called a field, contains a specific category of data within a record.

The Fitness database shown in Figure 3-9 consists of two tables: a Client table and a Trainer table. The Client table contains ten records (rows), each storing data about one client. The client data is grouped into eight fields (columns): Client Number, Last Name, First Name, Address, Telephone Number, Amount Paid, Balance, and Trainer Number. The Balance field, for instance, contains the balance due

Figure 3-9 This database contains two tables: one for the clients and one for the trainers. The Client table has ten records and eight fields; the Trainer table has three records and eight fields.

from the client. The Client and Trainer tables relate to one another through a common field, Trainer Number.

Users run queries to retrieve data. A query is a request for specific data from the database. For example, a query might request a list of clients whose balance is greater than $45. Database software can take the results of a query and present it in a window on the screen or send it to the printer.

Presentation Software

Presentation software is application software that allows users to create visual aids for presentations to communicate ideas, messages, and other information to a group. The presentations can be viewed as slides, sometimes called a slide show, that are displayed on a large monitor or on a projection screen (Figure 3-10).

Presentation software typically provides a variety of predefined presentation formats that define complementary colors for backgrounds, text, and graphical accents on the slides. This software also provides a variety of layouts for each individual slide such as a title slide, a two-column slide, and a slide with clip art, a chart, a table, or a diagram. In addition, you can enhance any text, charts, and graphical images on a slide with 3-D, animation, and other special effects such as shading, shadows, and textures.

When building a presentation, users can set the slide timing so that the presentation automatically displays the next slide after a preset delay. Presentation software allows you to apply special effects to the transition between slides. One slide, for example, might fade away as the next slide appears.

Presentation software typically includes a clip gallery that provides images, photos, video clips, and audio clips to enhance multimedia presentations. Some audio and video editing programs work with presentation software, providing users with an easy means to record and insert video, music, and audio commentary in a presentation.

You can view or print a finished presentation in a variety of formats, including an outline of text from each slide and audience handouts that show completed slides.

Presentation software incorporates features such as checking spelling, formatting, research, and creating Web pages from existing slide shows.

Figure 3-10
This presentation created with presentation software consists of five slides.

Note Taking Software

Note taking software is application software that enables users to enter typed text, handwritten comments, drawings, or sketches anywhere on a page and then save the page as part of a notebook (Figure 3-11). Users also can include audio recordings as part of their notes. Users find note taking software convenient during meetings, class lectures, conferences, in libraries, and other settings that previously required a pencil and tablet of paper for recording thoughts and discussions.

Figure 3-11 With note taking software, mobile users can handwrite notes, draw sketches, and type text.

Figure 3-12 With project management software, you plan and schedule a project.

Business Software Suite

A **software suite** is a collection of individual programs available together as a unit. Business software suites typically include, at a minimum, the following programs: word processing, spreadsheet, presentation, and e-mail. Popular software suites are Microsoft Office, Apple iWork, Corel WordPerfect Office, and Google Docs.

Software suites offer two major advantages: lower cost and ease of use. When you purchase a collection of programs as a software suite, the suite usually costs significantly less than purchasing them individually. Software suites provide ease of use because the programs in the suite normally use a similar interface and share features such as clip art and spelling checker.

Project Management Software

Project management software allows a user to plan, schedule, track, and analyze the events, resources, and costs of a project. Project management software helps users manage project variables, allowing them to complete a project on time and within budget. A customer service manager might use project management software to schedule the process of administering customer surveys, evaluating responses, and presenting recommendations (Figure 3-12).

Personal Information Manager Software

A **personal information manager** (**PIM**) is application software that includes an appointment calendar, address book, notepad, and other features to help users organize personal information.

Mobile devices such as smart phones and PDAs include, among many other features, PIM functionality. You can synchronize, or coordinate, information so that both the mobile device and your personal computer and/or organization's server have the latest version of any updated information.

Business Software for Phones

In addition to PIM software, a huge variety of business and other software is available for phones. Some software is preloaded on the phone, while other programs can be downloaded or accessed on memory cards. Business software for phones enables users to create documents and worksheets, manage databases and lists, create slide shows, take notes, manage budgets and finances, view and edit photos, read electronic books, plan travel routes, compose and read e-mail messages, send instant messages, send text and picture messages, view maps and directions, read the latest news articles, and browse the Web. Many of the programs discussed in this chapter have scaled-down versions that work with smart phones and other mobile devices.

Accounting Software

Accounting software helps companies record and report their financial transactions (Figure 3-13). With accounting software, business users perform accounting activities related to the general ledger, accounts receivable, accounts payable, purchasing, invoicing, and payroll functions. Accounting software also enables business users to write and print checks, track checking account activity, and update and reconcile balances on demand.

Most accounting software supports online credit checks, invoicing, bill payment, direct deposit, and payroll services. Some accounting software offers more complex features such as job costing and estimating, time tracking, multiple company reporting, foreign currency reporting, and forecasting the amount of raw materials needed for products. The cost of accounting software for small businesses ranges from less than one hundred to several thousand dollars. Accounting software for large businesses can cost several hundred thousand dollars.

Document Management Software

Document management software provides a means for sharing, distributing, and searching through documents by converting them into a format that can be viewed by any user. The converted document, which mirrors the original document's appearance, can be viewed and printed without the software that created the original document.

A popular file format that document management software uses to save converted documents is **PDF** (Portable Document Format), developed by Adobe Systems. To view and print a PDF file, you need Acrobat Reader software (Figure 3-14), which can be downloaded free from Adobe's Web site.

Enterprise Computing Software

A large organization, commonly referred to as an enterprise, requires special computing solutions because of its size and large geographical distribution. A typical enterprise consists of a wide variety of departments, centers, and divisions — collectively known as functional units. Nearly every enterprise has the following functional units: human resources, accounting and finance, engineering or product development, manufacturing, marketing, sales, distribution, customer service, and information technology. Each of these functional units has specialized software requirements.

Figure 3-13   Accounting software helps companies record and report their financial transactions.

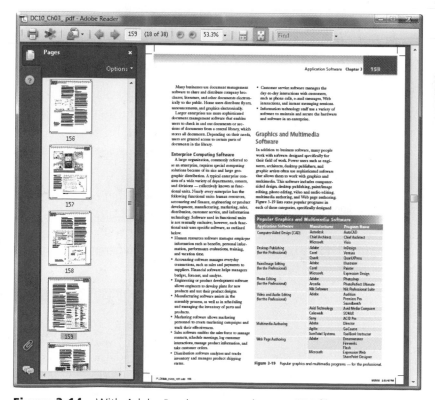

Figure 3-14   With Adobe Reader, you can view any PDF file.

Graphics and Multimedia Software

In addition to business software, many people work with software designed specifically for their field of work. Power users such as engineers, architects, desktop publishers, and graphic artists often use sophisticated software that allows them to work with graphics and multimedia. This software includes computer-aided design, desktop publishing, paint/image editing, photo editing, video and audio editing, multimedia authoring, and Web page authoring. Figure 3-15 lists the more popular programs for each of these categories, specifically designed for professional or more technically astute users.

Many graphics and multimedia programs incorporate user-friendly interfaces, or scaled-down versions, making it possible for the home and small business users to create documents using these programs. The following sections discuss the features and functions of graphics and multimedia software. Read Innovative Computing 3-1 to find out how fireworks shows can be produced using multimedia software.

Graphics Software
For more information, visit the Computer Concepts CourseMate Web site at www.cengagebrain.com, navigate to the Chapter 3 Web Link resource for this book, and then click Graphics Software.

Popular Graphics and Multimedia Software

Application Software	Manufacturer	Program Name	Application Software	Manufacturer	Program Name
Computer-Aided Design (CAD)	Autodesk	AutoCAD	Video and Audio Editing (for the Professional)	Adobe	Audition Premiere Pro Soundbooth
	Chief Architect	Chief Architect		Avid Technology	Avid Media Composer
	Microsoft	Visio		Cakewalk	SONAR
Desktop Publishing (for the Professional)	Adobe	InDesign		Sony	ACID Pro
	Corel	Ventura	Multimedia Authoring	Adobe	Director
	Quark	QuarkXPress		Agilix	GoCourse
Paint/Image Editing (for the Professional)	Adobe	Illustrator		SumTotal Systems	ToolBook Instructor
	Corel	Painter	Web Page Authoring	Adobe	Dreamweaver Fireworks Flash
	Microsoft	Expression Design			
Photo Editing (for the Professional)	Adobe	Photoshop		Microsoft	Expression Web SharePoint Designer
	Arcadia	PhotoPerfect Ultimate			
	Nik Software	Nik Professional Suite			

Figure 3-15   Popular graphics and multimedia programs — for the professional.

⚠ INNOVATIVE COMPUTING 3-1

Fireworks Software Creates a Real Blast

The "oohs" and "aahs" you hear at a fireworks show may be in response to the music and pyrotechnics synchronized with special multimedia software. Major fireworks productions on Independence Day and at theme parks are choreographed with programs designed to fire each shell, sometimes only one-hundredth of a second apart, at a specific beat of the music.

A 20-minute show can take 4 months to plan. Show choreographers estimate they spend at least four hours planning the firing order for each minute of music, not including testing and setting up the equipment. When the fireworks show operator starts the program, the computer sends a signal to the firing module, which connects to each shell.

The multimedia software can cost from $2,000 to $8,000, while the firing hardware that the computer synchronizes wirelessly or with wires can cost between $30,000 and $50,000.

For more information, visit the Computer Concepts CourseMate Web site at www.cengagebrain.com, navigate to the Chapter 3 Innovative Computing resource for this book, and then click Fireworks.

Computer-Aided Design

Computer-aided design (CAD) software is a sophisticated type of application software that assists a professional user in creating engineering, architectural, and scientific designs. For example, engineers create design plans for vehicles and security systems. Architects design building structures and floor plans (Figure 3-16). Scientists design drawings of molecular structures.

Figure 3-16 Architects use CAD software to design building structures.

Desktop Publishing Software (for the Professional)

Desktop publishing (DTP) software enables professional designers to create sophisticated documents that contain text, graphics, and many colors (Figure 3-17). Professional DTP software is ideal for the production of high-quality color documents such as textbooks, corporate newsletters, marketing literature, product catalogs, and annual reports. Designers and graphic artists can print finished publications on a color printer, take them to a professional printer, or post them on the Web in a format that can be viewed by those without DTP software.

Figure 3-17 Professional designers and graphic artists use DTP software to produce sophisticated publications such as a printed magazine article.

Paint/Image Editing Software (for the Professional)

Graphic artists, multimedia professionals, technical illustrators, and desktop publishers use paint software and image editing software to create and modify graphical images such as those used in DTP documents and Web pages. **Paint software**, also called illustration software, allows users to draw pictures (Figure 3-18), shapes, and other graphical images with various on-screen tools such as a pen, brush, eyedropper, and paint bucket. **Image editing software** provides the capabilities of paint software and also includes the capability to enhance and modify existing pictures and images. Modifications can include adjusting or enhancing image colors, adding special effects such as shadows and glows, creating animations, and image stitching, which is the process of combining multiple images into a larger image.

Professional photo editing software is a type of image editing software that allows photographers, videographers, engineers, scientists, and other high-volume digital photo users to edit and customize digital photos. With professional photo editing software, users can retouch photos, crop images, remove red-eye, change image shapes, color-correct images, straighten images, remove or rearrange objects in a photo, and apply filters.

Figure 3-18 This graphic artist uses paint software to draw characters in a computer game.

Video and Audio Editing Software (for the Professional)

Video editing software allows professionals to modify a segment of a video, called a clip. For example, users can reduce the length of a video clip, reorder a series of clips, or add special effects such as words that move horizontally across the screen. Video editing software typically includes audio editing capabilities. **Audio editing software** lets users modify audio clips, produce studio-quality soundtracks, and add audio to video clips (Figure 3-19). Most television shows and movies are created or enhanced using video and audio editing software.

Figure 3-19   With audio editing software, users modify audio clips.

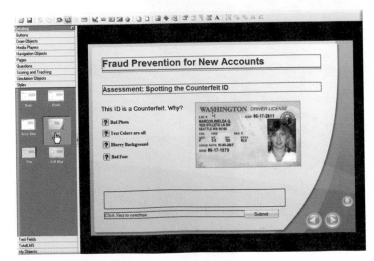

Figure 3-20   Multimedia authoring software allows you to create dynamic presentations that include text, graphics, video, sound, and animation.

Multimedia Authoring Software

Multimedia authoring software allows users to combine text, graphics, audio, video, and animation in an interactive application (Figure 3-20). With this software, users control the placement of text and images and the duration of sounds, video, and animation. Once created, multimedia presentations often take the form of interactive computer-based presentations or Web-based presentations designed to facilitate learning, demonstrate product functionality, and elicit direct-user participation. Training centers, educational institutions, and online magazine publishers all use multimedia authoring software to develop interactive applications. These applications may be available on an optical disc, over a local area network, or via the Internet.

Web Page Authoring Software

Web page authoring software helps users of all skill levels create Web pages that include graphical images, video, audio, animation, and special effects with interactive content. In addition, many Web page authoring programs allow users to organize, manage, and maintain Web sites.

Application software, such as Word and Excel, often includes Web page authoring features. This allows home and small business users to create basic Web pages using application software they already own. For more sophisticated Web pages, users work with Web page authoring software.

✔ QUIZ YOURSELF 3-2

Instructions: Find the true statement below. Then, rewrite the remaining false statements so that they are true.

1. Enterprise computing software provides the capabilities of paint software and also includes the capability to modify existing images.
2. Millions of people use spreadsheet software every day to develop documents such as letters, memos, reports, mailing labels, newsletters, and Web pages.
3. Professional accounting software is ideal for the production of high-quality color documents such as textbooks, corporate newsletters, marketing literature, product catalogs, and annual reports.
4. Database software is application software that allows users to create visual aids for presentations to communicate ideas, messages, and other information to a group.
5. Popular CAD programs include Microsoft Office, Apple iWork, Corel WordPerfect Office, and Google Docs.
6. Web page authoring software helps users of all skill levels create Web pages.

Quiz Yourself Online: To further check your knowledge of pages 112 through 122, visit the Computer Concepts CourseMate Web site at www.cengagebrain.com, navigate to the Chapter 3 Quiz Yourself resource for this book, and then click Objectives 3 – 4.

Software for Home, Personal, and Educational Use

A large amount of application software is designed specifically for home, personal, and educational use. Most of the programs in this category are relatively inexpensive, often priced less than $100. Figure 3-21 lists popular programs for many of these categories. The following pages discuss the features and functions of this application software.

Popular Programs for Home/Personal/Educational Use

Application Software	Manufacturer	Program Name	Application Software	Manufacturer	Program Name
Personal Finance	IGG Software	iBank	Clip Art/Image Gallery	Broderbund	ClickArt
	Intuit	Quicken		Nova Development	Art Explosion
Legal	Broderbund	Home and Business Lawyer WillWriter		CoolArchive	CoolArchive
			Video and Audio Editing (for Personal Use)	Corel	VideoStudio
	Cosmi	Perfect Attorney		Microsoft	Windows Live Movie Maker
	Nolo	Quicken Legal Business Quicken WillMaker		Pinnacle Systems	Studio
Tax Preparation	2nd Story Software	TaxACT		Roxio	Buzz
	H&R Block	TaxCut	Home Design/ Landscaping	Broderbund	Instant Architect
	Intuit	TurboTax		Chief Architect	Better Homes and Gardens Home Designer
Desktop Publishing (for Personal Use)	Broderbund	The Print Shop PrintMaster		IMSI/Design	TurboFLOORPLAN
	Microsoft	Publisher	Travel and Mapping	DeLorme	Street Atlas
Paint/Image Editing (for Personal Use)	Corel	CorelDRAW Painter Essentials		Microsoft	Streets & Trips
	The GIMP Team	The Gimp		Google	Earth Maps
Photo Editing and Photo Management (for Personal Use)	Adobe	Photoshop Elements Photoshop Express	Reference	Fogware Publishing	Merriam-Webster Collegiate Dictionary & Thesaurus
	Corel	Paint Shop Pro Photo Ulead PhotoImpact MediaOne Plus		Microsoft	MSN Encarta
	Yahoo!	Flickr			
	Google	Picasa			
	Microsoft	Windows Live Photo Gallery			
	Roxio	PhotoShow			

Figure 3-21 Many popular programs are available for home, personal, and educational use.

Personal Finance Software

Personal finance software is a simplified accounting program that helps home users and small office/home office users balance their checkbooks, pay bills, track personal income and expenses (Figure 3-22), track investments, and evaluate financial plans.

Most personal finance software includes financial planning features, such as analyzing home and personal loans, preparing income taxes, and managing retirement savings. Other features include managing home inventory and setting up budgets. Most of these programs also offer a variety of online services, such as online banking, which require access to the Internet.

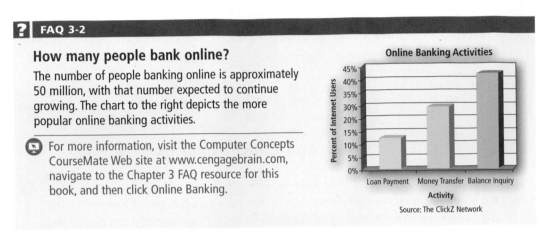

? FAQ 3-2

How many people bank online?

The number of people banking online is approximately 50 million, with that number expected to continue growing. The chart to the right depicts the more popular online banking activities.

For more information, visit the Computer Concepts CourseMate Web site at www.cengagebrain.com, navigate to the Chapter 3 FAQ resource for this book, and then click Online Banking.

Online Banking Activities

Source: The ClickZ Network

Figure 3-22 Personal finance software assists home users with tracking personal accounts.

Legal Software

Legal software assists in the preparation of legal documents and provides legal information to individuals, families, and small businesses (Figure 3-23). Legal software provides standard contracts and documents associated with buying, selling, and renting property; estate planning; marriage and divorce; and preparing a will or living trust. By answering a series of questions or completing a form, the legal software tailors the legal document to specific needs.

Figure 3-23 Legal software provides legal information and assists in record keeping and the preparation of legal documents.

Tax Preparation Software

Tax preparation software, which is available both as packaged software and Web applications, can guide individuals, families, or small businesses through the process of filing federal taxes (Figure 3-24). These programs forecast tax liability and offer money-saving tax tips, designed to lower your tax bill. After you answer a series of questions and complete basic forms, the software creates and analyzes your tax forms to search for missed potential errors and deduction opportunities.

Once the forms are complete, you can print any necessary paperwork, and then they are ready for filing. Some tax preparation programs also allow you to file your tax forms electronically.

Figure 3-24 Tax preparation software guides individuals, families, or small businesses through the process of filing federal taxes.

Desktop Publishing Software (for Personal Use)

Personal DTP software helps home and small business users create newsletters, brochures, flyers (Figure 3-25), advertisements, postcards, greeting cards, letterhead, business cards, banners, calendars, logos, and Web pages. Although many word processing programs include DTP features, users often prefer to create DTP documents using DTP software because of its enhanced features. For example, personal DTP programs provide hundreds of thousands of graphical images. You also can import (bring in) your own digital photos into the documents. These programs typically guide you through the development of a document by asking a series of questions. Then, you can print a finished publication on a color printer or post it on the Web.

Many personal DTP programs also include paint/image editing software and photo editing and photo management software.

Figure 3-25 With desktop publishing software, home and small business users can create flyers.

Paint/Image Editing Software (for Personal Use)

Personal paint/image editing software provides an easy-to-use interface; includes various simplified tools that allow you to draw pictures, shapes, and other images; and provides the capability of modifying existing graphics and photos. These products also include many templates to assist you in adding images to documents such as greeting cards, banners, calendars, signs, labels, business cards, and letterhead.

Personal photo editing software, a popular type of image editing software available both as packaged software and as Web applications, allows users to edit digital photos by removing red-eye, erasing blemishes, restoring aged photos, adding special effects, enhancing image quality, or creating electronic photo albums. When you purchase a digital camera, it usually includes photo editing software (Figure 3-26). Some digital cameras even have basic photo editing software built in so that you can edit the image directly on the camera. You can print edited photos on labels, calendars, business cards, and banners, or you can post them on the Web.

Figure 3-26 As shown here, home users adjust color on their digital photos with personal photo editing software.

With **photo management software**, you can view, organize, sort, catalog, print, and share digital photos. Some photo editing software includes photo management functionality.

Clip Art/Image Gallery

Application software often includes a **clip art/image gallery**, which is a collection of clip art and photos. Some programs have links to additional clips available on the Web or are available as Web applications. You also can purchase clip art/image gallery software that contains thousands of images (Figure 3-27).

Figure 3-27 Clip art/image gallery software contains thousands of images.

In addition to clip art, many clip art/image galleries provide fonts, animations, sounds, video clips, and audio clips. You can use the images, fonts, and other items from the clip art/image gallery in all types of documents, including word processing, desktop publishing, spreadsheet, and presentations.

Video and Audio Editing Software (for Personal Use)

Many home users work with easy-to-use video and audio editing software, which is much simpler to use than its professional counterpart, for small-scale movie making projects (Figure 3-28). With these programs, home users can edit home movies, add music or other sounds to the video, and share their movies on the Web. Some operating systems include video editing and audio editing software.

Figure 3-28 With personal video and audio editing software, home users can edit their home movies.

Home Design/Landscaping Software

Homeowners or potential homeowners can use **home design/landscaping software** to assist them with the design, remodeling, or improvement of a home, deck, or landscape (Figure 3-29). This software includes hundreds of predrawn plans that you can customize to meet your needs. These programs show changes to home designs and landscapes, allowing homeowners to preview proposed modifications.

Figure 3-29   Home design/landscaping software can help you design or remodel a home, deck, or landscape.

Travel and Mapping Software

Travel and mapping software enables users to view maps, determine route directions, and locate points of interest (Figure 3-30). Using travel and mapping software, which is available both as packaged software and as Web applications, you can display maps by searching for an address, postal code, telephone number, or point of interest (such as airports, lodging, and historical sites). Most programs also allow you to download construction reports and calculate mileage, time, and expenses. Read Looking Ahead 3-1 for a look at the next generation of navigation software.

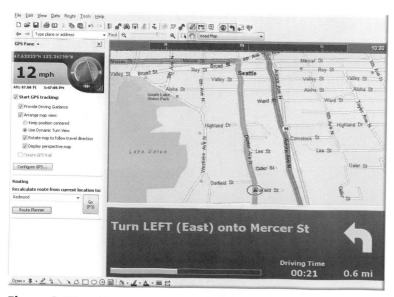

Figure 3-30   This software provides turn-by-turn directions, along with estimated travel times.

↗ **LOOKING AHEAD 3-1**

Sensors Help Drivers Find Their Way

Navigating through town may become less burdensome with products under development at Microsoft. Current devices are touted as being small enough to fit in a pocket, but this size can be a hindrance for people with large hands. When they attempt to place their fingers on the touch screen to press the commands, their fingers cover information they are trying to see. Microsoft's prototype LucidTouch solves this problem by allowing users to place their hands underneath the device, in-between it and a camera attached to the back. The camera captures an image of their hands, and the device overlays a semitransparent shadow of their fingers on the screen.

Microsoft also is developing sensors for a cell phone that collect data as a driver passes through town. These accelerometers sense speed, braking, and even when the driver hits a pothole, and the cell phone's microphone can detect the car's horn. Another potential use of Microsoft's sensors in cell phones is to monitor the behavior and health status of the elderly so that they can lead independent lives.

For more information, visit the Computer Concepts CourseMate Web site at www.cengagebrain.com, navigate to the Chapter 3 Looking Ahead resource for this book, and then click Mapping.

Reference and Educational Software

Reference software provides valuable and thorough information for all individuals. Popular reference software includes encyclopedias, dictionaries, and health/medical guides.

Educational software teaches a particular skill. Educational software exists for just about any subject, from learning how to type (Figure 3-31) to learning how to cook to preparing for college entrance exams. Educational software often includes games and other content to make the learning experience more fun. Many educational programs use a computer-based training approach. **Computer-based training (CBT)** is a type of education in which students learn by using and completing exercises with instructional software. CBT typically consists of self-directed, self-paced instruction about a topic.

Figure 3-31
Educational software can teach a skill.

Entertainment Software

Entertainment software for personal computers includes interactive games, videos, and other programs designed to support a hobby or provide amusement and enjoyment. For example, you might use entertainment software to play games individually (Figure 3-32) or with others online, make a family tree, or fly an aircraft. Many games are available as Web applications, allowing you to play individually or with other online players.

? FAQ 3-3

How popular is entertainment software?

The popularity of entertainment software has increased greatly during the past few years. More than 65 percent of American households play computer or video games. Further, more than 36 percent play games on a mobile device such as a smart phone or PDA.

For more information, visit the Computer Concepts CourseMate Web site at www.cengagebrain.com, navigate to the Chapter 3 FAQ resource for this book, and then click Entertainment Software.

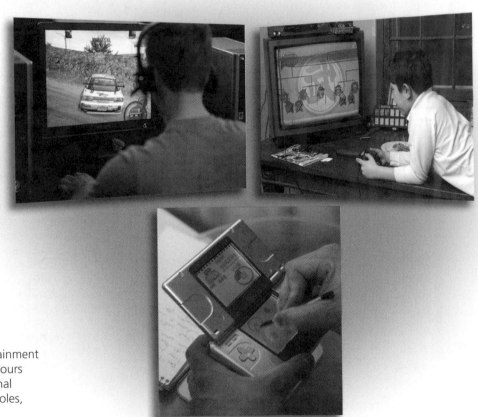

Figure 3-32 Entertainment software can provide hours of recreation on personal computers, game consoles, and mobile devices.

Web Applications

As previously mentioned, a Web application, or **Web app**, is a Web site that allows users to access and interact with software from any computer or device that is connected to the Internet. Users often interact with Web applications directly at the Web site, referred to as the host, through their Web browser. Some Web sites, however, require you download the software to your local computer or device. Web application hosts often store users' data and information on their servers. Some Web applications provide users with an option of storing data locally on their own personal computer or mobile device. Many of the previously discussed types of application software are available as Web applications (Figure 3-33). Read Ethics & Issues 3-2 for a related discussion.

Popular Web Applications

Program Name	Type of Application Software	Program Name	Type of Application Software
Britannica.com	Reference	Office Web Apps	Productivity Suite
Dictionary.com	Reference	Photoshop Express	Photo Editing
Flickr	Photo Editing and Photo Management	Picnik	Photo Editing
Gmail	E-Mail	TaxACT Online	Tax Preparation
Google Docs	Productivity Suite	TurboTax Online	Tax Preparation
Google Earth	Travel and Mapping	Windows Live Calendar	Personal Information Manager
Google Maps	Travel and Mapping	Windows Live Hotmail	E-Mail
MSN Encarta	Reference	YouSendIt	File Transfer and E-Mail

Figure 3-33   Some popular Web applications. For practice using Web applications, complete the last Learn It Online exercise in each chapter.

Many Web application hosts provide free access to their software, such as Google Docs shown in Figure 3-34. Others, such as Google Earth, offer part of their Web application free and charge for access to a more comprehensive program. Some Web applications allow you to use the Web application free and pay a fee when a certain action occurs. For example, you can prepare your tax return free, but if you elect to print it or file it electronically, you pay a minimal fee.

Experts often use the term Web 2.0 to describe Web applications. Recall that Web 2.0 refers to Web sites that provide users with a means to share personal information, allow users to modify Web site content, and/or have application software built into the site for visitors to use.

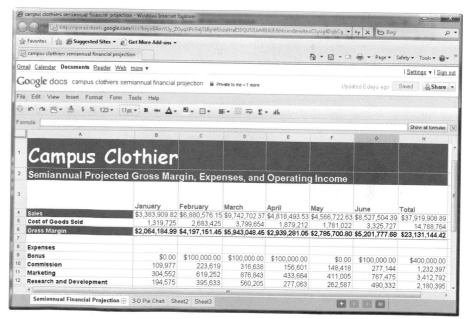

Figure 3-34   The spreadsheet shown here in Google Docs is the same Microsoft Excel spreadsheet that is shown in Figure 3-7 on page 115. Differences between the two figures are due to different features in the two programs.

as shown in Figure 3-7 on page 115.

ETHICS & ISSUES 3-2

Should Online Mapping Services Make You Feel More Secure or More Vulnerable?

Most Internet users find that online maps, such as Google Maps and Bing Maps, provide tremendous convenience and reliability. Instead of searching the house or car for maps or making phone calls for directions, a quick Web search results in a readable map with exact directions. Sometimes, even photos of the route and location are available. Some parents and advocacy groups, however, claim that the services allow predators to locate potential victims quickly. Google Maps, for example, provides photos for neighborhoods of entire cities. The opponents of the services believe that predators may find potential victims in the photos, or find likely locations where a crime may be easier to commit. Opponents of this point of view state that mapping services allow known predators and high-crime areas to be more readily identified. The services, therefore, increase personal security because the location of known predators can be pinpointed before they find victims. The services also provide much more positive value than any potential problems that they create, and, therefore, should thrive.

Do online mapping services make you feel more secure or more vulnerable? Why? Should parents and neighborhood associations have the legal right to have photos and personal information removed from mapping services? Why or why not? Would you feel comfortable if a service such as Google Maps showed a photo of you walking your normal route from home to work or school? Why?

Application Software for Communications

One of the main reasons people use computers is to communicate and share information with others. Some communications software is considered system software because it works with hardware and transmission media. Other communications software performs specific tasks for users, and thus, is considered application software. Chapter 2 presented a variety of application software for communications, which is summarized in the table in Figure 3-35.

? | **FAQ 3-4**

Does text messaging improve typing skills?

Although some individuals are able to send text messages from their phones quickly, the differences in layout between a phone keypad and a standard computer keyboard might not allow for their typing skills to improve at the same rate. Some individuals are able to send text messages more quickly than they can type. In fact, a 20-year-old college student won $50,000 in a text messaging competition when he typed more than 125 characters in 50 seconds with no mistakes.

 For more information, visit the Computer Concepts CourseMate Web site at www.cengagebrain.com, navigate to the Chapter 3 FAQ resource for this book, and then click Text Messaging.

Application Software for Communications

Web Browser
- Allows users to access and view Web pages on the Internet
- Requires a Web browser program
  - Integrated in some operating systems
  - Available for download on the Web free or for a fee

E-Mail
- Messages and files sent via a network such as the Internet
- Requires an e-mail program
  - Integrated in many software suites and operating systems
  - Available free at portals on the Web
  - Included with paid Internet access service
  - Can be purchased separately from retailers

Instant Messaging
- Real-time exchange of messages, files, audio, and/or video with another online user
- Requires instant messenger software
  - Integrated in some operating systems
  - Available for download on the Web, usually at no cost
  - Included with some paid Internet access services

Chat Room
- Real-time, online typed conversation
- Requires chat client software
  - Integrated in some operating systems, e-mail programs, and Web browsers
  - Available for download on the Web, usually at no cost
  - Included with some paid Internet access services
  - Built into some Web sites

Text, Picture, Video Messaging
- Short text, picture, or video messages sent and received, mainly on mobile devices
- Requires text, picture, video messenger software
  - Integrated in most mobile devices
  - Available for download on the Web, usually at no cost, for personal computers

RSS Aggregator
- Keeps track of changes made to Web sites by checking RSS feeds
- Requires RSS aggregator program
  - Integrated in some e-mail programs and Web browsers
  - Available for download on the Web, usually at no cost

Blogging
- Time-stamped articles, or posts, in a diary or journal format, usually listed in reverse chronological order
- Blogger needs blog software, or blogware, to create/ maintain blog
  - Some Web sites do not require installation of blog software

Newsgroup/Message Board
- Online area where users have written discussions
- Newsgroup may require a newsreader program
  - Integrated in some operating systems, e-mail programs, and Web browsers

FTP
- Method of uploading and downloading files with other computers on the Internet
- May require an FTP program
  - Integrated in some operating systems
  - Available for download on the Web for a small fee

VoIP (Internet Telephony)
- Allows users to speak to other users over the Internet
- Requires Internet connection, Internet telephone service, microphone or telephone, and Internet telephone software or telephone adapter

Video Conferencing
- Meeting between geographically separated people who use a network such as the Internet to transmit video/audio
- Requires video conferencing software, a microphone, speakers, and sometimes a video camera attached to your computer

 Figure 3-35 A summary of application software for home and business communications.

Learning Tools for Application Software

Learning how to use application software effectively involves time and practice. To assist in the learning process, many programs provide online Help (Figure 3-36) and Web-based Help.

Online Help is the electronic equivalent of a user manual. When working with a program, you can use online Help to ask a question or access the Help topics in subject or alphabetical order. Most online Help also links to Web sites that offer Web-based help, which provides updates and more comprehensive resources to respond to technical issues about software.

Many books are available to help you learn to use the features of personal computer programs. These books typically are available in bookstores and software stores.

Web-Based Training

Web-based training (WBT) is a type of CBT (computer-based training) that uses Internet technology and consists of application software on the Web. Similar to CBT, WBT typically consists of self-directed, self-paced instruction about a topic. WBT is popular in business, industry, and schools for teaching new skills or enhancing existing skills of employees, teachers, or students.

Many Web sites offer WBT to the general public. Such training covers a wide range of topics, from how to change a flat tire to creating documents in Word. Many of these Web sites are free. Others require registration and payment to take the complete Web-based course.

WBT often is combined with other materials for distance learning and e-learning. **Distance learning** is the delivery of education at one location while the learning takes place at other locations. **E-learning**, short for electronic learning, is the delivery of education via some electronic method such as the Internet, networks, or optical discs. To enhance communications, e-learning systems also may include video conferencing, e-mail, blogs, wikis, newsgroups, chat rooms, and groupware (Figure 3-37).

Figure 3-36 Many programs include online Help.

Figure 3-37 E-learning systems enable instructors to post course materials for their students.

✔ **QUIZ YOURSELF 3-3**

Instructions: Find the true statement below. Then, rewrite the remaining false statements so that they are true.

1. All Web application hosts provide free access to their software.

2. Computer-based training is a type of Web-based training that uses Internet technology and consists of application software on the Web.

3. E-mail and Web browsers are examples of communications software that are considered application software.

4. Legal software is a simplified accounting program that helps home users and small office/home office users balance their checkbooks, pay bills, track investments, and evaluate financial plans.

5. Personal DTP software is a popular type of image editing software that allows users to edit digital photos.

Quiz Yourself Online: To further check your knowledge of pages 123 through 131, visit the Computer Concepts CourseMate Web site at www.cengagebrain.com, navigate to the Chapter 3 Quiz Yourself resource for this book, and then click Objectives 5 – 8.

Chapter Summary

This chapter illustrated how to start and interact with application software. It presented an overview of a variety of business software, graphics and multimedia software, and home/personal/educational software. Finally, Web applications, application software for communications, and learning tools for application software were presented.

Computer Usage @ Work

Construction

Walking the streets, you stop to admire a new skyscraper with the most striking architectural features you ever have seen. You think to yourself that those responsible for designing the building are nothing less than brilliant. While a great deal of work goes into the design and construction of a building, computers and technology also play an important role in the process. In fact, the role of computers not only saves time and provides for more accurate results, it also allows us to preview how a building will look before construction even begins.

As mentioned in the chapter, computer-aided design (CAD) software is a sophisticated type of application software that assists a professional user in creating engineering, architectural, and scientific plans. During the preliminary design process, architects and design firms use CAD software to design the appearance and layout of a new building and can provide clients with a three-dimensional walkthrough of a building so that they can determine whether the proposed design will meet their needs. Later, the program can be used to include the placement of support beams, walls, roof shape, and so on, and also conform to building code.

CAD software allows engineers in various fields, such as mechanical and electrical, to design separate layers in a structure. The CAD software then can superimpose the designs to check for interactions and conflicts, such as if a structural beam in one layer covers a drain in another layer. The CAD software makes it easy to modify and correct the structure before it is built, which can save time and money during the construction process. This software also eliminates most, if not all, of the manual drafting required.

Engineers use computers to determine the type of foundation required to support the building and its occupants; the heating, ventilating, and air conditioning (HVAC); and the electrical requirements, as well as how the building may withstand external threats such as hurricanes and tornadoes.

During construction, contractors and builders are able to use computer software to estimate accurately the amount of materials and time required to complete the job. Without computers, determining materials and time required is a cumbersome and time-consuming task.

The next time you notice a building under construction, stop to think about how computer technology has increased the efficiency of the design and construction process.

For more information, visit the Computer Concepts CourseMate Web site at www.cengagebrain.com, navigate to the Chapter 3 Computer Usage @ Work resource for this book, and then click Construction.

Companies on the Cutting Edge

ADOBE SYSTEMS Design Software Leader

Practically all creative professionals involved with art and photography have a copy of Adobe Photoshop on their computer, and the leading computer manufacturers ship their products with a copy of Adobe Reader installed. The worldwide presence of Adobe Systems software attests to the company's success in developing programs that help people communicate effectively.

Charles Geschke and John Warnock founded the company in 1982 and named it after a creek that ran behind Warnock's house in California. Creative Suite contains the fundamental tools that help photographers, designers, and publishers develop and maintain their documents and Web sites, and it includes Dreamweaver, Flash, Fireworks, Contribute, InDesign, Illustrator, and Photoshop.

Recently, Adobe was voted one of the 100 Best Companies to Work For.

MICROSOFT Computer Technology Innovator

Internet users view Microsoft's Web site more than 2.4 million times each day, attesting to the company's presence as the largest software company in the world. Its Office and Internet Explorer programs dominate the computer industry, and it also has assets in the MSNBC cable television network, the Encarta multimedia encyclopedia, SharePoint, and gaming software, including Flight Simulator and Zoo Tycoon. Microsoft also manufactures hardware, such as the Xbox, Zune, mouse devices, keyboards, fingerprint readers, Web cams, and game controllers.

When Microsoft was incorporated in 1975, the company had three programmers, one product, and revenues of $16,000. The company now employs more than 92,000 people and has annual revenues in excess of $58 billion. Windows 7 is the latest version of Microsoft's flagship operating system.

 For more information, visit the Computer Concepts CourseMate Web site at www.cengagebrain.com and then navigate to the Chapter 3 Companies on the Cutting Edge resource for this book.

Technology Trailblazers

DAN BRICKLIN VisiCalc Developer

Dan Bricklin introduced wikiCalc in 2007 as a free software tool for Web pages that have data in lists and tables. This program is an offshoot of a prototype program he had developed 30 years earlier, named VisiCalc, that performed a series of calculations automatically when numbers were entered.

Bricklin and a friend founded a company, Software Arts, to develop VisiCalc, short for Visible Calculator. They programmed the software using Apple Basic on an Apple II computer. This small program was the first type of application software that provided a reason for businesses to buy Apple computers. It included many features found in today's spreadsheet software.

Bricklin founded a small consulting company, Software Garden, to develop and market software such as wikiCalc. The company also distributes resources to help programmers learn about licensing their products and about open source software.

MASAYOSHI SON Softbank President and CEO

In the 1970s, Masayoshi Son was convinced that the microchip was going to change people's lives. As an economics major at the University of California, Berkeley, each day he attempted to develop one original use for computer technology. One of these ideas made him a millionaire: a multilingual pocket translating device that he sold to Sharp Corporation.

At age 23, Son founded Softbank, which is one of Japan's largest telecommunications and media corporations. He now is one of the richest men in the world with a net worth of $3.7 billion.

Recently, Softbank partnered with Apple to develop a version of the iPhone for the Japanese market. In addition, Son's company collaborated with Tiffany & Co. to manufacture 10 cell phones, each worth more than $910,000, with 400 diamonds weighing more than 20 karats total.

For more information, visit the Computer Concepts CourseMate Web site at www.cengagebrain.com and then navigate to the Chapter 3 Technology Trailblazers resource for this book.

Chapter Review

The Chapter Review reinforces the main concepts presented in this chapter.

To listen to an audio version of this Chapter Review, visit the Computer Concepts CourseMate Web site at www.cengagebrain.com and then navigate to the Chapter 3 Chapter Review resource for this book.

1. What Are the Four Categories of Application Software? **Application software** consists of programs designed to make users more productive and/or assist them with personal tasks. The major categories of application software are business software; graphics and multimedia software; home, personal, and educational software; and communications software.

2. What Is the User Interface of Application Software? Personal computer operating systems often use the concept of a **desktop**, which is an on-screen work area that has a graphical user interface. One way to start a program in Windows is to move the **pointer** to the Start **button** on the taskbar and **click** the Start button by pressing and releasing a button on the mouse. Then, click the program name on the menu or in a list. Once loaded in memory, the program is displayed in a **window** on the desktop.

Visit the Computer Concepts CourseMate Web site at www.cengagebrain.com, navigate to the Chapter 3 Quiz Yourself resource for this book, and then click Objectives 1 – 2.

3. What Are the Key Features of Widely Used Business Programs? **Business software** assists people in becoming more effective and efficient while performing daily business activities. Business software includes the following programs. **Word processing software** allows users to **create** a document by entering text or numbers and inserting graphical images, **edit** the document by making changes to its existing content, and **format** the document by changing its appearance. **Spreadsheet software** allows users to organize data in rows and columns, perform calculations, recalculate when data changes, and chart the data in graphical form. **Database software** allows users to create a **database**, which is a collection of data organized in a manner that allows access, retrieval, and use of that data. **Presentation software** allows users to create slides that are displayed on a monitor or on a projection screen. **Note taking software** enables users to enter typed text, handwritten comments, drawings, and sketches. A **personal information manager (PIM)** includes an appointment calendar, address book, notepad, and other features to help users organize personal information. In addition to PIM software, a huge variety of business and other software is available for phones. A **software suite** is a collection of individual programs available together as a unit. **Project management software** allows users to plan, schedule, track, and analyze the events, resources, and costs of a project. **Accounting software** helps companies record and report their financial transactions. **Document management software** provides a means for sharing, distributing, and searching through documents by converting them into a format that can be viewed by any user.

4. What Are the Key Features of Widely Used Graphics and Multimedia Programs? Graphics and multimedia software includes the following. **Computer-aided design (CAD) software** assists a professional user in creating engineering, architectural, and scientific designs. **Desktop publishing (DTP) software** enables professional designers to create sophisticated documents that contain text, graphics, and colors. **Paint software** allows users to draw pictures, shapes, and other graphical images with various on-screen tools. **Image editing software** provides the capabilities of paint software and also includes the capability to modify existing images. **Professional photo editing software** is a type of image editing software that allows photographers, videographers, engineers, scientists, and other high-volume digital photo users to edit and customize digital photos. **Video editing software** allows professionals to modify a segment of a video, called a clip. **Audio editing software** lets users modify audio clips, produce studio-quality soundtracks, and add audio to video clips. **Multimedia authoring software** allows users to combine text, graphics, audio, video, and animation into an interactive application. **Web page authoring software** helps users create Web pages and organize and maintain Web sites.

Visit the Computer Concepts CourseMate Web site at www.cengagebrain.com, navigate to the Chapter 3 Quiz Yourself resource for this book, and then click Objectives 3 – 4.

5. What Are the Key Features of Widely Used Home, Personal, and Educational Programs? Software for home, personal, and educational use includes the following. **Personal finance software** is a simplified accounting program that helps users balance their checkbooks, pay bills, track personal income and expenses, track investments, and evaluate financial plans. **Legal software** assists in the preparation of legal documents and provides legal information. **Tax preparation software** can guide users through the process of filing federal taxes. **Personal DTP software** helps home and small business users create newsletters, brochures, flyers, advertisements, postcards, greeting cards, letterhead, business cards, banners, calendars, logos, and Web pages. **Personal paint/image editing software** provides an easy-to-use interface and includes various simplified tools that allow you to draw pictures, shapes, and other images and to modify existing graphics and photos. Application software often includes a **clip art/image gallery**, which is a collection of clip art and photos. **Home design/landscaping software** assists users with the design, remodeling, or improvement of a home, deck, or landscape. **Travel and mapping software** allows users to view maps, determine routes, and locate points of interest. **Reference software** provides valuable and thorough information for all individuals. **Educational software** teaches a particular skill. **Entertainment software** includes interactive games, video, and other programs.

6. What Are Web Applications?   A **Web application**, or **Web app**, is a Web site that allows users to access and interact with software from any computer or device that is connected to the Internet. Users often interact with Web applications directly at the Web site, referred to as the host, through their Web browser. Some Web sites require you to download the software to your computer or device.

7. What Are the Types of Application Software Used in Communications?   Application software for communications includes Web browsers to access and view Web pages; e-mail programs to transmit messages via a network; instant messaging software for real-time exchange of messages or files; chat room software to have real-time, online typed conversations; text, picture, and video messaging software; RSS aggregator program to keep track of changes made to Web sites; blog software, or blogware, to create and maintain a blog; newsgroup/message board programs that allow online written discussions; FTP programs to upload and download files on the Internet; VoIP (Internet telephony), which allows users to speak to other users over the Internet; and video conferencing software for meetings on a network.

8. What Learning Aids Are Available for Application Software?   To assist in the learning process, many programs provide **online Help,** which is the electronic equivalent of a user manual. Most online Help also links to Web-based Help, which provides updates and more comprehensive resources to respond to technical issues about software. Popular in business, industry, and schools, **Web-based training (WBT)** uses Internet technology and consists of application software on the Web.

Visit the Computer Concepts CourseMate Web site at www.cengagebrain.com, navigate to the Chapter 3 Quiz Yourself resource for this book, and then click Objectives 5 – 8.

Key Terms

You should know the Key Terms. The list below helps focus your study.

To see an example of and a definition for each term, and to access current and additional information from the Web, visit the Computer Concepts CourseMate Web site at www.cengagebrain.com and then navigate to the Chapter 3 Key Terms resource for this book.

accounting software (119)
application software (108)
audio editing software (122)
business software (112)
button (110)
click (110)
clip art (113)
clip art/image gallery (126)
command (110)
computer-aided design (CAD) software (121)
computer-based training (CBT) (127)
create (114)
custom software (108)
database (116)
database software (116)
desktop (110)
desktop publishing (DTP) software (121)
distance learning (131)
document management software (119)

edit (114)
educational software (127)
e-learning (131)
entertainment software (128)
file (110)
font (114)
font size (114)
font style (114)
format (114)
freeware (109)
home design/landscaping software (127)
icon (110)
image editing software (121)
legal software (125)
malware (110)
menu (110)
multimedia authoring software (122)
note taking software (118)
online Help (131)
open source software (109)
packaged software (108)

paint software (121)
PDF (119)
personal DTP software (125)
personal finance software (124)
personal information manager (PIM) (118)
personal paint/image editing software (126)
personal photo editing software (126)
photo management software (126)
pointer (110)
presentation software (117)
print (114)
professional photo editing software (121)
project management software (118)
public-domain software (109)
reference software (127)
save (114)

shareware (109)
software suite (118)
spreadsheet software (115)
system software (109)
tax preparation software (125)
title bar (110)
travel and mapping software (127)
video editing software (122)
Web app (128)
Web application (108)
Web page authoring software (122)
Web-based training (WBT) (131)
window (110)
word processing software (113)
worksheet (115)

Checkpoint

The Checkpoint exercises test your knowledge of the chapter concepts. The page number containing the answer appears in parentheses after each exercise.

To complete the Checkpoint exercises interactively, visit the Computer Concepts CourseMate Web site at www.cengagebrain.com and then navigate to the Chapter 3 Checkpoint resource for this book.

Multiple Choice   Select the best answer.

1. _____ is mass-produced, copyrighted retail software that meets the needs of a wide variety of users, not just a single user or company. (108)
   a. Custom software
   b. Open source software
   c. A Web application
   d. Packaged software

2. A feature, called _____, allows users of word processing software to type words continually without pressing the ENTER key at the end of each line. (113)
   a. AutoFormat
   b. clipboard
   c. AutoCorrect
   d. wordwrap

3. When using spreadsheet software, a function _____. (115)
   a. depicts data in graphical form
   b. changes certain values to reveal the effects of the changes
   c. is a predefined formula that performs common calculations
   d. contains the formatting necessary for a specific worksheet type

4. _____ combines application software such as word processing, spreadsheet, presentation graphics, and e-mail. (118)
   a. Shareware
   b. A software suite
   c. Packaged software
   d. Custom software

5. _____ software provides a means for sharing, distributing, and searching through documents by converting them into a format that can be viewed by any user. (119)
   a. Portable Document Format (PDF)
   b. Document management
   c. Database
   d. Word processing

6. With _____, you can view, organize, sort, catalog, print, and share digital photos. (126)
   a. spreadsheet software
   b. photo management software
   c. clip art
   d. desktop publishing software

7. A(n) _____ is an online area where users have written discussions. (130)
   a. FTP program
   b. text message
   c. newsgroup/message board
   d. Web browser

8. _____ is the electronic equivalent of a user manual. (131)
   a. Distance learning
   b. Online Help
   c. Web-based training
   d. E-learning

Matching   Match the terms with their definitions.

_____ 1. command (110)

_____ 2. format (114)

_____ 3. note taking software (118)

_____ 4. personal finance software (124)

_____ 5. Web app (128)

a. delivers applications to meet a specific business need

b. simplified accounting program that helps home users and small office/home office users balance their checkbooks, pay bills, track personal income and expenses, set up budgets, manage home inventory, track investments, and evaluate financial plans

c. an instruction that causes a program to perform a specific action

d. Web site that allows users to access and interact with software from any computer or device that is connected to the Internet

e. enables users to enter typed text, handwritten comments, drawings, or sketches anywhere on a page

f. change the appearance of a document

Short Answer   Write brief answer to each of the following questions.

1. Describe some types of utility programs. _____ What is malware? _____

2. What are the features of presentation software? _____ What types of media might a person use to enhance a presentation? _____

3. How is video editing software used? _____ How is multimedia authoring software used? _____

4. How is travel and mapping software used? _____ What are some examples of educational software? _____

5. Describe how many Web sites utilize Web-based training. _____ What are some ways that e-learning enhances communications? _____

Problem Solving

The Problem Solving exercises extend your knowledge of the chapter concepts by seeking solutions to practical computer problems that you may encounter at home, school, or work. The Collaboration exercise should be completed with a team.

In the real world, practical problems often can be solved in multiple ways. Provide one solution to each of the following problems using available resources, such as articles on the Web or in print, blogs, podcasts, videos, television, user guides, other individuals, and electronics and computer stores. You may need to use multiple resources to obtain an answer. Present your solutions in the form requested by your instructor (brief report, presentation, discussion, or other means).

@ Home

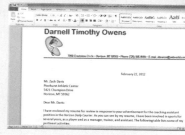

1. **Program Not Responding**   While working with a document, Microsoft Word suddenly fails to recognize when you click the mouse or type on the keyboard. The title bar also indicates that the program is not responding. What could be wrong?

2. **Unwanted Page**   A local charity in which you are active has asked you to design a one-page brochure. Each time you print the brochure, it prints the first page correctly, but a blank second page also comes out. What steps will you take to eliminate the blank second page?

3. **Audio Not Playing**   You are attempting for the first time to transfer video from your video recorder directly to your computer. When you save the file on your computer and play it back, the video quality is acceptable, but there is no audio. What is the first step you will take to troubleshoot this problem?

4. **Unusual File Size**   You are using photo editing software to remove red eye from a photo. After successfully removing the red eye, you save the file and notice that the size of the file nearly has doubled. What might be causing this?

@ Work

5. **Missing Font**   A coworker has sent you a document that was created in Microsoft Word. She asks you to format the heading of the document with a specific font; however, the font name does not appear in your list of fonts. What steps will you take to retrieve the font?

6. **Insufficient Permission**   When reviewing a document in your company's document management system, you attempt to correct a typographical error for the next person who views the file. The document management system prohibits this action and informs you that you do not have the proper permission. What will you do to resolve this problem?

7. **Trial Version Expired**   New job responsibilities require that you use Adobe Photoshop to create a new company logo. Your boss has been unable to purchase the latest version of the software for you, and recommends that you download and install the trial version until she is able to purchase the software. The trial period now has expired and you are unable to use the program. How might you be able to continue using the software?

8. **Web-Based Training Difficulties**   You have signed up for Web-based training that is designed to teach you how to use your company's new accounting system. During your training, you notice that the Web-based training Web site is not keeping track of your progress. Consequently, you have to start from the beginning each time you log in. What might be causing this?

Collaboration

9. **Computers in Construction**   As a student in a drafting class, your instructor has challenged you to design your dream home by using application software wherever possible. Form a team of three people that will determine how to accomplish this objective. One team member should compare and contrast two programs that can be used to create a two-dimensional floor plan, another team member should compare and contrast two computer-aided design programs that can create a more detailed design of the house, and the third team member should compare and contrast two programs that can assist with other aspects of the design process such as landscaping and interior design.

Learn How To

The Learn How To activities step you through fundamental technology skills when using a computer. The Learn How To exercises enable you to become more proficient with these skills.

Premium Activity: To relate this Learn How To activity to your everyday life, see a visual demonstration of the activity, and complete a short assessment, visit the Computer Concepts CourseMate Web site at www.cengagebrain.com and then navigate to the Chapter 3 Learn How To resource for this book.

Learn How To 1: Save a File in Application Software

When you use application software, most of the time you either will be creating a new file or modifying an existing file. For example, if you are using a word processor, when you create a new document, the document is a file.

When you create or modify a file, it is contained in RAM. If you turn off your computer or lose electrical power, the file will not be retained. In order to retain the file, you must save it on disk or other permanent storage, such as a USB flash drive.

As you create the file, you should save the file often. To save a new file, you must complete several tasks:

1. Initiate an action indicating you want to save the file, such as selecting Save on the File menu.
2. Designate where the file should be stored. This includes identifying both the device (such as drive C) and the folder or library.
3. Specify the name of the file, using the file name rules as specified by the application or operating system.
4. Click the Save button to save the file.

Tasks 2 through 4 normally can be completed using a dialog box such as the one shown in Figure 3-38.

If you use application software to create or modify a file and attempt to close the program prior to saving the new or modified file, the program may display a dialog box that asks if you want to save the file. If you click the Yes button, a modified file will be saved using the same file name in the same location from which it was retrieved. Saving a new file requires that you complete tasks 2 through 4.

Figure 3-38

Exercise

1a. Start the WordPad program from the Accessories list in the All Programs list. Type `Saving a file is the best insurance against losing work.`

1b. Click the Save button on the Quick Access Toolbar. What dialog box is displayed? Where will the file be saved? What is the default file name? If you wanted to save the file on the desktop, what would you do? Click the Cancel button in the dialog box. Submit your answers to your instructor.

1c. Click the Close button in the upper-right corner of the WordPad window. What happened? Click the Yes button in the WordPad dialog box. What happened? Connect a USB flash drive to one of the computer's USB ports. Select the USB flash drive as the location for saving the file. Save the file with the name, Chapter 3 Learn How To 1. What happened when you clicked the Save button? Submit your answers to your instructor.

Learn How To 2: Zip/Compress a File

When you zip or compress one or more files in Windows, it attempts to shrink the file size(s) by reducing the amount of unneeded space. Compressing a file is particularly useful when you attach files to an e-mail message and wish to keep the file size as small as possible. It also is useful when you compress multiple files simultaneously, because Windows compresses the multiple files into a single file. You can compress a file or folder by completing the following steps:

1. Locate the file(s) or folder(s) you want to compress. If the files or folders you wish to compress are located in multiple locations, it might be helpful to first move them so that they are in a single location.
2. Select the file(s) or folder(s) you would like to compress. If you are selecting multiple files or folders, click the first one and then hold down the CTRL key while you select the remaining files and/or folders. Once you are finished making your selections, release the CTRL key.

3. Right-click the selection to display a shortcut menu, point to Send to on the shortcut menu to display the Send to submenu (Figure 3-39), and then click Compressed (zipped) folder to create the compressed folder.

4. If necessary, type a new name for the compressed folder and then press the ENTER key.

Exercise

1. To better organize your hard disk, you decide to compress files you rarely use, but would like to keep as a backup. Click the Start button to display the Start menu, click Pictures to display the Pictures library, and then double-click the Sample Pictures folder to display sample pictures included with Windows 7. Select three pictures and compress them into one compressed folder. Use your first initial and last name as the name of the new compressed folder and then e-mail the folder to your instructor.

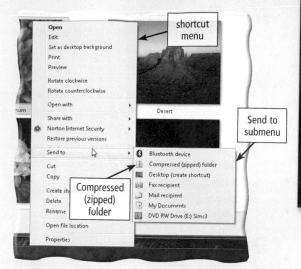

Figure 3-39

Learn It Online

The Learn It Online exercises are interactive Web exercises designed to reinforce and expand your understanding of the chapter concepts. The descriptions below briefly summarize each exercise.

To complete the Learn It Online exercises, visit the Computer Concepts CourseMate Web site at www.cengagebrain.com, navigate to the Chapter 3 resources for this book, click the link for the exercise you want to complete, and then read the instructions.

1 **At the Movies — MediaCell Video Converter**
Watch a movie to learn how to use the MediaCell Video Converter and then answer questions about the movie.

2 **Student Edition Labs — Word Processing, Spreadsheets, Databases, and Presentation Software**
Enhance your understanding and knowledge about business application software by completing the Word Processing, Spreadsheets, Databases, and Presentation Software Labs.

3 **Practice Test**
Take a multiple choice test that checks your knowledge of the chapter concepts and review the resulting study guide.

4 **Who Wants To Be a Computer Genius²?**
Play the Shelly Cashman Series version of this popular game by answering questions to find out if you are a computer genius. Panic buttons are available to provide assistance during game play.

5 **Crossword Puzzle Challenge**
Complete an interactive crossword puzzle to reinforce concepts presented in this chapter.

6 **Windows Exercises**
Step through the Windows 7 exercises to learn about working with application programs, creating a word processing document, using WordPad Help, and business software products.

7 **Exploring Computer Careers**
Read about a career as a help desk specialist, search for related employment advertisements, and then answer related questions.

8 **Web Apps — Britannica.com**
Learn how to browse world history and search for various encyclopedia articles using Britannica.com.

Web Research

The Web Research exercises broaden your understanding of chapter concepts by presenting questions that require you to search the Web for answers.

1 **Search Sleuth**

Use one of the search engines listed in Figure 2-8 in Chapter 2 on page 65 or your own favorite search engine to find the answers to the following questions. Copy and paste the Web address from the Web page where you found the answer. Some questions may have more than one answer. If required, submit your answers to your instructor. (1) What company did Bruce Artwick form in 1977, and what game did it license to Microsoft in 1982? (2) In what year did the United States Department of Revenue first provide tax forms and booklets in Adobe PDF format on its Web site? (3) What is the latest security incident listed on the United States Computer Emergency Readiness Team (US-CERT) Web site? (4) What is the name of the sans serif font the German Bauhaus movement developed in 1928? (5) What United States president's speech did Peter Norvig turn into a lighthearted PowerPoint presentation?

2 **Green Computing**

A typical desktop computer and 17-inch monitor that always are turned on release 750 pounds of carbon dioxide in one year, which is the same amount of carbon dioxide released by a car driven 820 miles. Power management software helps conserve a computer's electricity consumption while maintaining acceptable performance. The programs determine when a computer is inactive and, in turn, power down the computer. Use one of the search engines listed in Figure 2-8 in Chapter 2 on page 65 or your own favorite search engine to find information about power management software. What average return-on-investment do they promise? What features do they have, such as generating reports and exempting critical programs from powering down? What is their cost? Powering down the computer stresses critical components, such as the CPU and memory, so does this practice actually result in more waste because these parts must be replaced? Write a report summarizing your findings, and include a table of links to Web sites that you viewed.

3 **Social Networking**

Career-minded professionals have turned to LinkedIn as a resource for online networking. The more than 45 million registered users, who represent each of the FORTUNE 500 companies, create public profiles that recruiters scour in search of new talent. Users can link to work contacts who, in turn, give access to their work contacts. Visit the LinkedIn Web site (linkedin.com), click the What is LinkedIn? link at the top of the page, and then read the information about reconnecting with current and former colleagues and classmates, job hunting, and obtaining advice from experts. Click the LinkedIn Jobs link at the bottom of the page, type a keyword describing the type of job you would like to have, and then browse the listings. What tips for finding jobs does LinkedIn provide? Summarize the listings and job information you read.

4 **Blogs**

Vehicle buyers know that the Internet provides a wealth of information that helps direct them toward the best vehicle for their needs. Those consumers who research blogs can obtain price, safety, performance, and maintenance facts and then employ savvy negotiation techniques that help them make the purchase confidently. Visit several automotive blogs, including those from Popular Mechanics (popularmechanics.com/blogs/automotive_news), Autoblog (autoblog.com), Autoblog Green (autobloggreen.com), Autopia (blog.wired.com/cars), and Ask Patty — Car Advice for Women (caradvice.askpatty.com). What new hybrid, luxury, and high-performance vehicles are profiled? Which are promoted as being environmentally friendly? Write a report summarizing the vehicle information you read.

5 **Ethics in Action**

A hacker is someone who tries to access a computer or network illegally. Although hacking activity sometimes is a harmless prank, at times it causes extensive damage. Some hackers say their activities allow them to test their skills. Others say their activities are a form of civil disobedience that forces companies to make their products more secure. View online sites such as The Ethical Hacker Network (ethicalhacker.net) that provide information about when hackers provide some benefit to the Internet society. Write a report summarizing your findings and include a table of links to Web sites that provide additional details.

Digital Communications

DIGITAL COMMUNICATIONS, which factor largely in many people's personal and business lives, include any transmission of information from one computer or mobile device to another (Figure 1). This feature covers many forms of digital communications: e-mail; text messaging, instant messaging, and picture/video messaging; digital voice communications; blogs and wikis; online social networks, chat rooms, and Web conferences; and content sharing.

With the Internet, cell phone networks, and other wireless networks increasing in size and speed, digital communications have become more and more prevalent. The most common devices used to communicate digitally are desktop computers, notebook computers, smart phones, and other mobile devices.

Successful use of digital communications involves selecting both the proper communications device and the proper mode of communication for a given situation. Each computer or mobile device and communications method has advantages and disadvantages that you should consider.

The following pages describe how people use different types of digital communications in their personal and business lives to enhance collaboration and increase productivity. The final section of the feature includes an example of how you might use digital communications.

Figure 1   People use a variety of methods in their personal and business lives to engage in digital communications.

E-Mail

E-mail is the transmission of messages and files via a computer network. E-mail quickly has become one of the more widely used forms of digital communications. Although e-mail is primarily a text-based form of digital communications, it also can be used to share photos, videos, and other types of files by attaching files to e-mail messages.

E-Mail: The Personal Perspective

With a computer or mobile device connected to the Internet, you can use e-mail to keep in contact with friends, family, stores, companies, schools, and government agencies. Some people maintain several different e-mail addresses for use in different situations. Figure 2 lists some advantages, disadvantages, and good practices of personal e-mail use. Some e-mail programs are application programs that run on your computer, while others are Web applications (shown in Figure 3).

Personal E-Mail Use

Advantages
- One of the most preferred methods of online communications.
- Available on nearly any computer or mobile device with Internet access.
- Send files, called attachments, via e-mail messages to others.
- Fast, reliable, and proven technology.
- Allows messages to be sent anywhere free of charge or inexpensively.
- Allows communications with more than one person at a time.
- Provides an electronic forum for communications in which the originator has time to consider a thought before it is sent or spoken, unlike face-to-face meetings or telephone conversations.

Disadvantages
- Number of messages received can become overwhelming and unmanageable.
- Spam can overwhelm your e-mail inbox.
- Message tone can be misunderstood.
- Many computer viruses and other malicious programs are transmitted via e-mail messages.

Good practices
- Keep messages as short as possible.
- Check with the recipient before sending attachments, especially large attachments.
- Respond to messages promptly.
- Use a reputable Internet access provider that uses a spam filter, which is a program that detects and removes spam, and use an e-mail program that includes a spam filter.
- Never respond to unsolicited advertisements or spam.
- Informal language and shortcuts are acceptable when communicating with friends and family (e.g., suitable to use HRU? as a shortcut for How are you?).
- Always include a Subject line.
- Always reread your message and edit it before sending it.
- When replying to questions or comments included with a previous message, include the original message.

Figure 2   Personal e-mail remains one of the more popular reasons to use the Internet.

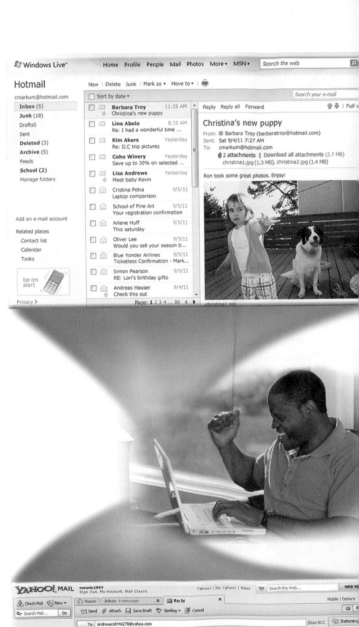

Figure 3   Many home users have e-mail Web applications.

E-Mail: The Business Perspective

Most businesses use e-mail for internal communications among employees and external communications with customers and business partners. E-mail gradually has replaced typed and copied memos, letters, and faxes while increasing the reliability, cost effectiveness, and speed of the communications. Figure 4 indicates some advantages, disadvantages, and good practices of e-mail use in business. Many of the notes listed in Figure 2 also apply to e-mail communications in business. Figure 5 shows an example of the inbox of a business e-mail program user and an example of an appropriate business e-mail message.

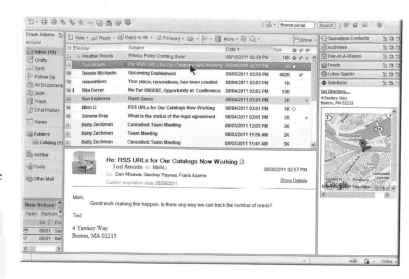

E-Mail Use in Business

Advantages

- Easily archive, or store long-term, all e-mail messages sent from or received by the business.
- Generally can guarantee delivery of any e-mail message that is sent within the business.
- A replacement for memos, letters, faxes, and other internal and external business communications when permitted by company policy.
- Communicate with someone who is not available at the time you need to communicate.

Disadvantages

- Volume of e-mail messages often becomes overwhelming.
- Often leads to overcommunication, which can result in important information being lost because it is ignored.
- Sometimes leads to avoidance of personal contact, such as a meeting or telephone call.

Good practices

- Because most companies archive, or save, all e-mail messages, use e-mail when you want a permanent record of a communication.
- Understand your company's e-mail policies. Many companies prohibit sending personal e-mail messages from a business computer.
- Never include any language that would be considered inappropriate in a business environment.
- Check your e-mail inbox regularly.
- Follow your company's or department's guidelines for formatting messages and including contact information and any appropriate disclaimers.
- In most cases, it is appropriate to send larger attachments in business e-mail messages as compared to those permissible in personal messages.
- Avoid sending messages to many people simultaneously or replying to large groups of people. For example, it is almost always inappropriate to send a message to the entire company.
- Avoid using e-mail messages when the content involves sensitive issues, such as a negotiation, legal matter, or employee review.
- When you need to know that the recipient has read your e-mail message, use the return receipt feature of your e-mail program to receive automatic notification as soon as the message is read.

Figure 4   Most businesses provide written policies and guidelines regarding use of e-mail programs.

Figure 5   Businesses often use more sophisticated e-mail programs than do home users.

Text Messaging, Instant Messaging, and Picture/Video Messaging

Text messaging, instant messaging, and picture/video messaging allow you to exchange short messages and small multimedia files with other online users. Text messaging is a wireless messaging service that allows users to send and receive short notes on a smart phone or other mobile device. Instant messaging is a real-time Internet communications service that notifies a user when one or more people are online and allows the user to exchange messages or files or join a private chat room with those people. Picture messaging is a wireless messaging service that allows users to send and receive photos and sound files, as well as short text messages, to and from a mobile device, or computer. Video messaging is a wireless messaging service that allows users to send and receive short video clips, usually up to 30 seconds, in addition to all picture messaging services.

Text Messaging, Instant Messaging, and Picture/Video Messaging: The Personal Perspective

Text messaging, instant messaging, and picture/video messaging typically are used on smart phones. Instant messaging often is used on desktop and notebook computers. Virtually instantaneous communication is possible with the various forms of messaging. Figure 6 indicates some advantages, disadvantages, and good practices of using instant messaging, text messaging, and picture/video messaging in your personal life. Figure 7 shows some examples of people using messaging.

Personal Text Messaging, Instant Messaging, and Picture/Video Messaging Use

Advantages
- Virtually instantaneous form of digital communications.
- Fast, reliable, and popular method of digital communications.
- Useful when you prefer an immediate response from the recipient.
- Allows you to carry on several conversations at any time.

Disadvantages
- Can be addictive in nature.
- Receiving a constant stream of messages can be distracting.
- May be very expensive on mobile devices.
- Text messaging: Overuse may result in repetitive stress injuries (RSIs).

Good practices
- Know the person with whom you are exchanging messages.
- Keep in mind that any text, picture, or video you send can be sent to others by the recipient.
- When messaging with a new contact, do not share personal information quickly.
- Always reread your text messages and preview your pictures and videos before you send them.
- Respect the status of others when they indicate they are busy.
- Instant messaging: If the program allows you to indicate your status to others, such as "Busy" or "Do not disturb," use these indicators to let others know when you are unavailable.
- Picture/video messaging: When sending picture/video messages, make sure the content is appropriate.

Figure 6   People use various types of messaging for different reasons. (Where noted, some bullet points apply only to particular technologies.)

Figure 7   Many people interact with messaging software both at home and while away from home or work.

Text Messaging, Instant Messaging, and Picture/Video Messaging: The Business Perspective

Businesses typically use more secure, feature-rich messaging programs that allow all messages to be archived. Archiving of messages often is required by law and allows old messages to be available for future reference. Messaging allows colleagues to collaborate, or work together, online. Figure 8 indicates some advantages, disadvantages, and good practices of text messaging, instant messaging, and picture/video messaging use in business. Many of the notes listed in Figure 6 also apply to the various forms of messaging in business. Figure 9 shows an example of business-level instant messaging software and video messaging at job sites.

Text Messaging, Instant Messaging, and Picture/Video Messaging Use in Business

Advantages
- When used properly, greatly increases collaboration and communications because users have instantaneous access to each other.
- All messages can be archived for retrieval at a later date or for meeting legal requirements.
- Immediate contact with customers when allowed by company policy and agreed to by the customer.
- Collaboration with geographically separated colleagues.
- Instant messaging: Some programs allow conferences of several people at one time, eliminating the need for scheduling meeting rooms or conference calls.
- Picture/video messaging: Provides instant views of remote locations, such as work sites or company assets.

Disadvantages
- Despite policies, business conversations often lead to personal conversations.
- Often leads to over-reliance on simply messaging a colleague for an answer to a question rather than determining the answer on your own.
- Can lead to a significant decline in important face-to-face contact with coworkers, customers, and business partners.
- Instant messaging: Because all messages can be archived, it can lead to difficult situations when inappropriate content is shared.

Good practices
- When beginning a messaging conversation, make your point quickly and keep messages concise.
- Separate your personal messaging habits from your business messaging habits, avoiding use of emoticons and shortcuts, such as "brb" as a shortcut for "Be right back."
- Use proper spelling, grammar, and punctuation, and avoid colloquialisms.
- Be aware of cultural differences that might arise during casual conversations.
- Acknowledge the end of a messaging conversation.
- Follow your company's policies regarding the type of information that can be conveyed in a message and with whom you may engage in messaging.
- Always try to meet or telephone a person to introduce yourself before sending a first message to him or her.
- Review all messages you send to colleagues to make sure that the contents are appropriate for the workplace.

Figure 8 Businesses use a variety of messaging methods to allow employees to collaborate in a timely and secure manner. (Where noted, some bullet points apply only to particular technologies.)

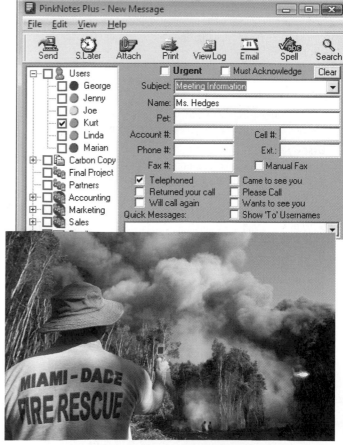

Figure 9 Business users employ instant messaging and video messaging to communicate ideas and multimedia information quickly.

Digital Voice Communications

Digital voice communications includes the use of cell phones, smart phones, and VoIP (Voice over IP). VoIP is a technology that allows users to speak to other users via the Internet. VoIP can be used as a replacement for the traditional telephone at work or in the home.

Digital Voice Communications: The Personal Perspective

With more than 200 million in use in the United States, cell phones are a primary source of digital voice communications. Cell phones can act as a suitable replacement for the traditional, wired, public switched telephone network. Smart phones offer features such as e-mail, text messaging, picture/video messaging, and playing or streaming multimedia.

Figure 10 indicates some advantages, disadvantages, and good practices of digital voice communications in your personal life. Figure 11 shows some examples of digital voice communications, including visual voice mail, which is a service that automatically translates voice mail into text messages or allows you to download voice messages to your smart phone and listen to them at your convenience.

Personal Digital Voice Communications Use

Advantages
- Increase productivity through greater and more timely communications.
- Both cell phones and VoIP offer more choice in providers than the public switched telephone network.
- Cell phones: Widespread coverage of cell phone networks provides voice communications nearly everywhere in the United States.
- Cell phones: Have been instrumental in saving lives in emergency situations.
- VoIP: Often offers free features, such as voice mail, unlimited in-country long distance calling, three-way calling, and call forwarding.
- VoIP: Typically is less expensive for both local and long distance calls than the public switched telephone network.

Disadvantages
- Cell phones: In some situations, such as while driving a car, can contribute to accidents.
- VoIP: Not as strictly regulated as the public switched telephone network, meaning that the quality of service may be lower.
- With many VoIP providers and some cell phone providers, connecting to a local service, such as 911 for emergencies, may be difficult or cumbersome.

Good practices
- Cell phones: Use a headset if you must use a cell phone while driving. Be aware of laws in your area that prohibit or limit cell phone use while driving.
- Cell phones: When using in public, be mindful of and courteous to those around you.
- Cell phones: Be aware of rules or policies at some locations, such as schools, medical facilities, or religious facilities.
- Cell phones: In public locations, use an alternative ring method, such as a vibration setting, to avoid interrupting others.

Figure 10   Cell phones and other forms of digital voice communications have become an essential means of communications throughout the world. (Where noted, some bullet points apply only to particular technologies.)

Figure 11   People use cell phones, VoIP, and visual voice mail in their everyday lives for contact with friends and family.

Digital Voice Communications: The Business Perspective

Businesses embrace digital voice communications because of increased collaboration and productivity, cost savings, and mobility. Figure 12 lists many of the advantages, disadvantages, and good practices of digital voice communications use in business. Many of the notes listed in Figure 10 also apply to the various forms of digital voice communications in business. Figure 13 shows an example of a simple VoIP system.

Digital Voice Communications Use in Business

Advantages
- Increased communications and collaboration can result in increased productivity and cost savings.
- Cell phones: Ability to contact a person almost anywhere at any time.
- VoIP: With some systems, employees can listen to and manage their voice messages on their personal computer.
- VoIP: A computer is not necessary to use a VoIP system.
- VoIP: Allows large companies to consolidate communications between geographically diverse locations.
- VoIP: Implement as an alternative to the public switched telephone network because VoIP allows businesses to use their existing network more efficiently and provides more features than the public switched telephone network.

Disadvantages
- With many VoIP providers and some cell phone providers, connecting to a local service, such as 911 for emergencies, may be difficult or cumbersome.
- The quality of calls may change at times due to excessive network usage.

- Cell phones: Misuse often leads to rude behavior or disruption of meetings.
- Cell phones: Using a cell phone provided by an employer for personal calls may have undesirable tax consequences.
- VoIP: Large companies may find it expensive and difficult to manage.
- VoIP: Unlike a public switched telephone network, many VoIP systems and equipment will not function during a power outage.

Good practices
- Cell phones: Follow company policy regarding the use for business communications. Limit personal calls on your cell phone during business hours.
- Cell phones: Disable the ringer when in meetings or during important discussions.
- Cell phones: Resist the need to answer every call at all times, such as when you are on breaks or when you are not at work.
- Cell phones: Avoid speaking loudly on the phone when walking through others' work areas.
- VoIP: When possible, use a VoIP telephone rather than a cell phone because it generally is less expensive for the company on a per-call basis.

Figure 12 Digital voice communications are used when a more personal form of communications than e-mail or messaging is required in real time. (Where noted, some bullet points apply only to particular technologies.)

Figure 13 VoIP allows businesses to connect their telephone system to their internal network and the Internet for voice telephone calls.

Blogs and Wikis

A blog is an informal Web site consisting of time-stamped articles, or posts, in a diary or journal format, usually listed in reverse chronological order. A wiki is a collaborative Web site that allows users to create, add to, modify, or delete the Web site content via their Web browser.

Blogs and Wikis: The Personal Perspective

Blog topics often include family life, social life, a personal project, or events during a vacation. You might read and contribute to a wiki regarding classical guitar techniques if your hobbies included playing classical guitar. While blogs can be modified only by the author, a wiki can be authored and edited by any user. Another difference between blogs and wikis is that blog entries typically are not included in search results from search engines, such as Google, while wiki entries are recognized by search engine queries. Figure 14 indicates some advantages, disadvantages, and good practices of using blogs and wikis in your personal life. Figure 15 shows examples of blog and wiki entries.

Personal Blog and Wiki Use

Advantages
- Some blogs and wikis provide secure access so that only a select group of qualified or desired individuals are allowed to read and write entries.
- Blogs: Easy, accessible, and often free method of keeping a group of people informed about events.
- Blogs: Easy way to keep up with an acquaintance or expand your knowledge about political or social points of view.
- Blogs: Often can be read or written using Internet-enabled mobile devices.
- Wikis: Provide free access to concise, almost encyclopedic, information about nearly any topic.

Disadvantages
- Vulnerable to fraudulent or biased entries placed by businesses or special interest groups in an effort to sway public opinion.
- Blogs: Often are biased towards a particular point of view.
- Blogs: Some blogging Web sites are often sources of malicious programs.
- Wikis: Publicly accessible wikis sometimes are vulnerable to vandalism or subject to errors.

Good practices
- Blogs: When writing a blog, be aware that the contents of your blog may be accessible publicly and associated with your identity for a long time.
- Blogs: When reading blogs, be aware of the source of the information and evaluate the credibility of the source.
- Wikis: When performing research using a wiki, check any provided sources and, if possible, check the editorial history of the entries.
- Wikis: If you locate an error, notify the author or editor of the wiki page, or, if possible, edit the page yourself to make the correction.
- Wikis: When possible, contribute your own knowledge to wikis that interest you, being sure to follow the guidelines of the wiki.

Figure 14 While blogs and wikis provide a great deal of information sharing, users and contributors alike should be aware of the risks involved. (Where noted, some bullet points apply only to particular technologies.)

Figure 15 Blogs and wikis allow people to share their knowledge, experience, viewpoints, and personal events on the Internet. People use mobile blogging while away from home or while in interesting locations.

Blogs and Wikis: The Business Perspective

Many businesses use blogs and wikis to share knowledge within the company. One large company claims to maintain more than 300,000 blogs and wikis internally. A key reason that blogs and wikis are so popular in business is that they can be written, read, and searched easily. As the company's resident expert regarding a particular topic, an employee may blog to keep others informed about topics relating to that expertise. A business-oriented wiki may contain a wealth of historical knowledge for a particular department in the company. Figure 16 indicates some advantages, disadvantages, and good practices of using blogs and wikis in business. Many of the notes listed in Figure 14 also apply to using blogs and wikis in business. Figure 17 shows examples of typical business-oriented blog and wiki entries.

Blog and Wiki Use in Business

Advantages

- Provide easy access to gained knowledge and experience.
- Easily can be searched by employees.
- Some may be made available to customers, business partners, or the general public.
- Blogs: Publicly accessible blogs often are used as an effective means to promote products or services.

Disadvantages

- Mistakes, inaccuracies, and inconsistencies in entries can lead to lost productivity and increased costs.
- Internal company blogs and wikis often contain proprietary company information that easily can be leaked to competitors or the press.
- Blogs: When contributing to a blog, some employees become engrossed with capturing every detail of their job.
- Wikis: Information often may become old, or stale, if it is not updated regularly.

Good practices

- Search your company's blogs and wikis for information before telephoning, instant messaging, or e-mailing a colleague with a question.
- If you do not find an answer to a question on your company's blogs or wikis, then contribute to a blog or wiki once you find the answer.
- When contributing to a blog or wiki entry, read your company's policies regarding content, formatting, and style. Some companies employ full-time bloggers and writers who can help you contribute a valuable entry.
- When contributing to a blog or wiki entry, stay on topic and create links within your entry to other related or relevant Web pages, including other blog and wiki entries.
- Blogs: When engaging in personal blogging, do not discredit your employer or potential future employers; many people have lost their jobs as a result of engaging in such behavior.
- Blogs: When engaging in personal blogging, be careful not to divulge proprietary company information.

Figure 16 Business blog and wiki use typically is governed by more guidelines and rules than those for personal blogs and wikis. (Where noted, some bullet points apply only to particular technologies.)

Figure 17 Increasingly more businesses use blogs and wikis to allow employees to share information with each other, customers, and business partners.

Online Social Networks, Chat Rooms, and Web Conferences

An online social network is a Web site that encourages members in its online community to share their interest, ideas, stories, photos, music, and videos with other registered users. A chat room is a location on the Internet that permits users to chat with one another. A Web conference allows two or more people to engage in an online meeting and often allows the attendees to access programs and digital content, such as documents, audio, and video, during the meeting.

Online Social Networks, Chat Rooms, and Web Conferences: The Personal Perspective

The popularity of online social networks such as Facebook continues to skyrocket. Most online social networks allow you to maintain a personal Web site that you can share with other registered users who, after being invited, may view or contribute content to your site. Those invited to your online social network often are known as friends. While chat rooms have decreased in popularity over the years, people often use them for targeted discussions about specific topics. Web conferences often are used by consumers to obtain technical support or assistance from companies and government agencies or in educational settings to engage in online learning. Figure 18 indicates some advantages, disadvantages, and good practices of using online social networks, chat rooms, and Web conferences in your personal life. Figure 19 shows an example of an online social network and a virtual chat room discussion.

Figure 19   Online social networks and virtual chat rooms allow groups of people with similar interests or lifestyles to enjoy real-time communications.

Personal Use of Online Social Networks, Chat Rooms, and Web Conferences

Advantages
- Online social networks/chat rooms: Easily find friends throughout the world with similar interests or traits.
- Online social networks/chat rooms: Can expand your knowledge about political or social points of view.
- Web conferences: Use Web conferencing when offered by a company for technical support issues because the tenor of the interaction is more personal than a telephone call.
- Web conferences: Often effectively provides the necessary communications to avoid a visit to a store location or a visit from a repair technician.

Disadvantages
- Online social networks/chat rooms: Some people are susceptible to overusing these forms of communications in lieu of real, in-person contacts and relationships. Overuse of these forms of communications may lead to addiction.

- Online social networks/chat rooms: People often hide their real identity to lure others into revealing too much personal information.
- Online social networks/chat rooms: Several high-profile incidents occurred in which people engaged in illegal activity using online social networks and chat rooms.

Good practices
- Online social networks: When submitting information, be aware that the information may be accessible publicly and associated with your identity for a long time.
- Online social networks: While many online social networks encourage the practice, do not try to gather too many friends in your social network. Some experts believe that a functional social network is limited to a maximum of 150 people.
- Chat rooms/Web conferences: Be as polite and courteous as you would be to someone in person.

Figure 18   People use online social networks, chat rooms, and Web conferences as a means of extending their social lives beyond their physical surroundings. (Where noted, some bullet points apply only to particular technologies.)

Online Social Networks, Chat Rooms, and Web Conferences: The Business Perspective

Online social networks, chat rooms, and Web conferences allow business users to interact and collaborate as teams. While online social networks have not been as popular as other forms of digital communications in business, their use is showing promise for many companies and groups who use it for business purposes. One company claims to have signed up more than five million business users for its business-oriented online social network. Chat rooms and Web conferences often serve as forums for online meetings. Figure 20 indicates some advantages, disadvantages, and good practices of using online social networks, chat rooms, and Web conferences in business. Many of the notes listed in Figure 6 on page 144 and Figure 18 also apply to these forms of digital communication in business. Figure 21 shows an example of a business-oriented online social network, chat room, and Web conference.

Online Social Network, Chat Room, and Web Conference Use in Business

Advantages

- Online social networks: Encourage people to collaborate with others with whom they typically would not collaborate.
- Online social networks/chat rooms: Often can be accessed using Internet-enabled mobile devices, providing instant collaboration almost anywhere.
- Online social networks/chat rooms: Provide forums for meeting potential customers, employers, and employees.
- Web conferences: Programs often allow application program sharing, which means that all participants can view the contents of one or more participant's computer screen.
- Online social networks/chat rooms: Some are located internally within a company and allow only employees access to the sites.
- Online social networks/chat rooms: Some are subscription-based and allow people to interact freely with others in related fields or industries.

Disadvantages

- Employees often over-rely on these means of online digital communications and do not interact with others in more personal ways.
- Online social networks: Can be cumbersome and expensive to maintain.

Good practices

- When engaging in online social networks, chat rooms, and Web conferences outside of your company, be careful not to divulge proprietary company information.
- Always maintain a professional demeanor. Often, those who use this technology in their personal lives are quick to behave more casually than is appropriate in a business setting.
- Divulge only that information about yourself that is relevant to the reasons you are participating in an online social network or chat room.

Figure 20 Businesses have embraced online social networks, chat rooms, and Web conferences to drive collaboration among geographically separated teams, employees, and other business contacts. (Where noted, some bullet points apply only to particular technologies.)

Figure 21 Businesses use online social networks, chat rooms, and Web conferences to allow employees and teams to communicate more effectively.

Content Sharing

Content sharing provides a means by which rich content, such as audio, video, photos, and documents, can be communicated digitally.

Content Sharing: The Personal Perspective

The prolific spread of digital cameras and digital video cameras combined with ever-increasing speeds of home and mobile Internet connections has resulted in the explosive growth of media sharing Web sites, such as YouTube and Flickr. In addition to sharing media, people are sharing documents, spreadsheets, and other content on Web sites. Figure 22 indicates some advantages, disadvantages, and

good practices of content sharing in your personal life. Figure 23 shows some examples of a video sharing Web site, a photo sharing group Web site, and a personal photo sharing Web site.

Figure 23 People share and view content on the Internet in a number of ways.

Personal Content Sharing Use

Advantages
- Ability to view broadcasts of events that may not be available through traditional broadcasts in your area.
- Media sharing Web sites provide almost limitless information and entertainment at little or no cost.
- Some services allow you to edit your content or the content of others directly on the site using a Web application.
- View or listen to live broadcasts of sporting events.
- View or listen to news stories.
- Much like online social networks, media sharing Web sites can provide a sense of community to a group of geographically separated individuals.

Disadvantages
- You may find it difficult to locate media and content that interests you.
- When sharing video and photos on a media sharing Web site, you may be giving up some of your rights to the media.
- Many people have been embarrassed by content posted by others to media sharing Web sites.

Good practices
- Before placing your content on a media sharing Web site, make a good effort to edit the content for brevity and clarity. For example, make certain that audio is clear in a video, and use photo editing software to remove red-eye.
- Take advantage of the fact that most media and content sharing Web sites allow you to limit who can access your media and content.
- Before you allow somebody to record video of you or take your picture, remember that the video or photo may end up on a media sharing Web site.
- Before placing your multimedia content on a media sharing Web site, check the terms of the service agreement and make certain you agree to give up certain legal rights to your multimedia content.
- Do not post pictures or videos that are protected by a copyright.

Figure 22 While most people act as consumers of content shared on the Internet, some share their own content.

Content Sharing: The Business Perspective

Media sharing Web sites allow business to interact creatively with employees, customers, and prospective customers. Video conferencing is the oldest form of real-time multimedia content sharing in business. Figure 24 outlines some advantages, disadvantages, and good practices of content sharing in business. Many of the notes listed in Figure 22 also apply to content sharing in business. Figure 25 shows examples of content shared in an educational setting and a document management system, which allows for secure storage and management of a company's documents.

Content Sharing Use in Business

Advantages

- Multimedia sharing sites allow companies to archive video conferences, advertisements, employee photos, and other multimedia content.
- Executives and managers create podcasts or vodcasts to spread their vision or message. Vodcasts are podcasts that contain video and usually audio.
- Video conferences allow geographically separate people to transmit audio and video and engage in a meeting remotely.
- Most business-based content sharing software provides for enhanced collaboration by making the content accessible and searchable.
- Multimedia content, such as videos and photos, can be stored in a document management system to archive information about important projects or events.

Disadvantages

- Production and distribution of multimedia content often is more expensive than traditional methods.
- Security on business content sharing systems often frustrates employees who are denied access to information without special approval.

Good practices

- Unless you have permission, do not share company-owned photos and videos on publicly available media sharing Web sites, such as YouTube or Flickr.
- When viewing or sharing photos and videos in the workplace, be certain that the content is appropriate for the workplace. Some businesses have a media department that manages all of the company's multimedia content.

Figure 24   Businesses provide secure content sharing repositories and real-time multimedia.

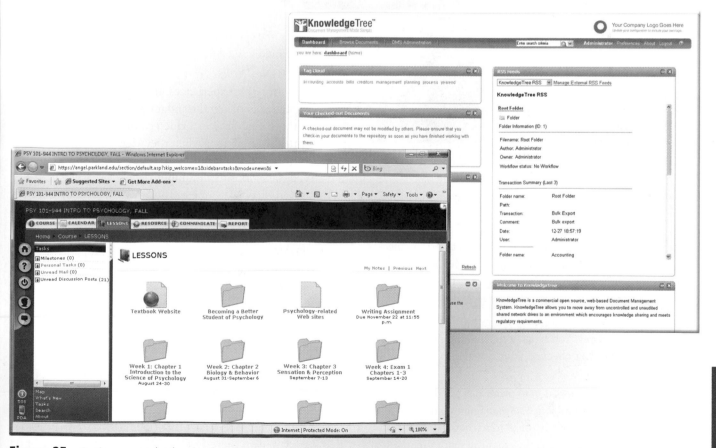

Figure 25   Businesses and other institutions share a variety of digital content in order to facilitate collaboration.

Digital Communications in Your Life

Many people use various forms of digital communications in both their personal and business lives. Imagine you are working in your chosen field and making decisions every day regarding how to communicate best with family, friends, and business contacts. The following scenario presents several situations and decisions regarding digital communications made during a single day.

8:15 a.m.

SITUATION: Before leaving for work, you remember that you are expecting an e-mail confirmation from your travel agent regarding plans for a trip to a friend's birthday party.

RESOLUTION: E-mail is a good tool when instant communication is not necessary. Personal business, such as travel arrangements, is negotiated or confirmed easily via e-mail messages, resulting in a permanent record of the communication.

You receive the e-mail message on your personal computer from your travel agent with the news that your trip is booked.

8:47 a.m.

SITUATION: While riding the bus to work, you use your smart phone to access wirelessly the newest song from your favorite band. The phone number of an incoming call appears on the smart phone's display, and you recognize it as your boss's phone number. Should you take the call?

RESOLUTION: Many people feel uncomfortable answering business calls while on personal time or in a public place. The decision whether to allow work life to interfere with personal life varies with each individual. You know that your boss calls your cell phone only for important reasons. You answer the call and your boss explains that she would like you to join a video conference with an important customer. After hanging up the phone, you resume listening to your song.

9:11 a.m.

SITUATION: After arriving at work, your first task is to check e-mail messages. You have more than 30 new e-mail messages since you last checked your e-mail inbox at 5:00 p.m. yesterday.

RESOLUTION: Business e-mail programs usually include several methods for organizing and managing your e-mail inbox. As you view your inbox, a few items have red exclamation marks next to them, indicating that the sender marked them as urgent. Your e-mail program also allows you to mark e-mail messages in your inbox with colored flags. You quickly flag the urgent items with a red flag, meaning that you will handle these immediately after you flag the remaining messages. You flag messages from customers with a yellow flag. By skimming the subject, you place blue, green, and black flags next to some messages. You use the colors to code messages based on the priority of the messages.

Good practices often suggest you respond by phone to urgent messages or messages from important customers. You put on your headset, and, using your VoIP phone, you begin the process of calling some of the people whose messages you marked with red and yellow flags. When you are finished talking on the phone, you respond to several of the other messages. By 9:45 a.m. your inbox is empty.

10:00 a.m.

SITUATION: By the time you arrive at your office's video conferencing room, five other coworkers already have gathered. After sitting down, you see a large monitor and a camera in front of you. A group of people in another conference room in London appears on the monitor. Your boss whispers that your shirt is a bit bright for the video conference. During the meeting, the cell phone in your pocket buzzes a number of times. Should you take the call?

RESOLUTION: At first, most people find video conferences to be uncomfortable experiences. In comparison to a typical meeting, some people tend to fidget more, tap their fingers, or speak more nervously in a video conference. People tend to recognize those actions when they view others on a monitor in a video conference, so experts suggest keeping these types of actions to a minimum.

You ignore the cell phone calls during the meeting. You plan to check your visual voice mail on your cell phone later.

9:15 p.m.

SITUATION: As you end the day at home, you log on to the online social network that you joined earlier in the year. When you add a friend to your list of contacts, you notice that she currently is logged on. You start your instant messaging program and begin instant messaging with your friend. Your friend reminds you that you still have a home page on another online social network from your days in school.

RESOLUTION: You log on to the old online social network that you used when you were in school. You decide to delete the site. People often forget that once they put content on an online social network, in a blog, or on a wiki that it may remain there forever unless they delete or edit it. Periodically, consider checking how others might perceive you based on content you have placed on the Internet.

Chapter Four

The Components of the System Unit

Objectives

After completing this chapter, you will be able to:

1 Differentiate among various styles of system units on desktop computers, notebook computers, and mobile devices

2 Describe the control unit and arithmetic logic unit components of a processor, and explain the four steps in a machine cycle

3 Define a bit and describe how a series of bits represents data

4 Differentiate among the various types of memory: RAM, cache, ROM, flash memory, and CMOS

5 Describe the purpose and types of expansion slots and adapter cards

6 Differentiate between a port and a connector, and explain the differences among a USB port and other ports

7 Describe the types of buses in a computer

8 Understand how to clean a system unit on a computer or mobile device

The System Unit

Whether you are a home user or a business user, you most likely will purchase a new computer or upgrade an existing computer at some time in the future. Thus, you should understand the purpose of each component in a computer. As Chapter 1 discussed, a computer includes devices used for input, processing, output, storage, and communications. Many of these components are part of the system unit.

The **system unit** is a case that contains electronic components of the computer used to process data. System units are available in a variety of shapes and sizes. The case of the system unit is made of metal or plastic and protects the internal electronic components from damage. All computers and mobile devices have a system unit (Figure 4-1).

On desktop personal computers, the electronic components and most storage devices are part of the system unit. Other devices, such as the keyboard, mouse, microphone, monitor, printer, USB flash drive, scanner, Web cam, and speakers, normally occupy space outside the system unit. An all-in-one desktop personal computer is an exception, which houses the monitor and the system unit in the same case. On most notebook computers, including netbooks, the keyboard and pointing device often occupy the area on the top of the system unit, and the display attaches to the system unit by hinges. The location of the system unit on a Tablet PC varies, depending on the design of the Tablet PC. With the slate Tablet PC (shown in Figure 4-23 on page 173), which typically does not include a keyboard, the system unit is behind the display. On a convertible Tablet PC (shown in lower-left corner of Figure 4-1), by contrast,

Figure 4-1 All sizes of computers and mobile devices have a system unit.

the system unit is positioned below a keyboard, and the display attaches to the system unit with a swivel-type hinge, which enables a user to rotate the display and fold it down over the keyboard to look like a slate Tablet PC. The system unit on an Ultra-Mobile PC, a smart phone, and a PDA usually consumes the entire device. On these mobile computers and devices, the display often is built into the system unit. With game consoles, the input and output devices, such as controllers and a television, reside outside the system unit. On handheld game consoles, portable media players, and digital cameras, by contrast, the packaging around the system unit houses the input devices and display.

At some point, you might have to open the system unit on a desktop personal computer to replace or install a new electronic component. For this reason, you should be familiar with the electronic components of a system unit. Figure 4-2 identifies some of these components, which include the processor, memory, adapter cards, drive bays, and the power supply.

The processor interprets and carries out the basic instructions that operate a computer. Memory typically holds data waiting to be processed and instructions waiting to be executed. The electronic components and circuitry of the system unit, such as the processor and memory, usually are part of or are connected to a circuit board called the motherboard. Many motherboards also integrate sound, video, and networking capabilities.

Adapter cards are circuit boards that provide connections and functions not built into the motherboard or expand on the capability of features integrated into the motherboard. For example, a sound card and a video card are two types of adapter cards found in some desktop personal computers today.

Devices outside the system unit often attach to ports on the system unit by a connector on a cable. These devices may include a keyboard, mouse, microphone, monitor, printer, scanner, USB flash drive, card reader/writer, Web cam, and speakers. A drive bay holds one or more disk drives. The power supply allows electricity to travel through a power cord from a wall outlet into a computer.

Figure 4-2 The system unit on a typical personal computer consists of numerous electronic components, some of which are shown in this figure. The sound card and video card are two types of adapter cards.

The Motherboard

The **motherboard**, sometimes called a system board, is the main circuit board of the system unit. Many electronic components attach to the motherboard; others are built into it. Figure 4-3 shows a photo of a current desktop personal computer motherboard and identifies its slots for adapter cards, the processor chip, and memory. Memory chips are installed on memory cards (modules) that fit in a slot on the motherboard.

A computer **chip** is a small piece of semiconducting material, usually silicon, on which integrated circuits are etched. An integrated circuit contains many microscopic pathways capable of carrying electrical current. Each integrated circuit can contain millions of elements such as resistors, capacitors, and transistors. Specific types of processor, memory, and other chips are discussed later in the chapter. Read Innovative Computing 4-1 to find out about chips implanted in animals.

❗ INNOVATIVE COMPUTING 4-1

Chip Implants Identify Animals

When Fido and Fluffy run away, their safe return home may be based on data stored on a chip that veterinarians have implanted under the skin, usually at the neck or shoulder blades. Other animals can be chipped, including horses, birds, and livestock.

Each chip is numbered uniquely and registered to the owner's name and address. This chip, sometimes called a microchip because it is the size of a grain of rice, contains an antenna and transponder encased in a glass tube. The antenna receives low-frequency radio waves when a scanning device passes over the chip, and the transponder sends a signal with the chip's number back to the scanner.

Shelters and animal control centers routinely scan runaway pets for chips in an attempt to reunite animals with their owners, and some animal hospitals scan pets to determine whether they have been reported lost or stolen. Most shelters require pets to have the implant before the animals are adopted. In addition, breeders, farmers, and animal associations implant the chips to thwart thieves. Researchers also use this technology to track migration of wild animals and fish.

🖥 For more information, visit the Computer Concepts CourseMate Web site at www.cengagebrain.com, navigate to the Chapter 4 Innovative Computing resource for this book, and then click ID Chips.

Figure 4-3   Many electronic components attach to the motherboard in a desktop personal computer, including a processor chip, memory modules, and adapter cards.

Processor

The **processor**, also called the **central processing unit** (**CPU**), interprets and carries out the basic instructions that operate a computer. The processor significantly impacts overall computing power and manages most of a computer's operations. On a personal computer, all functions of the processor usually are on a single chip. Some computer and chip manufacturers use the term **microprocessor** to refer to a personal computer processor chip.

Most processor chip manufacturers now offer multi-core processors. A processor core contains the circuitry necessary to execute instructions. The operating system views each processor core as a separate processor. A **multi-core processor** is a chip with two or more separate processor cores. Two common multi-core processors are dual-core and quad-core. A **dual-core processor** is a chip that contains two separate processor cores. Similarly, a **quad-core processor** is a chip with four separate processor cores.

Each processor core on a multi-core processor generally runs at a slower clock speed than a single-core processor, but multi-core processors typically increase overall performance. For example, although a dual-core processor does not double the processing speed of a single-core processor, it can approach those speeds. Multi-core processors also are more energy efficient than separate multiple processors, requiring lower levels of power consumption and emitting less heat in the system unit.

Processors contain a control unit and an arithmetic logic unit (ALU). These two components work together to perform processing operations. Figure 4-4 illustrates how other devices that are connected to the computer communicate with the processor to carry out a task.

Multi-Core Processors
For more information, visit the Computer Concepts CourseMate Web site at www.cengagebrain.com, navigate to the Chapter 4 Web Link resource for this book, and then click Multi-Core Processors.

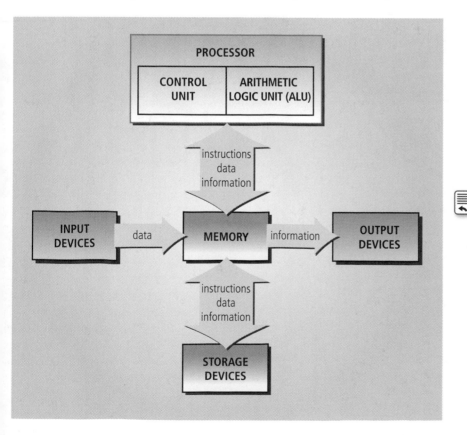

Figure 4-4 Most devices connected to the computer communicate with the processor to carry out a task. When a user starts a program, for example, its instructions transfer from a storage device to memory. Data needed by programs enters memory from either an input device or a storage device. The control unit interprets and executes instructions in memory, and the ALU performs calculations on the data in memory. Resulting information is stored in memory, from which it can be sent to an output device or a storage device for future access, as needed.

The Control Unit

The **control unit** is the component of the processor that directs and coordinates most of the operations in the computer. The control unit has a role much like a traffic cop: it interprets each instruction issued by a program and then initiates the appropriate action to carry out the instruction. Types of internal components that the control unit directs include the arithmetic/logic unit and buses, each discussed in this chapter.

The Arithmetic Logic Unit

The **arithmetic logic unit** (ALU), another component of the processor, performs arithmetic, comparison, and other operations. Arithmetic operations include basic calculations such as addition, subtraction, multiplication, and division. Comparison operations involve comparing one data item with another to determine whether the first item is greater than, equal to, or less than the other item. Depending on the result of the comparison, different actions may occur.

Machine Cycle

For every instruction, a processor repeats a set of four basic operations, which comprise a machine cycle (Figure 4-5): (1) fetching, (2) decoding, (3) executing, and, if necessary, (4) storing. Fetching is the process of obtaining a program instruction or data item from memory. The term decoding refers to the process of translating the instruction into signals the computer can execute. Executing is the process of carrying out the commands. Storing, in this context, means writing the result to memory (not to a storage medium).

The Steps in a Machine Cycle

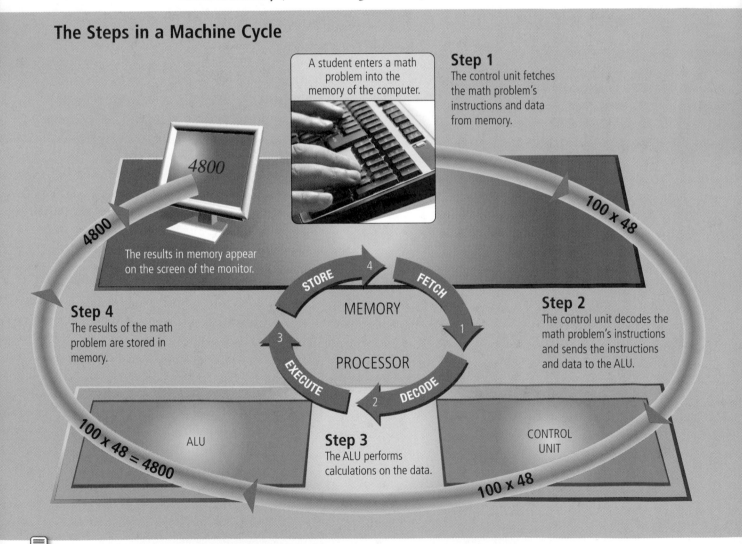

A student enters a math problem into the memory of the computer.

Step 1
The control unit fetches the math problem's instructions and data from memory.

Step 2
The control unit decodes the math problem's instructions and sends the instructions and data to the ALU.

Step 3
The ALU performs calculations on the data.

Step 4
The results of the math problem are stored in memory.

The results in memory appear on the screen of the monitor.

4800

100 x 48

100 x 48

100 x 48 = 4800

STORE 4 FETCH 1 DECODE 2 EXECUTE 3

MEMORY

PROCESSOR

ALU

CONTROL UNIT

Figure 4-5   This figure shows the steps in a machine cycle.

The System Clock

The processor relies on a small quartz crystal circuit called the **system clock** to control the timing of all computer operations. Just as your heart beats at a regular rate to keep your body functioning, the system clock generates regular electronic pulses, or ticks, that set the operating pace of components of the system unit.

The pace of the system clock, called the **clock speed**, is measured by the number of ticks per second. Current personal computer processors have clock speeds in the gigahertz range. Giga is a prefix that stands for billion, and a hertz is one cycle per second. Thus, one **gigahertz (GHz)** equals one billion ticks of the system clock per second. A computer that operates at 3 GHz has 3 billion (giga) clock cycles in one second (hertz). The faster the clock speed, the more instructions the processor can execute per second. The speed of the system clock is just one factor that influences a computer's performance. Other factors, such as the type of processor chip, amount of cache, memory access time, bus width, and bus clock speed, are discussed later in this chapter.

Comparison of Personal Computer Processors

The leading manufacturers of personal computer processor chips are Intel and AMD. These manufacturers often identify their processor chips by a model name or model number.

High-performance desktop personal computers today use a processor in the Intel Core family. Less expensive, basic personal computers today use a brand of Intel processor in the Pentium or Celeron family. The Xeon and Itanium families of processors are ideal for workstations and low-end servers.

AMD is the leading manufacturer of Intel-compatible processors, which have an internal design similar to Intel processors, perform the same functions, and can be as powerful, but often are less expensive.

In the past, chip manufacturers listed a processor's clock speed in marketing literature and advertisements. As previously mentioned, though, clock speed is only one factor that impacts processing speed in today's computers. To help consumers evaluate various processors, manufacturers such as Intel and AMD now use a numbering scheme that more accurately reflects the processing speed of their chips.

If you are ready to buy a new computer, the processor you select should depend on how you plan to use the computer. For detailed personal computer and mobile device purchasing guidelines, read the Buyer's Guide feature that follows Chapter 7.

? FAQ 4-1

Which PC vendors are the most popular with consumers?

Hewlett-Packard (HP) has the highest market share worldwide at approximately 20 percent, with Dell in second place with nearly 13 percent market share. HP accounts for nearly 21 percent of PC sales in the United States. The chart to the right compares the worldwide market share for various PC vendors.

Worldwide PC Market Share

Source: Gartner

- HP
- Dell
- Acer
- Lenovo
- Toshiba
- Others

For more information, visit the Computer Concepts CourseMate Web site at www.cengagebrain.com, navigate to the Chapter 4 FAQ resource for this book, and then click PC Vendor Market.

✔ QUIZ YOURSELF 4-1

Instructions: Find the true statement below. Then, rewrite the remaining false statements so that they are true.

1. A computer chip is a small piece of semiconducting material, usually silicon, on which integrated circuits are etched.
2. Four basic operations in a machine cycle are: (1) comparing, (2) decoding, (3) executing, and, if necessary, (4) pipelining.
3. Processors contain a motherboard and an arithmetic logic unit (ALU).
4. The central processing unit, sometimes called a system board, is the main circuit board of the system unit.
5. The leading processor chip manufacturers for personal computers are Microsoft and AMD.
6. The system unit is a case that contains mechanical components of the computer used to process data.

Quiz Yourself Online: To further check your knowledge of pages 156 through 161, visit the Computer Concepts CourseMate Web site at www.cengagebrain.com, navigate to the Chapter 4 Quiz Yourself resource for this book, and then click Objectives 1 – 2.

Data Representation

To understand how a computer processes data, you should know how a computer represents data. Most computers are **digital**. They recognize only two discrete states: on and off. The two digits, 0 and 1, easily can represent these two states (Figure 4-6). The digit 0 represents the electronic state of off (absence of an electronic charge). The digit 1 represents the electronic state of on (presence of an electronic charge).

The computer uses a binary system because it recognizes only two states. The **binary system** is a number system that has just two unique digits, 0 and 1, called bits. A **bit** (short for binary digit) is the smallest unit of data the computer can process. By itself, a bit is not very informative.

When 8 bits are grouped together as a unit, they form a **byte**. A byte provides enough different combinations of 0s and 1s to represent 256 individual characters. These characters include numbers, uppercase and lowercase letters of the alphabet, punctuation marks, and others, such as the letters of the Greek alphabet.

The combinations of 0s and 1s that represent characters are defined by patterns called a coding scheme. In one coding scheme, the number 4 is represented as 00110100, the number 6 as 00110110, and the capital letter E as 01000101 (Figure 4-7). ASCII (pronounced ASK-ee), which stands for American Standard Code for Information Interchange, is the most widely used coding scheme to represent data (Figure 4-8).

Coding schemes make it possible for humans to interact with a digital computer that processes only bits. When you press a key on a keyboard, a chip in the keyboard converts the key's electronic signal into a

BINARY DIGIT (BIT) | **ELECTRONIC CHARGE** | **ELECTRONIC STATE**

Figure 4-6 A computer circuit represents the 0 or the 1 electronically by the presence or absence of an electronic charge.

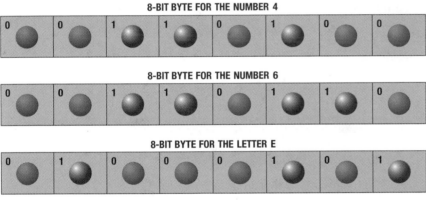

8-BIT BYTE FOR THE NUMBER 4

`0 0 1 1 0 1 0 0`

8-BIT BYTE FOR THE NUMBER 6

`0 0 1 1 0 1 1 0`

8-BIT BYTE FOR THE LETTER E

`0 1 0 0 0 1 0 1`

Figure 4-7 Eight bits grouped together as a unit are called a byte. A byte represents a single character in the computer.

Figure 4-8 ASCII is a widely used coding scheme.

ASCII	SYMBOL	ASCII	SYMBOL
00110000	0	01001110	N
00110001	1	01001111	O
00110010	2	01010000	P
00110011	3	01010001	Q
00110100	4	01010010	R
00110101	5	01010011	S
00110110	6	01010100	T
00110111	7	01010101	U
00111000	8	01010110	V
00111001	9	01010111	W
01000001	A	01011000	X
01000010	B	01011001	Y
01000011	C	01011010	Z
01000100	D	00100001	!
01000101	E	00100010	"
01000110	F	00100011	#
01000111	G	00100100	$
01001000	H	00100101	%
01001001	I	00100110	&
01001010	J	00101000	(
01001011	K	00101001	)
01001100	L	00101010	*
01001101	M	00101011	+

scan code that is sent to the system unit. Then, the system unit converts the scan code into a binary form the computer can process and is stored in memory. Every character is converted to its corresponding byte. The computer then processes the data as bytes, which actually is a series of on/off electrical states. When processing is finished, software converts the byte into a human-recognizable number, letter of the alphabet, or special character that is displayed on a screen or is printed (Figure 4-9). All of these conversions take place so quickly that you do not realize they are occurring.

Standards, such as those defined by ASCII, also make it possible for components in computers to communicate successfully with each other.

How a Letter Is Converted to Binary Form and Back

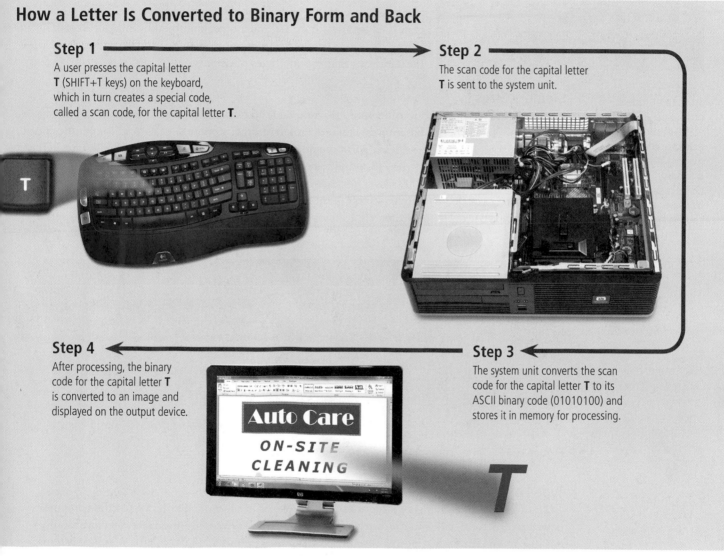

Step 1
A user presses the capital letter **T** (SHIFT+T keys) on the keyboard, which in turn creates a special code, called a scan code, for the capital letter **T**.

Step 2
The scan code for the capital letter **T** is sent to the system unit.

Step 4
After processing, the binary code for the capital letter **T** is converted to an image and displayed on the output device.

Step 3
The system unit converts the scan code for the capital letter **T** to its ASCII binary code (01010100) and stores it in memory for processing.

Figure 4-9 This figure shows how a letter is converted to binary form and back.

Memory

Memory consists of electronic components that store instructions waiting to be executed by the processor, data needed by those instructions, and the results of processing the data (information). Memory usually consists of one or more chips on the motherboard or some other circuit board in the computer.

Memory stores three basic categories of items: (1) the operating system and other system software that control or maintain the computer and its devices; (2) application programs that carry out a specific task such as word processing; and (3) the data being processed by the application programs and resulting information. This role of memory to store both data and programs is known as the stored program concept.

Figure 4-10
Seats in an opera house are similar to addresses in memory: a seat holds one person at a time, and a location in memory holds a single byte; and both a seat and a byte can be empty.

Bytes and Addressable Memory

A byte (character) is the basic storage unit in memory. When application program instructions and data are transferred to memory from storage devices, the instructions and data exist as bytes. Each byte resides temporarily in a location in memory that has an address. An address simply is a unique number that identifies the location of the byte in memory. The illustration in Figure 4-10 shows how seats in an opera house are similar to addresses in memory: (1) a seat, which is identified by a unique seat number, holds one person at a time, and a location in memory, which is identified by a unique address, holds a single byte; and (2) both a seat, identified by a seat number, and a byte, identified by an address, can be empty. To access data or instructions in memory, the computer references the addresses that contain bytes of data.

Memory Sizes

Manufacturers state the size of memory (Figure 4-11) and storage devices in terms of the number of bytes the chip or device has available for storage. Recall that storage devices hold data, instructions, and information for future use, while most memory holds these items temporarily. A **kilobyte** (**KB** or **K**) is equal to exactly 1,024 bytes. To simplify memory and storage definitions, computer users often round a kilobyte down to 1,000 bytes. For example, if a memory chip can store 100 KB, it can hold approximately 100,000 bytes (characters). A **megabyte** (**MB**) is equal to approximately 1 million bytes. A **gigabyte** (**GB**) equals approximately 1 billion bytes. A **terabyte** (**TB**) is equal to approximately 1 trillion bytes.

Memory Sizes

Term	Abbreviation	Approximate Number of Bytes	Exact Number of Bytes	Approximate Number of Pages of Text
Kilobyte	KB or K	1 thousand	1,024	1/2
Megabyte	MB	1 million	1,048,576	500
Gigabyte	GB	1 billion	1,073,741,824	500,000
Terabyte	TB	1 trillion	1,099,511,627,776	500,000,000

 Figure 4-11 Terms commonly used to define memory sizes.

Types of Memory

The system unit contains two types of memory: volatile and nonvolatile. When the computer's power is turned off, **volatile memory** loses its contents. **Nonvolatile memory**, by contrast, does not lose its contents when power is removed from the computer. Thus, volatile memory is temporary and nonvolatile memory is permanent. RAM is the most common type of volatile memory. Examples of nonvolatile memory include ROM, flash memory, and CMOS. The following sections discuss these types of memory.

RAM

Users typically are referring to RAM when discussing computer memory. **RAM** (random access memory), also called main memory, consists of memory chips that can be read from and written to by the processor and other devices. When you turn on power to a computer, certain operating system files (such as the files that determine how the desktop appears) load into RAM from a storage device such as a hard disk. These files remain in RAM as long as the computer has continuous power. As additional programs and data are requested, they also load into RAM from storage.

The processor interprets and executes a program's instructions while the program is in RAM. During this time, the contents of RAM may change (Figure 4-12). RAM can hold multiple programs simultaneously, provided the computer has enough RAM to accommodate all the programs.

Most RAM is volatile, which means it loses its contents when the power is removed from the computer. For this reason, you must save any items you may need in the future. Saving is the process of copying items from RAM to a storage device such as a hard disk.

How Program Instructions Transfer in and out of RAM

Step 1
When you start the computer, certain operating system files are loaded into RAM from the hard disk. The operating system displays the user interface on the screen.

Step 2
When you start a Web browser, the program's instructions are loaded into RAM from the hard disk. The Web browser and certain operating system instructions are in RAM. The Web browser window appears on the screen.

Step 3
When you start a paint program, the program's instructions are loaded into RAM from the hard disk. The paint program, along with the Web browser and certain operating system instructions, are in RAM. The paint program window appears on the screen.

Step 4
When you quit a program, such as the Web browser, its program instructions are removed from RAM. The Web browser no longer is displayed on the screen.

Figure 4-12 This figure shows how program instructions transfer in and out of RAM.

Three basic types of RAM chips exist: dynamic RAM, static RAM, and magnetoresistive RAM.
- Dynamic RAM (DRAM pronounced DEE-ram) chips must be re-energized constantly or they lose their contents. Many variations of DRAM chips exist, most of which are faster than the basic DRAM.
- Static RAM (SRAM pronounced ESS-ram) chips are faster and more reliable than any variation of DRAM chips. These chips do not have to be re-energized as often as DRAM chips, thus, the term static.
- A newer type of RAM, called magnetoresistive RAM (MRAM pronounced EM-ram), stores data using magnetic charges instead of electrical charges. Manufacturers claim that MRAM has greater storage capacity, consumes less power, and has faster access times than electronic RAM.

Figure 4-13 This photo shows a memory module being inserted in a motherboard.

RAM
For more information, visit the Computer Concepts CourseMate Web site at www.cengagebrain.com, navigate to the Chapter 4 Web Link resource for this book, and then click RAM.

RAM chips usually reside on a **memory module**, which is a small circuit board. **Memory slots** on the motherboard hold memory modules (Figure 4-13). To learn more about how to purchase RAM for a computer, complete the Learn How To 1 activity on pages 184 and 185.

RAM Configurations The amount of RAM necessary in a computer often depends on the types of software you plan to use. A computer executes programs that are in RAM. The more RAM a computer has, the faster the computer will respond.

Retail software typically indicates the minimum amount of RAM it requires. If you want the software to perform optimally, usually you need more than the minimum specifications for the software.

Generally, home users running the latest version of Windows and using basic application software such as word processing should have at least 1 GB of RAM. Most business users who work with accounting, financial, or spreadsheet programs, and programs requiring multimedia capabilities should have 2 to 8 GB of RAM. Users creating professional Web sites or using graphics-intensive applications will want 8 GB or more of RAM. The amount of RAM in computers purchased today ranges from 1 GB to 128 GB. Read Ethics & Issues 4-1 for a related discussion.

? FAQ 4-2

Can I add more RAM to my computer?

Check your computer documentation to see how much RAM you can add. RAM modules are relatively inexpensive and usually include easy-to-follow installation instructions. Be sure to purchase RAM that is compatible with your brand and model of computer.

For more information, visit the Computer Concepts CourseMate Web site at www.cengagebrain.com, navigate to the Chapter 4 FAQ resource for this book, and then click Upgrading RAM.

ETHICS & ISSUES 4-1

How Much Technology Should Be Provided to Students and Teachers?

Around the country and around the world, local and national governments have begun to supply schoolchildren with inexpensive notebook computers, including netbooks. Many school districts in the United States purchase notebook computers for each student and hope to recoup some of the cost by purchasing lower-cost CD-based textbooks. The United Nations endorses a plan known as One Laptop per Child to supply $100 notebook computers to developing countries, some of which already pledged to purchase millions of the devices for schoolchildren. The device, which recharges with a hand crank, includes Wi-Fi networking and a simple, intuitive user interface.

Supporters of these plans maintain that computer literacy and electronic communications are vital skills in today's world, and students should be introduced to computers as early in their school years as possible. Others claim that when students use notebook computers, instructors tend to lecture less, requiring students to engage in more research and independent study. Many people oppose plans to equip every student with a computer because they say that the technology detracts from traditional educational subjects, such as basic reading and math. Some believe that the best approach is to maintain dedicated computer lab rooms rather than allow computers in the classroom. Computers require maintenance, support, and instructional time to teach students how to use the devices. Young children may lack the responsibility to care for and use the computers properly.

Should schools supply computers to all students or teachers or both? Why or why not? What is the appropriate grade level at which to require computer literacy? Why? Should computers be relegated to a dedicated lab room? Why or why not?

Cache

Most of today's computers improve processing times with **cache** (pronounced cash). Two types of cache are memory cache and disk cache. This chapter discusses memory cache.

Memory cache helps speed the processes of the computer because it stores frequently used instructions and data. Most personal computers today have at least two types of memory cache: L1 cache and L2 cache.

- **L1 cache** is built directly in the processor chip. L1 cache usually has a very small capacity, ranging from 8 KB to 128 KB.
- **L2 cache** is slightly slower than L1 cache but has a much larger capacity, ranging from 64 KB to 16 MB. Current processors include **advanced transfer cache**, a type of L2 cache built directly on the processor chip. Processors that use advanced transfer cache perform at much faster rates than those that do not use it. Personal computers today typically have from 512 KB to 12 MB of advanced transfer cache.

Cache speeds up processing time because it stores frequently used instructions and data. When the processor needs an instruction or data, it searches memory in this order: L1 cache, then L2 cache, then RAM — with a greater delay in processing for each level of memory it must search. If the instruction or data is not found in memory, then it must search a slower speed storage medium such as a hard disk or optical disc.

ROM

Read-only memory (**ROM** pronounced rahm) refers to memory chips storing permanent data and instructions. The data on most ROM chips cannot be modified — hence, the name read-only. ROM is nonvolatile, which means its contents are not lost when power is removed from the computer.

Manufacturers of ROM chips often record data, instructions, or information on the chips when they manufacture the chips. These ROM chips, called **firmware**, contain permanently written data, instructions, or information.

Flash Memory

Flash memory is a type of nonvolatile memory that can be erased electronically and rewritten. Most computers use flash memory to hold their startup instructions because it allows the computer easily to update its contents. For example, when the computer changes from standard time to daylight savings time, the contents of a flash memory chip (and the real-time clock chip) change to reflect the new time.

Flash memory chips also store data and programs on many mobile computers and devices, such as smart phones, portable media players, PDAs, printers, digital cameras, automotive devices, digital voice recorders, and pagers. Some portable media players store music on flash memory chips (Figure 4-14). Others store music on tiny hard disks or flash memory cards. Flash memory cards contain flash memory on a removable device instead of a chip.

ROM
For more information, visit the Computer Concepts CourseMate Web site at www.cengagebrain.com, navigate to the Chapter 4 Web Link resource for this book, and then click ROM.

How a Portable Media Player Might Store Music in Flash Memory

Step 1
Purchase and download music tracks from a Web site. With one end of a special cable connected to a USB port on the system unit, connect the other end to the USB port in the portable media player.

Step 2
Instruct the computer to copy the music tracks to a flash memory chip in the portable media player.

flash memory chip

portable media player

USB port

Music

earbuds

from the computer

USB port

Step 3
Plug the earbuds in the portable media player, push a button on the portable media player, and listen to the music through the earbuds.

Figure 4-14 This figure shows how a portable media player might store music in flash memory.

? FAQ 4-3

How much music can I store on a portable media player?

Portable media players that store music on flash memory chips can hold up to 16,000 songs. Portable media players with tiny hard disks have a much greater storage capacity — from 1,000 to more than 80,000 songs.

For more information, visit the Computer Concepts CourseMate Web site at www.cengagebrain.com, navigate to the Chapter 4 FAQ resource for this book, and then click Portable Media Players.

CMOS

Some RAM chips, flash memory chips, and other types of memory chips use complementary metal-oxide semiconductor (**CMOS** pronounced SEE-moss) technology because it provides high speeds and consumes little power. CMOS technology uses battery power to retain information even when the power to the computer is off. Battery-backed CMOS memory chips, for example, can keep the calendar, date, and time current even when the computer is off. The flash memory chips that store a computer's startup information often use CMOS technology.

Memory Access Times

Access time is the amount of time it takes the processor to read data, instructions, and information from memory. A computer's access time directly affects how fast the computer processes data. Accessing data in memory can be more than 200,000 times faster than accessing data on a hard disk because of the mechanical motion of the hard disk.

Today's manufacturers use a variety of terminology to state access times (Figure 4-15). Some use fractions of a second, which for memory occurs in nanoseconds. A **nanosecond** (abbreviated ns) is one billionth of a second. A nanosecond is extremely fast (Figure 4-16). Other manufacturers state access times in MHz; for example, 800 MHz RAM.

While access times of memory greatly affect overall computer performance, manufacturers and retailers usually list a computer's memory in terms of its size, not its access time.

Access Time Terminology

Term	Abbreviation	Speed
Millisecond	ms	One-thousandth of a second
Microsecond	µs	One-millionth of a second
Nanosecond	ns	One-billionth of a second
Picosecond	ps	One-trillionth of a second

Figure 4-15   Access times are measured in fractions of a second. This table lists the terms used to define access times.

10 million operations = 1 blink

Figure 4-16   It takes about one-tenth of a second to blink your eye, which is the equivalent of 100 million nanoseconds. In the time it takes to blink your eye, a computer can perform some operations 10 million times.

✔ | **QUIZ YOURSELF 4-2**

Instructions: Find the true statement below. Then, rewrite the remaining false statements so that they are true.

1. A computer's memory access time directly affects how fast the computer processes data.
2. A gigabyte (GB) equals approximately 1 trillion bytes.
3. Memory cache helps speed the processes of the computer because it stores seldom used instructions and data.
4. Most computers are analog, which means they recognize only two discrete states: on and off.
5. Most RAM retains its contents when the power is removed from the computer.
6. Read-only memory (ROM) refers to memory chips storing temporary data and instructions.

Quiz Yourself Online: To further check your knowledge of pages 162 through 168, visit the Computer Concepts CourseMate Web site at www.cengagebrain.com, navigate to the Chapter 4 Quiz Yourself resource for this book, and then click Objectives 3 – 4.

Expansion Slots and Adapter Cards

An **expansion slot** is a socket on the motherboard that can hold an adapter card. An **adapter card**, sometimes called an **expansion card,** is a circuit board that enhances functions of a component of the system unit and/or provides connections to peripherals. A **peripheral** is a device that connects to the system unit and is controlled by the processor in the computer. Examples of peripherals are modems, disk drives, printers, scanners, and keyboards.

Figure 4-17 lists a variety of types of adapter cards. Sometimes, all functionality is built into the adapter card. With others, a cable connects the adapter card to a device, such as a digital video camera, outside the system unit. Some are a card that you insert in a slot on the computer. Figure 4-18 shows an adapter card being inserted in an expansion slot on a personal computer motherboard.

Some motherboards include all necessary capabilities and do not require adapter cards. Other motherboards may require adapter cards to provide capabilities such as sound and video. A **sound card** enhances the sound-generating capabilities of a personal computer by allowing sound to be input through a microphone and output through external speakers or headphones. A **video card,** also called a **graphics card,** converts computer output into a video signal that travels through a cable to the monitor, which displays an image on the screen.

Video Cards

For more information, visit the Computer Concepts CourseMate Web site at www.cengagebrain.com, navigate to the Chapter 4 Web Link resource for this book, and then click Video Cards.

Types of Adapter Cards

Adapter Card	Purpose
CableCARD	Allows viewing of digital cable television channels
Disk controller	Connects disk drives
FireWire	Connects to FireWire devices
HDTV tuner	Allows viewing of HDTV broadcasts on the monitor
MIDI	Connects musical instruments
Modem	Connects other computers through telephone lines, cable television lines, or other transmission media
Network	Connects other computers and peripherals
PC-to-TV converter	Connects a television
Sound	Connects speakers or a microphone
TV tuner	Allows viewing of television channels on the monitor
USB	Connects to USB devices
Video	Connects a monitor
Video capture	Connects an analog video camera or VCR

Figure 4-17 Currently used adapter cards and their functions.

Figure 4-18 An adapter card being inserted in an expansion slot on the motherboard of a personal computer.

Removable Flash Memory

Removable flash memory includes these devices: memory cards, USB flash drives, and PC Cards/ExpressCard modules.

- A **memory card** is a removable flash memory device, usually no bigger than 1.5" in height or width, that you insert and remove from a slot in a personal computer, game console, mobile device (Figure 4-19a), or card reader/writer. Many mobile and consumer devices, such as smart phones, digital cameras, and portable media players use memory cards. Some printers and computers have built-in card readers/writers or slots that read flash memory

Figure 4-19a (memory card)

memory card in camera slot

Figure 4-19 Examples of removable flash memory in use. *(continues on next page)*

Figure 4-19b (USB flash drive)

USB flash drive in USB port

Figure 4-19c (ExpressCard module)

ExpressCard module in an ExpressCard slot

Figure 4-19 Examples of removable flash memory in use. *(continued)*

cards. In addition, you can purchase an external card reader/writer that attaches to any computer.

- A **USB flash drive** is a flash memory storage device that plugs in a USB port on a computer or mobile device (Figure 4-19b). (A later section discusses USB ports.)
- Many desktop computers, traditional notebook computers, and Tablet PCs, have a PC Card slot or an **ExpressCard slot,** which is a special type of expansion slot that holds a PC Card or an ExpressCard module, respectively. Most netbooks do not have a PC Card slot or ExpressCard slot. A **PC Card** is a thin, credit card-sized removable flash memory device that primarily is used today to enable traditional notebook computers and Tablet PCs to access the Internet wirelessly. An **ExpressCard module**, which can be used as a removable flash memory device, is about one-half the size of a PC Card and adds memory, communications, multimedia, and security capabilities to computers (Figure 4-19c).

Ports and Connectors

A **port** is the point at which a peripheral attaches to or communicates with a system unit so that the peripheral can send data to or receive information from the computer. An external device, such as a keyboard, monitor, printer, mouse, and microphone, often attaches by a cable to a port on the system unit. Instead of port, the term jack sometimes is used to identify audio and video ports. The front and back of the system unit on a desktop personal computer contain many ports (Figure 4-20). On notebook computers, including netbooks and Tablet PCs, the ports are on the back, front, and/or sides (Figure 4-21).

built-in memory card readers

microphone port

headphones port (or jack)

keyboard port

digital audio (or S/PDIF) out port

serial port

FireWire port

USB ports

FireWire port

side surround sound port

microphone port

speaker port

DVI port

mouse port

digital audio (or S/PDIF) in port

network port

rear surround sound port

center surround sound/subwoofer port

audio in port

S-video port

HDMI port

Figure 4-20 A system unit on a desktop personal computer has many ports on its front and back.

Figure 4-21   Ports on a typical notebook computer.

A **connector** joins a cable to a port. A connector at one end of a cable attaches to a port on the system unit, and a connector at the other end of the cable attaches to a port on the peripheral.

The next section discusses the more widely used ports.

USB Ports

A **USB port**, short for universal serial bus port, can connect up to 127 different peripherals together with a single connector. Devices that connect to a USB port include the following: mouse, printer, digital camera, scanner, speakers, portable media player, optical disc drive, smart phone, PDA, game console, and removable hard disk. Personal computers typically have six to eight USB ports on the front and/or back of the system unit (Figure 4-20). USB ports on mobile devices usually are smaller than those on personal computers. Figure 4-22 shows a variety of USB ports and connectors.

	Connector	Port	Where Used
Type A			Desktop computers, traditional notebook computers, netbooks, and Tablet PCs
Type B			Peripherals (printers, scanners, external hard disks, etc.)
Mini-B			Mobile devices (cameras, phones, handheld game consoles)

Figure 4-22   A variety of USB ports and connectors are available.

USB Ports
 For more information, visit the Computer Concepts CourseMate Web site at www.cengagebrain.com, navigate to the Chapter 4 Web Link resource for this book, and then click USB Ports.

USB 2.0, or **Hi-Speed USB**, is a more advanced and faster USB, with speeds 40 times higher than that of its predecessor. USB 3.0 is even faster than USB 2.0. Both USB 2.0 and USB 3.0 are backward compatible, which means they support older USB devices as well as newer USB devices. Keep in mind, though, that older USB devices do not run any faster in a newer USB port.

To attach multiple peripherals using a single port, you can use a USB hub. A **USB hub** is a device that plugs in a USB port on the system unit and contains multiple USB ports in which you plug cables from USB devices. Some newer peripherals may attach only to a USB port. Others attach to either a serial or parallel port, as well as a USB port.

FireWire Ports

FireWire

For more information, visit the Computer Concepts CourseMate Web site at www.cengagebrain.com, navigate to the Chapter 4 Web Link resource for this book, and then click FireWire.

Previously called an IEEE 1394 port, a **FireWire port** is similar to a USB port in that it can connect multiple types of devices that require faster data transmission speeds, such as digital video cameras, digital VCRs, color printers, scanners, digital cameras, and DVD drives, to a single connector. A FireWire port allows you to connect up to 63 devices together. The three latest versions, FireWire 800, FireWire 1600, and FireWire 3200, have speeds faster than the original FireWire 400.

You can use a FireWire hub to attach multiple devices to a single FireWire port. A **FireWire hub** is a device that plugs in a FireWire port on the system unit and contains multiple FireWire ports in which you plug cables from FireWire devices.

Other Ports

Some ports not included in typical computers but sometimes used are Bluetooth, SCSI, eSATA, IrDA, and MIDI. For a computer to have these ports, you often must customize the computer purchase order.

Bluetooth Port   **Bluetooth** technology uses radio waves to transmit data between two devices. Bluetooth devices have to be within about 33 feet of each other. Many computers, peripherals, smart phones, PDAs, cars, and other consumer electronics are Bluetooth-enabled, which means they contain a small chip that allows them to communicate with other Bluetooth-enabled computers and devices. If you have a computer that is not Bluetooth enabled, you can purchase a Bluetooth wireless port adapter that will convert an existing USB port into a Bluetooth port. Also available are Bluetooth PC Cards and ExpressCard modules for traditional notebook computers and Tablet PCs, and Bluetooth cards for smart phones and PDAs.

SCSI Port   A special high-speed parallel port, called a **SCSI port**, allows you to attach SCSI (pronounced skuzzy) peripherals such as disk drives and printers. **SAS** (serial-attached SCSI) is a newer type of SCSI that transmits at much faster speeds than parallel SCSI. Some computers include a SCSI port. Others have a slot that supports a SCSI card.

eSATA Port   An **eSATA port**, or external SATA port, allows you to connect a high-speed external SATA (Serial Advanced Technology Attachment) hard disk to a computer.

IrDA Port   Some devices can transmit data via infrared light waves. For these wireless devices to transmit signals to a computer, both the computer and the device must have an **IrDA port.**

To ensure nothing obstructs the path of the infrared light wave, you must align the IrDA port on the device with the IrDA port on the computer, similarly to the way you operate a television remote control. Devices that use IrDA ports include a smart phone, PDA, keyboard, mouse, and printer.

MIDI Port   A special type of port that connects the system unit to a musical instrument, such as an electronic keyboard, is called a **MIDI port**. Short for Musical Instrument Digital Interface, MIDI (pronounced MID-dee) is the electronic music industry's standard that defines how devices, such as sound cards and synthesizers, represent sounds electronically. A synthesizer, which can be a peripheral or a chip, creates sound from digital instructions. A system unit with a MIDI port has the capability of recording sounds that have been created by a synthesizer and then processing the sounds (the data) to create new sounds.

Port Replicators and Docking Stations

Instead of connecting peripherals directly to ports on a mobile computer, some mobile users prefer the flexibility of port replicators and docking stations. A **port replicator** is an external device that provides connections to peripherals through ports built into the device. The mobile user accesses peripherals by connecting the port replicator to a USB port or a special port on the mobile computer.

A docking station is similar to a port replicator, but it has more functionality. A **docking station**, which is an external device that attaches to a mobile computer or device, contains a power connection and provides connections to peripherals; it usually also includes slots for memory cards, optical disc drives, and other devices (Figure 4-23). With the mobile computer or device in the docking station, users can work with a full-sized keyboard, a mouse, and other desktop peripherals from their traditional notebook computer, netbook, or Tablet PC. Read Looking Ahead 4-1 for a look at the next generation of notebook computers.

Tablet PC

docking station

Figure 4-23 To use a slate Tablet PC while working at a desk, insert the Tablet PC in a docking station. Devices such as a keyboard and an optical disc drive can be plugged in the docking station.

⬈ LOOKING AHEAD 4-1

Bendable Notebook Computers Will Slip in Your Pocket

Today's notebook computers are light and compact, but they will be enormous compared to what is being planned for the retail marketplace in the next 10 years. Top designers at Lenovo and Intel are designing flexible machines weighing less than one pound that are thin enough to fold and place in a pocket. Battery life will be nearly one week, and the 256-core processors will make current computers with quad-core processors seem like they are running at a snail's pace.

Notebook computer users will speak into a microphone, touch the screen, or type on a virtual keyboard that does not have actual keys but can give feedback that a letter or number has been selected. Thin screens will roll out to

any size needed and will be viewed easily outdoors. Users with sight impairments can coat their screens with a synthetic material that will create 3-D shapes for such tactile uses as reading Braille letters and blueprints.

For more information, visit the Computer Concepts CourseMate Web site at www.cengagebrain.com, navigate to the Chapter 4 Looking Ahead resource for this book, and then click Future Notebooks.

Buses

As explained earlier in this chapter, a computer processes and stores data as a series of electronic bits. These bits transfer internally within the circuitry of the computer along electrical channels. Each channel, called a **bus**, allows the various devices both inside and attached to the system unit to communicate with each other. Just as vehicles travel on a highway to move from one destination to another, bits travel on a bus (Figure 4-24).

Buses are used to transfer bits from input devices to memory, from memory to the processor, from the processor to memory, and from memory to output or storage devices. Buses consist of two parts: a data bus and an address bus. The data bus is used to transfer actual data and the address bus is used to transfer information about where the data should reside in memory.

The size of a bus, called the bus width, determines the number of bits that the computer can transmit at one time. For example, a 32-bit bus can transmit 32 bits (4 bytes) at a time. On a 64-bit bus, bits transmit from one location to another 64 bits (8 bytes) at a time. The larger the number of bits handled by the bus, the faster the computer transfers data. Most personal computers today use a 64-bit bus.

Every bus also has a clock speed. Just like the processor, manufacturers state the clock speed for a bus in hertz. Recall that one megahertz (MHz) is equal to one million ticks per second. Today's processors usually have a bus clock speed of 400, 533, 667, 800, 1066, 1333, or 1600 MHz. The higher the bus clock speed, the faster the transmission of data, which results in programs running faster.

A computer has these basic types of buses: a system bus, possibly a backside bus, and an expansion bus. A **system bus**, also called the **front side bus** (FSB), is part of the motherboard and connects the processor to main memory. When computer professionals use the term bus by itself, they usually are referring to the system bus. A **backside bus** (BSB) connects the processor to cache.

An **expansion bus** allows the processor to communicate with peripherals. Some peripherals outside the system unit connect to a port on an adapter card, which is inserted in an expansion slot on the motherboard. This expansion slot connects to the expansion bus, which allows the processor to communicate with the peripheral attached to the adapter card.

processor

bus

memory chips

Figure 4-24 Just as vehicles travel on a highway, bits travel on a bus. Buses are used to transfer bits from input devices to memory, from memory to the processor, from the processor to memory, and from memory to output or storage devices.

Bays

After you purchase a desktop or notebook computer, you may want to install an additional storage device such as a disk drive in the system unit. A **bay** is an opening inside the system unit in which you can install additional equipment. A bay is different from a slot on the motherboard, which is used for the installation of adapter cards. A **drive bay** is a rectangular opening that typically holds disk drives. Other bays house card readers and widely used ports such as USB, FireWire, and audio ports.

An external bay allows a user to access openings in the bay from outside the system unit (Figure 4-25). Optical disc drives are examples of devices installed in external bays. An internal bay is concealed entirely within the system unit. Hard disk drives are installed in internal bays.

card readers

optical disc drives

ports

Figure 4-25 External bays usually are located beside or on top of one another.

Power Supply

Many personal computers plug in standard wall outlets, which supply an alternating current (AC) of 115 to 120 volts. This type of power is unsuitable for use with a computer, which requires a direct current (DC) ranging from 5 to more than 15 volts. The **power supply** is the component of the system unit that converts the wall outlet AC power into DC power.

Built into the power supply is a fan that keeps the power supply cool. Some have variable speed fans that change speed or stop running, depending on temperature in the system unit.

Some external peripherals such as a cable modem, speakers, or a printer have an **AC adapter**, which is an external power supply. One end of the AC adapter plugs in the wall outlet and the other end attaches to the peripheral. The AC adapter converts the AC power into DC power that the peripheral requires.

Ethics & Issues

For the complete text of the Ethics & Issues boxes found in this chapter, visit the Computer Concepts CourseMate Web site at www.cengagebrain.com and then navigate to the Chapter 4 Ethics & Issues resource for this book.

Putting It All Together

When you purchase a computer, it is important to understand how the components of the system unit work. Many components of the system unit influence the speed and power of a computer. These include the type of processor, the clock speed of the processor, the amount of RAM, bus width, and the clock speed of the bus. The configuration you require depends on your intended use. Read Ethics & Issues 4-2 for a related discussion.

The table in Figure 4-26 lists the suggested minimum processor and RAM requirements based on the needs of various types of computer users.

ETHICS & ISSUES 4-2

Is Government Search and Seizure of Computers Ethical?

In the interest of national security, the Department of Homeland Security may search and seize any mobile computer or device from people arriving in the United States. The sometimes random searches may be done without a warrant or even a reason. Additionally, the government has taken computers from schools and libraries in a similar manner. Computers and mobile devices might be taken away for an off-site inspection for any amount of time. Sometimes, the devices are not returned and little or no reason is given for the seizure.

At airports and other points of entry to the country, the government considers computers and mobile devices to be containers, just as a piece of luggage is a container. Computers, therefore, can be searched and seized similarly to luggage without reasonable suspicion. Opponents claim that the data on a computer is like memories stored in the brain. They claim that the government should be able to inspect the hardware, but not the contents of memory or hard disk. Librarians and school administrators claim that the government is invading the privacy of patrons and students.

Is government search and seizure of computers without a warrant ethical? Why or why not? Would you allow a government employee to inspect the data on your mobile computer or device? Why or why not? If memories, thoughts, or intentions in one's mind could someday be deciphered by a computer at a security checkpoint, should the government be allowed to scan them? Why?

Suggested Minimum Configurations by User

User	Processor and RAM
Home	Intel Core i5 or Intel Core i3 or AMD Athlon II or AMD Sempron Minimum RAM: 2 GB
Small Office/Home Office	Intel Core i7 or Intel Core i7 Extreme or AMD Phenom II or AMD Athlon II Minimum RAM: 4 GB
Mobile	Intel Core i7 Extreme or Intel Core i7 or AMD Phenom II or AMD Turion II Minimum RAM: 2 GB
Power	Intel Xeon or Intel Itanium or AMD Opteron Minimum RAM: 8 GB
Enterprise	Intel Core i7 or Intel Core i7 Extreme or AMD Phenom II or AMD Athlon II Minimum RAM: 4 GB

Figure 4-26 Suggested processor and RAM configurations by user.

Keeping Your Computer or Mobile Device Clean

Over time, the system unit collects dust — even in a clean environment. Built up dust can block airflow in a computer or mobile device, which can cause it to overheat, corrode, or even stop working. By cleaning your computer or mobile device once or twice a year, you can help extend its life. This preventive maintenance requires a few basic products (Figure 4-27):

- can of compressed air — removes dust and lint from difficult-to-reach areas; removes sticky liquid spilled on keyboards
- lint-free antistatic wipes and swabs
- screen cleaning solution or 50/50 mix of rubbing alcohol and water (do not use ammonia-based solutions)
- small computer vacuum (or small attachments on your house vacuum)
- antistatic wristband — to avoid damaging internal components with static electricity
- small screwdriver (may be required to open the case or remove adapter cards)

Before cleaning the exterior of a computer or mobile device, turn it off, and if necessary, unplug it from the electrical outlet, remove its battery, and disconnect all cables from the ports. Use compressed air to blow away dust from any openings on the computer or device case, such as drives, slots, ports, and fan vents. Then, use an antistatic wipe to clean the exterior of the case and a cleaning solution on a soft cloth to clean the screen.

If you do not feel comfortable cleaning the inside of a desktop or notebook computer case, you can have a local professional or computer company clean it for you. Or, if you are familiar with electronics, you can clean it yourself if it will not void a warranty. While working inside the case, be sure to wear an antistatic wristband on your wrist. Use the antistatic wipes to clean inside the walls of the computer case. Vacuum as much dust as possible from the interior of the case, including the wires, chips, adapter cards, and fan blades. Release short blasts of compressed air in areas the vacuum cannot reach. If the motherboard and adapter cards still look dirty, gently clean them with lint-free wipes or swabs lightly dampened with alcohol. When finished, write down the date you cleaned the computer so that you have a record for your next cleaning.

Figure 4-27 With a few products, this computer user keeps his computer clean.

✔ **QUIZ YOURSELF 4-3**

Instructions: Find the true statement below. Then, rewrite the remaining false statements so that they are true.

1. A bus is the point at which a peripheral attaches to or communicates with a system unit so that the peripheral can send data to or receive information from the computer.
2. An AC adapter is a socket on the motherboard that can hold an adapter card.
3. eSATA ports can connect up to 127 different peripherals together with a single connector.
4. The higher the bus clock speed, the slower the transmission of data.
5. When cleaning the inside of the system unit, wear an antistatic wristband to avoid damaging internal components with static electricity.

Quiz Yourself Online: To further check your knowledge of pages 169 through 177, visit the Computer Concepts CourseMate Web site at www.cengagebrain.com, navigate to the Chapter 4 Quiz Yourself resource for this book, and then click Objectives 5 – 8.

Chapter Summary

Chapter 4 presented the components of the system unit; described how memory stores data, instructions, and information; and discussed the sequence of operations that occur when a computer executes an instruction. The chapter included a comparison of various personal computer processors on the market today. It also discussed how to clean the exterior and interior of a system unit.

Computer Usage @ Work

Sports

While watching your local football team play an out-of-state game on television, you watch various player and game statistics appear on the screen, alerting you to how many yards the offense must travel before making a first down. The camera then focuses on the large, colorful, high-resolution scoreboard at the stadium. While sports such as football have been around for many decades, the integration of computers has added significantly to the viewing experience.

While watching a baseball game, you notice that the scoreboard shows the number of balls and strikes for the player at bat, as well as the speed of each pitch. Behind home plate, an electronic radar gun calculates and records the speed of each pitch. This recorded data, along with the umpire's call (ball or strike) and the player's performance at bat (hit, home run, strike out, etc.) are entered in a computer, which updates the player's batting average automatically. During this entire time, the video display on the stadium's scoreboard plays audio and video to entertain the fans. The computer storing the player and game statistics, audio, and video communicates with the scoreboard and video display using either a wired or wireless connection. (If the computer communicates using wires, the scoreboard and

video display connect directly to a port on a system unit. Recall from the chapter that a port is the point at which a peripheral attaches to or communicates with a system unit.) At the same time, these computers send updated scores and statistics to Web pages and mobile devices.

Computers not only are used to keep track of athlete statistics and communicate with scoreboards, but also in NASCAR to help measure a vehicle's performance before a race. Sensors installed on a car can measure throttle inputs, airflow over the body, the distance between the car's frame and the track, and more. The NASCAR teams then can modify the car so that it achieves maximum performance during a race.

Overall, computers add enjoyment to various sporting events for many individuals. While waiting for a pitcher to throw the next ball or for a football team to start its next play, keep in mind that the integration of computers entertains you with interesting statistics and replays between the action.

For more information, visit the Computer Concepts CourseMate Web site at www.cengagebrain.com, navigate to the Chapter 4 Computer Usage @ Work resource for this book, and then click Sports.

Companies on the Cutting Edge

NVIDIA Visual Computing Technologies Leader

Serious gamers relish software with ultra-realistic graphics, while film producers need high-definition graphics. Both of these creative types of people likely have used a system unit equipped with an NVIDIA processor.

NVIDIA's technological specialty is developing high-performance processors that help generate graphics for personal computers, game consoles, and mobile devices. In the film and entertainment worlds, Sony Pictures, Sportvision, and Weather Central rely on NVIDIA's processor chips to produce imagery and animation. In medicine, the company's processors helped researchers to design a device that stabilizes the heart during bypass surgery and also to develop virtual reality simulations that help burn victims undergoing therapy.

Recently, NVIDIA's CUDA technology was used to enhance the historic *Apollo 11* video of Neil Armstrong walking on the moon.

INTEL World's Leading Chip Manufacturer

Turbochargers have a place in high-performance sports cars, but they have a new home residing in Intel's processors. Some of the company's chips have a turbo mode, which turns cores on and off depending upon when programs demand more processing power, all while conserving energy.

The company's chips have set the standard for personal computers since 1980 when IBM chose the Intel 8080 chip for its new product. Intel now is the world's largest chip manufacturer, with its processors found in approximately 80 percent of the world's personal computers.

Recently, Intel completed its acquisition of Wind River Systems, Inc., a leading software vendor in embedded devices. This acquisition will allow Intel to reach customers outside the traditional PC and server market.

 For more information, visit the Computer Concepts CourseMate Web site at www.cengagebrain.com and then navigate to the Chapter 4 Companies on the Cutting Edge resource for this book.

Technology Trailblazers

JACK KILBY Integrated Circuit Inventor

Jack Kilby is credited with being one of the more influential people in the world. He was awarded more than 60 patents during his lifetime, but none changed society as much as the one for his integrated circuit, or microchip, that made microprocessors possible. His Nobel Prize in physics, awarded in 2005, recognized his part in the invention of the integrated circuit.

Kilby started his work with miniature electrical components at Centralab, where he developed transistors for hearing aids. He then took a research position with Texas Instruments and developed a working model of the first integrated circuit, which was patented in 1959. Kilby applied this invention to various industrial, military, and commercial applications, including the first pocket calculator. Kilby died in 2005, but his legacy lives on.

GORDON MOORE Intel Cofounder

Moore's Law is a prediction made in 1965 by one of Intel's founders, Gordon Moore, that the number of transistors and resistors placed on a computer chip would double every year. This doubling would have a proportional increase in computing power and decrease in cost. This forecast proved amazingly accurate for 10 years, and then Moore revised the estimate to doubling every two years. A recent breakthrough in chip technology using photolithography, which uses light to imprint circuits on a chip, could perpetuate his estimate.

Moore cofounded Intel in 1968 with the conviction that silicon chips would change the world. His lifelong interest in technology is continuing with his contributions to the Large Binocular Telescope, the world's most technologically advanced optical telescope, in southeastern Arizona.

 For more information, visit the Computer Concepts CourseMate Web site at www.cengagebrain.com and then navigate to the Chapter 4 Technology Trailblazers resource for this book.

Chapter Review

The Chapter Review reinforces the main concepts presented in this chapter.

To listen to an audio version of this Chapter Review, visit the Computer Concepts CourseMate Web site at www.cengagebrain.com and then navigate to the Chapter 4 Chapter Review resource for this book.

1. **How Are Various Styles of System Units on Desktop Computers, Traditional Notebook Computers, and Mobile Devices Different?** The **system unit** is a case that contains electronic components of the computer used to process data. System units are available in a variety of shapes and sizes. The case of the system unit protects the internal electronic components from damage. All computers and mobile devices have a system unit. On desktop personal computers, most storage devices also are part of the system unit. On most notebook computers, including netbooks, the keyboard and pointing device often occupy the area on top of the system unit, and the display attaches to the system unit by hinges. The location of the system unit on a Tablet PC varies, depending on the design of the Tablet PC. On mobile computers and devices, the display often is built into the system unit. With game consoles, the input and output devices, such as controllers and a television, reside outside the system unit. On handheld game consoles, portable media players, and digital cameras, by contrast, the packaging around the system unit also houses the input devices and display.

2. **What Are the Control Unit and Arithmetic Logic Unit Components of a Processor, and What Are the Four Steps in a Machine Cycle?** The **processor**, also called the **central processing unit (CPU)**, interprets and carries out the basic instructions that operate a computer. The processor significantly impacts overall computing power and manages most of a computer's operations. Processors contain a control unit and an arithmetic logic unit, which work together to perform processing operations. A **control unit** directs and coordinates most of the operations in the computer, and an **arithmetic logic unit** (ALU) performs arithmetic, comparison, and other operations. The machine cycle is a set of four basic operations — fetching, decoding, executing, and storing — that the processor repeats for every instruction. Fetching obtains a program instruction or data item from memory. Decoding translates the instruction into signals the computer can execute. Executing carries out the commands. Storing writes the result to memory (not to a storage medium).

Visit the Computer Concepts CourseMate Web site at www.cengagebrain.com, navigate to the Chapter 4 Quiz Yourself resource for this book, and then click Objectives 1 – 2.

3. **What Is a Bit, and How Does a Series of Bits Represent Data?** Most computers are **digital** and recognize only two discrete states: off and on. To represent these two states, computers use the **binary system**, which is a number system that has just two unique digits — 0 (for off) and 1 (for on) — called bits. A **bit** (short for binary digit) is the smallest unit of data a computer can process. Grouped together as a unit, 8 bits form a **byte**, which provides enough different combinations of 0s and 1s to represent 256 individual characters. These characters include numbers, uppercase and lowercase letters of the alphabet, punctuation marks, and others, such as letters of the Greek alphabet. The combinations are defined by patterns, called coding schemes, such as ASCII.

4. **What Are the Various Types of Memory?** **Memory** consists of electronic components that store instructions waiting to be executed by the processor, data needed by those instructions, and the results of processing the data (information). The system unit contains volatile and nonvolatile memory. **Volatile memory** loses its contents when the computer's power is turned off. **Nonvolatile memory** does not lose its contents when the computer's power is turned off. RAM is the most common type of volatile memory. **RAM** (random access memory), also called main memory, consists of memory chips that can be read from and written to by the processor and other devices. The three basic types of RAM chips are dynamic RAM (DRAM), static RAM (SRAM), and magnetoresistive RAM (MRAM). ROM, flash memory, and CMOS are examples of nonvolatile memory. **ROM** (read-only memory) refers to memory chips storing permanent data and instructions that usually cannot be modified. **Flash memory** can be erased electronically and rewritten. **CMOS** (complementary metal-oxide semiconductor) technology uses battery power to retain information even when the power to the computer is turned off.

Visit the Computer Concepts CourseMate Web site at www.cengagebrain.com, navigate to the Chapter 4 Quiz Yourself resource for this book, and then click Objectives 3 – 4.

5. **What Are the Purposes and Types of Expansion Slots and Adapter Cards?** An **expansion slot** is a socket on the motherboard that can hold an adapter card. An **adapter card**, sometimes called an **expansion card**, is a circuit board that enhances functions of a component of the system unit and/or provides a connection to a **peripheral** such as a modem, disk drive, printer, scanner, or keyboard. Several types of adapter cards exist. A **sound card** enhances the sound-generating capabilities of a personal computer. A **video card**, also called a **graphics card**, converts computer output into a video signal that displays an image on the screen.

6. **What Is the Difference between a Port and a Connector, and What Are the Differences among a USB Port and Other Ports?** A **port** is the point at which a peripheral attaches to or communicates with a system unit so that the peripheral can send data to or receive information from the computer. A **connector** joins a cable to a port. A **USB port** (short for universal serial bus port) can connect up to 127 different peripherals together with a single connector. A **FireWire port** can connect multiple types of devices that require faster data transmission speeds. Other ports are Bluetooth, SCSI, eSATA, IrDA, and MIDI. **Bluetooth** technology uses radio waves to transmit data between two devices. A **SCSI port** attaches the system unit to SCSI peripherals, such as disk drives and printers. A **eSATA port** connects a high-speed external SATA hard disk to a computer. An **IrDA port** allows wireless devices to transmit signals to a computer via infrared light waves. A **MIDI port** connects the system unit to a musical instrument.

7. **What Are the Types of Buses in a Computer?** A **bus** is an electrical channel along which bits transfer within the circuitry of a computer, allowing devices both inside and attached to the system unit to communicate. The size of a bus, called the bus width, determines the number of bits that the computer can transmit at one time. The larger the bus width, the faster the computer transfers data. A computer has a **system bus**, also called the **front side bus** (FSB); possibly a **backside bus** (BSB); and an **expansion bus**.

8. **How Do You Clean a System Unit on a Computer or Mobile Device?** Before cleaning the exterior of a computer or mobile device, turn it off, and if necessary, unplug it from the electrical outlet, remove the battery, and disconnect all cables from the ports. Use compressed air to blow away dirt from any openings on the case, such as drives, slots, ports, and fan vents. Use an antistatic wipe to clean the exterior of the case and a cleaning solution on a soft cloth to clean the screen. While working inside the case, be sure to wear an antistatic wristband. If you do not feel comfortable cleaning the inside of the case, you can have a professional or computer company clean it for you. Use a vacuum and compressed air to remove dust inside the case.

Visit the Computer Concepts CourseMate Web site at www.cengagebrain.com, navigate to the Chapter 4 Quiz Yourself resource for this book, and then click Objectives 5 – 8.

Key Terms

You should know each key term. The list below helps focus your study.

To see an example of and a definition for each term, and to access current and additional information from the Web, visit the Computer Concepts CourseMate Web site at www.cengagebrain.com and then navigate to the Chapter 4 Key Terms resource for this book.

AC adapter (175)
access time (168)
adapter card (169)
advanced transfer cache (167)
arithmetic logic unit (160)
backside bus (174)
bay (175)
binary system (162)
bit (162)
Bluetooth (172)
bus (174)
byte (162)
cache (167)
central processing unit (CPU) (159)
chip (158)
clock speed (161)
CMOS (168)
connector (171)
control unit (159)

digital (162)
docking station (173)
drive bay (175)
dual-core processor (159)
eSATA port (172)
expansion bus (174)
expansion card (169)
expansion slot (169)
ExpressCard module (170)
ExpressCard slot (170)
FireWire hub (172)
FireWire port (172)
firmware (167)
flash memory (167)
front side bus (174)
gigabyte (GB) (164)
gigahertz (GHz) (161)
graphics card (169)
Hi-Speed USB (172)
IrDA port (172)

kilobyte (KB or K) (164)
L1 cache (167)
L2 cache (167)
megabyte (MB) (164)
memory (163)
memory cache (167)
memory card (169)
memory module (166)
memory slots (166)
microprocessor (159)
MIDI port (172)
motherboard (158)
multi-core processor (159)
nanosecond (168)
nonvolatile memory (164)
PC Card (170)
peripheral (169)
port (170)
port replicator (173)
power supply (175)

processor (159)
quad-core processor (159)
RAM (164)
read-only memory (ROM) (167)
SAS (172)
SCSI port (172)
sound card (169)
system bus (174)
system clock (160)
system unit (156)
terabyte (TB) (164)
USB flash drive (170)
USB hub (172)
USB port (171)
video card (169)
volatile memory (164)

Checkpoint

The Checkpoint exercises test your knowledge of the chapter concepts. The page number containing the answer appears in parentheses after each exercise.

To complete the Checkpoint exercises interactively, visit the Computer Concepts CourseMate Web site at www.cengagebrain.com and then navigate to the Chapter 4 Checkpoint resource for this book.

Multiple Choice   Select the best answer.

1. On _____, the display often is built into the system unit. (157)
   a. desktop personal computers
   b. mobile computers and devices
   c. notebook computers
   d. all of the above

2. The _____ is the component of the processor that directs and coordinates most of the operations in the computer. (159)
   a. register
   b. arithmetic logic unit
   c. control unit
   d. machine cycle

3. Each processor core on a multi-core processor generally runs at _____ clock speed than a single-core processor. (159)
   a. a faster   b. the same
   c. twice the   d. a slower

4. The term decoding refers to the process of _____. (160)
   a. obtaining a program instruction or data item from memory
   b. translating an instruction into signals a computer can execute
   c. carrying out commands
   d. writing a result to memory

5. ROM chips, called _____, contain permanently written data, instructions, or information. (167)
   a. memory cache   b. registers
   c. transistors   d. firmware

6. A(n) _____ is a socket on the motherboard that can hold an adapter card. (169)
   a. expansion slot
   b. parallel port
   c. drive bay
   d. front side bus

7. A(n) _____, which is an external device that attaches to a mobile computer or device, contains a power connection and provides connections to peripherals; it usually also includes slots for memory cards, optical disc drives, and other devices. (173)
   a. docking station
   b. port replicator
   c. peripheral
   d. expansion bus

8. A(n) _____ is part of the motherboard and connects the processor to main memory. (174)
   a. expansion bus
   b. system clock
   c. memory module
   d. front side bus

Matching   Match the terms with their definitions.

_____ 1. processor (159)
_____ 2. memory module (166)
_____ 3. read-only memory (ROM) (167)
_____ 4. expansion slot (169)
_____ 5. port replicator (173)
_____ 6. backside bus (174)

a. external device that provides connections to peripherals through ports built into the device
b. interprets and carries out the basic instructions that operate a computer
c. connects the processor to cache
d. small circuit board on which RAM chips usually reside
e. socket on the motherboard that can hold an adapter card
f. memory chips storing permanent data and instructions
g. most common type of volatile memory

Short Answer   Write a brief answer to each of the following questions.

1. What are two types of designs of Tablet PCs? _____ What are the differences in the designs of the two types of Tablet PCs? _____

2. What is the motherboard? _____ What is a computer chip? _____

3. What is memory cache? _____ How are the two types of cache (L1 cache and L2 cache) different? _____

4. What are four types of removable flash memory devices? _____ How are they different? _____

5. What is compressed air used for with regards to caring for your computer? _____ How should you prepare for cleaning your computer? _____

Problem Solving

The Problem Solving exercises extend your knowledge of the chapter concepts by seeking solutions to practical computer problems that you may encounter at home, school, or work. The Collaboration exercise should be completed with a team.

In the real world, practical problems often can be solved in multiple ways. Provide one solution to each of the following problems using available resources, such as articles on the Web or in print, blogs, podcasts, videos, television, user guides, other individuals, and electronics and computer stores. You may need to use multiple resources to obtain an answer. Present your solutions in the form requested by your instructor (brief report, presentation, discussion, or other means).

@ Home

1. **Malfunctioning Speakers**   While working on a homework assignment, you decide to listen to one of your favorite music CDs through your computer speakers. The media player program on your computer automatically starts when you insert the CD. Although it looks like the CD is playing, no sound is coming from your speakers. What might be causing this? What is the first step that you will take to correct this problem?

2. **Removing Germs**   While recovering from an illness, you realize that by using your computer during your illness, you probably left some germs behind on the keyboard and mouse. How will you clean these devices so that your family members will not become sick?

3. **Numerous Memory Types**   You have decided to purchase additional memory for your computer in order to better support the latest version of the Windows operating system. At the local computer store, you notice that not only are different types of memory for sale, but different sizes are available. What will you do to ensure that you get the proper memory for your computer?

4. **Missing Songs**   During the past several months, you downloaded more than 1,000 songs to your portable media player. Tonight, when you turn on your portable media player, it is not able to locate any of your songs and an error message displays on the screen. What might be causing this?

@ Work

5. **Printer Port Problem**   A colleague received a new printer and has delivered her old printer to your desk for your use. When attempting to plug the printer in a port on the back of your computer, you see that the connector will not fit in any of the available ports. You also notice that even the ports that are in use will not accept the connector. What steps will you take so that you can use the printer?

6. **USB Device Not Working**   You purchased a new USB external hard disk so that you can take work home. After plugging the hard disk in a USB port on your computer, the other USB devices stopped working, and the external hard disk does not work. You return to the store to exchange the hard disk, but the same problem occurs with the new device. Why might this be happening? What steps will you take to resolve this problem?

7. **Incorrect System Date and Time**   While using your computer, you notice that the date and time are incorrect. You correct the date and time settings, continue using your computer, and then power it off before leaving work. When you arrive to work the next morning and turn on the computer, the date and time once again are incorrect. What might be causing this, and what is the first step you might take to solve this problem?

8. **Dirty Fan**   While using your computer, you notice that the fan that removes the hot air from the inside of the computer has stopped running. You immediately turn off your computer to prevent it from overheating and notice that the fan is coated with dust. How will you clean the fan?

Collaboration

9. **Computers in Sports**   You serve as an assistant coach for your former high school's football team. The head coach, who has a computer that is more than five years old, informs you that he would like to create a program that will allow him to keep track of his players' statistics. For instance, he would like to track the quarterback's number of passing yards, rushing yards, and completions. Form a team of three people to determine the requirements for implementing his request. One team member will research the types of application software that can track this data, another team member will determine the specifications for a computer capable of running the software and storing the data, and the other team member will determine the best way to collect the data during the game.

Learn How To

The Learn How To activities step you through fundamental technology skills when using a computer. The Learn How To exercises enable you to become more proficient with these skills.

Learn How To 1: Purchase Memory for a Computer

One of the less expensive and more effective ways to speed up a computer, make it capable of processing more programs at the same time, and enable it to handle graphics, gaming, and other high-level programs is to increase the amount of memory. The process of increasing memory is accomplished in two phases — purchasing the memory and installing the memory. To purchase memory for a computer, complete the following steps:

1. Determine the amount of memory currently in the computer. The amount of memory in your computer is displayed in the Welcome Center when Windows starts.

2. Determine the maximum amount of memory your computer can contain. This value can change for different computers, based primarily on the number of slots on the motherboard available for memory and the size of the memory modules you can place in each slot. On most computers, different size memory modules can be inserted in slots. A computer, therefore, might allow a 128 MB, 256 MB, 512 MB, 1 GB, or 2 GB memory module to be inserted in each slot. To determine the maximum memory for a computer, in many cases you can multiply the number of memory slots on the computer by the maximum size memory module that can be inserted in each slot.

   For example, if a computer contains four memory slots and is able to accept memory modules of 128 MB, 256 MB, 512 MB, 1 GB, or 2 GB in each of its memory slots, the maximum amount of memory the computer can contain is 8 GB (4 x 2 GB).

   You can find the number of slots and the allowable sizes of each memory module by contacting the computer manufacturer, looking in the computer's documentation, or contacting sellers of memory such as Kingston (kingston.com) or Crucial (crucial.com) on the Web. These sellers have documentation for most computers, and even programs you can download to run on your computer that will specify how much memory your computer currently has and how much you can add.

3. Determine how much memory you want to add, which will be somewhere between the current memory and the maximum memory allowed on the computer.

4. Determine the current configuration of memory on the computer. For example, if a computer with four memory slots contains 1 GB of memory, it could be using one memory module of 1 GB in a single slot and the other three slots would be empty; two memory modules of 512 MB each in two slots with two slots empty; one memory module of 512 MB and two memory modules of 256 MB each in three slots with one slot empty; or four memory modules of 256 MB each in four slots with no slots empty. You may be required to look inside the system unit to make this determination. The current memory configuration on a computer will determine what new memory modules you should buy to increase the memory to the amount determined in Step 3.

   You also should be aware that a few computers require memory to be installed in the computer in matching pairs. This means that a computer with four slots could obtain 512 MB of memory with two memory modules of 256 MB each in two slots, or four memory modules of 128 MB each in four slots.

5. Determine the number of available memory slots on your computer and the number and size memory modules you must buy to fulfill your requirement. Several scenarios can occur (in the following examples, assume you can install memory one module at a time).

   a. Scenario 1: The computer has one or more open slots. In this case, you might be able to purchase a memory module that matches the amount of memory increase you desire. For example, if you want to increase memory by 2 GB, you should purchase a 2 GB memory module for insertion in the open slot. Generally, you should buy the maximum size module you can for an open slot. So, if you find two empty slots and wish to increase memory by 2 GB, it is smarter to buy one 2 GB module and leave one empty slot rather than buy two 1 GB memory modules and use both slots. This allows you to increase memory again without removing currently used modules.

   b. Scenario 2: Many other combinations can occur. You may have to perform arithmetic calculations to decide the combination of memory modules that will work for the number of slots on the computer and the desired additional memory.

6. Determine the type of memory to buy for the computer. Computer memory has many types and configurations, and it is critical that you buy the kind of memory for which the computer was designed. It is preferable to buy the same

type of memory that currently is found in the computer. That is, if the memory is DDR3 SDRAM with a certain clock speed, then that is the type of additional memory you should place in the computer. The documentation for the computer should specify the memory type. In addition, the Web sites cited in Step 2, and others as well, will present a list of memory modules that will work with your computer. Enough emphasis cannot be placed on the fact that the memory you buy must be compatible with the type of memory usable on your computer. Because so many types and configurations exist, you must be especially diligent to ensure you purchase the proper memory for your computer.

7. Once you have determined the type and size of memory to purchase, buy it from a reputable dealer. Buying poor or mismatched memory is a major reason for a computer's erratic performance and is one of the more difficult problems to troubleshoot.

Adding memory to a computer can extend its usefulness and increase its processing power.

Exercise

1. Assume you have a computer that contains 1 GB of memory. It contains four memory slots. Each slot can contain 128 MB, 256 MB, 512 MB, 1 GB, or 2 GB memory modules. Two of the slots contain 512 MB memory modules. What memory chip(s) would you buy to increase the memory on the computer to 4 GB? What is the maximum memory on the computer? Submit your answers to your instructor.

Learn It Online

The Learn It Online exercises are interactive Web exercises designed to reinforce and expand your understanding of the chapter concepts. The descriptions below briefly summarize each exercise.

To complete the Learn It Online exercises, visit the Computer Concepts CourseMate Web site at www.cengagebrain.com, navigate to the Chapter 4 resources for this book, click the link for the exercise you want to complete, and then read the instructions.

1 At the Movies — The Leopard with a Time Machine
Watch a movie to learn about Apple Computer's "Time Machine" software, which allows users to travel through time by scrolling through different windows that represent days, to help them find the files that they need and then answer questions about the movie.

2 Student Edition Labs — Understanding the Motherboard and Binary Numbers
Enhance your understanding and knowledge about the motherboard and binary numbers by completing the Understanding the Motherboard and Binary Numbers Labs.

3 Practice Test
Take a multiple choice test that checks your knowledge of the chapter concepts and review the resulting study guide.

4 Who Wants To Be a Computer Genius^2?
Play the Shelly Cashman Series version of this popular game by answering questions to find out if you are a computer genius. Panic buttons are available to provide assistance during game play.

5 Crossword Puzzle Challenge
Complete an interactive crossword puzzle to reinforce concepts presented in this chapter.

6 Windows Exercises
Step through the Windows 7 exercises to learn about installing new hardware, setting the system clock, using Calculator to perform number system conversion, and power management.

7 Exploring Computer Careers
Read about a career as a computer engineer, search for related employment advertisements, and then answer related questions.

8 Web Apps — Google Docs
Learn how to create, edit, and share documents, presentations, and spreadsheets using Google Docs.

Web Research

The Web Research exercises broaden your understanding of chapter concepts by presenting questions that require you to search the Web for answers.

1 **Search Sleuth**

Use one of the search engines listed in Figure 2-8 in Chapter 2 on page 65 or your own favorite search engine to find the answers to the following questions. Copy and paste the Web address from the Web page where you found the answer. Some questions may have more than one answer. If required, submit your answers to your instructor. (1) In nanometers, what is the current size of a quad-core processor? (2) What company holds the trademark for the term, FireWire? (3) What is the relationship between the names of the Itanium processors and the steamship *Titanic*? (4) What Intel chip powered the Busicom calculator? (5) What is the admission price to visit the Intel Museum in Santa Clara, California? (6) What term did Dr. Werner Buchholz coin while designing the IBM Stretch computer? (7) How was a Steckerverbindung used in an Enigma machine?

2 **Green Computing**

Greenpeace International's *Guide to Greener Electronics* ranks the major technology hardware companies in their manufacturing and recycling efforts. The goal is to urge these computer, television, mobile devices, and game console manufacturers to reduce the use of toxic chemicals and to implement recycling policies. View the *Guide* (greenpeace.org/electronics) and then use your word processing program to answer the following questions. Then, if required, submit your answers to your instructor. (1) The *Guide* has been updated every three months since June 2006. What is the version of this most current *Guide*? (2) Which company is at the top of the list for its better toxic waste, recycling, and climate change practices? What is this company's score, and why did this company receive this ranking? (3) Which company received the lowest ranking? Why? (4) What criteria are used to score the manufacturers? (5) Review the Toxics News links and read the article discussing the rankings from the previous year. Compare the companies' rankings between the past year and the current year. (6) How does Greenpeace obtain the data for its analysis? (7) What are Greenpeace's definitions of PVC-free and BFR-free?

3 **Social Networking**

Business creativity helps drive innovation and invention of new products. Oddpodz is an online meeting place for creative people to share ideas with like-minded professionals. This Web site includes a blog, a marketplace for unique products, job postings, and a forum to discuss current topics. Visit the Oddpodz Web site (Oddpodz.com) and then read the FAQs to get an overview of the Web site and to learn the definitions of an Oddpodz. Browse the company profiles in the Creative Services Marketplace. Read the profiles of some new members, who are called citizens, and view some of the creative projects featured. Read several articles in the Cylibrary about the advice given to plan a business. Review the topics in the blog, especially those discussing current advertising campaigns. Summarize the information you read and viewed.

4 **Blogs**

Technology news blogs offer information about new products, trends, and issues facing information technology professionals. Visit several technology blogs, including those from CNET (news.cnet.com), Geekzone (geekzone.co.nz/blogindex.asp), Good Morning Silicon Valley (blogs.siliconvalley.com/gmsv), Lifehacker (lifehacker.com), TechnoClicks (technoclicks.com), and WordPress (wordpress.com/tag/technology/). What are bloggers discussing in their more recent posts? What top news stories are featured? What products are reviewed? What questions are members asking about computer chips, flash memory, Bluetooth, and green computing products? Which stories have generated more than 20 comments?

5 **Ethics in Action**

Law enforcement agencies use handheld wireless devices to access commercial databases. For example, Massachusetts state police stationed at Logan International Airport use the LocatePLUS Holdings Corporation's database, which has information on 98 percent of Americans. Police say accessing this information helps them perform their jobs more efficiently. Privacy experts, in contrast, say that information collected for one purpose, such as checking credit or registering motor vehicles, should not be available in other contexts. View online sites that provide information about commercial databases for sale. Write a report summarizing your findings, and include a table of links to Web sites that provide additional details.

Chapter Five

Input and Output

Objectives

After completing this chapter, you will be able to:

1. Identify the keys and buttons commonly found on desktop computer keyboards, and describe how keyboards for mobile computers and devices differ from desktop computer keyboards

2. Describe different mouse types

3. Describe various types of touch screens and explain how a touch-sensitive pad works

4. Describe various types of pen input

5. Explain other types of input, including various game controllers, other input for smart phones, how resolution affects the quality of a picture captured on digital cameras, voice and video input,

scanners and reading devices, various biometric devices, and terminals

6. Explain the characteristics of LCD monitors, LCD screens, and CRT monitors

7. Summarize the various types of printers: ink-jet printers, photo printers, laser printers, multifunction peripherals, thermal printers, mobile printers, and plotters and large-format printers

8. Identify the purpose and features of speakers, headphones, and earbuds; data projectors; and interactive whiteboards

9. Identify input and output options for physically challenged users

What Is Input?

Input is any data and instructions entered into the memory of a computer. As shown in Figure 5-1, people have a variety of options for entering data and instructions into a computer.

An **input device** is any hardware component that allows users to enter data and instructions into a computer. The following pages discuss a variety of input devices.

touch-sensitive pad

touch screen

keyboard

mouse

input

biometric device

ACCESS GRANTED

RFID reader

MICR

magnetic stripe
card reader

Figure 5-1 Users can enter data and instructions into a computer in a variety of ways.

Keyboard and Pointing Devices

Two of the more widely used input devices are the keyboard and the mouse. Most computers include a keyboard or keyboarding capabilities.

The mouse is a **pointing device** because it allows a user to control a pointer on the screen. In a graphical user interface, a **pointer** is a small symbol on the screen whose location and shape change as a user moves a pointing device. A pointing device can select text, graphics, and other objects; and click buttons, icons, links, and menu commands.

The following pages discuss the keyboard and a variety of pointing devices.

game controller

graphics tablet

stylus

microphone

devices

Web cam

bar code reader

scanner

optical mark recognition

The Keyboard

Many people use a keyboard as one of their input devices. A **keyboard** is an input device that contains keys users press to enter data and instructions into a computer (Figure 5-2).

All desktop computer keyboards have a typing area that includes the letters of the alphabet, numbers, punctuation marks, and other basic keys. Many desktop computer keyboards also have a numeric keypad on the right side of the keyboard.

Most of today's desktop computer keyboards are enhanced keyboards. An enhanced keyboard has 12 or more function keys along the top and a set of arrow and additional keys between the typing area and the numeric keypad (Figure 5-2). Function keys are special keys programmed to issue commands to a computer.

Keyboards with media control buttons allow you to control your media player program, access the computer's optical disc drive, and adjust speaker volume. Internet controls allow you to open an e-mail program, start a Web browser, and search the Internet. Some keyboards include buttons and other features specifically for users that enjoy playing games on the computer.

Desktop computer keyboards often attach via a cable to a USB port on the system unit. Some keyboards, however, do not have any wires connecting the keyboard to the system unit. A wireless keyboard, or cordless keyboard, is a battery-powered device that transmits data to the system unit using wireless technology, such as radio waves (Bluetooth) or infrared light waves (IrDA).

Regardless of size, many keyboards have a rectangular shape with the keys aligned in straight, horizontal rows. Users who spend a lot of time typing on these keyboards sometimes experience repetitive strain injuries (RSI) of their wrists and hands. For this reason, some manufacturers offer ergonomic keyboards, which have a design that reduces the chance of wrist and hand injuries.

The goal of **ergonomics** is to incorporate comfort, efficiency, and safety in the design of the workplace. Employees can be injured or develop disorders of the muscles, nerves, tendons, ligaments, and joints from working in an area that is not designed ergonomically.

Ergonomics
For more information, visit the Computer Concepts CourseMate Web site at www.cengagebrain.com, navigate to the Chapter 5 Web Link resource for this book, and then click Ergonomics.

Figure 5-2 On a desktop computer keyboard, you type using keys in the typing area and on the numeric keypad.

Keyboards for Mobile Computers and Mobile Devices   On notebook and some handheld computers, smart phones, and other mobile devices, the keyboard is built in the top of the system unit. To fit in these smaller computers and devices, the keyboards usually are smaller and have fewer keys than desktop computer keyboards.

A variety of options are available for typing on a smart phone (Figure 5-3). Many can display an on-screen keyboard, where you press the on-screen keys using a stylus or your finger. Some smart phones have one key for each letter of the alphabet, often called a mini-keyboard. Other phones have keypads that contain fewer keys than there are letters in the alphabet. For these phones, each key on the keypad represents multiple characters, which are identified on the key.

mini-keyboard

on-screen keyboard

keypad

Figure 5-3   Users have a variety of options for typing on a phone.

? FAQ 5-1

What can I do to reduce chances of experiencing repetitive strain injuries?

If possible, use an ergonomic keyboard. Do not rest your wrists on the edge of a desk; use a wrist rest. Keep your forearms and wrists level so that your wrists do not bend. Take a break and do hand exercises every 15 minutes. Keep your shoulders, arms, hands, and wrists relaxed while you work. Maintain good posture. Keep feet flat on the floor, with one foot slightly in front of the other. Immediately stop using the computer if you begin to experience pain or fatigue.

For more information, visit the Computer Concepts CourseMate Web site at www.cengagebrain.com, navigate to the Chapter 5 FAQ resource for this book, and then click Repetitive Strain Injuries.

Mouse

A **mouse** is a pointing device that fits comfortably under the palm of your hand. With a mouse, users control the movement of the pointer. As you move a mouse, the pointer on the screen also moves. Generally, you use the mouse to move the pointer on the screen to an object such as a button, a menu, an icon, a link, or text. Then, you press a mouse button to perform a certain action associated with that object.

Most desktop computer users today have some type of **optical mouse**, which uses devices that emit and sense light to detect the mouse's movement. Some use optical sensors, and others use a laser. The latter, often referred to as a **laser mouse**, usually is more expensive than the former (Figure 5-4).

The mobile user who makes presentations may prefer a mouse that has additional buttons for running a slide show and controlling media, similar to a remote control. An **air mouse** is a newer type of motion-sensing mouse that, in addition to the typical buttons, allows you to control objects, media players, and slide shows by moving the mouse in predetermined directions through the air. For example, raising the mouse up might increase the volume on your media player.

left mouse button   wheel button   right mouse button

thumb buttons

Figure 5-4   This mouse uses a laser to detect movement of the mouse. It also includes buttons you push with your thumb that enable forward and backward navigation through Web pages.

A mouse connects to a computer in several ways. Many types connect with a cable that attaches to a USB port or a mouse port on the system unit. A wireless mouse, or cordless mouse, is a battery-powered device that transmits data using wireless technology, such as radio waves (Bluetooth) or infrared light waves (IrDA). Read Ethics & Issues 5-1 for a related discussion.

ETHICS & ISSUES 5-1

Are Employers Responsible for Computer-Related Repetitive Strain Injuries?

When you consider the causes of workplace injuries, you might not put clicking a mouse or using a cell phone in the same category with lifting a bag of concrete, but perhaps you should. According to the chairman of a National Academy of Sciences panel that investigated workplace injuries, every year one million Americans lose workdays because of repetitive strain injuries (RSIs), including the latest malady known as cell phone elbow. RSI is caused when muscle groups perform the same actions over and over again. Once, RSIs were common among factory workers who performed the same tasks on an assembly line for hours a day. Today, these injuries, which often result from prolonged use of a computer mouse and keyboard or overuse of cell phones and other mobile devices, are the largest job-related injury and illness problem in the United States and are almost completely avoidable with proper computer and mobile device use. OSHA proposed standards whereby employers would have to establish programs to prevent workplace injuries with respect to computer use. Yet, Congress rejected the standards, accepting the argument that the cost to employers would be prohibitive and unfair. Some argue that it is each employee's responsibility to be aware of preventative measures against RSI.

Should the government establish laws regarding computer use? Why or why not? Are employees, employers, or the government responsible for repetitive strain injuries? Why? Who should be responsible for the costs of prevention and medical care? Why?

Ethics & Issues

For the complete text of the Ethics & Issues boxes found in this chapter, visit the Computer Concepts CourseMate Web site at www.cengagebrain.com and then navigate to the Chapter 5 Ethics & Issues resource for this book.

Trackball

A **trackball** is a stationary pointing device with a ball on its top or side (Figure 5-5). To move the pointer using a trackball, you rotate the ball with your thumb, fingers, or the palm of your hand. In addition to the ball, a trackball usually has one or more buttons that work just like mouse buttons.

Touchpad

A **touchpad** is a small, flat, rectangular pointing device that is sensitive to pressure and motion (Figure 5-6). To move the pointer using a touchpad, slide your fingertip across the surface of the pad. Some touchpads have one or more buttons around the edge of the pad that work like mouse buttons. On most touchpads, you also can tap the pad's surface to imitate mouse operations such as clicking. Touchpads are found most often on notebook computers, including netbooks and many Tablet PCs.

Pointing Stick

A **pointing stick** is a pressure-sensitive pointing device shaped like a pencil eraser that is positioned between keys on a keyboard (Figure 5-7). To move the pointer using a pointing stick, you push the pointing stick with a finger. The pointer on the screen moves in the direction you push the pointing stick. By pressing buttons below the keyboard, users can click and perform other mouse-type operations with a pointing stick.

Figure 5-5 A trackball.

Figure 5-6 Most notebook computers have a touchpad that allows users to control the movement of the pointer.

Figure 5-7 Some notebook computers include a pointing stick to allow a user to control the movement of the pointer.

Touch Screens and Touch-Sensitive Pads

A **touch screen** is a touch-sensitive display device. Touch screens that recognize multiple points of contact at the same time are known as multi-touch. Users can interact with touch screens by touching areas of the screen. Because touch screens require a lot of arm or hand movements, you do not enter large amounts of data using a touch screen. Instead, users touch words, pictures, numbers, letters, or locations identified on the screen. Some touch screens also respond to finger motions such as sliding your finger to drag an object or pinching your fingers to zoom in or out. The latest version of the Windows operating system provides increased support for computers with touch screens. Support for touch screens makes it easier for users to interact with the operating system.

With some smart phones, portable media players, and other mobile devices, you can touch the screen to perform tasks such as dialing phone numbers, entering text, and making on-screen selections. Some handheld game consoles also have touch screens. A **kiosk**, which is a freestanding computer, usually includes a touch screen (Figure 5-8).

Figure 5-8   This traveler checks in using an airport kiosk.

A recently developed touch screen, called **Microsoft Surface**, is a 30-inch tabletop display that allows one or more people to interact with the screen using their fingers or hands (Figure 5-9). The Microsoft Surface display also allows devices that are not digital, such as an everyday paintbrush, to be used as an input device.

Figure 5-9   Guests explore photos of hotel amenities by touching and dragging them across the Microsoft Surface display.

Multi-Touch Screens
For more information, visit the Computer Concepts CourseMate Web site at www.cengagebrain.com, navigate to the Chapter 5 Web Link resource for this book, and then click Multi-Touch Screens.

Touch-Sensitive Pads

Portable media players that do not have touch screens typically have a **touch-sensitive pad**, which is an input device that enables users to scroll through and play music, view pictures, watch videos or movies, adjust volume, and/or customize settings. Touch-sensitive pads typically contain buttons and/or wheels that are operated with a thumb or finger. For example, users rotate a **Click Wheel** to browse through a portable media player's song, picture, or movie lists and press the Click Wheel's buttons to play or pause media, display a menu, and perform other actions (Figure 5-10).

touch-sensitive pad

Figure 5-10   You use your thumb to rotate or press buttons on a Click Wheel.

Which companies sell the most portable media players?

Apple has dominated the portable media player market for several years. A recent study shows that Apple holds 71 percent of the market share, with SanDisk in second place at 11 percent of the market. The chart to the right illustrates the market share for the top four portable media player manufacturers.

For more information, visit the Computer Concepts CourseMate Web site at www.cengagebrain.com, navigate to the Chapter 5 FAQ resource for this book, and then click Portable Media Players.

Portable Media Player Market Share

4%   12%   2%   11%   71%

☐Apple ☐SanDisk ■Creative ☐Microsoft ☐Other

Source: NPD Group

Pen Input

With **pen input**, you touch a stylus or digital pen on a flat surface to write, draw, or make selections. The flat surface may be a screen on a monitor or mobile device, a signature capture pad, or a graphics tablet (Figure 5-11). A **stylus** is a small metal or plastic device that looks like a tiny ink pen but uses pressure instead of ink. A **digital pen**, which is slightly larger than a stylus, typically provides more functionality than a stylus, featuring electronic erasers and programmable buttons. Most digital pens, often simply called pens, are pressure-sensitive.

Some desktop and mobile computers and nearly all mobile devices have touch screens that recognize pen input and thus include a pressure-sensitive digital pen or stylus.

To capture a handwritten signature, a user writes his or her name on a **signature capture pad** with a stylus or pen that is attached to the device. Software then transmits the signature via a cable connected to a USB or serial port on the computer. Signature capture pads often include a magnetic stripe card reader and work with POS terminals, both discussed later in the chapter.

To use pen input on a computer that does not have a touch screen, you can attach a graphics tablet to the computer. A **graphics tablet** is a flat, rectangular, electronic, plastic board. Architects, mapmakers, designers, artists, and home users create drawings and sketches by using a pressure-sensitive pen on a graphics tablet.

smart phone   stylus

signature capture pad   stylus

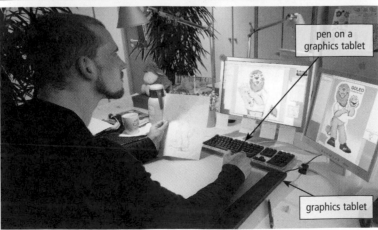

pen on a graphics tablet

graphics tablet

Figure 5-11   You use a stylus or a pen to write, draw, or make selections on a screen, signature capture pad, or graphics tablet.

Instructions: Find the true statement below. Then, rewrite the remaining false statements so that they are true.

1. A keyboard is an output device that contains keys users press to enter data and instructions into a computer.
2. A trackball is a small, flat, rectangular pointing device commonly found on notebook computers, including netbooks and many Tablet PCs.
3. Input is any data and instructions entered into the memory of a computer.
4. An optical mouse has moving mechanical parts inside.
5. A stylus is a flat, rectangular, electronic, plastic board.

Quiz Yourself Online: To further check your knowledge of pages 188 through 194, visit the Computer Concepts CourseMate Web site at www.cengagebrain.com, navigate to the Chapter 5 Quiz Yourself resource for this book, and then click Objectives 1 – 4.

Other Types of Input

In addition to the keyboard, mouse, and pointing devices just discussed, users have a variety of other options available to enter data and instructions into a computer. These include other input for smart phones, game controllers, digital cameras, voice input, video input, scanners and reading devices, biometric input, and terminals.

Other Input for Smart Phones

Previously discussed input devices such as mini-keyboards, keypads, touch screens, and a stylus are used with smart phones and PDAs. In addition to these input methods, a variety of alternatives for entering data and instructions is available for smart phones and mobile devices (Figure 5-12).

obtain maps and directions on the phone by attaching this navigation receiver to your vehicle's window

speak into the microphone that wirelessly communicates with the phone

take a picture using the digital camera built into the back of the phone

use one end of the stylus to write on the phone's screen and the other end as a ballpoint pen

transfer data and instructions to and from the computer and phone by connecting it to the computer with a cable

enter text-based messages via a wireless keyboard

Figure 5-12   Besides a touch screen and basic stylus, users have a variety of other options for entering data and instructions into a smart phone.

You can talk directly into the smart phone's microphone or into a Bluetooth headset that wirelessly communicates with the smart phone to receive audio. Some smart phones have digital cameras that take pictures and touch-sensitive pads that enable you to interact with media, such as music and photos. Others can receive navigation signals to provide users with maps and directions.

You also can transfer, or synchronize, data and information from a computer to a phone. With some phones, you synchronize wirelessly; with others, you attach the phone to the computer via a cable or a cradle that has a cable connected to the computer.

Figure 5-13
A variety of game controllers.

Game Controllers

Video games and computer games use a **game controller** as the input device that directs movements and actions of on-screen objects (Figure 5-13). Game controllers include gamepads, joysticks and wheels, light guns, dance pads, and a variety of motion-sensing controllers.

Gamepads A **gamepad**, which is held with both hands, controls the movement and actions of players or objects in video games or computer games. On the gamepad, users press buttons with their thumbs or move sticks in various directions to trigger events. Gamepads communicate with a game console or a personal computer via wired or wireless technology.

Joysticks and Wheels Users running game software or flight and driving simulation software often use a joystick or wheel to control an airplane, vehicle, or player. A **joystick** is a handheld vertical lever mounted on a base. You move the lever in different directions and press buttons to control the actions of the simulated vehicle or player. A **wheel** is a steering-wheel-type input device that you turn to simulate driving a car, truck, or other vehicle. Most wheels also include foot pedals for acceleration and braking actions. Joysticks and wheels typically attach via a cable to a personal computer or game console.

Light Guns A **light gun** is used to shoot targets and moving objects after you pull the trigger on the weapon. Light guns typically attach via a cable to a game console or personal computer.

Dance Pads A **dance pad** is a flat electronic device divided into panels that users press with their feet in response to instructions from a music video game. These games test the user's ability to step on the correct panel at the correct time, following a pattern that is synchronized with the rhythm or beat of a song. Dance pads communicate with a game console or a personal computer via wired or wireless technology.

Motion-Sensing Game Controllers Motion-sensing game controllers allow the user to guide on-screen elements by moving a handheld input device in predetermined directions through the air. Sports games, for example, use motion-sensing game controllers, such as baseball bats and golf clubs, as their input device. These types of controllers communicate with a game console or a personal computer via wired or wireless technology.

A popular general-purpose, motion-sensing game controller is Nintendo's Wii Remote. Shaped like a television remote control and operated with one hand, the **Wii Remote** is a motion-sensing input device that uses Bluetooth wireless technology to communicate with the Wii game console. Users point the Wii Remote in different directions and rotate it to control on-screen players, vehicles, and other objects.

Other Game Controllers   Other popular game controllers include musical instruments and balance boards. Controllers that resemble musical instruments, such as guitars, drums, and keyboards, work with music video games that enable game players to create sounds and music by playing the instrument. Fitness games often communicate with a balance board, which is shaped like a weight scale and contains sensors that measure a game player's balance and weight. Musical instrument and balance board controllers communicate with game consoles via wired or wireless technology.

Digital Cameras

As discussed in Chapter 1, a **digital camera** is a mobile device that allows users to take pictures and store the photographed images digitally, instead of on traditional film. The three basic types of digital cameras are studio cameras, field cameras, and point-and-shoot cameras. The most expensive and highest quality of the three is a studio camera, which is a stationary camera used for professional studio work. Often used by photojournalists, a field camera is a portable camera that has many lenses and other attachments. As with the studio camera, a field camera can be quite expensive. A point-and-shoot camera is much more affordable and lightweight and provides acceptable quality photographic images for the home or small business user. Figure 5-14 illustrates how one model of a point-and-shoot digital camera works.

Game Controllers

For more information, visit the Computer Concepts CourseMate Web site at www.cengagebrain.com, navigate to the Chapter 5 Web Link resource for this book, and then click Game Controllers.

How a Digital Camera Might Work

Step 1
Point to the image to photograph and take the picture. Light passes into the lens of the camera.

Step 2
The image is focused on a chip called a charge-coupled device (CCD).

Step 3
The CCD generates an analog signal that represents the image.

Step 4
The analog signal is converted to a digital signal by an analog-to-digital converter (ADC).

Step 5
A processor in the camera adjusts the quality of the image and usually stores the digital photo on media inserted in the camera.

Figure 5-14   This figure shows how a digital camera might work.

Often users prefer to download, or transfer a copy of, the images from the digital camera to the computer's hard disk, where the photos are available for editing with photo editing software, printing, faxing, sending via e-mail, including in another document, or posting to a Web site or photo community for everyone to see.

One factor that affects the quality of digital camera photos is its resolution. **Resolution** is the number of horizontal and vertical pixels in a display device. A digital camera's resolution is defined in pixels. A **pixel** (short for picture element) is the smallest element in an electronic image. The greater the number of pixels the camera uses to capture a picture, the better the quality of the picture. Digital camera resolutions range from about 4 million to more than 16 million pixels (MP).

Voice Input

Voice input is the process of entering input by speaking into a microphone. Uses of voice input include instant messaging that supports voice conversations, chat rooms that support voice chats, VoIP, and voice recognition. Recall that VoIP (Voice over IP) enables users to speak to other users over the Internet. **Voice recognition**, also called **speech recognition**, is the computer's capability of distinguishing spoken words. Voice recognition programs recognize a vocabulary of pre-programmed words. The vocabulary of voice recognition programs can range from two words to millions of words.

Audio Input   Voice input is part of a larger category of input called audio input. **Audio input** is the process of entering any sound into the computer such as speech, music, and sound effects. To enter high-quality sound into a personal computer, the computer must have a sound card. Users enter sound into a computer via devices such as microphones, tape players, CD/DVD/Blu-ray Disc players, or radios, each of which plugs in a port on the sound card.

Some users also record live music and other sound effects using external music devices such as an electronic keyboard (Figure 5-15), guitar, drums, harmonica, and microphones. Music production software allows users to record, compose, mix, and edit music and sounds.

Figure 5-15   An electronic keyboard can be connected to a computer, allowing users to record and store music in the computer.

Video Input

Video input is the process of capturing full-motion images and storing them on a computer's storage medium such as a hard disk or optical disc. Some video devices use analog video signals. A **digital video (DV) camera**, by contrast, records video as digital signals instead of analog signals. Many DV cameras have the capability of capturing still frames, as well as motion. To transfer recorded images to a hard disk or optical disc, users connect DV cameras directly to a USB port or a FireWire port on the system unit. After saving the video on a storage medium, such as a hard disk or DVD, you can play it or edit it using video editing software on a computer. For additional information about digital video, read the Digital Video Technology feature that follows this chapter.

Web Cams A **Web cam**, also called a **PC video camera**, is a type of digital video camera that enables a home or small business user to capture video and still images, send e-mail messages with video attachments, add live images to instant messages, broadcast live images over the Internet, and make video telephone calls (Figure 5-16). During a **video telephone call**, both parties see each other as they communicate over the Internet. The cost of Web cams usually is less than $100.

Figure 5-16 This student uses a notebook computer, which has a built-in Web cam, to watch a video of a lecture for her online class.

You can configure some Web cams to display their output on a Web page. This use of a Web cam attracts Web site visitors by showing images that change regularly. Home or small business users might use Web cams to show a work in progress, weather and traffic information, employees at work, photos of a vacation, and countless other images.

Video Conferencing A **video conference** is a meeting between two or more geographically separated people who use a network or the Internet to transmit audio and video data (Figure 5-17). To participate in a video conference using a computer, you need video conferencing software or use a video conferencing Web application, along with a microphone, speakers, and a video camera attached to or built into a computer. As you speak, members of the meeting hear your voice on their speakers. Any image in front of the video camera, such as a person's face, appears in a window on each participant's screen.

As the costs of video conferencing hardware and software decrease, increasingly more business meetings, corporate training, and educational classes will be conducted as video conferences.

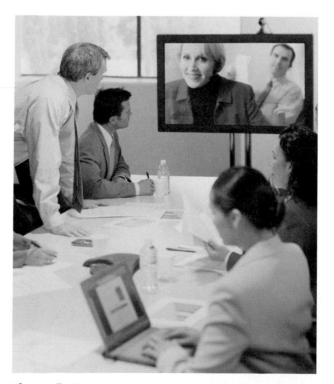

Figure 5-17 To save on travel expenses, many large businesses are turning to video conferencing.

Scanners and Reading Devices

Some input devices save users time by capturing data directly from a source document, which is the original form of the data. Examples of source documents include time cards, order forms, invoices, paychecks, advertisements, brochures, photos, inventory tags, or any other document that contains data to be processed.

Devices that can capture data directly from a source document include optical scanners, optical readers, bar code readers, RFID readers, magnetic stripe card readers, and magnetic-ink character recognition readers.

Optical Scanners   An optical scanner, usually called a **scanner**, is a light-sensing input device that reads printed text and graphics and then translates the results into a form the computer can process. A **flatbed scanner** works in a manner similar to a copy machine except it creates a file of the document in memory instead of a paper copy (Figure 5-18). Once you scan a picture or document, you can display the scanned object on the screen, modify its appearance, store it on a storage medium, print it, fax it, attach it to an e-mail message, include it in another document, or post it on a Web site or photo community for everyone to see.

Many scanners include OCR (optical character recognition) software, which can read and convert text documents into electronic files. OCR software converts a scanned image into a text file that can be edited, for example, with a word processing program.

Figure 5-18
A flatbed scanner.

Optical Readers   An optical reader is a device that uses a light source to read characters, marks, and codes and then converts them into digital data that a computer can process. Two technologies used by optical readers are optical character recognition and optical mark recognition.

- **Optical character recognition (OCR)** involves reading typewritten, computer-printed, or hand-printed characters from ordinary documents and translating the images into a form the computer can process. Most **OCR devices** include a small optical scanner for reading characters and sophisticated software to analyze what is read. OCR devices range from large machines that can read thousands of documents per minute to hand-held wands that read one document at a time.

Many companies use OCR characters on turnaround documents. A **turnaround document** is a document that you return (turn around) to the company that creates and sends it. For example, when consumers receive a bill, they often tear off a portion of the bill and send it back to the company with their payment (Figure 5-19). The portion of the bill they return usually has their payment amount, account number, and other information printed in OCR characters.

- **Optical mark recognition (OMR)** devices read hand-drawn marks such as small circles or rectangles. A person places these marks on a form, such as a test, survey, or questionnaire answer sheet.

this portion is returned with payment

CHASE Continental Airlines

ACCOUNT NUMBER: 24085 6105 0824 8058

name and address printed using OCR characters

OCR characters

new balance

minimum due

OCR characters

Figure 5-19   OCR characters frequently are used with turnaround documents. With this bill, you tear off the top portion and return it with a payment.

ISAAC NARO
1227 SOUTH HI ST
LOS ANGELES CA 90055

BOX 52064
PHOENIX AZ 85072-2064

Continental Airlines

Continental Airlines Visa® Signature Card from Chase
ACCOUNT NUMBER: 24085 6105 0824 8058

NEW BALANCE	REVOLVING LINE BALANCE	NON REVOLVING LINE BALANCE	STATEMENT CLOSING DATE
$1,165.15	$1,165.15	$0.00	02/18/11

REVOLVING LINE	AVAILABLE REVOLVING LINE	CASH ACCESS LINE	AVAILABLE CASH
$25,000	$23,834	$25,000	$23,834

ONEPASS® MILEAGE SUMMARY	
Miles Earned This Statement	Total Miles Earned Since 01/09
1,014	100,497

Here is your Account Summary:

	TOTAL
Previous Balance	$471.50
(-) Payments, Credits	471.50
(+) Purchases, Cash, Debits	1,165.15
(+) FINANCE CHARGES	0.00
(=) New Balance	1,165.15
Total Minimum Payment Due by 03/14/11	$23.00

Bar Code Readers   A **bar code reader**, also called a bar code scanner, is an optical reader that uses laser beams to read bar codes (Figure 5-20). A **bar code** is an identification code that consists either of a set of vertical lines and spaces of different widths or a two-dimensional pattern of dots, squares, and other images. The bar code represents data that identifies the manufacturer and the item. A newer type of bar code, called a 2-D bar code, can store much more data than the traditional linear bar code.

Manufacturers print a bar code either on a product's package or on a label that is affixed to a product.

 Figure 5-20   A bar code reader uses laser beams to read bar codes on products such as food and boarding passes.

RFID Readers   **RFID** (radio frequency identification) is a technology that uses radio signals to communicate with a tag placed in or attached to an object, an animal, or a person. RFID tags, which contain a memory chip and an antenna, are available in many shapes and sizes. An **RFID reader** reads information on the tag via radio waves. RFID readers can be handheld devices or mounted in a stationary object such as a doorway.

Many retailers see RFID as an alternative to bar code identification because it does not require direct contact or line-of-site transmission. Each product in a store would contain a tag that identifies the product (Figure 5-21). As consumers remove products from the store shelves and walk through a checkout area, an RFID reader reads the tag(s) and communicates with a computer that calculates the amount due.

Other uses of RFID include tracking times of runners in a marathon; tracking location of soldiers, employee wardrobes, airline baggage, and misplaced or stolen goods; checking lift tickets of skiers; managing inventory; gauging temperature and pressure of tires on a vehicle; checking out library books; and tracking payment as vehicles pass through booths on tollway systems.

Figure 5-21   RFID readers read information stored on an RFID tag and then communicate this information to computers, which instantaneously compute payments and update inventory records. In this example, the RFID tag is embedded in a label attached to the tire.

Magnetic Stripe Card Readers   A **magnetic stripe card reader**, often called a magstripe reader, reads the magnetic stripe on the back of credit cards, entertainment cards, bank cards, and other similar cards. The stripe contains information identifying you and the card issuer (Figure 5-22). Some information stored in the stripe includes your name, account number, the card's expiration date, and a country code.

Figure 5-22   A magnetic stripe card reader reads information encoded on the stripe on the back of your credit card.

When a consumer swipes a credit card through a magstripe reader, it reads the information stored on the magnetic stripe on the card. If the magstripe reader rejects the card, it is possible that the magnetic stripe is scratched, dirty, or erased. Exposure to a magnet or magnetic field can erase the contents of a card's magnetic stripe.

MICR Readers MICR (magnetic-ink character recognition) devices read text printed with magnetized ink. An **MICR reader** converts MICR characters into a form the computer can process. The banking industry almost exclusively uses MICR for check processing. Each check in your checkbook has precoded MICR characters beginning at the lower-left edge (Figure 5-23).

When a bank receives a check for payment, it uses an MICR inscriber to print the amount of the check in MICR characters in the lower-right corner. The check then is sorted or routed to the customer's bank, along with thousands of others. Each check is inserted in an MICR reader, which sends the check information — including the amount of the check — to a computer for processing.

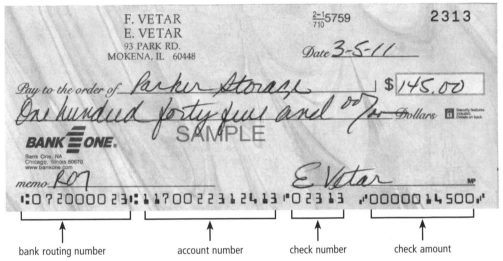

Figure 5-23 The MICR characters preprinted on the check represent the bank routing number, the customer account number, and the check number. The amount of the check in the lower-right corner is added after the check is cashed.

Biometric Input

Biometrics is the technology of authenticating a person's identity by verifying a personal characteristic. Biometric devices grant users access to programs, systems, or rooms by analyzing some physiological (related to physical or chemical activities in the body) or behavioral characteristic. Examples include fingerprints, hand geometry, facial features, voice, signatures, and eye patterns.

The most widely used biometric device today is a fingerprint reader. A **fingerprint reader** captures curves and indentations of a fingerprint (Figure 5-24). To save on desk space, some newer keyboards and notebook computers have a fingerprint reader attached to them, which allows users to log on to programs and Web sites via their fingerprint instead of entering a user name and password.

A face recognition system captures a live face image and compares it with a stored image to determine if the person is a legitimate user. Some buildings use face recognition systems to secure access to rooms. Law enforcement, surveillance systems, and airports use face recognition to protect the public. Read Ethics & Issues 5-2 for a related discussion.

Figure 5-24 A fingerprint reader.

ETHICS & ISSUES 5-2

How Often Should You Be Monitored in Public Locations?

Customers with yearly passes for a theme park in Japan enjoy a unique method of entering the park. A biometric face recognition system recognizes the customer's face and allows the visitor entry into the park. At large sporting events, airports, and other public areas, face recognition systems scan visitors' faces and compare the visitors' faces to wanted or known criminals. Those who match a known criminal's face are detained so that authorities can make a final determination if the person should be removed from the location or arrested. Some local governments support placing face recognition systems on streets and scanning everybody who walks by. Supporters state the use of these systems, rather than authorities trying to recognize criminals, is more efficient in finding wanted criminals and allows law enforcement personnel to focus their efforts elsewhere.

Opponents of the systems claim that they are an invasion of privacy and even may violate the fourth amendment to the Constitution, which provides protection from unreasonable searches. They also claim that the systems result in an increase in innocent people being detained because the systems are imperfect. In fact, at one large sporting event, more than a dozen people were detained, but none was found to be a match to a known criminal.

Would you mind constant monitoring by face recognition systems? Why? Which types of criminals should face recognition systems be used to locate? Why? How would you react if you were improperly detained due to a mistake made by a face recognition system?

Biometric devices measure the shape and size of a person's hand using a hand geometry system. Because their cost is more than $1,000, larger companies typically use these systems as time and attendance devices or as security devices.

A voice verification system compares a person's live speech with their stored voice pattern. Larger organizations sometimes use voice verification systems as time and attendance devices. Many companies also use this technology for access to sensitive files and networks.

A signature verification system recognizes the shape of your handwritten signature, as well as measures the pressure exerted and the motion used to write the signature. Signature verification systems use a specialized pen and tablet.

High security areas use iris recognition systems. The camera in an iris recognition system uses iris recognition technology to read patterns in the iris of the eye (Figure 5-25). These patterns are as unique as a fingerprint. Iris recognition systems are quite expensive and are used by government security organizations, the military, and financial institutions that deal with highly sensitive data. Some organizations use retinal scanners, which work similarly but instead scan patterns of blood vessels in the back of the retina.

Biometric Input

For more information, visit the Computer Concepts CourseMate Web site at www.cengagebrain.com, navigate to the Chapter 5 Web Link resource for this book, and then click Biometric Input.

Figure 5-25 An iris recognition system.

Terminals

A **terminal** is a computer, usually with limited processing power, that enables users to send data to and/or receive information from a host computer. Special-purpose terminals perform specific tasks and contain features uniquely designed for use in a particular industry. Three special-purpose terminals are point-of-sale (POS) terminals, automated teller machines, and DVD kiosks.

- The location in a retail or grocery store where a consumer pays for goods or services is the point of sale (POS). Most retail stores use a **POS terminal** to record purchases, process credit or debit cards, and update inventory.

  Many POS terminals handle credit card or debit card payments and thus also include a magstripe reader. Some have fingerprint readers (discussed in the next section) that read your fingerprint, which is linked to a payment method such as a checking account or credit card. Once the transaction is approved, the terminal prints a receipt for the customer. A self-service POS terminal allows consumers to perform all checkout-related activities (Figure 5-26). That is, they scan the items, bag the items, and pay for the items themselves.

- An **automated teller machine** (**ATM**) is a self-service banking machine that connects to a host computer through a network (Figure 5-27). Banks place ATMs in convenient locations, including grocery stores, convenience stores, retail outlets, shopping malls, sports and concert venues, and gas stations.

  Using an ATM, people withdraw cash, deposit money, transfer funds, or inquire about an account balance. Some ATMs have a touch screen; others have special buttons or keypads for entering input. To access a bank account, you insert a plastic bankcard in the ATM's magstripe reader. The ATM asks you to enter a password, called a personal identification number (PIN), which verifies that you are the holder of the bankcard. When your transaction is complete, the ATM prints a receipt for your records.

Figure 5-26 Many grocery stores offer self-serve checkouts, where the consumers themselves use the POS terminals to scan purchases, scan their store saver card and coupons, and then pay for the goods.

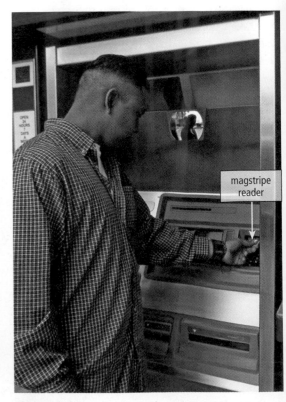

Figure 5-27 An ATM is a self-service banking terminal that allows customers to access their bank accounts.

- A **DVD kiosk** is a self-service DVD rental machine that connects to a host computer through a network (Figure 5-28). The DVD kiosks, some of which can hold more than 600 DVDs, are located nationwide at retail stores, fast-food restaurants, grocery stores, airports, and other convenient public locations

A DVD kiosk is associated with a particular vendor. To rent a movie online, for example, a customer visits the vendor's Web site, establishes an account or connects to an existing account, selects the desired movie, and then chooses a nearby DVD kiosk where the movie will be picked up. Customers also usually can select movies directly on the DVD kiosk via a touch screen or some other input device on the kiosk. After presenting identifying information and swiping a credit card through the reader, the DVD kiosk dispenses the rented movie to the customer. When finished viewing the movie, the customer returns it to any of the vendor's nationwide DVD kiosks, at which time the customer's account is charged a fee based on the time elapsed.

Figure 5-28   A DVD kiosk is a self-service DVD rental machine.

✔ **QUIZ YOURSELF 5-2**

Instructions: Find the true statement below. Then, rewrite the remaining false statements so that they are true.

1. A digital camera allows users to take pictures and store the photographed images digitally, instead of on traditional film.
2. A fingerprint reader captures curves and indentations of a signature.
3. After swiping a credit card through an MICR reader, it reads the information stored on the magnetic stripe on the card.
4. Video games and computer games use a Web cam as the input device that directs movements and actions of on-screen objects.
5. Many smart phones today have POS capabilities.
6. RFID is a technology that uses laser signals to communicate with a tag placed in an object, an animal, or a person.

🖳 **Quiz Yourself Online:** To further check your knowledge of pages 195 through 205, visit the Computer Concepts CourseMate Web site at www.cengagebrain.com, navigate to the Chapter 5 Quiz Yourself resource for this book, and then click Objective 5.

What Is Output?

Output is data that has been processed into a useful form. That is, computers process data (input) into information (output). Users view or watch output on a screen, print it, or hear it through speakers, headphones, or earbuds. While working with a computer, a user encounters four basic types of output: text, graphics, audio, and video (Figure 5-29). Very often, a single form of output, such as a Web page, includes more than one of these types of output.

An **output device** is any hardware component that conveys information to one or more people. Commonly used output devices include display devices; printers; speakers, headphones, and earbuds; data projectors; and interactive whiteboards.

Figure 5-29 Four types of output are text, graphics, audio, and video.

Display Devices

A **display device** is an output device that visually conveys text, graphics, and video information. Desktop computers typically use a monitor as their display device. A **monitor** is a display device that is packaged as a separate peripheral. Some monitors have a tilt-and-swivel base that allows users to adjust the angle of the screen to minimize neck strain and reduce glare from overhead lighting. With some, you can rotate the screen. Adjustable monitor stands allow you to adjust the height of the monitor. Some have integrated speakers and/or a built-in Web cam. Monitor controls permit users to adjust the brightness, contrast, positioning, height, and width of images.

Most mobile computers and devices integrate the display and other components into the same physical case.

GRAPHICS

VIDEO

Most display devices show text, graphics, and video information in color. Some, however, are monochrome. Monochrome means the information appears in one color (such as white, amber, green, black, blue, or gray) on a different color background (such as black or grayish-white). Some mobile devices use monochrome displays because they require less battery power.

Types of display devices include LCD monitors and LCD screens, plasma monitors, and CRT monitors. The following sections discuss each of these display devices.

LCD Monitors and LCD Screens

An **LCD monitor** is a desktop monitor that uses a liquid crystal display to produce images (Figure 5-30). These monitors produce sharp, flicker-free images. LCD monitors have a small footprint; that is, they do not take up much desk space. LCD monitors are available in a variety of sizes, with the more common being 19, 20, 22, 24, 26, 27, and 30 inches — some are 45 or 65 inches. Most are **widescreen,** which are wider than they are tall. You measure a monitor the same way you measure a television, that is, diagonally from one corner to the other.

Mobile computers and mobile devices often have built-in LCD screens (Figure 5-31). Many are widescreen; some are touch screen. Notebook computer screens are available in a variety of sizes, with the more common being 14.1, 15.4, 17, and 20.1 inches. Netbook screens typically range in size from 8.9 inches to 12.1 inches, and Tablet PC screens range from 8.4 inches to 14.1 inches. Portable media players usually have screen sizes from 1.5 inches to 3.5 inches. On smart phones, screen sizes range from 2.5 inches to 4.1 inches. Digital camera screen sizes usually range from 2.5 inches to 4 inches. Read Innovative Computing 5-1 to find out about another use of LCD screens.

Widescreen LCD Monitors

For more information, visit the Computer Concepts CourseMate Web site at www.cengagebrain.com, navigate to the Chapter 5 Web Link resource for this book, and then click Widescreen LCD Monitors.

speakers

Figure 5-30 This widescreen LCD monitor has built-in speakers.

notebook computer

PDA

smart phone

handheld game console

portable media player

digital camera

Figure 5-31 Many people use their computers and mobile devices to view photos or watch downloaded videos and home movies. To learn about creating and uploading videos to YouTube, complete the Learn How To 1 activity on pages 228 and 229.

Get the Picture with Digital Frames

Put away your photo albums filled with vacation pictures, baby portraits, and wedding reception candids. With digital photo frames, you constantly can display all the photos that capture the best times of your life.

Digital photo frames are becoming main stream as they drop in price and increase in quality. A correlation exists between price, photo quality, and features, so the higher priced frames generally have clearer displays with accurate color. They also have adjustments for brightness, contrast, tint, and color and may use rechargeable batteries instead of electricity to power the display and dissolve from one photo to the next. Look for frames with a resolution of at least 640 × 480.

Some frames integrate Wi-Fi so that you can send your photos to the frame via your home network or download them from photo sharing Web sites. Once the photos are stored, you can add transitions and set the mood by timing the presentation to your favorite songs.

For more information, visit the Computer Concepts CourseMate Web site at www.cengagebrain.com, navigate to the Chapter 5 Innovative Computing resource for this book, and then click Digital Frames.

LCD Technology and Quality   A **liquid crystal display** (**LCD**) uses a liquid compound to present information on a display device. Computer LCDs typically contain fluorescent tubes that emit light waves toward the liquid-crystal cells, which are sandwiched between two sheets of material.

The quality of an LCD monitor or LCD screen depends primarily on its resolution, response time, brightness, dot pitch, and contrast ratio.

- Resolution is the number of horizontal and vertical pixels in a display device. For example, a monitor that has a 1440 × 900 resolution displays up to 1440 pixels per horizontal row and 900 pixels per vertical row, for a total of 1,296,000 pixels to create a screen image. A higher resolution uses a greater number of pixels and thus provides a smoother, sharper, and clearer image. As the resolution increases, however, some items on the screen appear smaller.

  With LCD monitors and screens, resolution generally is proportional to the size of the device. That is, the resolution increases for larger monitors and screens. For example, a widescreen 19-inch LCD monitor typically has a resolution of 1440 × 900, while a widescreen 22-inch LCD monitor has a resolution of 1680 × 1050. LCDs are geared for a specific resolution.

- Response time of an LCD monitor or screen is the time in milliseconds (ms) that it takes to turn a pixel on or off. LCD monitors' and screens' response times range from 3 to 16 ms. The lower the number, the faster the response time.

- Brightness of an LCD monitor or LCD screen is measured in nits. A nit is a unit of visible light intensity. The higher the nits, the brighter the images.

- Dot pitch, sometimes called pixel pitch, is the distance in millimeters between pixels on a display device. Average dot pitch on LCD monitors and screens should be .30 mm or lower. The lower the number, the sharper the image.

- Contrast ratio describes the difference in light intensity between the brightest white and darkest black that can be displayed on an LCD monitor. Contrast ratios today range from 500:1 to 2000:1. Higher contrast ratios represent colors better.

Ports and LCD Monitors   A cable on a monitor plugs in a port on the system unit. LCD monitors use a digital signal to produce a picture. To display the highest quality images, an LCD monitor should plug in a DVI port, an HDMI port, or a DisplayPort. A DVI (Digital Video Interface) port enables digital signals to transmit directly to an LCD monitor. An HDMI (High-Definition Media Interface) port combines DVI with high-definition (HD) television and video. The DisplayPort is an alternative to DVI that also supports HDMI.

DVI

For more information, visit the Computer Concepts CourseMate Web site at www.cengagebrain.com, navigate to the Chapter 5 Web Link resource for this book, and then click DVI.

Plasma Monitors

A **plasma monitor** is a display device that uses gas plasma technology, which sandwiches a layer of gas between two glass plates (Figure 5-32).

Plasma monitors offer screen sizes up to 150 inches wide and richer colors than LCD monitors but are more expensive. Like LCD monitors, plasma monitors can hang directly on a wall.

Figure 5-32
Large plasma monitors can measure up to 150 inches wide.

? **FAQ 5-3**

What type of video content do users view on display devices?

Music videos and newscasts are the most widely viewed video content on display devices, as shown in the chart to the right.

For more information, visit the Computer Concepts CourseMate Web site at www.cengagebrain.com, navigate to the Chapter 5 FAQ resource for this book, and then click Video Output Content.

Video Output
(Breakdown by Content)

- Internet TV
- Film
- Music
- News
- Sports
- Other

5% 6% 11% 17% 28% 33%

Source: The ClickZ Network

CRT Monitors

A **CRT monitor** is a desktop monitor that contains a cathode-ray tube (Figure 5-33). A cathode-ray tube (CRT) is a large, sealed glass tube. The front of the tube is the screen. A CRT's viewable size is the diagonal measurement of the actual viewing area provided by the screen in the CRT monitor. A 21-inch monitor, for example, may have a viewable size of 20 inches.

Figure 5-33 The popularity of CRT monitors is declining.

CRT monitors produce a small amount of electromagnetic radiation. Electromagnetic radiation (EMR) is a magnetic field that travels at the speed of light. Excessive amounts of EMR can pose a health risk. To be safe, all high-quality CRT monitors comply with a set of standards that defines acceptable levels of EMR for a monitor. To protect yourself even further, sit at arm's length from the CRT monitor because EMR travels only a short distance.

✔| **QUIZ YOURSELF 5-3**

Instructions: Find the true statement below. Then, rewrite the remaining false statements so that they are true.

1. A lower resolution uses a greater number of pixels and thus provides a smoother image.

2. An output device is any type of software component that conveys information to one or more people.

3. Types of pixels include LCD monitors, LCD screens, plasma monitors, and CRT monitors.

4. You measure a monitor diagonally from one corner to the other.

Quiz Yourself Online: To further check your knowledge of pages 206 through 211, visit the Computer Concepts CourseMate Web site at www.cengagebrain.com, navigate to the Chapter 5 Quiz Yourself resource for this book, and then click Objective 6.

Printers

A **printer** is an output device that produces text and graphics on a physical medium such as paper. Many different types and styles of printers exist with varying speeds, capabilities, and printing methods. Figure 5-34 presents a list of questions to help you determine the printer best suited to your needs.

The following pages will help you to answer these questions by discussing various ways to produce printed output, as well as many different types of printers.

1. What is my budget?
2. How fast must my printer print?
3. Do I need a color printer?
4. What is the cost per page for printing?
5. Do I need multiple copies of documents?
6. Will I print graphics?
7. Do I want to print photos?
8. Do I want to print directly from a memory card?
9. What types of paper does the printer use?
10. What sizes of paper does the printer accept?
11. Do I want to print on both sides of the paper?
12. How much paper can the printer tray hold?
13. Will the printer work with my computer and software?
14. How much do supplies such as ink, toner, and paper cost?
15. Can the printer print on envelopes?
16. How many envelopes can the printer print at a time?
17. How much do I print now, and how much will I be printing in a year or two?
18. Will the printer be connected to a network?
19. Do I want wireless printing capability?

Figure 5-34   Questions to ask when purchasing a printer.

Producing Printed Output

Although many users today print by connecting a computer to a printer with a cable, a variety of printing options are available as shown in Figure 5-35.

Today, wireless printing technology makes the task of printing from a notebook computer, smart phone, or digital camera much easier. Two wireless technologies for printing are Bluetooth and infrared. With Bluetooth printing, a computer or other device transmits output to a printer via radio waves. With infrared printing, a printer communicates with a computer or other device using infrared light waves.

Instead of downloading photos from a digital camera to a computer, users can print these digital photos using a variety of techniques. Some cameras connect directly to a printer via a cable. Others store photos on memory cards that can be removed and inserted in the printer. Some printers have a docking station, into which the user inserts the camera to print photos stored in the camera.

Finally, many home and business users print to a central printer on a network. Their computer may communicate with the network printer via cables or wirelessly.

Various Ways Users Print Documents and Photos

printer cable connected to system unit

Notebook computer wirelessly communicates with system unit, which is connected to the printer on the home network.

digital camera

wireless printers

Digital camera communicates with printer wirelessly.

Smart phone communicates with printer wirelessly.

network printer

Printer connected to network prints documents from many computers.

Printer prints photos in camera when camera sits in docking station.

docking station

Printer connects to camera via cable.

cable

Printer prints images on memory card removed from camera and inserted in printer.

memory card

Figure 5-35 Users print documents and photos using a variety of printing methods.

Nonimpact Printers

A **nonimpact printer** forms characters and graphics on a piece of paper without actually striking the paper. Some nonimpact printers spray ink, while others use heat or pressure to create images. Commonly used nonimpact printers are ink-jet printers, photo printers, laser printers, thermal printers, mobile printers, plotters, and large-format printers.

Ink-Jet Printers

An **ink-jet printer** is a type of nonimpact printer that forms characters and graphics by spraying tiny drops of liquid ink onto a piece of paper. Ink-jet printers have become a popular type of color printer for use in the home. Ink-jet printers produce text and graphics in both black-and-white and color on a variety of paper types (Figure 5-36). A reasonable quality ink-jet printer costs less than $100.

As with many other input and output devices, one factor that determines the quality of an ink-jet printer is its resolution. Printer resolution is measured by the number of dots per inch (dpi) a printer can print. Most ink-jet printers can print from 1200 to 4800 dpi.

The speed of an ink-jet printer is measured by the number of pages per minute (ppm) it can print. Most ink-jet printers print from 12 to 36 ppm. Graphics and colors print at a slower rate.

Figure 5-36 Ink-jet printers are a popular type of color printer used in the home.

The print head mechanism in an ink-jet printer contains ink-filled cartridges. Each cartridge has fifty to several hundred small ink holes, or nozzles. The ink propels through any combination of the nozzles to form a character or image on the paper. When the ink cartridge runs out of ink, you simply replace the cartridge. Most ink-jet printers use two or more ink cartridges: one containing black ink and the other(s) containing colors. Consider the number of ink cartridges a printer requires, along with the cost of the cartridges, when purchasing a printer. To reduce the expense of purchasing cartridges, some users opt to purchase refilled cartridges or have empty cartridges refilled by a third party vendor.

Photo Printers

A **photo printer** is a color printer that produces photo-lab-quality pictures (Figure 5-37). Some photo printers print just one or two sizes of photos, for example, 3 × 5 inches and 4 × 6 inches. Others print up to letter size, legal size, or even larger. Many photo printers use ink-jet technology. With models that can print letter-sized documents, users connect the photo printer to their computer and use it for all their printing needs.

Most photo printers are PictBridge enabled, so that you can print photos without a computer. **PictBridge** is a standard technology that allows you to print photos directly from a digital camera by connecting a cable from the digital camera to a USB port on the printer.

Photo printers also usually have a built-in card slot(s) so that the printer can print digital photos directly from a memory card. Some photo printers have built-in LCD color screens, allowing users to view and enhance the photos before printing them.

prints 4 × 6, 5 × 7, 8 × 10, 8½ × 11, and panoramic sizes

Figure 5-37 Photo printers print in a range of sizes.

Photo Printers
For more information, visit the Computer Concepts CourseMate Web site at www.cengagebrain.com, navigate to the Chapter 5 Web Link resource for this book, and then click Photo Printers.

Laser Printers

A **laser printer** is a high-speed, high-quality nonimpact printer (Figure 5-38). Laser printers for personal computers ordinarily use individual sheets of paper stored in one or more removable trays that slide in the printer case.

Laser printers print text and graphics in high-quality resolutions, usually ranging from 1200 to 2400 dpi. While laser printers usually cost more than ink-jet printers, many models are available at affordable prices for the home user. Laser printers usually print at faster speeds than ink-jet printers. Printer manufacturers state that a laser printer for the home and small office user typically prints black-and-white text at speeds of 15 to 62 ppm. Color laser printers print 8 to 40 ppm. Laser printers for large business users print more than 150 ppm.

Depending on the quality, speed, and type of laser printer, the cost ranges from a few hundred to a few thousand dollars for the home and small office user, and several hundred thousand dollars for the large business user. Color laser printers are slightly higher priced than otherwise equivalent black-and-white laser printers.

Operating in a manner similar to a copy machine, a laser printer creates images using a laser beam and powdered ink, called **toner**. Black-and-white laser printers use one toner cartridge. Color laser printers use multiple cartridges — one for black and one or more for colors. When the toner runs out, you replace the toner cartridge.

black-and-white
laser printer

color laser printer

Figure 5-38 Laser printers are available in both black-and-white and color models.

Laser Printers
For more information, visit the Computer Concepts CourseMate Web site at www.cengagebrain.com, navigate to the Chapter 5 Web Link resource for this book, and then click Laser Printers.

? FAQ 5-4

How do I dispose of toner cartridges?

Do not throw them in the garbage. The housing contains iron, metal, and aluminum that is not biodegradable. The ink toner inside the cartridges contains toxic chemicals that pollute water and soil if discarded in dumps. Instead, recycle empty toner cartridges. Many stores that sell new toner cartridges also allow you to recycle your old ones. Recycling programs in which some schools and organizations participate offer discounts or cash to customers who bring in depleted cartridges. If you are unable to find a recycling program in your area, contact your printer manufacturer to see if it has a recycling program.

For more information, visit the Computer Concepts CourseMate Web site at www.cengagebrain.com, navigate to the Chapter 5 FAQ resource for this book, and then click Recycling Toner Cartridges.

Multifunction Peripherals

A **multifunction peripheral**, also called an **all-in-one device**, is a single device that looks like a printer or copy machine but provides the functionality of a printer, scanner, copy machine, and perhaps a fax machine (Figure 5-39). Some use color ink-jet printer technology, while others include a black-and-white or color laser printer. An advantage of these devices is they are significantly less expensive than if you purchase each device separately. If the device breaks down, however, you lose all four functions, which is the primary disadvantage.

Figure 5-39
This multifunction peripheral is a color printer, scanner, copy machine, and fax machine.

Thermal Printers

A **thermal printer** generates images by pushing electrically heated pins against heat-sensitive paper. Basic thermal printers are inexpensive, but the print quality is low and the images tend to fade over time. Self-service gas pumps often print gas receipts using a built-in lower-quality thermal printer. Many point-of-sale terminals in retail and grocery stores also print purchase receipts on thermal paper.

Some thermal printers have high print quality and can print at much faster rates than ink-jet and laser printers. A dye-sublimation printer, sometimes called a **digital photo printer**, uses heat to transfer colored dye to specially coated paper. Professional applications requiring high image quality, such

Figure 5-40 The printer shown in this figure uses dye-sublimation technology to create photographic-quality output for the home or small office user.

as photography studios, medical labs, and security identification systems, use dye-sublimation printers. These high-end printers cost thousands of dollars and print images in a wide range of sizes.

Dye-sublimation printers for the home or small business user, by contrast, typically print images in only one or two sizes and are much slower than their professional counterparts. These lower-end dye-sublimation printers are comparable in cost to a photo printer based on ink-jet technology (Figure 5-40).

Mobile Printers

A **mobile printer** is a small, lightweight, battery-powered printer that allows a mobile user to print from a notebook computer, or smart phone or other mobile device while traveling (Figure 5-41). Barely wider than the paper on which they print, mobile printers fit easily in a briefcase alongside a notebook computer. Mobile printers mainly use ink-jet or thermal technology.

Figure 5-41 A mobile printer.

Plotters and Large-Format Printers

Plotters are sophisticated printers used to produce high-quality drawings such as blueprints, maps, and circuit diagrams. These printers are used in specialized fields such as engineering and drafting and usually are very costly.

Using ink-jet printer technology, but on a much larger scale, a **large-format printer** creates photo-realistic-quality color prints. Graphic artists use these high-cost, high-performance printers for signs, posters, and other professional quality displays (Figure 5-42).

 Figure 5-42 Graphic artists use large-format printers to print signs, posters, and other professional quality displays.

Impact Printers

An **impact printer** forms characters and graphics on a piece of paper by striking a mechanism against an inked ribbon that physically contacts the paper. Impact printers are ideal for printing multipart forms because they easily print through many layers of paper. Two commonly used types of impact printers are dot-matrix printers and line printers.

A **dot-matrix printer** produces printed images when tiny wire pins on a print head mechanism strike an inked ribbon (Figure 5-43). When the ribbon presses against the paper, it creates dots that form characters and graphics. Dot-matrix printers typically use continuous-form paper, in which thousands of sheets of paper are connected together end to end. The pages have holes along the sides to help feed the paper through the printer. The speed of most dot-matrix printers ranges from 375 to 1100 characters per second (cps), depending on the desired print quality.

A **line printer** is a high-speed impact printer that prints an entire line at a time. The speed of a line printer is measured by the number of lines per minute (lpm) it can print. Some line printers print as many as 3,000 lpm.

continuous-form paper

Figure 5-43 A dot-matrix printer produces printed images when tiny pins strike an inked ribbon.

Other Output Devices

In addition to monitors and printers, other output devices are available for specific uses and applications. These include speakers, headphones, and earbuds; data projectors; and interactive whiteboards.

Speakers, Headphones, and Earbuds

An **audio output device** is a component of a computer that produces music, speech, or other sounds, such as beeps. Three commonly used audio output devices are speakers, headphones, and earbuds.

Most personal computers and mobile devices have a small internal speaker that usually emits only low-quality sound. Thus, many users attach surround sound **speakers** or speaker systems to their computers to generate higher-quality sounds (Figure 5-44). Most surround sound computer speaker systems include one or two center speakers and two or more satellite speakers that are positioned so that sound emits from all directions. Speakers typically have tone and volume controls, allowing users to adjust settings. To boost the low bass sounds, surround sound speaker systems also include a subwoofer. In many cases, a cable connects the speakers or the subwoofer to a port on the sound card. With wireless speakers, however, a transmitter connects to the sound card, which wirelessly communicates with the speakers.

Many users opt for a wireless music system, where you can play any optical disc or media file on your computer and transmit the audio to a home or office stereo or television. You also can plug a portable media player, such as an iPod, into the computer to hear its songs on the stereo or television speakers.

In a computer laboratory or other crowded environment, speakers might not be practical. Instead, users can listen through wireless headphones or earbuds or plug the device in a port on the sound card, in a speaker, or in the front of the system unit. With headphones or earbuds, only the individual

subwoofer

satellite speakers

satellite speakers

center speaker

Figure 5-44 Most personal computer users attach high-quality surround sound speaker systems to their computers.

Earbuds

 For more information, visit the Computer Concepts CourseMate Web site at www.cengagebrain.com, navigate to the Chapter 5 Web Link resource for this book, and then click Earbuds.

wearing the headphones or earbuds hears the sound from the computer. The difference is that **headphones** cover or are placed outside of the ear, whereas **earbuds**, or **earphones**, rest inside the ear canal.

A **headset** is a device that functions as both headphones and a microphone. Computer and smart phone users wear a headset to free their hands for typing and other activities while talking or listening to audio output.

Portable media players usually include a set of earbuds. As an alternative, you can listen to audio from the portable media player through speakers in a vehicle or on a stereo system at home or work. Or, you can purchase speakers specifically designed to play audio from a portable media player.

Electronically produced voice output is growing in popularity. **Voice output** occurs when you hear a person's voice or when the computer talks to you through the speakers on the computer. In some programs, the computer can speak the contents of a document through voice output. On the Web, you can listen to (or download and then listen to) interviews, talk shows, sporting events, news, recorded music, and live concerts from many radio and television stations. Some Web sites and programs, such as media players, dedicate themselves to providing voice output, such as those that allow you to listen to and then purchase and download songs. VoIP allows users to speak and listen to others over the Internet using their computer or mobile device.

Data Projectors

A **data projector** is a device that takes the text and images displaying on a computer screen and projects them on a larger screen so that an audience can see the image clearly. Some data projectors are large devices that attach to a ceiling or wall in an auditorium. Others, designed for the mobile user, are small portable devices that can be transported easily (Figure 5-45).

computer

data projector

Figure 5-45 Data projectors can produce sharp, bright images.

Interactive Whiteboards

An **interactive whiteboard** is a touch-sensitive device, resembling a dry-erase board, that displays the image on a connected computer screen. A presenter controls the computer program by clicking a remote control, touching the whiteboard, drawing on or erasing the whiteboard with a special digital pen and eraser, or writing on a special tablet. Notes written on the interactive whiteboard can be saved directly on the computer. Interactive whiteboards are used frequently in classrooms as a teaching tool (Figure 5-46), during meetings as a collaboration tool, and to enhance delivery of presentations.

Interactive whiteboards, which are hung on the wall or mounted on a stand, range in size from 48 to 94 inches. A widely used interactive whiteboard is the SMART Board.

Figure 5-46 Teachers and students can write directly on an interactive whiteboard, or they can write on a wireless slate that communicates with the whiteboard.

SMART Board

 For more information, visit the Computer Concepts CourseMate Web site at www.cengagebrain.com, navigate to the Chapter 5 Web Link resource for this book, and then click SMART Board.

Putting It All Together

Many factors influence the type of input and output devices you should use: the type of input and output desired, the hardware and software in use, and the anticipated cost. Figure 5-47 outlines several suggested input and output devices for various types of computer users.

Suggested Input and Output Devices by User

User	Input Device	Output Device
Home	• Enhanced keyboard or ergonomic keyboard • Mouse • Stylus for smart phone or other mobile device • Game controllers • Color scanner • 7 MP digital camera • Headphones that include a microphone (headset) • Web cam • Fingerprint reader	• 19- or 20-inch color LCD monitor, or 17-inch LCD screen on notebook computer • Ink-jet color printer; or • Photo printer • Speakers • Headphones or earbuds or headset
Small Office/Home Office	• Enhanced keyboard or ergonomic keyboard • Mouse • Stylus and portable keyboard for smart phone or other mobile device, or digital pen for Tablet PC • Color scanner • 8 MP digital camera • Headphones that include a microphone (headset) • Web cam	• 20- or 22-inch LCD monitor • LCD screen on smart phone or other mobile device • Multifunction peripheral; or • Ink-jet color printer; or • Laser printer (black-and-white or color) • Speakers
Mobile	• Wireless mouse for notebook computer • Touchpad or pointing stick on notebook computer • Stylus and portable keyboard for smart phone or other mobile device, or digital pen for Tablet PC • 7 or 8 MP digital camera • Headphones that include a microphone (headset) • Fingerprint reader for notebook computer	• 17-inch LCD screen on notebook computer • 8.9-inch screen on a netbook • LCD screen on smart phone or other mobile device • Mobile color printer • Ink-jet color printer; or • Laser printer, for in-office use (black-and-white or color) • Photo printer • Headphones or earbuds or headset • Data projector
Power	• Enhanced keyboard or ergonomic keyboard • Mouse • Stylus and portable keyboard for smart phone or other mobile device • Pen for graphics tablet • Color scanner • 9 to 12 MP digital camera • Headphones that include a microphone (headset) • Web cam	• 30-inch LCD monitor • Laser printer (black-and-white or color) • Plotter or large-format printer; or • Photo printer; or • Dye-sublimation printer • Speakers • Headphones or earbuds or headset
Enterprise	• Enhanced keyboard or ergonomic keyboard • Mouse • Stylus and portable keyboard for smart phone or other mobile device, or digital pen for Tablet PC • Touch screen • Color scanner • 9 to 12 MP digital camera • OCR/OMR readers, bar code readers, or MICR reader • Microphone • Video camera for video conferences • Fingerprint reader or other biometric device	• 20- or 22-inch LCD monitor • LCD screen on smart phone or other mobile device • High-speed laser printer • Laser printer, color • Line printer (for large reports from a mainframe) • Speakers • Headphones or earbuds or headset • Data projector • Interactive whiteboard

Figure 5-47 This table recommends suggested input and output devices for various types of users.

Input and Output Devices for Physically Challenged Users

The ever-increasing presence of computers in everyone's lives has generated an awareness of the need to address computing requirements for those who have or may develop physical limitations. The **Americans with Disabilities Act (ADA)** requires any company with 15 or more employees to make reasonable attempts to accommodate the needs of physically challenged workers. Read Ethics and Issues 5-3 for a related discussion.

Besides voice recognition, which is ideal for blind or visually impaired users, several other input devices are available. Users with limited hand mobility who want to use a keyboard have several options. Keyboards with larger keys are available. Still another option is the on-screen keyboard, in which a graphic of a standard keyboard is displayed on the user's screen. As the user clicks letters on the on-screen keyboard, they appear in the document at the location of the insertion point. An option for people with limited hand movement is a head-mounted pointer to control the pointer or insertion point (Figure 5-48). To simulate the functions of a mouse button, a user works with switches that control the pointer. The switch might be a hand pad, a foot pedal, a receptor that detects facial motions, or a pneumatic instrument controlled by puffs of air.

ⓨ ETHICS & ISSUES 5-3

Should Web Sites Be Held Accountable for Accessibility Levels for Physically Challenged People?

The World Wide Web Consortium (W3C) has published accessibility guidelines for Web sites. The guidelines specify measures that Web site designers can take to increase accessibility for physically challenged users. Among its guidelines, the W3C urges Web site designers to provide equivalent text for audio or visual content, include features that allow elements to be activated and understood using a variety of input and output devices, and make the user interface follow principles of accessible design. A recent report found that most Web sites do not meet all of the W3C guidelines. This failure is disappointing, because many physically challenged users could benefit from the Web's capability to bring products and services into the home. Ironically, a survey discovered that more than 50 percent of the

Web sites hosted by disability organizations also fail to meet the W3C guidelines. Critics contend that these Web sites neglect the needs of their users and fail to lead by example. The Web site supporters contend, however, that many sponsoring organizations lack the funding necessary to comply with the guidelines.

Should the government require that all Web sites meet the W3C accessibility guidelines? Why or why not? Do Web sites hosted by disability organizations have a moral obligation to meet the guidelines? Why? What can be done to encourage people and organizations to make their Web sites more accessible?

camera/receiver

reflective tracking surface attached to brim of hat

Figure 5-48 A camera/receiver mounted on the monitor tracks the position of the head-mounted pointer, which is reflective material that this user is wearing on the brim of her hat. As the user moves her head, the pointer on the screen also moves.

For users with mobility, hearing, or vision disabilities, many different types of output devices are available. Hearing-impaired users, for example, can instruct programs to display words instead of sounds. Read Looking Ahead 5-1 for a look at a tongue-powered input device.

Visually impaired users can change Windows settings, such as increasing the size or changing the color of the text to make the words easier to read. Instead of using a monitor, blind users can work with voice output. That is, the computer reads the information that appears on the screen. Another alternative is a Braille printer, which outputs information on paper in Braille (Figure 5-49).

Figure 5-49 A Braille printer.

 LOOKING AHEAD 5-1

Tongue May Become Joystick to Control Devices

Thousands of people are paralyzed from the neck down due to spinal cord damage, but they have full control of their tongue because it is controlled by a cranial nerve, not the spinal cord. For these people, Georgia Institute of Technology's Tongue Drive System may be the input device that helps them control their lives.

In the Georgia Tech prototype, the tongue serves as a joystick. A magnet less than one-eighth of an inch wide is surgically implanted under the tip of the tongue, and when a person moves his or her tongue, sensors on each cheek record the magnet's movements in one of six directions: left, right, forward, backward, single-click, and double-click. This data is sent to a receiver on top of the person's head, which, in turn, transmits a signal wirelessly to a computer that controls an electronic device. For example, if the tongue moves forward and to the left, lights in the room could turn on or a wheelchair could roll forward.

In a future development of the Tongue Drive System, an individual tooth could be designated as a specific letter, so teeth could function, in effect, as a keyboard.

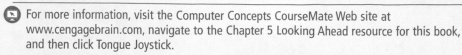

For more information, visit the Computer Concepts CourseMate Web site at www.cengagebrain.com, navigate to the Chapter 5 Looking Ahead resource for this book, and then click Tongue Joystick.

✔ **QUIZ YOURSELF 5-4**

Instructions: Find the true statement below. Then, rewrite the remaining false statements so that they are true.

1. A laser printer generates images by pushing electrically heated pins against heat-sensitive paper.
2. A photo printer creates images using a laser beam and powdered ink, called toner.
3. An ink-jet printer is a type of impact printer that forms characters and graphics by spraying tiny drops of liquid nitrogen onto a piece of paper.
4. Many personal computer users attach surround sound printer systems to their computers to generate a higher-quality sound.
5. Multifunction peripherals require more space than having a separate printer, scanner, copy machine, and fax machine.
6. The Americans with Disabilities Act (ADA) requires any company with 15 or more employees to make reasonable attempts to accommodate the needs of physically challenged workers.

Quiz Yourself Online: To further check your knowledge of pages 211 through 221, visit the Computer Concepts CourseMate Web site at www.cengagebrain.com, navigate to the Chapter 5 Quiz Yourself resource for this book, and then click Objectives 7 – 9.

Chapter Summary

Input is any data and instructions you enter into the memory of a computer. This chapter described the various techniques of entering input and several commonly used input devices. Topics included the keyboard, mouse and other pointing devices, touch screens, pen input, other input for smart phones, game controllers, digital cameras, voice input, video input, scanners and reading devices, biometric input, and terminals.

Computers process and organize data (input) into information (output). This chapter also described the various methods of output and several commonly used output devices. Output devices presented included display devices; printers; speakers, headphones, and earbuds; data projectors; and interactive whiteboards.

Computer Usage @ Work

Space Exploration

Watching the television closely, you hear the announcer count the seconds until the spacecraft lifts off from its launch pad: "Three, two, one, and we have liftoff." The engines ignite and the glow from the burning fuel illuminates the night sky as it begins its journey toward the International Space Station. As you sit back and watch, mesmerized by the thought that a group of astronauts are accomplishing something of which you only could dream, hundreds of individuals and computers are working behind the scenes to ensure a safe mission.

Because space exploration is fraught with danger, it is extremely important that all decisions be made with precision and that personnel become aware of problems before the problems become too serious. For instance, space vehicles contain a plethora of sensors that measure environmental variables such as temperature, velocity, position, and altitude. If the sensors return readings outside an acceptable range, computers correct any problems or notify mission managers as necessary. Employees work around the clock monitoring the output from the spacecraft sensors while it is in flight and communicating to astronauts any actions required to ensure a continued safe mission.

In addition to keeping the spacecraft safe while in orbit, computers also help guide the spacecraft into and out of orbit. To reach the International Space Station, spacecraft can be launched safely only during specified launch time frames. Once the spacecraft is launched, it must travel in a precise direction at an exact velocity to ensure a successful mission. As the mission nears completion and a capsule containing the astronauts reenters the atmosphere, onboard computers position the capsule precisely so that the extreme temperatures at the reentry interface do not cause catastrophic damage. Furthermore, these onboard computers help to ensure that the capsule touches down in a safe location.

With billions of dollars spent on space travel, computers play a vital role in guaranteeing the safety of the space vehicle, the astronauts, and those of us on Earth.

For more information, visit the Computer Concepts CourseMate Web site at www.cengagebrain.com, navigate to the Chapter 5 Computer Usage @ Work resource for this book, and then click Space Exploration.

Companies on the Cutting Edge

LOGITECH Personal Interface Products Leader

Design and innovation drive the development of Logitech products, and the company continues to win top industry awards for its imaginative personal peripheral, Internet communications, home entertainment, gaming, and digital music devices. Logitech has sold millions of mouse devices and wireless products in practically every country in the world.

Stanford computer science students Daniel Borel and Pierluigi Zappacosta, along with Giacomo Marini, founded Logitech in 1981 at Borel's father-in-law's farm in Apples, Switzerland. The company's name is derived from logiciel, which is the French word for software.

Many of Logitech's latest ventures have capitalized on consumers' growing interest in their digital homes. Recently, Logitech announced its one millionth Logitech Vid customer after only three months of being available publicly. Logitech Vid is Logitech's free video conferencing software.

HP Hardware and Software Products Leader

One of the more famous real estate parcels in the United States is the birthplace of the Silicon Valley: the garage where Stanford University friends William Hewlett and David Packard developed various electronic products. Their first success in 1938 was an oscillator used to test sound equipment.

Today HP (Hewlett-Packard) has become the world's top manufacturer of ink-jet and laser printers, multifunction peripherals, desktop and notebook computers, and servers. It also is a leading software company with products for networking and storage management.

Recently, HP introduced the first workstation with a six-core AMD Opteron processor, delivering high productivity for multi-threaded programs. HP also ranked ninth in the 2009 FORTUNE 500 ranking.

 For more information, visit the Computer Concepts CourseMate Web site at www.cengagebrain.com and then navigate to the Chapter 5 Companies on the Cutting Edge resource for this book.

Technology Trailblazers

DOUGLAS ENGELBART Creator of the Mouse

The ubiquitous mouse is a staple for desktop computers, but its evolution to becoming the most widely used pointing device was a slow process. Douglas Engelbart conceived the idea of the mouse in 1950 to help humans work more efficiently. Fourteen years later he developed the first prototype with the goal of making it easier for people to move a cursor around a computer screen. In 1974, engineers at Xerox refined Engelbart's prototype and showed the redesigned product to Apple's Steve Jobs, who applied the concept to his graphical Macintosh computer. The final product did not gain worldwide acceptance for another 10 years.

Engelbart is continuing his pursuits of helping people work smarter. His Bootstrap Institute is a California-based company that promotes collaboration, creativity, and competition to solve problems.

URSULA BURNS Xerox Chairman and CEO

When Ursula Burns was nominated to chair Xerox Corporation in 2010, two milestones were reached: she became the first African-American woman to lead a major American company and the first woman to succeed another woman in that role.

She began working at Xerox 30 years earlier as a mechanical engineering summer intern. After earning her bachelor's and master's degrees in that field, she worked in various areas of the corporation, including office network printing, global research, product development, manufacturing, and planning.

When Burns was named Xerox's president in 2007, her leadership role expanded to include the information technology, corporate marketing, and human resources departments.

Forbes and *Fortune* have named Burns as one of the most powerful women in the world. She serves as advisor to several educational and community organizations, including FIRST (For Inspiration and Recognition of Science and Technology) and the White House's STEM (Science, Technology, Engineering, and Math) program.

 For more information, visit the Computer Concepts CourseMate Web site at www.cengagebrain.com and then navigate to the Chapter 5 Technology Trailblazers resource for this book.

Chapter Review

The Chapter Review reinforces the main concepts presented in this chapter.

To listen to an audio version of this Chapter Review, visit the Computer Concepts CourseMate Web site at www.cengagebrain.com and then navigate to the Chapter 5 Chapter Review resource for this book.

1. **What Keys and Buttons Commonly Are Found on Desktop Computer Keyboards, and How Do Keyboards for Mobile Computers and Devices Differ from Desktop Computer Keyboards?** A **keyboard** is an input device that contains keys users press to enter data and instructions into a computer. Desktop computer keyboards have a typing area that includes letters of the alphabet, numbers, punctuation marks, and other basic keys. An enhanced keyboard also has function keys programmed to issue commands, a numeric keypad, arrow keys, and additional keys and buttons. On mobile computers and devices, the keyboard is built into the system unit. Keyboards on these devices usually are smaller and have fewer keys than desktop computer keyboards. Some smart phones have a mini-keyboard or on-screen keyboard.

2. **What Are the Different Mouse Types?** An **optical mouse** uses devices that emit and sense light to detect the mouse's movement. A **laser mouse** uses a laser to detect movement. An **air mouse** is a motion-sensing mouse that you can move through the air. A wireless, or cordless, mouse transmits data using wireless technology.

3. **What Are the Various Types of Touch Screens, and How Does a Touch-Sensitive Pad Work?** A **touch screen** is a touch-sensitive display device that you interact with by touching areas of the screen. A **kiosk** is a freestanding computer that includes a touch screen. **Microsoft Surface** is a tabletop display that allows users to interact with the screen using their fingers or hands. A **touch-sensitive pad** enables users to scroll through and play music, view pictures, watch videos or movies, adjust volume, and/or customize settings on a portable media player or other mobile device. Touch-sensitive pads typically contain buttons and/or wheels that are operated with a thumb or finger.

4. **What Are the Various Types of Pen Input?** With **pen input**, you touch a **stylus** or a **digital pen** on a flat surface to write, draw, or make selections. A **signature capture pad** captures handwritten signatures. A **graphics tablet** can be connected to a computer that does not include a touch screen in order to use pen input.

Visit the Computer Concepts CourseMate Web site at www.cengagebrain.com, navigate to the Chapter 5 Quiz Yourself resource for this book, and then click Objectives 1 – 4.

5. **What Are Other Types of Input?** Video and computer games use a **game controller** as the input device. Game controllers include a **gamepad**, which controls the movement and actions of players or objects in video games or computer games; a **joystick**, which is a handheld vertical lever mounted on a base; a **wheel**, which is a steering-wheel-type input device; a **light gun**, which is used to shoot targets; and a **dance pad**, which users press with their feet in response to instructions. The **Wii Remote** is a type of motion-sensing game controller. For smart phones, you can talk directly into the microphone or headset. Some smart phones have digital cameras and touch-sensitive pads. A digital camera's **resolution** is the number of horizontal and vertical pixels in a display device. **Video input** is the process of capturing full-motion pictures and storing them on a computer's storage medium. A **Web cam** is used for video input. A **video conference** is a meeting between two or more geographically separate people who use a network to transmit audio and video data. A **scanner** is a light-sensing input device that reads printed text and graphics and translates the results into a form a computer can process. An optical reader is a device that uses a light source to read characters, marks, and codes and converts them into digital data. **OCR (optical character recognition)** devices use a small optical scanner and software to analyze characters from ordinary documents. **OMR (optical mark recognition)** devices read hand-drawn marks on a form. A **bar code reader** uses laser beams to read bar codes. An **RFID device** reads information on an embedded tag via radio waves. A **magnetic stripe card reader** reads the magnetic stripe on the back of credit cards and other similar cards. **MICR** (magnetic-ink character recognition) devices read text printed with magnetized ink. Biometric input can include fingerprints, hand geometry, facial features, voice, signatures, and eye patterns.

Visit the Computer Concepts CourseMate Web site at www.cengagebrain.com, navigate to the Chapter 5 Quiz Yourself resource for this book, and then click Objective 5.

6. **What Are the Characteristics of LCD Monitors, LCD Screens, and CRT Monitors?** A **display device** is a commonly used **output device** that visually conveys text, graphics, and video information. An **LCD monitor** is a desktop monitor that uses a liquid crystal display. A **liquid crystal display (LCD)** uses a liquid compound to present information on a display device. A **CRT monitor** is a desktop monitor that contains a cathode-ray tube. The popularity of CRT monitors is declining.

Visit the Computer Concepts CourseMate Web site at www.cengagebrain.com, navigate to the Chapter 5 Quiz Yourself resource for this book, and then click Objective 6.

7. What Are Various Types of Printers? A **printer** is an output device that produces text and graphics on a physical medium. An **ink-jet printer** forms characters and graphics by spraying tiny drops of ink onto paper. A **photo printer** produces photo-lab-quality pictures. A **laser printer** is a high-speed, high-quality printer that operates in a manner similar to a copy machine. A **multifunction peripheral** is a single device that looks like a computer or copy machine but provides the functionality of a printer, scanner, copy machine, and possibly a fax machine. A **thermal printer** generates images by pushing electrically heated pins against heat-sensitive paper. A **mobile printer** is a small, battery-powered printer used to print from a notebook computer, or mobile device. **Plotters** are used to produce high-quality drawings in specialized fields. A **large-format printer** creates large, photo-realistic-quality color prints. A **dot-matrix printer** is an impact printer that produces an image when tiny wire pins on a print head strike an inked ribbon. A **line printer** prints an entire line at a time.

8. What Are the Purposes and Features of Speakers, Headphones, and Earbuds; Data Projectors; and Interactive Whiteboards? **Speakers** are a type of **audio output device** added to computers to generate higher-quality sounds. Only the individual wearing headphones or earbuds hears the sound from the computer. The difference is that **headphones** cover or are placed outside of the ear, whereas **earbuds** rest inside the ear canal. A **data projector** takes the text and images displaying on a computer screen and projects them on a larger screen for an audience. An **interactive whiteboard** is a touch-sensitive device, resembling a dry-erase board, that displays the image on a connected computer screen.

9. What Are Input and Output Options for Physically Challenged Users? **Voice recognition** is an input option for visually impaired users. Input options for people with limited hand mobility include keyboards with larger keys, on-screen keyboards, and head-mounted pointers. Hearing-impaired users can instruct programs to display words instead of sounds. Visually impaired users can change Windows settings to make words easier to read. Blind users can use voice output and a Braille printer.

Visit the Computer Concepts CourseMate Web site at www.cengagebrain.com, navigate to the Chapter 5 Quiz Yourself resource for this book, and then click Objectives 7 – 9.

Key Terms

You should know each key term. The list below helps focus your study.

To see an example of and a definition for each term, and to access current and additional information about the term from the Web, visit the Computer Concepts CourseMate Web site at www.cengagebrain.com and then navigate to the Chapter 5 Key Terms resource for this book.

air mouse (191)	flatbed scanner (200)	Microsoft Surface (193)	resolution (198)
all-in-one device (215)	game controller (196)	mobile printer (216)	RFID (201)
Americans with Disabilities Act (ADA) (220)	gamepad (196)	monitor (207)	RFID reader (201)
audio input (198)	graphics tablet (194)	mouse (191)	scanner (200)
audio output device (217)	headphones (218)	multifunction peripheral (215)	signature capture pad (194)
automated teller machine (ATM) (204)	headset (218)	nonimpact printer (213)	speakers (217)
bar code (201)	impact printer (217)	OCR devices (200)	speech recognition (198)
bar code reader (201)	ink-jet printer (213)	optical character recognition (OCR) (200)	stylus (194)
biometrics (202)	input (188)		terminal (204)
Click Wheel (193)	input device (188)	optical mark recognition (OMR) (200)	thermal printer (215)
CRT monitor (210)	interactive whiteboard (218)	optical mouse (191)	toner (214)
dance pad (196)	joystick (196)	output (206)	touch screen (193)
data projector (218)	keyboard (190)	output device (206)	touch-sensitive pad (193)
digital camera (197)	kiosk (193)	PC video camera (199)	touchpad (192)
digital pen (194)	large-format printer (216)	pen input (194)	trackball (192)
digital photo printer (215)	laser mouse (191)	photo printer (214)	turnaround document (200)
digital video (DV) camera (199)	laser printer (214)	PictBridge (214)	video conference (199)
display device (207)	LCD monitor (208)	pixel (198)	video input (199)
dot-matrix printer (217)	light gun (196)	plasma monitor (210)	video telephone call (199)
DVD kiosk (205)	line printer (217)	plotters (216)	voice input (198)
earbuds (218)	liquid crystal display (LCD) (209)	pointer (189)	voice output (218)
earphones (218)	magnetic stripe card reader (201)	pointing device (189)	voice recognition (198)
ergonomics (190)	MICR (202)	pointing stick (192)	Web cam (199)
fingerprint reader (202)	MICR reader (202)	POS terminal (204)	wheel (196)
		printer (211)	widescreen (208)
			Wii Remote (197)

Checkpoint

The Checkpoint exercises test your knowledge of the chapter concepts. The page number containing the answer appears in parentheses after each exercise.

To complete the Checkpoint exercises interactively, visit the Computer Concepts CourseMate Web site at www.cengagebrain.com and then navigate to the Chapter 5 Checkpoint resource for this book.

Multiple Choice Select the best answer.

1. An ergonomic keyboard _____. (190)
   a. has a design that reduces wrist and hand injuries
   b. transmits data using wireless technology
   c. is used to enter data into a biometric device
   d. is built into the top of a handheld computer

2. A _____ is a small metal or plastic device that looks like a tiny ink pen but uses pressure instead of ink. (194)
   a. touch screen
   b. stylus
   c. trackball
   d. pointing stick

3. Architects, mapmakers, designers, artists, and home users create drawings and sketches on a _____. (194)
   a. trackball
   b. smart terminal
   c. graphics tablet
   d. touchpad

4. _____ is the computer's capability of distinguishing spoken words. (198)
   a. Voice input
   b. VoIP
   c. MIDI
   d. Voice recognition

5. RFID is a technology that uses _____ to communicate with a tag placed in or attached to an object, an animal, or a person. (201)
   a. a thin wire
   b. pixels
   c. radio signals
   d. light waves

6. The speed of an ink-jet printer is measured by the number of _____ it can print. (213)
   a. lines per page (lpp)
   b. dots per inch (dpi)
   c. characters per second (cps)
   d. pages per minute (ppm)

7. The primary disadvantage of multifunction peripherals is that _____. (215)
   a. if the multifunction peripheral breaks down, all functions are lost
   b. they all use laser-printer technology
   c. they are significantly more expensive than purchasing each device separately
   d. all of the above

8. Basic _____ are inexpensive, but the print quality is low and the images tend to fade over time. (215)
   a. laser printers
   b. thermal printers
   c. dot-matrix printers
   d. line printers

Matching Match the terms with their definitions.

_____ 1. kiosk (193)

_____ 2. turnaround document (200)

_____ 3. biometrics (202)

_____ 4. POS terminal (204)

_____ 5. headset (218)

a. technology of authenticating a person's identity by verifying a personal characteristic

b. a device that functions as both headphones and a microphone

c. self-service banking machine that connects to a host computer through a network

d. freestanding computer that includes a touch screen

e. a document that you return to the company that creates and sends it

f. used by most retail stores to record purchases, process credit or debit cards, and update inventory

Short Answer Write a brief answer to each of the following questions.

1. How are an optical mouse, an air mouse, and a wireless mouse different? _____ How is a trackball used? _____

2. How does a signature capture pad work? _____ How is an RFID reader used? _____

3. What is a DVD kiosk? _____ How might a DVD kiosk function for a customer? _____

4. What type of monitor emits electromagnetic radiation? _____ What can you do to protect yourself from electromagnetic radiation from a monitor? _____

5. How does an ink-jet printer work? _____ What are the differences between dye-sublimation printers used by professionals as compared to home or small business users? _____

Problem Solving

The Problem Solving exercises extend your knowledge of the chapter concepts by seeking solutions to practical computer problems that you may encounter at home, school, or work. The Collaboration exercise should be completed with a team.

In the real world, practical problems often can be solved in multiple ways. Provide one solution to each of the following problems using available resources, such as articles on the Web or in print, blogs, podcasts, videos, television, user guides, other individuals, and electronics and computer stores. You may need to use multiple resources to obtain an answer. Present your solutions in the form requested by your instructor (brief report, presentation, discussion, or other means).

@ Home

1. **No Media Controls** You have purchased a new keyboard for your three-year-old computer. When you connect the keyboard to your computer's USB port, you are able to type, but the media controls do not work. What could be the problem?

2. **Smeared Printouts** Each time you print a picture on photo paper using your photo printer, the photo comes out of the printer smeared. What is one step you can take that might prevent the ink from smearing while the photo is printing?

3. **Dim Screen** While using your notebook computer, the screen suddenly becomes dim. You set the brightness to its highest setting before it dimmed, and wonder why it suddenly changed. After resetting the brightness to its highest setting, you continue working. What might have caused the screen to dim?

4. **Malfunctioning Earbud** While listening to music on your portable media player, one side of your earbuds suddenly stops working. What might have caused this?

@ Work

5. **Fingerprint Not Recognized** To increase security, your company now requires employees to log into their computers using a fingerprint reader instead of entering a user name and password. This past weekend, you cut the finger you use to log in, and your computer now does not recognize your fingerprint. As a result, you are unable to access your computer. What are your next steps?

6. **Access Denied** Your company uses security badges with embedded RFID tags to authenticate the rooms to which employees have access. This badge also grants employees access to the company's parking lot. When arriving at work one morning, you wave your badge in front of the RFID reader, but the gate that allows access to the parking lot does not rise. In addition, a red light blinks on the RFID reader. What are your next steps?

7. **Unrecognizable Characters** Because of budget cuts, you and your coworkers no longer have printers connected to your computers and must print to a printer connected to the company network. You started to print a 40-page document, but realized immediately that you needed to make one more change to the document, so you cancelled the print job. After making the correction and printing the document again, you walk to the printer only to find the printer printing many pages with unrecognizable characters. What might be wrong?

8. **Monitors Reversed** You have two monitors set up on your desk at work: the monitor on the left is your primary monitor and displays the taskbar, and you typically use the monitor on the right to display your e-mail program. When you arrive at work and log into Windows, you realize that the monitor on the right is now the primary monitor. What might have happened?

Collaboration

9. **Computers in Space Exploration** The space tourism industry is gaining worldwide attention. Many more people might express interest in experiencing outer space if prices become more reasonable and safety concerns are minimized. Computers help ensure safety by helping the space vehicles to fly with great precision, but human intervention also is necessary. Form a team of three people and determine how computer output can provide enough information to ensure a safe experience. One team member should research current space exploration and data returned from space vehicles that proved useful. Another team member should research how space vehicles collect this data and present it in a useful form, and the other team member should think of additional ways that computer output can assist in space exploration. Write a brief report summarizing your findings.

Learn How To

The Learn How To activities step you through fundamental technology skills when using a computer. The Learn How To exercises enable you to become more proficient with these skills.

Premium Activity: To relate this Learn How To activity to your everyday life, see a visual demonstration of the activity, and complete a short assessment, visit the Computer Concepts CourseMate Web site at www.cengagebrain.com and then navigate to the Chapter 5 Learn How To resources for this book.

Learn How To 1: Make a Video and Upload It to YouTube

As digital video cameras become smaller and more affordable, many individuals are choosing to create digital recordings of everyday events. In the past, video cameras were bulky, expensive, and required big VCR tapes. Video cameras now are digital and small enough to take anywhere. They also have the capability to transfer video footage to a computer, allowing you to reuse tapes. The increase in individuals storing videos on their computer has prompted companies to develop media sharing Web sites, such as YouTube, for people to post their videos online for others to view. This is especially helpful when you would like to share a video of a memorable event, such as your child's first steps, with a relative across the country who was unable to experience it in person.

Transferring a Video from a Digital Video Camera to a Computer

1. Connect the digital video camera to a computer using the provided USB or FireWire cable. If the camera does not have a cable and stores the digital video on a memory card, remove the memory card from the camera and then insert it into the computer.
2. You can transfer the video from the digital video camera to a computer in one or more of the following ways, depending upon the type of camera you own:
   a. Start the program that came with the digital video camera and follow the manufacturer's instructions for importing the video to a hard disk.
   b. When the digital video camera or memory card is displayed as a removable disk in Windows, copy the video file(s) to a hard disk.
   c. Open Windows Live Movie Maker and click the 'Import from device' command on the Movie Maker menu to import video from the digital video camera.
3. Your video should be less than 10 minutes, less than 2 GB in size, and one of the following file formats: .AVI, .MOV, .WMV, or .MPG. If your video does not meet these requirements, you either should create your video again or use software such as Windows Live Movie Maker to change its file format or reduce its length or size.
4. Double-click the video on the computer to make sure that it plays in its entirety and that you can hear audio.
5. If you would like to free space on a digital camera's media, delete the original video file(s) from the digital video camera or memory card.
6. Disconnect the digital video camera from the computer or remove the memory card from the computer.

Log into YouTube

1. Start a Web browser, type youtube.com in the Address bar, and then press the ENTER key to display the YouTube – Broadcast Yourself Web page.
2. Click the Sign In link.
3. Type your user name and password, and then click the Sign In button. If you do not have a YouTube account, click the Sign up for YouTube! link and follow the instructions to sign up for a new YouTube account.

Upload the Video

1. Click a Upload button to display the Video File Upload Web page.
2. Click the Upload Video button to display the 'Select file to upload' dialog box. Locate the video on your computer that you wish to upload and then click the Open button.
3. If necessary, change the title of the video to one you prefer.
4. Enter the description and tags for this video. If you would like to make it easy for people to find your video, enter a detailed description and several tags.
5. Select a video category from the Category drop-down list.
6. If you want to make the video private, click the 'Private (Viewable by you and up to 25 people)' option button.

7. Click the Save Changes button.

8. YouTube will save your changes once the video is finished uploading.

View the Video

1. Point to your user name at the top of the Video File Upload Web page and then click My Videos.

2. Click the Play button to preview the video. Once the video has finished playing, click the Sign Out link to sign out of YouTube.

Exercise

1. Use a digital video camera to create a short video that is less than 20 seconds in length. Save the video to your computer and then sign into YouTube. Upload the video you just created (if you do not have a digital video camera, upload a sample video that is included with Windows or another video on your computer that is not protected by copyright). Once the video has finished uploading, preview it and then send the Web address to your instructor.

Learn It Online

The Learn It Online exercises are interactive Web exercises designed to reinforce and expand your understanding of the chapter concepts. The descriptions below briefly summarize each exercise.

To complete the Learn It Online exercises, visit the Computer Concepts CourseMate Web site at www.cengagebrain.com, navigate to the Chapter 5 resources for this book, click the link for the exercise you want to complete, and then read the instructions.

1 At the Movies — Video Editing on Your Computer

Watch a movie to learn about simple editing tips for converting raw video footage into interesting videos.

2 Student Edition Labs — Peripheral Devices

Enhance your understanding and knowledge about the motherboard and binary numbers by completing the Peripheral Devices Lab.

3 Practice Test

Take a multiple choice test that checks your knowledge of the chapter concepts and review the resulting study guide.

4 Who Wants To Be a Computer Genius²?

Play the Shelly Cashman Series version of this popular game by answering questions to find out if you are a computer genius. Panic buttons are available to provide assistance during game play.

5 Crossword Puzzle Challenge

Complete an interactive crossword puzzle to reinforce concepts presented in this chapter.

6 Windows Exercises

Step through the Windows 7 exercises to learn about your computer, Accessibility options, Magnifier, and adjusting the sound on a computer.

7 Exploring Computer Careers

Read about a career as a graphic designer/illustrator, search for related employment advertisements, and then answer related questions.

8 Web Apps — YouSendIt

Learn how to use YouSendIt to create an e-mail message with an attachment and add options such as premium delivery, password-protected secure delivery, certified delivery with tracking, and return receipt.

Web Research

The Web Research exercises broaden your understanding of the chapter concepts by presenting questions that require you to search Web for answers.

1 Search Sleuth

Use one of the search engines listed in Figure 2-8 in Chapter 2 on page 65 or your own favorite search engine to find the answers to the following questions. Copy and paste the Web address from the Web page where you found the answer. Some questions may have more than one answer. If required, submit your answers to your instructor. (1) Which Haruhi Suzumiya games have been released for the Nintendo Wii? (2) Which two companies worked in partnership with Kodak to develop kiosks with digital image-making software? (3) Which countries have adopted the ENERGY STAR program? (4) What invention relating to the printing industry did Lord Kelvin patent in 1867? (5) Which output devices did Donald Bitzer design for the PLATO IV computer assisted instruction system at the University of Illinois? (6) Which country has imposed a maximum limit of 100 decibels on all headphones and earbuds sold?

2 Green Computing

Digital cameras use more battery power than film cameras because they operate electronic image sensors, LCD viewfinders, and flashes. They also write images to storage devices. The battery packs discharge whether you snap photos or not, but you can help extend your digital camera's battery life by following some conservation tips. View online Web sites, including The Battery Bank (batterybank.net), MalekTips (malektips.com/digital_camera_battery_help_and_tips.html), and Associated Content (associatedcontent.com) that provide information about charging battery packs, using cameras, and storing batteries. How do nickel cadmium (Ni-Cd), nickel metal hydride (Ni-MH), and lithium ion (Li-ion) batteries differ in charging time and discharge? How should batteries be stored if cameras are used infrequently? How does conditioning affect "memory effect"? Write a report summarizing your findings, and include a table of links to Web sites that provide additional details.

3 Social Networking

Each day, more than 100,000 people register for Friendster, which is one of the top three online social networking Web sites in the world. The San Francisco-based company is popular in more than 75 countries, particularly in Asia. Its mobile Web site, m.friendster.com, allows the more than 110 million registered users to receive and send messages using their smart phones. Visit the Friendster Web site (friendster.com). Follow the instructions to create a Friendster account, log in, and then click the Explore link at the top of the home page. Who are some musicians, athletes, and artists featured in the Fan Profiles section? Click the Classifieds link and then select a city in the Location area. What types of computer listings are shown in the Services area? Click the About Us link at the bottom of the page and then click the Testimonials link. What do members like about Friendster? Summarize the information you read and viewed.

4 Blogs

Whether you are listening to the radio, watching television, or drinking a beverage at the local coffee shop, the world of sports is likely to surface. People are passionate about their favorite athletes and sporting events, from the community Little League game to the NFL Super Bowl. Visit several sports blogs, including those from Fanblogs (fanblogs.com), BC Sports (blogcritics.org/sports), Deadspin (deadspin.com), Full Throttle (fullthrottle.cranialcavity .net), ESPN (sports.espn.go.com/espn/blog), and Fox Sports (community.foxsports.com/blogs). What are the more popular discussions? Which college football and basketball teams are featured? Who are the professional athletes receiving much discussion? Which NASCAR teams are analyzed?

5 Ethics in Action

"Netomania" is not a recognized disorder, but this popular name for Internet Addiction Disorder (IAD) may be affecting some Internet users who spend many hours gaming, blogging, shopping, and social networking. People may be addicted when they spend up to 10 hours a day online, they occasionally binge for extended Internet sessions, and they suffer withdrawal symptoms when they have not been online for some time. Some researchers, however, believe the Internet problem is just a symptom of other psychiatric disorders, such as manic depression. View online sites that provide information about IAD, including the Center for Internet Addiction Recovery (netaddiction.com). Write a report summarizing your findings, and include a table of links to Web sites that provide additional details.

Digital Video Technology

Everywhere you look, people are capturing moments they want to remember. They shoot movies of their vacations, birthday parties, activities, accomplishments, sporting events, weddings, and more. Because of the popularity of digital video cameras and mobile devices with built-in digital cameras, increasingly more people desire to capture their memories digitally, instead of on film. As shown in Figure 1, people have the ability to modify and share the digital videos they create. When you use special hardware and/or software, you can copy, manipulate, and distribute digital videos using your personal computer and the Internet. Amateurs can achieve professional quality results by using more sophisticated hardware and software. This feature describes how to select a video camera, record a video, transfer and manage videos, edit a video, and distribute a video.

Digital recordings deliver significant benefits over film-based movie making. With digital video cameras, recordings reside on storage media such as a hard disk, optical disc,

or memory card. Unlike film, storage media can be reused, which reduces costs, saves time, and provides immediate results. Digital technology allows greater control over the creative process, both while recording video and in the editing process. You can check results immediately after capturing a video to determine whether it meets your expectations. If you are dissatisfied with a video, you can erase it and recapture it, again and again. Today, many mobile devices, such as smart phones and PDAs, allow you to capture video.

As shown in Figure 1, digital video cameras, and mobile devices function as input devices when they transmit video to a personal computer. You can transmit video by connecting the video camera or mobile device to your personal computer using a USB or FireWire port, or by placing the storage media used on the camera or mobile device in the computer. Some cameras and devices also can transmit wirelessly to a computer or to the media sharing Web sites.

digital video-enabled smart phone

PDA

digital video camera

media sharing Web site

television

personal computer

optical disc drive

e-mail message

Figure 1   A variety of input, output, and storage devices are used by home users to process and edit digital video.

When you transmit video that was captured with a digital video camera or mobile device to a computer, you can edit the video using video editing software. If desired, you often can preview the video during the editing process on a television. Finally, you save the finished result to the desired media, such as an optical disc or, perhaps, e-mail the edited video or post it to a media sharing Web site. In this example, an optical disc drive also can be used to input video from an optical disc. Also in the example shown in Figure 1 on the previous page, a mobile device that includes a video camera sends a video directly to a media sharing Web site.

Digital video technology allows you to input, edit, manage, publish, and share your videos using a personal computer. With digital video technology, you can transform home videos into Hollywood-style movies by enhancing the videos with scrolling titles and transitions, cutting out or adding scenes, and adding background music and voice-over narration. The following sections outline the steps involved in the process of using digital video technology.

1 Select a Video Camera

Video cameras record in either analog or digital format. **Analog formats** include 8mm, Hi8, VHS-C, and Super VHS-C. **Digital formats** include Mini-DV, MICROMV, Digital8, DVD, Blu-ray, and HDV (high-definition video format). Some digital video cameras record on an internal hard disk. Others may allow you to record directly on an optical disc drive. Digital video cameras fall into three general categories: high-end consumer, consumer, and webcasting and monitoring (Figure 2). Consumer digital video cameras are by far the most popular type among consumers. High-end consumer models may support the Blu-ray or HDV standards. A video recorded in high-definition can be played back on a high-definition display. Many mobile devices allow you to record video that you later can transmit to your computer or e-mail from the device. Some devices allow you to upload video directly to video sharing Web sites. Digital video cameras provide more features than analog video cameras, such as a higher level of zoom, better sound, or greater control over color and lighting.

2 Record a Video

Most video cameras provide you with a choice of recording programs, which sometimes are called automatic settings. Each recording program includes a different combination of camera settings, so that you can adjust the exposure and other functions to match the recording environment. Usually, several different programs are available, such as point-and-shoot, point-and-shoot with manual adjustment, sports, portrait, spotlit scenes, and low light. You also have the ability to select special digital effects, such as fade, wipe, and black and white. If you are shooting outside on a windy day, then you can enable the windscreen to prevent wind noise. If you are shooting home videos or video meant for a Web site, then the point-and-shoot recording program is sufficient.

3 Transfer and Manage Videos

After recording the video, the next step is to transfer the video to your personal computer or to the Internet. Most video cameras connect directly to a USB or FireWire port on a personal computer (Figure 3). Transferring video with a

Figure 2 The high-end consumer digital video camera can produce professional-grade results. The consumer digital video camera produces amateur-grade results. The webcasting and monitoring digital video camera is appropriate for webcasting and security monitoring.

Figure 3 A digital video camera is connected to the personal computer or DVD/Blu-ray Disc recorder via a USB or FireWire port. No additional hardware is needed.

digital camera or mobile device is easy, because the video already is in a digital format that the computer can recognize. Many mobile devices include a special cable used to connect the device to a personal computer or allow you to transfer the videos to a media sharing Web site or your own Web site.

Some people own analog format video tapes that require additional hardware to convert the analog signals to a digital format before the video can be manipulated on a personal computer. The additional hardware includes a special video capture card using a standard RCA video cable or an S-video cable (Figure 4). **S-video** cables provide sharper images and greater overall quality. A personal computer also can record video to an optical disc, or it can be connected to an external DVD/Blu-ray Disc recorder to record videos. Video conversion services often specialize in converting older analog video to a variety of digital formats.

When transferring video, plan to use approximately 15 to 30 GB of hard disk storage per hour of digital video. High-definition formats may require much more storage per hour. A typical video project requires about four times the amount of raw footage as the final product. At the high end, therefore, a video that lasts an hour may require up to 120 GB of storage for the raw footage, editing process, and final video. This storage requirement can vary depending on the software you use to copy the video from the video camera to the hard disk and the format you select to save the video. For example, Microsoft's Windows Live Movie Maker can save 15 hours of standard video in 10 GB when creating video for playback on a computer, but saves only 1 hour of video in 10 GB when creating video for playback on a DVD. A high-definition video file may require more than 10 GB per hour.

The video transfer requires application software on the personal computer (Figure 5). The Windows Live Movie Maker software, available as a free download from Microsoft's Web site, allows you to transfer the video from

Figure 5   Some video editing software allows you to transfer a video from any video source to a hard disk.

a video camera. Depending on the length of video and the type of connection used, the video may take a long time to transfer. Make certain that no other programs are running on your personal computer while transferring the video.

The frame rate of a video refers to the number of frames per second (fps) that are captured in the video. The most widely used frame rate is 30 fps. A smaller frame rate results in a smaller file size for the video, but playback of the video will not be as smooth as one recorded with a higher frame rate.

When transferring video, the software may allow you to choose a file format and a codec to store the video. A video **file format** holds the video information in a manner specified by a vendor, such as Apple or Microsoft. Six of the more popular file formats are listed in Figure 6. The 3GP format is widely used on mobile devices.

File formats support codecs to encode the audio and video into the file formats. A **codec** specifies how the audio and video is compressed and stored within the file. A particular file format may be able to store audio and video in a number of

Figure 4   An analog camcorder or VCR is connected to the personal computer via an S-video port on a video capture card.

Popular Video File Formats

File Format	File Extensions
Apple QuickTime	.MOV or .QT
DivX	.DIVX
Microsoft Windows Media Video	.WMV or .ASF
MPEG-4 Part 4	.MP4
Real RealMedia	.RM or .RAM
3GP	.3GP or .3G2

Figure 6   Apple, DivX, Microsoft, and Real offer the more popular video file formats.

different codecs. Figure 7 shows some options available for specifying a file format and video quality settings in a video capture program. The file format and codec you choose often is based on what you plan to do with the movie. For example, if you plan to upload your video to the YouTube video sharing Web site, the best choices are DivX and MPEG-4 file formats. Many users find that they are unable to play their own or others' videos, and the problem often is that the proper codec is not installed on the user's personal computer. Video conversion software often allows the user to convert a video in a less popular format to a better supported format. Many of these programs are available as freeware.

After transferring the video to a personal computer or the Internet, and before manipulating the video, you should store the video files in appropriate folders, named correctly, and backed up. Most video transfer application software helps manage these tasks.

4 Edit a Video

Once the video is stored on your hard disk or the Internet, the next step is to edit, or manipulate, the video. If you used a video capture card to transfer analog video to the computer (Figure 4 on the previous page), the files may require extra initial processing. Some Web sites allow you to perform minor editing and other tasks on the Web site. When you use a video capture card, some of the video frames may be lost in the transfer process. Some video editing programs allow you to fix this problem with **frame rate correction** tools.

The first step in the editing process is to split the video into smaller pieces, or scenes, that you can manipulate more easily. This process is called splitting. Most video software automatically splits the video into scenes, thus sparing you the task. After splitting, you should delete unwanted scenes or portions of scenes. This process is called pruning.

After creating the scenes you want to use in the final production, you edit each individual scene. You can crop, or change the size of, scenes. That is, you may want to delete the top or a side of a scene that is irrelevant. You also can resize the scene. For example, you may be creating a video that will be displayed on a media sharing Web site. Making a smaller video, such as 320 × 200 pixels, instead of 640 × 480 pixels, results in a smaller file that transmits faster over the Internet. Some media sharing Web sites recommend smaller video resolutions, such as 320 × 200 pixels, and some will perform the conversion for you automatically.

Figure 7 Video editing software allows you to specify a combination of file format and video quality settings when saving a video.

If a video has been recorded over a long period, using different cameras or under different lighting conditions, the video may need color correction. Color correction tools analyze your video and match brightness, colors, and other attributes of video clips to ensure a smooth look to the video (Figure 8).

You can add logos, special effects, or titles to scenes. You can place a company logo or personal logo in a video to identify yourself or the company producing the video. Logos often are added on the lower-right corner of a video and remain for the duration of the video. Special effects include warping, changing from color to black and white, morphing, or zoom motion. Morphing is a special effect in which one video image is transformed into another image over the course of several frames of video, creating the illusion of metamorphosis. You usually add titles at the beginning and ending of a video to give the video context. A training video may have titles throughout the video to label a particular scene, or each scene may begin with a title.

The next step in editing a video is to add audio effects, including voice-over narration and background music. Many video editing programs allow you to add additional tracks, or layers, of sound to a video in addition to the sound that was recorded on the video camera or mobile device. You also can add special audio effects.

The final step in editing a video is to combine the scenes into a complete video (Figure 9). This process involves ordering scenes and adding transition effects between scenes. Video editing software allows you to combine scenes and separate each scene with a transition. Transitions include fading, wiping, blurry, bursts, ruptures, erosions, and more.

Figure 8 Color correction tools in video editing software allow a great deal of control over the mood of your video creation.

Figure 9 Scenes are combined into a sequence on the bottom of the screen.

5 Distribute the Video

After editing the video, the final step is to distribute it or save it on an appropriate medium. You can save video in a variety of formats. Video recorded on a mobile device often requires conversion to a more widely accepted format.

Video also can be stored in digital formats in any of several optical disc formats or on a media sharing Web site. **Optical disc creation software**, which often is packaged with video editing software, allows you to create, or master, optical discs. You can add interactivity to your optical disc creations. For example, you can allow viewers to jump to certain scenes using a menu.

You also can save your video creation in electronic format for distribution over the Web, via e-mail, or to a mobile device. Some cameras include a button that allows users to upload directly to a media sharing Web site. Popular media sharing Web sites, such as YouTube (Figure 10), have recommendations for the best file format and codecs to use

for video that you upload to them (Figure 11). Your video editing software must support the file format and codec you want to use. For example, Apple's iMovie software typically saves files in the QuickTime file format.

Professionals use hardware and software that allow them to create a film version of digital video that can be played in movie theaters. This technology is becoming increasingly popular. The cost of professional video editing software ranges from thousands to hundreds of thousands of dollars. Video editing software for the home user is available for a few hundred dollars or less. Some Hollywood directors believe that eventually all movies will be recorded and edited digitally.

After creating your final video for distribution or for your personal video collection, you should back up the final video file. You can save your scenes for inclusion in other video creations or create new masters using different effects, transitions, and ordering of scenes.

Figure 10 Media sharing Web sites allow you to share your videos with acquaintances or the entire world.

Figure 11 Media sharing Web sites, such as YouTube, provide tools that simplify the process of uploading videos to the site.

Chapter Six

Storage

Objectives

After completing this chapter, you will be able to:

1 Describe the characteristics of an internal hard disk including capacity, platters, read/write heads, cylinders, sectors and tracks, and revolutions per minute

2 Discuss the purpose of network attached storage devices, external and removable hard disks, and hard disk controllers

3 Describe the various types of flash memory storage: solid state drives, memory cards, USB flash drives, and ExpressCard modules

4 Describe cloud storage and explain its advantages

5 Describe the characteristics of optical discs

6 Differentiate among various types of optical discs: CDs, archive discs and Picture CDs, DVDs, and Blu-ray Discs

7 Identify the uses of tape, magnetic stripe cards, smart cards, microfilm and microfiche, and enterprise storage

Storage

Storage holds data, instructions, and information for future use. For example, all types of users store digital photos; appointments, schedules, and contact/address information; correspondence, such as letters, e-mail messages; tax records; and Web pages. A home user also might store budgets, bank statements, a household inventory, records of stock purchases, tax information, homework assignments, recipes, music, and videos. In addition or instead, a business user stores reports, financial records, travel records, customer orders and invoices, vendor payments, payroll records, inventory records, presentations, quotations, and contracts. Other users store diagrams, drawings, blueprints,

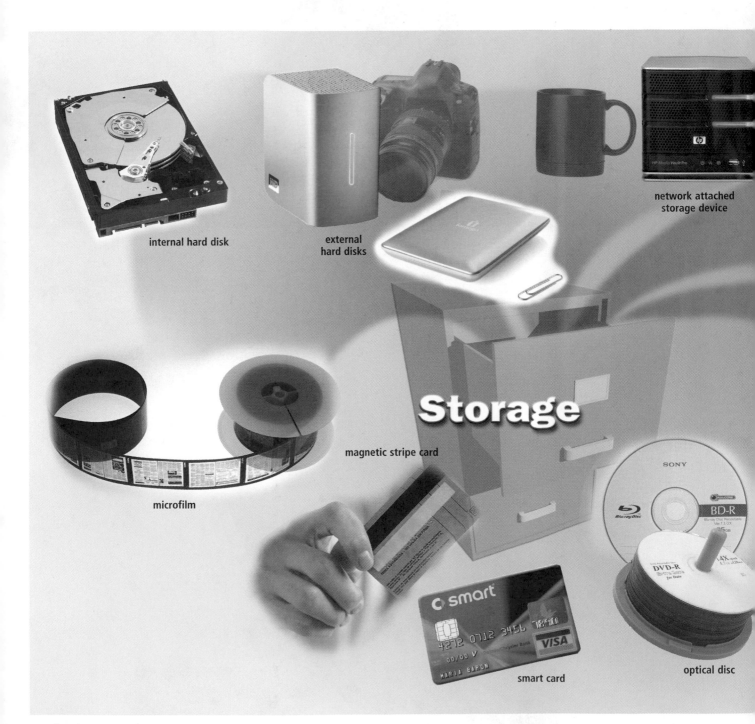

Figure 6-1 A variety of storage options.

designs, marketing literature, corporate newsletters, and product catalogs. All computers also store system and application software.

Storage requirements among users vary greatly. Home users typically have much smaller storage requirements than enterprise users. For example, a home user may need 320 GB (billion bytes) of storage, while enterprises may require 50 PB (quadrillion bytes) of storage.

A **storage medium** (media is the plural), also called **secondary storage**, is the physical material on which a computer keeps data, instructions, and information. Examples of storage media are hard disks, solid state drives, memory cards, USB flash drives, ExpressCard modules, optical discs, smart cards, magnetic stripe cards, and microfilm. Cloud storage is another storage option, in which the actual storage media used is transparent to the user. Figure 6-1 shows a variety of storage options.

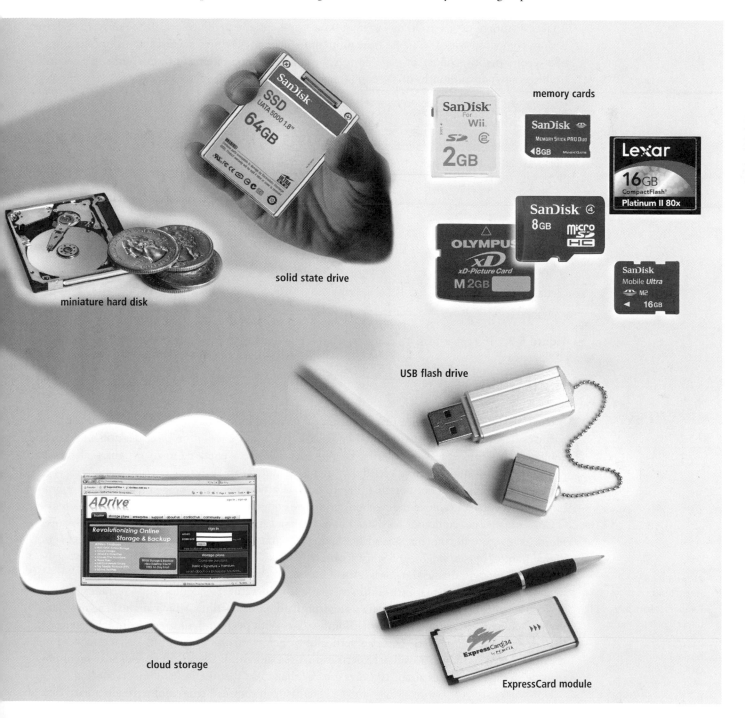

miniature hard disk

solid state drive

memory cards

USB flash drive

cloud storage

ExpressCard module

Capacity is the number of bytes (characters) a storage medium can hold. Figure 6-2 identifies the terms manufacturers use to define the capacity of storage media. For example, a reasonably priced USB flash drive can store up to 4 GB of data (approximately four billion bytes) and a typical hard disk has 320 GB (approximately 320 billion bytes) of storage capacity.

A **storage device** is the computer hardware that records and/or retrieves items to and from storage media. **Writing** is the process of transferring data, instructions, and information from memory to a storage medium. **Reading** is the process of transferring these items from a storage medium into memory. When storage devices write data on storage media, they are creating output. Similarly, when storage devices read from storage media, they function as a source of input. Nevertheless, they are categorized as storage devices, not as input or output devices.

The speed of storage devices is defined by access time. **Access time** measures the amount of time it takes a storage device to locate an item on a storage medium. The access time of storage devices is slow, compared with the access time of memory. Memory (chips) accesses items in billionths of a second (nanoseconds). Storage devices, by contrast, access items in thousandths of a second (milliseconds) or millionths of a second (microseconds).

Storage Terms

Storage Term	Approximate Number of Bytes	Exact Number of Bytes
Kilobyte (KB)	1 thousand	2^{10} or 1,024
Megabyte (MB)	1 million	2^{20} or 1,048,576
Gigabyte (GB)	1 billion	2^{30} or 1,073,741,824
Terabyte (TB)	1 trillion	2^{40} or 1,099,511,627,776
Petabyte (PB)	1 quadrillion	2^{50} or 1,125,899,906,842,624
Exabyte (EB)	1 quintillion	2^{60} or 1,152,921,504,606,846,976
Zettabyte (ZB)	1 sextillion	2^{70} or 1,180,591,620,717,411,303,424
Yottabyte (YB)	1 septillion	2^{80} or 1,208,925,819,614,629,174,706,176

Figure 6-2 The capacity of a storage medium is measured by the number of bytes it can hold.

Hard Disks

A **hard disk** is a storage device that contains one or more inflexible, circular platters that use magnetic particles to store data, instructions, and information. The system unit on most desktop and notebook computers contains at least one hard disk. The entire device is enclosed in an airtight, sealed case to protect it from contamination. A hard disk that is mounted inside the system unit sometimes is called a fixed disk because it is not portable (Figure 6-3). With respect to a storage medium, the term portable means you can remove the medium from one computer and carry it to another computer.

Current personal computer hard disks have storage capacities from 160 GB to 2 TB and more. Home users store documents, spreadsheets, presentations, databases, e-mail messages, Web pages, digital photos, music, videos, and software on hard disks. Businesses use hard disks to store correspondence, reports, financial records, e-mail messages, customer orders and invoices, payroll records, inventory records, presentations, contracts, marketing literature, schedules, and Web sites.

Traditionally, hard disks stored data using **longitudinal recording**, which aligned the magnetic particles horizontally around the surface of the disk. With **perpendicular recording**, by contrast, hard disks align the magnetic particles vertically, or perpendicular to the disk's surface, making much greater storage capacities possible. Experts estimate that hard disks using perpendicular recording provide storage capacities about 10 times greater than disks that use longitudinal recording.

Hard disks are read/write storage media. That is, you can read from and write on a hard disk any number of times. Read Ethics & Issues 6-1 for a related discussion.

Perpendicular Recording

For more information, visit the Computer Concepts CourseMate Web site at www.cengagebrain.com, navigate to the Chapter 6 Web Link resource for this book, and then click Perpendicular Recording.

hard disk
mounted inside
system unit

close-up of
hard disk

Figure 6-3 The hard disk in a desktop computer is enclosed inside an airtight, sealed case inside the system unit. (In this and other hard disk photos in the book, the top plate is removed from the hard disk for illustration purposes.)

? FAQ 6-1

To what degree are hard disk capacities increasing?

Hard disk capacities have increased at an exponential rate. Advancements in technology, such as perpendicular recording and enhanced read/write heads that can read and write denser areas on the platter, have resulted in a hard disk's capability of storing increasing amounts of data and information in a fixed amount of space. The chart to the right illustrates that the maximum hard disk size is growing.

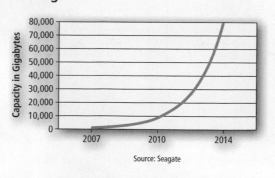

Source: Seagate

For more information, visit the Computer Concepts CourseMate Web site at www.cengagebrain.com, navigate to the Chapter 6 FAQ resource for this book, and then click Hard Disk Capacity.

Ethics & Issues

For the complete text of the Ethics & Issues boxes found in this chapter, visit the Computer Concepts CourseMate Web site at www.cengagebrain.com and then navigate to the Chapter 6 Ethics & Issues resource for this book.

ᚤ ETHICS & ISSUES 6-1

Should the Government Require Hard Disks to Be Cleaned?

An IT professional recently purchased a hard disk on an auction Web site only to find private banking records of several million people. Fortunately, the purchaser notified authorities, rather than use the data for nefarious purposes. In other incidents, taxpayer data and secret police tactics appeared on hard disks purchased on auction Web sites, donated to charitable organizations, or recovered from discarded computers. Most people do not realize that deleting files from a computer does not render the data permanently inaccessible. Deleted files can be recovered easily by a smart criminal or digital forensics examiner.

Experts recommend that special utility software, known as a wiping utility,

be used to clean the contents of a hard disk before it leaves possession of the owner. The government sets various disk wiping standards. For example, one standard requires that the software wipe the drive seven times, while a more stringent standard requires fourteen. Experts also recommend the use of full disk encryption, which is the process of encoding data and information into an unreadable form. Others recommend that any hard disk that at any time contained sensitive information be destroyed by a service company that specializes in hard disk destruction. Some companies now offer a service that allows you to keep a hard disk if it fails while covered by a warranty. Typically, companies

require that you return the damaged hard disk when you receive the replacement. Some people are not comfortable with this service, for fear of confidential information on the damaged hard disk falling into the wrong hands.

Should the government require that hard disks on sold, donated, or discarded computers be cleaned, encrypted, or destroyed? Why or why not? Would you make an extra effort to clean or encrypt the contents of hard disks on sold, donated, or discarded computers? Why or why not?

Characteristics of a Hard Disk

Characteristics of a hard disk include capacity, platters, read/write heads, cylinders, sectors and tracks, revolutions per minute, transfer rate, and access time. Figure 6-4 shows sample characteristics of a 1 TB hard disk. The following paragraphs discuss each of these characteristics.

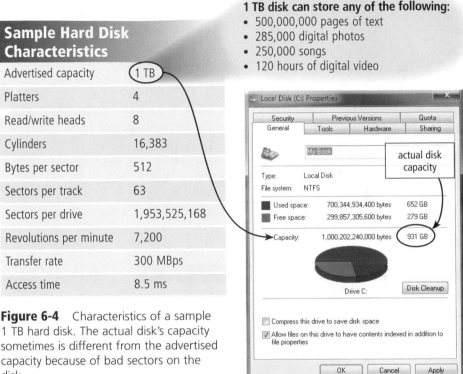

1 TB disk can store any of the following:
- 500,000,000 pages of text
- 285,000 digital photos
- 250,000 songs
- 120 hours of digital video

Sample Hard Disk Characteristics

Advertised capacity	1 TB
Platters	4
Read/write heads	8
Cylinders	16,383
Bytes per sector	512
Sectors per track	63
Sectors per drive	1,953,525,168
Revolutions per minute	7,200
Transfer rate	300 MBps
Access time	8.5 ms

Figure 6-4   Characteristics of a sample 1 TB hard disk. The actual disk's capacity sometimes is different from the advertised capacity because of bad sectors on the disk.

The capacity of a hard disk is determined from whether it uses longitudinal or perpendicular recording, the number of platters it contains, and the composition of the magnetic coating on the platters. A platter is made of aluminum, glass, or ceramic and is coated with an alloy material that allows items to be recorded magnetically on its surface. The coating usually is three millionths of an inch thick.

Magnetic disks store data and instructions in tracks and sectors (Figure 6-5). A track is a narrow recording band that forms a full circle on the surface of the disk. The disk's storage locations consist of pie-shaped sections, which break the tracks into small arcs called sectors. On a hard disk, a sector typically stores up to 512 bytes of data.

On desktop computers, platters most often have a size of approximately 3.5 inches in diameter. On notebook computers, mobile devices, and some servers, the diameter is 2.5 inches or less. A typical hard disk has multiple platters stacked on top of one another. Each platter has two read/write heads, one for each side. The hard disk has arms that move the read/write heads to the proper location on the platter (Figure 6-6).

The location of the read/write heads often is referred to by its cylinder. A cylinder is the vertical section of a track that passes through all platters (Figure 6-7). A single movement of the read/write head arms accesses all the platters in a cylinder. If a hard disk has two platters (four sides), each with 1,000 tracks, then it will have 1,000 cylinders with each cylinder consisting of 4 tracks (2 tracks for each platter).

Figure 6-5   Tracks form circles on the surface of a hard disk. The disk's storage locations are divided into pie-shaped sections, which break the tracks into small arcs called sectors.

While the computer is running, the platters in the hard disk rotate at a high rate of speed. This spinning, which usually is 5,400 to 15,000 revolutions per minute (rpm), allows nearly instant access to all tracks and sectors on the platters. The platters may continue to spin until power is removed from the computer, or more commonly today, they stop spinning or slow down after a specified time to save power. The spinning motion creates a cushion of air between the platter and its read/write head. This cushion ensures that the read/write head floats above the platter instead of making direct contact with the platter surface. The distance between the read/write head and the platter is about two millionths of one inch.

How a Hard Disk Works

Step 2
A small motor spins the platters while the computer is running.

Step 3 When software requests a disk access, the read/write heads determine the current or new location of the data.

Step 1
The circuit board controls the movement of the head actuator and a small motor.

Step 4
The head actuator positions the read/write head arms over the correct location on the platters to read or write data.

Figure 6-6   This figure shows how a hard disk works.

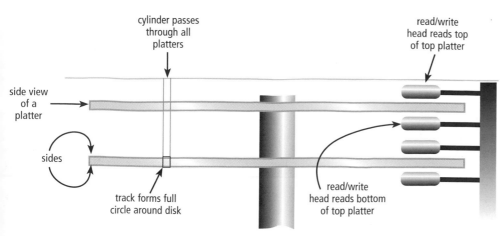

cylinder passes through all platters

read/write head reads top of top platter

side view of a platter

sides

track forms full circle around disk

read/write head reads bottom of top platter

Figure 6-7   A cylinder is the vertical section of track through all platters on a hard disk.

As shown in Figure 6-8, this close clearance leaves no room for any type of contamination. Dirt, hair, dust, smoke, and other particles could cause the hard disk to have a head crash. A head crash occurs when a read/write head touches the surface of a platter, usually resulting in a loss of data or sometimes loss of the entire disk. Thus, it is crucial that you back up your hard disk regularly. A **backup** is a duplicate of a file, program, or disk placed on a separate storage medium that you can use in case the original is lost, damaged, or destroyed. Chapter 7 discusses backup techniques. Access time for today's hard disks ranges from approximately 3 to 12 ms (milliseconds).

Figure 6-8 The clearance between a disk read/write head and the platter is about two millionths of an inch. A smoke particle, dust particle, human hair, or other contaminant could render the disk unusable.

RAID

Some personal computer manufacturers provide a hard disk configuration that connects multiple smaller disks into a single unit that acts like a single large hard disk. A group of two or more integrated hard disks is called a **RAID** (redundant array of independent disks). RAID is an ideal storage solution for users who must have the data available when they attempt to access it.

NAS

Network Attached Storage

For more information, visit the Computer Concepts CourseMate Web site at www.cengagebrain.com, navigate to the Chapter 6 Web Link resource for this book, and then click Network Attached Storage.

A **network attached storage** (NAS) device is a server connected to a network with the sole purpose of providing storage (shown in Figure 6-1 on page 238). Any user or device connected to the network can access files on the NAS device. These devices often use a RAID configuration. In the past, enterprises were the primary users of NAS. With the introduction of smaller, less expensive NAS devices, however, some home and small business users opt to add up to 6 TB or more of hard disk storage space to their network with a NAS device.

External and Removable Hard Disks

An **external hard disk**, shown in the left picture in Figure 6-9, is a separate freestanding hard disk that connects with a cable to a USB port or FireWire port on the system unit or communicates wirelessly. As with the internal hard disk, the entire hard disk is enclosed in an airtight, sealed case. External hard disks have storage capacities of up to 4 TB and more. Some external hard disk units include multiple hard disks that you can use for different purposes, if desired.

A **removable hard disk** is a hard disk that you insert and remove from a drive. A removable hard disk drive, shown in the right picture in Figure 6-9, reads from and writes on the removable hard disk. Removable hard disks have storage capacities up to 1 TB or more.

External and removable hard disks offer the following advantages over internal hard disks (fixed disks):

- Transport a large number of files
- Back up important files or an entire internal hard disk (several external hard disk models allow you to back up simply by pushing a button on the disk)
- Easily store large audio and video files
- Secure your data; for example, at the end of a work session, remove the hard disk and lock it up, leaving no data in the computer
- Add storage space to a notebook computer, including netbooks and Tablet PCs
- Add storage space to a desktop computer without having to open the system unit or connect to a network

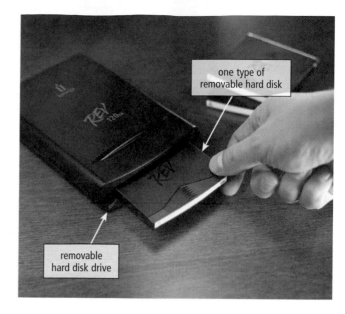

one type of
removable hard disk

removable
hard disk drive

external hard
disk

Figure 6-9   Examples of external and removable hard disks.

Miniature Hard Disks

Both internal and external hard disks are available in miniature sizes. These tiny hard disks have form factors of 1.8 inch, 1 inch, and 0.85 inch. Devices such as portable media players, digital cameras, and smart phones often have internal miniature hard disks, which provide greater storage capacities than flash memory (Figure 6-10). External hard disks that are smaller in size and capacity, which also contain miniature hard disks, are sometimes called a **pocket hard drive** because they enable mobile users easily to transport photos and other files from one computer to another (Figure 6-11). Miniature hard disks have storage capacities that range from 4 GB to 250 GB.

earbuds for portable
media player

Figure 6-10   This miniature hard disk is used in portable media players and other small devices, enabling users to store music, videos, movies, and any other type of files on the disk.

pocket hard drive

Figure 6-11   Users easily can transport data from one computer to another with a pocket hard drive.

Hard Disk Controllers

A **disk controller** consists of a special-purpose chip and electronic circuits that control the transfer of data, instructions, and information from a disk to and from the system bus and other components in the computer. That is, it controls the interface between the hard disk and the system bus. A disk controller for a hard disk, called the hard disk controller, may be part of a hard disk or the motherboard, or it may be a separate adapter card inside the system unit.

In their personal computer advertisements, vendors usually state the type of hard disk interface supported by the hard disk controller. Thus, you should understand the types of available hard disk interfaces. In addition to USB and FireWire, which can function as external hard disk interfaces, four other types of hard disk interfaces for use in personal computers are SATA, EIDE, SCSI, and SAS.

eSATA
For more information, visit the Computer Concepts CourseMate Web site at www.cengagebrain.com, navigate to the Chapter 6 Web Link resource for this book, and then click eSATA.

- SATA (Serial Advanced Technology Attachment) uses serial signals to transfer data, instructions, and information. The primary advantage of SATA interfaces is their cables are thinner, longer, more flexible, and less susceptible to interference than cables used by hard disks that use parallel signals. SATA interfaces also support connections to optical disc drives. External disks use the eSATA (external SATA) interface, which is much faster than USB and FireWire.
- EIDE (Enhanced Integrated Drive Electronics) is a hard disk interface that uses parallel signals to transfer data, instructions, and information. EIDE interfaces can support up to four hard disks at 137 GB per disk. EIDE interfaces also provide connections for optical disc drives and tape drives.
- SCSI interfaces, which also use parallel signals, can support up to eight or fifteen peripheral devices. Supported devices include hard disks, optical disc drives, tape drives, printers, scanners, network cards, and much more. Some computers have a built-in SCSI interface, while others use an adapter card to add a SCSI interface.
- SAS (serial-attached SCSI) is a newer type of SCSI that uses serial signals to transfer data, instructions, and information. Advantages of SAS over parallel SCSI include thinner, longer cables; reduced interference; less expensive; support for many more connected devices at once; and faster speeds. In addition to hard disks, SAS interfaces support connections to optical disc drives, printers, scanners, digital cameras, and other devices. Experts predict that SAS eventually will replace parallel SCSI.

Maintaining Data Stored on a Hard Disk

Most manufacturers guarantee their hard disks to last approximately three to five years. Many last much longer with proper care. To prevent the loss of items stored on a hard disk, you regularly should perform preventive maintenance such as defragmenting or scanning the disk for errors. To learn more about how to maintain a hard disk, complete the Learn How To 1 activity on pages 266 and 267. Chapter 7 discusses these and other utilities in depth.

✔ QUIZ YOURSELF 6-1

Instructions: Find the true statement below. Then, rewrite the remaining false statements so that they are true.

1. Hard disks contain one or more inflexible, circular platters that magnetically store data, instructions, and information.
2. SATA is a hard disk interface that uses parallel signals to transfer data, instructions, and information.
3. Storage media is the computer hardware that records and/or retrieves items to and from a storage device.
4. Users can move an internal hard disk from computer to computer as needed by connecting the disk to a USB port or FireWire port on the system unit.

Quiz Yourself Online: To further check your knowledge of pages 238 through 246, visit the Computer Concepts CourseMate Web site at www.cengagebrain.com, navigate to the Chapter 6 Quiz Yourself resource for this book, and then click Objectives 1 – 2.

Flash Memory Storage

As discussed in Chapter 4, flash memory is a type of nonvolatile memory that can be erased electronically and rewritten. Flash memory chips are a type of **solid state media**, which means they consist entirely of electronic components, such as integrated circuits, and contain no moving parts. The lack of moving parts makes flash memory storage more durable and shock resistant than other types of media such as magnetic hard disks or optical discs.

Types of flash memory storage include solid state drives, memory cards, USB flash drives, and ExpressCard modules.

Solid State Drives

A **solid state drive** (**SSD**) is a storage device that typically uses flash memory to store data, instructions, and information (Figure 6-12). With available sizes of 3.5 inches, 2.5 inches, and 1.8 inches, SSDs are used in all types of computers including servers, desktop computers, and mobile computers and devices such as portable media players and digital video cameras. Storage capacities of current SSDs range from 16 GB to 256 GB and more.

SSDs have several advantages over magnetic hard disks.

- Access times of SSDs are about 0.1 ms, which is more than 80 times faster than a hard disk.
- Transfer rates of SSDs are faster than comparable hard disks.
- SSDs generate less heat and consume less power than hard disks.
- Manufacturers claim that SSDs will last more than 50 years, which is much greater than the 3 to 5 year hard disk stated lifespan.

The disadvantages of SSDs are they currently have a higher failure rate than hard disks, and their cost is much higher per gigabyte. As the price of SSDs drops, experts estimate that increasingly more users will purchase computers and devices that use this media.

Solid State Drives

For more information, visit the Computer Concepts CourseMate Web site at www.cengagebrain.com, navigate to the Chapter 6 Web Link resource for this book, and then click Solid State Drives.

Figure 6-12   As the price of SSDs drops, experts estimate that increasingly more users will purchase computers and devices that use this media.

Memory Cards

Memory cards enable mobile users easily to transport digital photos, music, or files to and from mobile devices and computers or other devices. As mentioned in Chapter 4, a **memory card** is a removable flash memory device, usually no bigger than 1.5 inches in height or width, that you insert and remove from a slot in a computer, mobile device, or card reader/writer (Figure 6-13).

Common types of memory cards include **CompactFlash (CF)**, **Secure Digital (SD)**, **Secure Digital High Capacity (SDHC)**, **microSD**, **microSDHC**, **xD Picture Card**, **Memory Stick**, and **Memory Stick Micro (M2)**. The table in Figure 6-14 compares storage capacities and uses of

Figure 6-13   Many types of computers and devices have slots for memory cards.

these flash memory storage media. Depending on the device, manufacturers claim memory cards can last from 10 to 100 years.

To view, edit, or print images and information stored on memory cards, you transfer the contents to your desktop computer or other device. Some printers have slots to read flash memory cards. If your computer or printer does not have a built-in slot, you can purchase a **card reader/writer**, which is a device that reads and writes data, instructions, and information stored on memory cards. Card reader/writers usually connect to the USB port or FireWire port on the system unit. The type of card you have will determine the type of card reader/writer needed.

SDHC Cards
For more information, visit the Computer Concepts CourseMate Web site at www.cengagebrain.com, navigate to the Chapter 6 Web Link resource for this book, and then click SDHC Cards.

Various Memory Cards

Media Type		Storage Capacity	Use
CompactFlash (CF)		512 MB to 100 GB	Digital cameras, smart phones, PDAs, photo printers, portable media players, notebook computers, desktop computers
Secure Digital (SD)		512 MB to 8 GB	Digital cameras, digital video cameras, smart phones, PDAs, photo printers, portable media players
SDHC		4 to 32 GB	Digital cameras
microSD		1 to 2 GB	Smart phones, portable media players, handheld game consoles, handheld navigation devices
microSDHC		4 to 16 GB	Smart phones, portable media players, handheld game consoles, handheld navigation devices
xD Picture Card		256 MB to 2 GB	Digital cameras, photo printers
Memory Stick PRO Duo		1 to 16 GB	Digital cameras, smart phones, handheld game consoles
Memory Stick Micro (M2)		1 to 16 GB	Smart phones

Figure 6-14   A variety of memory cards.

USB Flash Drives

A **USB flash drive**, sometimes called a thumb drive, is a flash memory storage device that plugs in a USB port on a computer or mobile device (Figure 6-15). USB flash drives are convenient for mobile users because they are small and lightweight enough to be transported on a keychain or in a pocket. Current USB flash drives have storage capacities ranging from 512 MB to 64 GB, with the latter being extremely expensive.

Figure 6-15   A close-up of the flash memory and circuitry inside a USB flash drive.

? FAQ 6-2

Can airport security screening equipment damage or erase the data on my mobile media or hard disk?

The Transportation Security Administration's Web site states that their screening (X-ray) equipment will not damage or erase the data stored on flash memory mobile media, optical discs, or hard disks. Although your media is equally safe whether you carry it onto the airplane or leave it in checked baggage, packing it with your carry-on items is a better safeguard against physical damage. If you are uneasy about your media passing through the airport screening equipment, you may be able to request that the items be manually (hand) searched. It is important to note that the equipment used to screen checked baggage will not harm electronic media, but it may damage undeveloped film. As a safeguard, you should carry all film onto the airplane and request a manual search.

📺 For more information, visit the Computer Concepts CourseMate Web site at www.cengagebrain.com, navigate to the Chapter 6 FAQ resource for this book, and then click Airport Screening Equipment.

ExpressCard Modules

An **ExpressCard module** is a removable device, about 75 mm long and 34 mm wide or L-shaped with a width of 54 mm, that fits in an ExpressCard slot (Figure 6-16). ExpressCard modules can be used to add memory, storage, communications, multimedia, and security capabilities to a computer. ExpressCard modules commonly are used in notebook computers.

two sizes of ExpressCard modules

Figure 6-16   ExpressCard modules are available in two sizes.

Cloud Storage

Some users choose cloud storage instead of storing data locally on a hard disk or other media. **Cloud storage** is an Internet service that provides hard disk storage to computer users (Figure 6-17).

Types of services offered by cloud storage providers vary. Figure 6-18 identifies a variety of cloud storage providers. Read Innovative Computing 6-1 to find out about another type of cloud storage.

Fee arrangements vary. For example, one cloud storage service provides 25 GB of storage free to registered users; another charges $5 per month for 150 GB of storage. For enterprises, cloud storage services typically charge for storage on a per gigabyte basis, such as 15 cents per gigabyte.

Figure 6-17   An example of one Web site that provides cloud storage.

Cloud Storage Providers

Web Site Names	Type of Storage Provided	Other Services
Box.net, IDrive, Windows Live SkyDrive	Backup or additional storage for any type of file	
Flickr, Picasa	Digital photos	Photo editing and photo management
YouTube	Digital videos	
Facebook, MySpace	Digital photos, digital videos, messages, and personal information	Social networking
Google Docs, Office Web Apps	Documents, spreadsheets, presentations	Productivity suite
Gmail, Windows Live Hotmail, Yahoo! Mail	E-mail messages	
Amazon EC2, Amazon S3, Nirvanix	Enterprise-level storage	Web services, data center services

Figure 6-18   Some of the more widely used cloud storage providers.

Users subscribe to a cloud storage service for a variety of reasons:
- To access files on the Internet from any computer or device that has Internet access
- To allow others to access their files on the Internet so that others can listen to an audio file, watch a video clip, or view a photo — instead of e-mailing the file to them
- To view time-critical data and images immediately while away from the main office or location; for example, doctors can view X-ray images from another hospital, home, or office
- To store offsite backups of data
- To provide data center functions, relieving enterprises of this task

Read Ethics & Issues 6-2 for a related discussion.

Cloud Storage

For more information, visit the Computer Concepts CourseMate Web site at www.cengagebrain.com, navigate to the Chapter 6 Web Link resource for this book, and then click Cloud Storage.

ETHICS & ISSUES 6-2

Is Data Stored in the Cloud Free from Prying Eyes?

At an ever increasing rate, companies and individuals store Web sites and data in the cloud. For example, those who utilize Web-based e-mail store their sent and received e-mail messages in the e-mail provider's cloud environment. Those who use corporate or private e-mail servers do not store their communications in the cloud. Important legal rulings highlight the differences between the two approaches for storing e-mail. Law enforcement agencies consider e-mail stored in the cloud to belong to the company that owns the cloud service, often an Internet access provider. E-mail stored

on a private e-mail server, however, is the property of the company or individual who owns the server. When the law enforcement officials need to read someone's e-mail on a private e-mail server, they must obtain a warrant that outlines exactly the information being sought. In the cloud, however, law enforcement officials simply may need to request the information from the company that owns the cloud service. The user might not be notified of the search until up to 90 days later; further, the search may occur without limitations and may include continuous monitoring of an individual's

e-mail. While the government takes a liberal approach to viewing one's e-mail in the cloud, individuals who secretly read others' e-mail messages may be subject to felony computer crimes.

Should data kept in the cloud be treated the same way legally as items that are kept in one's home? Why? Should the government be able to access your data in the cloud without your knowledge or permission? Why or why not? What types and amount of personal data are you comfortable storing in the cloud? Why?

QUIZ YOURSELF 6-2

Instructions: Find the true statement below. Then, rewrite the remaining false statements so that they are true.

1. A USB flash drive is a flash memory storage device that plugs in a parallel port on a computer or mobile device.
2. CompactFlash and Memory Sticks are two types of flash memory cards.
3. Cloud storage is a storage device that typically uses flash memory to store data, instructions, and information.
4. An ExpressCard module is a removable RAID device that fits in an ExpressCard slot.

Quiz Yourself Online: To further check your knowledge of pages 247 through 252, visit the Computer Concepts CourseMate Web site at www.cengagebrain.com, navigate to the Chapter 6 Quiz Yourself resource for this book, and then click Objectives 3 – 4.

Optical Discs

An **optical disc** is a type of optical storage media that consists of a flat, round, portable disc made of metal, plastic, and lacquer. These discs usually are 4.75 inches in diameter and less than one-twentieth of an inch thick.

Optical discs primarily store software, data, digital photos, movies, and music. Some optical disc formats are read only, meaning users cannot write (save) on the media. Others are read/write, which allows users to save on the disc just as they save on a hard disk.

Nearly every personal computer today includes some type of optical disc drive installed in a drive bay. On some, you push a button to slide out a tray, insert the disc, and then push the same button to close the tray; others are slot loaded, which means you insert the disc in a narrow opening on the drive (Figure 6-19).

Figure 6-19 A slot-loaded optical disc drive.

With some discs, you can read and/or write on one side only. Manufacturers usually place a silk-screened label on the top layer of these single-sided discs. You insert a single-sided disc in the drive with the label side up. Other discs are double-sided. Simply remove the disc from the drive, flip it over, and reinsert it in the drive to use the other side of the disc. Double-sided discs often have no label; instead, each side of the disc is identified with small writing around the center of the disc. Some drives use **LightScribe technology**, which works with specially coated optical discs, to etch labels directly on the disc (as opposed to placing an adhesive label on the disc).

Optical discs store items by using microscopic pits (indentations) and lands (flat areas) that are in the middle layer of the disc. A high-powered laser light creates the pits. A lower-powered laser light reads items from the disc by reflecting light through the bottom of the disc. The reflected light is converted into a series of bits the computer can process.

Manufacturers claim that a properly cared for high-quality optical disc will last 5 years but could last up to 100 years. Figure 6-20 offers some guidelines for the proper care of optical discs.

Many different formats of optical discs exist today. Figure 6-21 identifies a variety of optical disc formats and specifies whether a user can read from the disc, write to the disc, and/or erase the disc. The following sections describe characteristics unique to each of these disc formats.

Figure 6-20 of image content:
DO store the disc in a jewel box when not in use.
DO NOT eat, smoke, or drink near a disc.
DO NOT expose the disc to excessive heat or sunlight.
DO hold a disc by its edges.
DO NOT touch the underside of the disc.
DO NOT stack discs.

Figure 6-20 Some guidelines for the proper care of optical discs.

Optical Disc Formats

Optical Disc	Read	Write	Erase
CD-ROM	Y	N	N
CD-R	Y	Y	N
CD-RW	Y	Y	Y
DVD-ROM BD-ROM	Y	N	N
DVD-R DVD+R BD-R	Y	Y	N
DVD-RW DVD+RW DVD-RAM BD-RE	Y	Y	Y

Figure 6-21 Manufacturers sell CD-ROM, DVD-ROM, and BD-ROM media prerecorded (written) with audio, video, and software. Users cannot change the contents of these discs. Users, however, can purchase the other formats of optical discs as blank media and record (write) their own data, instructions, and information on these discs.

? **FAQ 6-3**

Can I clean a disc?

Yes, you can remove dust, dirt, smudges, and fingerprints from the surface of an optical disc. Moisten a nonabrasive cloth with warm water or rubbing alcohol (do not use ammonia-based solutions) and then wipe the disc in straight lines from the center outward. You also can repair scratches on the bottom surface with a specialized disc repair kit.

For more information, visit the Computer Concepts CourseMate Web site at www.cengagebrain.com, navigate to the Chapter 6 FAQ resource for this book, and then click Cleaning and Repairing Discs.

CDs

A **CD-ROM**, or compact disc read-only memory, is a type of optical disc that users can read but not write (record) or erase — hence, the name read-only. Manufacturers write the contents of standard CD-ROMs. A standard CD-ROM is called a single-session disc because manufacturers write all items on the disc at one time. Software manufacturers often distribute programs using CD-ROMs (Figure 6-22).

A typical CD-ROM holds from 650 MB to 1 GB of data, instructions, and information. To read a CD-ROM, insert the disc in a **CD-ROM drive** or a CD-ROM player. Because audio CDs and CD-ROMs use the same laser technology, you may be able to use a CD-ROM drive to listen to an audio CD while using the computer.

Figure 6-22   Encyclopedias, games, simulations, and many other programs are distributed on CD-ROM.

CD-Rs and CD-RWs   Many personal computers today include either a CD-R or CD-RW drive, or a combination drive that includes CD-R or CD-RW capabilities, as a standard feature. Unlike standard CD-ROM drives, users record, or write, their own data on a disc with a CD-R or CD-RW drive. The process of writing on an optical disc is called **burning**.

A **CD-R** (compact disc-recordable) is a multisession optical disc on which users can write, but not erase, their own items such as text, graphics, and audio. Multisession means you can write on part of the disc at one time and another part at a later time. Each part of a CD-R can be written on only one time, and the disc's contents cannot be erased.

A **CD-RW** (compact disc-rewritable) is an erasable multisession disc you can write on multiple times. To write on a CD-RW disc, you must have CD-RW software and a **CD-RW drive**. A popular use of CD-RW and CD-R discs is to create audio CDs. For example, users can record their own music and save it on a CD, purchase and download songs from the Web, or rearrange tracks on a purchased music CD. The process of copying audio and/or video data from a purchased disc and saving it on digital media is called **ripping**.

Archive Discs and Picture CDs

Many people use archive discs or Picture CDs to preserve their photos. When you post and share photos online on a photo sharing community, you can choose to save your collection of online photos on an **archive disc**, which stores photos in the jpg file format (Figure 6-23). The cost of archive discs is determined by the number of photos being stored. One service, for example, charges $9.99 for the first hundred pictures.

A Kodak **Picture CD** stores digital versions of film using a jpg file format. Many photo centers offer Picture CD service for consumers when they drop off film to be developed. The additional cost for a Picture CD is about $3 per roll of film.

Most optical disc drives can read an archive disc and a Picture CD. You can print copies of the photos from the disc on paper with an ink-jet printer. If you do not have a printer to print the images, many stores have kiosks at which you can print pictures from an archive disc, a Picture CD, or other media.

How an Archive Disc Works

Step 1
Upload your digital photos to a photo sharing community for others to view.

Step 2
Select the photos to be stored on the archive disc and then place your order.

Step 3
Pick up your archive disc at a designated store or receive it in the mail. At home, edit and/or print images from the archive disc on your ink-jet or photo printer, or view the images on a monitor or television screen. At a store, edit and/or print images from the archive disc at a kiosk.

archive disc ➞

Figure 6-23   This figure shows how an archive disc works.

DVDs and Blu-ray Discs

Although the size and shape of a CD and DVD are similar, a DVD stores data, instructions, and information in a slightly different manner and thus achieves a higher storage capacity. DVD quality also far surpasses that of CDs because images are stored at higher resolution.

A **DVD-ROM** (digital versatile disc-read-only memory or digital video disc-read-only memory) is a high-capacity optical disc on which users can read but not write or erase. Manufacturers write the contents of DVD-ROMs and distribute them to consumers. DVD-ROMs store movies, music, huge databases, and complex software (Figure 6-24).

To read a DVD-ROM, you need a **DVD-ROM drive** or DVD player. Most DVD-ROM drives also can read audio CDs, CD-ROMs, CD-Rs, and CD-RWs. Some drives, called DVD/CD-RW drives, are combination drives that read and write DVD and CD media. Many of today's computers include these combination drives.

A DVD-ROM uses one of three storage techniques. The first involves making the disc denser by packing the pits closer together. The second involves using two layers of pits. For this technique to work, the lower layer of pits is semitransparent so that the laser can read through it to the upper layer. This technique doubles the capacity of the disc. Finally, some DVD-ROMs are double-sided.

A newer, more expensive DVD format is Blu-ray, which is a higher capacity and better quality than standard DVDs, especially for high-definition audio and video. A **Blu-ray Disc** (BD) has storage capacities of 100 GB, with expectations of exceeding 200 GB in the future. Blu-ray Disc drives and players are backward compatible with DVD and CD formats. Figure 6-25 compares the current storage capacities of DVD and Blu-ray media. Another high density format, called **HD VMD** (Versatile Multilayer Disc) potentially will contain up to 20 layers, each with a capacity of 5 GB. Current HD VMDs have capacities of 40 GB and more.

A mini-DVD that has grown in popularity is the UMD, which works specifically with the PlayStation Portable (PSP) handheld game console. The **UMD** (Universal Media Disc), which has a diameter of about 2.4 inches, can store up to 1.8 GB of games, movies, or music. Similarly, the mini Blu-ray Disc, which is used primarily in digital video recorders, stores approximately 7.5 GB.

Blu-ray

For more information, visit the Computer Concepts CourseMate Web site at www.cengagebrain.com, navigate to the Chapter 6 Web Link resource for this book, and then click Blu-ray.

Figure 6-24 A DVD-ROM is a high-capacity optical disc.

DVD and Blu-ray Storage Capacities

Sides	Layers	DVD	Blu-ray
1	1	4.7 GB	25 GB
1	2	8.5 GB	50 GB
2	1	9.4 GB	50 GB
2	2	17 GB	100 GB

Figure 6-25 Storage capacities of DVDs and Blu-ray Discs.

Recordable and Rewritable DVDs Many types of recordable and rewritable DVD formats are available. DVD-R, DVD+R and BD-R allow users to write on the disc once and read (play) it many times. **DVD-RW, DVD+RW**, and **DVD+RAM** are three competing rewritable DVD formats. Similarly, **BD-RE** is a high-capacity rewritable DVD format. To write on these discs, you must have a compatible drive or recorder.

Rewritable DVD drives usually can read a variety of DVD and CD media. Before investing in equipment, check to be sure it is compatible with the media on which you intend to record.

Other Types of Storage

In addition to the previously discussed types of storage, other options are available for specific uses and applications. These include tape, magnetic stripe cards and smart cards, microfilm and microfiche, and enterprise storage.

Tape

One of the first storage media used with mainframe computers was tape. **Tape** is a magnetically coated ribbon of plastic capable of storing large amounts of data and information at a low cost. Tape no longer is used as a primary method of storage. Instead, business users utilize tape most often for long-term storage and backup.

A **tape drive** reads and writes data and information on a tape. Although older computers used reel-to-reel tape drives, today's tape drives use tape cartridges. A tape cartridge is a small, rectangular, plastic housing for tape (Figure 6-26). Tape cartridges that contain quarter-inch-wide tape are slightly larger than audiocassette tapes.

Business users sometimes back up personal computer hard disks to tape, often using an external tape drive. On larger computers, tape cartridges are mounted in a separate cabinet called a tape library.

Tape storage requires sequential access, which refers to reading or writing data consecutively. As with a music tape, you must forward or rewind the tape to a specific point to access a specific piece of data.

Hard disks, flash memory storage, and optical discs all use direct access. Direct access means that the device can locate a particular data item or file immediately, without having to move consecutively through items stored in front of the desired data item or file. When writing or reading specific data, direct access is much faster than sequential access.

Figure 6-26   A tape drive and a tape cartridge.

Magnetic Stripe Cards and Smart Cards

A **magnetic stripe card** is a credit card, entertainment card, bank card, or other similar card, with a stripe that contains information identifying you and the card (shown in Figure 6-1 on page 238). Information stored in the stripe includes your name, account number, and the card's expiration date. A magnetic stripe card reader reads information stored on the stripe.

A **smart card**, which is similar in size to a credit card or ATM card (Figure 6-27), stores data on a thin microprocessor embedded in the card. Smart cards contain a processor and have input, process, output, and storage capabilities. When you insert the smart card in a specialized card reader, the information on the smart card is read and, if necessary, updated. Uses of smart cards include storing medical records, vaccination data, and other health care or identification information; tracking information, such as customer purchases or employee attendance; storing a prepaid amount of money, such as for student purchases on campus; and authenticating users, such as for Internet purchases or building access. In addition, a smart card can double as an ID card. Read Ethics & Issues 6-3 for a related discussion.

Figure 6-27   This user inserts the smart card to access the computer.

Should the World Become a Cashless Society?

Do you toss your loose change in a jar with the hopes of making a special purchase with the savings someday? This habit may become futile if the world goes cashless. One form of payment that could end the need for cash is the smart card, which can store a dollar amount on a thin microprocessor and update the amount whenever a transaction is made. Advocates claim that smart cards would eliminate muggings and robberies, make it difficult to

purchase illegal goods, and reduce taxes by identifying tax cheats. Also, payment using biometrics, such as fingerprints, is becoming more common. Several high-profile security breaches at credit reporting and credit card companies, however, have heightened concerns over privacy. In a recent survey, most Americans said that they would not use a smart card even if privacy was guaranteed. Another survey shows that most Americans believe that fingerprints are a

trustworthy form of identification. A cash purchase usually is anonymous. Yet, a smart card purchase preserves a record of the transaction that could become available to other merchants, advertisers, government agencies, or hackers.

Should the world become a cashless society? Why or why not? Would you be comfortable using a smart card or fingerprint instead of cash for all transactions? Why?

Figure 6-28   Images on microfilm can be read only with a microfilm reader.

Media Life Expectancies*
(when using high-quality media)

Media Type	Guaranteed Life Expectancy	Potential Life Expectancy
Magnetic disks	3 to 5 years	20 to 30 years
Optical discs	5 to 10 years	50 to 100 years
Solid state drives	50 years	140 years
Microfilm	100 years	500 years

*according to manufacturers of the media

 Figure 6-29   Microfilm is the medium with the longest life.

Microfilm and Microfiche

Microfilm and microfiche store microscopic images of documents on roll or sheet film. **Microfilm** is a 100- to 215-foot roll of film. **Microfiche** is a small sheet of film, usually about 4 × 6 inches. A computer output microfilm recorder is the device that records the images on the film. The stored images are so small that you can read them only with a microfilm or microfiche reader (Figure 6-28).

Microfilm and microfiche use is widespread, with many companies allowing you to search through and view microfilm images online. Libraries use these media to store back issues of newspapers, magazines, and genealogy records. Some large organizations use microfilm and microfiche to archive inactive files. Some banks use them to store transactions and canceled checks. The U.S. Army uses them to store personnel records.

The use of microfilm and microfiche provides a number of advantages. They greatly reduce the amount of paper firms must handle. They are inexpensive and have the longest life of any storage media (Figure 6-29). Read Looking Ahead 6-1 for a look at long-term storage.

LOOKING AHEAD 6-1

Rosetta Project a Storage Solution

The Rosetta Stone unlocked the secret of understanding Egyptian hieroglyphics. Created in 186 B.C., the carved stone contains translations of one hieroglyphic passage into three languages. Today, more than 2,500 human languages exist, but 50 to 90 percent of them are expected to become extinct by the end of this century. In an effort to preserve these languages using long-term storage technology, thousands of people collaborated on the Rosetta Project to create the Rosetta Disk.

Measuring only 3 inches wide, the nickel Rosetta Disk contains 15,000 etched pages documenting more than 1,000 known languages in the world. Each page is .019 inches wide, approximately the width of 5 human hairs. The pages are readable when the Disk is magnified 1,000 times. For protection, the Disk is housed in a 4-inch spherical container.

Five prototype Disks were created. The original Disk is attached to the European Space Agency's Rosetta Space Probe that was launched in 2004 and is expected to land on a comet in 2014. The Probe will measure the comet's molecular composition and then orbit the sun for millions of years.

 For more information, visit the Computer Concepts CourseMate Web site at www.cengagebrain.com, navigate to the Chapter 6 Looking Ahead resource for this book, and then click Long-Term Storage.

Enterprise Storage

A large business, commonly referred to as an enterprise, has hundreds or thousands of employees in offices across the country or around the world. Enterprises use computers and computer networks to manage and store huge volumes of data and information about customers, suppliers, and employees.

To meet their large-scale needs, enterprises use special hardware geared for heavy use, maximum availability, and maximum efficiency. One or more servers on the network have the sole purpose of providing storage to connected users. For high-speed storage access, entire networks are dedicated exclusively to connecting devices that provide storage to other servers. In an enterprise, some storage systems can provide more than 185 TB of storage capacity. Optical disc servers hold hundreds of optical discs.

An enterprise's storage needs usually grow daily. Thus, the storage solutions an enterprise chooses must be able to store its data and information requirements today and tomorrow. Read Ethics & Issues 6-4 for a related discussion.

ETHICS & ISSUES 6-4

Who Should Be Looking at Your Medical Records?

A medical transcriber based in a foreign country and hired by a U.S. medical center threatened to post private medical records to the Internet if she was not paid more. With the widespread use of computers and an explosion in data storage capacity around the world, private information, such as medical records, requires increased diligence by companies, governments, and individuals to maintain this privacy. The government would like most Americans' health care records available in privacy-protected electronic format by 2014. Although these records will be stored by a corporation or the government, individuals probably will have complete control, or ownership, of these electronic records.

The Health Insurance Portability and Accountability Act (HIPAA) sets rigorous standards for medical record privacy. The law does not cover financial records, education records, or employment records — each of which may contain medical information about you. Your medical information also may be examined by insurance companies, government agencies, the Medical Information Bureau (MIB), employers, and the courts. You also inadvertently may pass on medical information to direct marketers when you participate in informal health screenings or surveys. Some people have found that discussing medical conditions via Internet chat rooms or newsgroups has resulted in unwanted attention, and they later regret the disclosures. Proponents of greater electronic access to medical records claim that more access means that physicians can be better prepared when they see patients, physicians will make fewer errors, and insurance companies can better root out fraud.

Should more limits be placed on what other people can do with your medical information? Why or why not? What are the advantages of increased access to medical records? What are the disadvantages?

Putting It All Together

Many factors influence the type of storage devices you should use: the amount of data, instructions, and information to be stored; the hardware and software in use; and the desired cost. The table in Figure 6-30 outlines several suggested storage devices for various types of computer users.

Categories of Users

User	Typical Storage Devices	User	Typical Storage Devices
Home	• 500 GB hard disk • Cloud storage • Optical disc drive • Card reader/writer • USB flash drive	**Power**	• 2.5 TB hard disk • Cloud storage • Optical disc drive • Portable hard disk for backup • USB flash drive

Small Office/ Home Office	• 1 TB hard disk
	• Cloud storage
	• Optical disc drive
	• External hard disk for backup
	• USB flash drive
		Enterprise	• Desktop Computer
			  - 1 TB hard disk
			  - Optical disc drive
			  - Smart card reader
			  - Tape drive
			  - USB flash drive
			• Server or Mainframe
			  - Network storage server
			  - 40 TB hard disk system
			  - Optical disc server
			  - Microfilm or microfiche

Mobile	• 250 GB hard disk • Cloud storage • Optical disc drive • Card reader/writer • Portable hard disk for backup • USB flash drive		

Figure 6-30   Recommended storage devices for various users.

Instructions: Find the true statement below. Then, rewrite the remaining false statements so that they are true.

1. A CD-RW is a type of optical disc on which users can read but not write (record) or erase.
2. A DVD-RAM is a single-session disc that stores digital versions of film using a jpg file format.
3. DVDs have the same storage capacities as CDs.
4. Optical discs are written and read by mirrors.
5. Microfilm and microfiche have the shortest life of any media.

💻 **Quiz Yourself Online:** To further check your knowledge of pages 252 through 259 visit the Computer Concepts CourseMate Web site at www.cengagebrain.com, navigate to the Chapter 6 Quiz Yourself resource for this book, and then click Objectives 5 – 7.

Chapter Summary

Storage holds data, instructions, and information, which includes pictures, music, and videos, for future use. Users depend on storage devices to provide access to their storage media for years and decades to come.

This chapter identified and discussed various storage media and storage devices. Storage media covered included internal hard disks; external and removable hard disks; solid state drives; memory cards; USB flash drives; ExpressCard modules; cloud storage; CDs, DVDs, and Blu-ray Discs; tape; smart cards; and microfilm and microfiche.

Computer Usage @ Work

Meteorology

With the television tuned to the local weather station, you anxiously are awaiting to see the projected path of a hurricane in the tropics. Having experienced hurricanes in the past, you rely heavily on the accuracy of weather forecasts so that you can adequately prepare if a storm travels through the area. Computers allow meteorologists to better estimate the severity and path of storms, enabling people to make potentially life-saving preparations.

The National Hurricane Center uses multiple computer models to determine a storm's path. These models consider factors such as the storm's current strength, the effects of nearby weather systems, the storm's central pressure, and whether the storm may travel over land. These models also may consider previous storms that traveled a similar path. Historical weather and storm data are stored on large storage devices by the National Weather Service. While these models are not 100 percent accurate, they do ensure that everyone who may be affected by the storm has enough time to prepare.

Violent, rotating thunderstorms potentially can spawn tornadoes, which sometimes cause catastrophic damage. For this reason, it is important for everyone to closely watch or listen to the weather during the storm. Meteorologists can monitor weather systems on multiple radars and send additional severe weather warnings automatically to weather radios. Computer technology enables these messages to be broadcast automatically only to weather radios in areas that may be affected.

In addition to computers helping us stay safe during severe storms, they also assist with day-to-day weather forecasting. Several years ago, meteorologists could predict the weather for only a few days into the future. Beyond that point, the forecast was very uncertain. Meteorologists presently are able to predict the weather, including temperature and chance of precipitation, one week or more into the future with much greater accuracy because computers create models using historical weather data and behavior to predict the future path of various weather systems.

News and weather stations also post their weather forecasts online. In fact, several Web sites have interactive radars that allow visitors to zoom in and view how weather is affecting their immediate neighborhood.

The meteorology field has made significant advancements because of computer technologies. Weather forecasts are more meaningful, which not only helps us prepare on land but also helps to protect those traveling by air or by sea.

💻 For more information, visit the Computer Concepts CourseMate Web site at www.cengagebrain.com, navigate to the Chapter 6 Computer Usage @ Work resource for this book, and then click Meteorology.

Companies on the Cutting Edge

SEAGATE TECHNOLOGY Storage Solutions Supplier

The average household with a broadband Internet connection will need nearly 1 TB of storage for its personal media collections, and Seagate has the storage solutions for practically every digital need. The company offers more than 40 products for the personal computing, consumer electronics, and enterprise computing fields.

Seagate has been at the forefront of the digital storage world since it developed the first 5.25-inch hard disk for the personal computer in 1980. In 2008 it shipped its one billionth hard disk, making the company's

production for the past 30 years a total of 79 million terabytes. Seagate expects to ship its two billionth hard disk by 2013.

Seagate recently introduced the FreeAgent DockStar network adapter. This device allows users to access their digital media from anywhere in the world and share these files with anyone. The FreeAgent DockStar network adapter also enables users to link their digital content to online social networks such as Facebook, Twitter, and MySpace.

SANDISK CORPORATION Flash Memory Storage Supplier

The number of flash memory card formats is growing, and only one company has the rights to design, develop, manufacture, and market every one of them: SanDisk. The company is the world's largest supplier of flash memory storage products and also has lines of portable media players.

The company was founded in 1988, and one of its earliest flash drives was used on a U.S. space shuttle three years later. Today SanDisk is developing rewritable 3-D memory products that will store data vertically, and

company executives believe this technology will replace flash products in the next decade.

SanDisk recently introduced the world's fastest 32 GB SDHC card. The 32 GB SanDisk Extreme SDHC card boasts read and write speeds of 30 megabytes per second. The increased speeds enable photographers to take pictures quickly without having to wait long for the card to record the images. In addition, computer users also are able to transfer data to and from the card quickly.

For more information, visit the Computer Concepts CourseMate Web site at www.cengagebrain.com and then navigate to the Chapter 6 Companies on the Cutting Edge resource for this book.

Technology Trailblazers

AL SHUGART Storage Expert

Al Shugart said that his real goal in life was to have fun, and he spent his life doing the things that gave him the most pleasure. The day after receiving his bachelor's degree in engineering physics in 1951, he landed a job at IBM doing what he loved to do: fixing broken items and developing new technology. He was promoted to supervisor of the product development team that developed the first removable hard disk drive.

Shugart then left IBM, became vice president of Memorex, and then started Shugart Associates and

began developing floppy disks. In 1979 he founded Seagate Technology with a friend. As his company grew to become the world's largest hard disk manufacturer, he had fun placing his dog, Ernest, on the ballot for a Congressional seat.

Shugart served as president and CEO of Al Shugart International, a venture capital firm in California, until his death in 2006.

MARK DEAN IBM Inventor

Web 2.0 applications demand large, inexpensive storage, and Mark Dean is hard at work helping to meet this need. As vice president of IBM's Almaden Research Center lab in California, Dean is responsible for developing innovative products.

Dean joined IBM after graduating from Stanford University with a degree in electrical engineering. He led a team that developed the first CMOS microprocessor to operate at one gigahertz and has more than

40 patents or patents pending that are used in more than 40 million personal computers manufactured each year. Three of his patents are among the nine registered for the architecture of the original personal computer.

Dean is the first African-American to be appointed to IBM Fellow, the company's highest level of technical merit. He also was inducted in the National Inventors Hall of Fame.

For more information, visit the Computer Concepts CourseMate Web site at www.cengagebrain.com and then navigate to the Chapter 6 Technology Trailblazers resource for this book.

Chapter Review

The Chapter Review section reinforces the main concepts presented in this chapter.

To listen to an audio version of this Chapter Review, visit the Computer Concepts CourseMate Web site at www.cengagebrain.com and then navigate to the Chapter 6 Chapter Review resource for this book.

1. What Are the Characteristics of an Internal Hard Disk?   A **hard disk** is a storage device that contains one or more inflexible, circular platters that use magnetic particles to store data, instructions, and information. The system unit in most desktop and notebook computers contains at least one hard disk. **Capacity** is the number of bytes (characters) a storage medium can hold. Hard disk capacity is determined from whether it uses **longitudinal recording** or **perpendicular recording**, the number of platters it contains, and the composition of the magnetic coating on the platters. A platter is made of aluminum, glass, or ceramic and is coated with a material that allows items to be recorded magnetically on its surface. Each platter has two read/write heads, one for each side. The location of a read/write head often is referred to by its cylinder, which is the vertical section of a track that passes through all platters. Magnetic disks store data and instructions in tracks and sectors. A track is a narrow recording band that forms a full circle on the surface of the disk. The disk's storage locations consist of pie-shaped sections, which break the tracks into small arcs called sectors. While the computer is running, the platters rotate at 5,400 to 15,000 revolutions per minute (rpm), which allows nearly instant access to all tracks and sectors on the platters.

2. What Is the Purpose of Network Attached Storage Devices, External and Removable Hard Disks, and Hard Disk Controllers?   A **network attached storage** (NAS) device is a server connected to a network with the sole purpose of providing storage. Any user or device connected to the network can access files on the NAS device. These devices often use a **RAID** (redundant array of independent disks) configuration. A group of two or more integrated hard disks is called a RAID. An **external hard disk** is a separate freestanding hard disk that connects with a cable to a USB or FireWire port on the system unit or communicates wirelessly. External hard disks have storage capacities up to 4 TB or more. A **removable hard disk** can be inserted or removed from a drive. Removable hard disks have storage capacities up to 1 TB. A **disk controller** consists of a special-purpose chip and electronic circuits that control the transfer of data, instructions, and information from a disk to and from the system bus and other components in the computer. A hard disk controller may be part of a hard disk on the motherboard, or it may be a separate adapter card inside the system unit. In addition to USB and FireWire, which can function as hard disk interfaces, four other types of hard disk interfaces for use in personal computers are SATA (Serial Advanced Technology Attachment), EIDE (Enhanced Integrated Drive Electronics), SCSI, and SAS (serial-attached SCSI).

Visit the Computer Concepts CourseMate Web site at www.cengagebrain.com, navigate to the Chapter 6 Quiz Yourself resource for this book, and then click Objectives 1 – 2.

3. What Are the Various Types of Flash Memory Storage?   Flash memory chips are a type of **solid state media,** which means they consist entirely of electronic components and contain no moving parts. A **solid state drive** (SSD) is a storage device that uses flash memory to store data, instructions, and information. Although SSDs currently have a higher failure rate than hard disks and are more expensive, experts estimate that as the price of SSDs drops, increasingly more users will purchase computers and devices that contain this media. A **memory card** is a removable flash memory device that you insert and remove from a slot in a computer, mobile device, or card reader/writer. Common types of memory cards include **CompactFlash (CF), Secure Digital (SD), Secure Digital High Capacity (SDHC), microSD, microSDHC, xD Picture Card, Memory Stick,** and **Memory Stick Micro (M2).** A **USB flash drive** is a flash memory storage device that plugs in a USB port on a computer or mobile device. An **ExpressCard module** is a removable device that fits in an ExpressCard slot. ExpressCard modules add storage or other capabilities to a computer and commonly are used in notebook computers.

4. What Is Cloud Storage, and What Are Its Advantages?   **Cloud storage** is an Internet service that provides storage for computer users. Types of services offered by cloud storage providers vary. Available for all sizes of users, with various degrees of storage services available for home and business users, cloud storage fees vary, depending on the user's storage requirements. Advantages include accessing files on the Internet from any computer or device with Internet access; storing large audio, video, and graphics files on the Internet instantaneously; allowing others to access their files on the Internet; viewing time-critical data and images immediately; storing off-site backups of data; and providing data center functions.

Visit the Computer Concepts CourseMate Web site at www.cengagebrain.com, navigate to the Chapter 6 Quiz Yourself resource for this book, and then click Objectives 3 – 4.

Chapter Review

5. What Are the Characteristics of Optical Discs? An **optical disc** is a type of storage media that consists of a flat, round, portable disc made of metal, plastic, and lacquer. These discs usually are 4.75 inches in diameter and less than one-twentieth of an inch thick. Optical discs primarily store software, data, digital photos, movies, and music. Some are read only, which means users cannot write (save) on them; others are read/write, which allows users to save on the disc just as they save on a hard disk. Optical discs store items by using microscopic pits (indentations) and lands (flat areas). A high-powered laser light creates the pits, and a lower-powered laser light reads items by reflecting light through the bottom of the disc. The reflected light is converted into a series of bits the computer can process.

6. What Are the Various Types of Optical Discs? A **CD-ROM** is an optical disc that users can read but not write (record) or erase. A **CD-R** is a multisession disc on which users can write, but not erase. A **CD-RW** (compact disc-rewritable) is erasable and can be written on multiple times. An **archive disc** is used to store photos from a photo sharing community in the jpg file format. A **Picture CD** stores digital versions of film using a jpg file format. A **DVD-ROM** is a high-capacity disc which users can read but not write on or erase. A **Blu-ray Disc** (BD) currently has storage capacities of 100 GB. The **HD VMD** (Versatile Multilayer Disc) is a high-density format with a capacity of 40 GB or more. A mini-DVD that has grown in popularity is the UMD (Universal Media Disc), which works specifically with the PlayStation Portable handheld game console. Similarly, the mini Blu-ray Disc is used primarily in digital video recorders. DVD-R, DVD+R, BD-R formats can be written on once. **DVD-RW**, **DVD+RW**, and **DVD+RAM** are three competing high-capacity rewritable DVD formats. **BD-RE** is a high-capacity rewritable DVD format.

7. How Are Tape, Magnetic Stripe Cards, Smart Cards, Microfilm and Microfiche, and Enterprise Storage Used? **Tape** is a magnetically coated ribbon of plastic capable of storing large amounts of data and information at a low cost. A **tape drive** reads and writes data and information on tape. Business users utilize tape most often for long-term storage and backup. A **magnetic stripe card** is a credit card, entertainment card, bank card, or other similar card with a stripe that contains information identifying you and the card. A magnetic stripe card reader reads information stored on the stripe. A **smart card**, which is similar in size to a credit or ATM card, stores data on a thin microprocessor embedded in the card. Smart cards contain a processor and have input, process, output, and storage capabilities. **Microfilm** is a 100- to 215-foot roll of film. **Microfiche** is a small sheet of film, usually about 4 × 6 inches. Microfilm and microfiche greatly reduce the amount of paper firms must handle, are inexpensive, and have the longest life of any storage media. Enterprises use special hardware to meet their large-scale needs, including servers, entire networks, and optical disc servers. In an enterprise, some storage systems can provide more than 185 TB of storage capacity.

Visit the Computer Concepts CourseMate Web site at www.cengagebrain.com, navigate to the Chapter 6 Quiz Yourself resource for this book, and then click Objectives 5 – 7.

Key Terms
You should know each key term. The list below helps focus your study.

To see an example of and a definition for each term, and to access current and additional information from the Web, visit the Computer Concepts CourseMate Web site at www.cengagebrain.com and then navigate to the Chapter 6 Key Terms resource for this book.

access time (240)
archive disc (255)
backup (244)
BD-RE (256)
Blu-ray Disc (256)
burning (254)
capacity (240)
card reader/writer (249)
CD-R (254)
CD-ROM (254)
CD-ROM drive (254)
CD-RW (255)
CD-RW drive (255)
cloud storage (251)
CompactFlash (CF) (248)
disk controller (246)

DVD+RAM (256)
DVD-ROM (256)
DVD-ROM drive (256)
DVD+RW (256)
DVD-RW (256)
ExpressCard module (250)
external hard disk (244)
hard disk (240)
HD VMD (256)
LightScribe technology (253)
longitudinal recording (240)
magnetic stripe card (257)
memory card (248)
Memory Stick (248)
Memory Stick Micro (M2)
   (248)

microfiche (258)
microfilm (258)
microSD (248)
microSDHC (248)
network attached storage
   (244)
optical disc (252)
perpendicular recording
   (240)
Picture CD (255)
pocket hard drive (245)
RAID (244)
reading (240)
removable hard disk (244)
ripping (255)
secondary storage (239)

Secure Digital (SD) (248)
Secure Digital High Capacity
   (SDHC) (248)
smart card (257)
solid state drive (SSD) (247)
solid state media (247)
storage device (240)
storage medium (239)
tape (257)
tape drive (257)
UMD (256)
USB flash drive (250)
writing (240)
xD Picture Card (248)

Checkpoint

The Checkpoint exercises test your knowledge of the chapter concepts. The page number containing the answer appears in parentheses after each exercise.

To complete the Checkpoint exercises interactively, visit the Computer Concepts CourseMate Web site at www.cengagebrain.com and then navigate to the Chapter 6 Checkpoint resource for this book.

Multiple Choice Select the best answer.

1. _____ measures the amount of time it takes a storage device to locate an item on a storage medium. (240)
   a. Capacity   b. Access time
   c. A storage medium   d. Reading

2. A group of two or more integrated hard disks is called a _____. (244)
   a. backup   b. platter
   c. RAID   d. portable hard disk

3. A _____ consists of a special-purpose chip and electronic circuits that control the transfer of data, instructions, and information from a disk to and from the system bus and other components in the computer. (246)
   a. pocket hard drive
   b. removable hard disk
   c. magnetic disk
   d. disk controller

4. A _____ is a memory storage device that plugs in a USB port on a computer or mobile device. (250)
   a. smart card   b. USB flash drive
   c. UMD   d. Memory Stick

5. Users subscribe to a cloud storage service to _____. (252)
   a. access files from any computer that has Internet access
   b. allow others to access their files
   c. store offsite backups of data
   d. all of the above

6. _____ technology works with specially coated optical discs to etch labels directly on the disc. (253)
   a. LightScribe   b. SATA
   c. LightSaber   d. SCSI

7. _____ storage requires sequential access. (257)
   a. Hard disk   b. Tape
   c. Memory card   d. DVD

8. A(n) _____ card is a credit card, entertainment card, bank card, or other similar card, with a stripe that contains information identifying you and the card. (257)
   a. Secure Digital High Capacity
   b. magnetic stripe
   c. Secure Digital
   d. microSDHC

Matching Match the terms with their definitions.

_____ 1. backup (244)

_____ 2. external hard disk (244)

_____ 3. solid state media (247)

_____ 4. solid state drive (247)

_____ 5. card reader/writer (249)

a. media which consist entirely of electronic components, such as integrated circuits, and contain no moving parts

b. device that reads and writes data, instructions, and information stored on memory cards

c. portable, large-capacity magnetic medium that can store from 100 MB to 750 MB of data

d. duplicate of a file, program, or disk placed on a separate storage medium that you can use in case the original is lost, damaged, or destroyed

e. a storage device that typically uses flash memory to store data, instructions, and information

f. a separate freestanding hard disk that connects with a cable to a USB port or FireWire port on the system unit or communicates wirelessly

Short Answer Write a brief answer to each of the following questions.

1. What is longitudinal recording? _____ What is the benefit of perpendicular recording over longitudinal recording? _____

2. What is network attached storage? _____ How much hard disk storage can home and small business users add to their network with a NAS device? _____

3. How is a single-session disc different from a multisession disc? _____ What is a CD-RW? _____

4. Why do users use memory cards? _____ Name five types of memory cards and describe some of the characteristics of each card. _____

5. What is one difference between microfilm and microfiche? _____ What are some uses of microfilm and microfiche? _____

Problem Solving

The Problem Solving exercises extend your knowledge of the chapter concepts by seeking solutions to practical computer problems that you may encounter at home, school, or work. The Collaboration exercise should be completed with a team.

In the real world, practical problems often can be solved in multiple ways. Provide one solution to each of the following problems using available resources, such as articles on the Web or in print, blogs, podcasts, videos, television, user guides, other individuals, and electronics and computer stores. You may need to use multiple resources to obtain an answer. Present your solutions in the form requested by your instructor (brief report, presentation, discussion, or other means).

@ Home

1. **Old Movies**   During the past two decades, you have been recording home movies on VHS tapes. It is becoming more difficult to locate blank VHS tapes, and you are worried that if your current VCR breaks, it will be hard to find a store that sells them new. A friend suggests that you copy these movies to an optical disc. What steps will you take to convert these movies?

2. **Possible Head Crash**   When you turn on your computer, you hear a clicking sound coming from inside the computer. Furthermore, you realize that Windows is not starting automatically. You talk to a friend who said that your hard disk might have experienced a head crash. What might have caused this?

3. **Missing Cable**   You are attempting to install a new 1 TB hard disk in your computer. You have found the empty bay for the new hard disk, but you cannot locate the cable that connects it to the computer. What are your next steps?

4. **Memory Card Problems**   For the past two years, you have been using the same Secure Digital (SD) memory card to take pictures with your digital camera. When you insert the SD memory card in your computer's card reader to transfer the pictures, your computer does not display the contents of the card. When you put the card back into your digital camera, you can see that the pictures still are stored on the card. What might be wrong?

@ Work

5. **Disk Not Recognized**   The information technology manager at your company has purchased external hard disks for employees to use to back up their files. When you connect the external hard disk to the USB port on your computer, the computer displays a message stating that it cannot recognize the device. What might you do to correct this problem?

6. **File Will Not Open**   Your computer is unable to open a file on an optical disc that you just inserted into the optical disc drive. You have been able to access other files on the same disc, but one file in particular is not opening. What might be causing this?

7. **Backing Up Data**   It has been several years since your office computer was upgraded, and you just received an e-mail message stating that you finally will receive a new computer next week. The e-mail message also stated that all employees will be responsible for backing up their data. What files will you back up?

8. **Optical Disc Problem**   Your colleague gives you an optical disc containing some video files. When you insert the disc in your computer, the disc burning software asks if you would like to finalize the disc. How will you respond?

Collaboration

9. **Computers in Meteorology**   Your environmental sciences instructor is teaching a lesson about how computers have advanced the meteorology field. Form a team of three people to prepare a brief report about how computers and meteorology are connected. One team member should research how meteorologists predicted weather patterns before computer use became mainstream. Another team member should create a timeline illustrating when and how computers were introduced to the meteorology field, and the third team member should research the types of computer hardware and software required for a typical news station to forecast and present the weather.

Learn How To

The Learn How To activities step you through fundamental technology skills when using a computer. The Learn How To exercises enable you to become more proficient with these skills.

Premium Activity: To relate this Learn How To activity to your everyday life, see a visual demonstration of the activity, and complete a short assessment, visit the Computer Concepts CourseMate Web site at www.cengagebrain.com and then navigate to the Chapter 6 Learn How To resource for this book.

Learn How To 1: Maintain a Hard Disk

A computer's hard disk is used for the majority of storage requirements. It is important, therefore, to ensure that each hard disk on a computer is operating at peak efficiency, both to use the available storage space effectively and to make disk operations as fast as possible.

Two tasks that maximize disk operations are removing unused or unnecessary files and folders by using the Disk Cleanup utility program and consolidating files and folders into contiguous storage areas using the Disk Defragmenter utility program. Defragmenting allows your system to access stored files and folders more efficiently.

A. Cleanup Disk

To clean up the disk by removing any programs and data that are not required for the computer, complete the following steps:

1. Click the Start button on the Windows taskbar and then click Computer on the Start menu.
2. When the Computer window opens, right-click the hard disk icon for drive C (or any other hard disk you want to select) and then click Properties on the shortcut menu.
3. If necessary, click the General tab in the disk drive Properties dialog box to display the General sheet.
4. Click the Disk Cleanup button in the General sheet to display the Disk Cleanup Options dialog box.
5. The Disk Cleanup dialog box is displayed and contains a message that indicates the amount of space that can be freed up is being calculated.
6. After the calculation is complete, the Disk Cleanup dialog box specifies the amount of space that can be freed up and the files to delete, some of which are selected automatically (Figure 6-31). Select those items from which you wish to delete files.
7. Click the OK button in the Disk Cleanup dialog box.
8. A dialog box asks if you are sure you want to perform these actions. Click the Delete Files button. The Disk Cleanup dialog box illustrates the progress of the cleanup. When the cleanup is complete, the dialog box closes.

Disk Cleanup dialog box

amount of space to be freed up

Files to delete area

OK button

Figure 6-31

B. Defragment Disk

After removing all the unnecessary files from the hard disk, the next step in disk maintenance is to defragment all the files on the disk. When a file is stored on disk, the data in the file sometimes is stored contiguously, and other times is stored in a noncontiguous manner. The greater the amount of data on a disk, the more likely files will be stored noncontiguously. When a file is stored in a noncontiguous manner, it can take significantly longer to find and retrieve data from the file. One of the more useful utilities to speed up disk operations, therefore, is the defragmentation program, which combines all files so that no files are stored in a noncontiguous manner. To use the defragmentation program, complete the following steps:

1. If necessary, click the Tools tab in the Properties dialog box for the hard disk to be defragmented.
2. Click the Defragment now button in the Tools sheet to open the Disk Defragmenter window (Figure 6-32). This window displays the Disk Defragmenter schedule, when Disk Defragmenter was run last, and when Disk Defragmenter is scheduled to run next.
3. Click the Defragment disk button. The defragmentation process begins. During the defragmentation process, the Stop operation button replaces the Defragment disk button. The defragmentation process can consume more than one hour in some cases, depending on the size of the hard disk and the amount of processing that must occur. You can cancel the operation at any time by clicking the Stop operation button in the Disk Defragmenter window.
4. When the process is complete, the Defragment disk button will replace the Stop operation button.
5. Click the Close button to close the Disk Defragmenter window.

Proper disk maintenance is critically important so that disk operation is as efficient as possible.

Learn How To

Exercises

Caution: The exercises for this chapter that require actual disk maintenance are optional. If you are performing these exercises on a computer that is not your own, obtain explicit permission to complete these exercises. Keep in mind that these exercises can require significant computer time and the computer may be unusable during this time.

1. Display the Properties dialog box for a hard disk found on the computer. Display the General sheet. What is the capacity of the hard disk? How much space is used? How much free space is available? Click the Disk Cleanup button. How much space can be freed up if you use the Disk Cleanup program? Click the OK button to clean up the disk. How long did it take to perform the disk cleanup? Submit your answers to your instructor.

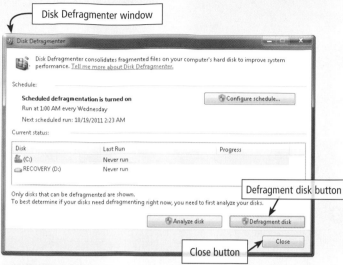

Figure 6-32

2. Display the Properties dialog box for a hard disk found on the computer. Display the Tools sheet. Click the Defragment now button. In the Disk Defragmenter window, click the Defragment disk button. How could you tell when the defragmentation process was completed? How long did defragmentation require? Submit your answers to your instructor.

Learn It Online

The Learn It Online exercises are interactive Web exercises designed to reinforce and expand your understanding of the chapter concepts. The descriptions below briefly summarize each exercise.

To complete the Learn It Online exercises, visit the Computer Concepts CourseMate Web site at www.cengagebrain.com, navigate to the Chapter 6 resources for this book, click the link for the exercise you want to complete, and then read the instructions.

1 At the Movies — Thumb-drive (USB Flash Drive) Encryption

Watch a movie to learn how people who store personal and confidential information on USB flash drives can use third-party programs to password-protect the files so that others cannot access them and then answer questions about the movie.

2 Student Edition Labs — Maintaining a Hard Drive (Hard Disk) and Managing Files and Folders

Enhance your understanding and knowledge about maintaining a hard disk and managing files and folders by completing the Maintaining a Hard Drive and Managing Files and Folders Labs.

3 Practice Test

Take a multiple choice test that checks your knowledge of the chapter concepts and review the resulting study guide.

4 Who Wants To Be a Computer Genius²?

Play the Shelly Cashman Series version of this popular game by answering questions to find out if you are a computer genius. Panic buttons are available to provide assistance during game play.

5 Crossword Puzzle Challenge

Complete an interactive crossword puzzle to reinforce concepts presented in this chapter.

6 Windows Exercises

Step through the Windows 7 exercises to learn about the Recycle Bin, working with files, the hard disk, and Disk Cleanup.

7 Exploring Computer Careers

Read about a career as a computer technician, search for related employment advertisements, and then answer related questions.

8 Web Apps — TurboTax Online

Learn how to use TurboTax Online to create an account, start a new tax return from scratch, review your tax return, and then print and file your tax return.

Web Research

The Web Research exercises broaden your understanding of chapter concepts by presenting questions that require you to search the Web for answers.

1 Search Sleuth

Use one of the search engines listed in Figure 2-8 in Chapter 2 on page 65 or your own favorite search engine to find the answers to the following questions. Copy and paste the Web address from the Web page where you found the answer. Some questions may have more than one answer. If required, submit your answers to your instructor. (1) What album did Hillsong United release in 2008 on a flash drive embedded in a rubber wristband? (2) What country uses the MyKad smart card for national identification? (3) What product did HP develop in 2004 based on the efforts of engineer Daryl Anderson? (4) What products are available for sale at the SanDisk Plaza? (5) For what storage medium are phase change alloys used? (6) What company introduced using a hard disk for accounting projects in 1956?

2 Green Computing

Data storage is doubling every 18 months according to some computer industry experts, and consumers and businesses are turning to environmentally sound methods of backing up and storing files. Accessing hard disks consumes 80 percent of a storage system's electrical consumption, so companies have developed products that reduce a system's energy usage. Businesses invest in cooling systems that dissipate the heat generated when servers and storage hardware operate. Locate Web sites that describe these products and how they operate efficiently to conserve energy. How much energy savings do they claim to make in one year? To what extent are carbon dioxide and other greenhouse gases reduced? How do they maximize the use of power and cooling resources? Review your search results and then write a 50-word summary of your findings.

3 Social Networking

Privacy on social networking Web sites such as MySpace and Facebook is an international concern, and the Electronic Privacy Information Center (epic.org/privacy/socialnet) features news, policies, and resources discussing safeguarding and controlling personal information. At least one-fourth of hiring managers admit to researching job applicants' "digital dirt" by searching social networks and blogs, and some employers search social networking Web sites for profiles of current employees. Visit the Reputation Defender (reputationdefender.com) and Defend My Name (defendmyname .com) Web sites and read about the services offered. Then view the standards posted on the MySpace and Facebook Web sites regarding privacy and allowable content. Summarize the information you read and viewed.

4 Blogs

Exercise and nutrition advice is available from experts who post firsthand experiences in their blogs. These authorities may be people who share a particular experience, such as losing weight or training for a marathon, or who have specialized training in the fitness field. For example, noted author Lou Schuler discusses nutrition, weight training, and issues of particular interest to men (malepatternfitness.com). Other popular fitness blogs are featured by The Families .com (fitness.families.com/blog) and Diet-Blog (diet-blog.com). Athlete Blog Central (yardbarker.com/athletes) lists blogs that professional and amateur athletes and their fans write. Visit these sites and read the posts. Which stories received more than 25 comments? Which food, exercises, and programs are featured?

5 Ethics in Action

The United States Federal Bureau of Investigation used a controversial program until January 2005 to monitor and store the e-mail and Internet activity of suspected criminals. Originally called Carnivore, the surveillance program was renamed DCS1000. The program was designed to track the activities of potential terrorists, spies, drug traffickers, and organized crime ring members. FBI agents needed to obtain a court order to monitor an individual, but privacy advocates claim the software tracked people not covered under the court order. View online sites that provide information about DCS1000 or Carnivore, including HowStuffWorks (howstuffworks.com/carnivore.htm). What commercial software has replaced Carnivore? Write a report summarizing your findings, and include a table of links to Web sites that provide additional details.

Chapter Seven

Operating Systems and Utility Programs

Objectives

After completing this chapter, you will be able to:

1 Define system software and identify the two types of system software

2 Describe each of these functions of an operating system: starting and shutting down a computer, providing a user interface, managing memory, coordinating tasks, configuring devices, establishing an Internet connection, monitoring performance, providing file management and other utilities, updating automatically, controlling a network, and administering security

3 Summarize the features of several stand-alone operating systems: Windows, Mac OS, UNIX, and Linux

4 Identify various server operating systems

5 Briefly describe several embedded operating systems: Windows Embedded CE, Windows Phone, Palm OS, iPhone OS, BlackBerry, Google Android, Embedded Linux, and Symbian OS

6 Explain the purpose of several utility programs: file manager, search utility, image viewer, uninstaller, disk cleanup, disk defragmenter, backup and restore utilities, screen saver, personal firewall, antivirus programs, spyware and adware removers, Internet filters, file compression, media player, disc burning, and personal computer maintenance

System Software

When you purchase a personal computer, it usually has system software installed on its hard disk. **System software** consists of the programs that control or maintain the operations of the computer and its devices. System software serves as the interface between the user, the application software, and the computer's hardware.

Two types of system software are operating systems and utility programs. This chapter discusses the operating system and its functions, as well as several types of utility programs for personal computers.

start and shut down the computer

administer security

control a network

update automatically

operating system functions

provide file management and other utilities

Figure 7-1 Most operating systems perform similar functions, which are illustrated with the latest version of Windows in this figure.

Operating Systems

An **operating system** (**OS**) is a set of programs containing instructions that work together to coordinate all the activities among computer hardware resources. Most operating systems perform similar functions that include starting and shutting down a computer, providing a user interface, managing programs, managing memory, coordinating tasks, configuring devices, establishing an Internet connection, monitoring performance, providing file management and other utilities, and automatically updating itself and certain utility programs. Some operating systems also allow users to control a network and administer security (Figure 7-1).

Although an operating system can run from an optical disc and/or flash memory mobile media, in most cases, the operating system is installed and resides on the computer's hard disk. On handheld computers and many mobile devices, the operating system may reside on a ROM chip.

provide a user interface

manage programs

manage memory

establish an Internet connection

monitor performance

coordinate tasks and configure devices

Different sizes of computers typically use different operating systems because operating systems generally are written to run on a specific type of computer. For example, a mainframe computer does not use the same operating system as a personal computer. Even the same types of computers, such as desktop computers, may not use the same operating system. Some, however, can run multiple operating systems. When purchasing application software, you must ensure that it works with the operating system installed on your computer or mobile device.

The operating system that a computer uses sometimes is called the platform. With purchased application software, the package or specifications identify the required platform (operating system). A cross-platform program is one that runs the same on multiple operating systems.

Operating System Functions

Many different operating systems exist; however, most operating systems provide similar functions. The following sections discuss functions common to most operating systems. The operating system handles many of these functions automatically, without requiring any instruction from a user.

Starting and Shutting Down a Computer

Booting is the process of starting or restarting a computer. When turning on a computer that has been powered off completely, you are performing a **cold boot**. A **warm boot**, by contrast, is the process of using the operating system to restart a computer. With Windows, for example, you can perform a warm boot by clicking a menu command (Figure 7-2).

When you install new software or update existing software, often an on-screen prompt instructs you to restart the computer. In this case, a warm boot is appropriate.

Each time you boot a computer, the kernel and other frequently used operating system instructions are loaded, or copied, from storage into the computer's memory (RAM). The kernel is the core of an operating system that manages memory and devices, maintains the computer's clock, starts programs, and assigns the computer's resources, such as devices, programs, data, and information. The kernel is memory resident, which means it remains in memory while the computer is running. Other parts of the operating system are nonresident, that is, these instructions remain on a storage medium until they are needed.

Shut down button menu

performs a warm boot

puts computer in a low-power consumption state

Figure 7-2 To reboot a running computer, click the Shut down button arrow and then click Restart.

When you boot a computer, a series of messages may appear on the screen. The actual information displayed varies depending on the make and type of the computer and the equipment installed. The boot process, however, is similar for large and small computers.

Although some users leave their computers running continually and never turn them off, others choose to shut them down. Shut down options including powering off the computer, placing the computer in sleep mode, and hibernating the computer. Both sleep mode and hibernate are designed to save time when you resume working on the computer. **Sleep mode** saves any open documents and programs to RAM, turns off all unneeded functions, and then places the computer in a low-power state. **Hibernate**, by contrast, saves any open documents and programs to a hard disk before removing power from the computer.

Providing a User Interface

You interact with software through its user interface. That is, a **user interface** controls how you enter data and instructions and how information is displayed on the screen. Two types of user interfaces are graphical and command-line (Figure 7-3). Operating systems sometimes use a combination of these interfaces to define how a user interacts with a computer.

Graphical User Interface   Most users today work with a graphical user interface. With a **graphical user interface** (**GUI**), you interact with menus and visual images such as buttons and other graphical objects to issue commands (Figure 7-3a). Many current GUI operating systems incorporate features similar to those of a Web browser.

Windows 7 offers two different GUIs, depending on your hardware configuration. Computers with less than 1 GB of RAM work with the Windows 7 Basic interface. Computers with more than 1 GB of RAM that have the required hardware may be able to work with the Windows 7 Aero interface, also known as **Windows Aero**, shown in Figure 7-3a, which provides an enhanced visual look, additional navigation options, and animation.

Command-Line Interface   To configure devices, manage system resources, and troubleshoot network connections, network administrators and other advanced users work with a command-line interface. In a **command-line interface**, a user types commands or presses special keys on the keyboard to enter data and instructions (Figure 7-3b). Some people consider command-line interfaces difficult to use because they require exact spelling, grammar, and punctuation.

Figure 7-3a   (graphical user interface)

Figure 7-3b   (command-line interface)

Figure 7-3   Examples of graphical user and command-line interfaces.

Managing Programs

Some operating systems support a single user and only one running program at a time. Others support thousands of users running multiple programs. How an operating system handles programs directly affects your productivity.

A single user/single tasking operating system allows only one user to run one program at a time. Smart phones and other mobile devices often use a single user/single tasking operating system.

A single user/multitasking operating system allows a single user to work on two or more programs that reside in memory at the same time. Users today typically run multiple programs concurrently. It is common to have an e-mail program and Web browser open at all times, while working with application programs such as word processing or graphics.

When a computer is running multiple programs concurrently, one program is in the foreground and the others are in the background. The one in the foreground is the active program, that is, the one you currently are using. The other programs running but not in use are in the background. In Figure 7-4, the Windows Live Movie Maker program is in the foreground, and three other programs are running in the background (Windows Media Player, Microsoft PowerPoint, and Chess Titans).

The foreground program typically is displayed on the desktop but the background programs often are hidden partially or completely behind the foreground program. You easily can switch between foreground and background programs. To make a program active (in the foreground) in Windows, click its program button on the taskbar. This causes the operating system to place all other programs in the background.

foreground program

taskbar

program button

background programs

Figure 7-4 The foreground program, Windows Live Movie Maker, is displayed on the desktop. The other programs (Windows Media Player, Microsoft PowerPoint, and Chess Titans) are in the background.

A **multiuser** operating system enables two or more users to run programs simultaneously. Networks, servers, mainframes, and supercomputers allow hundreds to thousands of users to connect at the same time, and thus are multiuser.

A **multiprocessing** operating system supports two or more processors running programs at the same time. Multiprocessing involves the coordinated processing of programs by more than one processor. Multiprocessing increases a computer's processing speed.

Managing Memory

The purpose of **memory management** is to optimize the use of random access memory (RAM). RAM consists of one or more chips on the motherboard that hold items such as data and instructions while the processor interprets and executes them. The operating system allocates, or assigns, data and instructions to an area of memory while they are being processed. Then, it carefully monitors the contents of memory. Finally, the operating system releases these items from being monitored in memory when the processor no longer requires them.

Virtual memory is a concept in which the operating system allocates a portion of a storage medium, usually the hard disk, to function as additional RAM. As you interact with a program, part of it may be in physical RAM, while the rest of the program is on the hard disk as virtual memory. Because virtual memory is slower than RAM, users may notice the computer slowing down while it uses virtual memory.

The operating system uses an area of the hard disk for virtual memory, in which it swaps (exchanges) data, information, and instructions between memory and storage. The technique of swapping items between memory and storage is called paging. When an operating system spends much of its time paging, instead of executing application software, it is said to be thrashing. If application software, such as a Web browser, has stopped responding and the hard disk's LED blinks repeatedly, the operating system probably is thrashing.

Instead of using a hard disk as virtual memory, Windows users can increase the size of memory through **Windows ReadyBoost**, which can allocate available storage space on removable flash memory devices as additional memory cache. Users notice better performance with Windows ReadyBoost versus hard disk virtual memory because the operating system accesses a flash memory device, such as a USB flash drive or SD memory card, more quickly than it accesses a hard disk.

Coordinating Tasks

The operating system determines the order in which tasks are processed. A task, or job, is an operation the processor manages. Tasks include receiving data from an input device, processing instructions, sending information to an output device, and transferring items from storage to memory and from memory to storage.

A multiuser operating system does not always process tasks on a first-come, first-served basis. Sometimes, one user may have a higher priority than other users. In this case, the operating system adjusts the schedule of tasks.

Sometimes, a device already may be busy processing one task when it receives a second task. This occurs because the processor operates at a much faster rate of speed than peripheral devices. For example, if the processor sends five documents to a printer, the printer can print only one document at a time and store as many documents as its memory can handle.

While waiting for devices to become idle, the operating system places items in buffers. A **buffer** is a segment of memory or storage in which items are placed while waiting to be transferred from an input device or to an output device.

The operating system commonly uses buffers with printed documents. This process, called **spooling**, sends documents to be printed to a buffer instead of sending them immediately to the printer. If a printer does not have its own internal memory or if its memory is full, the operating system's buffer holds the information waiting to print while the printer prints from the buffer at its own rate of speed. By spooling documents to a buffer, the processor can continue interpreting and executing instructions while the printer prints. This allows users to work on the computer for other

Spooling
For more information, visit the Computer Concepts CourseMate Web site at www.cengagebrain.com, navigate to the Chapter 7 Web Link resource for this book, and then click Spooling.

tasks while a printer is printing. Multiple print jobs line up in a **queue** (pronounced Q) in the buffer. A program, called a print spooler, intercepts documents to be printed from the operating system and places them in the queue (Figure 7-5).

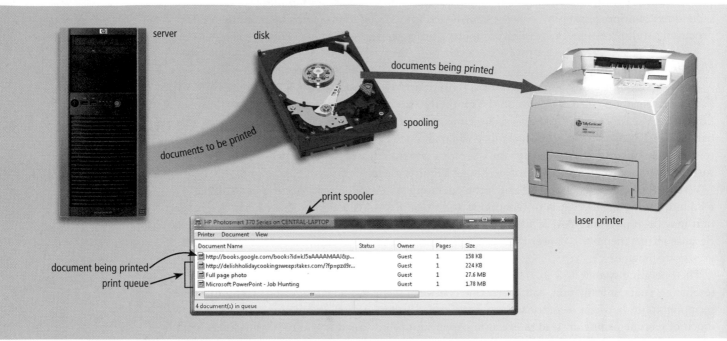

Figure 7-5   Spooling increases both processor and printer efficiency by placing documents to be printed in a buffer on disk before they are printed. This figure illustrates three documents in the queue with one document printing.

Configuring Devices

A **driver** is a small program that tells the operating system how to communicate with a specific device. Each device on a computer, such as the mouse, keyboard, monitor, printer, and scanner, has its own specialized set of commands and thus requires its own specific driver. When you boot a computer, the operating system loads each device's driver.

If you attach a new device to a computer, such as a printer or scanner, its driver must be installed before you can use the device. Today, most devices and operating systems support Plug and Play. **Plug and Play** means the operating system automatically configures new devices as you install them. With Plug and Play, a user can plug in a device, turn on the computer, and then use the device without having to configure the system manually.

Plug and Play

For more information, visit the Computer Concepts CourseMate Web site at www.cengagebrain.com, navigate to the Chapter 7 Web Link resource for this book, and then click Plug and Play.

Establishing an Internet Connection

Operating systems typically provide a means to establish Internet connections. For example, Windows includes a Set Up a Connection or Network wizard that guides users through the process of setting up a connection between a computer and an Internet access provider (Figure 7-6).

Some operating systems also include a Web browser and an e-mail program, enabling you to begin using the Web and communicate with others as soon as you set up the Internet connection. Some also include utilities to protect computers from unauthorized intrusions and unwanted software such as viruses and spyware.

Figure 7-6   To connect to a network using Windows, click the Start button, click Control Panel, click Network and Internet, click Network and Sharing Center, and then click 'Set up a new connection or network' to open the window shown here.

Monitoring Performance

Operating systems typically contain a performance monitor. A **performance monitor** is a program that assesses and reports information about various computer resources and devices (shown in Figure 7-1 on pages 270 and 271).

The information in performance reports helps users and administrators identify a problem with resources so that they can try to resolve any problems. If a computer is running extremely slow, for example, the performance monitor may determine that the computer's memory is being used to its maximum. Thus, you might consider installing additional memory in the computer. Read Looking Ahead 7-1 for a look at a future type of health-based performance monitor.

↗ LOOKING AHEAD 7-1

Contact Lenses Monitor Glaucoma

The future looks good for contact lenses that will help study and treat glaucoma. Biomedical engineers at the University of California – Davis are developing lenses that measure eye pressure and then flow if the readings are abnormal.

Glaucoma occurs when the fluid pressure inside the eye increases. This intraocular pressure can result in total blindness if the optic nerve, which sends messages from the eyes to the brain, is damaged. Doctors can measure the amount of pressure and then perform surgery to correct the blockage in the back of the eye that prevents the fluid from draining. As an alternative to the pressure measurement, the new contact lenses can perform the fluidic resistance evaluation for the drainage network of the eye, which prevents dangerously high levels in the early glaucomatous eyes.

Lasers, too, are expected to become part of a doctor's means of detecting glaucoma. A high-resolution laser can measure 28 million areas of the optic nerve, and then software can create a 3-D view of the eye and assess signs of the disease.

🖳 For more information, visit the Computer Concepts CourseMate Web site at www.cengagebrain.com, navigate to the Chapter 7 Looking Ahead resource for this book, and then click Contact Lenses.

Providing File Management and Other Utilities

Operating systems often provide users with the capability of managing files, searching for files, viewing images, securing a computer from unauthorized access, uninstalling programs, cleaning up disks, defragmenting disks, diagnosing problems, backing up files and disks, and setting up screen savers. A later section in the chapter discusses these and other utilities in depth.

Updating Software Automatically

Many popular programs, including most operating systems, include an **automatic update** feature that automatically provides updates to the program. With an operating system, these updates can include fixes to program bugs (errors), enhancements to security, modifications to device drivers, access to new or expanded components such as desktop themes or games, and even updates to application software on the computer such as a Web browser or an e-mail program.

Many software makers provide free downloadable updates, sometimes called a **service pack**, to users who have registered and/or activated their software. With operating systems, the automatic update feature automatically alerts users when an update is available; further, it can be configured to download and install the update automatically. Users without an Internet connection usually can order the updates on an optical disc for a minimal shipping fee. To learn about keeping Windows up-to-date, complete the Learn How To 2 exercise on pages 298 and 299.

Controlling a Network

Some operating systems are designed to work with a server on a network. A **server operating system** is an operating system that organizes and coordinates how multiple users access and share resources on a network. Resources include hardware, software, data, and information. For example, a server operating system allows multiple users to share a printer, Internet access, files, and programs.

Some operating systems have network features built into them. In other cases, the server operating system is a set of programs separate from the operating system on the client computers that access the network. When not connected to the network, the client computers use their own operating system. When connected to the network, the server operating system may assume some of the operating system functions.

The network administrator, the person overseeing network operations, uses the server operating system to add and remove users, computers, and other devices to and from the network. The network administrator also uses the server operating system to install software and administer network security.

Administering Security

Computer and network administrators typically have an **administrator account** that enables them to access all files and programs on the computer or network, install programs, and specify settings that affect all users on a computer or network. Settings include creating user accounts and establishing permissions. These permissions define who can access certain resources and when they can access those resources.

For each user, the network administrator establishes a user account, which enables a user to access, or **log on** to, a computer or a network (Figure 7-7). Each user account typically consists of a user name and password. A **user name**, or **user ID**, is a unique combination of characters, such as letters of the alphabet or numbers, that identifies one specific user. Many users select a combination of their first and last names as their user name. A user named Henry Baker might choose H Baker as his user name.

A **password** is a private combination of characters associated with the user name that allows access to certain computer resources. Some operating systems allow the computer or network administrator to assign passwords to files and commands, restricting access to only authorized users.

To prevent unauthorized users from accessing computer resources, keep your password confidential. While users type a password, most computers hide the actual password characters by displaying some other characters, such as asterisks (*) or dots. After entering a user name and password, the operating system compares the user's entry with a list of authorized user names and passwords. If the entry matches the user name and password kept on file, the operating system grants the user access. If the entry does not match, the operating system denies access to the user.

The operating system records successful and unsuccessful logon attempts in a file. This allows the computer or network administrator to review who is using or attempting to use the computer. The administrators also use these files to monitor computer usage.

To protect sensitive data and information as it travels over a network, the operating system may encrypt it. Encryption is the process of encoding data and information into an unreadable form. Administrators can specify that data be encrypted as it travels over a network to prevent unauthorized users from reading the data. When an authorized user attempts to read the data, it automatically is decrypted, or converted back into a readable form.

Figure 7-7   Most multiuser operating systems allow each user to log on, which is the process of entering a user name and a password into the computer.

? FAQ 7-1

What are the guidelines for selecting a good password?

Choose a password that is easy to remember, and that no one could guess. Do not use any part of your first or last name, your spouse's or child's name, telephone number, street address, license plate number, Social Security number, birthday, and so on. Be sure your password is at least eight characters long, mixed with uppercase and lowercase letters, numbers, and special characters. You also should avoid using single-word passwords that are found in the dictionary. Security experts also recommend using a passphrase, which is similar to a password, but comprised of several words separated by spaces.

For more information, visit the Computer Concepts CourseMate Web site at www.cengagebrain.com, navigate to the Chapter 7 FAQ resource for this book, and then click Passwords.

QUIZ YOURSELF 7-1

Instructions: Find the true statement below. Then, rewrite the remaining false statements so that they are true.

1. A buffer is a small program that tells the operating system how to communicate with a specific device.

2. A warm boot is the process of using the operating system to restart a computer.

3. A password is a public combination of characters associated with the user name that allows access to certain computer resources.

4. The program you currently are using is in the background, and the other programs running but not in use are in the foreground.

5. Two types of system software are operating systems and application programs.

Quiz Yourself Online: To further check your knowledge of pages 270 through 278, visit the Computer Concepts CourseMate Web site at www.cengagebrain.com, navigate to the Chapter 7 Quiz Yourself resource for this book, and then click Objectives 1 – 2.

Types of Operating Systems

When you purchase a new computer or mobile device, it typically has an operating system preinstalled. As new versions of the operating system are released, users upgrade their existing computers and mobile devices to incorporate features of the new version. Purchasing an operating system upgrade usually costs less than purchasing the entire operating system.

New versions of an operating system usually are backward compatible. That is, they recognize and work with application software written for an earlier version of the operating system (or platform). By contrast, the application software may or may not be upward compatible, meaning it may or may not run on new versions of the operating system.

The three basic categories of operating systems that exist today are stand-alone, server, and embedded. The table in Figure 7-8 lists names of operating systems in each category. The following pages discuss a variety of operating systems.

Categories of Operating Systems

Category	Operating System Name
Stand-alone	• DOS • Early Windows versions (Windows 3.x, Windows 95, Windows NT Workstation, Windows 98, Windows 2000 Professional, Windows Millennium Edition, Windows XP, Windows Vista) • Windows 7 • Mac OS X • UNIX • Linux
Server	• Early Windows Server versions (Windows NT Server, Windows 2000 Server, Windows Server 2003) • Windows Server 2008 • UNIX • Linux • Solaris • NetWare
Embedded	• Windows Embedded CE • Windows Phone 7 • Palm OS • iPhone OS • BlackBerry • Google Android • Embedded Linux • Symbian OS

Figure 7-8 Examples of stand-alone, server, and embedded operating systems. Some stand-alone operating systems include the capability of configuring small home or office networks.

FAQ 7-2

Which operating systems have the most market share?
The Windows operating system family currently dominates the operating system market with more than 93 percent market share. The Mac operating system is in second place with nearly 5 percent market share. The chart to the right illustrates the market share for various operating systems.

For more information, visit the Computer Concepts CourseMate Web site at www.cengagebrain.com, navigate to the Chapter 7 FAQ resource for this book, and then click Operating System Market Share.

Operating System Market Share

Source: Market Share by Net Applications

Stand-Alone Operating Systems

A **stand-alone operating system** is a complete operating system that works on a desktop computer, notebook computer, or mobile computing device. Some stand-alone operating systems are called client operating systems because they also work in conjunction with a server operating system. Client operating systems can operate with or without a network. Other stand-alone operating systems include networking capabilities, allowing the home and small business user to set up a small network. Examples of currently used stand-alone operating systems are Windows 7, Mac OS X, UNIX, and Linux.

Windows 7

In the mid-1980s, Microsoft developed its first version of Windows, which provided a graphical user interface (GUI). Since then, Microsoft continually has updated its Windows operating system, incorporating innovative features and functions with each new version. **Windows 7** is Microsoft's fastest, most efficient operating system to date, offering quicker program start up, built-in diagnostics, automatic recovery, improved security, enhanced searching and organizing capabilities, and an easy-to-use interface (Figure 7-9).

Most users choose one of these Windows 7 editions: Windows 7 Starter, Windows 7 Home Premium, Windows 7 Ultimate, or Windows 7 Professional.

- Windows 7 Starter, designed for netbooks and other small notebook computers, uses the Windows 7 Basic interface and allows users easily to search for files, connect to printers and devices, browse the Internet, join home networks, and connect to wireless networks. This edition of Windows typically is preinstalled on new computers and not available for purchase in retail stores.
- Windows 7 Home Premium, which includes all the capabilities of Windows 7 Starter, also includes Windows Aero with its Aero Flip 3D feature and provides tools to create and edit high-definition movies, record and watch television shows, connect to a game console, and read from and write on Blu-ray Discs.
- Windows 7 Ultimate, which includes all features of Windows 7 Home Premium, provides additional features designed to keep your files secure and support for 35 languages.
- With Windows 7 Professional, users in all sizes of businesses are provided a secure operating environment that uses Windows Aero where they easily can search for files, protect their computers from unauthorized intruders and unwanted programs, use improved backup technologies, securely connect to Wi-Fi networks, quickly view messages on a powered-off, specially equipped notebook computer, easily share documents and collaborate with other users, and watch and record live television.

Windows 7 adapts to the hardware configuration on which it is installed. Thus, two users with the same edition of Windows 7 may experience different functionality and interfaces.

Windows 7

For more information, visit the Computer Concepts CourseMate Web site at www.cengagebrain.com, navigate to the Chapter 7 Web Link resource for this book, and then click Windows 7.

 Figure 7-9 Windows 7 has a new interface, easier navigation a searching techniques, and improv security.

Mac OS X

Since it was released with Macintosh computers in 1984, Apple's **Macintosh operating system** has set the standard for operating system ease of use and has been the model for most of the new GUIs developed for non-Macintosh systems. The latest version, **Mac OS X**, is a multitasking operating system available only for computers manufactured by Apple (Figure 7-10).

Mac OS X

 For more information, visit the Computer Concepts CourseMate Web site at www.cengagebrain.com, navigate to the Chapter 7 Web Link resource for this book, and then click Mac OS X.

Figure 7-10   Mac OS X is the operating system used with Apple Macintosh computers.

UNIX

UNIX (pronounced YOU-nix) is a multitasking operating system. Several versions of this operating system exist, each slightly different. Although some versions of UNIX have a command-line interface, most versions of UNIX offer a graphical user interface (Figure 7-11). Today, a version of UNIX is available for most computers of all sizes. Power users often work with UNIX because of its flexibility and power.

Figure 7-11   Many versions of UNIX have a graphical user interface.

Linux

For more information, visit the Computer Concepts CourseMate Web site at www.cengagebrain.com, navigate to the Chapter 7 Web Link resource for this book, and then click Linux.

Linux

Linux is one of the faster growing operating systems. **Linux** (pronounced LINN-uks), introduced in 1991, is a popular, multitasking UNIX-type operating system. In addition to the basic operating system, Linux also includes many free programming languages and utility programs. Linux is not proprietary software like the operating systems discussed thus far. Instead, Linux is open source software, which means its code is available to the public for use, modification, and redistribution. Read Ethics & Issues 7-1 for a related discussion.

Linux is available in a variety of forms, known as distributions. Some distributions of Linux are command-line. Others are GUI (Figure 7-12). Users obtain Linux in a variety of ways. Some people download it free from the Web. Others purchase it from vendors, who bundle their own software with the operating system. Linux optical discs are included in many Linux books and also are available for purchase from vendors. For purchasers of new personal computers, some retailers such as Dell will preinstall Linux on the hard disk on request. If you want to preview the Linux operating system, you can obtain a Live CD or Live USB.

Figure 7-12   This distribution of Linux has a graphical user interface.

ETHICS & ISSUES 7-1

Closed Source vs. Open Source Operating Systems

One of the features that make Linux different from other operating systems is that Linux is open source and its source code, along with any changes, remains public. Often, when closed source operating system developers refuse to share some or all of the operating system code, third-party software developers become hindered when developing application software for the operating system. Supporters of open source maintain that source code should be open to the public so that it can be scrutinized, corrected, and enhanced. In light of concerns about security and fears of possible virus problems, however, some people are not sure open source software is a good idea. Besides, they argue, companies and programmers should be able to control, and profit from, the operating systems they create. On the other hand, open source software can be scrutinized for errors by a much larger group of people and changes can be made immediately, resulting in better software.

Are open source operating systems a good idea? Why or why not? How can the concerns about open source software be addressed? What are the advantages and disadvantages of open versus closed source operating systems? Does the open source model lead to better software?

Ethics & Issues

For the complete text of the Ethics & Issues boxes found in this chapter, visit the Computer Concepts CourseMate Web site at www.cengagebrain.com and then navigate to the Chapter 7 Ethics & Issues resource for this book.

Server Operating Systems

As discussed earlier in this chapter, a server operating system is an operating system that is designed specifically to support a network. A server operating system typically resides on a server. The client computers on the network rely on the server(s) for resources.

Many of the stand-alone operating systems discussed in the previous section function as clients and work in conjunction with a server operating system. Some of these stand-alone operating systems do include networking capability; however, server operating systems are designed specifically to support all sizes of networks, including medium- to large-sized businesses and Web servers.

Following are examples of server operating systems:

- Windows Server 2008 is an upgrade to Windows Server 2003.
- UNIX and Linux often are called multipurpose operating systems because they are both stand-alone and server operating systems.
- Solaris, a version of UNIX developed by Sun Microsystems, is a server operating system designed specifically for e-commerce applications.
- Novell's NetWare is a server operating system designed for client/server networks.

Embedded Operating Systems

The operating system on most mobile devices and many consumer electronics, called an **embedded operating system**, resides on a ROM chip. Popular embedded operating systems include Windows Embedded CE, Windows Phone 7, Palm OS, iPhone OS, BlackBerry, Google Android, embedded Linux, and Symbian OS.

- Windows Embedded CE is a scaled-down Windows operating system designed for use on communications, entertainment, and computing devices with limited functionality. Examples of devices that use Windows Embedded CE include VoIP telephones, digital cameras, point-of-sale terminals, automated teller machines, digital photo frames, fuel pumps, handheld navigation devices, portable media players, ticket machines, and computerized sewing machines.
- Windows Phone 7, which is a successor to Windows Mobile, works on specific types of smart phones. With the Windows Phone 7 operating system and a compatible device, users have access to the basic PIM (personal information manager) functions such as contact lists, schedules, tasks, calendars, and notes. These devices also can check e-mail, browse the Web, listen to music, take pictures or record video, watch a video, send and receive text messages and instant messages, record a voice message, manage finances, view a map, read an e-book, or play a game.
- Palm OS, a competing operating system to Windows Phone 7, runs on smart phones and PDAs. With Palm OS and a compatible device, users manage schedules and contacts, phone messages, notes, tasks and address lists, and appointments. Many Palm OS devices allow users to connect wirelessly to the Internet; browse the Web; send and receive e-mail messages, text messages, and instant messages; listen to music; record voice messages; and view digital photos.
- iPhone OS is an operating system for the iPhone and iPod touch. With finger motions, users can manage contacts and notes, send and receive e-mail and text messages, take pictures, record videos, record voice messages, view a compass, connect to the Internet wirelessly and browse the Web, check stocks, access maps and obtain directions, listen to music, watch movies and videos, and display photos. iPhone OS devices also provide Wi-Fi access to the iTunes Music Store.
- The BlackBerry operating system runs on handheld devices supplied by RIM (Research In Motion), shown in Figure 7-13. BlackBerry devices provide PIM, phone, and wireless capabilities such as sending e-mail messages, text messages, and instant messages; connecting to the Internet and browsing the Web; and accessing Bluetooth devices. Some also allow you to take pictures, play music, and access maps and directions.
- Google Android is an operating system designed by Google for mobile devices. Used on more than 20 different types of mobile devices, Google Android allows programmers to design programs specifically for devices supporting this operating system. Google Android contains features such as access to e-mail accounts, an alarm clock, video capture, access to Google Apps, Wi-Fi access, and easy Web browsing.
- Embedded Linux is a scaled-down Linux operating system designed for smart phones, PDAs, portable media players, Internet telephones, and many other types of devices and computers requiring an embedded operating system. Devices with embedded Linux offer calendar and address book and other PIM functions, touch screens, and handwriting recognition.
- Symbian OS is an open source multitasking operating system designed for smart phones. Users enter data by pressing keys on the keypad or keyboard, touching the screen, and writing on the screen with a stylus.

Figure 7-13 A smart phone that uses the BlackBerry operating system.

✓ **QUIZ YOURSELF 7-2**

Instructions: Find the true statement below. Then, rewrite the remaining false statements so that they are true.

1. Pocket PCs use Palm OS as their operating system.
2. Examples of embedded operating systems include Windows Server 2008, UNIX, Linux, Solaris, and NetWare.
3. Windows 7 Starter uses Windows Aero.
4. Mac OS X is a multitasking operating system available only for computers manufactured by Apple.
5. Aero Flip 3D is a UNIX-type operating system that is open source software.

Quiz Yourself Online: To further check your knowledge of pages 279 through 283, visit the Computer Concepts CourseMate Web site at www.cengagebrain.com, navigate to the Chapter 7 Quiz Yourself resource for this book, and then click Objectives 3 – 5.

Utility Programs

A **utility program**, also called a **utility**, is a type of system software that allows a user to perform maintenance-type tasks, usually related to managing a computer, its devices, or its programs. Most operating systems include several built-in utility programs (Figure 7-14). Users often buy stand-alone utilities, however, because they offer improvements over those included with the operating system.

Functions provided by utility programs include the following: managing files, searching for files, uninstalling programs, viewing images, cleaning up disks, defragmenting disks, backing up files and disks, setting up screen savers, securing a computer from unauthorized access, protecting against viruses, removing spyware and adware, filtering Internet content, compressing files, playing media files, burning optical discs, and maintaining a personal computer. The following sections briefly discuss each of these utilities. Read Innovative Computing 7-1 to find out about utility programs that can help you recover deleted files.

Figure 7-14   To display the utilities available in the Windows System Tools list, click the Start button, click All Programs, click Accessories, and then click System Tools.

System Tools command

utility for managing files

utility for removing unwanted files

utility for defragmenting disks

utility for restoring backed up files

! **INNOVATIVE COMPUTING 7-1**

Utility Programs Locate Deleted Files

If you delete a file mistakenly from a USB flash drive, removable flash memory device, or hard disk, you easily can recover that erased file with utility programs. A few of the more popular utility programs have names that explain their purpose: Recuva, Recover My Files, FreeUndelete, FileMakerRecovery, R-Studio, and Recovery Toolbox. Most can be downloaded from the Web, often free of charge.

Data recovery experts offer advice on actions to take immediately when you realize you have erased files, even if you have emptied the Recycle Bin.

Although the file name does not appear in the list of files on that storage medium, the file actually remains intact on the storage medium. The computer marks the space on the disk as free so that another file can overwrite the contents of the deleted file. As long as you do not save any file, no matter how small, the utility program generally can locate the marked space and then retrieve the contents of the file.

For more information, visit the Computer Concepts CourseMate Web site at www.cengagebrain.com, navigate to the Chapter 7 Innovative Computing resource for this book, and then click Recovering Deleted Files.

File Manager

A **file manager** is a utility that performs functions related to file management. Some of the file management functions that a file manager performs are displaying a list of files on a storage medium (Figure 7-15); organizing files in folders; and copying, renaming, deleting, moving, and sorting files. A **folder** is a specific named location on a storage medium that contains related documents. Operating systems typically include a file manager.

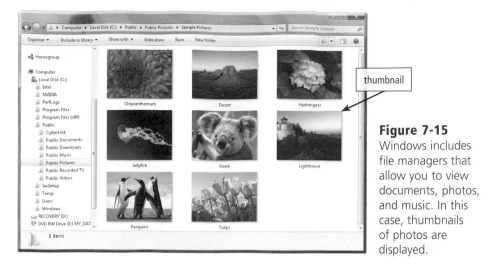

Figure 7-15
Windows includes file managers that allow you to view documents, photos, and music. In this case, thumbnails of photos are displayed.

Search Utility

A **search utility** is a program that attempts to locate a file on your computer based on criteria you specify (Figure 7-16). The criteria could be a word or words contained in a file, date the file was created or modified, size of the file, location of the file, file name, author/artist, and other similar properties. Search utilities can look through documents, photos, music, and other files. Operating systems typically include a built-in search utility.

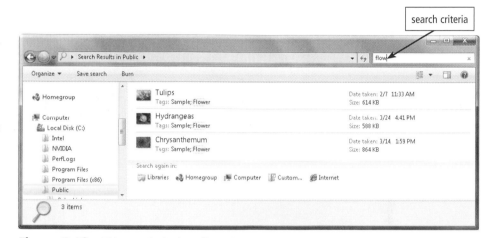

Figure 7-16 This search displays files whose name or contents contain the text, flow.

Uninstaller

An **uninstaller** is a utility that removes a program, as well as any associated entries in the system files. When you install a program, the operating system records the information it uses to run the software in the system files. The uninstaller deletes files and folders from the hard disk, as well as removes program entries from the system files.

Image Viewer

An **image viewer** is a utility that allows users to display, copy, and print the contents of a graphics file. With an image viewer, users can see images without having to open them in a paint or image editing program. Most operating systems include an image viewer. Windows image viewer is called Windows Photo Viewer (Figure 7-17).

Figure 7-17
Windows Photo Viewer allows users to see the contents of a photo file.

Disk Cleanup

A **disk cleanup** utility searches for and removes unnecessary files. Unnecessary files may include downloaded program files, temporary Internet files, deleted files, and unused program files. Operating systems, such as Windows, include a disk scanner utility.

Disk Defragmenter

A **disk defragmenter** is a utility that reorganizes the files and unused space on a computer's hard disk so that the operating system accesses data more quickly and programs run faster. When an operating system stores data on a disk, it places the data in the first available sector on the disk. It attempts to place data in sectors that are contiguous (next to each other), but this is not always possible. When the contents of a file are scattered across two or more noncontiguous sectors, the file is fragmented.

Fragmentation slows down disk access and thus the performance of the entire computer. **Defragmenting** the disk, or reorganizing it so that the files are stored in contiguous sectors, solves this problem (Figure 7-18). Operating systems usually include a disk defragmenter. Windows Disk Defragmenter is available in the System Tools list.

Figure 7-18   A fragmented disk has many files stored in noncontiguous sectors. Defragmenting reorganizes the files so that they are located in contiguous sectors, which speeds access time.

Backup and Restore Utilities

A **backup utility** allows users to copy, or back up, selected files or an entire hard disk to another storage medium such as another hard disk, optical disc, USB flash drive, or tape. During the backup process, the backup utility monitors progress and alerts you if it needs additional media, such as another disc. Many backup programs compress, or shrink the size of, files during the backup process. By compressing the files, the backup program requires less storage space for the backup files than for the original files.

Because they are compressed, you usually cannot use backup files in their backed up form. In the event you need to use a backup file, a **restore utility** reverses the process and returns backed up files to their original form. Backup utilities work with a restore utility.

You should back up files and disks regularly in the event your originals are lost, damaged, or destroyed. Operating systems include backup and restore utilities. Instead of backing up to a local disk storage device, some users opt to use cloud storage to back up their files. Cloud storage is a service on the Web that provides storage to computer users, usually for free or for a minimal monthly fee.

Screen Saver

A **screen saver** is a utility that causes a display device's screen to show a moving image or blank screen if no keyboard or mouse activity occurs for a specified time. When you press a key on the keyboard or move the mouse, the screen saver disappears and the screen returns to the previous state.

Screen savers originally were developed to prevent a problem called ghosting, in which images could be etched permanently on a monitor's screen. Although ghosting is not as severe of a problem with today's displays, manufacturers continue to recommend that users install screen savers for this reason. Screen savers also are popular for security, business, and entertainment purposes. To secure a computer, users configure their screen saver to require a password to deactivate. In addition to those included with the operating system, many screen savers are available for a minimal fee in stores and on the Web.

Personal Firewall

A **personal firewall** is a utility that detects and protects a personal computer from unauthorized intrusions. Personal firewalls constantly monitor all transmissions to and from a computer.

When connected to the Internet, your computer is vulnerable to attacks from a hacker. A hacker is someone who tries to access a computer or network illegally. Users with broadband Internet connections, such as through DSL and cable Internet service, are even more susceptible than those with dial-up access because the Internet connection always is on.

Operating systems often include a personal firewall. Windows automatically enables its built-in personal firewall, called Windows Firewall, upon installation of the operating system. If your operating system does not include a personal firewall or you want additional protection, you can purchase a stand-alone personal firewall utility (Figure 7-19) or a hardware firewall, which is a device such as a router that has a built-in firewall.

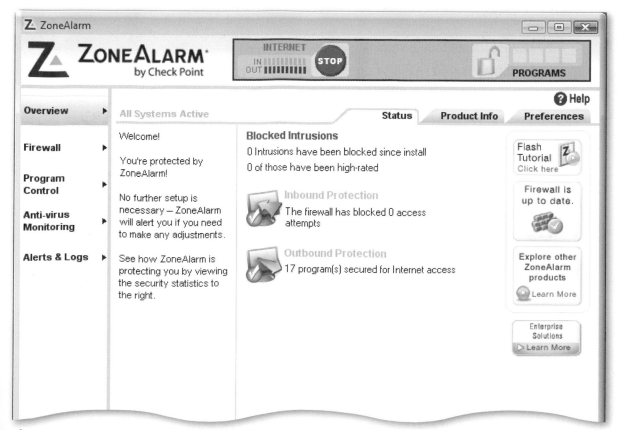

Figure 7-19   A stand-alone personal firewall utility.

Antivirus Programs

The term, computer **virus**, describes a potentially damaging computer program that affects, or infects, a computer negatively by altering the way the computer works without the user's knowledge or permission. Once the virus is in a computer, it can spread throughout and may damage your files and operating system.

Computer viruses do not generate by chance. The programmer of a virus, known as a virus author, intentionally writes a virus program. Some virus authors find writing viruses a challenge. Others write them to cause destruction. Writing a virus program usually requires significant programming skills.

Some viruses are harmless pranks that simply freeze a computer temporarily or display sounds or messages. The Music Bug virus, for example, instructs the computer to play a few chords of music. Other viruses destroy or corrupt data stored on the hard disk of the infected computer. If you notice any unusual changes in your computer's performance, it may be infected with a virus (Figure 7-20).

A **worm** copies itself repeatedly, for example, in memory or over a network, using up system resources and possibly shutting the system down. A **Trojan horse** hides within or looks like a legitimate program such as a screen saver. A certain condition or action usually triggers the Trojan horse. Unlike a virus or worm, a Trojan horse does not replicate itself to other computers. Currently, more than one million known threats to your computer exist.

To protect a computer from virus attacks, users should install an antivirus program and update it frequently. An **antivirus program** protects a computer against viruses by identifying and removing any computer viruses found in memory, on storage media, or on incoming files (Figure 7-21). Most antivirus programs also protect against worms and Trojan horses. When you purchase a new computer, it often includes antivirus software.

Three more popular antivirus programs are McAfee VirusScan, Norton AntiVirus, and Windows Live OneCare, most of which also contains spyware removers, Internet filters, and other utilities. As an alternative to purchasing these products on disc, both McAfee and Norton offer Web-based antivirus programs.

? | **FAQ 7-3**

What steps should I take to prevent virus infections on my computer?

Set up the antivirus program to scan on a regular basis. Never open an e-mail attachment unless you are expecting the attachment and it is from a trusted source. Set macro security in programs such as word processing and spreadsheet so that you can enable or disable macros. Write-protect your recovery disk. Back up files regularly.

For more information, visit the Computer Concepts CourseMate Web site at www.cengagebrain.com, navigate to the Chapter 7 FAQ resource for this book, and then click Virus Infections.

Signs of Virus Infection

- An unusual message or image is displayed on the computer screen
- An unusual sound or music plays randomly
- The available memory is less than what should be available
- A program or file suddenly is missing
- An unknown program or file mysteriously appears
- The size of a file changes without explanation
- A file becomes corrupted
- A program or file does not work properly
- System properties change
- The computer operates much slower than usual

Figure 7-20 Viruses attack computers in a variety of ways. This list indicates some of the more common signs of virus infection.

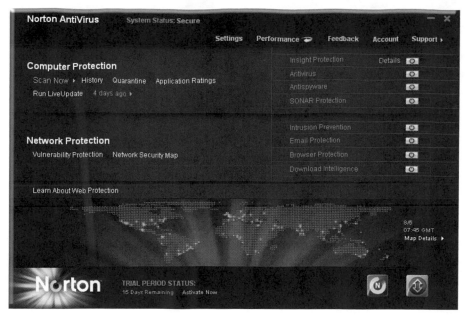

Figure 7-21   An antivirus program scans memory, disks, and incoming e-mail messages and attachments for viruses and attempts to remove any viruses it finds.

Spyware and Adware Removers

Spyware is a program placed on a computer without the user's knowledge that secretly collects information about the user, often related to Web browsing habits. The spyware program communicates information it collects to some outside source while you are online. Adware is a program that displays an online advertisement in a banner or pop-up window on Web pages, e-mail, or other Internet services. Sometimes, spyware is hidden in adware.

A **spyware remover** is a program that detects and deletes spyware, and similar programs. An **adware remover** is a program that detects and deletes adware. Most spyware and adware removers cost less than $50; some are available on the Web at no cost. Some operating systems include spyware and adware removers.

Internet Filters

Filters are programs that remove or block certain items from being displayed. Four widely used Internet filters are anti-spam programs, Web filters, phishing filters, and pop-up blockers.

Anti-Spam Programs   **Spam** is an unsolicited e-mail message or newsgroup posting sent to many recipients or newsgroups at once. Spam is Internet junk mail. An **anti-spam program** is a filtering program that attempts to remove spam before it reaches your inbox. Internet access providers often filter spam as a service for their subscribers.

Where does spam originate?

Research indicates that spam originates from various countries throughout the world. Symantec Corporation found that in a 30-day period, the United States was responsible for more spam than any other country. The chart to the right illustrates the countries responsible for the most spam worldwide.

For more information, visit the Computer Concepts CourseMate Web site at www.cengagebrain.com, navigate to the Chapter 7 FAQ resource for this book, and then click Spam.

Spam Origin

Source: Symantec

United States, Brazil, South Korea, Turkey, India, Colombia, Poland, China, Vietnam, Argentina, Other

Web Filters   **Web filtering software** is a program that restricts access to certain material on the Web. Some restrict access to specific Web sites; others filter sites that use certain words or phrases. Many businesses use Web filtering software to limit employee's Web access. Some schools, libraries, and parents use this software to restrict access to minors. Windows 7 contains parental controls, which allow parents to record and control the types of content their children can access on the Internet.

Phishing Filters   **Phishing** is a scam in which a perpetrator attempts to obtain your personal and/or financial information. A **phishing filter** is a program that warns or blocks you from potentially fraudulent or suspicious Web sites. Some Web browsers include phishing filters.

Pop-Up Blockers   A pop-up ad is an Internet advertisement that suddenly appears in a new window in the foreground of a Web page displayed in your browser. A **pop-up blocker** is a filtering program that stops pop-up ads from displaying on Web pages. Many Web browsers include a pop-up blocker. You also can download pop-up blockers from the Web at no cost.

File Compression

A **file compression utility** shrinks the size of a file(s). A compressed file takes up less storage space than the original file. Compressing files frees up room on the storage media and improves system performance. Attaching a compressed file to an e-mail message, for example, reduces the time needed for file transmission. Uploading and downloading compressed files to and from the Internet reduces the file transmission time.

Compressed files sometimes are called **zipped files**. When you receive or download a compressed file, you must uncompress it. To **uncompress**, or unzip, a file, you restore it to its original form. Some operating systems such as Windows include file compression and uncompression capabilities. Two popular stand-alone file compression utilities are PKZIP and WinZip.

WinZip
For more information, visit the Computer Concepts CourseMate Web site at www.cengagebrain.com, navigate to the Chapter 7 Web Link resource for this book, and then click WinZip.

Media Player

A **media player** is a program that allows you to view images and animation, listen to audio, and watch video files on your computer (Figure 7-22). Media players may also include the capability to organize media files, convert them to different formats, connect to and purchase media from an online media store, download podcasts and vodcasts, burn audio CDs, and transfer media to portable media players. Windows includes Windows Media Player. Three other popular media players are iTunes, RealPlayer, and Rhapsody. Read Ethics & Issues 7-2 for a related discussion.

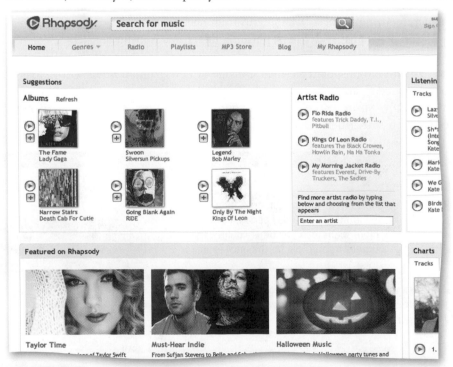

Figure 7-22
A popular media player.

Should the Government Tax Media Downloads?

When you purchase a DVD or Blu-ray Disc that contains a season or two of your favorite television show, chances are that you also pay a state and/or local sales tax. If you purchase and download the same material online in a digital format, however, chances are that you do not pay a sales tax. Some government taxing bodies seek to change that discrepancy. Two main reasons for the pressure to tax include: state and local governments feeling the pinch of lost revenue to legally downloaded digital content because consumers purchase less taxable, physical media; and pressure from the media industry to recoup lost sales due to illegally downloaded digital content. Some governments go as far as funneling collected taxes directly to the multimedia industry as compensation for illegally downloaded content that occurs in a region. Critics of the new taxes claim that government should not tax the greenest form of media purchases. Digitally downloaded content eliminates packaging, optical discs, trips to the store, and use of delivery vehicles. Critics also claim that governments single out multimedia content due to pressure from the multimedia industry. For example, some governments tax the purchase of newspapers, magazines and books, but often the same content is sold online and is not taxed. Typically, government taxing bodies tax goods, but not food and services.

Should the government tax media downloads, such as music, video, e-books, newspaper articles, and magazine articles? Why or why not? Should digital content delivery be considered a service rather than a good by taxing bodies? Why?

Disc Burning

Disc burning software writes text, graphics, audio, and video files on a recordable or rewritable CD, DVD, or Blu-ray Disc. This software enables the home user easily to back up contents of their hard disk on an optical disc and make duplicates of uncopyrighted music or movies. Disc burning software usually also includes photo editing, audio editing, and video editing capabilities (Figure 7-23). To learn about burning files to a disc, complete the Learn How To 1 exercise on page 298.

When you buy a recordable or rewritable disc, it typically includes burning software. You also can buy disc burning software for a cost of less than $100.

Figure 7-23 You can copy text, graphics, audio, and video files to discs using the digital media suite shown here, provided you have the correct type of drive and media.

Personal Computer Maintenance

Operating systems typically include a diagnostic utility that diagnoses computer problems but does not repair them. A **personal computer maintenance utility** identifies and fixes operating system problems, detects and repairs disk problems, and includes the capability of improving a computer's performance. Additionally, some personal computer maintenance utilities continuously monitor a computer while you use it to identify and repair problems before they occur. Norton SystemWorks is a popular personal computer maintenance utility designed for Windows operating systems (Figure 7-24).

Figure 7-24 A popular maintenance program for Windows users.

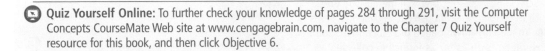

✔ QUIZ YOURSELF 7-3

Instructions: Find the true statement below. Then, rewrite the remaining false statements so that they are true.

1. A pop-up blocker shrinks the size of a file(s).

2. An anti-spam program protects a computer against viruses.

3. A personal firewall is a utility that detects and protects a personal computer from unauthorized intrusions.

4. You should uninstall files and disks regularly in the event your originals are lost, damaged, or destroyed.

5. Web filtering software writes text, graphics, audio, and video files to a recordable or rewritable disc.

Quiz Yourself Online: To further check your knowledge of pages 284 through 291, visit the Computer Concepts CourseMate Web site at www.cengagebrain.com, navigate to the Chapter 7 Quiz Yourself resource for this book, and then click Objective 6.

Chapter Summary

This chapter defined an operating system and then discussed the functions common to most operating systems. The chapter introduced a variety of stand-alone operating systems, server operating systems, and embedded operating systems. Finally, the chapter described several utility programs.

Computer Usage @ Work

Education

Teachers and students have been using computers in education for many years. Teachers have been taking advantage of advances in computer technology to help provide a better educational experience for their students.

Many grade schools throughout the United States, as well as other countries, enable parents to track their child's performance online. In the past, parents would rely solely on their child bringing home graded assignments and tests to know how he or she was doing. In some cases, parents would be surprised when they saw their child's grades on report cards every two to three months. Teachers now have the opportunity to engage parents in their child's education not only by giving them an up-to-the-minute snapshot of grades, but also by posting lesson plans online so that parents know what their child is learning.

Computers and technology also benefit students in the classroom. Schools now have one or more computers in almost every classroom, enabling students to access the Internet to do research that they otherwise would have had to visit the library to perform. Schools also are able to offer additional technology courses such as Web page design, digital media, and computer programming.

At the college level, many instructors today rely heavily on e-learning systems to provide students with Web-based access to course materials and assessments, discussion forums, chat rooms, and e-mail. Once used mainly in online classes, e-learning systems provide instructors with an easy way to allow students access to the class at any time of the day.

Most instructors go beyond e-learning systems and use additional technologies to enhance their classes. For example, digital media instructors might require students to upload their assignments to a photo sharing community, and an English instructor might save paper by requiring students to upload research papers to Google Docs and share them with the instructor.

Computer use in education not only enhances the teaching experience for instructors and learning experience for students, it also provides students with technological knowledge that will benefit them for the rest of their lives.

For more information, visit the Computer Concepts CourseMate Web site at www.cengagebrain.com, navigate to the Chapter 7 Computer Usage @ Work resource for this book, and then click Education.

Companies on the Cutting Edge

VERISIGN Internet Infrastructure Services

Technology users desire immediate access to information and services. Their ability to communicate and conduct commerce securely is aided in large part by VeriSign. More than 30 billion times a day, people interact on the Internet, and their purchases, text messages, downloads, and other transactions are enabled and protected by VeriSign's infrastructure services.

Computer security company Semantic acquired VeriSign's Authentication division business in 2010 to strengthen encryption and identity services and help protect businesses and consumers by protecting information and detecting online fraud. Its domain name services department registers all .com, .net, .cc, and .tv domain names. The VeriSign Secured Seal, which has been issued to more than 100,000 domains in 145 countries, ensures companies and consumers that the Web site is secure.

The California-based company was founded in 1995 and has more than 2,200 employees worldwide.

RESEARCH IN MOTION (RIM) Wireless Mobile Communications Devices Manufacturer

By 2012, 800 million people worldwide are expected to access social networking Web sites on smart phones, up from 82 million in 2007. Research in Motion (RIM) helped fuel this networking frenzy by partnering with MySpace in 2008 to help connect networkers on the go. They can access MySpace Mobile on a BlackBerry smart phone, which is RIM's key product.

The Canadian company was founded in 1984 by Mike Lazaridis, who serves as its president and co-CEO. Lazaridis's vision for wireless technology developed in high school when he was a member of the local amateur radio and television club. He developed RIM's first major product, the Inter@active Pager, which was integrated in the first BlackBerry product in 1998. The BlackBerry gained attention for having the capability to combine a wireless mailbox with a corporate mailbox so that users could assess e-mail continuously.

Recently, Research in Motion launched BlackBerry App World, an application store that allows BlackBerry users to download personal and business programs.

 For more information, visit the Computer Concepts CourseMate Web site at www.cengagebrain.com and then navigate to the Chapter 7 Companies on the Cutting Edge resource for this book.

Technology Trailblazers

STEVE WOZNIAK Apple Cofounder

Mixing fun with work comes naturally for Steve Wozniak. As Apple's cofounder, he says his computer designing career began and still continues to be a hobby filled with creativity, humor, games, and education. In his opinion, Apple's success evolved because he designed computers that had minimal parts and maximum performance.

Wozniak designed the original Apple computer in 1975 with Apple's current CEO, Steve Jobs, and wrote most of the software. Ten years later he cofounded Pixar, the award winning animation studio. He left Apple in 1985 to spend time with his family, work on community projects, and teach, but he still serves as an advisor to the corporation.

Wozinak was inducted into the Consumer Electronics Hall of Fame and the National Inventors Hall of Fame. One of his current passions is applying artificial intelligence to the area of robotics. He also is a member of the Silicon Valley Aftershocks, a polo team that plays using Segway electric transportation devices.

LINUS TORVALDS Linux Creator

Inductees to the Computer History Museum in Mountain View, CA, are noted for their contribution to computer technology. Linus Torvalds joined the Museum's Hall of Fellows in 2008 for his creation of the open source operating system, Linux.

When he developed an operating system in 1991, he announced his project in an Internet newsgroup. He made the source code available and asked readers for suggestions to enhance the product. Computer users responded by reviewing the system and offering enhancements. Three years later he released a greatly enhanced version he called Linux.

Torvalds developed this innovative operating system when he was a 21-year-old computer science student in Finland. Today, he leads the development of Linux as a fellow at OSDL (Open Source Development Labs), a not-for-profit consortium of companies dedicated to developing and promoting the operating system. Torvalds says his daily involvement with Linux involves coordinating and merging the lines of code submitted by users so that the software runs smoothly.

 For more information, visit the Computer Concepts CourseMate Web site at www.cengagebrain.com and then navigate to the Chapter 7 Technology Trailblazers resource for this book.

Chapter Review

The Chapter Review reinforces the main concepts presented in this chapter.

To listen to an audio version of this Chapter Review, visit the Computer Concepts CourseMate Web site at www.cengagebrain.com and then navigate to the Chapter 7 Chapter Review resource for this book.

1. **What Is System Software, and What Are the Two Types of System Software?** **System software** consists of the programs that control or maintain the operations of a computer and its devices. Two types of system software are operating systems and utility programs. System software serves as the interface between the user, the application software, and the computer's hardware. An **operating system (OS)** is a set of programs that contains instructions that work together to coordinate all the activities among computer hardware resources. Different sizes of computers typically use different operating systems because operating systems generally are written to run on a specific type of computer. A **utility program,** or **utility,** performs maintenance-type tasks, usually related to managing a computer, its devices, or its programs.

2. **What Are the Functions of an Operating System?** The operating system starts and shuts down a computer, provides a user interface, manages programs, manages memory, coordinates tasks, configures devices, establishes an Internet connection, monitors performance, provides file management and other utilities, updates automatically, controls a network, and administers security. The **user interface** controls how data and instructions are entered and how information is displayed. Two types of user interfaces are a **graphical user interface (GUI)** and a **command-line interface**. Managing programs refers to how many users, and how many programs, an operating system can support at one time. An operating system can be single user/single tasking, single user/multitasking, **multiuser,** or **multiprocessing**. **Memory management** optimizes the use of random access memory (RAM). **Virtual memory** is a concept in which the operating system allocates a portion of a storage medium, usually the hard disk, to function as additional RAM. Coordinating tasks determines the order in which tasks are processed. Configuring devices involves loading each device's driver when a user boots the computer. A **driver** is a small program that tells the operating system how to communicate with a specific device. Establishing an Internet connection sets up a connection between a computer and an Internet access provider. A **performance monitor** is a program that assesses and reports information about computer resources and devices. Operating systems often provide the capability of managing and searching for files, viewing images, securing a computer from unauthorized access, uninstalling programs, and other tasks. Most operating systems include an **automatic update** feature that provides updates to the program. A **server operating system** is an operating system that organizes and coordinates how multiple users access and share network resources. Network administrators typically have an **administrator account** that enables them to access files, install programs, and specify network settings.

Visit the Computer Concepts CourseMate Web site at www.cengagebrain.com, navigate to the Chapter 7 Quiz Yourself resource for this book, and then click Objectives 1 – 2.

3. **What Are Features of Windows 7, Mac OS X, UNIX, and Linux Operating Systems?** **Windows 7** is Microsoft's fastest, most efficient operating system to date, offering quicker program start up, built-in diagnostics, automatic recovery, improved security, enhanced searching and organizing capabilities, and an easy-to-use interface. Most users choose between Windows 7 Starter, Windows 7 Home Premium, Windows 7 Ultimate, or Windows 7 Professional editions. **Mac OS X** is a multitasking GUI operating system available only for Apple computers. **UNIX** is a multitasking operating system that is flexible and powerful. **Linux** is a popular, multitasking UNIX-type operating system that is open source software, which means its code is available to the public for use, modification, and redistribution.

4. **What Are the Various Server Operating Systems?** Server operating systems are designed to support all sizes of networks, including medium- to large-sized businesses and Web servers. An example of a server operating system is Windows Server 2008. UNIX and Linux often are called multipurpose operating systems because they are both stand-alone and server operating systems. Solaris is a server operating system designed specifically for e-commerce applications. Novell's NetWare is a server operating system designed for client/server networks.

5. **What Are Several Embedded Operating Systems?** Most mobile devices and many consumer electronics have an **embedded operating system** that resides on a ROM chip. Popular embedded operating systems include the following. Windows Embedded CE is a scaled-down Windows operating system designed for use on communications, entertainment, and computing devices with limited functionality, such as VoIP telephones, digital cameras, point-of-sale terminals, automated teller machines, digital photo frames, handheld navigation devices, and portable media players. Windows Phone 7, which is a successor to Windows Mobile, works on specific types of smart phones. Palm OS is an operating system used

on smart phones and PDAs. iPhone OS is an operating system for iPhone and iPod touch. The BlackBerry operating system runs on handheld devices supplied by RIM. Google Android is an operating system developed by Google for mobile devices. Embedded Linux is a scaled-down Linux operating system for smart phones, PDAs, portable media players, and other devices. Symbian OS is an open source multitasking operating system designed for smart phones.

Visit the Computer Concepts CourseMate Web site at www.cengagebrain.com, navigate to the Chapter 7 Quiz Yourself resource for this book, and then click Objectives 3 – 5.

6. **What Is the Purpose of Several Utility Programs?** Most operating systems include several built-in utility programs. A **file manager** performs functions related to file management. A **search utility** attempts to locate a file on your computer based on criteria you specify. An **image viewer** displays, copies, and prints the contents of a graphics file. An **uninstaller** removes a program and any associated entries in the system files. A **disk cleanup** utility searches for and removes unnecessary files. A **disk defragmenter** reorganizes the files and unused space on a computer's hard disk. A **backup utility** is used to copy, or back up, selected files or an entire hard disk to another storage medium. A **restore utility** reverses the backup process and returns backed up files to their original form. A **screen saver** displays a moving image or blank screen if no keyboard or mouse activity occurs for a specified time. A **personal firewall** detects and protects a personal computer from unauthorized intrusions. An **antivirus program** protects computers against a **virus**, or potentially damaging computer program, by identifying and removing any computer viruses. A **spyware remover** detects and deletes spyware and similar programs. An **adware remover** detects and deletes adware. An **anti-spam program** attempts to remove **spam** before it reaches your inbox. **Web filtering software** restricts access to certain material on the Web. A **phishing filter** warns or blocks you from potentially fraudulent or suspicious Web sites. A **pop-up blocker** stops pop-up ads from displaying on Web pages. A **file compression utility** shrinks the size of a file. A **media player** allows you to view images and animation, listen to audio, and watch video files on a computer. **Disc burning software** writes on a recordable or rewritable CD, DVD, or Blu-ray Disc. A **personal computer maintenance utility** identifies and fixes operating system or disk problems and improves a computer's performance.

Visit the Computer Concepts CourseMate Web site at www.cengagebrain.com, navigate to the Chapter 7 Quiz Yourself resource for this book, and then click Objective 6.

Key Terms

You should know each key term. The list below helps focus your study.

To see an example of and a definition for each term, and to access current and additional information from the Web, visit the Computer Concepts CourseMate Web site at www.cengagebrain.com and then navigate to the Chapter 7 Key Terms resource for this book.

administrator account (278)
adware remover (289)
anti-spam program (289)
antivirus program (288)
automatic update (277)
backup utility (286)
booting (272)
buffer (275)
cold boot (272)
command-line interface (273)
defragmenting (286)
disc burning software (291)
disk cleanup (286)
disk defragmenter (286)
driver (276)
embedded operating system (283)
file compression utility (290)
file manager (285)

folder (285)
graphical user interface (GUI) (273)
hibernate (272)
image viewer (285)
Linux (282)
log on (278)
Mac OS X (281)
Macintosh operating system (281)
media player (290)
memory management (275)
multiprocessing (275)
multiuser (275)
operating system (OS) (271)
password (278)
performance monitor (277)
personal computer maintenance utility (291)

personal firewall (287)
phishing (290)
phishing filter (290)
Plug and Play (276)
pop-up blocker (290)
queue (276)
restore utility (286)
screen saver (287)
search utility (285)
server operating system (277)
service pack (277)
sleep mode (272)
spam (289)
spooling (275)
spyware remover (289)
stand-alone operating system (280)
system software (270)
Trojan horse (288)

uncompress (290)
uninstaller (285)
UNIX (281)
user ID (278)
user interface (272)
user name (278)
utility (284)
utility program (284)
virtual memory (275)
virus (288)
warm boot (272)
Web filtering software (290)
Windows 7 (280)
Windows Aero (273)
Windows ReadyBoost (275)
worm (288)
zipped files (290)

Checkpoint

The Checkpoint exercises test your knowledge of the chapter concepts. The page number containing the answer appears in parentheses after each exercise.

To complete the Checkpoint exercises interactively, visit the Computer Concepts CourseMate Web site at www.cengagebrain.com and then navigate to the Chapter 7 Checkpoint resource for this book.

Multiple Choice Select the best answer.

1. In the Windows 7 operating system, _____ provides an enhanced visual look, additional navigation options, and animation. (273)
   a. Windows Aero
   b. Plug and Play
   c. Mac OS X
   d. Windows 7 Starter

2. Windows users can increase the size of memory through _____, which can allocate available storage space on removable flash memory devices as additional memory cache. (275)
   a. Windows Aero
   b. Plug and Play
   c. Windows ReadyBoost
   d. a disk defragmenter

3. A _____ is a small program that tells the operating system how to communicate with a specific device. (276)
   a. buffer
   b. driver
   c. performance monitor
   d. device

4. Computer and network administrators typically have a(n) _____ that enables them to access all files and programs on the computer or network, install programs, and specify settings that affect all users on a computer or network. (278)
   a. file manager
   b. personal computer maintenance utility
   c. administrator account
   d. graphical user interface

5. The operating system on most mobile devices and many consumer electronics, called a(n) _____, resides on a ROM chip. (283)
   a. network operating system
   b. embedded operating system
   c. stand-alone operating system
   d. stand-alone utility program

6. A _____ is a specific named location on a storage medium that contains related documents. (285)
   a. file
   b. buffer
   c. utility
   d. folder

7. A(n) _____ is a program that warns or blocks you from potentially fraudulent or suspicious Web sites. (290)
   a. phishing filter
   b. adware remover
   c. Web filter
   d. Trojan horse

8. A(n) _____ is a program that allows you to view images and animation, listen to audio, and watch video files on your computer. (290)
   a. file manager
   b. media player
   c. service pack
   d. image viewer

Matching Match the terms with their definitions.

_____ 1. sleep mode (272)

_____ 2. hibernate (272)

_____ 3. virus (288)

_____ 4. worm (288)

_____ 5. spam (289)

a. a potentially damaging computer program that affects, or infects, a computer negatively by altering the way the computer works without the user's knowledge or permission

b. copies itself repeatedly using up system resources and possibly shutting the system down

c. saves any open documents and programs to a hard disk before removing power from the computer

d. hides within or looks like a legitimate program such as a screen saver

e. saves any open documents and programs to RAM, turns off all unneeded functions, and then places the computer in a low-power state

f. an unsolicited e-mail message or newsgroup posting sent to many recipients or newsgroups at once

Short Answer Write a brief answer to each of the following questions.

1. How is a cold boot different from a warm boot? _____ How is a memory-resident part of an operating system different from a nonresident part of an operating system? _____

2. What is the purpose of an automatic update feature? _____ Why and when might a user receive a service pack? _____

3. How does a file become fragmented? _____ How does a disk defragmenter work? _____

4. What are the differences between Windows 7 Starter and Windows 7 Home Premium? _____ What is the difference between Windows 7 Ultimate and Windows 7 Professional? _____

5. What is a backup utility, and what happens during a backup? _____ What is the purpose of a restore utility? _____

Problem Solving

The Problem Solving exercises extend your knowledge of the chapter concepts by seeking solutions to practical computer problems that you may encounter at home, school, or work. The Collaboration exercise should be completed with a team.

In the real world, practical problems often can be solved in multiple ways. Provide one solution to each of the following problems using available resources, such as articles on the Web or in print, blogs, podcasts, videos, television, user guides, other individuals, and electronics and computer stores. You may need to use multiple resources to obtain an answer. Present your solutions in the form requested by your instructor (brief report, presentation, discussion, or other means).

@ Home

1. **Computer Cannot Boot**   You recently purchased a computer from your friend. When you turn on the computer, a message displays that says, "Operating system not found." What steps will you take before calling technical support?

2. **Incorrect Display Settings**   You have been using the same display settings since purchasing your computer several months ago. You recently turn on your computer and notice that the screen resolution, desktop background, and color scheme has changed, even though you have not changed the display settings. What might have caused Windows to change your display settings? What are your next steps?

3. **Maximum CPU Usage**   Because your computer is performing slowly, you start the Windows Task Manager to investigate. You see that the CPU usage is near 100%. You are not aware of any other programs currently running. What might be causing this?

4. **Unwanted Programs**   The new computer that you ordered online arrived today. You anxiously unpack it, connect all the components, and then turn it on. After answering a series of questions to set up the computer, you notice it includes programs that you do not want. How will you remove these unwanted programs?

@ Work

5. **Password Required**   After turning on your computer, it prompts you to type a password to continue the boot process; however, you forgot the password. What are your next steps to allow the computer to continue the boot process, start Windows, and access the files on the hard disk?

6. **Automatic Updates**   Two or three times per month, your coworker receives a notification on his computer that the computer recently has been updated. You ask your coworker about these messages, and he says that Microsoft periodically installs updates automatically to protect the computer from various threats, as well as to improve performance. You never have seen this message appear on your computer. Does this mean that your computer does not update automatically? How can you configure your computer to update automatically?

7. **Antivirus Schedule**   You recently changed your work schedule so that you work until 6:00 p.m. instead of 5:00 p.m. At 5:00 p.m. each day, you notice that the antivirus program on your computer automatically begins scanning all files on your hard disk. This process slows your computer, and the program usually still is scanning when you leave the office. How can you change the configuration so that the antivirus program does not start until after you leave?

8. **Minimum Battery Power**   When you use your notebook computer and it is not plugged in, the battery lasts for only one hour, but the documentation states that the computer can last for two hours on battery power. What are some ways that you can increase the battery life?

Collaboration

9. **Computers in Education**   A private elementary school in your neighborhood has received a grant to create a computer lab with Internet access so that students can learn about computers and related technologies. Your neighbor, who also is a teacher at the school, asks for advice regarding how they should spend the grant money. Form a team of three people to determine the best configuration for the lab. One team member should research whether a PC or Mac is more beneficial. Another team member should research the application software that should be installed on these computers, and the other team member should determine what, if any, peripheral devices should be attached to the computers in the lab. Compile your findings and submit them to your instructor.

STUDENT ASSIGNMENTS

Learn How To

The Learn How To activities step you through fundamental technology skills when using a computer. The Learn How To exercises enable you to become more proficient with these skills.

Premium Activity: To relate this Learn How To activity to your everyday life, see a visual demonstration of the activity, and complete a short assessment, visit the Computer Concepts CourseMate Web site at www.cengagebrain.com and then navigate to the Chapter 7 Learn How To resource for this book.

Learn How To 1: Burn Files to an Optical Disc

Many people use USB flash drives to transport files from one location to another. If they wish to share files with someone else, however, they might choose to distribute these files on an optical disc. To learn how to burn files to an optical disc using Windows 7, complete the following steps:

1. Insert a blank optical disc into the optical disc drive.
2. When the AutoPlay dialog box is displayed, click the Burn files to disc using Windows Explorer link.
3. If necessary, change the Disc title, click the 'Like a USB flash drive' option button, and then click the Next button in the Burn a Disc dialog box to prepare the blank disc.
4. Drag the files you wish to burn to the empty window that opens.
5. Click the 'Burn to disk' button.
6. Click the Next button to burn the files to the disc. When the disc has finished burning, remove the disc from the optical disc drive.

Exercise

1. Locate photos on your computer that you are willing to share with others. If you are unable to locate any photos or are using someone else's computer, download at least three photos from the Internet. Insert a blank optical disc into your optical disc drive and then burn the photos to the disc. Once you have finished burning the disc, eject it, write your name on it, and then submit it to your instructor.

Learn How To 2: Keep Windows Up-to-Date

Keeping Windows up-to-date is a critical part of keeping your computer in working order. The updates made available by Microsoft for no charge over the Internet can help to keep errors from occurring on your computer and attempt to ensure that all security safeguards are in place. To update Windows, complete the next steps:

1. Click the Start button on the Windows taskbar, click All Programs, and then click Windows Update in the All Programs list (Figure 7-25) to open the Windows Update window.
2. Click the link indicating that updates are available.
3. If necessary, select those updates you wish to install and then click the OK button. Be aware that some updates might take 20 minutes or more to download and install, based primarily on your Internet access speed.
4. Often, after installation of updates, you must restart your computer to allow those updates to take effect. Be sure to save any open files before restarting your computer.

Figure 7-25

You also can schedule automatic updates for your computer. To do so, complete the following steps:

1. Click the Start button on the Windows taskbar and then click Control Panel on the Start menu.
2. In the Control Panel window, click System and Security to open the System and Security window.
3. In the System and Security window, click 'Turn automatic updating on or off' to open the Change settings window (Figure 7-26).
4. Select the option you want to use for Windows updates. Microsoft, together with all security and operating system experts, strongly recommends you select 'Install updates automatically' so that updates will be installed on your computer automatically. Notice that if you select 'Install updates automatically', you also should select a time when your computer will be on and be connected to the Internet. A secondary choice is to download the suggested updates and then choose when you want to install them, and a third choice allows you to check for updates and then choose when you want to download and install them.
5. When you have made your selection, click the OK button in the Change settings window.

Updating Windows on your computer is vital to maintain security and operational integrity.

Exercises

1. Open the Windows Update window. Make a list of the important updates to Windows on the computer you are using. Add to the list the optional updates that are available. If you are using your own computer, install the updates of your choice on your computer. Submit the list of updates to your instructor.

2. **Optional: If you are not using your own computer, do not complete this exercise.** Open the Control Panel, click System and Security, and then click 'Turn automatic updating on or off'. Select the level of automatic updates you want to use. Write a report justifying your choice of automatic updates and then submit the report to your instructor.

Figure 7-26

Learn It Online

The Learn It Online exercises are interactive Web exercises designed to reinforce and expand your understanding of the chapter concepts. The descriptions below briefly summarize each exercise.

To complete the Learn It Online exercises, visit the Computer Concepts CourseMate Web site at www.cengagebrain.com, navigate to the Chapter 7 resources for this book, click the link for the exercise you want to complete, and then read the instructions.

1 At the Movies — Free Online Antivirus

Watch a movie to learn why it is important to run antivirus software on your computer and how to scan your computer for malware online for no cost and then answer questions about the movie.

2 Student Edition Labs — Installing and Uninstalling Software and Keeping Your Computer Virus Free

Enhance your understanding and knowledge about installing and uninstalling software and keeping your computer virus free by completing the Installing and Uninstalling Software and Keeping Your Computer Virus Free Labs.

3 Practice Test

Take a multiple choice test that checks your knowledge of the chapter concepts and review the resulting study guide.

4 Who Wants To Be a Computer Genius^2?

Play the Shelly Cashman Series version of this popular game by answering questions to find out if you are a computer genius. Panic buttons are available to provide assistance during game play.

5 Crossword Puzzle Challenge

Complete an interactive crossword puzzle to reinforce concepts presented in this chapter.

6 Windows Exercises

Step through the Windows 7 exercises to learn about Windows, using a screen saver, changing desktop colors, customizing the desktop for multiple users, and backing up a computer.

7 Exploring Computer Careers

Read about a career as a systems programmer, search for related employment advertisements, and then answer related questions.

8 Web Apps — Photoshop Express

Learn how to use Photoshop Express to upload new photos as well as photos stored on other photo sharing communities, edit photos, create new pictures, and share them with others.

Web Research

The Web Research exercises broaden your understanding of chapter concepts by presenting questions that require you to search the Web for answers.

1 **Search Sleuth**

Use one of the search engines listed in Figure 2-8 in Chapter 2 on page 65 or your own favorite search engine to find the answers to the following questions. Copy and paste the Web address from the Web page where you found the answer. Some questions may have more than one answer. If required, submit your answers to your instructor. (1) Who are the "goons" who attend DEFCON? What color shirts do they wear? (2) Which product does IBM propose in its "Reincarnating PCs with Portable SoulPads" paper? (3) Which bird is the mascot for Linux? What is the mascot's name? (4) Why do some computer experts consider the term, spool, a backronym? (5) Who invented the Control-Alt-Delete (CTRL+ALT+DEL) key combination used to reboot a computer? (6) Which virus did the Farooq Alvi brothers invent? (7) Why would a programmer use the EICAR test file? (8) Why are UNIX programmers concerned about the "Year 2038 problem"?

2 **Green Computing**

Operating systems can help monitor computer energy use and suggest methods of reducing electricity through efficient power management. Experts claim monitoring systems can save each computer user at least $60 per year in electricity costs. Suggestions include not using a screen saver, turning down a monitor's brightness level, maximizing the standby and sleep settings, and using a power saver or high performance power setting that balances processing power with notebook computer battery life. View online Web sites that provide information about power management. Which methods are effective in reducing power consumption, especially for notebook computers? Which sleep state setting gives significant power savings? Which power management settings are recommended for balanced, power saver, and high performance? Write a report summarizing your findings, and include a table of links to Web sites that provide additional details.

3 **Social Networking**

Social networking Web site advertisers in the United States spent $108 million in 2009, an increase of 119 percent in one year. General Motors and Proctor & Gamble are two of the larger marketers exploring the placement of advertising on social networking Web sites. Millions of registered online social networking users have posted demographic information about themselves, including age, gender, and geographical location. This data helps marketing managers deliver specific advertisements to each user in an attempt to raise revenue to support their Web sites. Adknowledge (adknowledge.com) is one of the primary companies that gathers and studies data regarding online users and then sells targeted ads on social networking, e-mail, and gaming Web sites. Visit the Adknowledge Web site, view the information about targeting social network consumers, and then read articles in the About Us and Press Room sections. How are advertisers using virtual currency? How do traffic networks help advertisers create marketing campaigns? View the posts in the Adverblog Web site (adverblog.com) to read about interactive marketing trends. Summarize the information you read and viewed.

4 **Blogs**

Search engines help locate Web pages about certain topics based on the search text specified. A number of the search engine Web sites feature blogs describing popular search topics. For example, Ask.com's blog (blog.ask.com) lists its Blogroll, which gives recommended research and search engine Web sites. The Yahoo! Search blog (ysearchblog.com) includes news about consumer search trends (Yahoo! Buzz) and innovations in Web search technology. Google Blog Search (blogsearch.google.com) has search engines to help users find blogs about particular topics, including politics, technology, sports, and business. Visit these sites and read the posts. What topics are discussed? Compose search queries about issues and products discussed in this chapter, such as personal firewalls or antivirus programs, and read a few of the blogs describing these topics. Summarize the information you read and viewed.

5 **Ethics in Action**

Several automobile insurers, including Progressive Casualty Insurance Company, are promising drivers insurance premium discounts if they install a data recorder in their cars to track their driving and then exercise good driving behavior. Progressive customers voluntarily using the MyRate wireless device hope to decrease their insurance bills by a maximum of 25 percent. Privacy experts predict more insurance companies will offer this monitoring system and that it eventually will become mandatory. These critics fear that negative data will be used against poor drivers and possibly be subpoenaed in litigation. View online sites that provide information about vehicle monitoring devices. Write a report summarizing your findings, and include a table of links to Web sites that provide additional details.

Buyer's Guide:
How to Purchase Computers and Mobile Devices

AT SOME POINT, perhaps while you are taking this course, you may decide to buy a computer or mobile device (Figure 1). The decision is an important one and will require an investment of both time and money. Like many buyers, you may have little experience with technology and find yourself unsure of how to proceed. You can start by talking to your friends, coworkers, and instructors about their computers and mobile devices. What type of computers and mobile devices did they buy? Why? For what purposes do they use their computers and mobile devices?

desktop computer

notebook computer

portable media player

smart phone

digital camera

Figure 1 Computers and mobile devices.

How to Purchase a Desktop Computer

A desktop computer sits on or below a desk or table in a stationary location such as a home, office, or dormitory room. Desktop computers are a good option if you work mostly in one place and have plenty of space in a work area. Desktop computers generally provide more performance for your money. Today, manufacturers are placing more emphasis on style by offering bright colors, stylish displays, and theme-based displays so that the computer looks attractive if it is in an area of high visibility. Once you have decided that a desktop computer is most suited to your computing needs, the next step is to determine specific software, hardware, peripheral devices, and services to purchase, as well as where to buy the computer.

❶ Determine the specific software to use on your computer.

Before deciding to purchase software, be sure it contains the features necessary for the tasks you want to perform. Rely on the computer users in whom you have confidence to help you decide on the software to use. In addition, consider purchasing software that might help you perform tasks at home that you otherwise would perform at another location, such as at school or at work. The minimum requirements of the software you select may determine the operating system (Microsoft Windows, Mac OS, Linux) you need. If you decide to use a particular operating system that does not support software you want to use, you may be able to purchase similar software from other manufacturers.

Many Web sites and trade magazines provide reviews of software products. These Web sites frequently have articles that rate computers and software on cost, performance, and support.

Your hardware requirements depend on the minimum requirements of the software you will run on your computer. Some software requires more memory and disk space than others, as well as additional input, output, and storage devices. For example, suppose you want to run software that can copy one optical disc's contents directly to another optical disc, without first copying the data to the hard disk. To support that, you should consider a desktop computer or a high-end notebook computer, because the computer will need two optical disc drives: one that reads from an optical disc, and one that writes on an optical disc. If you plan to run software that allows your computer to function as an entertainment system, then you will need an optical disc drive, quality speakers, and an upgraded sound card.

❷ Know the system requirements of the operating system.

After determining the software you want to run on your new computer, the next step is to determine the operating system to use. If, however, you purchase a new computer, chances are it will have the latest version of your preferred operating system (Windows, Mac OS, Linux).

❸ Look for bundled software.

When you purchase a computer, it may include bundled software. Some sellers even let you choose which software you want. Remember, however, that bundled software has value only if you would have purchased the software even if it had not been included with the computer. At the very least, you probably will want word processing software and an antivirus program. If you need additional programs, such as a spreadsheet, a database, or presentation software, consider purchasing or downloading Microsoft Office, Microsoft Works, OpenOffice.org, or Sun StarOffice, which include several programs at a reduced price or at no cost.

❹ Avoid buying the least powerful computer available.

Once you know the application software you want to use, then consider the following important criteria about the computer's components: (1) processor speed, (2) size and types of memory (RAM) and storage, (3) types of input/output devices, (4) types of ports and adapter cards, and (5) types of communications devices. You also should consider if the computer is upgradeable and to what extent you are able to upgrade. For example, all manufacturers limit the amount of memory you can add. The information in Figure 2 on pages 303 and 304 can help you determine which computer components are best for you and outlines considerations for specific hardware components. For a sample Base Components worksheet that lists PC recommendations for each category of user discussed in this

Considerations for Hardware Components

Card Reader/Writer: A card reader/writer is useful for transferring data directly to and from a memory card, such as the type used in a digital camera, smart phone, or portable media player. Make sure the card reader/writer can read from and write on the memory cards that you use.

Digital Video Capture Device: A digital video capture device allows you to connect a computer to a video camera or VCR and record, edit, manage, and then write video back on an optical disc or VCR tape. To create quality video (true 30 frames per second, full-sized TV), the digital video capture device should have a USB or FireWire port.

External Hard Disk: An external hard disk can serve many purposes: it can serve as extra storage for your computer, provide a way to store and transport large files or large quantities of files, and provide a convenient way to back up data on other internal and external hard disks. External hard disks can be purchased with the same capacity as any internal disk.

Fingerprint Reader: For added security, you may want to consider purchasing a fingerprint reader. It helps prevent unauthorized access to your computer and also allows you to log onto Web sites quickly via your fingerprint, rather than entering a user name and password each time you access the site. Most use a USB connection and require software installation.

Hard Disk: It is recommended that you buy a computer with at least a 320 GB hard disk if your primary interests are browsing the Web and using e-mail and Office suite-type programs; 1 TB if you also want to edit digital photos or if you plan to edit digital video or manipulate large audio files even occasionally; and 2 TB if you will edit digital video, movies, or photos often; store audio files and music; or consider yourself to be a power user. Internal hard disk controllers are available with the RAID option for added data protection.

Joystick/Wheel: If you use the computer to play games, then you will want to purchase a joystick or a wheel. These devices, especially the more expensive ones, provide for realistic game play with force feedback, programmable buttons, and specialized levers and wheels.

Keyboard: The keyboard is one of the more important devices used to communicate with the computer. For this reason, make sure the keyboard you purchase has 101 to 105 keys, is comfortable and easy to use, and has a USB connection. A wireless keyboard should be considered, especially if you have a small desk area.

Microphone: If you plan to record audio or use speech recognition to enter text and commands, then purchase a close-talk headset with gain adjustment support.

Modem: Most computers include a modem so that you can use a telephone line to access the Internet. Some modems also have fax capabilities. Your modem should be rated at 56 Kbps.

Monitor: The monitor is where you will view documents, read e-mail messages, and view pictures. A minimum of a 19" LCD flat-panel monitor is recommended, but if you plan to use the computer for graphic design or game playing, then you may want to purchase a 22" or 27" monitor. Instead of a single large, widescreen monitor, you may want to consider a side-by-side monitor setup.

Mouse: While working with a desktop computer, you use the mouse constantly. Make sure the mouse has a wheel, which acts as a third button in addition to the top two buttons on the left and right. An ergonomic design also is important because your hand is on the mouse most of the time when you are using the computer. A wireless mouse should be considered to eliminate the cord and allow you to work at short distances from the computer.

Optical Disc Drives: Most computers include a DVD±RW combination drive and/or DVD/Blu-ray Disc drive. A DVD±RW or a Blu-ray Disc drive allows you to read optical discs and to write data on (burn) an optical disc. It also will allow you to store and share video files, digital photos, and other large files with other people who have access to a DVD/Blu-ray Disc drive. A Blu-ray Disc has a capacity of at least 25 GB, and a DVD has a capacity of at least 4.7 GB, versus the 650 MB capacity of a CD.

Figure 2 Hardware guidelines. *(continues)*

Considerations for Hardware Components

Ports: Depending on how you are using the computer, you may need anywhere from 4 to 10 USB ports. USB ports have become the connection of choice in the computer industry. They offer an easy way to connect peripheral devices such as printers, digital cameras, and portable media players. Many computers intended for home or professional audio/video use have built-in FireWire ports. Most personal computers include a minimum of six USB ports, two FireWire ports, and an Ethernet port.

Printer: Your two basic printer choices are ink-jet and laser. Color ink-jet printers cost on average between $50 and $300. Laser printers cost from $200 to $2,000. In general, the less expensive the printer, the lower the resolution and speed, and the more often you are required to change the ink cartridges or toner. Laser printers print faster and with a higher quality than an ink-jet, and their toner on average costs less.

Processor: For a personal computer, an Intel Core i7 processor at 2.93 GHz is more than enough processor power for most home and small office/home office users. Game home, enterprise, and power users should upgrade to faster, more powerful processors.

RAM: RAM plays a vital role in the speed of a computer. Make sure the computer you purchase has at least 2 GB of RAM. If you have extra money to invest in a computer, consider increasing the RAM. The extra money for RAM will be well spent because more RAM typically translates into more speed.

Scanner: The most popular scanner purchased with a computer today is the flatbed scanner. When evaluating a flatbed scanner, check the color depth and resolution. Do not buy anything less than a color depth of 48 bits and a resolution of 1200 x 2400 dpi. The higher the color depth, the more accurate the color. A higher resolution picks up the more subtle gradations of color.

Sound Card: Many computers include a standard sound card that supports Dolby 5.1 surround and are capable of recording and playing digital audio. Make sure they are suitable in the event you decide to use the computer as an entertainment or gaming system.

Speakers: Once you have a good sound card, quality speakers and a separate subwoofer that amplifies the bass frequencies of the speakers can turn the computer into a premium stereo system.

USB Flash Drive: If you work on different computers and need access to the same data and information, then this portable flash memory device is ideal. USB flash drive capacity varies from 1 GB to 16 GB.

USB Hub: If you plan to connect several peripheral devices to the computer at the same time, then you need to be concerned with the number of ports available on the computer. If the computer does not have enough ports, then you should purchase a USB hub. A USB hub plugs into a single USB port and provides several additional ports.

Video Card: Most standard video cards satisfy the monitor display needs of most home and small office users. If you are a game home user or a graphic designer, you will want to upgrade to a higher quality video card. The higher refresh rates will further enhance the display of games, graphics, and movies.

Web Cam: A Web cam is a small digital video camera that can capture and display live video on a Web page. You also can capture, edit, and share video and still photos. Recommended minimum specifications include 640 x 480 resolution, a video with a rate of 30 frames per second, and a USB or FireWire port. Some Web cams are built into computer monitors.

Wireless LAN Access Point: A wireless LAN access point allows you to network several computers, so that multiple users can share files and access the Internet through a single broadband connection. Each device that you connect requires a wireless card. A wireless LAN access point can offer a range of operations up to several hundred feet, so be sure the device has a high-powered antenna.

Figure 2   Hardware guidelines. *(continued)*

book, visit the Computer Concepts CourseMate Web site at www.cengagebrain.com and then navigate to the Buyer's Guide Feature resource for this book. In the worksheet, the Home User category is divided into two groups: Application Home User and Game Home User.

Computer technology changes rapidly, meaning a computer that seems powerful enough today may not serve your computing needs in several years. In fact, studies show that many users regret not buying a more powerful computer. To avoid this, plan to buy a computer that will last for at least two to three years. You can help delay obsolescence by purchasing the fastest processor, the most memory, and the largest hard disk you can afford. If you must buy a less powerful computer, be sure you can upgrade it with additional memory, components, and peripheral devices as your computer requirements grow.

5 Consider upgrades to the mouse, keyboard, monitor, printer, microphone, and speakers.

You use these peripheral devices to interact with the computer, so make sure they are up to your standards. Review the peripheral devices listed in Figure 2 and then visit both local computer dealers and large retail stores to test the computers and devices on display. Ask the salesperson which input and output devices would be best for you and whether you should upgrade beyond the standard product. Consider purchasing a wireless keyboard and wireless mouse to eliminate wires on your desktop. A few extra dollars spent on these components when you initially purchase a computer can extend its usefulness by years.

6 Determine whether to use a broadband or dial-up connection to access the Internet.

If your computer has a modem, you can access the Internet using a standard telephone line. Ordinarily, you call a local or toll-free 800 number to connect to an Internet access provider. Using a dial-up Internet connection usually is relatively inexpensive but slow.

Broadband connections provide much faster Internet connections, which are ideal if you want faster file download speeds for software, digital photos, digital video, and music. As you would expect, they can be more expensive than a dial-up connection. If you want to use a broadband connection, your computer should have an Ethernet card installed, unless you are using a wireless broadband connection such as WiMax or 3G. If you will be using a dial-up connection, your computer should have a modem installed.

7 Use a worksheet to compare computers, services, and other considerations.

You can use a separate sheet of paper to take notes about each vendor's computer and then summarize the information on a worksheet. For a sample worksheet that compares prices for a PC or a Mac, visit the Computer Concepts CourseMate

Web site at www.cengagebrain.com and then navigate to the Buyer's Guide Feature resource for this book. Most companies advertise a price for a base computer that includes components housed in the system unit (processor, RAM, sound card, video card, network card), hard disks, optical disc drives, a keyboard, mouse, monitor, printer, speakers, and modem. Be aware, however, that some advertisements list prices for computers with only some of these components. Monitors and printers, for example, often are not included in a base computer's price. Depending on how you plan to use the computer, you may want to invest in additional or more powerful components. When comparing the prices of computers, make sure you are comparing identical or similar configurations.

8 If you are buying a new computer, you have several purchasing options: buying from a school bookstore, a local computer dealer, a local large retail store, or ordering by mail via telephone or the Web.

Each purchasing option has certain advantages. Many college bookstores, for example, sign exclusive pricing agreements with computer manufacturers and, thus, can offer student discounts. Local dealers and local large retail stores, however, more easily can provide hands-on support. Mail-order companies that sell computers by telephone or online via the Web (Figure 3) often provide the lowest prices, but extend less personal service. Some major mail-order companies, however, have started to provide next-business-day, on-site services. A credit card usually is required to buy from a mail-order company.

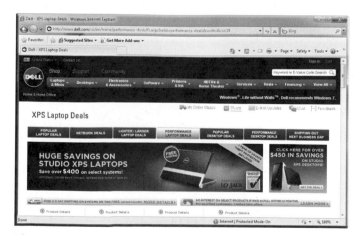

Figure 3   Mail-order companies, such as Dell, sell computers online.

9 If you are buying a used computer, stay with name brands such as Dell, Apple, HP, and Gateway.

Although brand-name equipment can cost more, most brand-name computers have longer, more comprehensive warranties, are better supported, and have more authorized centers for repair services. As with new computers, you can purchase a used computer from local computer dealers, local large retail stores, or mail order via the telephone or the Web. Classified ads and used computer sellers offer additional outlets for purchasing used computers.

10 If you have a computer and are upgrading to a new one, then consider selling or trading in the old one.

If you are a replacement buyer, your older computer still may have value. If you cannot sell the computer through the classified ads, via a Web site, or to a friend, then ask if the computer dealer will buy your old computer.

An increasing number of companies are taking trade-ins, but do not expect too much money for your old computer. Other companies offer to recycle your old computer free or for a fee.

11 Be aware of hidden costs.

Before purchasing, be sure to consider any additional costs associated with buying a computer, such as an additional telephone line, a broadband modem, an uninterruptible power supply (UPS), computer furniture, a USB flash drive, paper, and computer training classes you may want to take. Depending on where you buy the computer, the seller may be willing to include some or all of these in the computer purchase price.

12 Consider more than just price.

The lowest-cost computer may not be the best long-term buy. Consider such intangibles as the vendor's time in business, regard for quality, and reputation for support. If you need to upgrade a computer often, you may want to consider a leasing arrangement, in which you pay monthly lease fees, but can upgrade or add on to your computer as your equipment needs change. No matter what type of buyer you are, insist on a 30-day, no-questions-asked return policy on the computer.

13 Avoid restocking fees.

Some companies charge a restocking fee of 10 to 20 percent as part of their money-back return policy. In some cases, no restocking fee for hardware is applied, but it is applied for software. Ask about the existence and terms of any restocking policies before you buy.

14 Use a credit card to purchase a new computer.

Many credit cards offer purchase protection and extended warranty benefits that cover you in case of loss of or damage to purchased goods. Paying by credit card also gives you time to install and use the computer before you have to pay for it. Finally, if you are dissatisfied with the computer and are unable to reach

an agreement with the seller, paying by credit card gives you certain rights regarding withholding payment until the dispute is resolved. Check your credit card terms for specific details.

15 Consider purchasing an extended warranty or service plan.

If you use your computer for business or require fast resolution to major computer problems, consider purchasing an extended warranty or a service plan through a local dealer or third-party company. Most extended warranties cover the repair and replacement of computer components beyond the standard warranty. Most service plans ensure that your technical support calls receive priority response from technicians. You also can purchase an on-site service plan that states that a technician will arrive at your home, work, or school within 24 hours. If your computer includes a warranty and service agreement for a year or less, consider extending the service for two or three years when you buy the computer.

How to Purchase a Notebook Computer

If you need computing capability when you travel or to use in lectures or meetings, you may find a notebook computer to be an appropriate choice. The guidelines mentioned in the previous section also apply to the purchase of a notebook computer. The following are additional considerations unique to notebook computers, including netbooks and Tablet PCs.

1 Determine which computer fits your mobile computing needs.

Before purchasing a notebook computer, you need to determine whether a traditional notebook computer, netbook, or Tablet PC will meet your needs. If you spend most of your time working on spreadsheets, writing and/or editing documents, e-mail, or using the Internet, then a traditional notebook computer will suffice. If your primary use will be to access the Internet while traveling and you are not concerned as much with processing power or hard disk capacity, consider a netbook. If you find yourself in need of a computer in class or that you spend more time in meetings than in your office, then the Tablet PC may be the answer. Before you invest money in a Tablet PC, however, determine which programs you plan to use on it. You should not buy a Tablet PC simply because it is an interesting type of computer.

❷ Purchase a notebook computer with a sufficiently large screen.

Active-matrix screens display high-quality color that is viewable from all angles. Less expensive, passive-matrix screens sometimes are difficult to see in low-light conditions and cannot be viewed from an angle.

Notebook computers typically include a 12.1-inch, 13.3-inch, 14.1-inch, 15.4-inch, or 17-inch display. Netbooks have screens as small as 7 inches. For most users, a 14.1-inch display is satisfactory. If you intend to use the notebook computer as a desktop computer replacement, however, you may opt for a 15.4-inch or 17-inch display. The WSXGA+ standard (1680 × 1050) is popular with 17-inch displays, so if you intend to watch HD movies on the computer, take this into consideration. Dell offers a notebook computer with a 20.1-inch display that looks like a briefcase when closed. Some notebook computers with these larger displays weigh more than 10 pounds, however, so if you travel a lot and portability is essential, you might want a lighter computer with a smaller display. The lightest notebook computers, which weigh less than 3 pounds, are equipped with a 12.1-inch display.

Regardless of size, the resolution of the display should be at least 1024 × 768 pixels. To compare the screen size on various notebook computers, including netbooks and Tablet PCs, visit the company Web sites. Tablet PCs use a digitizer below a standard 10.4-inch motion-sensitive LCD display to make the writing experience on the screen feel like writing on paper. To ensure you experience the maximum benefits from the ClearType technology, make sure the LCD display has a resolution of 800 × 600 in landscape mode and a 600 × 800 in portrait mode.

❸ Experiment with different keyboards, pointing devices, and digital pens.

Notebook computer keyboards, especially netbook keyboards, are far less standardized than those for desktop computers. Some notebook computers, for example, have wide wrist rests, while others have none, and keyboard layouts on notebook computers often vary. Notebook computers also use a range of pointing devices, including touchpads, pointing sticks, trackballs, and, in the case of Tablet PCs, digital pens.

Before purchasing a notebook computer, try various types of keyboards and pointing devices to determine which is easiest for you to use. Regardless of the device you select, you also may want to purchase a standard mouse to use when you are working at a desk or other large surface. Figure 4 compares the standard point-and-click of a mouse with the gestures made with a digital pen. Other gestures with the digital pen replicate some of the commonly used keys on a keyboard.

Mouse and Digital Pen Operations

Mouse	Digital Pen
Point	Point
Click	Tap
Double-click	Double-tap
Right-click	Tap and hold
Click and drag	Drag

Figure 4 Standard point-and-click of a mouse compared with the gestures made with a digital pen.

❹ Make sure the notebook computer you purchase has an optical disc drive.

Most mobile computers include an optical disc drive. Although DVD/Blu-ray Disc drives are slightly more expensive, they allow you to play CDs, DVDs, and Blu-ray Discs using your notebook computer and hear the sound through earbuds. If you decide to purchase a netbook, it might not include an optical disc drive. Instead, you might need to purchase an external optical disc drive.

❺ If necessary, upgrade the processor, memory, and disk storage at the time of purchase.

As with a desktop computer, upgrading a notebook computer's memory and disk storage usually is less expensive at the time of initial purchase. Some disk storage is custom designed for notebook computer manufacturers, meaning an upgrade might not be available in the future. If you are purchasing a lightweight notebook computer or Tablet PC, then it should include at least an Intel Core 2 Quad processor, 2 GB RAM, and 250 GB of storage. If you are purchasing a netbook, it should have an Intel Atom processor, at least 1 GB RAM, and 120 GB of storage.

❻ The availability of built-in ports and slots and a USB hub on a notebook computer is important.

A notebook computer does not have much room to add adapter cards. If you know the purpose for which you plan to use the notebook computer, then you can determine the ports you will need. Netbooks typically have fewer ports than traditional notebook computers and Tablet PCs. Most notebook computers include common ports, such as a video port, audio port, network port, FireWire port, and multiple USB ports. If you plan to connect the notebook computer to a television, however, then you will need a PC to TV port. To optimize television viewing, you may want to consider DisplayPort, DVI, or HDMI ports. If you want to connect to networks at school or in various offices via a network cable, make sure the notebook computer you purchase has a network port. If the notebook computer does not contain a network port, you will have to purchase an external network card that slides into an expansion slot in your computer, as well as a network cable. You also may want to consider adding a card reader.

⑦ If you plan to use your notebook computer for note-taking at school or in meetings, consider a convertible Tablet PC.

Some computer manufacturers have developed convertible Tablet PCs that allow the screen to rotate 180 degrees on a central hinge and then fold down to cover the keyboard (Figure 5). You then can use a digital pen to enter text or drawings into the computer by writing on the screen. Some notebook computers have wide screens for better viewing and editing, and some even have a screen on top of the unit in addition to the regular screen. If you spend much of your time attending lectures or meetings, then the slate Tablet PC is ideal. With a slate Tablet PC, users can attach a removable keyboard.

Figure 5
A convertible Tablet PC.

⑧ If you purchase a Tablet PC, determine whether you require multi-touch technology.

Newer operating systems now support hardware with multi-touch technology. If you choose an operating system that supports this technology, the Tablet PC also must support this technology.

⑨ Purchase a notebook computer with an integrated Web cam.

If you will be using a notebook computer to connect to the Internet and chat with friends online, consider purchasing one with an integrated Web cam.

⑩ Check with your wireless carrier to see if it offers netbooks for sale.

Most wireless carriers now offer wireless data plans allowing you to connect to the Internet from almost anywhere with a cell phone signal. Some wireless carriers now are selling netbooks with built-in capability to connect wirelessly to the Internet using a wireless data plan.

⑪ Purchase a notebook computer with a built-in wireless network connection.

A wireless network connection (Bluetooth, Wi-Fi a/b/g/n, WiMAX, etc.) can be useful when you travel or as part of a home network. Increasingly more airports, hotels, schools, and cafés have wireless networks that allow you to connect to the Internet. Many users today are setting up wireless home networks. With a wireless home network, your notebook computer can access the Internet, as well as other computers in the house, from any location to share files and hardware, such as a printer, and browse the Web. Most home wireless networks allow connections from distances of 150 to 800 feet.

⑫ If you plan to use your notebook computer for long periods without access to an electrical outlet, purchase a second battery.

The trend among notebook computer users today is power and size over battery life. Many notebook computer users today are willing to give up longer battery life for a larger screen, faster processor, and more storage. In addition, some manufacturers typically sell the notebook computer with the lowest capacity battery. For this reason, be careful in choosing a notebook computer if you plan to use it without access to electrical outlets for long periods, such as an airplane flight. You also might want to purchase a second battery as a backup. If you anticipate running the notebook computer on batteries frequently, choose a computer that uses lithium-ion batteries, which last longer than nickel cadmium or nickel hydride batteries.

⑬ Purchase a well-padded and well-designed carrying case.

An amply padded carrying case will protect your notebook computer from the bumps it will receive while traveling. A well-designed carrying case will have room for accessories such as spare optical discs, pens, and paperwork (Figure 6). Although a netbook may be small enough to fit in a handbag, make sure that the bag has sufficient padding to protect the computer.

Figure 6
A well-designed notebook computer carrying case.

⑭ **If you plan to connect your notebook computer to a video projector, make sure the notebook computer is compatible with the video projector.**

You should check, for example, to be sure that your notebook computer will allow you to display an image on the computer screen and projection device at the same time. Also, ensure that the notebook computer has the ports required to connect to the video projector. You also may consider purchasing a notebook computer with a built-in Web cam for video conferencing purposes.

⑮ **For improved security and convenience, consider a fingerprint reader.**

More than half a million notebook computers are stolen or lost each year. If you have critical information stored on your notebook computer, consider purchasing one with a fingerprint reader (Figure 7) to protect the data if your computer is stolen or lost. Fingerprint security offers a level of protection that extends well beyond the standard password protection. If your notebook computer is stolen, the odds of recovering it improve dramatically with anti-theft tracking software. Manufacturers claim recovery rates of 90 percent or more for notebook computers using their product. For convenience, fingerprint readers also allow you to log onto several Web sites in lieu of entering user name and password information.

Figure 7 Fingerprint reader technology offers greater security than passwords.

⑯ **Review the docking capabilities of the Tablet PC.**

The Tablet Technology in the Windows operating system supports a grab-and-go form of docking, so that you can pick up and take a docked Tablet PC with you, just as you would pick up a notepad on your way to a meeting (Figure 8).

Figure 8 A Tablet PC docked to create a desktop computer with the Tablet PC as the monitor.

How to Purchase a Smart Phone

You probably will use a smart phone more often than other mobile devices. For this reason, it is important to choose a phone that is available through your preferred wireless carrier, available in your price range, and offers access to the features you will use most frequently. This section lists guidelines you should consider when purchasing a smart phone.

❶ **Choose a wireless carrier and plan that satisfies your needs and budget.**

Multiple wireless carriers exist today, and each one offers a different line of smart phones. For example, the Samsung Alias is available only through Verizon Wireless. Alternatively, some smart phones, such as the BlackBerry line of smart phones, are available from multiple wireless carriers. Before deciding on a smart phone, you first should research the wireless carriers in your area, and be sure to ascertain whether the coverage is acceptable. Additionally, compare the calling plans for the various carriers and determine which one best meets your needs. Once you have determined the wireless carrier to use, you then can choose from one of their available smart phones. Once you purchase a smart phone, most carriers allow you to perform a risk-free evaluation for 30 days. If you are not satisfied with the phone or its performance, you can return the phone and pay only for the service you have used.

❷ **Decide on the size, style, and weight of the smart phone that will work best for you.**

Smart phones are available in various sizes, weights, shapes, and colors. Some people prefer larger, heavier phones because they feel that they are more durable, while others prefer smaller, lightweight phones for easy portability. Some smart phones are flip phones, meaning that you have to open the phone (like a clamshell) to display the screen and keypad, some open by sliding the phone, and others do not need to be opened to use them. Figure 9 shows the various smart phone styles.

Figure 9 Various smart phone styles.

③ Determine whether you prefer a touch screen, keypad, or mini-keyboard.

Modern smart phones provide various ways to enter text. During the past several years, smart phones with touch screens as their primary input device have been penetrating the market. Some smart phone users prefer touch screens because the phone does not require additional space for a keypad or mini-keyboard, but others find it more difficult to type on a touch screen. Most newer smart phones with touch screens also include handwriting recognition. Smart phones with keypads might make it easier to type for some users, but others do not like the unfamiliar feeling of keys arranged in alphabetical order. In addition, you often have to press the keys multiple times before reaching the letter you want to type. Mini-keyboards are available on some smart phones, such as the BlackBerry and Samsung Alias. Mini-keyboards provide a key for each letter, but the keys are significantly smaller than those on a standard keyboard. Most smart phone users type on mini-keyboards using their thumbs.

④ If you will be synchronizing your smart phone with a program on your computer, select a smart phone that is compatible with the program you wish to use.

Programs such as Microsoft Outlook allow you to synchronize your e-mail messages, contacts, and calendar with your smart phone. If you would like this functionality, purchase a smart phone that can synchronize with Microsoft Outlook. Similarly, if your company uses a BlackBerry Enterprise server or Microsoft Exchange server, you should consider purchasing a smart phone that can synchronize, either using wires or wirelessly, with those servers.

⑤ Compare battery life.

Any smart phone is useful only if it has the power required to run. Talking and using the Internet on your smart phone will shorten battery life more quickly than when the phone is powered on but not in use. If you have a choice, be sure to purchase a battery that will allow the phone to function all day. Pay particular attention to the talk time and standby time. If you plan to talk on the phone more than the advertised talk time, you might consider purchasing a second battery or an extended battery if your phone supports it.

⑥ Make sure your smart phone has enough memory and storage.

If you are using the smart phone to send and receive picture, video, and e-mail messages, and to store music, purchase a memory card that not only is compatible with your computer and smart phone, but also has adequate storage space for your messages and files. If you purchase a memory card and eventually fill it, you easily can transfer the data to a larger memory card.

⑦ Check out the accessories.

Determine which accessories you want for the smart phone. Accessories include carrying cases, screen protectors, synchronization cradles and cables, and car chargers.

How to Purchase a Portable Media Player

Portable media players are becoming the preferred device for listening to music and watching videos on the go. When choosing a portable media player, it is important to consider features and characteristics other than the physical size and amount of storage space. This section lists guidelines you should consider when purchasing a portable media player.

① Choose a device with sufficient storage capacity.

Audio and video files can consume a great deal of storage space, so be sure to purchase a portable media player that has enough capacity to store your audio and video files. You also should consider approximately how many media files you acquire each year, and make sure that your device has enough storage space to accommodate these files for years to come.

② Determine which file formats your new portable media player should support and how you will add files to your library.

Some portable media players are designed to accept new audio and video files only through a program installed on a computer. For example, it is easiest to add media files to an iPod using the iTunes program. Other portable media players connect to a computer using a cable and are displayed in Windows as a removable disk. You then can add files to the media player by dragging the files to the removable disk icon in Windows. The portable media player must support the file formats you are using. You can determine the file format by looking at the file extension on the media files you wish to transfer to your portable media player. Before purchasing a portable media player, make sure that it can support the file formats you are using.

③ Consider a portable media player that can play video.

Some users prefer to watch videos on their portable media player in addition to playing music. You typically can download videos for portable media players less expensively than purchasing the movie on a DVD/Blu-ray Disc. Although the display on a portable media player is small, many still find entertainment value because they are able to watch videos and stay occupied while waiting for a bus, on an airplane, or at other locations where they otherwise might not have anything to occupy them.

4 Read reviews about the sound quality on the portable media players you are considering.

Sound quality may vary greatly among portable media players. If you are unable to try the portable media player before buying it, read reviews and make sure that those reviewing the devices find the sound quality to be acceptable. You also may consider purchasing higher-quality earbuds or headphones to enhance the sound quality.

5 Select a size and style that works best for you.

Portable media players are available in various shapes and styles. For example, Apple offers the iPod shuffle, iPod nano, iPod classic, and iPod touch (Figure 10). Each type of iPod varies in size and style, and some have capabilities (such as video) that others do not. Choose a size and style that meets your needs and fits your personality.

Figure 10 Portable media players are available in different shapes, styles, and colors.

6 Check out additional memory cards.

Most portable media players have internal storage for your media files. If you wish to increase the available storage, consider purchasing a portable media player that allows you to increase storage capacity by inserting memory cards. Similar to most computers, it is less expensive initially to purchase the largest amount of storage that you can afford, but it is helpful to be able to increase your storage at a later date.

7 Consider rechargeable batteries.

Although most portable media players include rechargeable batteries, some still use traditional alkaline batteries. Portable media players sometimes can last for only a few hours on alkaline batteries, and battery replacement can be costly. Rechargeable batteries often last longer and create less waste. If you are not near a power source, you are unable to recharge the batteries when they die. With alkaline batteries, you simply can insert new ones and continue enjoying your player.

8 Stay within your budget.

As previously mentioned, portable media players are available in a variety of shapes and sizes, and they also are available with various storage capacities. When shopping for a portable media player, be realistic when you consider how you will use the device, as well as how much storage you require. Purchasing the latest and greatest device is not always the best option, and the cost can exceed what you care to spend.

How to Purchase a Digital Camera

Both amateur and professional photographers now are mostly purchasing digital cameras to meet their photography needs. Because digital cameras with new and improved features regularly are introduced to the marketplace, consumers should know how to compare the differences among the multiple cameras that are available. This section lists guidelines you should consider when purchasing a digital camera.

1 Determine the type of digital camera that meets your needs.

Various types of digital cameras exist, including point-and-shoot cameras, field cameras, and studio cameras. Point-and-shoot cameras typically fit in your pocket and meet the needs of most general consumers. Field cameras, which often are used by photojournalists, are portable but flexible. Field cameras allow photographers to change lenses and use other attachments, and also are more customizable than point-and-shoot cameras. Studio cameras are used in photo studios and are stationary. These cameras give you the widest range of lenses and settings.

2 The digital camera with the highest resolution is not always the best.

Many consumers mistakenly believe that the digital camera with the highest resolution is the best camera for their needs. A higher resolution increases quality and clarity of your photos, as well as the size at which you can print the photos before noticing degradation in quality. If you never plan to print photos larger than 8" × 10", for example, you do not need a camera with a resolution greater than 5 megapixels. Many cameras available today advertise higher resolutions, but taking pictures at these high resolutions can use valuable storage space. Just because your camera can take a 10-megapixel photo does not mean that you always should set the resolution to 10 megapixels.

❸ Consider size and weight.

Digital cameras are available in various sizes and weights. Some people prefer smaller, lighter cameras because they are easier to transport and take up less space. Others prefer bulkier, heavier cameras because the weight helps steady them to take a clearer picture. Many digital cameras also include an image stabilization feature that reduces the possibility of a blurry picture if you move your hands slightly while taking the picture. Some also believe that heavier cameras are of better quality, although that seldom is true. When choosing a digital camera, practice taking pictures with it and select one that feels comfortable and natural.

❹ Different cameras require different memory cards.

When purchasing a digital camera, pay careful attention to the type of memory card the camera uses. Many use SD cards, some use xD Picture cards, and some use CompactFlash memory cards. Some memory cards are more expensive to replace than others, and some have a higher capacity than other cards. If you take a lot of pictures, purchase a camera that supports a memory card with a higher storage capacity so that you can avoid carrying multiple memory cards. You also might consider purchasing a camera that uses a memory card that is compatible with your other mobile devices.

❺ Photo editing features can save you time.

Some digital cameras have integrated tools that allow you to edit photos directly from the camera. For instance, you may be able to crop photos, change the brightness, or remove red eye effects. Editing photos directly on the camera after taking them can save you from editing multiple photos at once when you transfer them to a computer. The photo editing capabilities available on digital cameras are limited when compared to photo editing programs, but in many cases they can edit a photo to your satisfaction.

❻ Make sure that you can see the LCD screen easily.

LCD screens on digital cameras allow you to configure the settings, frame a shot before taking it, and preview photos after taking them. LCD screens vary by inches, so select a camera with a screen that does not require you to strain your eyes to view. This is especially important if the camera you are considering does not have a viewfinder, because you then will be required to use the display to frame your shots.

❼ Determine whether your pictures will require you to zoom.

If you plan to take pictures of people or objects that require you to zoom in, select a digital camera that has a high optical zoom. An optical zoom enlarges the subject by adjusting the camera lens, whereas a digital zoom uses algorithms built into the camera to magnify images. Optical zooms, as opposed to digital zooms, often result in a higher quality photo. While a digital zoom might be capable of magnifying objects that are 100 feet away, the photo will suffer a loss of quality.

❽ Price is important.

As with all other devices, locate a digital camera that does not exceed your budget. If you find a great camera that is available for more than you are willing to spend, consider locating a camera with a slightly lower resolution, an alternate brand, or a smaller screen. Digital cameras can last well beyond five years if properly maintained, so consider this a longer-term investment that will create memories lasting you a lifetime.

❾ Know your batteries.

Some digital cameras require replaceable alkaline or rechargeable batteries (often AA or AAA), and others have a rechargeable battery. Similar to batteries in portable media players, using disposable batteries in digital cameras can get expensive, and they may not last as long as rechargeable battery packs. Digital camera battery life is not measured in hours (as is the case with smart phones and portable media players); instead, it is measured in how many pictures can be taken on a single charge or set of batteries. Turning off the LCD screen and flash when you take pictures can help to extend battery life.

❿ Purchase accessories.

Accessories that are available for digital cameras include carrying cases, extra batteries and battery chargers, and extra memory cards (Figure 11). Carrying cases can help protect your digital camera, especially while traveling, and the extra batteries and chargers can stay inside your carrying case so that they are readily available should you need them. Screen protectors can help protect the LCD screen on your digital camera.

Figure 11 Digital camera accessories include memory cards, cases, batteries, and battery chargers.

Multiple Web sites on the Internet allow you to purchase computers and mobile devices. For a list of Web sites that sell computers and mobile devices, visit the Computer Concepts CourseMate Web site at www.cengagebrain.com and then navigate to the Buyer's Guide Feature resource for this book.

Chapter Eight

Communications and Networks

Objectives

After completing this chapter, you will be able to:

1 Discuss the purpose of the components required for successful communications: sending device, communications device, communications channel, and receiving device

2 Describe these uses of computer communications: wireless messaging services, wireless Internet access points, cybercafés, global positioning systems, collaboration, groupware, voice mail, and Web services

3 Differentiate among types of networks: LANs, MANs, and WANs

4 Explain the purpose of communications software

5 Describe various types of lines for communications over the telephone network: dial-up, ISDN, DSL, FTTP, T-carrier, and ATM

6 Describe commonly used communications devices: dial-up modems, digital modems, wireless modems, network cards, wireless access points, and routers

7 Discuss different ways to set up a home network

8 Describe various physical and wireless transmission media: twisted-pair cable, coaxial cable, fiber-optic cable, infrared, broadcast radio, cellular radio, microwaves, and communications satellite

Communications

Computer **communications** describes a process in which two or more computers or devices transfer data, instructions, and information. Figure 8-1 shows a sample communications system. Some communications involve cables and wires; others are sent wirelessly through the air. As illustrated in this figure, communications systems contain all types of computers and computing devices. For successful communications, you need the following:

- A **sending device** that initiates an instruction to transmit data, instructions, or information.
- A communications device that connects the sending device to a communications channel.
- A **communications channel**, or transmission media on which the data, instructions, or information travel.
- A communications device that connects the communications channel to a receiving device.
- A **receiving device** that accepts the transmission of data, instructions, or information.

communications system

Figure 8-1 An example of a communications system. The communications channel consists of telephone and power lines, cable television and other underground lines, microwave stations, and satellites.

All types of computers and mobile devices serve as sending and receiving devices in a communications system. This includes mainframe computers, servers, desktop computers, notebook computers, smart phones, portable media players, handheld game consoles, and GPS receivers. One type of communications device that connects a communications channel to a sending or receiving device such as a computer is a modem. Two examples of communications channels are cable television lines and telephone lines.

Uses of Computer Communications

Computer communications are everywhere. Many require that users subscribe to an Internet access provider. With other computer communications, an organization such as a business or school provides communications services to employees, students, or customers. The following pages discuss a variety of computer communications.

Blogs, Chat Rooms, E-Mail, Fax, FTP, Instant Messaging, Internet, Newsgroups, RSS, Video Conferencing, VoIP, Web, Web 2.0, Web Folders, and Wikis

Previous chapters discussed many uses of computer communications as they related to a particular topic. In the course of a day, it is likely you use, or use information generated by, one or more of the previously discussed communications technologies, which are outlined in Figure 8-2.

The following pages discuss a variety of other uses of communications that have not been discussed in depth previously. These include wireless messaging services, wireless Internet access points, cybercafés, global positioning systems, collaboration, groupware, voice mail, and Web services.

Summary of Communications Discussed in Previous Chapters

Communications Type	Brief Description
Blogs	Time-stamped articles on a network that reflect the author's interests, opinions, and personality
Chat Rooms	Real-time typed conversation among two or more people that takes place on a compute connected to a network that also may allow the exchange of messages, photos, files, audio, and video
E-Mail	Transmission of messages and files via a computer network
Fax	Transmits and receives documents over telephone lines
FTP	Internet standard that permits users to upload and download files to and from FTP servers on the Internet
Instant Messaging	Real-time one-on-one Internet communications service that notifies you when one or more people are online and then allows you to exchange messages, photos, files, audio, and video
Internet	Worldwide collection of networks that links millions of businesses, government agencie educational institutions, and individuals
Newsgroups	Online areas in which users have written discussions about a particular subject
RSS	Specification that enables Web content to be distributed to subscribers
Video Conferencing	Real-time meeting between two or more geographically separated people who use a network to transmit audio and video data
VoIP	Conversation that takes place over the Internet using a telephone connected to a computer, mobile device, or telephone adapter
Web	Worldwide collection of electronic documents on the Internet that users access through a Web browser
Web 2.0	Web sites that provide a means for users to share personal information, allow users to modify Web site content, and/or have application software built into the site for visitors to use
Web Folders	Location on a Web server to which users publish documents and other files
Wikis	Collaborative Web sites that allow users to create, add to, modify, or delete Web site conte

Wikis

 For more information, visit the Computer Concepts CourseMate Web site at www.cengagebrain.com, navigate to the Chapter 8 Web Link resource for this book, and then click Wikis.

Figure 8-2 Uses of communications discussed in earlier chapters.

? FAQ 8-1

How many households are using cell phones as their primary telephone?

A recent study indicates that approximately 20 percent of households use cell phones as their primary telephone. Some families choose to save money by disconnecting their home telephone and using their cell phone for all calls, although they tend to make more telephone calls than families with a traditional telephone line.

For more information, visit the Computer Concepts CourseMate Web site at www.cengagebrain.com, navigate to the Chapter 8 FAQ resource for this book, and then click Wireless Households.

Wireless Messaging Services

Users can send and receive wireless messages to and from smart phones, cell phones, handheld game consoles, and other mobile devices and computers using three techniques: text messaging, picture/video messaging, and wireless instant messaging (Figure 8-3).

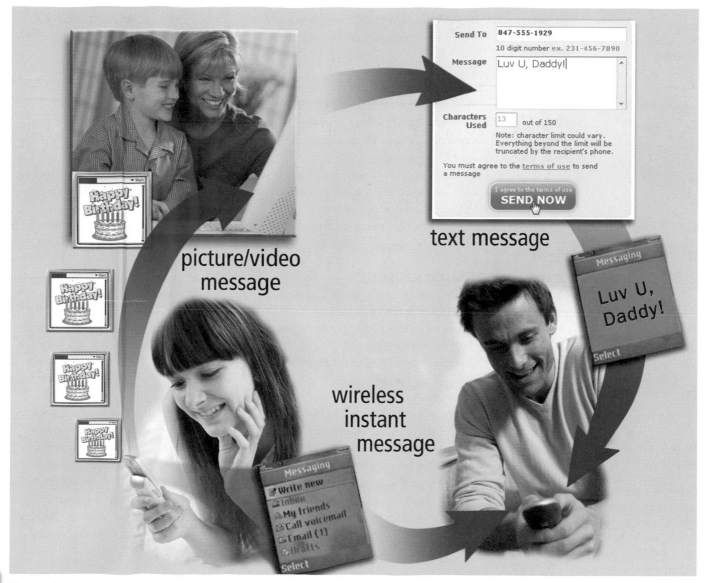

picture/video message

text message

wireless instant message

Send To 847-555-1929
10 digit number ex. 231-456-7890
Message Luv U, Daddy!
Characters Used 13 out of 150
Note: character limit could vary. Everything beyond the limit will be truncated by the recipient's phone.
You must agree to the terms of use to send a message
I agree to the terms of use SEND NOW

Luv U, Daddy!

Figure 8-3 Users can send and receive text messages, picture/video messages, and wireless instant messages to and from their smart phones and other computers and devices.

Text Messaging A mobile device with **text messaging**, also called SMS (short message service), capability allows users to send and receive short text messages, typically fewer than 300 characters, on a phone or other mobile device or computer. Text messaging services typically provide users with several options for sending and receiving messages:

• Mobile to Mobile: send a message from your mobile device to another mobile device
• Mobile to E-Mail: send a message from your mobile device to an e-mail address anywhere in the world
• Web to Mobile: send a message from a text messaging Web site to a mobile device, or request that a Web site alert a mobile device with breaking news and other updates, such as sports scores, stock prices, and weather forecasts
• Mobile to Provider: send a message by entering a four- or five-digit number assigned to a specific content or wireless service provider, followed by the message, such as a vote for a television program contestant

Video Messaging

For more information, visit the Computer Concepts CourseMate Web site at www.cengagebrain.com, navigate to the Chapter 8 Web Link resource for this book, and then click Video Messaging.

Picture/Video Messaging   With **picture messaging**, users can send pictures and sound files, as well as short text messages, to a phone or other mobile device, or a computer. With **video messaging**, users can send short video clips, usually about 30 seconds in length, in addition to all picture messaging services. Picture/video messaging service, also called MMS (multimedia message service), typically provides users these options for sending and receiving messages:

- Mobile to Mobile: send the picture/video from your mobile device to another mobile device
- Mobile to E-Mail: send the picture/video from your mobile device to an e-mail address anywhere in the world

Wireless Instant Messaging   Wireless instant messaging (IM) is a real-time Internet communications service that allows wireless mobile devices to exchange messages with one or more mobile devices or online users. Some wireless Internet service providers partner with IM services so that you can use your smart phone or other mobile device to send and receive wireless instant messages. With a compatible IM service, users have these IM options:

- Mobile to Mobile: use a wireless instant messenger to communicate between two mobile devices
- Mobile to Personal Computer: use a wireless instant messenger to communicate between a mobile device and a desktop or notebook computer
- Web to Mobile: send or forward messages from a desktop or notebook computer's instant messenger to a mobile device

Wireless Internet Access Points

At home, work, school, and in many public locations, people connect wirelessly to the Internet through a **wireless Internet access point** using notebook computers, smart phones, handheld game consoles, or other devices. Users access wireless Internet access points with computers or devices that have the necessary built-in wireless capability or the appropriate wireless network card, USB network adapter, ExpressCard module, or PC Card (Figure 8-4). Two types of wireless Internet access points are hot spots and mobile wireless networks.

A **hot spot** is a wireless network that provides Internet connections to mobile computers and devices. Through the hot spot, mobile users check e-mail, browse the Web, and access any service on the Internet. Three hot spot technologies are Wi-Fi, WiMAX, and Bluetooth. Wi-Fi hot spots provide wireless network connections to users in public locations such as airports and airplanes, train stations, hotels, convention centers, schools, campgrounds, shopping malls, bookstores, libraries, restaurants, and coffee shops. The coverage range for WiMAX hot spots, can be much wider than Wi-Fi; for example, they can cover an entire city. Bluetooth hot spots provide location-based services, such as sending coupons or menus, to users whose enabled devices enter the coverage range. Sections later in this chapter discuss Wi-Fi, WiMAX, and Bluetooth in more detail. Read Ethics & Issues 8-1 for a related discussion.

Ethics & Issues

For the complete text of the Ethics & Issues boxes found in this chapter, visit the Computer Concepts CourseMate Web site at www.cengagebrain.com and then navigate to the Chapter 8 Ethics & Issues resource for this book.

ETHICS & ISSUES 8-1

Will Widespread Wireless Broadband Connections Kill Print Media?

Airlines around the world recently started offering Wi-Fi hot spots on some flights. Communications companies also began offering WiMax coverage throughout entire cities. Even smart phones deliver high-speed Web browsing. With the proliferation of high-speed wireless Internet access, some experts believe that the end is near for print media, such as newspapers and magazines. The traditional airport and city newspaper and magazine stands' days may be numbered. Instead of buying a newspaper and a couple of magazines before a flight, travelers choose from thousands of searchable publications on their mobile devices while traveling. Even the morning newspaper delivery is at risk as more people choose to use mobile devices to wirelessly access their favorite newspapers from home. Some experts dispute this claim, stating that the print media industry perfected the centuries-old hard copy delivery of newspapers and magazines, and that, when given the choice, most people prefer print reading.

For now, people prefer the style, quality, and portability of print media.

Will widespread wireless broadband connections, such as Wi-Fi, put an end to printed newspapers and magazines? Why or why not? Would you prefer to read newspapers and magazines in print or on a mobile device that provides similar or better readability as compared to print media? Why or why not? How can the media industry take advantage of the wireless Internet trend?

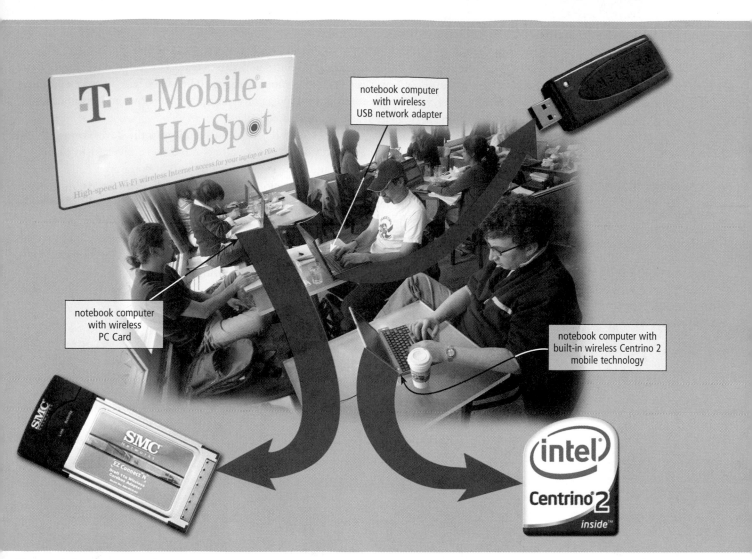

Figure 8-4 Mobile users in this hot spot access the Internet through their notebook computers. One computer uses a wireless USB network adapter; another uses a wireless PC Card. Others have Intel's built-in wireless Centrino 2 mobile technology.

Some hot spots provide free Internet access, some charge a per-use fee, and others require users to subscribe to a wireless Internet service provider, to which they pay per-access fees, daily fees, or a monthly fee. Per-access fees average $3, daily fees range from $5 to $20, and monthly fees range from $20 to $60 for unlimited access, with the higher monthly fee providing greater coverage areas.

A mobile wireless network provides users with high-speed Internet connections, as long as they are in the network's range. A mobile wireless network usually includes most major cities and airports. Subscription fees for unlimited monthly Internet access to a mobile wireless network through a cell phone usually range from $30 to $50. Fees for notebook computer access are higher, usually ranging from $60 to $80 per month.

Cybercafés

When mobile users travel without their notebook computer or Internet-enabled mobile device, they can visit a cybercafé to access e-mail, the Web, and other Internet services. A **cybercafé**, or Internet cafe, is a coffeehouse, restaurant, or other location that provides personal computers with Internet access to its customers. Cybercafés exist in cities around the world. Although some provide free Internet access, most charge a per-hour or per-minute fee. Some cybercafés also are hot spots.

Global Positioning Systems

A **global positioning system** (**GPS**) is a navigation system that consists of one or more earth-based receivers that accept and analyze signals sent by satellites in order to determine the receiver's geographic location (Figure 8-5). A GPS receiver is a handheld, mountable, or embedded device that contains an antenna, a radio receiver, and a processor. Many include a screen display that shows an individual's location on a map. Some also function as a portable media player.

Many mobile devices such as smart phones have GPS capability built into the device or as an add-on feature. Some users carry a handheld GPS receiver; others mount a receiver to an object such as an automobile, boat, airplane, farm and construction equipment, or computer.

The first and most used application of GPS technology is to assist people with determining where they are located. The data obtained from a GPS, however, can be applied to a variety of other uses: creating a map, ascertaining the best route between two points, locating a lost person or stolen object, monitoring the movement of a person or object, determining altitude, and calculating speed. Many vehicles use GPSs to provide drivers with directions or other information. Read Innovative Computing 8-1 to find out about a hobby that uses GPS technology.

GPS

For more information, visit the Computer Concepts CourseMate Web site at www.cengagebrain.com, navigate to the Chapter 8 Web Link resource for this book, and then click GPS.

How a GPS Works

Step 1
GPS satellites orbit Earth. Every thousandth of a second, each satellite sends a signal that indicates its current position to the GPS receiver.

Step 2
A GPS receiver (such as in a car, a wearable device, a smart phone, a handheld device, or a collar) determines its location on Earth by analyzing at least 3 separate satellite signals from the 24 satellites in orbit.

Figure 8-5 This figure shows how a GPS works.

Geocaching for Hidden Treasure

Treasure hunting for all ages has gone high-tech. Geocaching is a form of outdoor recreation, discovery, and fun, and the only requirements are a GPS receiver, Internet access, and a sense of adventure.

Participants bury or hide a small container, called a cache, that has a logbook and writing instrument and usually a small novelty trinket such as a coin, button, toy, or CD. They then log on to a geocaching Web site and post details of the container's location using latitudinal and longitudinal coordinates. Cachers then use their GPS receivers to find the container, note their discovery in the logbook, and write about their adventure on the Web site.

The first cache with GPS coordinates was documented in 2000. Today, more than 900,000 geocaches in more than 100 countries and on all 7 continents are registered on a variety of Web sites, such as geocaching.com. The locations range from under water to mountain peaks. Cachers generally follow the Geocacher's Creed, which encourages ethical behavior and preservation of natural resources.

💻 For more information, visit the Computer Concepts CourseMate Web site at www.cengagebrain.com, navigate to the Chapter 8 Innovative Computing resource for this book, and then click Geocaching.

Collaboration

Many software products provide a means to **collaborate**, or work online, with other users connected to a server. Two methods of collaboration include collaborative software and document management systems. **Collaborative software** includes tools that enable users to share documents via online meetings and communicate with other connected users. An online meeting allows users to share documents with others in real time (Figure 8-6). When the online meeting takes place on the Web, it is called a **Web conference**. In an online meeting, all participants see a document(s) at the same time. As someone changes the document, everyone in the meeting sees the changes being made. Collaborative software often has chat, whiteboard, and video/audio conferencing capabilities.

Some organizations use document management systems to make collaboration possible among employees. A **document management system** provides for storage and management of a company's documents, such as word processing documents, presentations, and spreadsheets. Users then access these documents, depending on their needs. A document management system can track all changes made to a document. It also can store additional information such as the document's creation date, the user who created the document, a summary of the document, and any keywords associated with the document. Google Docs is a Web-based document management system that provides basic services to its subscribers at no cost. With Google Docs, multiple users can work on the same document at the same time, viewing each others edits as they are entered.

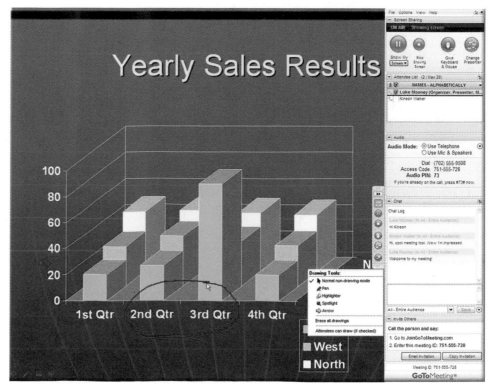

Figure 8-6   Through an online meeting, all participants see a document at the same time.

Groupware

Groupware is software that helps groups of people work together on projects and share information over a network. Groupware is a component of a broad concept called workgroup computing, which includes network hardware and software that enables group members to communicate, manage projects, schedule meetings, and make group decisions. To assist with these activities, most groupware provides personal information manager (PIM) functions, such as an electronic appointment calendar, an address book, and a notepad. A major feature of groupware is group scheduling, in which a group calendar can track the schedules of multiple users and help coordinate appointments and meeting times.

Voice Mail

Voice mail, which functions much like an answering machine, allows someone to leave a voice message for one or more people. Unlike answering machines, however, a computer in the voice mail system converts an analog voice message into digital form. Once digitized, the message is stored in a voice mailbox. A voice mailbox is a storage location on a hard disk in the voice mail system.

To help users manage voice mail messages, some systems offer visual voice mail. With **visual voice mail**, users can view message details such as the length of calls and, in some cases, read message contents instead of listening to them. Some voice mail systems can send digital voice mail files to e-mail addresses. Others can convert a voice mail message to a text message for display on a computer or mobile device.

Web Services

Web services describe standardized software that enables programmers to create applications that communicate with other remote computers over the Internet or over an internal business network. Businesses are the primary users of Web services because this technology provides a means for departments to communicate with each other, suppliers, vendors, and with clients. For example, third-party vendors can use Web services to communicate with their online retailer's Web site to manage their inventory levels.

Web services often provide content for mashups. A **mashup** is a Web application that combines services from two or more sources, creating a new application. An e-commerce business, for example, might determine the address of its closest retail store from its Web site and combine (mash) the location with a map from a travel and mapping Web site to provide the Web site visitor with driving directions.

✔ QUIZ YOURSELF 8-1

Instructions: Find the true statement below. Then, rewrite the remaining false statements so that they are true.

1. A cybercafé is a wireless network that provides Internet connections to mobile computers and devices.
2. GPS is a navigation system that consists of one or more earth-based receivers that accept and analyze signals sent by satellites in order to determine the receiver's geographic location.
3. Receiving devices initiate an instruction to transmit data, instructions, or information.
4. Users can send pictures and sound files, as well as short text messages, with text messaging.

Quiz Yourself Online: To further check your knowledge of pages 314 through 322, visit the Computer Concepts CourseMate Web site at www.cengagebrain.com, navigate to the Chapter 8 Quiz Yourself resource for this book, and then click Objectives 1 – 2.

Networks

As discussed in Chapter 1, a **network** is a collection of computers and devices connected together via communications devices and transmission media. Many businesses network their computers together to facilitate communications, share hardware, share data and information, share software, and transfer funds.

A network can be internal to an organization or span the world by connecting to the Internet. Instead of using the Internet or an internal network, some companies hire a value-added network provider for network functions. A **value-added network** (**VAN**) is a third-party business that provides networking services for a fee.

Networks facilitate communications among users and allow users to share resources with other users. Some examples of resources are data, information, hardware, and software.

LANs, MANs, and WANs

Networks usually are classified as a local area network, metropolitan area network, or wide area network. The main differentiation among these classifications is their area of coverage, as described in the following pages. Read Looking Ahead 8-1 for a look at another type of network.

↗ LOOKING AHEAD 8-1

Body Area Networks Sense Intentions

Local area networks literally can move over when a body area network (BAN) makes the scene in a few years. This set of wearable or implanted body sensors will turn the body into a human router. The devices will communicate wirelessly and transmit data from the body to another device that performs an action.

For example, you can save a word processing document to a device on your wrist, walk to a printer, and just touch the printer with your hand to print. Or, merely by shaking hands, you can transfer information from a business card stored on your wrist device to another device worn by a business colleague.

Researchers actively are pursuing the BAN architecture and applications. Many of the uses are being developed for physical rehabilitation, interactive games, and human interaction with computers. Each year experts in the fields of computer science, electrical engineering, bio-medical engineering, and medicine meet at the BodyNet conference to exchange ideas.

For more information, visit the Computer Concepts CourseMate Web site at www.cengagebrain.com, navigate to the Chapter 8 Looking Ahead resource for this book, and then click Body Area Networks.

LAN   A **local area network** (**LAN**) is a network that connects computers and devices in a limited geographical area such as a home, school computer laboratory, office building, or closely positioned group of buildings. Each computer or device on the network, called a node, often shares resources such as printers, large hard disks, and programs. Often, the nodes are connected via cables. A **wireless LAN** (**WLAN**) is a LAN that uses no physical wires. Very often, a WLAN communicates with a wired LAN for access to its resources (Figure 8-7).

Figure 8-7   Computers and mobile devices on a wireless LAN often communicate via an access point with a wired LAN to access its software, printer, the Internet, and other resources.

MAN A **metropolitan area network** (**MAN**) is a high-speed network that connects local area networks in a metropolitan area such as a city or town and handles the bulk of communications activity across that region. A MAN typically includes one or more LANs, but covers a smaller geographic area than a WAN.

A MAN usually is managed by a consortium of users or by a single network provider that sells the service to the users. Local and state governments, for example, regulate some MANs. Telephone companies, cable television operators, and other organizations provide users with connections to the MAN.

WAN A **wide area network** (**WAN**) is a network that covers a large geographic area (such as a city, country, or the world) using a communications channel that combines many types of media such as telephone lines, cables, and radio waves (Figure 8-8). A WAN can be one large network or can consist of two or more LANs connected together. The Internet is the world's largest WAN.

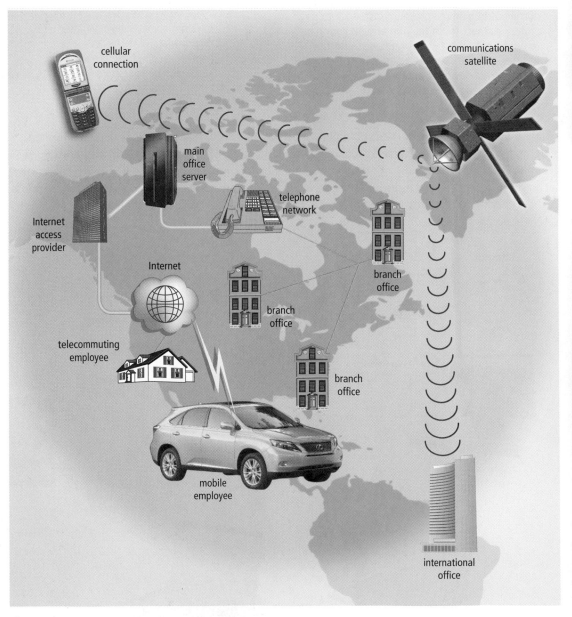

Figure 8-8   An example of a WAN.

Network Architectures

The design of computers, devices, and media in a network, sometimes called the network architecture, is categorized as either client/server or peer-to-peer.

Client/Server On a **client/server network**, one or more computers act as a server; the other computers on the network request services from the server (Figure 8-9). A **server** controls access to the hardware, software, and other resources on the network and provides a centralized storage area for programs, data, and information. The **clients** are other computers and mobile devices on the network that rely on the server for its resources. For example, a server might store a database of customers. Clients on the network (company employees) access the customer database on the server.

Some servers, called dedicated servers, perform a specific task and can be placed with other dedicated servers to perform multiple tasks. For example, a file server stores and manages files. A print server manages printers and documents being printed. A database server stores and provides access to a database. A network server manages network traffic (activity). A Web server is a computer that delivers requested Web pages to your computer.

A client/server network typically provides an efficient means to connect 10 or more computers. Most client/server networks require a person to serve as a network administrator because of the large size of the network.

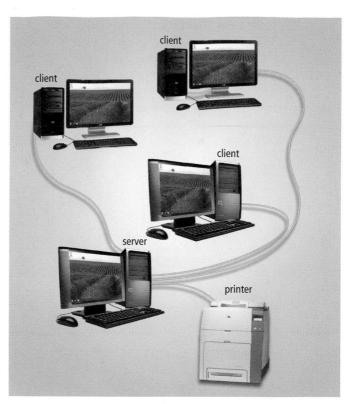

Figure 8-9 On a client/server network, one or more computers act as a server, and the clients access the server(s).

Peer-to-Peer One type of **peer-to-peer network** is a simple, inexpensive network that typically connects fewer than 10 computers. Each computer, called a peer, has equal responsibilities and capabilities, sharing hardware (such as a printer), data, or information with other computers on the peer-to-peer network (Figure 8-10). Each computer stores files on its own storage devices. Thus, each computer on the network contains both the server operating system and application software. All computers on the network share any peripheral device(s) attached to any computer. For example, one computer may have a laser printer and a scanner, while another has an ink-jet printer and an external hard disk. Peer-to-peer networks are ideal for very small businesses and home users.

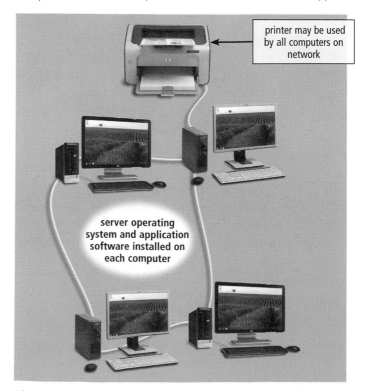

Figure 8-10 Each computer on a peer-to-peer network shares its hardware and software with other computers on the network.

P2P

For more information, visit the Computer Concepts CourseMate Web site at www.cengagebrain.com, navigate to the Chapter 8 Web Link resource for this book, and then click P2P.

Internet Peer-to-Peer   Another type of peer-to-peer, called **P2P**, describes an Internet network on which users access each other's hard disks and exchange files directly (Figure 8-11). This type of peer-to-peer network sometimes is called a file sharing network because users with compatible software and an Internet connection copy files from someone else's hard disk to their hard disks. As more users connect to the network, each user has access to shared files on other users' hard disks. When users log off, others no longer have access to their hard disks.

Examples of networking software that support P2P are BitTorrent, Gnutella, Kazaa, and LimeWire, which allow users to swap music and other files via the Web.

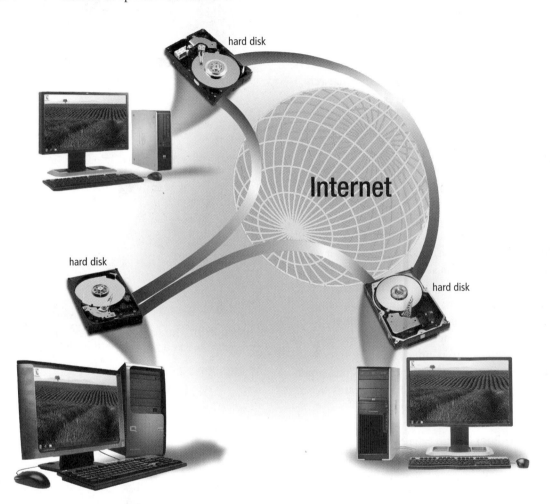

Figure 8-11   P2P describes an Internet network on which users connect to each other's hard disks and exchange files directly.

Network Topologies

A **network topology** refers to the layout of the computers and devices in a communications network. Three commonly used network topologies are star, bus, and ring. Most networks, including the Internet, use combinations of these topologies.

Star Network   On a **star network**, all of the computers and devices (nodes) on the network connect to a central device, thus forming a star (Figure 8-12). Two types of devices that provide a common central connection point for nodes on the network are a hub and a switch. All data that transfers from one node to another passes through the hub or switch.

Star networks are fairly easy to install and maintain. Nodes can be added to and removed from the network with little or no disruption to the network.

On a star network, if one node fails, only that node is affected. The other nodes continue to operate normally. If the hub or switch fails, however, the entire network is inoperable until the device is repaired.

Figure 8-12   A star network contains a single, centralized hub or switch through which all the devices in the network communicate.

Bus Network   A **bus network** consists of a single central cable, to which all computers and other devices connect (Figure 8-13). The bus is the physical cable that connects the computers and other devices. The bus in a bus network transmits data, instructions, and information in both directions. When a sending device transmits data, the address of the receiving device is included with the transmission so that the data is routed to the appropriate receiving device.

Bus networks are popular on LANs because they are inexpensive and easy to install. One advantage of the bus network is that computers and other devices can be attached and detached at any point on the bus without disturbing the rest of the network. Another advantage is that failure of one device usually does not affect the rest of the bus network. The greatest risk to a bus network is that the bus itself might become inoperable. If that happens, the network remains inoperative until the bus is back in working order.

Figure 8-13   Devices in a bus network share a single data path.

Ring Network On a **ring network**, a cable forms a closed loop (ring) with all computers and devices arranged along the ring (Figure 8-14). Data transmitted on a ring network travels from device to device around the entire ring, in one direction. When a computer or device sends data, the data travels to each computer on the ring until it reaches its destination.

If a computer or device on a ring network fails, the entire network potentially could stop functioning. A ring network can span a larger distance than a bus network, but it is more difficult to install. The ring topology primarily is used for LANs, but also is used in WANs.

Figure 8-14 On a ring network, all connected devices form a continuous loop.

Intranets

Recognizing the efficiency and power of the Internet, many organizations apply Internet and Web technologies to their internal networks. An **intranet** (intra means within) is an internal network that uses Internet technologies. Intranets generally make company information accessible to employees and facilitate working in groups.

Simple intranet applications include electronic publishing of organizational materials such as telephone directories, event calendars, procedure manuals, employee benefits information, and job postings. Additionally, an intranet typically includes a connection to the Internet. More sophisticated uses of intranets include groupware applications such as project management, chat rooms, newsgroups, group scheduling, and video conferencing.

An intranet essentially is a small version of the Internet that exists within an organization. Users update information on the intranet by creating and posting a Web page, using a method similar to that used on the Internet.

Sometimes a company uses an extranet, which allows customers or suppliers to access part of its intranet. Package shipping companies, for example, allow customers to access their intranet to print air bills, schedule pickups, and even track shipped packages as the packages travel to their destinations.

Network Communications Standards

Today's networks connect terminals, devices, and computers from many different manufacturers across many types of networks, such as wide area, local area, and wireless. For the different devices on various types of networks to be able to communicate, the network must use similar techniques of moving data through the network from one application to another.

To alleviate the problems of incompatibility and ensure that hardware and software components can be integrated into any network, various organizations such as ANSI and IEEE (pronounced I triple E) propose, develop, and approve network standards. A **network standard** defines guidelines that specify the way computers access the medium to which they are attached, the type(s) of medium used, the speeds used on different types of networks, and the type(s) of physical cable and/or the wireless technology used. A standard that outlines characteristics of how two network devices communicate is called a protocol. Hardware and software manufacturers design their products to meet the guidelines specified in a particular standard, so that their devices can communicate with the network.

The following sections discuss some of the more widely used network communications standards for both wired and wireless networks including Ethernet, token ring, TCP/IP, Wi-Fi, Bluetooth, UWB, IrDA, RFID, WiMAX, and WAP. As data moves through a network from one program to another, it may use one or more of these standards.

Ethernet   **Ethernet** is a network standard that specifies no central computer or device on the network (nodes) should control when data can be transmitted; that is, each node attempts to transmit data when it determines the network is able to receive communications. If two computers on an Ethernet network attempt to send data at the same time, a collision occurs, and the computers must attempt to send their messages again.

Ethernet is based on a bus topology, but Ethernet networks can be wired in a star pattern. The Ethernet standard defines guidelines for the physical configuration of the network, e.g., cabling, network cards, and nodes. Today, Ethernet is the most popular LAN standard because it is relatively inexpensive and easy to install and maintain. Ethernet networks often use cables to transmit data.

Token Ring   The **token ring** standard specifies that computers and devices on the network share or pass a special signal, called a token, in a unidirectional manner and in a preset order. A token is a special series of bits that function like a ticket. The device with the token can transmit data over the network. Only one token exists per network. This ensures that only one computer transmits data at a time. Token ring is based on a ring topology (although it can use a star topology). The token ring standard defines guidelines for the physical configuration of a network. Some token ring networks connect up to 72 devices. Others use a special type of wiring that allows up to 260 connections.

TCP/IP   Short for Transmission Control Protocol/Internet Protocol, **TCP/IP** is a network standard, specifically a protocol, that defines how messages (data) are routed from one end of a network to the other. TCP/IP describes rules for dividing messages into small pieces, called packets; providing addresses for each packet; checking for and detecting errors; sequencing packets; and regulating the flow of messages along the network.

TCP/ IP has been adopted as a network standard for Internet communications. Thus, all hosts on the Internet follow the rules defined in this standard. Internet communications also use other standards, such as the Ethernet standard, as data is routed to its destination.

When a computer sends data over the Internet, the data is divided into packets. Each packet contains the data, as well as the recipient (destination), the origin (sender), and the sequence information used to reassemble the data at the destination. Each packet travels along the fastest individual available path to the recipient's computer via communications devices called routers.

Wi-Fi   Computers and devices that have the appropriate wireless capability can communicate via radio waves with other computers or devices using **Wi-Fi** (wireless fidelity), which identifies any network based on the 802.11 standards. Developed by IEEE, **802.11** is a series of network standards that specifies how two wireless devices communicate over the air with each other. Wi-Fi uses techniques similar to the Ethernet standard to specify how physically to configure a wireless network. Most of today's computers and many mobile devices, such as smart phones and handheld game consoles, are Wi-Fi enabled.

One popular use of the Wi-Fi standard is in hot spots that offer mobile users the ability to connect to the Internet with their Wi-Fi enabled wireless computers and devices. Many homes and small businesses also use Wi-Fi to network computers and devices together wirelessly.

Bluetooth   **Bluetooth** is a standard, specifically a protocol, that defines how two Bluetooth devices use short-range radio waves to transmit data. To communicate with each other, Bluetooth devices often must be within about 10 meters (about 33 feet) but can be extended to 100 meters with additional equipment. Examples of Bluetooth devices can include desktop computers, notebook computers, handheld computers, smart phones, headsets, microphones, digital cameras, GPS receivers, and printers.

Ethernet
For more information, visit the Computer Concepts CourseMate Web site at www.cengagebrain.com, navigate to the Chapter 8 Web Link resource for this book, and then click Ethernet.

UWB **UWB**, which stands for **ultra-wideband**, is a network standard that specifies how two UWB devices use short-range radio waves to communicate at high speeds with each other. For optimal communications, the devices should be within 2 to 10 meters (about 6.5 to 33 feet) of each other. Examples of UWB uses include wirelessly transferring video from a digital video camera, printing pictures from a digital camera, downloading media to a portable media player, or displaying a slide show on a projector.

IrDA Some computers and devices use the **IrDA** specification to transmit data wirelessly to each other via infrared (IR) light waves. Infrared requires a line-of-sight transmission; that is, the sending device and the receiving device must be in line with each other so that nothing obstructs the path of the infrared light wave.

RFID

For more information, visit the Computer Concepts CourseMate Web site at www.cengagebrain.com, navigate to the Chapter 8 Web Link resource for this book, and then click RFID.

RFID **RFID** (radio frequency identification) is a standard, specifically a protocol, that defines how a network uses radio signals to communicate with a tag placed in or attached to an object, an animal, or a person. The tag consists of an antenna and a memory chip that contains the information to be transmitted via radio waves. Through an antenna, an RFID reader reads the radio signals and transfers the information to a computer or computing device. Readers can be handheld or embedded in an object such as a doorway or tollbooth.

WiMAX **WiMAX** (Worldwide Interoperability for Microwave Access), also known as **802.16**, is a newer network standard developed by IEEE that specifies how wireless devices communicate over the air in a wide area. Using the WiMAX standard, computers or devices with the appropriate WiMAX wireless capability communicate via radio waves with other computers or devices via a WiMAX tower. The WiMAX tower, which can cover up to a 30-mile radius, connects to the Internet or to another WiMAX tower.

Two types of WiMAX specifications are fixed wireless and mobile wireless. With fixed wireless WiMAX, a customer accesses the Internet from a desktop computer at home or other permanent location. Mobile wireless WiMAX, by contrast, enables users to access the WiMAX network with mobile computers and mobile devices such as smart phones.

The WiMAX standard provides wireless broadband Internet access at a reasonable cost over long distances to business and home users. WiMAX, similar to Wi-Fi, connects mobile users to the Internet via hot spots. Some game consoles also support the WiMAX standard.

WAP The **Wireless Application Protocol (WAP)** is a standard, specifically a protocol, that specifies how some mobile devices such as smart phones can display the content of Internet services such as the Web, e-mail, and chat rooms. To display a Web page on a smart phone, the phone should contain a microbrowser. WAP uses a client/server network. The wireless device contains the client software, which connects to the Internet access provider's server.

Communications Software

Communications software consists of programs that (1) help users establish a connection to another computer or network; (2) manage the transmission of data, instructions, and information; and (3) provide an interface for users to communicate with one another. The first two are system software and the third is application software. Chapter 3 presented a variety of examples of application software for communications: e-mail, FTP, Web browser, newsgroup/message boards, chat rooms, instant messaging, video conferencing, and VoIP.

Some communications devices are preprogrammed to accomplish communications tasks. Other communications devices require separate communications software to ensure proper transmission of data. Communications software works with the network standards and protocols defined earlier to ensure data moves correctly through a network. Communications software usually is bundled with the operating system or purchased network devices.

Often, a computer has various types of communications software, each serving a different purpose. One type of communications software helps users establish a connection to the Internet using wizards, dialog boxes, and other on-screen messages. Communications software also allows home and small office users to configure wired and wireless networks and connect devices to an existing network.

Communications over the Telephone Network

The public switched telephone network (PSTN) is the worldwide telephone system that handles voice-oriented telephone calls (Figure 8-15). Nearly the entire telephone network today uses digital technology, with the exception of the final link from the local telephone company to a home, which often is analog.

The telephone network is an integral part of computer communications. Data, instructions, and information are transmitted over the telephone network using dial-up lines or dedicated lines. The following sections discuss various types of lines that use the telephone network for data communications.

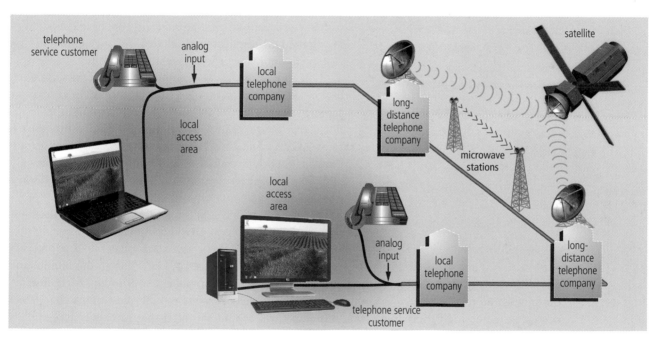

Figure 8-15   A sample telephone network configuration.

Dial-Up Lines

A **dial-up line** is a temporary connection that uses one or more analog telephone lines for communications. A dial-up connection is not permanent. Using a dial-up line to connect computers costs no more than making a regular telephone call.

Dedicated Lines

A **dedicated line** is a type of always-on connection that is established between two communications devices (unlike a dial-up line where the connection is reestablished each time it is used). The quality and consistency of the connection on a dedicated line are better than a dial-up line because dedicated lines provide a constant connection.

Businesses often use dedicated lines to connect geographically distant offices. Dedicated lines can be either analog or digital. Digital lines increasingly are connecting home and business users to networks around the globe because they transmit data and information at faster rates than analog lines.

Five types of digital dedicated lines are ISDN lines, DSL, FTTP, T-carrier lines, and ATM. Although cable television (CATV) lines and fixed wireless are not a type of telephone line, they are very popular ways for the home user to connect to the Internet. Fixed wireless Internet connections use an antenna on your house or business to communicate with a tower location via radio signals. Later sections in this chapter discuss the use of CATV lines and radio signals to connect to the Internet.

The table in Figure 8-16 lists the approximate monthly costs of various types of Internet connections and transfer rates (speeds), as compared with dial-up lines. The following sections discuss ISDN lines, DSL, FTTP, T-carrier lines, and ATM.

Speeds of Various Internet Connections

Type of Line	Approximate Monthly Cost	Transfer Rates*
Dial-up	Local or long-distance rates	Up to 56 Kbps
ISDN	$10 to $40	Up to 1.54 Mpbs
DSL	$13 to $70	128 Kbps to 8.45 Mbps
Cable TV (CATV)	$20 to $50	128 Kbps to 52 Mbps
FTTP	$35 to $180	5 Mbps to 100 Mbps
Fixed Wireless	$35 to $80	256 Kbps to 10 Mbps
Fractional T1	$200 to $700	128 Kbps to 768 Kbps
T1	$400 to $1,600	1.544 Mbps
T3	$5,000 to $15,000	44.736 Mbps
ATM	$3,000 or more	155 Mbps to 622 Mbps, can reach 10 Gbps

*Kbps = thousand bits per second
Mbps = million bits per second
Gbps = billion bits per second

Figure 8-16 The speeds of various lines that can be used to connect to the Internet.

ISDN Lines For the small business and home user, an ISDN line provides faster transfer rates than dial-up telephone lines. Not as widely used today as in the past, **ISDN** (Integrated Services Digital Network) is a set of standards for digital transmission of data over standard copper telephone lines.

DSL DSL is a popular digital line alternative for the small business or home user. **DSL** (Digital Subscriber Line) transmits at fast speeds on existing standard copper telephone wiring. Some DSL installations include a dial tone, providing users with both voice and data communications.

ADSL is one of the more popular types of DSLs. ADSL (asymmetric digital subscriber line) is a type of DSL that supports faster transfer rates when receiving data (the downstream rate) than when sending data (the upstream rate). ADSL is ideal for Internet access because most users download more information from the Internet than they upload.

FTTP **FTTP**, which stands for **Fiber to the Premises**, uses fiber-optic cable to provide extremely high-speed Internet access to a user's physical permanent location. Two specific types of FTTP are FTTH (Fiber to the Home) and FTTB (Fiber to the Building). With FTTP service, an optical terminal at your premises receives the signals and transfers them to a router connected to your computer. As the cost of installing fiber decreases, increasingly more homes and businesses will opt for this high-speed Internet access.

T-Carrier Lines A **T-carrier line** is any of several types of long-distance digital telephone lines that carry multiple signals over a single communications line. T-carrier lines provide very fast data transfer rates. Only medium to large companies usually can afford the investment in T-carrier lines because these lines are so expensive.

The most popular T-carrier line is the **T1 line**. Businesses often use T1 lines to connect to the Internet. Many Internet access providers use T1 lines to connect to the Internet backbone. Home and small business users purchase fractional T1, in which they share a connection to the T1 line with other users. Fractional T1 is slower than a dedicated T1 line, but it also is less expensive.

A T3 line is equal in speed to 28 T1 lines. T3 lines are quite expensive. Main users of T3 lines include large corporations, telephone companies, and Internet access providers connecting to the Internet backbone. The Internet backbone itself also uses T3 lines.

ATM **ATM** (Asynchronous Transfer Mode) is a service that carries voice, data, video, and multimedia at extremely high speeds. Telephone networks, the Internet, and other networks with large amounts of traffic use ATM. Some experts predict that ATM eventually will become the Internet standard for data transmission, replacing T3 lines.

✔ | QUIZ YOURSELF 8-2

Instructions: Find the true statement below. Then, rewrite the remaining false statements so that they are true.

1. A wireless LAN is a LAN that uses physical wires.
2. An intranet is an internal network that uses video conferencing technologies.
3. Five types of digital dial-up lines are ISDN lines, DSL, FTTP, T-carrier lines, and ATM.
4. In a client/server network, servers on the network access resources on the client.
5. P2P describes an Internet network on which users access each other's hard disks and exchange files directly over the Internet.

Quiz Yourself Online: To further check your knowledge of pages 322 through 332, visit the Computer Concepts CourseMate Web site at www.cengagebrain.com, navigate to the Chapter 8 Quiz Yourself resource for this book, and then click Objectives 3 – 5.

Communications Devices

A **communications device** is any type of hardware capable of transmitting data, instructions, and information between a sending device and a receiving device. One type of communications device that connects a communications channel to a sending or receiving device such as a computer is a modem. Computers process data as digital signals. Data, instructions, and information travel along a communications channel in either analog or digital form, depending on the communications channel.

The following pages describe the following types of communications devices: dial-up modems, digital modems, wireless modems, network cards, wireless access points, and routers.

Dial-Up Modems

A **dial-up modem** is a communications device that can convert digital signals to analog signals and analog signals to digital signals, so that data can travel along an analog telephone line. An analog signal consists of a continuous electrical wave, and a digital signal consists of individual electrical pulses that represent bits grouped together into bytes. A dial-up modem usually is in the form of an adapter card that you insert in an expansion slot on a computer's motherboard. One end of a standard telephone cord attaches to a port on the modem card and the other end plugs into a telephone outlet.

Digital Modems: ISDN, DSL, and Cable

A **digital modem** is a communications device that sends and receives data and information to and from a digital line. Three types of digital modems are ISDN modems, DSL modems, and cable modems.

An **ISDN modem** sends digital data and information from a computer to an ISDN line and receives digital data and information from an ISDN line. A **DSL modem** sends digital data and information from a computer to a DSL line and receives digital data and information from a DSL line. ISDN and DSL modems usually are external devices, in which one end connects to the telephone line and the other end connects to a port on the system unit.

A **cable modem** is a digital modem that sends and receives digital data over the cable television (CATV) network (Figure 8-17). With more than 110 million homes wired for cable television, cable modems provide a faster Internet access alternative to dial-up for the home user and can have speeds similar to DSL.

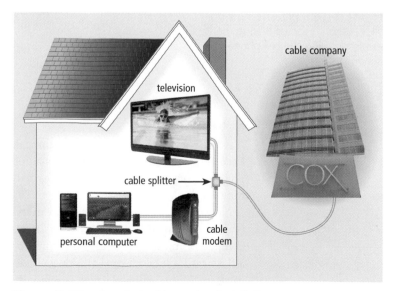

Figure 8-17 A typical cable modem installation.

? **FAQ 8-2**

Which is better, DSL or cable Internet service?

Each has its own advantages. DSL uses a line that is not shared with other users in the neighborhood. With cable Internet service, by contrast, users might share the node with up to hundreds of other cable Internet users. Simultaneous access by many users can cause the cable Internet service to slow down. Cable Internet service, however, has widespread availability.

For more information, visit the Computer Concepts CourseMate Web site at www.cengagebrain.com, navigate to the Chapter 8 FAQ resource for this book, and then click DSL and Cable Internet Service.

Wireless Modems

Some mobile users have a **wireless modem** that uses the cell phone network to connect to the Internet wirelessly from a notebook computer, a smart phone, or other mobile device (Figure 8-18). Wireless modems, which have an external or built-in antenna, are available as USB flash drive, ExpressCard modules, PC Cards, and flash cards. Some smart phones also can function as a wireless modem when connected with a special cable to a personal computer.

wireless modem communicates with wireless Internet access provider

wireless modem inserted in notebook computer

Figure 8-18 Wireless modems allow users to access the Internet wirelessly using the cell phone network.

Network Cards

A **network card** is a communications device that enables a computer or device that does not have networking capability to access a network. The network card coordinates the transmission and receipt of data, instructions, and information to and from the computer or device containing the network card.

Network cards are available in a variety of styles (Figure 8-19). A network card for a desktop computer is an adapter card that has a port to which a cable connects. A network card for mobile computers and devices is in the form of a USB network adapter, ExpressCard module, PC Card, or a flash card. Network cards that provide wireless data transmission also are available. This type of card, sometimes called a wireless network card, often has an antenna.

A network card follows the guidelines of a particular network communications standard, such as Ethernet or token ring. An Ethernet card is the most common type of network card.

network card for desktop computer, for wired network communications

ExpressCard module, for wireless network communications

Figure 8-19 Network cards are available for both desktop and notebook computers.

Wireless Access Points

A **wireless access point** is a central communications device that allows computers and devices to transfer data wirelessly among themselves or to transfer data wirelessly to a wired network (Figure 8-7 on page 323). Wireless access points have high-quality antennas for optimal signals.

Routers

A **router** is a communications device that connects multiple computers or other routers together and transmits data to its correct destination on a network. A router can be used on any size of network. On the largest scale, routers along the Internet backbone forward data packets to their destination using the fastest available path. For smaller business and home networks, a router allows multiple computers to share a single high-speed Internet connection such as a cable modem or DSL modem (Figure 8-20). These routers connect from 2 to 250 computers.

To prevent unauthorized users from accessing files and computers, many routers are protected by a built-in firewall, called a hardware firewall. Some also have built-in antivirus protection. Today's routers or combination wireless access point/routers are easy to configure and secure against unauthorized access.

Internet

router

cable or DSL modem

Figure 8-20 Through a router, home and small business networks can share access to a high-speed Internet connection such as through a cable or DSL modem.

Home Networks

Many home users are connecting multiple computers and devices together in a **home network**. Each networked computer in the house has the following capabilities:

- Connect to the Internet at the same time
- Share a single high-speed Internet connection
- Access files and programs on the other computers in the house
- Share peripherals such as a printer, scanner, external hard disk, or optical disc drive
- Play multiplayer games with players on other computers in the house
- Connect game consoles to the Internet
- Subscribe to and use VoIP

Many vendors offer home networking packages that include all the necessary hardware and software to network your home using wired or wireless techniques. Some of these packages also offer intelligent networking capabilities. An intelligent home network extends the basic home network to include features such as lighting control, thermostat adjustment, and a security system. You no longer need extensive knowledge of networks to set up a home network. For example, the latest version of Windows allows you to connect all computers in your house to a home network easily.

Wired Home Networks

As with other networks, a home network can use wires, be wireless, or use a combination of wired and wireless. Three types of wired home networks are Ethernet, powerline cable, and phoneline.

Ethernet Network   As discussed earlier in this chapter, traditional Ethernet networks require that each computer have built-in networking capabilities or contain a network card, which connects to a central network hub or similar device with a physical cable. This may involve running cable through walls, ceilings, and floors in the house. For the average home user, the hardware and software of an Ethernet network can be difficult to configure.

Powerline Cable Network   A home powerline cable network is a network that uses the same lines that bring electricity into the house. This network requires no additional wiring. One end of a cable plugs in the computer's USB port and the other end of the cable plugs in a wall outlet. The data transmits through the existing power lines in the house.

Phoneline Network   A phoneline network is an easy-to-install and inexpensive network that uses existing telephone lines in the home. With this network, one end of a cable connects to an adapter card or PC Card in the computer and the other end plugs in a wall telephone jack. The phoneline network does not interfere with voice and data transmissions on the telephone lines. That is, you can talk on the telephone and use the same line to connect to the Internet.

Wireless Home Networks

To network computers and devices that span multiple rooms or floors in a home, it may be more convenient to use a wireless strategy. One advantage of wireless networks is that you can take a mobile computer outside, for example in the backyard, and connect to the Internet through the home network as long as you are in the network's range.

Most home networks use a Wi-Fi network, which sends signals through the air at distances of up to 1,500 feet in some configurations. Wi-Fi networks are fairly easy to configure. Each computer that accesses the network must have the appropriate built-in wireless networking capabilities or a wireless network card, which communicates with a wireless access point or a combination router/wireless access point (Figure 8-21). To learn more about setting up a Wi-Fi network, complete the Learn How To 1 activity on pages 348 and 349.

Home Networks
For more information, visit the Computer Concepts CourseMate Web site at www.cengagebrain.com, navigate to the Chapter 8 Web Link resource for this book, and then click Home Networks.

How to Set Up Hardware for a Wi-Fi Home Network

Step 1
Sign up for high-speed Internet service, such as through a cable or DSL modem.

Step 2
Using a cable, connect the network card in a desktop computer to the combination router/wireless access point.

Step 3
Using a cable, connect the combination router/wireless access point to the cable/DSL modem.

Step 6
Purchase a smart phone with built-in wireless capabilities.

Step 4
Install a wireless network card or network adapter in other desktop computers in the home network.

Step 5
Insert a wireless USB network adapter, ExpressCard module, or PC Card in each notebook computer that will access the home network or purchase a notebook computer with built-in wireless networking capabilities.

Internet

cable/DSL modem

desktop computer

smart phone

router/wireless access point

wireless desktop computer

wireless notebook computer

Figure 8-21 This figure shows how to set up hardware for a Wi-Fi home network.

Communications Channel

As described at the beginning of the chapter, a communications channel is the transmission media on which data, instructions, or information travel in a communications system. The amount of data, instructions, and information that can travel over a communications channel sometimes is called the **bandwidth**. The higher the bandwidth, the more the channel transmits. For example, a cable modem has more bandwidth than a dial-up modem.

For transmission of text only, a lower bandwidth is acceptable. For transmission of music, graphics, photos, virtual reality images, or 3-D games, however, you need a higher bandwidth. When the bandwidth is too low for the application, you will notice a considerable slow-down in system performance.

A communications channel consists of one or more transmission media. **Transmission media** consist of materials or substances capable of carrying one or more signals. When you send data from a computer, the signal that carries the data may travel over various transmission media. This is especially true when the transmission spans a long distance.

Figure 8-22 illustrates a typical communications channel and shows the variety of transmission media used to complete the connection.

Broadband media transmit multiple signals simultaneously. Home and business users today opt for broadband Internet access because of the fast transfer rates. Two previously discussed services that offer broadband transmission are DSL and the cable television Internet service. Satellites also offer broadband transmission.

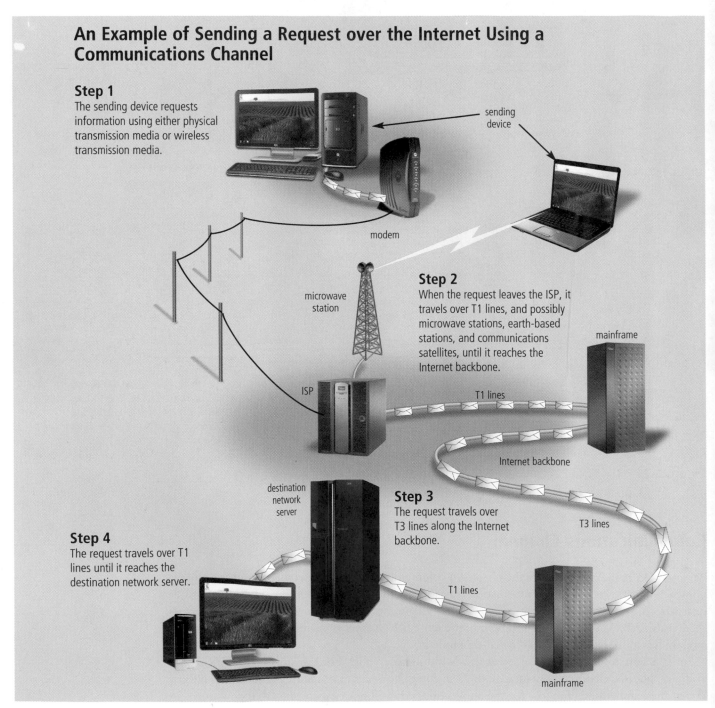

An Example of Sending a Request over the Internet Using a Communications Channel

Step 1
The sending device requests information using either physical transmission media or wireless transmission media.

sending device

modem

microwave station

Step 2
When the request leaves the ISP, it travels over T1 lines, and possibly microwave stations, earth-based stations, and communications satellites, until it reaches the Internet backbone.

mainframe

ISP

T1 lines

Internet backbone

destination network server

Step 3
The request travels over T3 lines along the Internet backbone.

T3 lines

Step 4
The request travels over T1 lines until it reaches the destination network server.

T1 lines

mainframe

Figure 8-22 This figure shows an example of sending a request over the Internet using a communications channel.

Transmission media are one of two types: physical or wireless. Physical transmission media use wire, cable, and other tangible materials to send communications signals. Wireless transmission media send communications signals through the air or space using radio, microwave, and infrared signals. The following sections discuss these types of media.

? FAQ 8-3

Is home broadband adoption increasing?

Home broadband Internet is increasing overall. The chart to the right illustrates broadband adoption for various categories of users.

For more information, visit the Computer Concepts CourseMate Web site at www.cengagebrain.com, navigate to the Chapter 8 FAQ resource for this book, and then click Broadband Adoption.

Physical Transmission Media

Physical transmission media used in communications include twisted-pair cable, coaxial cable, and fiber-optic cable. These cables typically are used within or underground between buildings. Ethernet and token ring LANs often use physical transmission media.

Twisted-Pair Cable

One of the more commonly used transmission media for network cabling and telephone systems is twisted-pair cable. **Twisted-pair cable** consists of one or more twisted-pair wires bundled together (Figure 8-23). Each twisted-pair wire consists of two separate insulated copper wires that are twisted together. The wires are twisted together to reduce noise. **Noise** is an electrical disturbance that can degrade communications.

Coaxial Cable

Coaxial cable, often referred to as coax (pronounced KO-ax), consists of a single copper wire surrounded by at least three layers: (1) an insulating material, (2) a woven or braided metal, and (3) a plastic outer coating (Figure 8-24).

Cable television (CATV) network wiring often uses coaxial cable because it can be cabled over longer distances than twisted-pair cable. Most of today's computer networks, however, do not use coaxial cable because other transmission media such as fiber-optic cable transmit signals at faster rates.

Figure 8-23 A twisted-pair cable consists of one or more twisted-pair wires. Each twisted-pair wire usually is color coded for identification. Telephone networks and LANs often use twisted-pair cable.

Figure 8-24 On a coaxial cable, data travels through a copper wire. This illustration shows computers networked together with coaxial cable.

Fiber-Optic Cable

The core of a **fiber-optic cable** consists of dozens or hundreds of thin strands of glass or plastic that use light to transmit signals. Each strand, called an optical fiber, is as thin as a human hair. Inside the fiber-optic cable, an insulating glass cladding and a protective coating surround each optical fiber (Figure 8-25).

outer covering jacket

cable contains many optical fibers

optical fiber core

glass cladding

protective coating

fiber-optic cable between floors of a building

Figure 8-25 A fiber-optic cable consists of hair-thin strands of glass or plastic that carry data as pulses of light.

Fiber-optic cables have the following advantages over cables that use wire, such as twisted-pair and coaxial cables:

- Capability of carrying significantly more signals than wire cables
- Faster data transmission
- Less susceptible to noise (interference) from other devices such as a copy machine
- Better security for signals during transmission because they are less susceptible to noise
- Smaller size (much thinner and lighter weight)

Disadvantages of fiber-optic cable are it costs more than twisted-pair or coaxial cable and can be difficult to install and modify. Despite these limitations, many local and long-distance telephone companies are replacing existing telephone lines with fiber-optic cables, enabling them to offer fibe Internet access to home and business users.

Wireless Transmission Media

Many users opt for wireless transmission media because it is more convenient than installing cables. In addition, businesses use wireless transmission media in locations where it is impossible to install cables. Types of wireless transmission media used in communications include infrared, broadcast radio, cellular radio, microwaves, and communications satellites. Read Ethics & Issues 8-2 for a related discussion.

ETHICS & ISSUES 8-2

Should You Worry about Cell Phone, Cellular Antenna, and Wi-Fi Device Radiation?

Billions of people use cell phones, and more than 80 percent of the world's population has access to cell phone service from cellular antennas. Wi-Fi signals permeate businesses, public areas, and homes everywhere. These numbers are expected to rise sharply in coming years, and many are concerned about potential health effects from cell phones, cellular antennas, and Wi-Fi devices. Some cell phone users who suffered rare illnesses have filed lawsuits against cell phone companies, but the cases usually are lost due to lack of scientific evidence linking the use of the phones to the illnesses. While debates rage

in communities over placement of cellular antennas, the consideration of health effects on residents is muted because the federal government's Telecommunications Act of 1996 prohibits local governments from considering health effects when making decisions about cellular antenna placement. The law does not apply to Wi-Fi antennas, and some municipalities reject municipal Wi-Fi deployments due to residents' health concerns. It generally is agreed that no studies conclusively demonstrate negative health effects from cell phones, cellular antennas, and Wi-Fi devices, but skeptics claim that the

technology is too new to have endured long-term studies on humans. Long-term studies that are underway may not provide results for decades.

Are you concerned about cell phone, cellular antenna, and Wi-Fi radiation? Why or why not? Do you or does anyone you know minimize use of cell phones or other wireless devices due to health concerns? Should governments be required to consider health concerns when making decisions about wireless deployments? Why? Would you live next to a cellular antenna? Why or why not?

Infrared

As discussed earlier in the chapter, infrared (IR) is a wireless transmission medium that sends signals using infrared light waves. Mobile computers and devices, such as a mouse, printer, and smart phone, often have an IrDA port that enables the transfer of data from one device to another using infrared light waves.

Broadcast Radio

Broadcast radio is a wireless transmission medium that distributes radio signals through the air over long distances such as between cities, regions, and countries and short distances such as within an office or home. Bluetooth, UWB, Wi-Fi, and WiMAX communications technologies discussed earlier in this chapter use broadcast radio signals.

Cellular Radio

Cellular radio is a form of broadcast radio that is used widely for mobile communications, specifically wireless modems and cell phones. A cell phone is a telephone device that uses high-frequency radio waves to transmit voice and digital data messages.

Some mobile users connect their notebook computer or other mobile computer to a cell phone to access the Web, send and receive e-mail, enter a chat room, or connect to an office or school network while away from a standard telephone line. Others watch mobile TV, which is a service that provides television programs over the cellular network.

Personal Communications Services (**PCS**) is the term used by the United States Federal Communications Commission (FCC) to identify all wireless digital communications. Devices that use PCS include cell phones, PDAs, pagers, and fax machines.

Mobile TV
For more information, visit the Computer Concepts CourseMate Web site at www.cengagebrain.com, navigate to the Chapter 8 Web Link resource for this book, and then click Mobile TV.

Microwaves

Microwaves are radio waves that provide a high-speed signal transmission. Microwave transmission, often called fixed wireless, involves sending signals from one microwave station to another (shown in Figure 8-1 on page 314). Microwaves can transmit data at rates up to 4,500 times faster than a dial-up modem.

A microwave station is an earth-based reflective dish that contains the antenna, transceivers (which both send and receive signals from wireless devices), and other equipment necessary for microwave communications. Microwaves use line-of-sight transmission. To avoid possible obstructions, such as buildings or mountains, microwave stations often sit on the tops of buildings, towers, or mountains.

Microwave transmission is used in environments where installing physical transmission media is difficult or impossible and where line-of-sight transmission is available. For example, microwave transmission is used in wide-open areas such as deserts or lakes; between buildings in a close geographic area; or to communicate with a satellite. Current users of microwave transmission include universities, hospitals, city governments, cable television providers, and telephone companies. Home and small business users who do not have other high-speed Internet connections available in their area also opt for lower-cost fixed wireless plans.

Communications Satellite

A **communications satellite** is a space station that receives microwave signals from an earth-based station, amplifies (strengthens) the signals, and broadcasts the signals back over a wide area to any number of earth-based stations (shown in Figure 8-1).

These earth-based stations often are microwave stations. Other devices, such as smart phones and GPS receivers, also can function as earth-based stations. Transmission from an earth-based station to a satellite is an uplink. Transmission from a satellite to an earth-based station is a downlink.

Applications such as air navigation, television and radio broadcasts, weather forecasting, video conferencing, paging, global positioning systems, and Internet connections use communications satellites. With the proper satellite dish and a satellite modem card, consumers access the Internet using satellite technology. With satellite Internet connections, however, uplink transmissions usually are slower than downlink transmissions. This difference in speeds usually is acceptable to most Internet satellite users because they download much more data than they upload. Although a satellite Internet connection is more expensive than cable Internet or DSL connections, sometimes it is the only high-speed Internet option in remote areas.

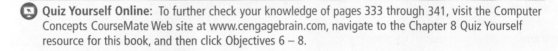

✔ | **QUIZ YOURSELF 8-3**

Instructions: Find the true statement below. Then, rewrite the remaining false statements so that they are true.

1. A cable modem converts a computer's digital signals to analog signals before they are transmitted over standard telephone lines.

2. A network card is an adapter card, USB network adapter, ExpressCard module, PC Card, or flash card that enables the computer or device to access a network.

3. Analog signals consist of individual electrical pulses that represent bits grouped together into bytes.

4. Physical transmission media send communications signals through the air or space using radio, microwave, and infrared signals.

5. Most wireless home networks use powerline cables.

💻 **Quiz Yourself Online:** To further check your knowledge of pages 333 through 341, visit the Computer Concepts CourseMate Web site at www.cengagebrain.com, navigate to the Chapter 8 Quiz Yourself resource for this book, and then click Objectives 6 – 8.

Chapter Summary

This chapter provided an overview of communications terminology and applications. It also discussed how to join computers into a network, allowing them to communicate and share resources such as hardware, software, data, and information. It also explained various types of communications devices, media, and procedures as they relate to computers.

Computer Usage @ Work

Agriculture

The world's dependence on the agriculture industry is enormous. The demand to keep food prices affordable encourages those working in this industry to operate as efficiently as possible. Although people have worked in agriculture for more than 10,000 years, advances in technology assist with maintaining and protecting land, crops, and animals.

Almost all companies in this industry have many acres of land that they must maintain, and it is not always feasible for farmers to take frequent trips around the property to perform basic tasks such as watering soil in the absence of rain. The number of people-hours required to water soil manually on several thousand acres of land might result in businesses spending thousands of dollars in labor and utility costs. If an irrigation system is installed instead, one or more individuals still are responsible for deciding when to water and how long to water. If the irrigation process is automated, sensors detect how much rain has fallen recently, as well as whether the soil is in need of watering. The sensors then send this data to a computer that processes it and decides when and how much to water. Many automated home irrigation systems also are programmable and use rain sensors, which keep the irrigation system from turning on, or turn it off when rainfall occurs.

In addition to keeping the soil moist and reducing maintenance costs, computers also can utilize sensors to analyze the condition of crops in the field and determine whether pests or diseases are affecting the crops. If sensors detect pests and/or diseases, computers send a notification to the appropriate individual to take corrective action. In some cases, the discovery of pests might trigger a pesticide to discharge in the affected area automatically.

Until recently, the lack of adequate cellular and wireless network signals in the fields made communications difficult for farmers. Mobile cellular antennas and amplifiers stretch mobile broadband coverage across entire farms, enabling farmers to receive wireless signals up to eight times farther from the cellular tower than they would without the antennas and amplifiers. Wireless access throughout the farm also allows farmers to monitor their farms and communicate with colleagues from remote locations.

The next time you take a bite of a delicious carrot or juicy cucumber, you can appreciate how technology has helped to maintain an ideal environment for these vegetables to grow and protected them from unwanted pests, all for a reasonable price when you purchase them from your local supermarket.

💻 For more information, visit the Computer Concepts CourseMate Web site at www.cengagebrain.com, navigate to the Chapter 8 Computer Usage @ Work resource for this book, and then click Agriculture.

Companies on the Cutting Edge

CISCO SYSTEMS Networking the Internet

Green networking practices have given Cisco Systems top ranking on the Vendor Matrix, a research tool used to assess companies' innovation and implementation of environmentally sound initiatives. Low power consumption, green power supplies and switching tools, and sound recycling efforts are part of the reason for Cisco's high marks and for the company's success.

Cisco manufactures a broad line of networking equipment for transporting data within a building, across a campus, and across the globe. A group of computer scientists at Stanford University founded Cisco in 1984. From the start,

the company focused on communicating over networks. Today, Cisco's Internet Protocol-based (IP) networking equipment is the basis of the Internet and most private networks.

The company's TelePresence video conferencing system is installed in more than 100 cities worldwide and serves a variety of audiences, ranging from corporate board members to soldiers stationed at military bases overseas. More than 2.5 million students in 160 countries have received certification credentials through the company's Cisco Academy.

VERIZON Communications Network Leader

One of the largest mergers in United States' history occurred when Bell Atlantic acquired GTE in 2000. The company was renamed Verizon, a combination of the words Veritas, the Roman goddess of truth, and horizon. Verizon's famous "Can you hear me now?" tagline has become synonymous with the cell phone industry's connectivity issues.

More than 87 million customers nationwide subscribe to Verizon's wireless network, which is managed through the company's Wireless division. Its other units are Verizon Telecom and Verizon Business, which offer local telephone, nationwide long distance, broadband

Internet services, networking, and security services. The company's global fiber-optic network serves more than 150 countries on 6 continents, and its United States network, FiOS, was the first in the country to offer Internet, television, and telephone service.

Verizon is the only telecommunications company that has been named repeatedly to *Working Mother* magazine's 100 Best Companies for Working Mothers list. Recently, it was ranked 17th among FORTUNE 500 companies. Verizon Wireless also boasts the highest customer loyalty, profitability, and cost efficiency.

 For more information, visit the Computer Concepts CourseMate Web site at www.cengagebrain.com and then navigate to the Chapter 8 Companies on the Cutting Edge resource for this book.

Technology Trailblazers

ROBERT METCALFE Ethernet Inventor

Robert Metcalfe promised to eat his words if his prediction of the Internet's collapse in 1996 was wrong. During his keynote speech at the WWW International Conference in 1997, he placed the paper containing his prediction in a blender, mixed it with liquid, and drank the pulp. Metcalfe certainly has been correct in predicting many other aspects of the Internet, however, primarily the vision that his Ethernet invention would one day connect millions of computers worldwide.

Metcalfe's fascination with linking computers developed while he was in college. At Harvard's Project

MAC, he connected the university's computers to the ARPANET. Then, at Xerox's Palo Alto Research Center (PARC), he coinvented Ethernet in 1973. Xerox managers did not see how the Ethernet fit with the company's primary business of photocopying, so he left the company in 1979 to found 3Com Corporation and make Ethernet the standard for computer communications.

After his retirement from 3Com, he became a general partner in Polaris Venture Partners, a venture capital firm that invests in the early stages of information technology and life sciences companies.

PATRICIA RUSSO Communications Industry Leader

The ability to lead teams and solve problems is important for any top corporate leader, and Patricia Russo has used these skills in her career in the communications industry.

After graduating from Georgetown University, she held positions in sales and marketing at IBM and then in management at AT&T for more than 20 years. She also served as CEO and president of Eastman Kodak. Forbes.com has listed Russo as one of the most powerful

women in the world and noted that she has the skills to lead a company through difficult financial times.

Russo was instrumental in forming Lucent Technologies in 1996 and was appointed CEO in 2002. Under her leadership, Lucent merged with Alcatel in 2006 to become a major worldwide communications services equipment manufacturer. She served as CEO until 2008, and during her tenure Alcatel-Lucent was one of the largest corporations in the world run by a woman.

 For more information, visit the Computer Concepts CourseMate Web site at www.cengagebrain.com and then navigate to the Chapter 8 Technology Trailblazers resource for this book.

Chapter Review

The Chapter Review reinforces the main concepts presented in this chapter.

To listen to an audio version of this Chapter Review, visit the Computer Concepts CourseMate Web site at www.cengagebrain.com and then navigate to the Chapter 8 Chapter Review resource for this book.

1. What Is the Purpose of the Components Required for Successful Communications? Computer **communications** describes a process in which two or more computers or devices transfer data, instructions, and information. Successful communications require a **sending device** that initiates a transmission instruction, a communications device that connects the sending device to a communications channel, a **communications channel** on which the data travels, a communications device that connects the communications channel to a receiving device, and a **receiving device** that accepts the transmission.

2. How Are Computer Communications Used? Communications technologies include blogs, chat rooms, e-mail, instant messaging, Internet, newsgroups, RSS, video conferencing, VoIP, Web, Web folders, and wikis. People also use communications for other purposes. Users send and receive wireless messages to and from smart phones, cell phones, handheld game consoles, and other mobile devices using **text messaging, picture messaging, video messaging,** and wireless instant messaging. At home, work, school, and in many public locations, people connect wirelessly to the Internet through a **wireless Internet access point**, either a **hot spot** or a mobile wireless network. A **cybercafé** is a coffeehouse, restaurant, or other location that provides personal computers with Internet access. A **global positioning system** (GPS) analyzes signals sent by satellites to determine an earth-based receiver's geographic location. Many software products allow users to **collaborate**, or work online, with other users connected to a server. **Groupware** is software that helps groups of people work together and share information over a network. **Voice mail** allows someone to leave a voice message for one or more people. **Web services** describe standardized software that enables programmers to create applications that communicate with other remote computers over a network.

Visit the Computer Concepts CourseMate Web site at www.cengagebrain.com, navigate to the Chapter 8 Quiz Yourself resource for this book, and then click Objectives 1 – 2.

3. What Are Different Types of Networks? A **network** is a collection of computers and devices connected together via communications devices and media. Networks usually are classified as a local area network, metropolitan area network, or wide area network. A **local area network** (**LAN**) connects computers and devices in a limited geographical area or closely positioned group of buildings. A **wireless LAN** (**WLAN**) is a LAN that uses no physical wires. A **metropolitan area network** (**MAN**) connects local area networks in a metropolitan area and handles the bulk of communications activity across that region. A **wide area network** (**WAN**) covers a large geographic area using a communications channel that combines many types of media.

4. What Is the Purpose of Communications Software? **Communications software** helps users establish a connection to another computer or network, manages the transmission of data, and provides an interface for users to communicate with one another.

5. What Are Various Types of Lines for Communications Over the Telephone Network? The telephone network uses dial-up lines or dedicated lines. A **dial-up line** is a temporary connection that uses one or more analog telephone lines for communications. A **dedicated line** is an always-on connection established between two communications devices. Dedicated lines include ISDN lines, DSL, FTTP, T-carrier lines, and ATM. **ISDN** is a set of standards for digital transmission over standard copper telephone lines. **DSL** transmits at fast speeds on existing standard copper telephone wiring. **FTTP** (**Fiber to the Premises**) uses fiber-optic cable to provide extremely high-speed Internet access to a user's physical permanent location. A **T-carrier line** is a long-distance digital telephone line that carries multiple signals over a single communications line. **ATM** (Asynchronous Transfer Mode) is a service that carries voice, data, video, and multimedia at extremely high speeds.

Visit the Computer Concepts CourseMate Web site at www.cengagebrain.com, navigate to the Chapter 8 Quiz Yourself resource for this book, and then click Objectives 3 – 5.

6. What Are Commonly Used Communications Devices? A **communications device** is any hardware capable of transmitting data between a sending device and a receiving device. A **dial-up modem** converts digital signals to analog signals and analog signals to digital signals so that data can travel along an analog telephone line. A **digital modem** sends and receives data and information to and from a digital line. An **ISDN modem** transmits digital data to and from an ISDN line, while a **DSL**

modem transmits digital data to and from a DSL line. A **cable modem** is a digital modem that sends and receives digital data over the cable television network. A **wireless modem** uses the cell phone network to connect to the Internet wirelessly from a mobile device. A **network card** enables a computer or device that does not have networking capability to access a network. A **wireless access point** allows computers and devices to transfer data wirelessly. A **router** connects multiple computers or routers together and transmits data to its correct destination on the network.

7. How Can a Home Network Be Set Up? A **home network** connects multiple computers and devices in a home. An Ethernet network connects each computer to a central hub with a physical cable. A home powerline cable network uses the same lines that bring electricity into the house. A phoneline network uses existing telephone lines in a home. Most home networks use a Wi-Fi network, which sends signals through the air at distances of up to 1,500 feet in some configurations.

8. What Are Various Physical and Wireless Transmission Media? **Transmission media** consist of materials or substances capable of carrying one or more signals. Physical transmission media use tangible materials to send communications signals. **Twisted-pair cable** consists of one or more twisted-pair wires bundled together. **Coaxial cable** consists of a single copper wire surrounded by at least three layers: an insulating material, a woven or braided metal, and a plastic outer coating. **Fiber-optic cable** consists of thin strands of glass or plastic that use light to transmit signals. Wireless transmission media send communications signals through the air or space. Infrared (IR) sends signals using infrared light waves. **Broadcast radio** distributes radio signals through the air over long and short distances. **Cellular radio** is a form of broadcast radio that is used widely for mobile communications. **Microwaves** are radio waves that provide a high-speed signal transmission. A **communications satellite** is a space station that receives microwave signals from an earth-based station, amplifies the signals, and broadcasts the signals back over a wide area.

Visit the Computer Concepts CourseMate Web site at www.cengagebrain.com, navigate to the Chapter 8 Quiz Yourself resource for this book, and then click Objectives 6 – 8.

Key Terms

You should know each key term. The list below helps focus your study.

To see an example of and a definition for each term, and to access current and additional information from the Web, visit the Computer Concepts CourseMate Web site at www.cengagebrain.com and then navigate to the Chapter 8 Key Terms resource for this book.

802.11 (329)
802.16 (330)
ATM (332)
bandwidth (337)
Bluetooth (329)
broadband (338)
broadcast radio (341)
bus network (327)
cable modem (333)
cellular radio (341)
client/server network (325)
clients (325)
coaxial cable (339)
collaborate (321)
collaborative software (321)
communications (314)
communications channel (314)
communications device (333)
communications satellite (341)
communications software (330)
cybercafé (319)

dedicated line (331)
dial-up line (331)
dial-up modem (333)
digital modem (333)
document management system (321)
DSL (332)
DSL modem (333)
Ethernet (329)
fiber-optic cable (340)
FTTP (Fiber to the Premises) (332)
global positioning system (GPS) (320)
groupware (321)
home network (336)
hot spot (318)
intranet (328)
IrDA (330)
ISDN (332)
ISDN modem (333)
local area network (LAN) (323)
mashup (322)

metropolitan area network (MAN) (324)
microwaves (341)
network (322)
network card (334)
network standard (328)
network topology (326)
noise (339)
P2P (326)
PCS (341)
peer-to-peer network (325)
picture messaging (318)
receiving device (314)
RFID (330)
ring network (328)
router (335)
sending device (314)
server (325)
star network (326)
T1 line (332)
T-carrier line (332)
TCP/IP (329)
text messaging (317)
token ring (329)

transmission media (338)
twisted-pair cable (339)
UWB (ultra-wideband) (330)
value-added network (VAN) (322)
video messaging (318)
visual voice mail (322)
voice mail (322)
Web conference (321)
Web services (322)
wide area network (WAN) (324)
Wi-Fi (329)
WiMAX (330)
wireless access point (335)
Wireless Application Protocol (WAP) (330)
wireless Internet access point (318)
wireless LAN (WLAN) (323)
wireless modem (334)

Checkpoint

The Checkpoint exercises test your knowledge of the chapter concepts. The page number containing the answer appears in parentheses after each exercise.

To complete the Checkpoint exercises interactively, visit the Computer Concepts CourseMate Web site at www.cengagebrain.com and then navigate to the Chapter 8 Checkpoint resource for this book.

Multiple Choice Select the best answer.

1. When an online meeting takes place on the Web, it is called _____. (321)
   a. video messaging
   b. a peer-to-peer network
   c. a Web meeting
   d. a Web conference

2. With _____, users can view message details such as the length of calls and, in some cases, read message contents instead of listening to them. (322)
   a. Web services
   b. Internet telephony
   c. video messaging
   d. visual voice mail

3. A _____ network is a third-party business that provides networking services for a fee. (322)
   a. value-added
   b. client/server
   c. star
   d. file sharing

4. A _____ is a Web application that combines services from two or more sources, creating a new application. (322)
   a. document management system
   b. peer-to-peer network
   c. Web service
   d. mashup

5. _____ is a standard, specifically a protocol, that defines how a network uses radio signals to communicate with a tag placed in or attached to an object, an animal, or a person. (330)
   a. RFID   b. WiMAX
   c. Bluetooth   d. UWB

6. _____ is a newer network standard developed by IEEE that specifies how wireless devices communicate over the air in a wide area. (330)
   a. Wi-Fi
   b. WiMAX
   c. 802.16
   d. Both b and c

7. DSL, cable television Internet service, and satellites offer _____ transmission. (338)
   a. baseband
   b. IrDA
   c. microwave
   d. broadband

8. _____ consists of a single copper wire surrounded by at least three layers. (339)
   a. Fiber-optic cable
   b. Twisted-pair cable
   c. Coaxial cable
   d. Infrared

Matching Match the terms with their definitions.

_____1. collaborate (321)
_____2. Bluetooth (329)
_____3. dedicated line (331)
_____4. dial-up modem (333)
_____5. noise (339)

a. online area in which users have written discussions about a subject
b. electrical disturbance that can degrade communications
c. work online with other users connected to a server
d. type of always-on connection that is established between two communications devices
e. communications device that can convert digital signals to analog signals and analog signals to digital signals, so that data can travel along an analog telephone line
f. a protocol that defines how two devices use short-range radio waves to transmit data

Short Answer Write a brief answer to each of the following questions.

1. What is text messaging? _____ What are some options for sending and receiving text messages? _____

2. Describe how the global positioning system (GPS) works. _____ How do individuals use GPS technology? _____

3. What is a network topology? _____ How are a star network, a bus network, and a ring network different? _____

4. What is UWB and what are its benefits? _____ What are some uses of UWB? _____

5. What are three different types of digital modems? _____ How does each one function? _____

Problem Solving

The Problem Solving exercises extend your knowledge of the chapter concepts by seeking solutions to practical computer problems that you may encounter at home, school, or work. The Collaboration exercise should be completed with a team.

In the real world, practical problems often can be solved in multiple ways. Provide one solution to each of the following problems using available resources, such as articles on the Web or in print, blogs, podcasts, videos, television, user guides, other individuals, and electronics and computer stores. You may need to use multiple resources to obtain an answer. Present your solutions in the form requested by your instructor (brief report, presentation, discussion, or other means).

@ Home

1. **Text Messages Not Received**   Although you have sent your friend multiple text messages from a cell phone, he is not receiving them. What might be the problem?

2. **Intermittent Network Connection**   While using your computer, you intermittently lose the network connection. The computer is connected to a wired network using an Ethernet cable. What might be causing this loss of connection?

3. **Telephone Noise**   Recently, you installed DSL service in your house. Your computers can connect to the Internet successfully, but your home telephone now experiences noise. Before the DSL service was installed, your telephone had no noise problem. What steps will you take to eliminate the noise?

4. **No Network Activity**   Your computer has a network card installed to access the wired network in your house. Upon plugging the Ethernet cable into the network card and the network port on the wall, the activity lights on the network card do not illuminate. What might be causing this?

@ Work

5. **Slow Network Connection**   You subscribed to an Internet service for your home business. After performing several tests, you realize that the Internet connection speed you were promised by your Internet access provider is higher than the speed you currently are experiencing. What might be causing this? What are your next steps?

6. **WEP Key Required**   The information technology team has provided you with a new notebook computer. When you attempt to connect to the wireless network, Windows asks you for a WEP key. How will you proceed?

7. **Trouble Accessing Wired Network**   In an effort to save money spent in commuting to and from your office, your boss has agreed to provide you with a notebook computer so that you can work from home. When you work in the office, you bring the notebook computer and regularly retrieve files from your desktop computer. When you attempt to use the corporate network to connect to the notebook computer to the desktop computer, an error message appears stating that the connection is unsuccessful. What might be wrong?

8. **No GPS Signal**   As a traveling sales representative for a startup company, your boss provided you with a GPS receiver so that you can locate your customers when driving to meet them at various locations. When you travel to certain areas, the GPS receiver has a difficult time receiving signals from the GPS satellites. What might be wrong? How can you make sure that you are able to locate your customers' addresses?

Collaboration

9. **Computers in Agriculture**   Your employer owns hundreds of acres of orange groves and realizes that labor and utility costs can be decreased by installing automated systems to manage the property. As a computer-literate employee of the organization, your supervisor asks you to research automated systems that can help decrease expenses. Form a team of three people to research automated agricultural solutions. One team member should research automated irrigation systems that water the trees only as needed. Another team member should research solutions that can keep the trees healthy and free from pests, and the third team member should create a list of reasons why these automated systems can decrease costs, bolster efficiency, and increase profit. Compile your findings and submit them to your instructor.

Learn How To

The Learn How To activities step you through fundamental technology skills when using a computer. The Learn How To exercises enable you to become more proficient with these skills.

Premium Activity: To relate this Learn How To activity to your everyday life, see a visual demonstration of the activity, and complete a short assessment, visit the Computer Concepts CourseMate Web site at www.cengagebrain.com and then navigate to the Chapter 8 Learn How To resource for this book.

Learn How To 1: Set Up and Install a Wi-Fi Home Network

In this chapter you learned about home networks and their advantages (see page 336, Home Networks). Creating a Wi-Fi home network consists of four phases: 1) subscribe to a high-speed Internet access provider, 2) purchase the Wi-Fi equipment, 3) connect the physical devices, and 4) create the network through the use of software.

Subscribe to a High-Speed Internet Access Provider   A high-speed Internet access provider is advisable to connect all computers on the home network to the Internet. The three primary ways for home users to obtain a fast connection to the Internet are DSL, cable, and satellite. DSL is provided by telephone companies, cable is provided by cable TV companies, and satellite connections are provided by satellite TV providers. Each has its advantages and disadvantages, including the minimum and maximum speed of Internet access, cost, and availability.

Determining the optimal high-speed Internet access provider depends largely on where the network will be located, local costs, and service availability. The way to obtain the best high-speed Internet access provider is to research the options available in your area.

Purchase the Wi-Fi Equipment   As part of the service when you subscribe to a high-speed Internet access provider, you receive a modem that is capable of connecting to the Internet. In most cases, the modem is not a wireless transmitter. So, in order to establish a wireless connection between the Internet and the home network, you will need a wireless router that establishes the wireless access point.

You can visit any retail electronics store and find a wide variety of wireless routers. A key to purchasing the correct router is to ensure it will work with your modem and Internet access provider. Some Internet access providers support only certain brands of routers and, while it is true that other routers may work, you might be taking a risk if you purchase an unsupported router. With the popularity of wireless home networks, though, some Internet access providers now provide a wireless router as part of the subscription service, often for an additional fee. You should investigate closely the needs for the Wi-Fi router to ensure compatibility with your Internet access provider.

In addition to the router, each computer that is to be part of the Wi-Fi network needs a wireless network adapter. This device allows the computers to communicate with one another. Most external wireless network adapters plug in either a PC Card slot, ExpressCard slot, or a USB connection. Many notebook computers have a built-in wireless network adapter.

Finally, some home networks have a combination of wired and wireless devices. In these networks, the modem connects to the wireless router, and computers on the network either connect to the wireless router using a wireless or wired connection.

Once the Wi-Fi equipment is assembled, you are ready to connect your home network.

Connect the Physical Devices   Once you have assembled your equipment, you can connect the devices in the network. Usually, the modem will be connected to the source of the Internet transmission (DSL, cable, or satellite). Then the modem is connected to the wireless router, which in turn is connected to the computers on your network.

After these connections are completed, each of the computers that will be used in the network that do not have a built-in wireless network adapter must have the adapter attached, often by using a USB connection. Once these connections are made, the computers can join the network.

Create the Homegroup   To establish a homegroup and share files with other computers on your network, complete the following steps:
1. Click the Start button on the Windows taskbar and then click Control Panel on the Start menu.
2. Click the 'Choose homegroup and sharing options' link below the Network and Internet heading to display the HomeGroup dialog box.
3. Click the 'Create a homegroup' button to display the Create a Homegroup dialog box.
4. In the Create a Homegroup dialog box, place a check mark next to each item you wish to share with other computers connected to the same homegroup and then click the Next button.
5. Once Windows sets up the homegroup, it will display a password that other computer users will need to know to join your homegroup.

6. Click the 'Print password and instructions' link to open the 'View and print your homegroup password' window, which contains your homegroup password and instructions about how other computers on your network can join your homegroup.

7. Ready the printer according to the printer instructions and then click the 'Print this page' button to display the Print dialog box. Select the printer to which you want to print and then click the Print button to print these instructions.

8. Click the Close button on the title bar to close the 'View and print your homegroup password' window.

9. Click the Finish button to open the HomeGroup window.

10. If necessary, make changes to your homegroup settings and then click the Save changes button. If you have no changes, click the Close button on the title bar to close the HomeGroup window.

11. Follow the instructions you printed in Step 7 to join other computers to the homegroup.

Exercise

1. Assume you live near Coeur d'Alene, Idaho. You have decided that a high-speed Internet access provider and a Wi-Fi network would be advantageous for your at-home business. Find answers to the following questions for this Idaho town or a town specified by your instructor: What high-speed Internet access providers are available? Which provides the best service? Which is the cheapest? Based on the information you gather, write a plan for subscribing to a high-speed Internet access provider. Submit the answers to the questions and your plan to your instructor.

Learn It Online

The Learn It Online exercises are interactive Web exercises designed to reinforce and expand your understanding of the chapter concepts. The descriptions below briefly summarize each exercise.

To complete the Learn It Online exercises, visit the Computer Concepts CourseMate Web site at www.cengagebrain.com, navigate to the Chapter 8 resources for this book, click the link for the exercise you want to complete, and then read the instructions.

1 At the Movies — Got Your Video Right Here
Watch a movie to see why the Sling Media Slingbox is the best way to beam your favorite shows to any broadband-connected computer or Windows Mobile device in the world and then answer questions about the movie.

2 Student Edition Labs — Networking Basics and Wireless Networking
Enhance your understanding and knowledge about networking basics and wireless networking by completing the Networking Basics and Wireless Networking Labs.

3 Practice Test
Take a multiple choice test that checks your knowledge of the chapter concepts and review the resulting study guide.

4 Who Wants To Be a Computer Genius²?
Play the Shelly Cashman Series version of this popular game by answering questions to find out if you are a computer genius. Panic buttons are available to provide assistance during game play.

5 Crossword Puzzle Challenge
Complete an interactive crossword puzzle to reinforce concepts presented in this chapter.

6 Windows Exercises
Step through the Windows 7 exercises to learn about understanding your modem, Windows Firewall, viewing network connections, and using Help and Support to understand networks.

7 Exploring Computer Careers
Read about a career as a network specialist, search for related employment advertisements, and then answer related questions.

8 Web Apps — Gmail
Learn how to use Gmail to send and receive e-mail messages, label e-mail messages, chat with others, and search for e-mail messages.

Web Research

The Web Research exercises broaden your understanding of chapter concepts by presenting questions that require you to search the Web for answers.

① Search Sleuth

Use one of the search engines listed in Figure 2-8 in Chapter 2 on page 65 or your own favorite search engine to find the answers to the following questions. Copy and paste the Web address from the Web page where you found the answer. Some questions may have more than one answer. If required, submit your answers to your instructor. (1) Which product is manufactured in the modified chemical vapor deposition (MCVD) process? (2) In what city is the IrDA corporate office located? How many companies are IrDA members? (3) Which agency funds and controls the global positioning system? In how many hours does one satellite orbit the earth? (4) Which California county built a crime lab in 2008 that uses passive RFID tags to track evidence? (5) Who sent the first text message in 1989?

② Green Computing

As the speed of Ethernet routers, switches, and servers increases, so does the amount of electricity consumed. Engineers are working to reduce the power requirements in various ways, including a technology called Rapid PHY Selection (RPS), which could save $1.2 billion during computer systems' lifetimes. Critics say RPS would slow the networks' performance and cause connectivity problems. Consumers, too, can benefit from using green Wi-Fi routers that adjust power consumption and shut down automatically. View online Web sites that provide information about reducing networks' electricity consumption. How does RPS adjust Ethernet speed and corresponding power usage? What technological challenges are engineers facing when developing this RPS technology? Which companies are manufacturing Wi-Fi routers for home networks? How much energy do they claim to save? Write a report summarizing your findings, and include a table of links to Web sites that provide additional details.

③ Social Networking

Conversations, experiences, photos, videos, and other aspects of a person's life can be preserved for future generations using LifeNaut, an online social network funded by the Terasem Movement Foundation, Inc. More than 9,000 people have created a personal space, called a mindfile, to create a profile, build a 3-D virtual avatar, upload files, and then share these personal life memories. Members can meet new people by browsing the online mindfiles. As biotechnology advances, scientists predict that these preserved memories could be added to a person's mind, not necessarily the mind of the person who originally created these mindfiles. Visit the LifeNaut Web site (lifenaut.com) and then click the About and FAQ links on the left side of the home page. Could viewing the LifeNaut mindfiles be useful to people who have lost their memory? Would parents desire to preserve aspects of their lives for their children to view and hear? Would you desire to record your life? Summarize the information you read and viewed.

④ Blogs

Avoiding information overload is difficult in today's world, with more than 80 million live Web sites available at all times of the day. Managing blogs, news feeds, and podcasts can be accomplished by subscribing to Bloglines, a free service that tracks Web sites tailored to a person's specific interests. More than 10,000 subscribers monitor an average of 20 news feeds, which are updated hourly. Visit Bloglines (bloglines.com) and then read the information in the About link at the bottom of the home page. What are Bloglines' key features? How does Bloglines examine RSS feeds? How does the Web site help readers organize their subscriptions? What is the purpose of a Clip Blog? Summarize the information you read and viewed.

⑤ Ethics in Action

Consumers may welcome customized advertisements, but they may be unaware of how they have become targeted to receive these messages. When people visit some Web sites, their IP address, browser software, operating system, and viewing habits are tracked and recorded along with their wish lists and purchase histories. These details are collected and shared among advertisers without the users' consent. The Center for Digital Democracy (CDD) filed a complaint with the Federal Trade Commission stating that these targeted advertisements and user profiles can constitute an invasion of privacy. Visit the CDD Web site (democraticmedia.org) and other Web sites discussing online ads and privacy concerns. How are the CDD and other organizations working to protect consumers from being exploited by digital advertisers? What steps can Web users take to avoid sharing personal data with marketers? Write a report summarizing your findings, and include a table of links to Web sites that provide additional details.

Chapter Nine

Database Management

After completing this chapter, you will be able to:

1 Define the term, database, and explain how a database interacts with data and information

2 Describe the qualities of valuable information

3 Discuss the terms character, field, record, and file

4 Describe file maintenance techniques (adding records, modifying records, deleting records) and validation techniques

5 Differentiate between a file processing approach and the database approach

6 Discuss the functions common to most database management systems: data dictionary, file retrieval and maintenance, data security, and backup and recovery

7 Describe characteristics of relational, object-oriented, and multidimensional databases

8 Explain how to access Web databases

9 Discuss the responsibilities of database analysts and administrators

Databases, Data, and Information

A **database** is a collection of data organized in a manner that allows access, retrieval, and use of that data. **Data** is a collection of unprocessed items, which can include text, numbers, images, audio, and video. **Information** is processed data; that is, it is organized, meaningful, and useful.

Computers process data in a database into information. A database at a school, for example, contains data about students, e.g., student data, class data, etc. As shown in Figure 9-1, a computer at the school processes new student data and then sends advising appointment and ID card information to the printers.

With **database software**, often called a **database management system** (**DBMS**), users create a computerized database; add, modify, and delete data in the database; sort and retrieve data from the database; and create forms and reports from the data in the database. Database software includes many powerful features, as you will discover later in this chapter.

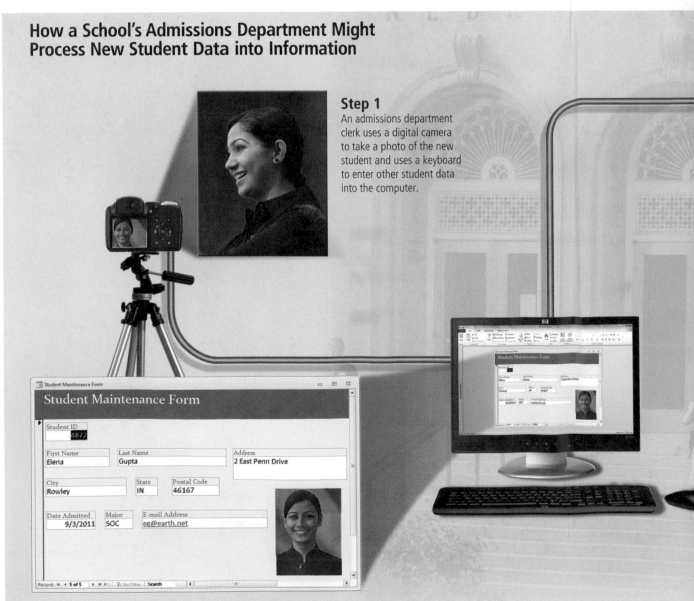

How a School's Admissions Department Might Process New Student Data into Information

Step 1
An admissions department clerk uses a digital camera to take a photo of the new student and uses a keyboard to enter other student data into the computer.

Student Maintenance Form

Student Maintenance Form

Student ID
4872

First Name
Elena

Last Name
Gupta

Address
2 East Penn Drive

City
Rowley

State
IN

Postal Code
46167

Date Admitted
9/3/2011

Major
SOC

E-mail Address
eg@earth.net

Record: 5 of 5   No Filter   Search

 Figure 9-1 This figure shows how a school's admissions department might process new student data into information.

Data Integrity

Most organizations realize that data is one of their more valuable assets — because data is used to generate information. Many business transactions take less time when employees have instant access to information. To ensure that data is accessible on demand, an organization must manage and protect its data just as it would any other resource. Thus, it is vital that the data has integrity and is kept secure.

For a computer to produce correct information, the data that is entered into a database must have integrity. Data integrity identifies the quality of the data. An erroneous student address in a student database is an example of incorrect data. When a database contains this type of error, it loses integrity. Data integrity is very important because computers and people use information to make decisions and take actions.

Garbage in, garbage out (GIGO) is a computing phrase that points out the accuracy of a computer's output depends on the accuracy of the input. If you enter incorrect data into a computer (garbage in), the computer will produce incorrect information (garbage out).

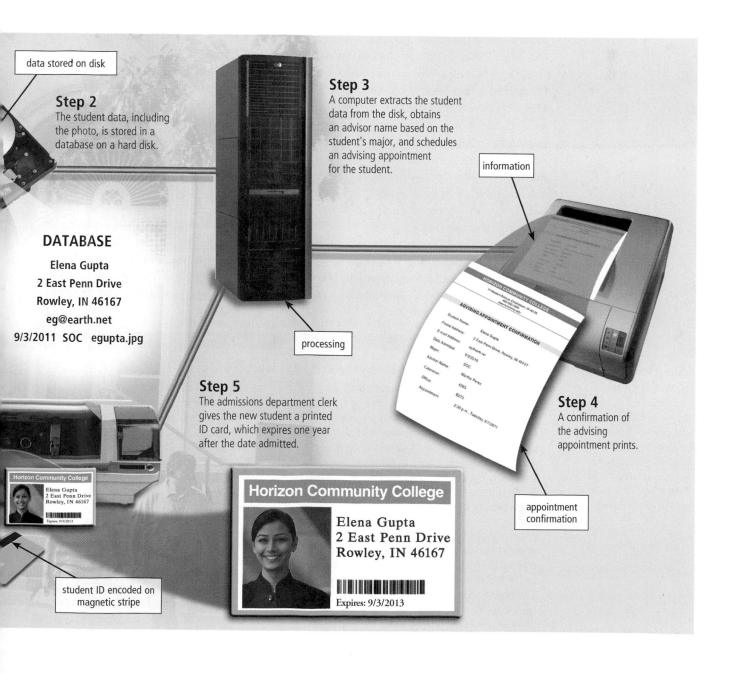

data stored on disk

Step 2
The student data, including the photo, is stored in a database on a hard disk.

Step 3
A computer extracts the student data from the disk, obtains an advisor name based on the student's major, and schedules an advising appointment for the student.

information

DATABASE

Elena Gupta

2 East Penn Drive

Rowley, IN 46167

eg@earth.net

9/3/2011 SOC   egupta.jpg

processing

Step 5
The admissions department clerk gives the new student a printed ID card, which expires one year after the date admitted.

Step 4
A confirmation of the advising appointment prints.

appointment confirmation

student ID encoded on magnetic stripe

Horizon Community College

Elena Gupta
2 East Penn Drive
Rowley, IN 46167

Expires: 9/3/2013

Qualities of Valuable Information

The information that data generates also is an important asset. People make decisions daily using all types of information such as receipts, bank statements, pension plan summaries, stock analyses, transcripts, and credit reports. At school, students use grade reports and degree audits to make decisions. In a business, managers make decisions based on sales trends, competitors' products and services, production processes, and even employee skills. Read Ethics & Issues 9-1 for a related discussion.

To assist with sound decision making, information must have value. For it to be valuable, information should be accurate, verifiable, timely, organized, accessible, useful, and cost-effective.

- Accurate information is error free. Inaccurate information can lead to incorrect decisions. For example, consumers assume their credit report is accurate. If your credit report incorrectly shows past due payments, a bank may not lend you money for a car or house.
- Verifiable information can be proven as correct or incorrect. For example, security personnel at an airport usually request some type of photo identification to verify that you are the person named on the ticket.
- Timely information has an age suited to its use. A decision to build additional schools in a particular district should be based on the most recent census report — not on one that is 20 years old. Most information loses its value with time. Some information, however, such as information about trends, gains value as time passes and more information is obtained.
- Organized information is arranged to suit the needs and requirements of the decision maker. Different people may need the same information presented in a different manner. For example, an inventory manager may want an inventory report to list out-of-stock items first. The purchasing agent, instead, wants the report alphabetized by vendor.
- Accessible information is available when the decision maker needs it. Having to wait for information may delay an important decision.
- Useful information has meaning to the person who receives it. Most information is important only to certain people or groups of people.
- Cost-effective information should give more value than it costs to produce. An organization occasionally should review the information it produces to determine if it still is cost-effective to produce. Sometimes, it is not easy to place a value on information. For this reason, some organizations create information only on demand, that is, as people request it, instead of on a regular basis. Many make information available online. Users then can access and print online information as they need it.

𝓎 ETHICS & ISSUES 9-1

Ethics & Issues

For the complete text of the Ethics & Issues boxes found in this chapter, visit the Computer Concepts CourseMate Web site at www.cengagebrain.com and then navigate to the Chapter 9 Ethics & Issues resource for this book.

Do Internet Databases Mean the End of Privacy?

The amount of data and information about individuals that is stored anywhere on the Internet increases every day. Photos, financial records, employment history, personal relationship details, and purchases are just a few of the types of data and information available to others for free or for a fee. Any type of data and information placed on the Internet is almost instantly indexed, and often copied, by a vast number of search engines, such as Google and Yahoo!. Older data stored on paper is scanned, digitized, indexed, and stored in databases available on the Internet. Marketing companies gather and sell information about consumer habits and detailed transaction information. Cell phone records can track not only a person's calls but also from where the call was made and other activities performed using the phone. Many people find it almost impossible to purge details about themselves from any of these sources. Even incorrect or embarrassing information regarding past indiscretions can damage one's reputation for decades. Privacy advocates fear that because of the pervasive and permanent nature of data and information stored on the Internet, nobody can expect privacy. They encourage people not to share personal information online and to be judicious when engaging in financial transactions.

Do Internet databases mean the end of privacy? Why or why not? Should the government enact laws to prevent the sale of personal information gathered in Internet databases? Why? How can people change their behaviors so that less personal data is available in Internet databases?

The Hierarchy of Data

Data is organized in layers. In the computer profession, data is classified in a hierarchy. Each higher level of data consists of one or more items from the lower level. For example, a student has an address, and an address consists of letters and numbers. Depending on the application and the user, different terms describe the various levels of the hierarchy.

As shown in Figure 9-2, a database contains files (sometimes called tables), a file contains records, a record contains fields, and a field is made up of one or more characters. This sample School database contains four files: Student, Instructor, Schedule of Classes, and Student Schedule. The Student file contains records about enrolled students. The Instructor file contains records about current instructors. The Schedule of Classes file contains records about class offerings in a particular semester, and the Student Schedule file contains records about the classes in which a student is enrolled for a given semester. Each field in a record contains many characteristics, one of which is the field size.

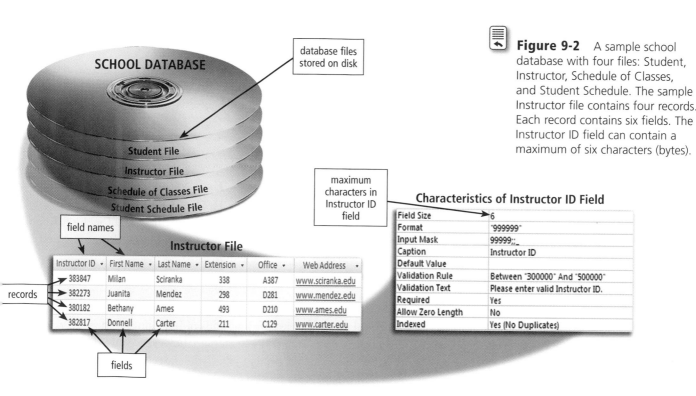

Figure 9-2   A sample school database with four files: Student, Instructor, Schedule of Classes, and Student Schedule. The sample Instructor file contains four records. Each record contains six fields. The Instructor ID field can contain a maximum of six characters (bytes).

Characters

As Chapter 4 discussed, a bit is the smallest unit of data the computer can process. Eight bits grouped together in a unit comprise a byte. In the ASCII coding scheme, each byte represents a single **character**, which can be a number (4), letter (R), space, punctuation mark (?), or other symbol (&).

Fields

A **field** is a combination of one or more related characters or bytes and is the smallest unit of data a user accesses. A **field name** uniquely identifies each field. When searching for data in a database, you often specify the field name. Field names for the data in the Instructor file are Instructor ID, First Name, Last Name, Extension, Office, and Web Address.

A database uses a variety of characteristics, such as field size and data type, to define each field. The **field size** defines the maximum number of characters a field can contain. For example, the Instructor ID field contains 6 characters and thus has a field size of 6 (shown in Figure 9-2).

Instructor file

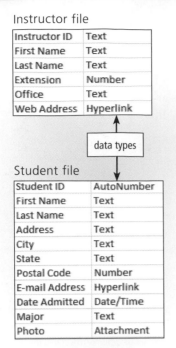

Figure 9-3 Data types of fields in the Instructor and Student files.

The type of data in a field is an important consideration. Figure 9-3 identifies the data types for fields in the Instructor and Student files. The **data type** specifies the kind of data a field can contain and how the field is used. Common data types include:

- Text (also called alphanumeric) — letters, numbers, or special characters
- Numeric (also called number) — numbers only
- AutoNumber — unique number automatically assigned by the DBMS to each added record
- Currency — dollar and cent amounts or numbers containing decimal values
- Date (also called date/time) — month, day, year, and sometimes time
- Memo — lengthy text entries
- Yes/No — only the values Yes or No (or True or False)
- Hyperlink — E-mail address or Web address that links to a Web page on the Internet or document on a local network
- Object — photo, audio, video, or a document created in other programs and stored as a bitmap in the database
- Attachment — document or image that is attached to the field, which can be opened in the program that created the document or image (functioning similarly to e-mail attachments)

Records

A **record** is a group of related fields. For example, a student record includes a set of fields about one student. A **primary key** is a field that uniquely identifies each record in a file. The data in a primary key is unique to a specific record. For example, the Student ID field uniquely identifies each student because no two students can have the same Student ID. In some tables, the primary key consists of multiple fields, called a **composite key**. For example, the primary key for the Schedule of Classes file could consist of the fields Semester Code, Class Code, and Class Section, which together would uniquely identify each class listed in a schedule.

Files

A **data file** is a collection of related records stored on a storage medium such as a hard disk or optical disc. A Student file at a school might consist of thousands of individual student records. Each student record in the file contains the same fields. Each field, however, contains different data. Figure 9-4 shows a small sample Student file that contains four student records, each with eleven fields. A database includes a group of related data files.

Sample Student File

Student ID	First Name	Last Name	Address	City	State	Postal Code	E-mail Address	Date Admitted	Major	Photo
2295	Milton	Brewer	54 Lucy Court	Charlestown	IN	46176		6/10/2010	EE	mbrew
3876	Louella	Drake	33 Timmons Place	Bonner	IN	45208	lou@world.com	8/9/2010	BIO	ldrake.
3928	Adelbert	Ruiz	99 Tenth Street	Sheldon	IN	46033		10/8/2010	CT	aruiz.jp
2872	Benjamin	Tu	2204 Elm Court	Rowley	IN	46167	tu@indi.net	11/6/2010	GEN	btu.jpg

records   key field   fields   fields

Figure 9-4 A sample data file, stored on a hard disk, that contains four records, each with eleven fields.

Maintaining Data

File maintenance refers to the procedures that keep data current. File maintenance procedures include adding records to, modifying records in, and deleting records from a file.

Adding Records

Users add new records to a file when they obtain new data. If a new student is admitted to the school, an admissions department clerk adds a new record to the Student file. The process required to add this record to the file might include the following steps:

1. An admissions department clerk uses the database management system (DBMS) to display a Student Maintenance Form that gives him or her access to the Student file. The clerk then clicks the New button, which begins the process of adding a record to the Student file.
2. The clerk fills in the fields of the student record with data (except for the Student ID, which automatically is assigned by the DBMS).
3. The clerk takes a picture of the student using a digital camera. The DBMS stores this picture in the Student file and prints it on a student ID card.
4. The admissions department clerk verifies the data on the screen and then instructs the DBMS to add the new student record to the Student file. The system software determines where to write the record on the disk (Figure 9-5).

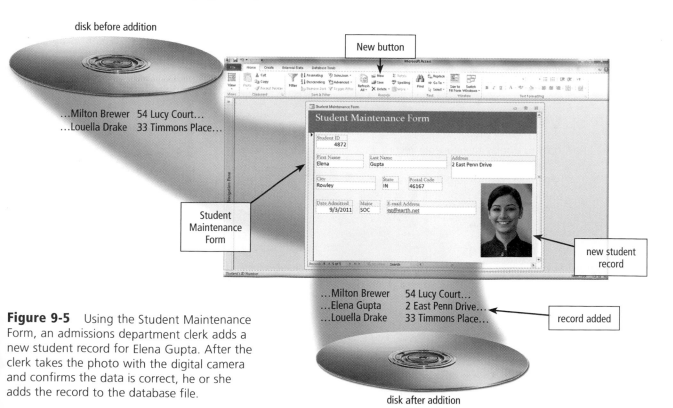

Figure 9-5 Using the Student Maintenance Form, an admissions department clerk adds a new student record for Elena Gupta. After the clerk takes the photo with the digital camera and confirms the data is correct, he or she adds the record to the database file.

Modifying Records

Generally, users modify a record in a file for two reasons: (1) to correct inaccurate data or (2) to update old data with new data.

Suppose, for example, that Elena Gupta moves from 2 East Penn Drive to 76 Ash Street. The process to change the address and update Elena Gupta's record might include the following steps:

1. The admissions department clerk displays the Student Maintenance Form.
2. Assuming Elena Gupta is present, the clerk inserts Elena's student ID card in a card reader to display her student record on the screen. If Elena did not have her ID card or was not present, the clerk could enter Elena's student ID number — if Elena knew it. Otherwise, the clerk could

enter Gupta in the Last Name field, which would retrieve all students with that same last name. The clerk then would scroll through all of the retrieved records to determine which one is Elena's.

3. The DBMS displays data about Elena Gupta so that the clerk can confirm the correct student record is displayed.

4. The clerk enters the new street address, 76 Ash Street.

5. The admissions department clerk verifies the data on the screen and then, if required, clicks the Save button to modify the record in the Student file. The DBMS modifies the record on the disk (Figure 9-6).

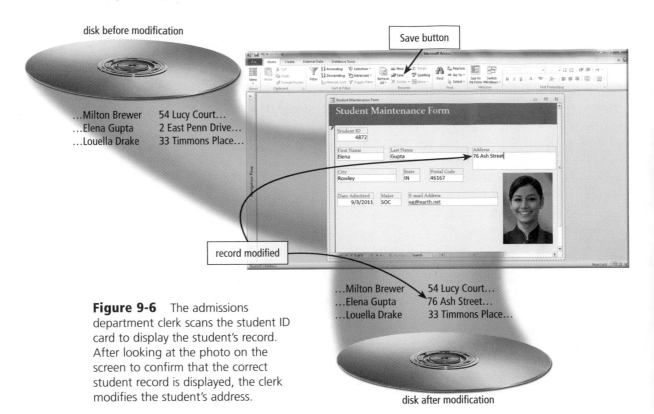

Figure 9-6 The admissions department clerk scans the student ID card to display the student's record. After looking at the photo on the screen to confirm that the correct student record is displayed, the clerk modifies the student's address.

Deleting Records

When a record no longer is needed, a user deletes it from a file. Assume a student named Benjamin Tu is moving out of the country. The process required to delete a record from a file includes the following steps:

1. The admissions department clerk displays the Student Maintenance Form.

2. The clerk displays Benjamin Tu's student record on the screen.

3. The clerk confirms the correct student record is displayed. Then, the clerk clicks the Delete button to delete the record from the Student file and then, if required, clicks the Save button to save the modified file.

DBMSs use a variety of techniques to manage deleted records. Sometimes, the DBMS removes the record from the file immediately, which means the deleted record cannot be restored. Other times, the record is flagged, or marked, so the DBMS will not process it again. In this case, the DBMS places an asterisk (*) or some other character at the beginning of the record (Figure 9-7).

DBMSs that maintain inactive data for an extended period commonly flag records. For example, a school might flag inactive students. When a DBMS flags a deleted record, the record remains physically on the disk. The record, however, is deleted logically because the DBMS will not process it.

From time to time, users should run a utility program that removes the flagged records and reorganizes current records. For example, the school may remove from disk any students who have not taken classes in five years.

disk after deletion

Delete button

record flagged

... Adelbert Ruiz   99 Tenth Street...
... *Benjamin Tu   2204 Elm Court...

Figure 9-7 The admissions department clerk displays the student's record on the screen. After the clerk verifies that the correct student record is displayed, he or she deletes the record. The DBMS flags the student record on disk by placing an asterisk in the first position of the record.

Validating Data

Validation is the process of comparing data with a set of rules or values to find out if the data is correct. Many programs perform a validity check that analyzes data, either as you enter it or after you enter it, to help ensure that it is correct. For instance, when an admissions department clerk adds or modifies data in a student record, the DBMS tests the entered data.

With a per credit hour fee, you would expect to see numbers before and after a decimal point. For example, a valid per credit hour fee is 220.25. An entry of 2DW.8I clearly is not correct. If the entered data fails a validity check, the computer either should not allow the invalid data to be entered, or it should display an error message that instructs the user to enter the data again. Validity checks reduce data entry errors. Read Innovative Computing 9-1 to find out how data validation is used in baseball.

Various types of validity checks include alphabetic checks, numeric checks, range checks, consistency checks, and completeness checks. Check digits also validate data accuracy. The paragraphs on the next page describe the purpose of these validity checks. The table in Figure 9-8 illustrates several of these validity checks and shows valid data that passes the check and invalid data that fails the check.

Sample Valid and Invalid Data

Validity Check	Field(s) Being Checked	Valid Data	Invalid Data
Alphabetic Check	First Name	Karen	Ka24n
Numeric Check	Postal Code	46322	4tr22
Range Check	Per Credit Hour Fee	$220.25	$2,120.00
Consistency Check	Date Admitted and Birth Date	9/20/2010 8/27/1985	9/20/2010 8/27/2011
Completeness Check	Last Name	Gupta	

Figure 9-8 In this table of sample valid and invalid data, the first column lists commonly used validity checks. The second column lists the name of the field that contains data being checked. The third column shows valid data that passes the validity checks. The fourth column shows invalid data that fails the validity checks.

⚠ **INNOVATIVE COMPUTING 9-1**

America's Favorite Pastime Adds Authentic Twist

Validating baseball memorabilia has been simplified with the help of holograms and an online database. Each game uniform, bat, and other licensed Major League Baseball (MLB) merchandise is issued a specific hologram with a tracking number. More than 135 carefully trained authenticators enter this number and other data into the database's fields for all 30 MLB teams.

Obtaining data for significant home run balls is a bit more challenging. MLB authenticators are assigned to the bleachers where they must track the home run ball and identify the person who caught it. They immediately glue a hologram to the ball and record the specific details in the database.

Another innovative use of databases in baseball is found in Baseball Boss, a free game that meshes players from the past with today's stars. Each gamer becomes a manager who randomly is assigned 40 players. This team is paired with another team, and the computer determines, in an inning-by-inning contest, the final score in minutes. The box score is determined by analyzing actual player statistics in the database's fields and with chance. Ultimately, gamers will be able to determine how Babe Ruth would fare against today's power pitchers.

 For more information, visit the Computer Concepts CourseMate Web site at www.cengagebrain.com, navigate to the Chapter 9 Innovative Computing resource for this book, and then click Baseball Databases.

Alphabetic/Numeric Check   An **alphabetic check** ensures that users enter only alphabetic data into a field. A **numeric check** ensures that users enter only numeric data into a field. For example, data in a First Name field should contain only characters from the alphabet. Data in a Postal Code field should contain numbers (with the exception of the special characters such as a hyphen).

Range Check   A **range check** determines whether a number is within a specified range. Assume the lowest per credit hour fee at the school is $75.00 and the highest is $370.75. A range check for the Credit Hour Fee field ensures it is a value between $75.00 and $370.75.

Consistency Check   A **consistency check** tests the data in two or more associated fields to ensure that the relationship is logical and their data is in the correct format. For example, the value in a Date Admitted field cannot occur earlier in time than a value in a Birth Date field.

Completeness Check   A **completeness check** verifies that a required field contains data. For example, some fields cannot be left blank; others require a minimum number of characters. One completeness check can ensure that data exists in a Last Name field. Another can ensure that a day, month, and year are included in a Birth Date field.

Check Digit   A **check digit** is a number(s) or character(s) that is appended to or inserted in a primary key value. A check digit often confirms the accuracy of a primary key value. Bank account, credit card, and other identification numbers often include one or more check digits.

A program determines the check digit by applying a formula to the numbers in the primary key value. An oversimplified illustration of a check digit formula is to add the numbers in the primary key. For example, if the primary key is 1367, this formula would add these numbers (1 + 3 + 6 + 7) for a sum of 17. Next, the formula would add the numbers in the result (1 + 7) to generate a check digit of 8. The primary key then is 13678.

When a data entry clerk enters the primary key of 13678, for example, to look up an existing record, the program determines whether the check digit is valid. If the clerk enters an incorrect primary key, such as 13778, the check digit entered (8) will not match the computed check digit (9). In this case, the program displays an error message that instructs the user to enter the primary key value again.

Data Validation
For more information, visit the Computer Concepts CourseMate Web site at www.cengagebrain.com, navigate to the Chapter 9 Web Link resource for this book, and then click Data Validation.

Other Checks   DBMSs that include hyperlink and attachment data types can perform validity checks on data entered in those fields. Hyperlink entries can be tested to ensure that the Web address follows the correct format and that the link works. Similarly, an attachment entry can be validated by confirming that the file exists.

✔ **QUIZ YOURSELF 9-1**

Instructions: Find the true statement below. Then, rewrite the remaining false statements so that they are true.

1. A database is a combination of one or more related characters or bytes and is the smallest unit of data a user accesses.
2. A record is a collection of data organized in a manner that allows access, retrieval, and use of that data.
3. Data is processed information.
4. Hierarchy of data procedures include adding records to, modifying records in, and deleting records from a file.
5. To be valuable, information should be accurate, verifiable, timely, organized, accessible, useful, and cost-effective.

Quiz Yourself Online: To further check your knowledge of pages 352 through 360, visit the Computer Concepts CourseMate Web site at www.cengagebrain.com, navigate to the Chapter 9 Quiz Yourself resource for this book, and then click Objectives 1 – 4.

File Processing versus Databases

Almost all application programs use the file processing approach, the database approach, or a combination of both approaches to store and manage data. The following pages discuss these two approaches.

File Processing Systems

In the past, many organizations exclusively used file processing systems to store and manage data. In a typical **file processing system**, each department or area within an organization has its own set of files. The records in one file may not relate to the records in any other file.

Organizations have used file processing systems for many years. Many of these systems, however, have two major weaknesses: they have redundant data and they isolate data.

- Data Redundancy — Each department or area in an organization has its own files in a file processing system. Thus, the same fields are stored in multiple files. If a file processing system is used at a school, for example, the Student file and the Student Schedule file both might store the same students' names and addresses.

   Duplicating data in this manner wastes resources such as storage space and people's time. When new students are added or student data is modified, file maintenance tasks consume additional time because people must update multiple files that contain the same data.

   Data redundancy also can increase the chance of errors. If a student changes his or her address, for example, the school must update the address wherever it appears. If the Address field is not changed in all the files where it is stored, then discrepancies among the files exist.

- Isolated Data — Often it is difficult to access data stored in separate files in different departments. Sharing data from multiple, separate files is a complicated procedure and usually requires the experience of a computer programmer.

The Database Approach

When an organization uses the **database approach**, many programs and users share the data in the database. A school's database most likely at a minimum contains data about students, instructors, schedule of classes, and student schedules. As shown in Figure 9-9, various areas within the school share and interact with the data in this database. The database does secure its data, however, so that only authorized users can access certain data items. While a user is working with the database, the DBMS resides in the memory of the computer.

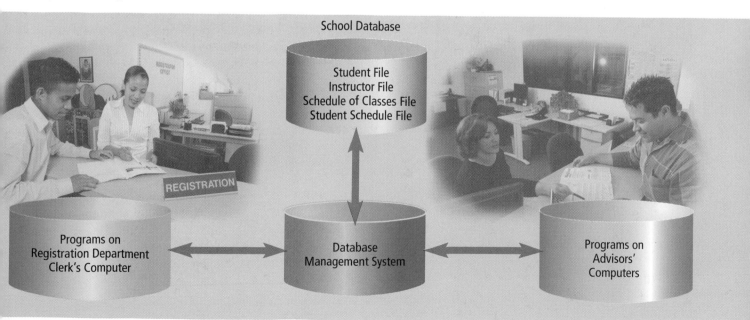

School Database

Student File
Instructor File
Schedule of Classes File
Student Schedule File

Programs on Registration Department Clerk's Computer

Database Management System

Programs on Advisors' Computers

Figure 9-9   In a school that uses a database, the computer used by a registration department clerk and the computers used by advisors access data in a single database through the DBMS.

The database approach addresses many of the weaknesses associated with file processing systems. The following list presents some strengths of the database approach.

- Reduced Data Redundancy — Most data items are stored in only one file, which greatly reduces duplicate data. Figure 9-10 demonstrates the differences between how a file processing application and a database application might store data.
- Improved Data Integrity — When users modify data in the database, they make changes to one file instead of multiple files. Thus, the database approach increases the data's integrity by reducing the possibility of introducing inconsistencies.
- Shared Data — The data in a database environment belongs to and is shared, usually over a network, by the entire organization. Organizations that use databases typically have security settings to define who can access, add, modify, and delete the data in a database.
- Easier Access — The database approach allows nontechnical users to access and maintain data, providing they have the necessary privileges.
- Reduced Development Time — It often is easier and faster to develop programs that use the database approach.

Databases have many advantages as well as some disadvantages. A database can be more complex than a file processing system. People with special training usually develop larger databases and their associated applications. Databases also require more memory, storage, and processing power than file processing systems.

Data in a database can be more vulnerable than data in file processing systems. A database can store a lot of data in a single file. Many users and programs share and depend on this data. If the database is not operating properly or is damaged or destroyed, users may not be able to perform their jobs. Furthermore, unauthorized users potentially could gain access to a single database file that contains personal and confidential data. To protect their valuable database resource, individuals and companies should establish and follow security procedures. Despite these limitations, many business and home users work with databases because of their tremendous advantages.

? FAQ 9-1

Can a database eliminate redundant data completely?

No, a database reduces redundant data — it does not eliminate it. Key fields link data together in a database. For example, a Student ID field will exist in any database table that requires access to student data. Thus, a Student ID is duplicated (exists in many tables) in the database.

For more information, visit the Computer Concepts CourseMate Web site at www.cengagebrain.com, navigate to the Chapter 9 FAQ resource for this book, and then click Database Relationships.

Figure 9-10 In the file processing environment, both files contain all six instructor data fields. In a database environment, only the Instructor file contains the First Name, Last Name, Extension, Office, and Web Address fields. Other files, however, such as the Schedule of Classes file, contain the Instructor ID, which links to the Instructor file when instructor data is needed.

Database Management Systems

As previously discussed, a database management system (DBMS), or database program, is software that allows you to create, access, and manage a database. DBMSs are available for many sizes and types of computers (Figure 9-11). Whether designed for a small or large computer, most DBMSs perform common functions. The following pages discuss functions common to most DBMSs.

Popular Database Management Systems

Database	Manufacturer	Computer Type
Access	Microsoft Corporation	Personal computer, server, mobile devices
Adabas	Software AG	Server, mainframe
D³	Raining Data	Personal computer, server
DB2	IBM Corporation	Personal computer, server, mainframe
Essbase	Oracle Corporation	Personal computer, server, mobile devices
FastObjects	Versant Corporation	Personal computer, server
FileMaker	FileMaker, Inc.	Personal computer, server
GemFire	GemStone Systems	Server
Informix	IBM Corporation	Personal computer, server, mainframe
Ingres	Ingres Corporation	Personal computer, server, mainframe
InterBaseSMP	Embarcadero Technologies	Personal computer, server
KE Texpress	KE Software, Inc.	Personal computer, server
MySQL	Oracle Corporation	Personal computer, server
ObjectStore	Progress Software Corporation	Personal computer, server
Oracle Database	Oracle Corporation	Personal computer, server, mainframe, mobile devices
SQL Server	Microsoft Corporation	Server, personal computer
SQL Server Compact Edition	Microsoft Corporation	Mobile devices
Sybase	Sybase Inc.	Personal computer, server, mobile devices
Teradata Database	Teradata	Server
Versant	Versant Corporation	Personal computer, server
Visual FoxPro	Microsoft Corporation	Personal computer, server

Figure 9-11 Many database management systems run on multiple types of computers.

MySQL

For more information, visit the Computer Concepts CourseMate Web site at www.cengagebrain.com, navigate to the Chapter 9 Web Link resource for this book, and then click MySQL.

? FAQ 9-2

Which database vendors have the largest revenue market share?

As shown in the chart to the right, Oracle has the largest market share in terms of revenue, followed by IBM and Microsoft.

For more information, visit the Computer Concepts CourseMate Web site at www.cengagebrain.com, navigate to the Chapter 9 FAQ resource for this book, and then click Database Market Share.

Market Share

3% 9% 4% 44% 19% 21%

☐ Oracle ☐ IBM ☐ Microsoft ☐ Sybase ☐ Teradata ☐ Other

Source: IDC

Data Dictionary

A **data dictionary** contains data about each file in the database and each field within those files. For each file, it stores details such as the file name, description, the file's relationship to other files, and the number of records in the file. For each field, it stores details such as the field name, description, field type, field size, default value, validation rules, and the field's relationship to other fields. Figure 9-12 shows how a data dictionary might list data for a Student file.

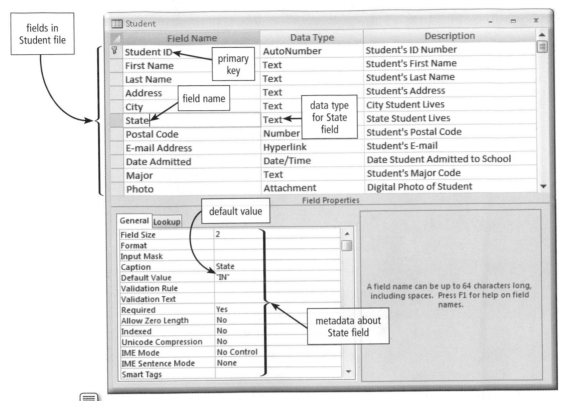

Figure 9-12 A sample data dictionary entry shows the fields in the Student file and the properties of the State field.

File Retrieval and Maintenance

A DBMS provides several tools that allow users and programs to retrieve and maintain data in the database. To retrieve or select data in a database, you query it. A **query** is a request for specific data from the database. Users can instruct the DBMS to display, print, or store the results of a query. The capability of querying a database is one of the more powerful database features.

A DBMS offers several methods to retrieve and maintain its data. The four more commonly used are query languages, query by example, forms, and report generators. The following sections describe each of these methods. To learn about organizing files on a computer, complete the Learn How To 1 activity on pages 378 and 379. Read Looking Ahead 9-1 for a look at a future use of databases.

Query Language A **query language** consists of simple, English-like statements that allow users to specify the data to display, print, or store. Users can retrieve actual data in a query or display the results of calculations performed on the data. Each query language has its own grammar and vocabulary. A person without a programming background usually can learn a query language in a short time.

To simplify the query process, many DBMSs provide wizards to guide users through the steps of creating a query. Figure 9-13 shows how to use the Simple Query Wizard in Microsoft Access to display the First Name, Last Name, and E-mail Address fields from the Student file. Instead of using the wizard, you could enter the query language statement shown in Figure 9-13 directly in the DBMS to display the results shown in Step 3. SQL, which is a widely used query language, is discussed later in the chapter.

SQL

For more information, visit the Computer Concepts CourseMate Web site at www.cengagebrain.com, navigate to the Chapter 9 Web Link resource for this book, and then click SQL.

↗ **LOOKING AHEAD 9-1**

DNA Barcoding Identifies World's Species

Taxonomists have been collecting and cataloging the world's 1.7 million known species of plants, animals, and microbes for the past 300 years. Each of these species has a unique DNA sequence, called the barcode of life, that researchers can extract from tissue samples.

The Consortium for the Barcode of Life is attempting to build three separate databases with data obtained from analyzing the tissues: GenBank at the National Institutes of Health

in the United States, the European Molecular Biology Laboratory (EMBL) in Germany, and the DNA Data Bank of Japan (DDBJ). These global databases will contain records with the DNA sequence, data on the specimen, and the species' name. The data will be available to researchers worldwide free of charge.

Researchers hope the databases will help protect endangered species, provide basic research in taxonomy, sustain natural resources, explore marine

biodiversity, control agricultural pests, monitor environmental quality, and stop the spread of disease-bearing mosquitoes.

For more information, visit the Computer Concepts CourseMate Web site at www.cengagebrain.com, navigate to the Chapter 9 Looking Ahead resource for this book, and then click DNA Barcode.

How to Use the Simple Query Wizard

Step 1

Select the fields from the Available Fields list you want to be displayed in the resulting query.

Step 2

Assign a name to the query, so that you can open it later.

SELECT FIRST NAME, LAST NAME, E-MAIL ADDRESS FROM STUDENT

query language statement generated by wizard

Step 3

View the query results on the screen.

Figure 9-13 This figure shows how to use the Simple Query Wizard.

Query by Example Most DBMSs include a **query by example** (**QBE**) feature that has a graphical user interface to assist users with retrieving data. Figure 9-14 shows a sample QBE screen for a query that searches for and lists students majoring in sociology; that is, their Major field value is equal to SOC.

Figure 9-14a (all records in Student table)

Major field

criteria

Figure 9-14b (query by example screen showing query that will search for students whose Major is equal to SOC, for sociology)

Figure 9-14c (query results list students whose Major is equal to SOC)

Figure 9-14 Access has many QBE capabilities. One QBE technique is Filter by Form, which uses a form to show available fields. The database program retrieves records that match criteria you enter in the form fields. This example searches for students whose major is sociology.

Form A **form**, sometimes called a data entry form, is a window on the screen that provides areas for entering or modifying data in a database. You use forms (such as the Student Maintenance Form in Figure 9-5 on page 357) to retrieve and maintain the data in a database.

To reduce data entry errors, well-designed forms should validate data as it is entered. When designing a form using a DBMS, you can make the form attractive and easy to use by incorporating color, shading, lines, boxes, and graphics; varying the fonts and font styles; and using other formatting features.

Student List by Major

Major	Last Name	Student ID	First Name	Address	City	Date Admitted
BIO						
	Drake	3876	Louella	33 Timmons Place	Bonner	8/9/2010
CT						
	Ruiz	3928	Adelbert	99 Tenth Street	Sheldon	10/8/2010
GEN						
	Tu	2928	Benjamin	2204 Elm Court	Rowley	9/4/2010
SOC						
	Brewer	2295	Milton	54 Lucy Court	Charlestown	6/10/2010
	Gupta	4872	Elena	76 Ash Street	Rowley	9/3/2011

Figure 9-15 This report, created in Microsoft Access, displays student information by major.

Report Generator A **report generator**, also called a report writer, allows users to design a report on the screen, retrieve data into the report design, and then display or print the report (Figure 9-15). Report generators usually allow you to format page numbers and dates; titles and column headings; subtotals and totals; and fonts, font sizes, color, and shading. Many allow you to include images, for example, a product catalog with photos and descriptions of products.

Data Security

A DBMS provides means to ensure that only authorized users access data at permitted times. In addition, most DBMSs allow different levels of access privileges to be identified for each field in the database. These access privileges define the actions that a specific user or group of users can perform. Access privileges for data involve establishing who can enter new data, modify existing data, delete unwanted data, and view data. Many organizations adopt the **principle of least privilege** policy, where users' access privileges are limited to the lowest level necessary to perform required tasks. Read Ethics & Issues 9-2 for a related discussion.

ETHICS & ISSUES 9-2

Should People Be Punished for Accidently Accessing Stolen Data?

A university student discovered a file containing private student information, including Social Security numbers and student grades, on a publicly accessible area of a university computer. Instead of notifying authorities, he took the file to the student newspaper in the hopes of making sure that the security breach was made public. After the newspaper published an article about the situation, the student was nearly expelled and the newspaper's adviser was fired for violating the university's computer policies. Some privacy advocates felt that the outcome was a case of shooting the messenger.

More and more often, institutions attempt to resolve security breaches as quietly as possible, fearing that publicity may cause financial loss and loss of public confidence, and may encourage hackers to target the institution. In some cases, an institution may file lawsuits against those who make security breaches public, including reporters. Some states require computer technicians to report illegally obtained data that they encounter in the course of their jobs.

If you find a USB flash drive left behind by someone that contains inappropriate or illegally obtained data, should you be required to report the incident to pertinent authorities? Why or why not? In the university computer situation described, should the student and newspaper be praised or punished for making the security breach public knowledge? Why? Should people who inadvertently receive illegal photos or videos on their cell phones be prosecuted? Why or why not?

Backup and Recovery

Occasionally a database is damaged or destroyed because of hardware failure, a problem with the software, human error, or a catastrophe such as fire or flood. A DBMS provides a variety of techniques to restore the database to a usable form in case it is damaged or destroyed.

- A **backup**, or copy, of the entire database should be made on a regular basis. Some DBMSs have their own built-in backup utilities. Others require users to purchase a separate backup utility, or use one included with the operating system.
- More complex DBMSs maintain a **log**, which is a listing of activities that change the contents of the database.
- A DBMS that creates a log usually provides a recovery utility. A **recovery utility** uses the logs and/or backups to restore a database when it becomes damaged or destroyed.
- **Continuous backup** is a backup plan in which all data is backed up whenever a change is made. This backup technique can cost more than other backup strategies but is growing in popularity because of its benefits.

✔ QUIZ YOURSELF 9-2

Instructions: Find the true statement below. Then, rewrite the remaining false statements so that they are true.

1. A DBMS is hardware that allows you to create, access, and manage an operating system.
2. A query contains data about each file in the database and each field in those files.
3. Access privileges for data involve establishing who can enter new data, modify existing data, delete unwanted data, and view data.
4. Strengths of the database approach include increased data redundancy, reduced data integrity, shared data, easier access, and increased development time.

Quiz Yourself Online: To further check your knowledge of pages 361 through 367, visit the Computer Concepts CourseMate Web site at www.cengagebrain.com, navigate to the Chapter 9 Quiz Yourself resource for this book, and then click Objectives 5 – 6.

Relational, Object-Oriented, and Multidimensional Databases

Every database and DBMS is based on a specific data model. A **data model** consists of rules and standards that define how the database organizes data. A data model defines how users view the organization of the data. It does not define how the operating system actually arranges the data on the disk.

Three popular data models in use today are relational, object-oriented, and multidimensional. A database typically is based on one data model. Some databases, however, combine features of the relational and object-oriented data models. The following sections discuss relational, object-oriented, and multidimensional databases.

Relational Databases

A **relational database** is a database that stores data in tables that consist of rows and columns. Each row has a primary key and each column has a unique name.

As discussed earlier in this chapter, a file processing environment uses the terms file, record, and field to represent data. A relational database uses terms different from a file processing system. A developer of a relational database refers to a file as a **relation,** a record as a **tuple**, and a field as an **attribute**. A user of a relational database, by contrast, refers to a file as a **table**, a record as a **row**, and a field as a **column**. Figure 9-16 summarizes this varied terminology.

In addition to storing data, a relational database also stores data relationships. A **relationship** is a link within the data. In a relational database, you can set up a relationship between tables at any time. The tables must have a common column (field). For example, you would relate the Schedule of Classes table and the Instructor table using the Instructor ID column. Figure 9-17 illustrates

Data Terminology

File Processing Environment	Relational Database Developer	Relational Database User
File	Relation	Table
Record	Tuple	Row
Field	Attribute	Column

Figure 9-16 Varied terminology for relational databases.

Figure 9-17 This figure shows relationships among some tables in the School database. For example, the Schedule of Classes table is related to the Instructor table through the Instructor ID column.

these relational database concepts. In a relational database, the only data redundancy (duplication) exists in the common columns (fields). The database uses these common columns for relationships.

Many organizations use relational databases for payroll, accounts receivable, accounts payable, general ledger, inventory, order entry, invoicing, and other business-related functions.

SQL Structured Query Language (**SQL**) is a popular query language that allows users to manage, update, and retrieve data. SQL has special keywords and rules that users include in SQL statements. For example, the SQL statement in Figure 9-18a creates the results shown in Figure 9-18b.

Most relational database products for servers and mainframes include SQL. Many personal computer databases also include SQL.

Figure 9-18a   (SQL statement)

```
SELECT CLASS_TITLE, CLASS_CODE, MAXIMUM_ENROLLMENT -
   CURRENT_ENROLLMENT AS SEATS_REMAINING
FROM SCHEDULE_OF_CLASSES, CLASS_CATALOG
WHERE SCHEDULE_OF_CLASSES.CLASS_CODE =
   CLASS_CATALOG.CLASS_CODE
ORDER BY CLASS_TITLE
```

Figure 9-18b   (SQL statement results)

Class Title	Class Section	Seats Remaining
Algebra 1	51	14
Art Appreciation	52	19
English Composition 1	02	5
Introduction to Sociology	01	14

Figure 9-18   A sample SQL statement and its results.

Object-Oriented Databases

An **object-oriented database** (**OODB**) stores data in objects. An **object** is an item that contains data, as well as the actions that read or process the data. A Student object, for example, might contain data about a student such as Student ID, First Name, Last Name, Address, and so on. It also could contain instructions about how to print a student transcript or the formula required to calculate a student's grade point average.

Object-oriented databases have several advantages compared with relational databases: they can store more types of data, access this data faster, and allow programmers to reuse objects. An object-oriented database stores unstructured data more efficiently than a relational database. Unstructured data includes photos, video clips, audio clips, and documents. When users query an object-oriented database, the results often are displayed more quickly than the same query of a relational database. If an object already exists, programmers can reuse it instead of recreating a new object — saving on program development time.

? FAQ 9-3

Are my portable media player's playlists stored in a database?

Most programs that manage your playlist, such as iTunes and Windows Media Player, use a database to store details about your playlists. Storing this data in a database makes it easier and faster for you to search for songs that you wish to play or add to a playlist.

For more information, visit the Computer Concepts CourseMate Web site at www.cengagebrain.com, navigate to the Chapter 9 FAQ resource for this book, and then click Media Player Databases.

Object Query Language   Object-oriented databases often use a query language called object query language (OQL) to manipulate and retrieve data. OQL is similar to SQL. OQL and SQL use many of the same rules, grammar, and keywords. Because OQL is a relatively new query language, not all object databases support it.

Multidimensional Databases

A **multidimensional database** stores data in dimensions. Whereas a relational database is a two-dimensional table, a multidimensional database can store more than two dimensions of data. These multiple dimensions allow users to access and analyze any view of the database data.

A Webmaster at a retail business may want information about product sales and customer sales for each region spanning a given time. A manager at the same business may want information about product sales by department for each sales representative spanning a given time. A multidimensional database can consolidate this type of data from multiple dimensions at very high rates of speed. Nearly every multidimensional database has a dimension of time. The content of other dimensions varies depending on the subject.

No standard query language exists for multidimensional databases. Each database uses its own language. Most are similar to SQL.

Data Warehouses One application that typically uses multidimensional databases is a data warehouse. A **data warehouse** is a huge database that stores and manages the data required to analyze historical and current transactions. Through a data warehouse, managers and other users access transactions and summaries of transactions quickly and efficiently. Some major credit card companies monitor and manage customers' credit card transactions using a data warehouse. Additionally, consumers can access their own transactions in the data warehouse via the Web. A data warehouse typically has a user-friendly interface, so that users easily can interact with its data.

A smaller version of a data warehouse is the data mart. A data mart contains a database that helps a specific group or department make decisions. Marketing and sales departments may have their own separate data marts. Individual groups or departments often extract data from the data warehouse to create their data marts.

Data Warehouses
For more information, visit the Computer Concepts CourseMate Web site at www.cengagebrain.com, navigate to the Chapter 9 Web Link resource for this book, and then click Data Warehouses.

Web Databases

One of the more profound features of the Web is the vast amount of information it provides. The Web offers information about jobs, travel destinations, television programming, photos, movies, videos, local and national weather, sporting events, and legislative information. You can shop for just about any product or service, buy or sell stocks, search for a job, make airline reservations, register for college classes, and check semester grades. Much of this and other information exists in databases that are stored on the Web or are accessible through the Web. Some Web databases are **collaborative databases**, where users store and share photos, videos, recordings, and other personal media with other registered users (Figure 9-19). Read Ethics & Issues 9-3 for a related discussion.

ETHICS & ISSUES 9-3

Who Should Be Held Accountable for the Rash of Database Security Breaches?

Over the course of three years, a privacy advocacy group documented the fact that more than 160 million records that contain personal information were accessed illegally or stolen. The records were allowed to be accessed because of carelessness by government agencies, educational institutions, and corporations. Often database software is not updated properly with security-related bug fixes. Information such as credit card numbers, credit history, and employment information often are involved in such security breaches. In one case, a security breach resulted in more than 45 million customer records being stolen with an estimated cost to the company of more than $4 billion. Institutions typically have their own set of guidelines to manage the security of such information, yet the number of security breaches is escalating.

While some have proposed laws requiring stricter controls for how institutions handle private data and provide for harsher penalties for those not properly securing data, corporations resist such efforts. They claim that the costs involved in such measures would hurt their capability of competing with corporations in other states and countries that are not bound by the same rules. Many institutions voluntarily notify individuals whose information was breached, and some even compensate victims; for example, some provide credit monitoring for free.

Who should be held accountable for the rash of database security breaches? Why? Should the government enact stronger laws regarding data security? Why or why not? Should institutions be required to notify individuals whose data has been breached? Why or why not?

To access data in a Web database, you fill in a form or enter search text on a Web page. Many search engines such as Yahoo! use databases to store Web site descriptions. To access the database, you enter search text into the search engine. A Web database usually resides on a database server. A database server is a computer that stores and provides access to a database.

In addition to accessing information, users provide information to Web databases. Many Web sites request users to enter personal information, such as name, address, telephone number, and preferences, into an e-form (electronic form). The database then stores this personal information for future use. An organization, for example, may send e-mail messages to certain groups of customers.

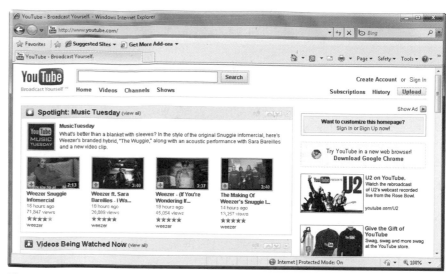

Figure 9-19 Media sharing Web sites store users' digital videos, photos, and other media in a collaborative database, the contents of which are shared with other registered users.

Database Administration

Managing a company's database requires a great deal of coordination. The role of coordinating the use of the database belongs to the database analysts and administrators. To carry out their responsibilities, these IT (information technology) professionals follow database design guidelines and need cooperation from all database users.

Database Design Guidelines

A carefully designed database makes it easier for a user to query the database, modify the data, and create reports. The guidelines shown in Figure 9-20 apply to databases of all sizes.

Database Design Guidelines

For more information, visit the Computer Concepts CourseMate Web site at www.cengagebrain.com, navigate to the Chapter 9 Web Link resource for this book, and then click Database Design Guidelines.

Database Design Guidelines

1. Determine the purpose of the database.

2. Design the tables or files.
   - Design tables or files on paper first.
   - Each table or file should contain data about one subject. The Student table, for example, contains data about students.

3. Design the records and fields for each table or file.
   - Be sure every record has a unique primary key.
   - Use separate fields for logically distinct items. For example, a name could be stored in six fields: Title (Mr., Mrs., Dr., etc.), First Name, Middle Name, Last Name, Suffix (Jr., Sr., etc.), and Nickname.
   - Do not create fields for information that can be derived from entries in other fields. For example, do not include a field for Age. Instead, store the birth date and compute the age.
   - Allow enough space for each field.
   - Set default values for frequently entered data.

4. Determine the relationships among the tables or files.

Figure 9-20 Guidelines for designing a database.

Role of the Database Analysts and Administrators

The database analysts and administrators are responsible for managing and coordinating all database activities. The **database analyst (DA)** decides on the proper placement of fields, defines the relationships among data, and identifies users' access privileges. The **database administrator (DBA)** requires a more technical inside view of the data. The DBA creates and maintains the data dictionary, manages security of the database, monitors the performance of the database, and checks backup and recovery procedures.

In small companies, one person often is both the DA and DBA. In larger companies, the responsibilities of the DA and DBA are split among two or more people.

Role of the Employee as a User

Employees should learn how to use the data in the database effectively. The amount of information available often amazes first-time database users. Instant access to information helps employees perform their jobs more effectively. Today, employees access databases from their office desktop computers, notebook computers, or even smart phones and other mobile devices.

The maintenance of a database is an ongoing task that organizations measure constantly against their overall goals.

✔ **QUIZ YOURSELF 9-3**

Instructions: Find the true statement below. Then, rewrite the remaining false statements so that they are true.

1. Object-oriented databases store data in tables.
2. Relational database users refer to a file as a table, a field as a column, and a record as a row.
3. SQL is a data modeling language that allows users to manage, update, and retrieve data.
4. The database analyst requires a more technical inside view of the data than does the database administrator.

Quiz Yourself Online: To further check your knowledge of pages 368 through 372, visit the Computer Concepts CourseMate Web site at www.cengagebrain.com, navigate to the Chapter 9 Quiz Yourself resource for this book, and then click Objectives 7 – 9.

Chapter Summary

This chapter discussed how data and information are valuable assets to an organization. The chapter also presented methods for maintaining high-quality data and assessing the quality of valuable information. It then discussed the advantages of organizing data in a database and described various types of databases. It also presented the roles of the database analysts and administrators.

Computer Usage @ Work

Health Sciences

During an intramural volleyball game, you suffer an injury that requires a trip to the emergency room. Upon check-in, you notice that the emergency room is extremely crowded, so the employee at the front desk uses a computer to record your personal data and symptoms. She also uses the computer to verify that your insurance coverage is current and informs you of your co-payment amount. After waiting several minutes, a triage nurse takes your temperature and blood pressure and then asks a series of questions about your symptoms. The nurse also records this data in a computer and asks you to remain in the waiting room until someone from the radiology department is available to perform a CT scan. The radiology department is located in a different area of the hospital, so the technicians watch a computer monitor that displays a list of patients who currently are waiting for their services.

About 30 minutes later, a technician calls your name and escorts you to the radiology department for your CT scan. As she is performing the scan, a computer records the images that later will be reviewed by a physician. When the CT scan is complete, you return to the waiting room until a physician reviews the results. Once he receives the results and reviews them, a hospital employee takes you to a consultation room.

The physician informs you that other than a few bumps and bruises, he believes that you have sustained no permanent damage and prescribes medication to help ease the pain. He then returns to a computer at the nurse's station and adds his diagnosis to the database that stores your medical records. He also sends your prescription electronically to the hospital's pharmacy. Once discharged, you visit the cashier to pay the bill. You then sign an electronic version of your discharge paperwork using a Tablet PC so that the hospital can store it electronically. The hospital bills your insurance company electronically. If you owe a balance after the insurance company has paid its portion, a computer at the hospital will generate a bill that will be mailed to you.

After purchasing your medication and leaving the hospital, you realize that despite the hospital being busy, computers decreased the time of your visit by automating processes that otherwise would have been performed manually.

For more information, visit the Computer Concepts CourseMate Web site at www.cengagebrain.com, navigate to the Chapter 9 Computer Usage @ Work resource for this book, and then click Health Sciences.

Companies on the Cutting Edge

ORACLE Database Software Developer

One hundred terabytes of data may seem impossible to manage, but Oracle can handle a database of this size with its recent products. The company is the world's second largest independent software company and is the world's largest enterprise software company.

Larry Ellison, the company's CEO, founded Oracle in 1977 with the help of two partners. They envisioned developing a commercially viable relational database, and their efforts were an instant success. Their first Oracle database changed the way companies stored and managed information because, for the first time, users could connect separate data tables by using a common field.

More than one-half of the FORTUNE 100 companies use an Oracle database. Its latest products feature online social networking and collaboration. Oracle's acquisitions and growth dominate the database community. Recently, Oracle acquired Sun Microsystems, another pioneer in the IT industry, for $7.4 billion.

SYBASE Unwired Enterprise Database and Services Leader

Wireless banking and messaging technology are two areas in demand today, and Sybase is helping companies meet consumers' demands for these services. The company provides mobile software for wireless applications and services, especially in the customer service and emergency response areas of the financial, telecommunications, health care, and government sectors.

Mark Hoffman and Bob Epstein founded Sybase more than 25 years ago out of Epstein's Berkeley, CA, home. Their company was the first to develop a client/server relational database; one of the first tests of this product was for the Human Genome Project, a 13-year study sponsored by the U.S. Department of Energy and the National Institutes of Health to identify more than 20,000 genes in human DNA and then store the findings in a database.

Sybase recently made the *InformationWeek* 500 list for the fifth year in a row. The *InformationWeek* 500 lists the most innovative technology users, including companies such as Kimberly-Clark, National Semiconductor, and Hilton Hotels.

 For more information, visit the Computer Concepts CourseMate Web site at www.cengagebrain.com and then navigate to the Chapter 9 Companies on the Cutting Edge resource for this book.

Technology Trailblazers

E. F. CODD Relational Database Model Inventor

Organized data is the key to effective database design, and the normalization process that helps structure data and eliminate redundancy is credited to Edgar Frank (E. F.) Codd. His relational database design is the structure for most of the small and large databases used today, and this concept is considered one of the greatest technological inventions of the twentieth century.

After attending college in England and serving in the Royal Air Force, he immigrated to New York and began working at IBM as a programming mathematician. He developed and promoted his relational model in a series of research papers beginning with his 1969 IBM report, "Derivability, Redundancy, and Consistency of Relations Stored in Large Data Banks." As a result of his research, IBM introduced in 1982 the first version of Structured Query Language (SQL).

Among his achievements is earning the prestigious A. M. Turing Award, which is the Association for Computing Machinery's highest technical achievement honor given to an individual.

LARRY ELLISON Oracle Cofounder and CEO

E. F. Codd's research had a profound effect on Larry Ellison. During the 1970s, Ellison modeled Codd's relational database theories and then developed a database named Oracle for the Central Intelligence Agency. In 1977, he invested $2,000 to form his company, Software Development Laboratories, and renamed the company Oracle two years later.

Ellison called his company's first database Oracle 2. He hoped this name gave the impression that an earlier version of the software had existed and that the second edition eliminated programming errors. This relational database system used IBM's Structured Query Language (SQL).

His compensation from Oracle and investments have made him one of the wealthiest men in the United States with an estimated net worth of $22.5 billion. In 2000, he was considered the richest man in the world. Among his hobbies are racing sailboats, flying jet planes, and playing guitar and tennis. He sits on the board of the Dian Fossey Gorilla Fund.

 For more information, visit the Computer Concepts CourseMate Web site at www.cengagebrain.com and then navigate to the Chapter 9 Technology Trailblazers resource for this book.

Chapter Review

The Chapter Review reinforces the main concepts presented in this chapter.

To listen to an audio version of this Chapter Review, visit the Computer Concepts CourseMate Web site at www.cengagebrain.com and then navigate to the Chapter 9 Chapter Review resource for this book.

1. **What Is a Database, and How Does a Database Interact with Data and Information?** A **database** is a collection of data organized in a manner that allows access, retrieval, and use of that data. **Data** is a collection of unprocessed items, which can include text, numbers, images, audio, and video. **Information** is processed data; that is, it is organized, meaningful, and useful. **Database software**, often called a **database management system** (**DBMS**), allows users to create a computerized database; add, modify, and delete the data; sort and retrieve the data; and create forms and reports from the data.

2. **What Are the Qualities of Valuable Information?** Most organizations realize that data is one of their more valuable assets — because data is used to generate information. It is vital that the data has integrity and is kept secure. Data integrity identifies the quality of the data. For information to be valuable, it should be accurate, verifiable, timely, organized, accessible, useful, and cost-effective. Accurate information is error free. Verifiable information can be proven as correct or incorrect. Timely information has an age suited to its use. Organized information is arranged to suit the needs and requirements of the decision maker. Accessible information is available when the decision maker needs it. Useful information has meaning to the person who receives it. Cost-effective information should give more value than it costs to produce.

3. **What Is Meant by Character, Field, Record, and File?** Data is classified in a hierarchy, with each level of data consisting of one or more items from the lower level. A bit is the smallest unit of data a computer can process. Eight bits grouped together in a unit form a byte, and each byte represents a single **character**, which can be a number, letter, space, punctuation mark, or other symbol. A **field** is a combination of one or more related characters and is the smallest unit of data a user accesses. A **record** is a group of related fields. A **data file** is a collection of related records stored on a storage medium.

4. **What Are File Maintenance Techniques and Validation Techniques?** **File maintenance** refers to the procedures that keep data current. File maintenance procedures include adding records when new data is obtained, modifying records to correct inaccurate data or to update old data with new data, and deleting records when they no longer are needed. **Validation** is the process of comparing data with a set of rules or values to find out if the data is correct. Many programs perform a validity check that analyzes data, either as you enter it or after you enter it, to help ensure that it is correct. Types of validity checks include an **alphabetic check**, a **numeric check**, a **range check**, a **consistency check**, a **completeness check**, and a **check digit**.

Visit the Computer Concepts CourseMate Web site at www.cengagebrain.com, navigate to the Chapter 9 Quiz Yourself resource for this book, and then click Objectives 1 – 4.

5. **How Is a File Processing Approach Different from a Database Approach?** In a **file processing system**, each department or area within an organization has its own set of data files. Two major weaknesses of file processing systems are redundant data (duplicated data) and isolated data. With a **database approach**, many programs and users share the data in a database. The database approach reduces data redundancy, improves data integrity, shares data, permits easier access, and reduces development time. A database, however, can be more complex than a file processing system, requiring special training and more computer memory, storage, and processing power. Data in a database also can be more vulnerable than data in file processing systems.

6. **What Functions Are Common to Most Database Management Systems?** With a database management system (DBMS), users can create, access, and manage a computerized database. Most DBMSs perform common functions. A **data dictionary** contains data about each file in the database and each field within those files. A DBMS offers several methods to retrieve and maintain data, such as query languages, query by example, forms, and report generators. A **query language** consists of simple, English-like statements that allow users to specify the data to display, print, or store. **Query by example** (**QBE**) has a graphical user interface that assists users with retrieving data. A **form** is a window on the screen that provides areas for entering or modifying data. A **report generator** allows users to design a report on the screen, retrieve data into the report design, and then display or print the report. To supply security, most DBMSs can identify different levels of access privileges that define the actions a specific user or group of users can perform for each field in a database. If a database is damaged or destroyed, a DBMS provides techniques to return the database to a usable form. A **backup** is a copy of the database.

A **log** is a listing of activities that change the contents of the database. A **recovery utility** uses the logs and/or backups to restore the database. **Continuous backup** is a backup plan in which all data is backed up whenever a change is made.

Visit the Computer Concepts CourseMate Web site at www.cengagebrain.com, navigate to the Chapter 9 Quiz Yourself resource for this book, and then click Objectives 5 – 6.

7. **What Are Characteristics of Relational, Object-Oriented, and Multidimensional Databases?** A **data model** consists of rules and standards that define how the database organizes data. Three popular data models are relational, object-oriented, and multidimensional. A **relational database** stores data in tables that consist of rows and columns. A relational database developer refers to a file as a **relation**, a record as a **tuple**, and a field as an **attribute**. A relational database user refers to a file as a **table**, a record as a **row**, and a field as a **column**. A **relationship** is a link within the data in a relational database. **Structured Query Language (SQL)** allows users to manage, update, and retrieve data in a relational database. An **object-oriented database (OODB)** stores data in objects. An **object** is an item that contains data, as well as the actions that read or process the data. Object-oriented databases often use an object query language (OQL) to manipulate and retrieve data. A **multidimensional database** stores data in dimensions. These multiple dimensions allow users to access and analyze any view of the database data. No standard query language exists for multidimensional databases. One application that uses multidimensional databases is a **data warehouse**, which is a huge database system that stores and manages the data required to analyze historical and current transactions. A smaller version of a data warehouse is the data mart.

8. **How Do You Interact with Web Databases?** A Web database links to a form on a Web page. To access data in a Web database, you fill in the form or enter search text on a Web page. A Web database usually resides on a database server, which is a computer that stores and provides access to a database.

9. **What Are the Responsibilities of Database Analysts and Administrators?** Database analysts and database administrators are responsible for managing and coordinating all database activities. A **database analyst (DA)** focuses on the meaning and usage of data. The DA decides on the placement of fields, defines the relationships among data, and identifies users' access privileges. A **database administrator (DBA)** requires a more technical inside view of the data. The DBA creates and maintains the data dictionary, manages database security, monitors database performance, and checks backup and recovery procedures. In small companies, one person often is both the DA and DBA. In larger companies, the responsibilities of the DA and DBA are split among two or more people.

Visit the Computer Concepts CourseMate Web site at www.cengagebrain.com, navigate to the Chapter 9 Quiz Yourself resource for this book, and then click Objectives 7 – 9.

Key Terms

You should know each key term. The list below helps focus your study.

To see an example of and a definition for each term, and to access current and additional information from the Web, visit the Computer Concepts CourseMate Web site at www.cengagebrain.com and then navigate to the Chapter 9 Key Terms resource for this book.

alphabetic check (360)
attribute (368)
backup (367)
character (355)
check digit (360)
collaborative databases (370)
column (368)
completeness check (360)
composite key (356)
consistency check (360)
continuous backup (367)
data (352)
data dictionary (364)
data file (356)
data model (368)
data type (356)

data warehouse (370)
database (352)
database administrator (DBA) (371)
database analyst (DA) (371)
database approach (361)
database management system (DBMS) (352)
database software (352)
field (355)
field name (355)
field size (355)
file maintenance (357)
file processing system (361)
form (366)

garbage in, garbage out (GIGO) (353)
information (352)
log (367)
multidimensional database (370)
numeric check (360)
object (369)
object-oriented database (OODB) (369)
primary key (356)
principle of least privilege (367)
query (364)
query by example (QBE) (366)

query language (364)
range check (360)
record (356)
recovery utility (367)
relation (368)
relational database (368)
relationship (368)
report generator (366)
row (368)
Structured Query Language (SQL) (369)
table (368)
tuple (368)
validation (359)

Checkpoint

The Checkpoint exercises test your knowledge of the chapter concepts. The page number containing the answer appears in parentheses after each exercise.

To complete the Checkpoint exercises interactively, visit the Computer Concepts CourseMate Web site at www.cengagebrain.com and then navigate to the Chapter 9 Checkpoint resource for this book.

Multiple Choice Select the best answer.

1. A _____ is a field that uniquely identifies each record in a file. (356)
   a. data type
   b. data file
   c. primary key
   d. data character

2. In some tables, the primary key consists of multiple fields, called a _____. (356)
   a. composite key
   b. secondary key
   c. key field
   d. column

3. _____ procedures include adding records to, modifying records in, and deleting records from a file. (357)
   a. Range check
   b. File maintenance
   c. Backup
   d. Validation

4. A _____ verifies that a required field contains data. (360)
   a. completeness check
   b. range check
   c. consistency check
   d. numeric check

5. When an organization uses _____, many programs and users share the data in the database. (361)
   a. a data model
   b. a file processing system
   c. the database approach
   d. a check digit

6. All of the following are strengths of the database approach, except _____. (362)
   a. less complexity
   b. improved data integrity
   c. reduced development time
   d. easier access

7. Many organizations adopt the _____ policy, where users' access privileges are limited to the lowest level necessary to perform required tasks. (367)
   a. golden rule
   b. principle of least privilege
   c. principle of highest access
   d. least order

8. The database analyst (DA) _____. (371)
   a. monitors the performance of the database
   b. creates and maintains the data dictionary
   c. decides on the proper placement of fields
   d. checks backup and recovery procedures

Matching Match the terms with their definitions.

_____ 1. field name (355)

_____ 2. field size (355)

_____ 3. query language (364)

_____ 4. recovery utility (367)

_____ 5. database administrator (371)

a. consists of simple, English-like statements that allow users to specify the data to display, print, or store
b. item that contains data and the actions that read or process the data
c. defines the maximum number of characters a field can contain
d. uses the logs and/or backups to restore a database when it becomes damaged or destroyed
e. uniquely identifies each field
f. creates and maintains the data dictionary, manages security of the database, monitors the performance of the database, and checks backup and recovery procedures

Short Answer Write a brief answer to each of the following questions.

1. What is data integrity and why is it important? _____ What does the computing phrase, garbage in, garbage out (GIGO), mean? _____

2. What is validation? _____ What are five types of validity checks? _____

3. Why is data redundancy a weakness of file processing systems? _____ Why is isolated data a weakness of file processing systems? _____

4. What is the database approach? _____ Describe five strengths of the database approach. _____

5. What is contained in a data dictionary? _____ How does a query language differ from query by example (QBE)? _____

Problem Solving

The Problem Solving exercises extend your knowledge of the chapter concepts by seeking solutions to practical computer problems that you may encounter at home, school, or work. The Collaboration exercise should be completed with a team.

In the real world, practical problems often can be solved in multiple ways. Provide one solution to each of the following problems using available resources, such as articles on the Web or in print, blogs, podcasts, videos, television, user guides, other individuals, and electronics and computer stores. You may need to use multiple resources to obtain an answer. Present your solutions in the form requested by your instructor (brief report, presentation, discussion, or other means).

@ Home

1. **Value Too Long**   As a teacher's assistant at a local high school, you keep track of student grades in a Microsoft Access database. When you enter the last name of one of the students, you receive an error message stating that the value is too long for the field. What are your next steps?

2. **Account Already Exists**   While registering for an account on an online photo sharing community, you receive an error message stating that an account with your e-mail address already exists. You are unable to remember whether you have registered for an account on that Web site previously, and want to access the other account, if it exists. What are your next steps?

3. **Cannot Access Web Database**   To prepare for your upcoming wedding, you have been using a Web application to maintain your guest list. This Web application stores each guest's name, contact information, and whether he or she will attend. Today when you attempt to access this information, the Web site is unavailable. How can you ensure access to your guest list if the site is unavailable in the future?

@ Work

4. **Error Opening Database**   While attempting to open a database, you receive an error message stating that the database is damaged. What are your next steps?

5. **Accidentally Deleted Records**   While working in Microsoft Access, you select all records to copy them to another table in the database. Instead of copying the records, you accidentally press another key combination that removes all records from the table. Your attempt to paste the records back into the table is unsuccessful and the records appear to have been removed permanently. What steps will you take to restore the records?

6. **Incorrect Password**   At work, your company's database requires a password to access it. When you attempt to open the database, a dialog box requesting the database password is displayed. After typing your password and pressing the ENTER key, an error message states that your password is invalid. The same message appears on your next attempt. What are your next steps?

7. **Duplicate Records Exist**   A search of your company's employee database reveals that duplicate records exist for multiple employees. You notice minor differences between each record and believe that you should remove duplicate records to decrease data redundancy; however, you do not want to lose data that might be valuable. What steps will you take to back up the database before removing the duplicate records?

Collaboration

8. **Computers in Health Sciences**   Your physician, who once shared an office with three other physicians, has decided to open his own practice. Because his former colleagues will not allow him to take patient data to his new office, he needs to establish a method of recording and tracking patient data. Form a team of three people to determine a good strategy to collect and maintain data. One team member should research various database management systems and provide a recommendation on the most useful one for this practice. Another team member should research which specific patient data the database should store, and the third team member should research the computer hardware necessary to store, update, maintain, and properly back up the data. Compile your findings in a report and submit it to your instructor.

Learn How To

The Learn How To activities step you through fundamental technology skills when using a computer. The Learn How To exercises enable you to become more proficient with these skills.

Premium Activity: To relate this Learn How To activity to your everyday life, see a visual demonstration of the activity, and complete a short assessment, visit the Computer Concepts CourseMate Web site at www.cengagebrain.com and then navigate to the Chapter 9 Learn How To resource for this book.

Learn How To 1: Organize and Manage Files on a Computer

Introduction   In Learn How To 1 in Chapter 3 (page 138), you learned the procedure for saving a file. In this Learn How To activity, you will learn how to manage files using folders and how to find a file if you cannot remember where you saved it.

Folders   A folder is a virtual container where you can store a file on media. When you store any file, the file must be stored in a folder. The folder symbol, together with the folder name, identifies a folder.

You can create folders in a variety of ways. To create a folder on the desktop, complete the following steps:

1. Right-click the desktop in a location that does not contain an icon or toolbar.
2. Point to New on the shortcut menu that is displayed (Figure 9-21).
3. Click Folder on the New submenu.
4. When the folder icon is displayed on the desktop, type the name you want to assign to the folder and then press the ENTER key. You should choose a name that identifies the contents of the folder.

A folder can contain other folders. This allows you to organize your files in a hierarchical manner so that the highest-level folder contains all the folders for a given subject, and lower-level folders contain more specific files and folders. For example, your highest-level folder could be named Fall Semester. For each class, such as Computer Information Systems 110, you could define a folder within the Fall Semester folder. Within each class folder, you could define folders for each week of the class, or for each project or assignment within the class. In this manner, you would have a set of folders, each designated for a specific use. You then would save your files in the appropriate folder.

Figure 9-21

To create a folder within a folder, complete the following steps:

1. Double-click the folder name either on the desktop or in the window or dialog box in which the folder name appears.
2. Click the New folder button.
3. When the folder icon is displayed, type the name you want to assign to the folder, and then press the ENTER key.

To delete a folder, complete the following steps:

1. Right-click the folder.
2. On the shortcut menu that is displayed (Figure 9-22), click Delete.
3. In the Delete Folder dialog box, click the Yes button.

When you delete a folder, all the files and folders contained in the folder you are deleting, together with all files and folders on the lower hierarchical levels, are deleted.

Figure 9-22

If you accidentally delete a folder, complete the following steps:
1. Double-click the Recycle Bin icon on the desktop.
2. In the Recycle Bin window, select the folder you wish to restore.
3. Click the 'Restore this item' button.

Using folders effectively will aid you in keeping track of files you create for your classes.

Exercises

1. Assume you are taking the following courses: Computer Information Systems 120, History 210, English 145, Marketing 221, and Business Law 120. Define the hierarchy of folders you would create for these classes. In which folder would you store an assignment from English 145 that was assigned in the sixth week of class? Submit your answers to your instructor.

2. Windows creates a collection of folders that is associated with each user account. For example, each user might have a My Pictures folder that stores pictures, and a My Documents folder that stores documents. What subfolders exist in your My Documents folder? In addition to the subfolders already present, what subfolders might you add in the future to help organize your files? What subfolders, if any, exist in your My Pictures folder? What is your hierarchy of subfolders in the My Pictures folder? Finally, explain why organizing your files is important.

Learn It Online

The Learn It Online exercises are interactive Web exercises designed to reinforce and expand your understanding of the chapter concepts. The descriptions below briefly summarize each exercise.

To complete the Learn It Online exercises, visit the Computer Concepts CourseMate Web site at www.cengagebrain.com, navigate to the Chapter 9 resources for this book, click the link for the exercise you want to complete, and then read the instructions.

1 At the Movies — How a Photo Sharing Site Keeps Its Data
Watch a movie to visit Equinix, the data storage site for Smugmug.com, and learn how photos are uploaded and shared on the Web, and then answer questions about the movie.

2 Student Edition Labs — Advanced Databases and Advanced Spreadsheets
Enhance your understanding and knowledge about advanced databases and advanced spreadsheets by completing the Advanced Databases and Advanced Spreadsheets Labs.

3 Practice Test
Take a multiple choice test that checks your knowledge of the chapter concepts and review the resulting study guide.

4 Who Wants To Be a Computer Genius²?
Play the Shelly Cashman Series version of this popular game by answering questions to find out if you are a computer genius. Panic buttons are available to provide assistance during game play.

5 Crossword Puzzle Challenge
Complete an interactive crossword puzzle to reinforce concepts presented in this chapter.

6 Windows Exercises
Step through the Windows 7 exercises to learn about managing files and folders, creating folders, and moving and deleting files.

7 Exploring Computer Careers
Read about a career as a database administrator, search for related employment advertisements, and then answer related questions.

8 Web Apps — Windows Live Calendar
Learn how to use Windows Live Calendar to create events, display a list of recent and upcoming events, share your calendar, and display items in your to-do list.

Web Research

The Web Research exercises broaden your understanding of chapter concepts by presenting questions that require you to search the Web for answers.

1 Search Sleuth

Use one of the search engines listed in Figure 2-8 in Chapter 2 on page 65 or your own favorite search engine to find the answers to the following questions. Copy and paste the Web address from the Web page where you found the answer. Some questions may have more than one answer. If required, submit your answers to your instructor. (1) How many seconds did it take Google's 1,000 computers to sort 1 TB of data in 2008? (2) Which company has built data centers in Kronstorf, Austria; Goose Creek, South Carolina; and Dalles, Oregon? (3) Which energy source do Ormat and Raser Technologies use? (4) What is the name of the database system Charles Bachman helped create? (5) What geographic information system (GIS) functions does ArcExplorer perform? (6) What are the ACID rules for executed transactions?

2 Green Computing

Corporations are building eco-friendly data centers to help reduce power consumption while they are exploring alternative energy sources. AMD, Intel, IBM, Sun Microsystems, and Microsoft have formed The Green Grid to explore data center

efficiency worldwide. Google has publicized its commitment to develop clean energy solutions for its power-hungry data centers. The U.S. Green Building Council awards certifications to data centers meeting rigorous energy-efficiency standards. View online Web sites that provide information about companies that are making strides to reduce their data centers' power consumption. Which companies are developing geothermal power plants to run the data centers? In which areas of the world is Google exploring and building data centers to take advantage of favorable geographical and environmental factors, including renewable energy sources? Which companies are planning to build data centers driven by tidal and wave power? Which companies have earned a U.S. Green Building Council certification? Write a report summarizing your findings, and include a table of links to Web sites that provide additional details.

3 Social Networking

Bebo is the third largest online social network and has a strong presence in the United Kingdom. It has an active instant messaging partnership with Microsoft Windows Live Messenger and AOL's AIM. The online social network also partners with iTunes to allow Bebo users to buy music directly from the 700,000 musicians with a Bebo profile and whose music is available on iTunes. Visit the Bebo site (bebo.com) and view several profiles in the Video, Music, Authors, Groups, and Applications categories. Which features, news, and polls are listed in the More Fun Stuff group? Which weekly highlights from the Gap Year are available? Click the Safety link at the bottom of the home page and read the advice regarding safe online social networking. Summarize the information you read and viewed.

4 Blogs

Dave Winer developed the Scripting News Web site in 1997 before the term "Weblog" had been coined, and he continues to post to his blog on a regular basis. Scripting News is the longest-running blog on the Internet. Visit the Scripting News blog (scripting.com) and read Winer's biographical information on the home page. What technological breakthroughs did he develop? What are his employment and educational backgrounds? What are the three most recent topics discussed? Locate the article posted on or closest to your most recent birthday and then summarize the article. Which podcasts are listed in the Morning Coffee Notes? Click the Archive link at the top of the page and then click the year and month three years ago from today. What topics were posted at that time? Summarize the information you read and viewed.

5 Ethics in Action

Businesses automatically store data about you and your transactions in a marketing database when you shop online, enter contests, and complete warranty registration cards. They often use this data to analyze sales and develop advertising campaigns. Unbeknownst to many consumers, some companies also sell this data to third parties for financial gain. Consumers can refuse to receive targeted e-mail messages and marketing materials, but they actively must search the Web sites or paper forms for check boxes to indicate these opt-out preferences. Some privacy experts, however, view this practice as unethical and urge businesses to default to not adding consumers' information to databases unless the consumer opts in to receive additional materials. View online sites that include opt-in or opt-out provisions. Write a report summarizing your findings, and include a table of links to Web sites that provide additional details about protecting consumers' data.

Chapter Ten

Computer Security and Safety, Ethics, and Privacy

Objectives

After completing this chapter, you will be able to:

1 Describe various types of Internet and network attacks (computer viruses, worms, Trojan horses, rootkits, botnets, denial of service attacks, back doors, and spoofing), and identify ways to safeguard against these attacks, including firewalls and intrusion detection software

2 Discuss techniques to prevent unauthorized computer access and use

3 Identify safeguards against hardware theft and vandalism

4 Explain the ways to protect against software theft and information theft

5 Discuss the types of devices available that protect computers from system failure

6 Identify risks and safeguards associated with wireless communications

7 Discuss ways to prevent health-related disorders and injuries due to computer use

8 Discuss issues surrounding information privacy, including electronic profiles, cookies, spyware and adware, spam, phishing, privacy laws, social engineering, employee monitoring, and content filtering

Computer Security Risks

Today, people rely on computers to create, store, and manage critical information. Thus, it is crucial that users take measures to protect their computers and data from loss, damage, and misuse.

A **computer security risk** is any event or action that could cause a loss of or damage to computer hardware, software, data, information, or processing capability. While some breaches to computer security are accidental, many are intentional. Some intruders do no damage; they merely access data, information, or programs on the computer. Other intruders indicate some evidence of their presence either by leaving a message or by deliberately altering or damaging data.

An intentional breach of computer security often involves a deliberate act that is against the law. Any illegal act involving a computer generally is referred to as a **computer crime**. The term **cybercrime** refers to online or Internet-based illegal acts. Today, cybercrime is one of the FBI's top three priorities.

Perpetrators of cybercrime and other intrusions fall into seven basic categories: hacker, cracker, script kiddie, corporate spy, unethical employee, cyberextortionist, and cyberterrorist.

- The term **hacker**, although originally a complimentary word for a computer enthusiast, now has a derogatory meaning and refers to someone who accesses a computer or network illegally. Some hackers claim the intent of their security breaches is to improve security.

- A **cracker** also is someone who accesses a computer or network illegally but has the intent of destroying data, stealing information, or other malicious action. Both hackers and crackers have advanced computer and network skills.

- A **script kiddie** has the same intent as a cracker but does not have the technical skills and knowledge. Script kiddies often use prewritten hacking and cracking programs to break into computers.

- Some corporate spies have excellent computer and networking skills and are hired to break into a specific computer and steal its proprietary data and information. Unscrupulous companies hire corporate spies, a practice known as corporate espionage, to gain a competitive advantage.

- Unethical employees break into their employers' computers for a variety of reasons. Some simply want to exploit a security weakness. Others seek financial gains from selling confidential information. Disgruntled employees may want revenge.

- A **cyberextortionist** is someone who uses e-mail as a vehicle for extortion. These perpetrators send an organization a threatening e-mail message indicating they will expose confidential information, exploit a security flaw, or launch an attack that will compromise the organization's network — if they are not paid a sum of money.

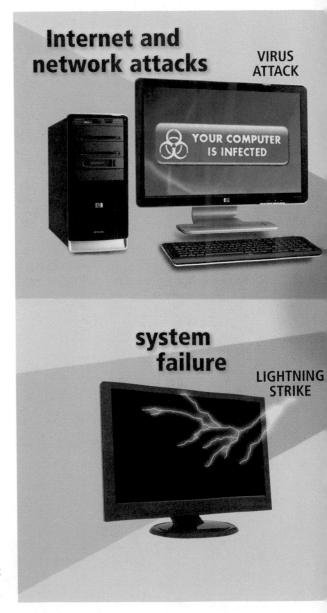

Internet and network attacks

VIRUS ATTACK

YOUR COMPUTER IS INFECTED

system failure

LIGHTNING STRIKE

- A **cyberterrorist** is someone who uses the Internet or network to destroy or damage computers for political reasons. The cyberterrorist might target the nation's air traffic control system, electricity-generating companies, or a telecommunications infrastructure. Cyberterrorism usually requires a team of highly skilled individuals, millions of dollars, and several years of planning.

Business and home users must protect, or safeguard, their computers from breaches of security and other computer security risks. Some organizations hire individuals previously convicted of computer crimes to help identify security risks and implement safeguards because these individuals know how criminals attempt to breach security.

The more common computer security risks include Internet and network attacks, unauthorized access and use, hardware theft, software theft, information theft, and system failure (Figure 10-1). The following pages describe these computer security risks and also discuss safeguards users might take to minimize or prevent their consequences.

unauthorized access and use

INTERCEPTING WIRELESS COMMUNICATIONS

hardware theft

STOLEN COMPUTER

SECURITY RISKS

software theft

information theft

STOLEN IDENTITY

ILLEGAL COPYING

Figure 10-1 Computers and computer users are exposed to several types of security risks.

Internet and Network Attacks

Information transmitted over networks has a higher degree of security risk than information kept on an organization's premises. In an organization, network administrators usually take measures to protect a network from security risks. On the Internet, where no central administrator is present, the security risk is greater.

Internet and network attacks that jeopardize security include computer viruses, worms, Trojan horses, and rootkits; botnets; denial of service attacks; back doors; and spoofing. The following sections address these computer security risks and suggest measures organizations and individuals can take to protect their computers while on the Internet or connected to a network.

Computer Viruses, Worms, Trojan Horses, and Rootkits

Every unprotected computer is susceptible to the first type of computer security risk — a computer virus, worm, Trojan horse, and/or rootkit.

- A computer **virus** is a potentially damaging computer program that affects, or infects, a computer negatively by altering the way the computer works without the user's knowledge or permission. Once the virus infects the computer, it can spread throughout and may damage files and system software, including the operating system.
- A **worm** is a program that copies itself repeatedly, for example in memory or on a network, using up resources and possibly shutting down the computer or network.
- A **Trojan horse** (named after the Greek myth) is a program that hides within or looks like a legitimate program. A certain condition or action usually triggers the Trojan horse. Unlike a virus or worm, a Trojan horse does not replicate itself to other computers.
- A **rootkit** is a program that hides in a computer and allows someone from a remote location to take full control of the computer. Once the rootkit is installed, the rootkit author can execute programs, change settings, monitor activity, and access files on the remote computer.

Computer viruses, worms, Trojan horses, and rootkits are classified as **malware** (short for malicious software), which are programs that act without a user's knowledge and deliberately alter the computer's operations. Unscrupulous programmers write malware and then test it to ensure it can deliver its payload. The **payload** is the destructive event or prank the program is intended to deliver. A computer infected by a virus, worm, Trojan horse, or rootkit often has one or more of the following symptoms:

- Operating system runs much slower than usual
- Available memory is less than expected
- Files become corrupted
- Screen displays unusual message or image
- Unknown programs or files mysteriously appear
- Music or unusual sound plays randomly
- Existing programs and files disappear
- Programs or files do not work properly
- System properties change
- Operating system does not start up
- Operating system shuts down unexpectedly

Currently, more than 300,000 Web sites can infect your computer with known viruses, worms, Trojan horses, rootkits, and other malware. These malicious programs deliver their payload on a computer in a variety of ways: when a user (1) opens an infected file, (2) runs an infected program, (3) boots the computer with infected removable media inserted in a drive or plugged in a port, (4) connects an unprotected computer to a network, or (5) when a certain condition or event occurs, such as the computer's clock changing to a specific date. A common way computers become infected with viruses and other malware is through users opening infected e-mail attachments (Figure 10-2).

How a Virus Can Spread through an E-Mail Message

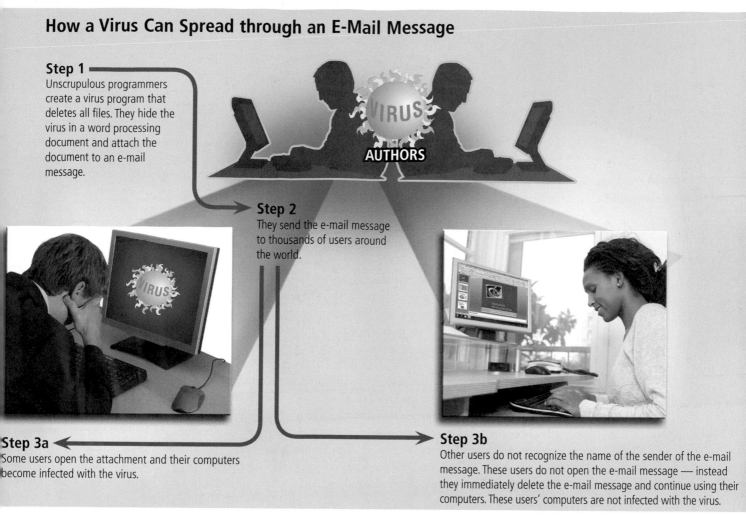

Step 1
Unscrupulous programmers create a virus program that deletes all files. They hide the virus in a word processing document and attach the document to an e-mail message.

Step 2
They send the e-mail message to thousands of users around the world.

Step 3a
Some users open the attachment and their computers become infected with the virus.

Step 3b
Other users do not recognize the name of the sender of the e-mail message. These users do not open the e-mail message — instead they immediately delete the e-mail message and continue using their computers. These users' computers are not infected with the virus.

Figure 10-2   This figure shows how a virus can spread through an e-mail message.

? | **FAQ 10-1**

Can multimedia files be infected with a virus?

Yes. The increase in popularity of media sharing Web sites provides a great opportunity to distribute malicious programs. During one year, approximately 500,000 people downloaded what they thought was a media file from the Internet. In fact, the file was a Trojan horse that infected many computers with spyware. For this reason, it is important to scan all media files for malware before playing them.

For more information, visit the Computer Concepts CourseMate Web site at www.cengagebrain.com, navigate to the Chapter 10 FAQ resource for this book, and then click Infected Media Files.

Safeguards against Computer Viruses and Other Malware

Users can take several precautions to protect their home and work computers and mobile devices from these malicious infections. The following paragraphs discuss these precautionary measures.

Do not start a computer with removable media, such as optical discs and USB flash drives, in the drives or ports — unless you are certain the media are uninfected or from a trusted source. A **trusted source** is an organization or person you believe will not send a virus infected file knowingly. Never open an e-mail attachment unless you are expecting the attachment *and* it is from a trusted source. If the e-mail message is from an unknown source, delete the e-mail message immediately — without opening or executing any attachments. If the e-mail message is from a trusted source, but you were not expecting an attachment, carefully check the spelling of the e-mail address and contents of the message for errors because perpetrators often make typographical errors. If the message is error-free, verify with the source that they intended to send you an attachment — before opening it.

Some viruses are hidden in macros, which are instructions saved in software such as a word processing or spreadsheet program. In programs that allow users to write macros, you should set the macro security level so that the application software warns users that a document they are attempting to open contains a macro. From this warning, a user chooses to disable or enable the macro. If the document is from a trusted source, the user can enable the macro. Otherwise, it should be disabled.

Users should install an antivirus program and update it frequently. An **antivirus program** protects a computer against viruses by identifying and removing any computer viruses found in memory, on storage media, or on incoming files. Most antivirus programs also protect against other malware. When you purchase a new computer, it often includes antivirus software. Many e-mail servers also have antivirus programs installed to check incoming and outgoing e-mail messages for malware.

An antivirus program scans for programs that attempt to modify the boot program, the operating system, and other programs that normally are read from but not modified. In addition, many antivirus programs automatically scan files downloaded from the Web, e-mail attachments, opened files, and all removable media inserted in the computer.

One technique that antivirus programs use to identify a virus is to look for virus signatures. A **virus signature**, also called a **virus definition**, is a known specific pattern of virus code. Computer users should update their antivirus program's signature files regularly (Figure 10-3). This extremely important activity allows the antivirus program to protect against viruses written since the antivirus program was released and/or its last update. Most antivirus programs contain an automatic update feature that regularly prompts users to download the virus signature, usually at least once a week. The vendor usually provides this service to registered users at no cost for a specified time.

If an antivirus program identifies an infected file, it attempts to remove the malware. If the antivirus program cannot remove the infection, it often quarantines the infected file. A **quarantine** is a separate area of a hard disk that holds the infected file until the infection can be removed. This step ensures other files will not become infected. Quarantined files remain on your computer until you delete them or restore them.

Some users also install a personal firewall program to protect a computer and its data from unauthorized intrusions. A section later in this chapter discusses firewalls.

Figure 10-3
This antivirus program, which protects a computer from a variety of malware, regularly checks for the latest virus signatures and other important updates.

Finally, stay informed about new virus alerts and virus hoaxes. A **virus hoax** is an e-mail message that warns users of a nonexistent virus or other malware. Often, these virus hoaxes are in the form of a chain letter that requests the user to send a copy of the e-mail message to as many people as possible. The content of the hoax message, for example, may inform users that an important operating system file on their computer is a virus and encourage them to delete the file, which could make their computer unusable. Instead of forwarding the message, visit a Web site that publishes a list of virus alerts and virus hoaxes.

The list in Figure 10-4 summarizes important tips for protecting your computer from viruses and other malware.

Tips for Preventing Viruses and Other Malware

1. Never start a computer with removable media inserted in the drives or plugged in the ports, unless the media are uninfected.

2. Never open an e-mail attachment unless you are expecting it *and* it is from a trusted source.

3. Set the macro security in programs so that you can enable or disable macros. Enable macros only if the document is from a trusted source and you are expecting it.

4. Install an antivirus program on all of your computers. Update the software and the virus signature files regularly.

5. Scan all downloaded programs for viruses and other malware.

6. If the antivirus program flags an e-mail attachment as infected, delete or quarantine the attachment immediately.

7. Before using any removable media, scan the media for malware. Follow this procedure even for shrink-wrapped software from major developers. Some commercial software has been infected and distributed to unsuspecting users.

8. Install a personal firewall program.

9. Stay informed about new virus alerts and virus hoaxes.

Figure 10-4 With the growing number of new viruses and other malware, it is crucial that users take steps to protect their computers.

Botnets

A **botnet** is a group of compromised computers connected to a network such as the Internet that are used as part of a network that attacks other networks, usually for nefarious purposes. A compromised computer, known as a **zombie**, is one whose owner is unaware the computer is being controlled remotely by an outsider. Cybercriminals use botnets to send spam via e-mail, spread viruses and other malware, or commit a denial of service attack.

? **FAQ 10-2**

How can I tell if my computer is a zombie or in a botnet?

The number of zombie computers is increasing at a rapid rate. Your computer may be a zombie or part of a botnet if you notice unusually high disk activity, a slower than normal Internet connection, or devices connected to your computer becoming increasingly unresponsive. The chances of your computer becoming a zombie or part of a botnet greatly increase if you do not have an effective firewall.

For more information, visit the Computer Concepts CourseMate Web site at www.cengagebrain.com, navigate to the Chapter 10 FAQ resource for this book, and then click Zombies and Botnets.

Denial of Service Attacks

A **denial of service attack**, or **DoS attack**, is an assault whose purpose is to disrupt computer access to an Internet service such as the Web or e-mail. Perpetrators carry out a DoS attack in a variety of ways. For example, they may use an unsuspecting computer to send an influx of confusing data messages or useless traffic to a computer network. The victim computer network slows down considerably and eventually becomes unresponsive or unavailable, blocking legitimate visitors from accessing the network.

Perpetrators have a variety of motives for carrying out a DoS attack. Those who disagree with the beliefs or actions of a particular organization claim political anger motivates their attacks. Some perpetrators use the attack as a vehicle for extortion. Others simply want the recognition, even though it is negative.

DoS Attacks

For more information, visit the Computer Concepts CourseMate Web site at www.cengagebrain.com, navigate to the Chapter 10 Web Link resource for this book, and then click DoS Attacks.

Back Doors

A **back door** is a program or set of instructions in a program that allow users to bypass security controls when accessing a program, computer, or network. Once perpetrators gain access to unsecure computers, they often install a back door or modify an existing program to include a back door, which allows them to continue to access the computer remotely without the user's knowledge.

Spoofing

Spoofing is a technique intruders use to make their network or Internet transmission appear legitimate to a victim computer or network. E-mail spoofing occurs when the sender's address or other components of the e-mail header are altered so that it appears the e-mail originated from a different sender. E-mail spoofing commonly is used for virus hoaxes, spam, and phishing scams. IP spoofing occurs when an intruder computer fools a network into believing its IP address is associated with a trusted source. Perpetrators of IP spoofing trick their victims into interacting with a phony Web site.

Safeguards against Botnets, DoS Attacks, Back Doors, and Spoofing

To defend against botnets, DoS attacks, improper use of back doors, and spoofing, users can implement firewall solutions and install intrusion detection software. The following sections discuss these safeguards.

Firewalls

A **firewall** is hardware and/or software that protects a network's resources from intrusion by users on another network such as the Internet (Figure 10-5). All networked and online computer users should implement a firewall solution.

Figure 10-5 A firewall is hardware and/or software that protects a network's resources from intrusion by users on another network such as the Internet.

Organizations use firewalls to protect network resources from outsiders and to restrict employees' access to sensitive data such as payroll or personnel records. They can implement a firewall solution themselves or outsource their needs to a company specializing in providing firewall protection. Large organizations often route all their communications through a proxy server, which is a component of the firewall. A proxy server is a server outside the organization's network that controls which communications pass into the organization's network.

Home and small office/home office users often protect their computers with a personal firewall utility. A **personal firewall** is a utility program that detects and protects a personal computer and its data from unauthorized intrusions. Some operating systems, such as Windows, include personal firewalls.

Some small office/home office users purchase a hardware firewall, such as a router or other device that has a built-in firewall, in addition to or instead of personal firewall software. Hardware firewalls stop intrusions before they attempt to affect your computer maliciously.

Firewalls

For more information, visit the Computer Concepts CourseMate Web site at www.cengagebrain.com, navigate to the Chapter 10 Web Link resource for this book, and then click Firewalls.

Intrusion Detection Software

To provide extra protection against hackers and other intruders, large organizations sometimes use intrusion detection software to identify possible security breaches. **Intrusion detection software** automatically analyzes all network traffic, assesses system vulnerabilities, identifies any unauthorized access (intrusions), and notifies network administrators of suspicious behavior patterns or system breaches.

To utilize intrusion detection software requires the expertise of a network administrator because the programs are complex and difficult to use and interpret. These programs also are quite expensive.

Unauthorized Access and Use

Another type of computer security risk is unauthorized access and use. **Unauthorized access** is the use of a computer or network without permission. **Unauthorized use** is the use of a computer or its data for unapproved or possibly illegal activities. Unauthorized use includes a variety of activities: an employee using an organization's computer to send personal e-mail messages, an employee using the organization's word processing software to track his or her child's soccer league scores, or someone gaining access to a bank computer and performing an unauthorized transfer.

Safeguards against Unauthorized Access and Use

Organizations take several measures to help prevent unauthorized access and use. At a minimum, they should have a written acceptable use policy (AUP) that outlines the computer activities for which the computer and network may and may not be used. An organization's AUP should specify the acceptable use of computers by employees for personal reasons. Some organizations prohibit such use entirely. Others allow personal use on the employee's own time such as a lunch hour.

Other measures that safeguard against unauthorized access and use include firewalls and intrusion detection software, which were discussed in the previous section, and identifying and authenticating users.

Identifying and Authenticating Users

Many organizations use access controls to minimize the chance that a perpetrator intentionally may access or an employee accidentally may access confidential information on a computer. An **access control** is a security measure that defines who can access a computer, when they can access it, and what actions they can take while accessing the computer. In addition, the computer should maintain an **audit trail** that records in a file both successful and unsuccessful access attempts. An unsuccessful access attempt could result from a user mistyping his or her password, or it could result from a hacker trying thousands of passwords.

Organizations should investigate unsuccessful access attempts immediately to ensure they are not intentional breaches of security. They also should review successful access for irregularities, such as use of the computer after normal working hours or from remote computers.

Many systems implement access controls using a two-phase process called identification and authentication. Identification verifies that an individual is a valid user. Authentication verifies that the individual is the person he or she claims to be. Three methods of identification and authentication include user names and passwords, possessed objects, and biometric devices. The technique(s) an organization uses should correspond to the degree of risk associated with the unauthorized access.

User Names and Passwords A **user name**, or user ID (identification), is a unique combination of characters, such as letters of the alphabet or numbers, that identifies one specific user. A **password** is a private combination of characters associated with the user name that allows access to certain computer resources.

Most multiuser (networked) operating systems require that users correctly enter a user name and a password before they can access the data, information, and programs stored on a computer or network (Figure 10-6).

Multiuser systems typically require that users select their own passwords. Users typically choose an easy-to-remember word or series of characters for passwords. If your password is too obvious, however, such as your initials or birthday, others can guess it easily. Easy passwords make it simple for hackers and other intruders to break into a system. Hackers use computer automated tools to assist them with guessing passwords. Thus, you should select a password carefully. Longer passwords provide greater security than shorter ones. Each character added to a password significantly increases the number of possible combinations and the length of time it might take for someone or for a hacker's computer to guess the password (Figure 10-7).

In addition to a user name and password, some systems ask users to enter one of several pieces of personal information. Such items can include a spouse's first name, a birth date, a place of birth, or a mother's maiden name. As with a password, if the user's response does not match the information on file, the system denies access.

Some Web sites use a CAPTCHA to further protect a user's password. A **CAPTCHA**, which stands for Completely Automated Public Turing test to tell Computers and Humans Apart, is a program that verifies user input is not computer generated. A CAPTCHA displays a series of distorted characters and requires the user to enter the characters correctly to continue using the Web site. For visually impaired users, the CAPTCHA text can be read aloud. Because unscrupulous individuals attempt to circumvent or decode CAPTCHAs, developers continually are seeking ways to make them more secure or develop alternative authentication techniques.

Figure 10-6 Many Web sites that maintain personal and confidential data require a user to enter a user name and password.

Password Protection

Number of Characters	Possible Combinations	AVERAGE TIME TO DISCOVER	
		Human	Computer
1	36	3 minutes	.000018 second
2	1,300	2 hours	.00065 second
3	47,000	3 days	.02 second
4	1,700,000	3 months	1 second
5	60,000,000	10 years	30 seconds
10	3,700,000,000,000,000	580 million years	59 years

- Possible characters include the letters A–Z and numbers 0–9
- Human discovery assumes 1 try every 10 seconds
- Computer discovery assumes 1 million tries per second
- Average time assumes the password would be discovered in approximately half the time it would take to try all possible combinations

Figure 10-7   This table shows the effect of increasing the length of a password that consists of letters and numbers. The longer the password, the more effort required to discover it. Long passwords, however, are more difficult for users to remember.

Possessed Objects   A **possessed object** is any item that you must carry to gain access to a computer or computer facility. Examples of possessed objects are badges, cards, smart cards, and keys. The card you use in an automated teller machine (ATM) is a possessed object that allows access to your bank account.

Possessed objects often are used in combination with personal identification numbers. A **personal identification number (PIN)** is a numeric password, either assigned by a company or selected by a user. PINs provide an additional level of security. An ATM card typically requires a four-digit PIN. PINs are passwords. Select them carefully and protect them as you do any other password.

Biometric Devices   A **biometric device** authenticates a person's identity by translating a personal characteristic, such as a fingerprint, into a digital code that is compared with a digital code stored in the computer verifying a physical or behavioral characteristic. If the digital code in the computer does not match the personal characteristic code, the computer denies access to the individual.

Biometric devices grant access to programs, computers, or rooms using computer analysis of some biometric identifier. Examples of biometric devices and systems include fingerprint readers (Figure 10-8), hand geometry systems, face recognition systems, voice verification systems, signature verification systems, iris recognition systems, and retinal scanners. Many grocery stores, retail stores, and gas stations now use **biometric payment**, where the customer's fingerprint is read by a fingerprint reader that is linked to a specific payment method such as a checking account or credit card.

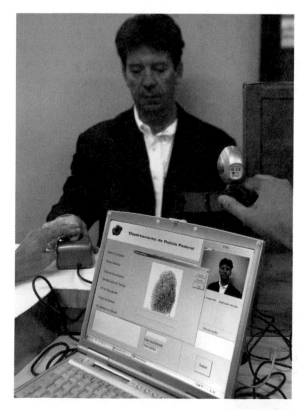

Figure 10-8
A fingerprint reader verifies this traveler's identity.

? FAQ 10-3

How many people are victims of identity theft each year?

Studies reveal that identity theft is the fastest growing crime in the United States. In fact, identity theft costs banks, victims, and the government millions of dollars each year, with that amount continually increasing. The chart to the right illustrates the reported number of identity theft cases grouped by age.

Identity Theft — Complaints by Victim Age

50–59 13%
60 and over 9%
Under 18 5%
18–29 29%
40–49 20%
30–39 24%

Source: FTC.gov

📮 For more information, visit the Computer Concepts CourseMate Web site at www.cengagebrain.com, navigate to the Chapter 10 FAQ resource for this book, and then click Identity Theft.

Digital Forensics

Digital forensics, also called computer forensics, network forensics, or cyberforensics, is the discovery, collection, and analysis of evidence found on computers and networks. Digital forensics involves the examination of computer media, programs, data and log files on computers, servers, and networks. Many areas use digital forensics, including law enforcement, criminal prosecutors, military intelligence, insurance agencies, and information security departments in the private sector.

A digital forensics examiner must have knowledge of the law, technical experience with many types of hardware and software products, superior communication skills, familiarity with corporate structures and policies, a willingness to learn and update skills, and a knack for problem solving. For a look at the next generation of forensics, read Looking Ahead 10-1.

↗ LOOKING AHEAD 10-1

Brain Waves, Behavior Tracked to Prevent and Solve Crimes

The brain may one day become part of a crime scene investigation. When a person has committed a criminal or fraudulent act, his brain generates unique waves involuntarily when confronted with pictures, sounds, and words related to the crime scene. Computers can capture and analyze this brain fingerprint of distinctive brain waves to determine if a person has stored critical details of a particular felony or misdemeanor situation.

Similarly, behavior detection systems study a person's body language, facial expressions, speech, and emotions to isolate specific patterns that criminals commonly exhibit. The surveillance systems can recognize microexpressions, which are the split-second emotions lasting one-fifteenth of a second, on a person's face.

The U.S. Department of Homeland Security is testing its Future Attribute Screening Technologies (FAST) program, which uses cameras, infrared heat sensors, and lasers to measure pulse and breathing rates. The trial technology is being tested for use at airports and sporting and music events.

📮 For more information, visit the Computer Concepts CourseMate Web site at www.cengagebrain.com, navigate to the Chapter 10 Looking Ahead resource for this book, and then click Brain Fingerprinting.

✔ QUIZ YOURSELF 10-1

Instructions: Find the true statement below. Then, rewrite the remaining false statements so that they are true.

1. A back door attack is an assault whose purpose is to disrupt computer access to an Internet service such as the Web or e-mail.

2. All networked and online computer users should implement a firewall solution.

3. Computer viruses, worms, Trojan horses, and rootkits are malware that acts with a user's knowledge.

4. Shorter passwords provide greater security than longer ones.

5. Updating an antivirus program's quarantine protects a computer against viruses written since the antivirus program was released.

📮 **Quiz Yourself Online:** To further check your knowledge of pages 382 through 392, visit the Computer Concepts CourseMate Web site at www.cengagebrain.com, navigate to the Chapter 10 Quiz Yourself resource for this book, and then click Objectives 1 – 2.

Hardware Theft and Vandalism

Hardware theft and vandalism are other types of computer security risks. **Hardware theft** is the act of stealing computer equipment. **Hardware vandalism** is the act of defacing or destroying computer equipment. Hardware vandalism takes many forms, from someone cutting a computer cable to individuals breaking into a business or school computer lab and aimlessly smashing computers.

Companies, schools, and other organizations that house many computers are at risk of hardware theft and vandalism, especially those that have smaller system units that easily can fit in a backpack or briefcase. Mobile users also are susceptible to hardware theft. It is estimated that more than 600,000 notebook computers are stolen each year. The size and weight of these computers, especially netbooks, make them easy to steal.

Safeguards against Hardware Theft and Vandalism

To help reduce the chances of theft, companies and schools use a variety of security measures. Physical access controls, such as locked doors and windows, usually are adequate to protect the equipment. Many businesses, schools, and some homeowners install alarm systems for additional security. School computer labs and other areas with a large number of semifrequent users often attach additional physical security devices such as cables that lock the equipment to a desk (Figure 10-9), cabinet, or floor. Small locking devices also exist that require a key to access a hard disk or optical disc drive.

Some businesses use a **real time location system** (**RTLS**) to track and identify the location of high-risk or high-value items. One implementation of RTLS places RFID tags in items to be tracked.

RTLS
For more information, visit the Computer Concepts CourseMate Web site at www.cengagebrain.com, navigate to the Chapter 10 Web Link resource for this book, and then click RTLS.

Mobile computer users must take special care to protect their equipment. Some users attach a physical device such as a cable to lock a mobile computer temporarily to a stationary object. Other mobile users install a mini-security system in the notebook computer. Some of these security systems shut down the computer and sound an alarm if the computer moves outside a specified distance. Others can be configured to photograph the thieves when they use the computer. Notebook computer security systems and tracking software also can track the location of a stolen notebook computer.

Some notebook computers use passwords, possessed objects, and biometrics as methods of security. When you start these computers, you must enter a password, slide a card in a card reader, or press your finger on a fingerprint reader before the hard disk unlocks. This type of security does not prevent theft, but it renders the computer useless if it is stolen.

Figure 10-9 Using cables to lock computers can help prevent the theft of computer equipment.

Software Theft

Another type of computer security risk is software theft. **Software theft** occurs when someone steals software media, intentionally erases programs, illegally copies a program, or illegally registers and/or activates a program. One form of software theft involves someone physically stealing the media that contain the software or the hardware that contains the media, as described in the previous section. Another form of software theft occurs when software is stolen from software manufacturers. This type of theft, called piracy, is by far the most common form of software theft. Software **piracy** is the unauthorized and illegal duplication of copyrighted software. A related form of software theft involves users illegally obtaining registration numbers and/or activation codes.

Safeguards against Software Theft

To protect software media from being stolen, owners should keep original software boxes and media in a secure location. All computer users should back up their files and disks regularly, in the event of theft.

To protect themselves from software piracy, software manufacturers issue users license agreements. A **license agreement** is the right to use the software. That is, you do not own the software. The license agreement provides specific conditions for use of the software, which a user must accept before using the software (Figure 10-10). These terms usually are displayed when you install the software.

Figure 10-10 A user must accept the terms in the license agreement before using the software.

The most common type of license included with software purchased by individual users is a single-user license agreement, also called an end-user license agreement (EULA). A single-user license agreement typically includes many of the following conditions that specify a user's responsibility upon acceptance of the agreement.

Users are permitted to:
- Install the software on only one computer. (Some license agreements allow users to install the software on one desktop computer and one notebook computer.)
- Make one copy of the software as a backup.
- Give or sell the software to another individual, but only if the software is removed from the user's computer first.

Users are not permitted to:
- Install the software on a network, such as a school computer lab.
- Give copies to friends and colleagues, while continuing to use the software.
- Export the software.
- Rent or lease the software.

Unless otherwise specified by a license agreement, you do not have the right to copy, loan, borrow, rent, or in any way distribute software. Doing so is a violation of copyright law. It also is a federal crime. Despite this, some experts estimate for every authorized copy of software in use, at least one unauthorized copy exists. Read Ethics & Issues 10-1 for a related discussion.

In an attempt to prevent software piracy, Microsoft and other manufacturers have incorporated an activation process into many of its consumer products. During the **product activation**, which is conducted either online or by telephone, users provide the software product's 25-character identification number to receive an installation identification number unique to the computer on which the software is installed.

If you are not completely familiar with your school or employer's policies governing installation of software, check with the information technology department or your school's technology coordinator.

ETHICS & ISSUES 10-1

Should Online Auctions Be Liable for Pirated Software Sales?

Currently, software companies patrol online auction sites looking for pirated copies of their software that might be for sale. When they find such activity, the software company takes legal action against the seller of the pirated software. With the explosion of online auctions, however, the companies are fighting an uphill battle given the amount of time it takes to discover the sales, find the perpetrators, and then individually bring each perpetrator to justice. Many software companies have joined forces to demand that auction sites, such as eBay, legally be held liable for pirated software sold on their Web sites, and they have offered more than 20 suggestions as to how auction sites could better police their Web sites for pirated software. Online auction Web sites claim that the law clearly states they are not responsible for such sales, but that the software companies legally are responsible for controlling pirated sales. For its part, eBay claims already to enforce more than 13,000 rules to check for suspicious activity on its Web site, and offers trademark holders a special program in which they can enroll and have additional rules enforced.

Should online auctions be liable for pirated software sales on their Web sites? Why or why not? Should new or clearer laws be written to force online auctions to check whether software for sale on their Web sites is pirated? Why? Would you purchase software at an online auction being sold at a substantial discount to prices offered elsewhere? Why or why not?

Information Theft

Information theft is yet another type of computer security risk. **Information theft** occurs when someone steals personal or confidential information. An unethical company executive may steal or buy stolen information to learn about a competitor. A corrupt individual may steal credit card numbers to make fraudulent purchases.

Safeguards against Information Theft

Most companies attempt to prevent information theft by implementing the user identification and authentication controls discussed earlier in this chapter. These controls are best suited for protecting information on computers located on an organization's premises. Information transmitted over networks offers a higher degree of risk because unscrupulous users can intercept it during transmission. To protect information on the Internet and networks, companies and individuals use a variety of encryption techniques.

Encryption

Encryption is the process of converting readable data into unreadable characters to prevent unauthorized access. You treat encrypted data just like any other data. That is, you can store it or send it in an e-mail message. To read the data, the recipient must **decrypt**, or decipher, it into a readable form.

In the encryption process, the unencrypted, readable data is called plaintext. The encrypted (scrambled) data is called ciphertext. An **encryption algorithm** is a set of steps that can convert readable plaintext into unreadable ciphertext. Figure 10-11 shows examples of some simple encryption algorithms. Encryption programs typically use more than one encryption algorithm, along with an encryption key. An **encryption key** is a programmed formula that the originator of the data uses to encrypt the plaintext and the recipient of the data uses to decrypt the ciphertext.

Simple Encryption Algorithms

Name	Algorithm	Plaintext	Ciphertext	Explanation
Transposition	Switch the order of characters	SOFTWARE	OSTFAWER	Adjacent characters swapped
Substitution	Replace characters with other characters	INFORMATION	WLDIMXQUWIL	Each letter replaced with another
Expansion	Insert characters between existing characters	USER	UYSYEYRY	Letter Y inserted after each character
Compaction	Remove characters and store elsewhere	ACTIVATION	ACIVTIN	Every third letter removed (T, A, O)

Figure 10-11   This table shows four simple encryption algorithms. Most encryption keys use a combination of algorithms.

Some operating systems and e-mail programs allow you to encrypt the contents of files and messages that are stored on your computer. You also can purchase an encryption program, such as Pretty Good Privacy (PGP).

A **digital signature** is an encrypted code that a person, Web site, or organization attaches to an electronic message to verify the identity of the message sender. Digital signatures often are used to ensure that an impostor is not participating in an Internet transaction. That is, digital signatures help to prevent e-mail forgery. A digital signature also can verify that the content of a message has not changed.

Many Web browsers and Web sites use encryption. A Web site that uses encryption techniques to secure its data is known as a **secure site** (Figure 10-12). Secure sites often use digital certificates. A **digital certificate** is a notice that guarantees a user or a Web site is legitimate. A **certificate authority** (CA)

Figure 10-12   Web addresses of secure sites often begin with https instead of http. Browsers also often display a lock symbol in the window.

is an authorized person or a company that issues and verifies digital certificates. Users apply for a digital certificate from a CA. The digital certificate typically contains information such as the user's name, the issuing CA's name and signature, and the serial number of the certificate. The information in a digital certificate is encrypted.

System Failure

System failure is yet another type of computer security risk. A **system failure** is the prolonged malfunction of a computer. System failure can cause loss of hardware, software, data, or information. A variety of causes can lead to system failure. These include aging hardware; natural disasters such as fires, floods, or hurricanes; random events such as electrical power problems; and even errors in computer programs.

One of the more common causes of system failure is an electrical power variation. Electrical power variations can cause loss of data and loss of equipment. If the computer equipment is networked, a single power disturbance can damage multiple systems.

Safeguards against System Failure

To protect against electrical power variations, use a surge protector. A **surge protector** uses special electrical components to provide a stable current flow to the computer and other electronic equipment (Figure 10-13). Sometimes resembling a power strip, the computer and other devices plug in the surge protector, which plugs in the power source.

No surge protectors are 100 percent effective. Typically, the amount of protection offered by a surge protector is proportional to its cost. That is, the more expensive, the more protection the protector offers.

If your computer connects to a network or the Internet, also be sure to have protection for your modem, telephone lines, DSL lines, Internet cable lines, and network lines. Many surge protectors include plug-ins for telephone lines and other cables.

For additional electrical protection, some users connect an uninterruptible power supply to the computer. An **uninterruptible power supply (UPS)** is a device that contains surge protection circuits and one or more batteries that can provide power during a loss of power (Figure 10-14). A UPS connects between your computer and a power source.

As another measure of protection, some companies use duplicate components or computers as a safeguard against system failure.

Figure 10-13
Circuits inside a surge protector safeguard against electrical power variations.

Figure 10-14 If power fails, an uninterruptible power supply (UPS) uses batteries to provide electricity for a limited amount of time.

Backing Up — The Ultimate Safeguard

To protect against data loss caused by a system failure or hardware/software/information theft, computer users should back up files regularly. A **backup** is a duplicate of a file, program, or disk that can be used if the original is lost, damaged, or destroyed. Thus, to **back up** a file means to make a copy of it. In the case of a system failure or the discovery of corrupted files, you **restore** the files by copying the backed up files to their original location on the computer.

You can use just about any media to store backups. A good choice for a home user might be optical discs or external hard disks. Keep backup copies in a fireproof and heatproof safe or vault, or offsite. Offsite means in a location separate from the computer site. A growing trend is to use cloud storage as an offsite location. Recall that cloud storage is an Internet service that provides storage to computer users. To learn more about how to back up files using an Internet service, complete the Learn How To 1 activity on pages 414 and 415.

Most backup programs for the home user provide for a full backup and a selective backup. A full backup copies all of the files in the computer. With a selective backup, users choose which folders and files to include in a backup.

Some users implement a three-generation backup policy to preserve three copies of important files. The grandparent is the oldest copy of the file. The parent is the second oldest copy of the file. The child is the most recent copy of the file. Others use RAID to duplicate the contents of a disk. Instead of multiple backup copies, some users choose continuous backup, where data is backed up whenever a change is made.

Most operating systems include a backup program. Backup devices, such as external disk drives, also include backup programs. Numerous stand-alone backup utilities exist. Many of these can be downloaded from the Web at no cost.

Wireless Security

Wireless technology has made dramatic changes in the way computer users communicate worldwide. Billions of home and business users have notebook computers, smart phones, and other mobile devices to access the Internet, send e-mail and instant messages, chat online, or share network connections — all without wires. Home users set up wireless home networks. Mobile users access wireless networks in hot spots at airports, hotels, shopping malls, bookstores, restaurants, and coffee shops. Schools have wireless networks so that students can access the school network using their mobile computers and devices as they move from building to building.

Although wireless access provides many conveniences to users, it also poses additional security risks. One study showed that about 80 percent of wireless networks have no security protection. Some perpetrators connect to other's wireless networks to gain free Internet access; others may try to access an organization's confidential data.

To access the network, the individual must be in range of the wireless network. Some intruders intercept and monitor communications as they transmit through the air. Others connect to a network through an unsecured wireless access point (WAP). In one technique, called **war driving**, individuals attempt to detect wireless networks via their notebook computer or mobile device while driving a vehicle through areas they suspect have a wireless network.

In addition to using firewalls, some safeguards that improve the security of wireless networks include reconfiguring the wireless access point and ensuring equipment uses one or more wireless security standards such as Wi-Fi Protected Access and 802.11i.

- A wireless access point (WAP) should be configured so that it does not broadcast a network name. The WAP also can be programmed so that only certain devices can access it.
- **Wi-Fi Protected Access** (WPA) is a security standard that improves on older security standards by authenticating network users and providing more advanced encryption techniques.
- An **802.11i** network, sometimes called WPA2, the most recent network security standard, conforms to the government's security standards and uses more sophisticated encryption techniques than WPA.

By implementing these security measures, you can help to prevent unauthorized access to wireless networks.

✔ QUIZ YOURSELF 10-2

Instructions: Find the true statement below. Then, rewrite the remaining false statements so that they are true.

1. An end-user license agreement (EULA) permits users to give copies to friends and colleagues, while continuing to use the software.
2. Encryption is a process of converting ciphertext into plaintext to prevent unauthorized access.
3. Mobile users are not susceptible to hardware theft.
4. Two wireless security standards are Wi-Fi Protected Access and 802.11i.
5. To protect against data loss caused by a system failure, computer users should restore files regularly.

Quiz Yourself Online: To further check your knowledge of pages 393 through 397, visit the Computer Concepts CourseMate Web site at www.cengagebrain.com, navigate to the Chapter 10 Quiz Yourself resource for this book, and then click Objectives 3 – 6.

Health Concerns of Computer Use

Users are a key component in any information system. Thus, protecting users is just as important as protecting hardware, software, and data.

The widespread use of computers has led to some important user health concerns. The following sections discuss health risks and preventions, along with measures users can take to keep the environment healthy.

Computers and Health Risks

A **repetitive strain injury** (**RSI**) is an injury or disorder of the muscles, nerves, tendons, ligaments, and joints. Computer-related RSIs include tendonitis and carpal tunnel syndrome. RSIs are the largest job-related injury and illness problem in the United States today.

Tendonitis is inflammation of a tendon due to some repeated motion or stress on that tendon. Carpal tunnel syndrome (CTS) is inflammation of the nerve that connects the forearm to the palm of the wrist. Repeated or forceful bending of the wrist can cause CTS or tendonitis of the wrist. Symptoms of tendonitis of the wrist include extreme pain that extends from the forearm to the hand, along with tingling in the fingers. Symptoms of CTS include burning pain when the nerve is compressed, along with numbness and tingling in the thumb and first two fingers.

Long-term computer work can lead to tendonitis or CTS. Factors that cause these disorders include prolonged typing, prolonged mouse usage, or continual shifting between the mouse and the keyboard. If untreated, these disorders can lead to permanent physical damage.

You can take many precautions to prevent these types of injuries. Take frequent breaks during the computer session to exercise your hands and arms (Figure 10-15). To prevent injury due to typing, place a wrist rest between the keyboard and the edge of your desk. To prevent injury while using a mouse, place the mouse at least six inches from the edge of the desk. In this position, your wrist is flat on the desk. Finally, minimize the number of times you switch between the mouse and the keyboard, and avoid using the heel of your hand as a pivot point while typing or using the mouse.

Another type of health-related condition due to computer usage is **computer vision syndrome** (**CVS**). You may have CVS if you have sore, tired, burning, itching, or dry eyes; blurred or double vision; distance blurred vision after prolonged staring at a display device; headache or sore neck; difficulty shifting focus between a display device and documents; difficulty focusing on the screen image; color fringes or after-images when you look away from the display device; and increased sensitivity to light. Eyestrain associated with CVS is not thought to have serious or long-term consequences. Figure 10-16 outlines some techniques you can follow to ease eyestrain.

People who spend their workday using the computer sometimes complain of lower back pain, muscle fatigue, and emotional fatigue. Lower back pain sometimes is caused from poor posture. Always sit

Hand Exercises

- Spread fingers apart for several seconds while keeping wrists straight.
- Gently push back fingers and then thumb.
- Dangle arms loosely at sides and then shake arms and hands.

Figure 10-15 To reduce the chance of developing tendonitis or carpal tunnel syndrome, take frequent breaks during computer sessions to exercise your hands and arms.

Techniques to Ease Eyestrain

- Every 10 to 15 minutes, take an eye break.
  - Look into the distance and focus on an object for 20 to 30 seconds.
  - Roll your eyes in a complete circle.
  - Close your eyes and rest them for at least one minute.
- Blink your eyes every five seconds.
- Place your display device about an arm's length away from your eyes with the top of the screen at eye level or below.
- Use large fonts.
- If you wear glasses, ask your doctor about computer glasses.
- Adjust the lighting.

Figure 10-16 Following these tips may help reduce eyestrain while working on a computer.

properly in the chair while you work. To alleviate back pain, muscle fatigue, and emotional fatigue, take a 15- to 30-minute break every 2 hours — stand up, walk around, stretch, and relax. Another way to help prevent these injuries is to be sure your workplace is designed ergonomically.

Ergonomics and Workplace Design

Ergonomics is an applied science devoted to incorporating comfort, efficiency, and safety into the design of items in the workplace. Ergonomic studies have shown that using the correct type and configuration of chair, keyboard, display device, and work surface helps users work comfortably and efficiently and helps protect their health. For the computer work space, experts recommend an area of at least two feet by four feet. Figure 10-17 illustrates additional guidelines for setting up the work area.

viewing angle: 20°
to center of screen
viewing distance:
18 to 28 inches

arms: elbows at about 90° and arms and hands approximately parallel to floor

adjustable height chair with 4 or 5 legs for stability

keyboard height:
23 to 28 inches
depending on
height of user

feet flat on floor

Figure 10-17   A well-designed work area should be flexible to allow adjustments to the height and build of different individuals. Good lighting and air quality also are important considerations.

Computer Addiction

Computers can provide entertainment and enjoyment. Some computer users, however, become obsessed with the computer and the Internet. **Computer addiction** occurs when the computer consumes someone's entire social life. Computer addiction is a growing health problem but can be treated through therapy and support groups. Symptoms of a user with computer addiction include the following:

- Craves computer time
- Overjoyed when at the computer
- Neglects family and friends
- Irritable when not at the computer
- Unable to stop computer activity
- Problems at work or school

Ethics and Society

As with any powerful technology, computers can be used for both good and bad intentions. The standards that determine whether an action is good or bad are known as ethics.

Computer ethics are the moral guidelines that govern the use of computers and information systems. Six frequently discussed areas of computer ethics are unauthorized use of computers and networks, software theft (piracy), information accuracy, intellectual property rights, green computing, and information privacy.

Previous sections in this chapter discussed unauthorized use of computers and networks, and software theft (piracy). The following sections discuss issues related to information accuracy, intellectual property rights, green computing, and information privacy. The questionnaire in Figure 10-18 raises issues in each of these areas.

Your Thoughts?

		Ethical	Unethical
1.	An organization requires employees to wear badges that track their whereabouts while at work.	☐	☐
2.	A supervisor reads an employee's e-mail.	☐	☐
3.	An employee uses his computer at work to send e-mail messages to a friend.	☐	☐
4.	An employee sends an e-mail message to several coworkers and blind copies his supervisor.	☐	☐
5.	An employee forwards an e-mail message to a third party without permission from the sender.	☐	☐
6.	An employee uses her computer at work to complete a homework assignment for school.	☐	☐
7.	The vice president of your Student Government Association (SGA) downloads a photo from the Web and uses it in a flyer recruiting SGA members.	☐	☐
8.	A student copies text from the Web and uses it in a research paper for his English Composition class.	☐	☐
9.	An employee sends political campaign material to individuals on her employer's mailing list.	☐	☐
10.	As an employee in the registration office, you have access to student grades. You look up grades for your friends, so that they do not have to wait for delivery of grade reports from the postal service.	☐	☐
11.	An employee makes a copy of software and installs it on her home computer. No one uses her home computer while she is at work, and she uses her home computer only to finish projects from work.	☐	☐
12.	An employee who has been laid off installs a computer virus on his employer's computer.	☐	☐
13.	A person designing a Web page finds one on the Web similar to his requirements, copies it, modifies it, and publishes it as his own Web page.	☐	☐
14.	A student researches using only the Web to write a report.	☐	☐
15.	In a society in which all transactions occur online (a cashless society), the government tracks every transaction you make and automatically deducts taxes from your bank account.	☐	☐
16.	Someone copies a well-known novel to the Web and encourages others to read it.	☐	☐
17.	A person accesses an organization's network and reports to the organization any vulnerabilities discovered.	☐	☐
18.	Your friend uses a neighbor's wireless network to connect to the Internet and check e-mail.	☐	☐
19.	A company uses recycled paper to print a 50-page employee benefits manual that is distributed to 425 employees.	☐	☐
20.	Your friend donates her old computers and mobile devices to local schools when she purchases newer models.	☐	☐

Figure 10-18   Indicate whether you think the situation described is ethical or unethical. Discuss your answers with your instructor and other students.

Information Accuracy

Information accuracy today is a concern because many users access information maintained by other people or companies, such as on the Internet. Do not assume that because the information is on the Web that it is correct. Users should evaluate the value of a Web page before relying on its content. Be aware that the organization providing access to the information may not be the creator of the information.

In addition to concerns about the accuracy of computer input, some individuals and organizations raise questions about the ethics of using computers to alter output, primarily graphical output such as retouched photos. Using graphics equipment and software, users easily can digitize photos and then add, change, or remove images (Figure 10-19).

One group that completely opposes any manipulation of an image is the National Press Photographer Association. It believes that allowing even the slightest alteration could lead to misrepresentative photos. Others believe that digital photo retouching is acceptable as long as the significant content or meaning of the photo does not change. Digital retouching is an area in which legal precedents so far have not been established.

Figure 10-19 A digitally altered photo shows the movie character Forrest Gump (1994) meeting President John F. Kennedy (who died in 1963).

Intellectual Property Rights

Intellectual property (IP) refers to unique and original works such as ideas, inventions, art, writings, processes, company and product names, and logos. **Intellectual property rights** are the rights to which creators are entitled for their work. Certain issues arise surrounding IP today because many of these works are available digitally.

A **copyright** gives authors and artists exclusive rights to duplicate, publish, and sell their materials. A copyright protects any tangible form of expression.

A common infringement of copyright is piracy. People pirate (illegally copy) software, movies, and music. Many areas are not clear-cut with respect to the law, because copyright law gives the public fair use to copyrighted material. The issues surround the phrase, fair use, which allows use for educational and critical purposes.

This vague definition is subject to widespread interpretation and raises many questions:

- Should individuals be able to download contents of your Web site, modify it, and then put it on the Web again as their own?
- Should a faculty member have the right to print material from the Web and distribute it to all members of the class for teaching purposes only?
- Should someone be able to scan photos or pages from a book, publish them to the Web, and allow others to download them?
- Should students be able to post term papers they have written on the Web, making it tempting for other students to download and submit them as their own work?

These issues with copyright law led to the development of **digital rights management** (DRM), a strategy designed to prevent illegal distribution of movies, music, and other digital content.

Green Computing

Green computing involves reducing the electricity and environmental waste while using a computer. People use, and often waste, resources such as electricity and paper while using a computer.

The United States government developed the **ENERGY STAR program** to help reduce the amount of electricity used by computers and related devices. This program encourages manufacturers to create energy-efficient devices that require little power when they are not in use. Computers and devices that meet the ENERGY STAR guidelines display an ENERGY STAR label.

Digital Rights Management

For more information, visit the Computer Concepts CourseMate Web site at www.cengagebrain.com, navigate to the Chapter 10 Web Link resource for this book, and then click Digital Rights Management.

Green Computing Suggestions

1. Use computers and devices that comply with the ENERGY STAR program.
2. Do not leave the computer running overnight.
3. Turn off the monitor, printer, and other devices when not in use.
4. Use LCD monitors instead of CRT monitors.
5. Use paperless methods to communicate.
6. Recycle paper.
7. Buy recycled paper.
8. Recycle toner cartridges.
9. Recycle old computers, printers, and other devices.
10. Telecommute (saves gas).
11. Use video conferencing and VoIP for meetings.

Figure 10-20 A list of suggestions to make computing healthy for the environment.

Users should not store obsolete computers and devices in their basement, storage room, attic, warehouse, or any other location. Computers, monitors, and other equipment contain toxic materials and potentially dangerous elements including lead, mercury, and flame retardants. In a landfill, these materials release into the environment. Recycling and refurbishing old equipment are much safer alternatives for the environment.

Experts estimate that more than 700 million personal computers are obsolete. Because of the huge volumes of electronic waste, the U.S. federal government has proposed a bill that would require computer recycling across the country. Many state and local governments have methods in place to make it easy for consumers to recycle this type of equipment.

To reduce the environmental impact of computing further, users simply can alter a few habits. Figure 10-20 lists the ways you can contribute to green computing. To learn more about green computing, complete the Green Computing exercise on the Web Research page in each chapter of this book.

Information Privacy

Information privacy refers to the right of individuals and companies to deny or restrict the collection and use of information about them. In the past, information privacy was easier to maintain because information was kept in separate locations. Each retail store had its own credit files. Each government agency maintained separate records. Doctors had their own patient files.

Today, huge databases store this data online. Much of the data is personal and confidential and should be accessible only to authorized users. Many individuals and organizations, however, question whether this data really is private.

Figure 10-21 lists measures you can take to make your personal data private. The following pages address techniques companies and employers use to collect your personal data. Read Innovative Computing 10-1 to find out how merchants watch shoppers' behaviors.

! INNOVATIVE COMPUTING 10-1

Customers' Behavior, Conversations Monitored

Deciding whether to display peanut butter next to jelly on a supermarket shelf is made easier with consumer-monitoring technology. Leading stores, including Best Buy, Walmart, Walgreens, Office Depot, and Abercrombie & Fitch, have installed video cameras and recorders, heat sensors, and sometimes microphones to track customers' movement throughout the store and their buying patterns.

One system, called Smartlane, counts the number of people, known as "hot blobs," entering and exiting the store and records how quickly clerks are completing transactions at cash registers. It alerts management when many hot blobs are waiting in checkout lanes or have entered the store in a short period of time so that additional clerks can be made available to reduce checkout waiting times.

Another system, BehaviorIQ, collects data on where customers walk throughout the store, when and for how long they stop to browse, and what they take from shelves and racks. Some stores claim information

gleaned from these monitoring systems has increased sales 300 percent.

Privacy experts warn that consumers might object to being recorded and analyzed. The monitoring companies, however, dispel these concerns by explaining that the data actually resembles audio recordings made when calling customer-service hotlines and when being observed for loss prevention purposes.

For more information, visit the Computer Concepts CourseMate Web site at www.cengagebrain.com, navigate to the Chapter 10 Innovative Computing resource for this book, and then click Shopping Behavior.

How to Safeguard Personal Information

1. Fill in only necessary information on rebate, warranty, and registration forms.	12. Obtain your credit report once a year from each of the three major credit reporting agencies (Equifax, Experian, and TransUnion) and correct any errors.
2. Do not preprint your telephone number or Social Security number on personal checks.	13. Request a free copy of your medical records once a year from the Medical Information Bureau.
3. Have an unlisted or unpublished telephone number.	14. Limit the amount of information you provide to Web sites. Fill in only required information.
4. If Caller ID is available in your area, find out how to block your number from displaying on the receiver's system.	15. Install a cookie manager to filter cookies.
5. Do not write your telephone number on charge or credit receipts.	16. Clear your history file when you are finished browsing.
6. Ask merchants not to write credit card numbers, telephone numbers, Social Security numbers, and driver's license numbers on the back of your personal checks.	17. Set up a free e-mail account. Use this e-mail address for merchant forms.
7. Purchase goods with cash, rather than credit or checks.	18. Turn off file and printer sharing on your Internet connection.
8. Avoid shopping club and buyer cards.	19. Install a personal firewall.
9. If merchants ask personal questions, find out why they want to know before releasing the information.	20. Sign-up for e-mail filtering through your Internet access provider or use an anti-spam program such as Brightmail.
10. Inform merchants that you do not want them to distribute your personal information.	21. Do not reply to spam for any reason.
11. Request, in writing, to be removed from mailing lists.	22. Surf the Web anonymously with a program such as Freedom WebSecure or through an anonymous Web site such as Anonymizer.com.

Figure 10-21   Techniques to keep personal data private.

Electronic Profiles

When you fill out a form such as a magazine subscription, product warranty registration card, or contest entry form, the merchant that receives the form usually enters it into a database. Likewise, every time you click an advertisement on the Web or register software online, your information and preferences enter a database. Merchants then sell the contents of their databases to national marketing firms and Internet advertising firms. By combining this data with information from public sources such as driver's licenses and vehicle registrations, these firms create an electronic profile of individuals.

Critics contend that the information in an electronic profile reveals more about an individual than anyone has a right to know. They also claim that companies should inform people if they plan to provide personal information to others. Many companies today allow people to specify whether they want their personal information distributed.

Cookies

E-commerce and other Web applications often rely on cookies to identify users. A **cookie** is a small text file that a Web server stores on your computer. Cookie files typically contain data about you, such as your user name or viewing preferences.

Many commercial Web sites send a cookie to your browser, and then your computer's hard disk stores the cookie. The next time you visit the Web site, your browser retrieves the cookie from your hard disk and sends the data in the cookie to the Web site.

Web sites use cookies for a variety of purposes:

• Most Web sites that allow for personalization use cookies to track user preferences. On such sites, users may be asked to fill in a form requesting personal information, such as their name, postal code, or site preferences. A news Web site, for example, might allow users to customize their viewing preferences to display certain stock quotes or local weather forecasts. The Web site stores their preferences in a cookie on the users' hard disks.

- Some Web sites use cookies to store users' passwords, so that they do not need to enter it every time they log in to the Web site.
- Online shopping sites generally use a session cookie to keep track of items in a user's shopping cart. This way, users can start an order during one Web session and finish it on another day in another session. Session cookies usually expire after a certain time, such as a week or a month.
- Some Web sites use cookies to track how often users visit a site and the Web pages they visit while at the site.
- Web sites may use cookies to target advertisements. These sites store a user's interests and browsing habits in the cookie.

You can set a browser to accept cookies automatically, prompt you if you want to accept a cookie, or disable cookie use altogether. Keep in mind if you disable cookie use, you will not be able to use many of the e-commerce Web sites. Figure 10-22 illustrates how Web sites work with cookies.

Cookies

For more information, visit the Computer Concepts CourseMate Web site at www.cengagebrain.com, navigate to the Chapter 10 Web Link resource for this book, and then click Cookies.

How Cookies Work

Step 1
When you type the Web address of a Web site in a browser window, the browser program searches your hard disk for a cookie associated with the Web site.

cookies

Step 2
If the browser finds a cookie, it sends information in the cookie file to the Web site.

identification number
cookie information

INTERNET

www.omahasteaks.com

Web server for www.omahasteaks.com

Step 3
If the Web site does not receive cookie information, and is expecting it, the site creates an identification number for you in its database and sends that number to your browser. The browser in turn creates a cookie file based on that number and stores the cookie file on your hard disk. The Web site now can update information in the cookie file whenever you access the site.

Figure 10-22 This figure shows how cookies work.

Spyware and Adware

Spyware is a program placed on a computer without the user's knowledge that secretly collects information about the user. Some vendors or employers use spyware to collect information about program usage or employees. Internet advertising firms often collect information about users' Web browsing habits by hiding spyware in adware. **Adware** is a program that displays an online advertisement in a banner or pop-up window on Web pages, e-mail messages, or other Internet services. To remove spyware and adware, you can obtain a spyware and adware remover that can detect and delete spyware and adware. Some operating systems and Web browsers include spyware removers.

Spam

Spam is an unsolicited e-mail message or newsgroup posting sent to multiple recipients or newsgroups at once. Spam is Internet junk mail (Figure 10-23). The content of spam ranges from selling a product or service, to promoting a business opportunity, to advertising offensive material. One study indicates more than 92 percent of e-mail is spam.

Users can reduce the amount of spam they receive with a number of techniques. Some e-mail programs have built-in settings that allow users to delete spam automatically. Users also can sign up for e-mail filtering from their Internet access provider. **E-mail filtering** is a service that blocks e-mail messages from designated sources. An alternative to e-mail filtering is to purchase an **anti-spam program** that attempts to remove spam before it reaches your inbox. The disadvantage of e-mail filters and anti-spam programs is that sometimes they remove valid e-mail messages. Thus, users should review the contents of the spam messages periodically to ensure they do not contain valid messages.

Phishing

Phishing is a scam in which a perpetrator sends an official looking e-mail message that attempts to obtain your personal and financial information (Figure 10-24). Some phishing e-mail messages ask you to reply with your information; others direct you to a phony Web site, or a pop-up window that looks like a Web site, that collects the information.

If you receive an e-mail that looks legitimate and requests you update credit card numbers, Social Security numbers, bank account numbers, passwords, or other private information, the FTC recommends you visit the Web site directly to determine if the request is valid. Never click a link in an e-mail message; instead retype the Web address in your browser.

A **phishing filter** is a program that warns or blocks you from potentially fraudulent or suspicious Web sites. Some Web browsers include phishing filters.

Pharming is a scam, similar to phishing, where a perpetrator attempts to obtain your personal and financial information, except they do so via spoofing. That is, when you type a Web address in the Web browser, you are redirected to a phony Web site that looks legitimate. The phony Web site requests you enter confidential information.

Clickjacking is yet another similar scam. With **clickjacking**, an object that can be clicked on a Web site, such as a button, image, or link, contains a malicious program. When users click the disguised object, for example, they may be redirected to a phony Web site that requests personal information, or a virus may download to their computer.

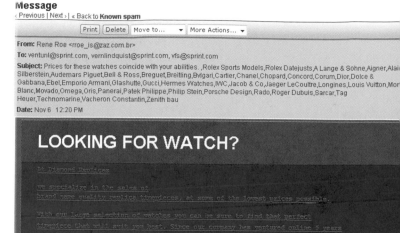

Figure 10-23   An example of spam.

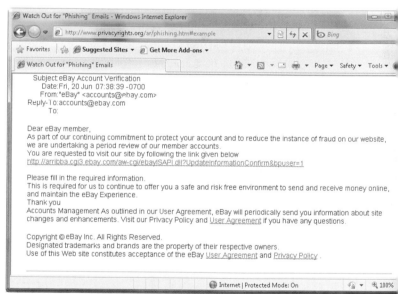

Figure 10-24   An example of a phishing e-mail message.

Social Engineering

As related to the use of computers, **social engineering** is defined as gaining unauthorized access or obtaining confidential information by taking advantage of the trusting human nature of some victims and the naivety of others. Some social engineers trick their victims into revealing confidential information such as user names and passwords on the telephone, in person, or on the Internet. Techniques they use include pretending to be an administrator or other authoritative figure, feigning an emergency situation, or impersonating an acquaintance. Social engineers also obtain information from users who do not destroy or conceal information properly. These perpetrators sift through company dumpsters, watch or film people dialing telephone numbers or using ATMs, and snoop around computers looking for openly displayed confidential information.

Privacy Laws

The concern about privacy has led to the enactment of federal and state laws regarding the storage and disclosure of personal data (Figure 10-25).

Common points in some of these laws include the following:

1. Information collected and stored about individuals should be limited to what is necessary to carry out the function of the business or government agency collecting the data.

Date	Law	Purpose
2006	Telephone Records and Privacy Protection Act	Makes it illegal to use fraudulent means to obtain someone's telephone records.
2003	CAN-SPAM Act	Gives law enforcement the right to impose penalties on people using the Internet to distribute spam.
2002	Sarbanes-Oxley Act	Requires corporate officers, auditors, and attorneys of publicly-traded companies follow strict financial reporting guidelines.
2001	Children's Internet Protection Act (CIPA)	Protects minors from inappropriate content when accessing the Internet in schools and libraries.
2001	Provide Appropriate Tools Required to Intercept and Obstruct Terrorism (PATRIOT) Act	Gives law enforcement the right to monitor people's activities, including Web and e-mail habits.
1999	Gramm-Leach-Bliley Act (GLBA) or Financial Modernization Act	Protects consumers from disclosure of their personal financial information and requires institutions to alert customers of information disclosure policies.
1998	Children's Online Privacy Protection Act (COPPA)	Requires Web sites protect personal information of children under 13 years of age.
1998	Digital Millennium Copyright Act (DMCA)	Makes it illegal to circumvent antipiracy schemes in commercial software; outlaws sale of devices that copy software illegally.
1997	No Electronic Theft (NET) Act	Closes a narrow loophole in the law that allowed people to give away copyrighted material (such as software) on the Internet without legal repercussions.
1996	Health Insurance Portability and Accountability Act (HIPAA)	Protects individuals against the wrongful disclosure of their health information.
1996	National Information Infrastructure Protection Act	Penalizes theft of information across state lines, threats against networks, and computer system trespassing.
1994	Computer Abuse Amendments Act	Amends 1984 act to outlaw transmission of harmful computer code such as viruses.
1992	Cable Act	Extends the privacy of the Cable Communications Policy Act of 1984 to include cellular and other wireless services.
1991	Telephone Consumer Protection Act	Restricts activities of telemarketers.
1988	Computer Matching and Privacy Protection Act	Regulates the use of government data to determine the eligibility of individuals for federal benefits.
1988	Video Privacy Protection Act	Forbids retailers from releasing or selling video-rental records without customer consent or a court order.
1986	Electronic Communications Privacy Act (ECPA)	Provides the same right of privacy protection for the postal delivery service and telephone companies to the new forms of electronic communications, such as voice mail, e-mail, and cell phones.
1984	Cable Communications Policy Act	Regulates disclosure of cable television subscriber records.
1984	Computer Fraud and Abuse Act	Outlaws unauthorized access of federal government computers.
1978	Right to Financial Privacy Act	Strictly outlines procedures federal agencies must follow when looking at customer records in banks.
1974	Privacy Act	Forbids federal agencies from allowing information to be used for a reason other than that for which it was collected.
1974	Family Educational Rights and Privacy Act	Gives students and parents access to school records and limits disclosure of records to unauthorized parties.
1970	Fair Credit Reporting Act	Prohibits credit reporting agencies from releasing credit information to unauthorized people and allows consumers to review their own credit records.

Figure 10-25 Summary of the major U.S. government laws concerning privacy.

2. Once collected, provisions should be made to restrict access to the data to those employees within the organization who need access to it to perform their job duties.
3. Personal information should be released outside the organization collecting the data only when the person has agreed to its disclosure.
4. When information is collected about an individual, the individual should know that the data is being collected and have the opportunity to determine the accuracy of the data.

Employee Monitoring

Employee monitoring involves the use of computers to observe, record, and review an employee's use of a computer, including communications such as e-mail messages, keyboard activity (used to measure productivity), and Web sites visited. Many programs exist that easily allow employers to monitor employees. Further, it is legal for employers to use these programs.

A frequently debated issue is whether an employer has the right to read employee e-mail messages. Actual policies vary widely. Some companies declare that they will review e-mail messages regularly, and others state that e-mail is private. In some states, if an organization does not have a formal e-mail policy, it can read e-mail messages without employee notification. Several lawsuits have been filed against employers because many believe that such internal communications should be private. Read Ethics & Issues 10-2 for a related discussion.

Another controversial issue relates to the use of cameras to monitor employees, customers, and the public. Many people feel that this use of video cameras is a violation of privacy.

ETHICS & ISSUES 10-2

Should Text Messages Sent by Employees Be Private?

When an employee sends or receives an e-mail message using his or her employer's e-mail server, the company most likely retains a backup of the message, which can be used as evidence against the employee if the employee is suspected of engaging in unscrupulous activity. When an employee sends a text message using a company-issued smart phone for such activity, however, the smart phone provider may store a record of the message. If an employer's workplace policy requires an employee to disclose all text message communications with customers, vendors,

and competitors, the employee is required legally to divulge those communications. The U.S. Supreme Court ruled that an employer can read workers' text messages if there is reason to believe the texts violate workplace rules. The Court held that employees can purchase their own cell phones if they need to make personal calls or text messages. Employees may believe they have an expectation of privacy and the right of self-expression when they use an employer's cell phone. Employers argue, however, that because they provide the devices and service to the employee, they

should have a right to view the content of the messages.

Should text messages sent by employees be private? Why or why not? How can employers create and enforce policies regarding the content of text messages sent on employer-issued smart phones? Should employers demand that smart phone providers offer the option to send all employee text message communications to the company on a monthly basis? Why or why not?

Content Filtering

One of the more controversial issues that surround the Internet is its widespread availability of objectionable material, such as racist literature, violence, and obscene pictures. Some believe that such materials should be banned. Others believe that the materials should be filtered, that is, restricted. **Content filtering** is the process of restricting access to certain material on the Web. Content filtering opponents argue that banning any materials violates constitutional guarantees of free speech and personal rights.

Many businesses use content filtering to limit employees' Web access. These businesses argue that employees are unproductive when visiting inappropriate or objectionable Web sites. Some schools, libraries, and parents use content filtering to restrict access to minors.

Web filtering software is a program that restricts access to specified Web sites. Some also filter sites that use specific words. Others allow you to filter e-mail messages, chat rooms, and programs. Many Internet security programs include a firewall, antivirus program, and filtering capabilities combined (Figure 10-26).

Figure 10-26 Many Internet security programs include content filtering capabilities, where users can block specified Web sites and applications.

✔ **QUIZ YOURSELF 10-3**

Instructions: Find the true statement below. Then, rewrite the remaining false statements so that they are true.

1. Factors that cause CVS include prolonged typing, prolonged mouse usage, or continual shifting between the mouse and the keyboard.
2. Phishing is the discovery, collection, and analysis of evidence found on computers and networks.
3. Spam is Internet junk mail.
4. You can assume that information on the Web is correct.

Quiz Yourself Online: To further check your knowledge of pages 398 through 407, visit the Computer Concepts CourseMate Web site at www.cengagebrain.com, navigate to the Chapter 10 Quiz Yourself resource for this book, and then click Objectives 7 – 8.

Chapter Summary

This chapter identified some potential computer risks and the safeguards that organizations and individuals can implement to minimize these risks. Wireless security risks and safeguards also were discussed.

The chapter presented computer-related health issues and their preventions. The chapter ended with a discussion about ethical issues surrounding information accuracy, intellectual property rights, green computing, and information privacy.

Computer Usage @ Work

National and Local Security

Since 2001, the federal government, local governments, businesses, and individuals have been implementing aggressive new security measures because of the increase in terrorist activity. A security threat can exist anywhere, and it is nearly impossible for humans alone to protect the country. As a result, computers now assist governments, law enforcement officials, business owners, and other individuals with monitoring and maintaining security.

Advancements in computer vision enable computers to monitor indoor and outdoor areas that might be subject to a high amount of criminal activity. For example, some cities are installing cameras in problematic areas. A computer program analyzes the output from the camera and can determine whether two or more people in close proximity to one another might be engaged in a physical confrontation. If the computer detects suspicious behavior, it automatically notifies local law enforcement.

Computers also use facial recognition to identify individuals who do not belong in a particular area. For example, one theme park in Florida often takes a picture of individuals they escort out of and ban from the park. As visitors walk from their cars to the park, surveillance cameras positioned in strategic locations scan visitors' faces and compare them to the database containing images of those who are banned from the park. If the computer finds a match, it alerts a security officer who then can investigate the situation. Thousands of people visit theme parks each day, and computers make it easier to perform the otherwise impossible task of identifying those who might be trespassing.

The federal government, particularly the Department of Homeland Security, uses a computerized No Fly List to track individuals who are not authorized to travel on commercial flights within the United States. When an individual makes a reservation, a computer compares his or her name to the names on the No Fly List. If the computer finds a match, the individual must prove that he or she is not the person on the list before being allowed to board an aircraft.

Whether you are walking outside, visiting an attraction, or traveling, the chances are good that computers are, in some way, ensuring your safety.

For more information, visit the Computer Concepts CourseMate Web site at www.cengagebrain.com, navigate to the Chapter 10 Computer Usage @ Work resource for this book, and then click National and Local Security.

Companies on the Cutting Edge

MCAFEE Intrusion Prevention Products Developer

The McAfee Initiative to Fight Cybercrime is a global effort to thwart security threats and criminal activity. The world's largest dedicated security technology company has partnered with experts in law enforcement, education, government, and society to investigate, prosecute, and attempt to prevent security breaches.

McAfee products protect more than 60 million consumers, small- and medium-sized businesses, governmental agencies, and large corporations from malware, spam, and unauthorized access. In addition, more than 100 million mobile devices are protected with McAfee software. The corporation takes its name from its founder, John McAfee, who started the company in 1987 from his Santa Clara, California, home.

Recently, McAfee launched a new online backup service with unlimited capacity that allows consumers to back up and encrypt their important files such as documents, photos, music, and e-mail messages.

SYMANTEC Computer Security Solutions Leader

Symantec's programmers analyzed every line of code, rewrote programs, and developed a new security model to create its latest versions of Norton AntiVirus and Norton Internet Security. The results are programs that use less hard disk space, decrease starting and scanning time, and average less than 7 MB of memory. The more than 100 performance improvements offer advanced protection for millions of computer users worldwide.

The California-based company is one of the ten largest software corporations in the world. It was founded in 1982 and has offices in more than 40 countries. Its primary manufacturing facility is located in Dublin, Ireland.

Symantec recently released the latest version of its Norton Internet Security software. A rating service tested the level of protection provided by 10 different security products and gave Norton Internet Security the only perfect score.

 For more information, visit the Computer Concepts CourseMate Web site at www.cengagebrain.com and then navigate to the Chapter 10 Companies on the Cutting Edge resource for this book.

Technology Trailblazers

RICHARD STALLMAN Software Freedom Advocate

The relationship between software and freedom is key to Richard Stallman's philosophy. Since his days as a physics student at Harvard University, he has advocated free software and campaigned against software patents and copyright laws. His pioneering work developed the concept of copyleft, which gives each person who has purchased a software product the ability to copy, adapt, and distribute the program as long as the new software also has the same lack of restrictions.

Stallman began the GNU/Linux Project in 1983 as an effort to develop and use the copyleft concept. Linux is an outgrowth of this project, which continues to be a forum for software development, ethical practices, and political campaigning. He also started the Free Software Foundation (FSF) in 1985 to promote writing free software for the GNU Project. The Free Software Directory catalogs more than 5,300 packages that run on the Linux and GNU operating systems.

GENE SPAFFORD Computer Security Expert

The Morris Worm, also called the MBDF virus, is considered the first computer worm distributed on the Internet, and Gene Spafford gained fame for deconstructing and analyzing this 1988 attack. His work led to the conviction of a Cornell University student, Robert Morris. Today, Spafford, who also is known as Spaf, is recognized as one of the world's foremost experts in the computer security, intelligence, cybercrime, and software engineering fields.

For 30 years, he has advised major corporations, including Microsoft, Intel, and Unisys, the U.S. Air Force, the Federal Bureau of Investigation, and two U.S. presidents. He is noted for several firsts in the computer security field. For example, he defined the terms, software forensics and firewall, wrote the first English-language book on the topics of viruses and malware, and founded the world's first multidisciplinary academic security awareness group: the Center for Education and Research in Information Assurance and Security (CERIAS).

 For more information, visit the Computer Concepts CourseMate Web site at www.cengagebrain.com and then navigate to the Chapter 10 Technology Trailblazers resource for this book.

Chapter Review

The Chapter Review reinforces the main concepts presented in this chapter.

To listen to an audio version of this Chapter Review, visit the Computer Concepts CourseMate Web site at www.cengagebrain.com and then navigate to the Chapter 10 Chapter Review resource for this book.

1. **What Are Various Internet and Network Attacks, and How Can Users Safeguard against These Attacks?** A computer **virus** is a potentially damaging program that infects a computer and negatively affects the way the computer works. A **worm** is a program that copies itself repeatedly, using up resources and possibly shutting down the computer or network. A **Trojan horse** is a program that hides within or looks like a legitimate program. A **rootkit** is a program that hides in a computer and allows someone from a remote location to take full control of the computer. Users can take precautions to guard against this **malware**. Do not start a computer with removable media in the drives or ports unless the media are uninfected. Never open an e-mail attachment unless it is from a **trusted source**. Disable macros in documents that are not from a trusted source. Install an **antivirus program** and a personal firewall program. Stay informed about any new virus alert or **virus hoax**. To defend against a **botnet**, a **denial of service attack**, improper use of a **back door**, and **spoofing**, users can install a **firewall** and install **intrusion detection software**.

2. **What Are Techniques to Prevent Unauthorized Access and Use?** **Unauthorized access** is the use of a computer or network without permission. **Unauthorized use** is the use of a computer or its data for unapproved or illegal activities. A written acceptable use policy (AUP) outlines the activities for which the computer and network may and may not be used. Other measures include firewalls and intrusion detection software. An **access control** defines who can access a computer, when they can access it, and what actions they can take. An **audit trail** records in a file both successful and unsuccessful access attempts. Access controls include a **user name** and **password**, a **possessed object**, and a **biometric device**.

Visit the Computer Concepts CourseMate Web site at www.cengagebrain.com, navigate to the Chapter 10 Quiz Yourself resource for this book, and then click Objectives 1 – 2.

3. **What Are Safeguards against Hardware Theft and Vandalism?** **Hardware theft** is the act of stealing computer equipment. **Hardware vandalism** is the act of defacing or destroying computer equipment. Physical devices and practical security measures, passwords, possessed objects, and biometrics can reduce the risk of theft or render a computer useless if it is stolen.

4. **How Do Software Manufacturers Protect against Software Theft and Information Theft?** **Software theft** occurs when someone steals software, intentionally erases programs, illegally copies programs, or illegally registers/activates a program. Software **piracy** is the unauthorized and illegal duplication of copyrighted software. To protect themselves from software piracy, manufacturers issue a **license agreement** that provides specific conditions for use of the software. During **product activation**, users provide the product's identification number to receive an installation identification number unique to their computer. Companies attempt to prevent **information theft** through user identification and authentication controls, **encryption**, a **digital signature**, a **digital certificate**, or a **certificate authority**.

5. **What Types of Devices Are Available to Protect Computers from System Failure?** A **system failure** is the prolonged malfunction of a computer. A common cause of system failure is an electrical power variation. A **surge protector** uses special electrical components to provide a stable current flow to the computer. An **uninterruptible power supply** (**UPS**) contains surge protection circuits and one or more batteries that can provide power during a power loss.

6. **What Risks and Safeguards Are Associated with Wireless Communications?** Wireless access poses additional security risks. Intruders connect to other wireless networks to gain free Internet access or to access an organization's confidential data. Some individuals intercept and monitor communications as they are transmitted. Others connect to a network through an unsecured wireless access point (WAP). Some safeguards include firewalls, reconfiguring the WAP, and ensuring equipment uses a wireless security standard, such as **Wi-Fi Protected Access** and **802.11i**.

Visit the Computer Concepts CourseMate Web site at www.cengagebrain.com, navigate to the Chapter 10 Quiz Yourself resource for this book, and then click Objectives 3 – 6.

7. **How Can Health-Related Disorders and Injuries Due to Computer Use Be Prevented?** A **repetitive strain injury** (**RSI**) is an injury or disorder of the muscles, nerves, tendons, ligaments, and joints. Computer-related RSIs include tendonitis and carpal tunnel syndrome (CTS). Another health-related condition is eyestrain associated with **computer vision**

syndrome (CVS). To prevent health-related disorders, take frequent breaks, use precautionary exercises and techniques, and incorporate ergonomics when planning the workplace. **Computer addiction** occurs when the computer consumes someone's entire social life.

8. **What Are Issues Surrounding Information Privacy?**   **Information privacy** is the right of individuals and companies to restrict the collection and use of information about them. An electronic profile combines data about an individual's Web use with data from public sources. A **cookie** is a file that a Web server stores on a computer to collect data about the user. **Spyware** is a program placed on a computer that secretly collects information about the user. **Adware** is a program that displays an online advertisement in a banner or pop-up window. **Spam** is an unsolicited e-mail message or newsgroup posting sent to many recipients. **Phishing** is a scam in which a perpetrator sends an official looking e-mail message that attempts to obtain a user's personal and financial information. The concern about privacy has led to the enactment of many federal and state laws regarding the storage and disclosure of data. As related to the use of computers, **social engineering** is defined as gaining unauthorized access or obtaining confidential information by taking advantage of the trusting human nature of some victims and the naivety of others. **Employee monitoring** uses computers to observe, record, and review an employee's computer use. **Content filtering** restricts access to certain material on the Web.

Visit the Computer Concepts CourseMate Web site at www.cengagebrain.com, navigate to the Chapter 10 Quiz Yourself resource for this book, and then click Objectives 7 – 8.

Key Terms

You should know each key term. The list below helps focus your study.

To see an example of and a definition for each term, and to access current and additional information from the Web, visit the Computer Concepts CourseMate Web site at www.cengagebrain.com and then navigate to the Chapter 10 Key Terms resource for this book.

802.11i (397)
access control (389)
adware (404)
anti-spam program (405)
antivirus program (386)
audit trail (389)
back door (388)
back up (396)
backup (396)
biometric device (391)
biometric payment (391)
botnet (387)
CAPTCHA (390)
certificate authority (395)
clickjacking (405)
computer addiction (399)
computer crime (382)
computer ethics (399)
computer security risk (382)
computer vision syndrome (398)
content filtering (407)
cookie (403)
copyright (401)
cracker (382)
cybercrime (382)

cyberextortionist (382)
cyberterrorist (383)
decrypt (395)
denial of service attack (387)
digital certificate (395)
digital forensics (392)
digital rights management (401)
digital signature (395)
DoS attack (387)
e-mail filtering (405)
employee monitoring (407)
encryption (395)
encryption algorithm (395)
encryption key (395)
ENERGY STAR program (401)
firewall (388)
green computing (401)
hacker (382)
hardware theft (393)
hardware vandalism (393)
information privacy (402)
information theft (395)
intellectual property rights (401)

intrusion detection software (389)
license agreement (394)
malware (384)
password (390)
payload (384)
personal firewall (389)
personal identification number (PIN) (391)
pharming (405)
phishing (405)
phishing filter (405)
piracy (393)
possessed object (391)
product activation (394)
quarantine (386)
real time location system (RTLS) (393)
repetitive strain injury (RSI) (398)
restore (396)
rootkit (384)
script kiddie (382)
secure site (395)
social engineering (405)
software theft (393)

spam (404)
spoofing (388)
spyware (404)
surge protector (396)
system failure (396)
Trojan horse (384)
trusted source (385)
unauthorized access (389)
unauthorized use (389)
uninterruptible power supply (UPS) (396)
user name (390)
virus (384)
virus definition (386)
virus hoax (387)
virus signature (386)
war driving (397)
Web filtering software (407)
Wi-Fi Protected Access (397)
worm (384)
zombie (387)

Checkpoint

The Checkpoint exercises test your knowledge of the chapter concepts. The page number containing the answer appears in parentheses after each exercise.

To complete the Checkpoint exercises interactively, visit the Computer Concepts CourseMate Web site at www.cengagebrain.com and then navigate to the Chapter 10 Checkpoint resource for this book.

Multiple Choice Select the best answer.

1. A _____ is a program that hides in a computer and allows someone from a remote location to take full control of the computer. (384)
   a. worm
   b. rootkit
   c. payload
   d. cookie

2. Malware is a term that can be used to describe _____. (384)
   a. viruses
   b. rootkits
   c. Trojan horses
   d. all of the above

3. The _____ is the destructive event or prank that malware is intended to deliver. (384)
   a. hash
   b. payload
   c. cookie
   d. spam

4. A _____ is an assault whose purpose is to disrupt computer access to an Internet service such as the Web or e-mail. (387)
   a. zombie
   b. denial of service attack
   c. Trojan horse
   d. virus hoax

5. _____ involves the examination of computer media, programs, data and log files on computers, servers, and networks. (392)
   a. Encryption key
   b. E-mail filtering
   c. Digital forensics
   d. Trusted source

6. Physical access controls, such as locked doors and windows, usually are adequate to protect against _____. (393)
   a. software piracy
   b. unauthorized access
   c. hardware theft
   d. all of the above

7. A(n) _____ is a programmed formula that the originator of the data uses to encrypt the plaintext and the recipient of the data uses to decrypt the ciphertext. (395)
   a. botnet
   b. certificate authority
   c. encryption algorithm
   d. encryption key

8. As related to the use of computers, _____ is defined as gaining unauthorized access or obtaining confidential information by taking advantage of the trusting human nature of some victims and the naivety of others. (405)
   a. phishing
   b. a virus hoax
   c. social engineering
   d. pharming

Matching Match the terms with their definitions.

_____ 1. virus (384)

_____ 2. trusted source (385)

_____ 3. spoofing (388)

_____ 4. encryption algorithm (395)

_____ 5. surge protector (396)

a. organization or person you believe will not send a virus infected file knowingly

b. set of steps that can convert readable plaintext into unreadable ciphertext

c. potentially damaging computer program that affects, or infects, a computer negatively by altering the way the computer works without the user's knowledge or permission

d. technique intruders use to make their network or Internet transmission appear legitimate to a victim computer or network

e. uses special electrical components to provide a stable current flow to the computer and other electronic equipment

f. service that blocks e-mail messages from designated sources

Short Answer Write a brief answer to each of the following questions.

1. How do antivirus programs detect and identify a virus? _____ What is a virus hoax? _____

2. Describe the ENERGY STAR program. _____ How should users handle obsolete computers? _____

3. What is information privacy? _____ List five ways to safeguard your personal information. _____

4. What are two methods for avoiding phishing attacks? _____ How does clickjacking work? _____

5. What is content filtering, and who uses it? _____ Why is content filtering controversial? _____

Problem Solving

The Problem Solving exercises extend your knowledge of the chapter concepts by seeking solutions to practical computer problems that you may encounter at home, school, or work. The Collaboration exercise should be completed with a team.

In the real world, practical problems often can be solved in multiple ways. Provide one solution to each of the following problems using available resources, such as articles on the Web or in print, blogs, podcasts, videos, television, user guides, other individuals, and electronics and computer stores. You may need to use multiple resources to obtain an answer. Present your solutions in the form requested by your instructor (brief report, presentation, discussion, or other means).

@ Home

1. **Infected File Detected**   A message appears on your computer screen stating that your antivirus program detected an infected file on your computer and is unable to move it to quarantine. What are your next steps?

2. **Product Key in Use**   While installing the latest version of Microsoft Office, the installation program prompts you to enter the product key. Once you finish entering the product key, you receive an error message stating that the product key already is in use. What might be causing this?

3. **Questionable Fair Use**   A media company's attorney has sent you a letter stating that you are violating their rights by including a short movie clip from one of their movies in one of your videos posted on YouTube. You believe that you are within fair use guidelines by including the movie clip but also feel that you should respond to the attorney's letter. What are your next steps?

4. **Verifying Photo Validity**   You are writing a research paper for your history class and have found a photo on the Web that you would like to use. You are cautious about using photos on the Web because of copyright issues and photos that have been altered digitally. How might you verify the validity of a photo on the Web?

@ Work

5. **Password Management**   You must remember multiple user names and passwords to access various computer resources within your company. Each time your company introduces a new system, you must remember a new user name and password, some of which you are unable to customize. What steps will you take to manage your passwords?

6. **Problem Reinstalling Software**   After recovering from a computer crash, you attempt to reinstall a program that was previously installed. When you insert the installation media, begin the installation, and type the product key, you receive an indication that you are unable to continue installing the software because you have installed it the maximum number of allowable times. What are your next steps?

7. **Missing Security Cable Key**   To protect your notebook computer from theft, you use a security cable to secure it to the desk in your cubicle. Your boss assigns you some work to take home and suggests that you take home your notebook computer. You discover, however, that you are unable to locate the key that releases the security cable from the computer. What are your next steps?

8. **Monitored Computer Activities**   You receive an e-mail message from the IT department stating that it randomly will monitor employee computers throughout the workday to ensure that they are being used for legitimate purposes. Shortly thereafter, you begin to notice that your computer slows significantly at random times once or twice per week. You suspect the performance decrease is a result of the computer monitoring. How will you address this?

Collaboration

9. **Computers in National and Local Security**   National and local security agencies often use computers to protect citizens. For example, computers are used to maintain a list of individuals not cleared to board a commercial aircraft. Form a team of three people to create a list of the various ways computers help to keep us safe. One team member should research how local agencies, such as police departments, use computers to ensure security. Another team member should research ways national security agencies use computers to protect us from threats, and the last team member should research ways that private businesses use computers to guarantee security. Compile these findings into a report and submit it to your instructor.

Learn How To

The Learn How To activities step you through fundamental technology skills when using a computer. The Learn How To exercises enable you to become more proficient with these skills.

Premium Activity: To relate this Learn How To activity to your everyday life, see a visual demonstration of the activity, and complete a short assessment, visit the Computer Concepts CourseMate Web site at www.cengagebrain.com and then navigate to the Chapter 10 Learn How To resource for this book.

Learn How To 1: Back Up Files on an Offsite Internet Server

Note: The service described in this exercise allows 15 days of free access. After that time, you may be billed automatically for service unless you cancel your service in the given time frame.

Backing up files stored on your computer on another disk or computer located in a different geographical location is the ultimate safeguard for data on your computer. A good way to back up data is to use one of the services available on the Web. A leading service is found at IBackup.com. To subscribe to the IBackup service, complete the following steps:

1. Start a Web browser, type the Web address IBackup.com in the Address bar and then press the ENTER key.
2. When the IBackup Web page is displayed, click Signup on the top horizontal toolbar.
3. Enter your e-mail address in the E-mail Address text box and then click the Continue with Registration button to display a form (Figure 10-27).
4. Fill in the form. Select the plan you want in the Select a Storage Plan list. If you want to try the service for a short period of time before subscribing, select 5 GB 15 day Free Trial Plan.
5. To continue to the next pages, you must enter credit card information. If you select the 15-day trial, your credit card will not be charged at this time, and an automatic billing at the end of 15 days will occur. After entering the required information, click the Continue button at the bottom of the page.
6. A message is displayed that confirms that you have signed up with IBackup and also provides a link for you to download the IBackup for Windows program.
7. Click the DOWNLOAD button to download the IBackup for Windows program and then follow the instructions to install the program on your computer.

Figure 10-27

After establishing an account, you can use it for the time for which you subscribed. Complete the following steps to use the service:

1. Start the IBackup for Windows program.
2. Enter your user name and password and then click the Connect button to open a window containing your files, as well as the contents of your My IBackup folder (Figure 10-28).
3. To upload a file, locate the file in the left pane of the IBackup window and drag it to the right pane. The Backup Progress dialog box will be displayed while the file is uploading. The file will be placed in the My IBackup folder.

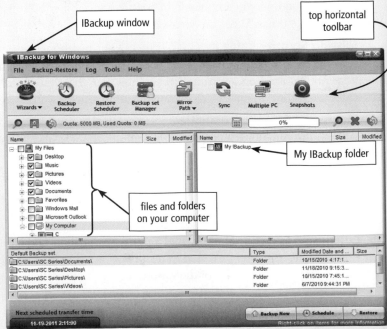

Figure 10-28

STUDENT ASSIGNMENTS

4. For further activities you can accomplish in this program for backing up your files, click the buttons on the top horizontal toolbar and experiment.

Exercises

1. Visit the IBackup Web site. Click View Demo and then follow the screen prompts to view all the services offered by IBackup. Which service is most appropriate for your home computer? Which service is most useful for the server that is used in the computer lab at your school? If you had critical data you needed to back up, would you use a service like this? Why or why not? Submit your answers to your instructor.

2. **Optional: Perform this exercise only for your own computer. Do not perform this exercise on a school computer.** Establish an account on IBackup.com. Upload two or more files from your computer. Download the files you uploaded back to your computer. Is this an efficient way to back up your files? Do you think the IBackup service would be useful for businesses? Submit your answers to your instructor.

Learn It Online

The Learn It Online exercises are interactive Web exercises designed to reinforce and expand your understanding of the chapter concepts. The descriptions below briefly summarize each exercise.

To complete the Learn It Online exercises, visit the Computer Concepts CourseMate Web site at www.cengagebrain.com, navigate to the Chapter 10 resources for this book, click the link for the exercise you want to complete, and then read the instructions.

❶ At the Movies — Attack of the Mobile Viruses

Watch a movie to learn about the recent wave of viruses plaguing mobile device users and then answer questions about the movie.

❷ Student Edition Labs — Protecting Your Privacy Online and Computer Ethics

Enhance your understanding and knowledge about online privacy and computer ethics by completing the Protecting Your Privacy Online and Computer Ethics Labs.

❸ Practice Test

Take a multiple choice test that checks your knowledge of the chapter concepts and review the resulting study guide.

❹ Who Wants To Be a Computer Genius²?

Play the Shelly Cashman Series version of this popular game by answering questions to find out if you are a computer genius. Panic buttons are available to provide assistance during game play.

❺ Crossword Puzzle Challenge

Complete an interactive crossword puzzle to reinforce concepts presented in this chapter.

❻ Windows Exercises

Step through the Windows 7 exercises to learn about playing audio compact discs, understanding multimedia properties, dragging and dropping Windows objects, and checking for system updates.

❼ Exploring Computer Careers

Read about a career as a digital forensics examiner, search for related employment advertisements, and then answer related questions.

❽ Web Apps — Dictionary.com

Learn how to use Dictionary.com to search for a dictionary entry, translate a word to other languages, and search for Web pages containing your search term.

Web Research

The Web Research exercises broaden your understanding of chapter concepts by presenting questions that require you to search the Web for answers.

1 Search Sleuth

Use one of the search engines listed in Figure 2-8 in Chapter 2 on page 65 or your own favorite search engine to find the answers to the following questions. Copy and paste the Web address from the Web page where you found the answer. Some questions may have more than one answer. If required, submit your answers to your instructor. (1) Which five words are among the most commonly used passwords? (2) What do e-mail messages with the subject lines "Sending You All My Love," "Laughing Kitty," and "You've Received a Postcard from a Family Member" have in common? (3) T'ai chi, yoga, and the Alexander technique might offer some relief to computer users suffering from which injury? (4) For which purpose is a gas discharge arrestor used? (5) How many computers in the business world have antivirus software that has been disabled or never was installed properly?

2 Green Computing

The more than 1 billion computers in the world each emit an average of 1,000 pounds of carbon dioxide each year. Many home computer users can help reduce their carbon footprint with the help of devices that monitor energy consumption. Computers are not the only home devices that draw a lot of current; the average home has 27 products that always are turned on, including the television, appliances, and heating and cooling systems. Verdiem's free download, Edison, helps consumers manage their computer power usage. Smart metering devices made by Control4, Colorado vNet, and ZigBee track power usage and give automated tips on how to reduce energy costs. View online Web sites that provide information about reducing home electricity consumption. How do the monitoring devices work? How much do they cost? How do they calculate the money and energy saved per year? Write a report summarizing your findings, and include a table of links to Web sites that provide additional details.

3 Social Networking

People with unique and special talents often desire to share their passions and pastimes with others. Online social networks provide them an opportunity to share their hobbies and creations. In fact, 69 percent of online social networking members say they have a connection with special-interest Web sites. For example, members of the Sports MatchMaker (sportsmatchmaker.com) community can find people who want to play any sport or participate in any hobby at a specific date and time. ShowOffDemo (showoffdemo.com) members spotlight their talents on a virtual stage, and the Instructables community (instructables.com) collaborates to provide instructions for arts, crafts, food, electronics, and games. Visit these Web sites and view the members' products. Which items are popular? Which are unusual? Which photos provide details on documenting the steps necessary to complete a project? How do members share project ideas and requests for information? Summarize the information you read and viewed.

4 Blogs

More than 80,000 blogs are created daily according to Umbria Communications, a service that tracks new Internet media. Many information technology (IT) professionals maintain these blogs to tout companies' products and express personal observations. IT bloggers include Robert Scoble on video (scobleizer.com); Jeff Jaffe, Novell's chief technical officer (novell.com/ctoblog); Ed Brill on IBM (edbrill.com); and Tom Kyte on Oracle (tkyte.blogspot.com). Visit these blogs and read some of the posts. What new products are mentioned? What are the bloggers' backgrounds? What controversial topics are discussed? What personal views do the bloggers express?

5 Ethics in Action

Radio frequency identification (RFID) tags are expected to help merchants in many ways. By placing these tags on such items as prescriptions, computer peripherals, and clothing, retailers hope to reduce theft, track inventory, reduce labor costs, and keep their shelves stocked. Privacy experts, however, claim the tags can store information about consumers' shopping habits and whereabouts. Law enforcement officials, lawyers, marketers, and even thieves could use this detailed electronic data to track people at all times of the day. View Web sites that discuss using RFID tags in stores and the privacy issues that arise from their use. Write a report summarizing your findings, and include a table of links to Web sites that provide additional details.

Chapter Eleven

Information System Development and Programming Languages

Objectives

After completing this chapter, you will be able to:

1 Discuss the importance of project management, feasibility assessment, documentation, and data and information gathering techniques

2 Discuss the purpose of each system development phase

3 Differentiate between low-level languages and procedural languages

4 Identify the benefits of object-oriented programming languages and program development tools

5 List other programming languages and other program development tools

6 Describe various ways to develop Web pages

7 List the six program development steps

8 Explain the basic control structures used in designing solutions to programming problems

System Development

A **system** is a set of components that interact to achieve a common goal. Businesses use many types of systems. A billing system allows a company to send invoices and receive payments from customers. Through a payroll system, employees receive paychecks. A manufacturing system produces the goods that customers order. An inventory system keeps track of the items in a warehouse. Very often, these systems also are information systems.

An **information system** (**IS**) is a collection of hardware, software, data, people, and procedures that work together to produce quality information. An information system supports daily, short-term, and long-range activities of users.

The type of information that users need often changes. When this occurs, the information system must meet the new requirements. In some cases, members of the system development team modify the current information system. In other cases, they develop an entirely new information system.

As a computer user in a business, you someday may participate in the modification of an existing system or the development of a new system. Thus, it is important that you understand system development. **System development** is a set of activities used to build an information system.

System development activities often are grouped into larger categories called **phases**. This collection of phases sometimes is called the **system development life cycle** (**SDLC**). Many SDLCs contain five phases:

1. Planning
2. Analysis
3. Design
4. Implementation
5. Operation, Support, and Security

As shown in Figure 11-1, each system development phase consists of a series of activities, and the phases form a loop. In theory, the five system development phases often appear sequentially, as shown in Figure 11-1. In reality, activities within adjacent phases often interact with one another — making system development a dynamic iterative process.

System Development

1. Planning
- Review project requests
- Prioritize project requests
- Allocate resources
- Form project development team

2. Analysis
- Conduct preliminary investig
- Perform detailed analysis act
  - Study current system
  - Determine user requiren
  - Recommend solution

3. Design
- Acquire hardware and software, if necessary
- Develop details of system

4. Implementation
- Develop programs, if necessary
- Install and test new system
- Train users
- Convert to new system

5. Operation, Support, and Security
- Perform maintenance activities
- Monitor system performance
- Assess system security

Ongoing Activities
- Project management
- Feasibility assessment
- Documentation
- Data/information gathering

Figure 11-1
System development often consists of five phases that form a loop. Several ongoing activities also take place throughout system development.

System development should follow three general guidelines: group activities into phases, involve the users, and define standards.

1. Group activities into phases: Many SDLCs contain the same phases shown in Figure 11-1. Others have more or fewer phases. Regardless, all system development cycles have similar activities and tasks.
2. Involve users: **Users** include anyone for whom the system is being built. Customers, employees, students, data entry clerks, accountants, sales managers, and owners all are examples of users. Users are more apt to accept a new system if they contribute to its design.
3. Define standards: **Standards** are sets of rules and procedures an organization expects employees to accept and follow. Standards help people working on the same project produce consistent results.

Who Participates in System Development?

System development should involve representatives from each department in which the proposed system will be used. This includes both nontechnical users and IT professionals. During system development, the systems analyst meets and works with a variety of people (Figure 11-2). A **systems analyst** is responsible for designing and developing an information system. The systems analyst is the users' primary contact person.

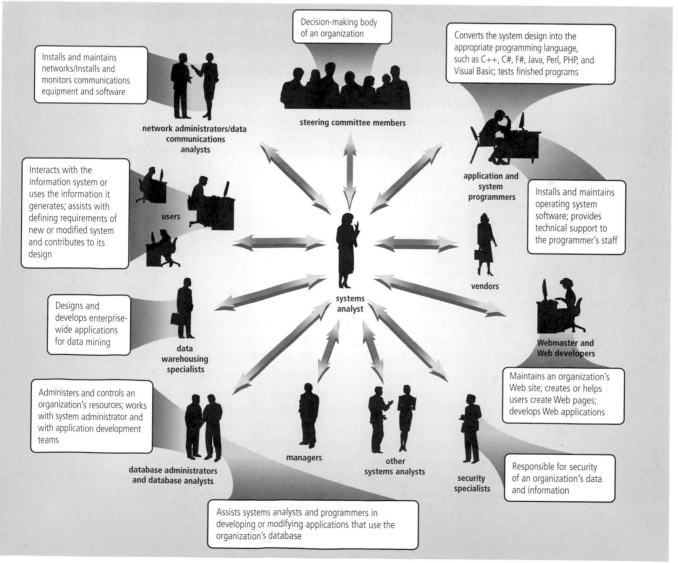

Installs and maintains networks/Installs and monitors communications equipment and software

network administrators/data communications analysts

Decision-making body of an organization

steering committee members

Converts the system design into the appropriate programming language, such as C++, C#, F#, Java, Perl, PHP, and Visual Basic; tests finished programs

application and system programmers

Interacts with the information system or uses the information it generates; assists with defining requirements of new or modified system and contributes to its design

users

Installs and maintains operating system software; provides technical support to the programmer's staff

vendors

Designs and develops enterprise-wide applications for data mining

data warehousing specialists

systems analyst

Webmaster and Web developers

Maintains an organization's Web site; creates or helps users create Web pages; develops Web applications

Administers and controls an organization's resources; works with system administrator and with application development teams

database administrators and database analysts

managers

other systems analysts

security specialists

Responsible for security of an organization's data and information

Assists systems analysts and programmers in developing or modifying applications that use the organization's database

Figure 11-2 A systems analyst meets with a variety of people during a system development project.

Smaller organizations may have one systems analyst or even one person who assumes the roles of both systems analyst and programmer. Larger organizations often have multiple systems analysts. Some refer to a systems analyst as a **system developer**.

Systems analysts are the liaison between the users and the IT professionals. They convert user requests into technical specifications. They must be familiar with business operations, be able to solve problems, have the ability to introduce and support change, and possess excellent communications and interpersonal skills. Systems analysts prepare many reports, drawings, and diagrams. They discuss various aspects of the development project with users, management, other analysts, database analysts, database administrators, network administrators, Web developers, programmers, vendors, and the steering committee. The **steering committee** is a decision-making body in an organization.

For each system development project, an organization usually forms a **project team** to work on the project from beginning to end. The project team consists of users, the systems analyst, and other IT professionals.

Project Management

Project management is the process of planning, scheduling, and then controlling the activities during system development. The goal of project management is to deliver an acceptable system to the user in an agreed-upon time frame, while maintaining costs.

In smaller organizations or projects, one person manages the entire project. For larger projects, the project management activities often are separated between a project manager and a project leader. In this case, the **project leader** manages and controls the budget and schedule of the project, and the **project manager** controls the activities during system development. Project leaders and/or project managers are part of the project team. If the systems analyst is not the project manager, he or she works closely with the project manager.

To plan and schedule a project effectively, the project leader identifies the following elements for the project:
- Goal, objectives, and expectations of the project, collectively called the **scope**
- Required activities
- Time estimates for each activity
- Cost estimates for each activity
- Order of activities
- Activities that can take place at the same time

Gantt Charts

For more information, visit the Computer Concepts CourseMate Web site at www.cengagebrain.com, navigate to the Chapter 11 Web Link resource for this book, and then click Gantt Charts.

PERT Charts

For more information, visit the Computer Concepts CourseMate Web site at www.cengagebrain.com, navigate to the Chapter 11 Web Link resource for this book, and then click PERT Charts.

After these items are identified, the project leader usually records them in a project plan. Project leaders can use **project management software** to assist them in planning, scheduling, and controlling development projects (Figure 11-3).

A popular tool used to plan and schedule the time relationships among project activities is a Gantt chart (Figure 11-3a). A Gantt chart, developed by Henry L. Gantt, is a bar chart that uses horizontal bars to show project phases or activities. The left side, or vertical axis, displays the list of required activities. A horizontal axis across the top or bottom of the chart represents time.

A tool used for planning and scheduling large, complex projects is the PERT chart (Figure 11-3b). A PERT chart, short for Program Evaluations and Review Technique chart, analyzes the time required to complete a task and identifies the minimum time required for an entire project.

When the project features and deadlines have been determined, the project leader monitors and controls the project. Some activities take less time than originally planned. Others take longer. Project leaders should use **change management**, which is the process of recognizing when a change in the project has occurred and taking actions to react to the change. It is crucial that everyone is aware of and agrees on any changes made to the project plan.

Figure 11-3a (Gantt chart)

Figure 11-3b (PERT chart)

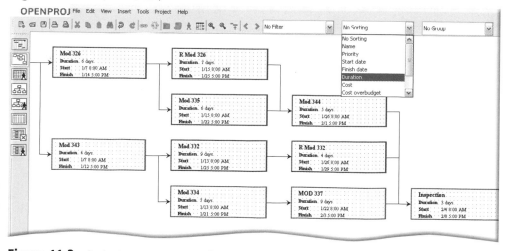

Figure 11-3 Project management software.

Feasibility Assessment

Feasibility is a measure of how suitable the development of a system will be to the organization. A project that is feasible at one point during system development might become infeasible at a later point. Thus, systems analysts frequently reevaluate feasibility during the system development project.

Four tests to evaluate feasibility are:

- Operational feasibility: Measures how well the proposed information system will work. Will the users like the new system? Will they use it? Will it meet their requirements? Is it secure?
- Schedule feasibility: Measures whether the established deadlines for the project are reasonable. If a deadline is not reasonable, the project leader might make a new schedule. If a deadline cannot be extended, then the scope of the project might be reduced to meet a mandatory deadline.
- Technical feasibility: Measures whether the organization has or can obtain the hardware, software, and people needed to deliver and then support the proposed information system.
- Economic feasibility, also called cost/benefit feasibility: Measures whether the lifetime benefits of the proposed information system will be greater than its lifetime costs.

? | FAQ 11-1

How can systems analysts build relationships with users?

Systems analysts have much more credibility with users if the analysts understand user concerns and have empathy for how the workers are feeling. If users are involved, they are more likely to accept and use the new system — called user buy-in. One reason systems fail is because some systems analysts create or modify systems with little or no user participation.

 For more information, visit the Computer Concepts CourseMate Web site at www.cengagebrain.com, navigate to the Chapter 11 FAQ resource for this book, and then click Systems Analyst.

Documentation

During system development, project members produce much documentation. **Documentation** is the collection and summarization of data and information. It includes reports, diagrams, programs, or any other information generated during system development.

It is important that all documentation be well written, thorough, consistent, and understandable. The final information system should be reflected accurately and completely in documentation developed throughout the development project. Maintaining up-to-date documentation should be an ongoing part of system development.

Data and Information Gathering Techniques

Systems analysts and other IT professionals use several techniques to gather data and information. They review documentation, observe, survey, interview, conduct joint-application design sessions, and research.

- Review Documentation — By reviewing documentation such as an organization chart, memos, and meeting minutes, systems analysts learn about the history of a project. Documentation also provides information about the organization such as its operations, weaknesses, and strengths.
- Observe — Observing people helps systems analysts understand exactly how they perform a task. Likewise, observing a machine allows you to see how it works. Read Ethics & Issues 11-1 for a related discussion.
- Survey — To obtain data and information from a large number of people, systems analysts distribute surveys.
- Interview — The interview is the most important data and information gathering technique for the systems analyst. It allows the systems analyst to clarify responses and probe during face-to-face feedback. To learn more about how to conduct an interview, complete the Learn How To 1 activity on pages 460 and 461.

γ | ETHICS & ISSUES 11-1

Do You Work Harder When Someone Is Watching?

While gathering data and information during system development, employees are involved actively in the process. They complete surveys, participate in interviews, and are observed while performing their jobs. Many researchers suggest that during observation, employees may not exhibit everyday behavior and may perform above and beyond their normal workday activities. They base this premise on the Hawthorne Effect, which is the result of a study performed in the 1920s in the Western Electric Company plant in Hawthorne, Illinois. The study discovered that productivity improved during observation, whether conditions were made better or worse. Researchers concluded that productivity seemed to improve whenever the workers knew they were being observed.

Do you believe that you work harder when someone is watching? Why or why not? What is your opinion of the Hawthorne Effect? Do you agree with the research? Is such observation ethical, and can it have other psychological effects on employees? If productivity increases during observation, is observation a good data gathering technique in a system study? Why or why not?

Ethics & Issues

 For the complete text of the Ethics & Issues boxes found in this chapter, visit the Computer Concepts CourseMate Web site at www.cengagebrain.com and then navigate to the Chapter 11 Ethics & Issues resource for this book.

- JAD Sessions — Instead of a single one-on-one interview, analysts often use joint-application design sessions to gather data and information. **Joint-application design (JAD)** sessions, or **focus groups**, are a series of lengthy, structured, group meetings in which users and IT professionals work together to design or develop an application (Figure 11-4).
- Research — Newspapers, computer magazines, reference books, trade shows, the Web, vendors, and consultants are excellent sources of information. These sources can provide the systems analyst with information such as the latest hardware and software products and explanations of new processes and procedures.

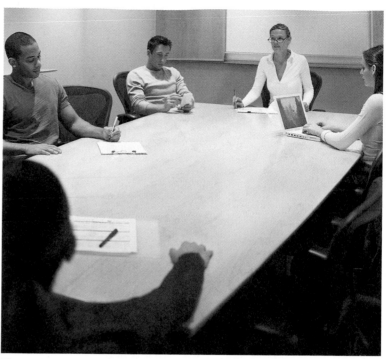

Figure 11-4   During a JAD session, the systems analyst is the moderator, or leader, of the discussion. Another member, called the scribe, records facts and action items assigned during the session.

What Initiates System Development?

A user may request a new or modified information system for a variety of reasons. The most obvious reason is to correct a problem such as an incorrect calculation or a security breach. Another reason is to improve the information system. Organizations may want to improve hardware, software, or other technology to enhance an information system.

Sometimes situations outside the control of an organization require a modification to an information system. Corporate management or some other governing body may mandate a change. Competition also can lead to change. Another source of change results from one organization merging with or acquiring another.

A user may request a new or modified information system verbally in a telephone conversation or written as an e-mail message. Read Ethics & Issues 11-2 for a related discussion. In larger organizations, users write a formal request for a new or modified information system, which is called a request for system services or **project request**. The project request becomes the first item of documentation for the project. It also triggers the first phase of the SDLC: planning.

ETHICS & ISSUES 11-2

Does E-Mail Make You Lie More?

A recent study found that people lied 50 percent more when writing business related e-mail messages than they did when writing with pen and paper. Fortunately, a second study found that the more familiarity between the e-mail sender and recipient, the level of untruths becomes less significant. Another study, though, showed that people are more likely to lie to coworkers than to strangers. Researchers offer a number of reasons for the results of the various studies. For example, one researcher found that people act in self-serving ways when typing as opposed to writing by hand. Others claim that the anonymous nature of sitting, perhaps, miles away from a faceless e-mail recipient simply makes people colder, or that the lack of facial cues, tone, and eye contact

largely are to blame. For some reason, many people find it easier to protect their sense of self-worth and self-esteem when sending e-mail messages. While the effects of the studies are clear, however, researchers provide few suggestions as how to fix the problem.

Does e-mail make you lie more? Why or why not? Given the results of the studies, should readers of e-mail messages be more skeptical of e-mail content? Why? Does knowing that e-mail makes some people lie more make you reconsider how you interact with others? Why or why not? Do you find the results of some of the studies to be truthful in your own experience?

Horizon Community College — A Case Study

This chapter includes a case study to help you understand real-world system development applications. The case study appears shaded in light orange immediately after the discussion of each phase in the chapter. The case is about Horizon Community College (HCC), a fictitious school.

Approximately 15,000 students are enrolled at HCC each year in its varied programs. Students can earn A.S. (Associate of Science) or A.A. (Associate of Arts) degrees in many areas: accounting, anthropology, childcare, computer technology, electronics, construction technology, forensic science, graphic design, history, management, marketing, nursing, and sociology. The school also offers certificates and adult education classes in each of these areas. Some classes are taken on campus, while others are offered online.

Currently, instructors use their own method for recording assignment grades and calculating semester grades. At semester end, the registration department distributes via e-mail a class semester grade form, which contains a list of all students in a class and an area for the instructor to record each student's final semester grade. As instructors send in their class semester grade forms, registration clerks enter each student's grade into the school's database program. After grades are entered, the quality control group compares the original class semester grade forms with the entered grades to check for any errors that may have occurred during the data entry process. Then, report cards are printed and mailed to students.

With the number of enrolled students on the rise, Chad Goldstein, registrar, has noticed that it takes a considerable amount of time for the registration clerks to enter semester grades and for quality control to verify entered grades for accuracy. Lately, quality control has been finding an excessive number of data entry errors, in part due to the excessive workload on the registration clerks. For this reason, Chad would like the instructors to use an online grade book, so that report cards could be printed directly from the instructor's grade book. This change in procedure would save the registration department a great deal of time and money and eliminate data entry errors.

Chad realizes this task will require substantial school resources. He believes a systems study is necessary. He sends an e-mail message to the IT director (Figure 11-5a). She agrees and asks him to fill out a Request for System Services form (Figure 11-5b) and submit it to Juanita Mendez, chair of the steering committee at HCC.

Figure 11-5a (informal project request)

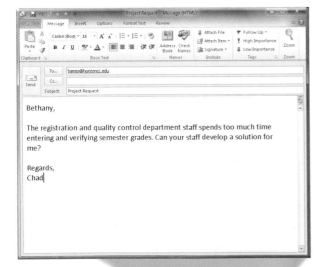

Figure 11-5
Sometimes users informally communicate a project request verbally or as an e-mail message. In larger organizations, requests often are documented on a form such as this Request for System Services.

Figure 11-5b
(formal project request)

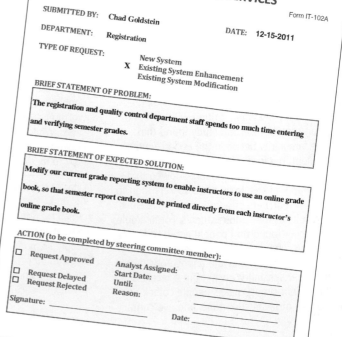

Planning Phase

The **planning phase** for a project begins when the steering committee receives a project request. This committee usually consists of five to nine people. It typically includes a mix of vice presidents, managers, nonmanagement users, and IT personnel.

During the planning phase, four major activities are performed: (1) review and approve the project requests; (2) prioritize the project requests; (3) allocate resources such as money, people, and equipment to approved projects; and (4) form a project development team for each approved project.

The projects that receive the highest priority are those mandated by management or some other governing body. These requests are given immediate attention. The steering committee evaluates the remaining project requests based on their value to the organization. The steering committee approves some projects and rejects others. Of the approved projects, it is likely that only a few will begin system development immediately. Others will have to wait for additional funds or resources to become available.

Planning at Horizon Community College

After receiving the project request (Figure 11-5b) from Chad, Juanita Mendez distributes it to all members of the steering committee. They will discuss the request at their next meeting. The steering committee members of HCC are Juanita Mendez, controller and chair of the steering committee; Milan Sciranka, professor; Suzy Zhao, Web developer; Donnell Carter, training specialist; Karl Schmidt, systems analyst; and Bethany Ames, IT director. Juanita also invites Chad Goldstein to the next steering committee meeting. Because he originated the project request, Chad will have the knowledge to answer questions.

During the meeting, the committee decides the project request identifies an improvement to the system, instead of a problem. They feel the nature of the improvement (to print report cards directly from instructors' online grade books) could lead to considerable savings for the school. It also will reduce data entry errors made by registration clerks.

The steering committee approves the request. Juanita points out that the school has enough funds in its budget to begin the project immediately. Thus, Bethany assembles a system development project team. She assigns Karl Schmidt, systems analyst, as the project leader. Karl and his team immediately begin the next phase: analysis.

Analysis Phase

The **analysis phase** consists of two major activities: (1) conduct a preliminary investigation and (2) perform detailed analysis. The following sections discuss these activities.

The Preliminary Investigation The main purpose of the **preliminary investigation**, sometimes called the **feasibility study**, is to determine the exact nature of the problem or improvement and decide whether it is worth pursuing. Should the organization continue to assign resources to this project? To answer this question, the systems analyst conducts a general study of the project.

The first activity in the preliminary investigation is to interview the user who submitted the project request. Depending on the nature of the request, project team members may interview other users, too.

In addition to interviewing, members of the project team may use other data gathering techniques, such as reviewing existing documentation. Often, the preliminary investigation is completed in just a few days.

Upon completion of the preliminary investigation, the systems analyst writes the feasibility report. This report presents the team's findings to the steering committee. The feasibility report contains these major sections: introduction, existing system, benefits of a new or modified system, feasibility of a new or modified system, and the recommendation (Figure 11-6).

In some cases, the project team may recommend not to continue the project. If the steering committee agrees, the project ends at this point. If the project team recommends continuing and the steering committee approves this recommendation, then detailed analysis begins.

Horizon Community College
MEMORANDUM

To: Steering Committee
From: Karl Schmidt, Project Leader
Date: December 29, 2011
Subject: Feasibility Report of Grade Reporting System

Following is the feasibility report in response to the request for a modification to our Grade Reporting System. Your approval is necessary before the next phase of the project will begin.

Introduction

The purpose of this feasibility report is to determine whether it is beneficial for Horizon Community College to continue studying the Grade Reporting System. The registrar has indicated registration and quality control department staff spends too much time entering and verifying semester grades. This project would affect the registration department, quality control, and instructors. Students also will notice a change.

Existing System

Background

Currently, instructors use their own method for recording assignment grades and calculating semester grades. At semester end, the registration department distributes via e-mail a class semester grade form, which contains a list of all students in a class and an area for the instructor to record each student's final semester grade. As instructors send in their class semester grade forms, registration clerks enter each student's grade using the school's database. After grades are entered, the quality control group compares the original semester grade forms with the entered grades to check for any errors that may have occurred during the data entry process. Then, report cards are printed and mailed to students.

Problems

As the number of enrolled students continues to rise, the following problems have been identified with the current Grade Reporting System at Horizon Community College:

- Registration clerks and quality control spend too much time entering semester grades and verifying entered grades.

- Quality control has been finding an excessive number of data entry errors in part due to the increased workload on the registration clerks.

FEASIBILITY REPORT
Page 2

Benefits of a New or Modified System

Following is a list of benefits that could be realized if the Grade Reporting System at Horizon Community College were modified to enable instructors to use an online grade book, so that report cards could be printed directly from each instructor's grade book:

- Data entry errors of semester grades by registration clerks would be eliminated.

- Cost of supplies, such as paper and ink, would be reduced by 10 percent.

- Through a more efficient use of registration and quality control staff time, the college could achieve a 50 percent reduction in temporary clerks in the registration department.

Feasibility of a New or Modified System

Operational

A modified Grade Reporting System will require instructors enter all semester grades online. In addition to report cards being generated automatically from each instructor's grade book, students will be able to check their class progress throughout the semester.

Schedule

The established deadline for the Grade Reporting System is reasonable.

Technical

Horizon Community College already has a functional database and server. To handle the increased volume and usage of data, however, it will need to purchase a larger database server.

Economic

A detailed summary of the costs and benefits, including all assumptions, is available on our FTP server. The potential costs of the proposed solution could range from $15,000 to $20,000. The estimated savings in temporary clerks and supplies will exceed $30,000.

If you have any questions about the detailed cost/benefit summary or require further information, please contact me.

Recommendation

Based on the findings presented in this report, we recommend a continued study of the Grade Reporting System.

Figure 11-6   A feasibility report presents the results of the preliminary investigation. The report must be prepared professionally and be well organized to be effective.

Preliminary Investigation at Horizon Community College

Karl Schmidt, systems analyst and project leader, meets with Chad Goldstein to discuss the project request. During the interview, Karl looks at the class semester grade forms. He asks Chad how many data entry errors that quality control identified during the last batch of report cards. Then Karl interviews the controller, Juanita Mendez, to obtain some general cost and benefit figures for the feasibility report. He also talks to several registration clerks, quality control clerks, instructors, and students. He wants to know their opinion of the current report card process.

Next, Karl prepares the feasibility report (Figure 11-6). After the project team members review it, Karl submits it to the steering committee. The report recommends proceeding to the detailed analysis phase of this project. The steering committee agrees. Karl and his team begin detailed analysis.

Detailed Analysis   Detailed analysis involves three major activities: (1) study how the current system works; (2) determine the users' wants, needs, and requirements; and (3) recommend a solution. Detailed analysis sometimes is called logical design because the systems analysts develop the proposed solution without regard to any specific hardware or software. That is, they make no attempt to identify the procedures that should be automated and those that should be manual.

During these activities, systems analysts use all of the data and information gathering techniques. They review documentation, observe employees and machines, distribute surveys, interview employees, conduct JAD sessions, and research.

While studying the current system and identifying user requirements, the systems analyst collects a great deal of data and information. A major task for the systems analyst is to document these findings in a way that can be understood by everyone. Systems analysts use diagrams to describe the processes that transform inputs into outputs and diagrams that graphically show the flow of data in the system. Both users and IT professionals refer to this documentation.

The System Proposal   After the systems analyst has studied the current system and determined all user requirements, the next step is to communicate possible solutions for the project in a system proposal. The purpose of the **system proposal** is to assess the feasibility of each alternative solution and then recommend the most feasible solution for the project, which often involves modifying or building on the current system. The systems analyst presents the system proposal to the steering committee. If the steering committee approves a solution, the project enters the design phase.

When the steering committee discusses the system proposal and decides which alternative to pursue, it considers whether to modify the existing system, buy packaged software from an outside source, build its own custom software, and/or outsource some or all of its IT needs to an outside firm. The final decision often is a mix of these options.

- **Packaged software** is mass-produced, copyrighted, prewritten software available for purchase. Packaged software is available for different types of computers. Chapter 3 presented many types of application software available for personal computers. These include word processing, spreadsheet, database, document management, note taking, desktop publishing, paint/image editing, Web page authoring, personal finance, legal, tax preparation, educational/reference, e-mail, and Web browser software.

  Vendors offer two types of packaged software: horizontal and vertical. Horizontal market software meets the needs of many different types of organizations. The programs discussed in Chapter 3 were horizontal. If an organization has a unique way of accomplishing activities, then it also may require vertical market software. Vertical market software specifically is designed for a particular business or industry. Examples of organizations that use vertical market software include banks, schools, hospitals, real estate offices, libraries, and insurance companies. Each of these industries has unique information processing requirements.

- Instead of buying packaged software, some organizations write their own applications using programming languages such as C++, C#, F#, Java, JavaScript, and Visual Basic. Application software developed by the user or at the user's request is called **custom software**.

Vertical Market Software

For more information, visit the Computer Concepts CourseMate Web site at www.cengagebrain.com, navigate to the Chapter 11 Web Link resource for this book, and then click Vertical Market Software.

The main advantage of custom software is that it matches the organization's requirements exactly. The disadvantages usually are that it is more expensive and takes longer to design and implement than packaged software.

- Organizations can develop custom software in-house using their own IT personnel or **outsource** its development, which means having an outside source develop it for them. Some organizations outsource just the software development aspect of their IT operation. Others outsource more or all of their IT operation. Depending on an organization's needs, outside firms can handle as much or as little of the IT requirements as desired. A trend that has caused much controversy relates to organizations that outsource to firms located outside their homeland.

Detailed Analysis at Horizon Community College

Karl and his team begin performing the activities in the detailed analysis phase of the Grade Reporting System. As part of the study and requirements activities, they use several of the data and information gathering techniques available to them. They interview employees throughout the school and meet with some students. They observe instructors recording grades. They prepare documents that become part of the project documentation. Members of the project team refer to these documents during the remainder of system development.

After two months of studying the existing system and obtaining user requirements, Karl discusses his findings with his supervisor, Bethany Ames. In addition to semester grades being printed from the online grade book, Karl recommends that students be granted access to the online grade book so that they can check their progress in a class at any given time.

Based on Karl's findings, Bethany writes a system proposal for the steering committee to review. Suzy Zhao, Web developer at Horizon Community College, developed the current Web site. Thus, Bethany recommends that Suzy's staff modify the Web site in-house. Bethany also recommends that the school invest in a larger database server to handle the additional grade book information.

The steering committee agrees with Bethany's proposal. Karl and his team begin the design phase of the project.

Design Phase

The **design phase** consists of two major activities: (1) if necessary, acquire hardware and software and (2) develop all of the details of the new or modified information system. The systems analyst often performs these two activities at the same time instead of sequentially.

Acquiring Necessary Hardware and Software   When the steering committee approves a solution, the systems analyst begins the activity of obtaining additional hardware or software or evaluating cloud providers that offer the hardware or software to meet the organization's needs. The systems analyst may skip this activity if the approved solution does not require new hardware or software. If this activity is required, it consists of four major tasks: (1) identify technical specifications, (2) solicit vendor proposals, (3) test and evaluate vendor proposals, and (4) make a decision.

Identifying Technical Specifications   The first step in acquiring necessary hardware and software is to identify all the hardware and software requirements of the new or modified system. To do this, systems analysts use a variety of research techniques. They talk with other systems analysts, visit vendors' stores, and search the Web. Many trade journals, newspapers, and magazines provide some or all of their printed content as e-zines. An **e-zine** (pronounced ee-zeen), or **electronic magazine**, is a publication available on the Web.

After the systems analyst defines the technical requirements, the next step is to summarize these requirements for potential vendors. The systems analyst can use three basic types of documents for this purpose: an RFQ, an RFP, or an RFI. A request for quotation (RFQ) identifies the required product(s). With an RFQ, the vendor quotes a price for the listed product(s). With a request for proposal (RFP), the vendor selects the product(s) that meets specified requirements and then quotes the price(s). A request for information (RFI) is a less formal method that uses a standard form to request information about a product or service.

E-Zines
For more information, visit the Computer Concepts CourseMate Web site at www.cengagebrain.com, navigate to the Chapter 11 Web Link resource for this book, and then click E-Zines.

Soliciting Vendor Proposals   Systems analysts send the RFQ, RFP, or RFI to potential hardware and software vendors. Another source for hardware and software products is a value-added reseller. A **value-added reseller (VAR)** is an organization that purchases products from manufacturers and then resells these products to the public — offering additional services with the product (Figure 11-7).

Instead of using vendors, some organizations hire an IT consultant or a group of IT consultants. An **IT consultant** is a professional who is hired based on computer expertise, including service and advice. IT consultants often specialize in configuring hardware and software for businesses of all sizes.

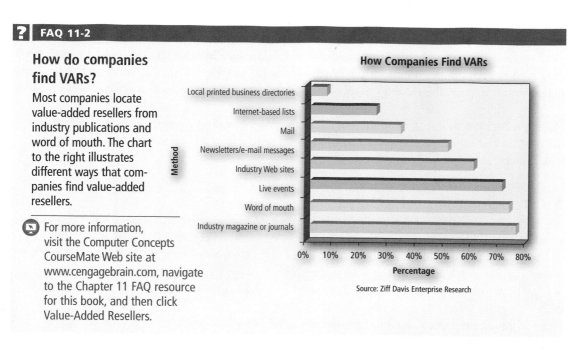

? FAQ 11-2

How do companies find VARs?

Most companies locate value-added resellers from industry publications and word of mouth. The chart to the right illustrates different ways that companies find value-added resellers.

For more information, visit the Computer Concepts CourseMate Web site at www.cengagebrain.com, navigate to the Chapter 11 FAQ resource for this book, and then click Value-Added Resellers.

How Companies Find VARs

Source: Ziff Davis Enterprise Research

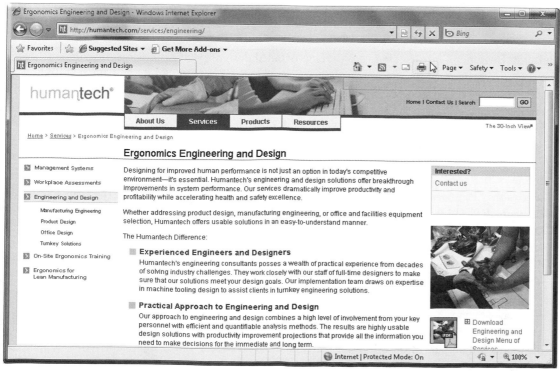

Figure 11-7   Many VARs provide complete systems, often called turnkey solutions.

Testing and Evaluating Vendor Proposals   After sending RFQs and RFPs to potential vendors, the systems analyst will receive completed quotations and proposals. Evaluating the proposals and then selecting the best one often is a difficult task. It is important to be as objective as possible while evaluating each proposal.

Systems analysts use many techniques to test the various software products from vendors. They obtain a list of user references from the software vendors. They also talk to current users of the software to solicit their opinions. Some vendors will give a demonstration of the product(s) specified. Other vendors provide demonstration copies or trial versions, allowing the organizations to test the software themselves.

Sometimes it is important to know whether the software can process a certain volume of transactions efficiently. In this case, the systems analyst conducts a benchmark test. A **benchmark test** measures the performance of hardware or software. For example, a benchmark test could measure the time it takes a payroll program to print 50 paychecks. Comparing the time it takes various accounting programs to print the same 50 paychecks is one way of measuring each program's performance.

Making a Decision   Having rated the proposals, the systems analyst presents a recommendation to the steering committee. The recommendation could be to award a contract to a vendor or to not make any purchases at this time.

Hardware Acquisition at Horizon Community College

Karl and his team compile a requirements list for the database server. They prepare an RFP and submit it to twelve vendors eight through the Web and four local computer stores. Ten vendors reply within the three-week deadline.

Of the ten replies, the development team selects two to evaluate. They eliminate the other eight because these vendors did not offer adequate warranties for the database server. The project team members ask for benchmark test results for each server. In addition, they contact two current users of this database server for their opinions about its performance. After evaluating these two servers, the team selects the best one.

Karl summarizes his team's findings in a report to the steering committee. The committee gives Karl authorization to award a contract to the proposed vendor. As a courtesy and to maintain good working relationships, Karl sends a letter to all twelve vendors informing them of the commitee's decision.

Detailed Design   The next step is to develop detailed design specifications for the components in the proposed solution. The activities to be performed include developing designs for the databases, inputs, outputs, and programs.

- During database design, the systems analyst works closely with the database analysts and database administrators to identify those data elements that currently exist within the organization and those that are new.

   The systems analyst also addresses user access privileges. This means that the systems analyst defines which data elements each user can access, when they can access the data elements, what actions they can perform on the data elements, and under what circumstances they can access the elements. Read Looking Ahead 11-1 for a look at a future database design.

- During detailed design of inputs and outputs, the systems analyst carefully designs every menu, screen, and report specified in the requirements. The outputs often are designed first because they help define the requirements for the inputs. Thus, it is very important that outputs are identified correctly and that users agree to them.

   The systems analyst typically develops two types of designs for each input and output: a mockup and a layout chart. A mockup is a sample of the input or output that contains actual data (Figure 11-8). The systems analyst shows mockups to users for their approval. Because users will work with the inputs and outputs of the system, it is crucial to involve users during input and output design.

   After users approve the mockup, the systems analyst develops a layout chart for the programmer. A layout chart is more technical and contains programming-like notations. Many database programs provide tools for technical design (Figure 11-9).

↗ **LOOKING AHEAD 11-1**

Remote Solar System Objects Mapped in Database

Exploding supernovas, neutron stars, and black holes will become more than faint astronomical objects when the Large Synoptic Survey Telescope (LSST) becomes fully operable in 2016. The LSST is being constructed atop an 8,800-foot mountain in Chile.

Managing the telescope's 200,000 images of the billions of remote galaxies is a massive undertaking. A single minute of observation time generates 72 GB of data, which will be saved in a 150 PB database. Each year, 60 PB of the stored images in this world's largest nonproprietary database will be released to researchers. Each night, 30 TB of data will be sent to the United States so that astronomy buffs can view the night sky via their computers. In addition, astronomers will be able to log on to the Data Access Center at any time to view all the data collected.

Software billionaires Bill Gates and Charles Simonyi have donated $30 million for the project. Researchers are hopeful the LSST ultimately will give a graphical view of the universe's evolution from its birth to the present day.

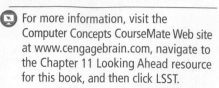 For more information, visit the Computer Concepts CourseMate Web site at www.cengagebrain.com, navigate to the Chapter 11 Looking Ahead resource for this book, and then click LSST.

Figure 11-8 Users must give their approval on all inputs and outputs. This input screen is a mockup (containing actual sample data) for users to review.

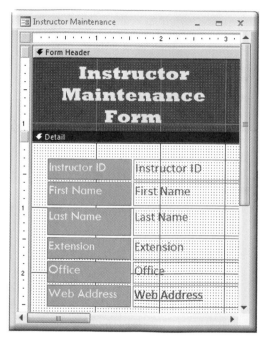

Figure 11-9 Shown here is a technical view in Access of the mockup in Figure 11-8.

Other issues that must be addressed during input and output design include the types of media to use (paper, video, audio); formats (graphical or narrative); and data entry validation techniques, which include making sure the entered data is correct (for example, a state code has to be one of the fifty valid two-letter state abbreviations).

• During program design, the systems analyst prepares the program specification package, which identifies required programs and the relationship among each program, as well as the input, output, and database specifications.

Prototyping Many systems analysts today use prototypes during detailed design. A **prototype** is a working model of the proposed system. The systems analyst actually builds a functional form of the solution during design. The main advantage of a prototype is users can work with the system before it is completed — to make sure it meets their needs. As soon as users approve a prototype, system analysts can implement a solution more quickly than without a prototype.

Case Tools Many systems analysts use computer software to assist during system development. **Computer-aided software engineering (CASE)** software tools are designed to support one or more activities of system development (Figure 11-10).

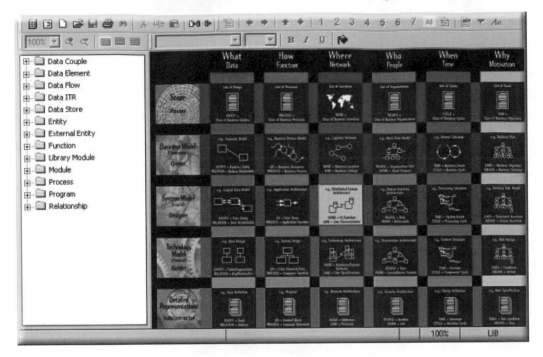

Figure 11-10
Computer-aided software engineering (CASE) programs assist analysts in the development of an information system. Visible Analyst by Visible Systems Corporation enables analysts to create diagrams, as well as to build the project dictionary.

Quality Review Techniques Many people should review the detailed design specifications before they are given to the programming team. Reviewers should include users, systems analysts, managers, IT staff, and members of the system development team. If the steering committee decides the project still is feasible, which usually is the case, the project enters the implementation phase.

Detailed Design at Horizon Community College

As approved by the steering committee, Karl and his team begin designing the Grade Reporting System. After studying current vendor information and interviewing more users and vendors, the team designs changes to the school's database, Web site, and the associated programs. They prepare several documents including a mockup (Figure 11-8 on the previous page) and a technical view in Access (Figure 11-9 on the previous page).

After completing the detailed design, Karl meets with several users and IT personnel to walk through the design. They locate two errors. He corrects the errors and then presents the design to the steering committee. The committee agrees with the design solution and consents to implement it.

Implementation Phase

The purpose of the **implementation phase** is to construct, or build, the new or modified system and then deliver it to the users. Members of the system development team perform four major activities in this phase: (1) develop programs, (2) install and test the new system, (3) train users, and (4) convert to the new system.

Develop Programs If the organization purchases packaged software and no modifications to the software are required, the development team may skip this activity. For custom software or packaged software that requires modification, however, programs are developed or modified either by an outside firm or in-house. Programmers write or modify programs from the program specification package created during the analysis phase. Just as system development follows an organized set of activities, so does program development. These program development activities are known as the program development life cycle.

The last sections of this chapter identify various programming languages and explain program development. An important concept to understand is that program development is part of the implementation phase.

Install and Test the New System

If the organization acquires new hardware or software, someone must install and test it. The systems analysts should test individual programs. They also should be sure that all the programs work together in the system.

Systems analysts and users develop test data so that they can perform various tests. A unit test verifies that each individual program or object works by itself. A systems test verifies that all programs in an application work together properly. An integration test verifies that an application works with other applications. An acceptance test is performed by end-users and checks the new system to ensure that it works with actual data.

Train Users

Training involves showing users exactly how they will use the new hardware and software in the system. Some training takes place as one-on-one sessions or classroom-style lectures (Figure 11-11). Other organizations use Web-based training, which is a self-directed, self-paced online instruction method. Whichever technique is used, it should include hands-on sessions with realistic sample data. Users should practice on the actual system during training. Users also should receive user manuals for reference. It is the systems analyst's responsibility to create user manuals, both printed and electronic.

Figure 11-11
Organizations must ensure that users are trained properly on the new system. One training method uses hands-on classes to learn the new system.

Convert to the New System

The final implementation activity is to change from the old system to the new system. This change can take place using one or more of the following conversion strategies: direct, parallel, phased, or pilot.

With **direct conversion**, the user stops using the old system and begins using the new system on a certain date. The advantage of this strategy is that it requires no transition costs and is a quick implementation technique. The disadvantage is that it is extremely risky and can disrupt operations seriously if the new system does not work correctly the first time.

Parallel conversion consists of running the old system alongside the new system for a specified time. Results from both systems are compared. The advantage of this strategy is that you can fix any problems in the new system before you terminate the old system. The disadvantage is that it is costly to operate two systems at the same time.

Larger systems with multiple sites may use a phased conversion. In a **phased conversion**, each location converts at a separate time. For example, an accounting system might convert its accounts receivable, accounts payable, general ledger, and payroll sites in separate phases. Each site can use a direct or parallel conversion.

With a **pilot conversion**, only one location in the organization uses the new system — so that it can be tested. After the pilot site approves the new system, other sites convert using one of the other conversion strategies.

Implementation at Horizon Community College

Upon receiving the program specification package, Karl forms an implementation team of Suzy Zhao, Web developer; Adam Rosen, programmer; and Stephan Davis, data modeler. The team works together to implement the Grade Reporting System.

Karl works closely with the team to answer questions about the design and to check the progress of their work. When the team completes its work, they ask Karl to test it. He does and it works great!

Karl arranges a training class for all instructors and also the employees of the registration department. During the training session, he shows them how to use the new online grade book on the school's Web site. Karl gives each attendee a printed user guide and indicates that he will e-mail them the electronic file. Karl also modifies the Web site informing students of the new online grade checking service.

Operation, Support, and Security Phase

The purpose of the **operation, support, and security phase** is to provide ongoing assistance for an information system and its users after the system is implemented. The support phase consists of three major activities: (1) perform maintenance activities, (2) monitor system performance, and (3) assess system security.

Information system maintenance activities include fixing errors in, as well as improving, a system's operations. To determine initial maintenance needs, the systems analyst should meet with users. The purpose of this meeting, called the post-implementation system review, is to discover whether the information system is performing according to the users' expectations. In some cases, users would like the system to do more. Maybe they have enhancements or additional requirements that involve modifying or expanding an existing information system.

During this phase, the systems analyst monitors performance of the new or modified information system. The purpose of performance monitoring is to determine whether the system is inefficient or unstable at any point. If it is, the systems analyst must investigate solutions to make the information system more efficient and reliable — back to the planning phase.

Most organizations must deal with complex computer security issues. All elements of an information system — hardware, software, data, people, and procedures — must be secure from threats both inside and outside the enterprise.

Organizations today often have a **chief security officer** (CSO) who is responsible for the physical security of an organization's property and people and also is in charge of securing its computing resources. It is critical that the CSO is included in all system development projects to ensure that all projects adequately address information security. The CSO uses many of the techniques discussed in Chapter 10 to maintain confidentiality or limited access to information, ensure integrity and reliability of systems, ensure uninterrupted availability of systems, ensure compliance with laws, and cooperate with law enforcement agencies.

An important responsibility of the CSO is to develop a computer security plan. A **computer security plan** summarizes in writing all of the safeguards that are in place to protect an organization's information assets. The CSO should evaluate the computer security plan annually or more frequently for major changes in information assets, such as the addition of a new computer or the implementation of a new application. In developing the plan, the CSO should recognize that some degree of risk is unavoidable; further, the more secure a system is, the more difficult it is for everyone to use. The goal of a computer security plan is to match an appropriate level of safeguards against the identified risks. Fortunately, most organizations never will experience a major information system disaster.

? FAQ 11-3

Are financial Web sites vulnerable?

Yes. Research indicates that vulnerabilities are common among financial Web sites. Some vulnerabilities include insecure login forms, confidential information displayed on insecure pages, and weak rules for user name and password selection. Before performing a transaction on a financial Web site, you should make sure that the Web site is secure and that the Web site has no known problems or vulnerabilities.

For more information, visit the Computer Concepts CourseMate Web site at www.cengagebrain.com, navigate to the Chapter 11 FAQ resource for this book, and then click Web Site Vulnerabilities.

Operation, Support, and Security at Horizon Community College

During the post-implementation system review, Karl learns that the new Grade Reporting System is working well. Instructors find it easy to use, and students appreciate being able to check grades online. The registration department is saving time and money because they no longer have to enter or check class semester grades. Chad says his staff is working efficiently on other registration tasks, now that the Grade Reporting System has been automated. Data in the system has been accessed only by authorized users, leading him to conclude security measures work as planned.

Six months after the Grade Reporting System has been in operation, Chad would like to add the capability for students to request transcripts online. He sends an e-mail message to Karl requesting the change. Karl asks him to fill out a Request for System Services and puts him on the agenda of the next steering committee meeting. Back to the planning phase again!

✔ QUIZ YOURSELF 11-1

Instructions: Find the true statement below. Then, rewrite the remaining false statements so that they are true.

1. A computer security plan summarizes in writing all of the safeguards that are in place to protect an organization's information assets.

2. Feasibility is the process of planning, scheduling, and then controlling the activities during system development.

3. The five phases in most SDLCs are programming, analysis, design, sampling, and recording.

4. The purpose of the design phase is to provide ongoing assistance for an information system and its users after the system is implemented.

5. Upon completion of the preliminary investigation, the systems analyst writes the system proposal.

6. Users should not be involved throughout system development.

Quiz Yourself Online: To further check your knowledge of pages 418 through 435, visit the Computer Concepts CourseMate Web site at www.cengagebrain.com, navigate to the Chapter 11 Quiz Yourself resource for this book, and then click Objectives 1 – 2.

Programming Languages and Program Development Tools

The previous sections discussed the system development phases. One activity during the implementation phase is to develop programs. Although you may never write a computer program, information you request may require a programmer to create or modify a program. Thus, you should understand how programmers develop programs to meet information requirements. A **computer program** is a series of instructions that directs a computer to perform tasks. A computer **programmer**, often called a **developer**, creates and modifies computer programs.

To create a program, programmers sometimes write, or code, a program's instructions using a programming language. A **programming language** is a set of words, abbreviations, and symbols that enables a programmer to communicate instructions to a computer. Other times, programmers use a program development tool to create a program. A program that provides a user-friendly environment for building programs often is called a **program development tool**. Programmers use a variety of programming languages and tools to create programs (Figure 11-12).

Several hundred programming languages exist today. Each language has its own rules for writing the instructions. Languages often are designed for specific purposes, such as scientific applications, business solutions, or Web page development. When solving a problem or building a solution, programmers often use more than one language; that is, they integrate the languages.

Two types of languages are low-level and high-level. A low-level language is a programming language that is machine dependent. A machine-dependent language runs on only one particular type of computer. Each instruction in a low-level language usually equates to a single machine instruction, discussed further in the next section. With a high-level language, by contrast, each instruction typically equates to multiple machine instructions. High-level languages often are machine independent. A machine-independent language can run on many different types of computers and operating systems.

The following pages discuss low-level languages, as well as several types of high-level languages.

Figure 11-12 Programmers must decide which programming languages and program development tools to use when they create programs.

```
0000DE   5A50   35AA                      015AC
0000E2   47F0   2100           00102
000102   1B77
000104   5870   304E                      01050
000108   1C47
00010A   4E50   30D6                      010D8
00010E   F075   30D6    003E   010D8      0003E
000114   4F50   30D6                      010D8
000118   5050   3052                      01054
00011C   58E0   30B6                      010B8
000120   07FE
                                          00122
000122   50E0   30BA                      010BC
000126   1B55
000128   5A50   304E                      01050
00012C   5B50   3052                      01054
000130   5050   305A                      0105C
000134   58E0   30BA                      010BC
000138   07FE
```

Low-Level Languages

Two types of low-level languages are machine languages and assembly languages. **Machine language**, known as the first generation of programming languages, is the only language the computer directly recognizes (Figure 11-13). Machine language instructions use a series of binary digits (1s and 0s) or a combination of numbers and letters that represents binary digits. The binary digits correspond to the on and off electrical states. As you might imagine, coding in machine language is tedious and time-consuming.

Figure 11-13 A sample machine language program, coded using the hexadecimal number system. A hexadecimal number system can be used to represent binary numbers using letters of the alphabet and decimal numbers.

With an **assembly language**, the second generation of programming languages, a programmer writes instructions using symbolic instruction codes (Figure 11-14). Examples of these codes include A for addition, C for compare, L for load, and M for multiply.

Assembly languages also use symbolic addresses. A symbolic address is a meaningful name that identifies a storage location. For example, a programmer can use the name RATE to refer to the storage location that contains a pay rate.

Despite these advantages, assembly languages can be difficult to learn. In addition, programmers must convert an assembly language program into machine language before the computer can execute, or run, the program. That is, the computer cannot execute the assembly source program. A **source program** is the program that contains the language instructions, or code, to be converted to machine language. To convert the assembly language source program into machine language, programmers use a program called an assembler.

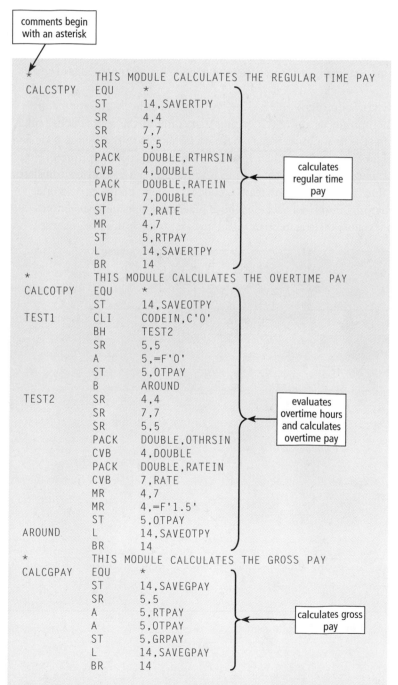

comments begin with an asterisk

```
*             THIS MODULE CALCULATES THE REGULAR TIME PAY
CALCSTPY   EQU      *
           ST       14,SAVERTPY
           SR       4,4
           SR       7,7
           SR       5,5
           PACK     DOUBLE,RTHRSIN
           CVB      4,DOUBLE
           PACK     DOUBLE,RATEIN
           CVB      7,DOUBLE
           ST       7,RATE
           MR       4,7
           ST       5,RTPAY
           L        14,SAVERTPY
           BR       14
*             THIS MODULE CALCULATES THE OVERTIME PAY
CALCOTPY   EQU      *
           ST       14,SAVEOTPY
TEST1      CLI      CODEIN,C'O'
           BH       TEST2
           SR       5,5
           A        5,=F'O'
           ST       5,OTPAY
           B        AROUND
TEST2      SR       4,4
           SR       7,7
           SR       5,5
           PACK     DOUBLE,OTHRSIN
           CVB      4,DOUBLE
           PACK     DOUBLE,RATEIN
           CVB      7,RATE
           MR       4,7
           MR       4,=F'1.5'
           ST       5,OTPAY
AROUND     L        14,SAVEOTPY
           BR       14
*             THIS MODULE CALCULATES THE GROSS PAY
CALCGPAY   EQU      *
           ST       14,SAVEGPAY
           SR       5,5
           A        5,RTPAY
           A        5,OTPAY
           ST       5,GRPAY
           L        14,SAVEGPAY
           BR       14
```

calculates regular time pay

evaluates overtime hours and calculates overtime pay

calculates gross pay

Figure 11-14   An excerpt from an assembly language payroll program. The code shows the computations for regular time pay, overtime pay, and gross pay and the decision to evaluate the overtime hours.

Procedural Languages

The disadvantages of machine and assembly (low-level) languages led to the development of procedural languages in the late 1950s and 1960s. In a **procedural language**, the programmer writes instructions that tell the computer what to accomplish and how to do it.

With a procedural language, often called a **third-generation language (3GL)**, a programmer uses a series of English-like words to write instructions. For example, ADD stands for addition or PRINT means to print. Many 3GLs also use arithmetic operators such as * for multiplication and + for addition. These English-like words and arithmetic symbols simplify the program development process for the programmer.

As with an assembly language program, the 3GL code (instructions) is called the source program. Programmers must convert this source program into machine language before the computer can execute the program. This translation process often is very complex, because one 3GL source program instruction translates into many machine language instructions. For 3GLs, programmers typically use either a compiler or an interpreter to perform the translation.

A **compiler** is a separate program that converts the entire source program into machine language before executing it. The machine language version that results from compiling the 3GL is called the object code or object program. The compiler stores the object code on storage media for execution later.

While it is compiling the source program into object code, the compiler checks the source program for errors. The compiler then produces a program listing that contains the source code and a list of any errors. This listing helps the programmer make necessary changes to the source code and correct errors in the program. Figure 11-15 shows the process of compiling a source program.

A compiler translates an entire program before executing it. An interpreter, by contrast, translates and executes one statement at a time. An **interpreter** reads a code statement, converts it to one or more machine language instructions, and then executes those machine language instructions. It does this all before moving to the next code statement in the program. Each time the source

 Figure 11-15 A compiler converts the source program into a machine language object program. If the compiler encounters any errors, it records them in a program-listing file, which the programmer may print when the entire compilation is complete. When a user wants to run the program, the object program is loaded into the memory of the computer and the program instructions begin executing.

```
*      COMPUTE REGULAR TIME PAY
       MULTIPLY REGULAR-TIME-HOURS BY HOURLY-PAY-RATE
           GIVING REGULAR-TIME-PAY.

*      COMPUTE OVERTIME PAY
       IF OVERTIME-HOURS > 0
          COMPUTE OVERTIME-PAY = OVERTIME-HOURS * 1.5 * HOURLY-PAY-RATE
       ELSE
          MOVE 0 TO OVERTIME-PAY.

*      COMPUTE GROSS PAY
       ADD REGULAR-TIME-PAY TO OVERTIME-PAY
           GIVING GROSS-PAY.
```

program runs, the interpreter translates and executes it, statement by statement. An interpreter does not produce an object program. Figure 11-16 shows the process of interpreting a program.

One advantage of an interpreter is that when it finds errors, it displays feedback immediately. The programmer can correct any errors before the interpreter translates the next line of code. The disadvantage is that interpreted programs do not run as fast as compiled programs.

Hundreds of procedural languages exist. Only a few, however, are used widely enough for the industry to recognize them as standards. These include C and COBOL. To illustrate the similarities and differences among these programming languages, the figures on the following pages show program code in these languages. The code solves a simple payroll problem — computing the gross pay for an employee.

The process used to compute gross pay can vary from one system to another. The examples on the following pages use a simple algorithm, or set of steps, to help you easily compare one programming language with another. Read Innovative Computing 11-1 to find out about some useful and fun online programs.

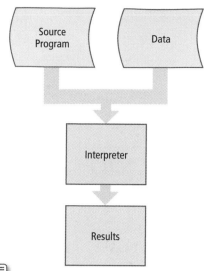

Figure 11-16 With an interpreter, one line of the source program at a time is converted into machine language and then immediately executed by the computer. If the interpreter encounters an error while converting a line of code, an error message immediately is displayed on the screen and the program stops.

! INNOVATIVE COMPUTING 11-1

Online Calculators Answer Life's Questions

At practically every phase of life, people can benefit from some sort of calculator. For example, one program can help expectant parents calculate the date their child will be born, and another can generate possible baby names. Once the child is born, they can use another calculator that attempts to estimate the total cost of raising the child through the teenage years.

One Web site has collected a wide variety of calculators: Your Life, Calculated. This MSN-sponsored site organizes the calculators in a variety of categories. The Career section includes a millionaire calculator to determine how much money will need to be saved each month to reach $1 million, and it also includes amortization tables and mortgage and car loan calculators.

Other tools are the tip calculator, a calculator that determines the chances of a successful personal relationship, the body mass index to measure body fat based on height and weight, the college cost calculator, and the financial aid calculator. When using online calculators, keep in mind that some are subjective in nature, and the results reflect the thoughts and/or opinions of the calculator's author.

For more information, visit the Computer Concepts CourseMate Web site at www.cengagebrain.com, navigate to the Chapter 11 Innovative Computing resource for this book, and then click Online Calculators.

C The **C** programming language, developed in the early 1970s by Dennis Ritchie at Bell Laboratories, originally was designed for writing system software. Today, many programs are written in C (Figure 11-17). C runs on almost any type of computer with any operating system, but it is used most often with the UNIX and Linux operating systems.

comments begin with a slash followed by an asterisk

calculates regular time pay

evaluates overtime hours and calculates overtime pay

prints gross pay

calculates gross pay

```
/* Compute Regular Time Pay                    */
rt_pay = rt_hrs * pay_rate;

/* Compute Overtime Pay                         */
if (ot_hrs > 0)
    ot_pay = ot_hrs * 1.5 * pay_rate;
else
    ot_pay = 0;

/* Compute Gross Pay                            */
gross = rt_pay + ot_pay;

/* Print Gross Pay                              */
printf("The gross pay is %d\n", gross);
```

Figure 11-17 An excerpt from a C payroll program. The code shows the computations for regular time pay, overtime pay, and gross pay; the decision to evaluate the overtime hours; and the output of the gross pay.

COBOL   COBOL (**CO**mmon **B**usiness-**O**riented **L**anguage) evolved out of a joint effort between the United States government, businesses, and major universities in the early 1960s. Naval officer Grace Hopper, a pioneer in computer programming, was a prime developer of COBOL.

COBOL is a programming language designed for business applications. Although COBOL programs often are lengthy, their English-like statements make the code easy to read, write, and maintain (Figure 11-18). COBOL especially is useful for processing transactions, such as payroll and billing, on mainframe computers.

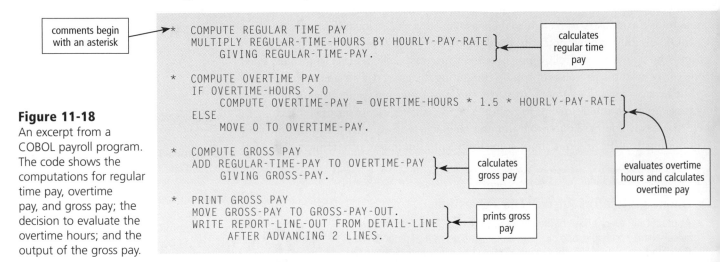

Figure 11-18
An excerpt from a COBOL payroll program. The code shows the computations for regular time pay, overtime pay, and gross pay; the decision to evaluate the overtime hours; and the output of the gross pay.

Object-Oriented Programming Languages and Program Development Tools

Programmers use an **object-oriented programming** (**OOP**) **language** or object-oriented program development tool to implement objects in a program. An object is an item that can contain both data and the procedures that read or manipulate that data. An object represents a real person, place, event, or transaction.

A major benefit of OOP is the ability to reuse and modify existing objects. For example, once a programmer creates an Employee object, it is available for use by any other existing or future program. Thus, programmers repeatedly reuse existing objects. For example, the payroll program and health benefits program both use the Employee object. That is, the payroll program would use it to process employee paychecks and the health benefits program would use it to process health insurance payments.

Programs developed using the object-oriented approach have several advantages. The objects can be reused in many systems, are designed for repeated use, and become stable over time. In addition, programmers create applications faster because they design programs using existing objects. Programming languages, such as Java, C#, F#, C++, and the latest versions of Visual Basic are complete object-oriented languages.

Object-oriented programming languages and program development tools work well in a RAD environment. **RAD** (rapid application development) is a method of developing software, in which the programmer writes and implements a program in segments instead of waiting until the entire program is completed. An important concept in RAD is the use of prebuilt components. For example, programmers do not have to write code for buttons and text boxes on Windows forms because they already exist in the programming language or tools provided with the language.

Most object-oriented program development tools are IDEs. An **IDE** (**integrated development environment**) includes tools for building graphical interfaces, an editor for entering program code, a compiler and/or interpreter, and a debugger (to remove errors, which is discussed later in the chapter). Some IDEs work with a single programming language, others support multiple languages.

Java   **Java** is an object-oriented programming language developed by Sun Microsystems. Figure 11-19 shows a portion of a Java program and the window that the program displays.

When programmers compile a Java program, the resulting object code is machine independent. Java uses a just-in-time (JIT) compiler to convert the machine-independent code into machine-dependent code that is executed immediately. Programmers use various Java Platform implementations, developed by Sun Microsystems, which provide development tools for creating programs for all sizes of computers.

Java Platforms

For more information, visit the Computer Concepts CourseMate Web site at www.cengagebrain.com, navigate to the Chapter 11 Web Link resource for this book, and then click Java Platforms.

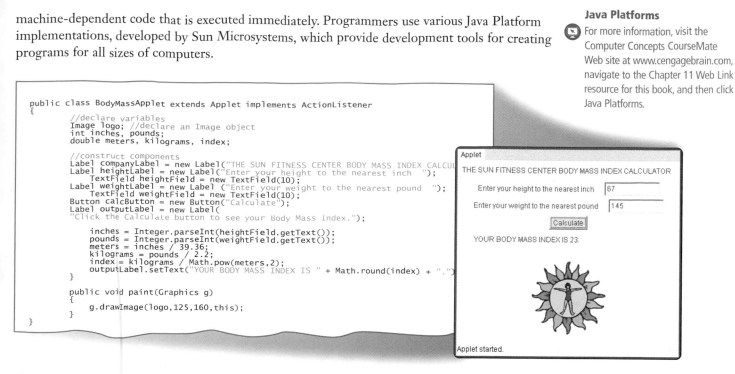

```
public class BodyMassApplet extends Applet implements ActionListener
{
        //declare variables
        Image logo; //declare an Image object
        int inches, pounds;
        double meters, kilograms, index;

        //construct components
        Label companyLabel = new Label("THE SUN FITNESS CENTER BODY MASS INDEX CALCUL
        Label heightLabel = new Label("Enter your height to the nearest inch  ");
            TextField heightField = new TextField(10);
        Label weightLabel = new Label ("Enter your weight to the nearest pound  ");
            TextField weightField = new TextField(10);
        Button calcButton = new Button("Calculate");
        Label outputLabel = new Label(
        "Click the Calculate button to see your Body Mass Index.");

        inches = Integer.parseInt(heightField.getText());
        pounds = Integer.parseInt(weightField.getText());
        meters = inches / 39.36;
        kilograms = pounds / 2.2;
        index = kilograms / Math.pow(meters,2);
        outputLabel.setText("YOUR BODY MASS INDEX IS " + Math.round(index) + ".")
    }

    public void paint(Graphics g)
    {
        g.drawImage(logo,125,160,this);
    }
}
```

Figure 11-19 A portion of a Java program and the window the program displays.

.NET The Microsoft .NET Framework, or **.NET** (pronounced dot net), is a set of technologies that allows almost any type of program to run on the Internet or an internal business network, as well as stand-alone computers and mobile devices. Similarly, ASP.NET is a Web application framework that provides the tools necessary for the creation of dynamic Web sites.

Using .NET and/or ASP.NET, programmers easily can develop Web applications, Web services, and Windows programs. Examples of languages that support .NET include C++, C#, F#, Visual Basic, Delphi, and PowerBuilder. The following sections discuss each of these languages.

C++ Developed in the 1980s by Bjarne Sroustrup at Bell Laboratories, **C++** (pronounced SEE-plus-plus) is an object-oriented programming language that is an extension of the C programming language. C++ includes all the elements of the C language (shown in Figure 11-17 on page 439), plus it has additional features for working with objects. Programmers commonly use C++ to develop database and Web applications.

C# Based on C++, **C#** (pronounced SEE-sharp) is an object-oriented programming language that was developed primarily by Anders Hejlsberg, Microsoft chief architect and distinguished engineer. C# has been accepted as a standard for Web applications and XML-based Web services.

F# **F#** (pronounced EFF-sharp), which is included with the latest version of Visual Studio (discussed in the next section), is a programming language that combines the benefits of an object-oriented language with the benefits of a functional language. A functional language is a programming language whose natural programming structure is useful in mathematical programs. Benefits of programs written in F# include easy access to .NET libraries and performance similar to that of C# programs.

Visual Studio **Visual Studio** is Microsoft's suite of program development tools that assists programmers in building programs for Windows, Windows Mobile, or any operating systems that support .NET. Visual Studio includes enhanced support for building security and reliability into applications through its programming languages, RAD tools, IDE, a specialized query language, and other resources that reduce development time. For example, Visual Studio includes **code snippets**, which are prewritten code and templates associated with common programming tasks. Visual Studio also includes a set of tools for developing programs that work with Microsoft's Office suite. The following paragraphs discuss these programming languages in the Visual Studio suite: Visual Basic, Visual C++, and Visual C#.

- Visual Basic is based on the BASIC programming language, which was developed by Microsoft Corporation in the early 1990s. This language is easy to learn and use. Thus, Visual Basic is ideal for beginning programmers.

  The first step in building a Visual Basic program often is to design the graphical user interface using Visual Basic objects (Steps 1 and 2 in Figure 11-20). Visual Basic objects include items such as buttons, text boxes, and labels. Next, the programmer writes instructions (code) to define any actions that should occur in response to specific events (Step 3 in Figure 11-20). Finally, the programmer generates and tests the final program (Step 4 in Figure 11-20).

Figure 11-20 This figure shows how to create a Visual Basic program.

- Visual C++ is a programming language based on C++. Not only is Visual C++ a powerful object-oriented programming language, it enables programmers to write Windows, Windows Mobile, and .NET applications quickly and efficiently.
- Visual C# combines the programming elements of C++ with an easier visual programming environment. The purpose of Visual C# is to take the complexity out of Visual C++.

Visual Programming Languages   A **visual programming language** is a language that uses a visual or graphical interface for creating all source code. The graphical interface, called a **visual programming environment** (**VPE**), allows programmers to drag and drop objects to build programs. Examples of visual programming languages include Alice, Mindscript, and Prograph.

Delphi   Borland's **Delphi** is a powerful program development tool that is ideal for building large-scale enterprise and Web applications in a RAD environment. Programmers use Delphi to develop programs quickly for Windows, Linux, and .NET platforms.

PowerBuilder   **PowerBuilder**, developed by Sybase, is another powerful program development RAD tool best suited for Web-based, .NET, and large-scale enterprise object-oriented applications. Programmers also use PowerBuilder to develop small- and medium-scale client/server applications.

Other Programming Languages and Development Tools

The following sections discuss a variety of other programming languages and program development tools.

4GLs   A **4GL** (fourth-generation language) is a nonprocedural language that enables users and programmers to access data in a database. With a **nonprocedural language**, the programmer writes English-like instructions or interacts with a graphical environment to retrieve data from files or a database. Many object-oriented program development tools use 4GLs.

One popular 4GL is SQL. **SQL** is a query language that allows users to manage, update, and retrieve data in a relational DBMS (Figure 11-21).

? FAQ 11-4

Why is it necessary for programmers to know SQL?

Programmers often write programs that interact with a database in some fashion. For this reason, programmers must know SQL so that their programs can communicate with the database.

For more information, visit the Computer Concepts CourseMate Web site at www.cengagebrain.com, navigate to the Chapter 11 FAQ resource for this book, and then click SQL.

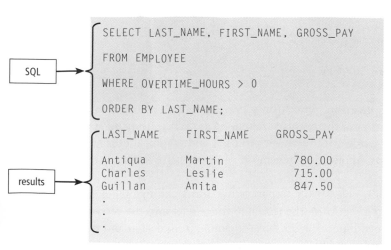

Figure 11-21   SQL is a 4GL that can be used to query database tables. This query produces an alphabetical list of those employees who receive overtime pay; that is, their overtime hours are greater than 0.

Classic Programming Languages In addition to the programming languages discussed on the previous pages, programmers sometimes use the languages listed in Figure 11-22, which were more popular in the past than today.

Ada	Derived from Pascal, developed by the U.S. Department of Defense, named after Augusta Ada Lovelace Byron, who is thought to be the first female computer programmer
ALGOL	ALGOrithmic Language, the first structured procedural language
APL	A Programming Language, a scientific language designed to manipulate tables of numbers
BASIC	Beginners All-purpose Symbolic Instruction Code, developed by John Kemeny and Thomas Kurtz as a simple, interactive problem-solving language
Forth	Similar to C, used for small computerized devices
FORTRAN	FORmula TRANslator, one of the first high-level programming languages used for scientific applications
HyperTalk	An object-oriented programming language developed by Apple to manipulate cards that can contain text, graphics, and sound
LISP	LISt Processing, a language used for artificial intelligence applications
Logo	An educational tool used to teach programming and problem solving to children
Modula-2	A successor to Pascal used for developing system software
Pascal	Developed to teach students structured programming concepts, named in honor of Blaise Pascal, a French mathematician who developed one of the earliest calculating machines
PILOT	Programmed Inquiry Learning Or Teaching, used to write computer-aided instruction programs
PL/1	Programming Language One, a business and scientific language that combines many features of FORTRAN and COBOL
Prolog	PROgramming LOGic, used for development of artificial intelligence applications
RPG	Report Program Generator, used to assist businesses with generating reports and to access/update data in databases
Smalltalk	Object-oriented programming language

Figure 11-22 Classic programming languages.

Application Generators An **application generator** is a program that creates source code or machine code from a specification of the required functionality. When using an application generator, a programmer or user works with menu-driven tools and graphical user interfaces to define the desired specifications. Application generators most often are bundled with or are included as part of a DBMS.

An application generator typically consists of a report writer, form, and menu generator. A report writer allows you to design a report on the screen, retrieve data into the report design, and then display or print the report. Figure 11-23 shows a sample form design and the resulting form it generates showing sample data a user may enter in the form. A menu generator enables you to create a menu for the application options.

Figure 11-23a (form design)

Figure 11-23b (resulting filled-in form)

Figure 11-23 A form design and the resulting filled-in form created with Microsoft Access.

Macros A **macro** is a series of statements that instructs a program how to complete a task. Macros allow users to automate routine, repetitive, or difficult tasks in application software such as word processing, spreadsheet, or database programs. That is, users can create simple programs within the software by writing macros. You usually create a macro in one of two ways: (1) record the macro or (2) write the macro.

If you want to automate a routine or repetitive task such as formatting or editing, you would record a macro. A macro recorder is similar to a movie camera because both record all actions until turned off. To record a macro, start the macro recorder in the software. Then, perform the steps to be part of the macro, such as clicks of the mouse or keystrokes. Once the macro is recorded, you can run it anytime you want to perform that same sequence of actions. For example, if you always print three copies of certain documents, you could record the actions required to print three copies. To print three copies, you would run the macro called PrintThreeCopies.

When you become familiar with programming techniques, you can write your own macros instead of recording them. Read Ethics & Issues 11-3 for a related discussion.

Macros
For more information, visit the Computer Concepts CourseMate Web site at www.cengagebrain.com, navigate to the Chapter 11 Web Link resource for this book, and then click Macros.

ETHICS & ISSUES 11-3

Who Should Be Held Accountable for Macro Security Threats?

Years ago, an individual downloaded and opened a small document that contained a virus from an Internet newsgroup. Upon opening the document, a macro was executed that sent the same document to the first 50 e-mail addresses in the person's e-mail contact list. The simple action of opening the document started a chain reaction that resulted in more than 100,000 infected computers and more than $80 million in damage. Today, such viruses, known as macro viruses, are the most common type of virus. Malware authors find that one of the easiest ways to spread viruses and worms is by distributing documents containing macro viruses. The convenience and simplicity of macros are both their greatest strengths and weaknesses. These are weaknesses because hackers find it easy to exploit technologies with such traits.

As a result of damaging macro viruses, antivirus companies and software companies have strengthened their efforts against macro viruses. Companies often prohibit employees from running macros on their computers. Both responses have made the use of macros more difficult and confusing for users, who prefer the convenience and simplicity of the earlier days. Many claim that software companies that include the capability to use macros should be responsible for making it impossible for malware authors to take advantage of security problems in the software. Software companies and others blame users who open documents from unknown sources.

Should users or software companies be held accountable for macro security threats? Why? Should a macro in a word processing document have the capability to access a person's e-mail contact list? Why or why not? How can users best be educated regarding handling documents from unknown sources?

Web Page Development

The designers of Web pages, known as **Web developers**, use a variety of techniques to create Web pages. The following sections discuss these techniques.

HTML and XHTML   **HTML** (Hypertext Markup Language) is a special formatting language that programmers use to format documents for display on the Web. You view a Web page written with HTML in a Web browser such as Internet Explorer, Mozilla, Safari, Firefox, Opera, or Google Chrome. Similarly, **XHTML** (extensible HTML) is a markup language that enables Web sites to be displayed more easily on microbrowsers in smart phones and other mobile devices, as well as on desktop and notebook computers. Figure 11-24a shows part of the XHTML code used to create the Web page shown in Figure 11-24b. XHTML includes features of HTML and XML, which is discussed in the next section.

HTML and XHTML are not actually programming languages. They are, however, languages that have specific rules for defining the placement and format of text, graphics, video, and audio on a Web page. HTML and XHTML use tags or elements, which are words, abbreviations, and symbols that specify links to other documents and indicate how a Web page is displayed when viewed on the Web.

Figure 11-24a (portion of XHTML program)

Figure 11-24b
(portion of resulting Web page)

Figure 11-24 The portion of the XHTML code in the top figure generates a portion of a Web page shown in the bottom figure.

XML and WML   **XML** (Extensible Markup Language) is an increasingly popular format for sharing data that allows Web developers to create customized tags, as well as use predefined tags, used for developing a single Web site whose content can be formatted to display appropriately on various devices. XML separates the Web page content from its format, allowing the Web browser to display the contents of a Web page in a form appropriate for the display device. For example, a smart phone, a PDA, and a notebook computer all could display the same XML page or use different formats or sections of the XML page.

Wireless devices use a subset of XML called WML. **WML** (wireless markup language) allows Web developers to design pages specifically for microbrowsers. Many smart phones and other mobile devices use WML as their markup language.

Two applications of XML are the RSS 2.0 and ATOM specifications. **RSS 2.0**, which stands for Really Simple Syndication, and **ATOM** are specifications that content aggregators use to distribute content to subscribers. The online publisher creates an RSS or ATOM document, called a Web feed, that is made available to Web sites for publication. News Web sites, blogs, and podcasts often use Web feeds to publish headlines and stories. Most Web browsers can read Web feeds, meaning they automatically download updated content from Web pages identified in the feed.

XML
For more information, visit the Computer Concepts CourseMate Web site at www.cengagebrain.com, navigate to the Chapter 11 Web Link resource for this book, and then click XML.

Scripts, Applets, Servlets, and ActiveX Controls   Markup languages tell a browser how to display text and images, set up lists and option buttons, and establish links on a Web page. By adding dynamic content and interactive elements such as scrolling messages, animated graphics, forms, pop-up windows, and interaction, Web pages become much more interesting. To add these elements, Web developers write small programs called scripts, applets, servlets, and ActiveX controls. These programs run inside of another program. This is different from programs discussed thus far, which are executed by the operating system. In this case, the Web browser executes these short programs.

One reason for using scripts, applets, servlets, and ActiveX controls is to add special multimedia effects to Web pages. Examples include animated graphics, scrolling messages, calendars, and advertisements. Another reason to use these programs is to include interactive capabilities on Web pages.

Scripting Languages   Programmers write scripts, applets, servlets, or ActiveX controls using a variety of languages. These include some of the languages previously discussed, such as Java, C++, C#, F#, and Visual Basic. Some programmers use scripting languages. A **scripting language** is an interpreted language that typically is easy to learn and use. Popular scripting languages include JavaScript, Perl, PHP, Rexx, Tcl, and VBScript.

- **JavaScript** is an interpreted language that allows a programmer to add dynamic content and interactive elements to a Web page (Figure 11-25). These elements include alert messages, scrolling text, animations, drop-down menus, data input forms, pop-up windows, and interactive quizzes.

Figure 11-25a (JavaScript code)

Figure 11-25b (Web page)

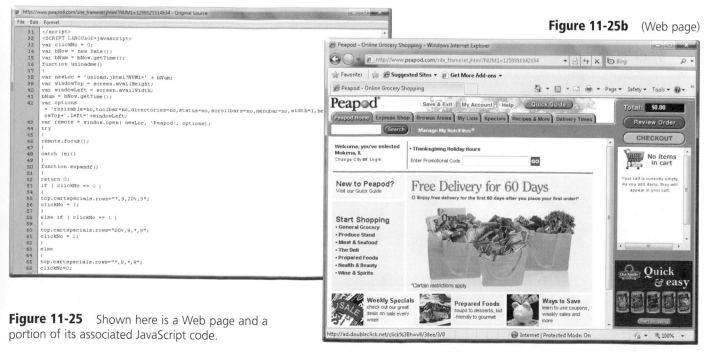

Figure 11-25   Shown here is a Web page and a portion of its associated JavaScript code.

PHP

For more information, visit the Computer Concepts CourseMate Web site at www.cengagebrain.com, navigate to the Chapter 11 Web Link resource for this book, and then click PHP.

- **Perl** (Practical Extraction and Report Language) originally was developed by Larry Wall at NASA's Jet Propulsion Laboratory as a procedural language similar to C and C++. The latest release of Perl, however, is an interpreted scripting language. Because Perl has powerful text processing capabilities, it has become a popular language for writing scripts.
- **PHP**, which stands for PHP: Hypertext Preprocessor, is a free, open source scripting language. PHP is similar to C, Java, and Perl.
- **Rexx** (REstructured eXtended eXecutor) was developed by Mike Cowlishaw at IBM as a procedural interpreted scripting language for both the professional programmer and the nontechnical user.
- **Tcl** (Tool Command Language) is an interpreted scripting language created by Dr. John Ousterhout and maintained by Sun Microsystems Laboratories.
- **VBScript** (Visual Basic, Scripting Edition) is a subset of the Visual Basic language that allows programmers to add intelligence and interactivity to Web pages. As with JavaScript, Web developers embed VBScript code directly into an HTML document.

Dynamic HTML **Dynamic HTML (DHTML)** is a newer type of HTML that allows Web developers to include more graphical interest and interactivity in a Web page. Typically, Web pages created with DHTML are more animated and responsive to user interaction. Colors change, font sizes grow, objects appear and disappear as a user moves the mouse, and animations dance around the screen.

Ruby on Rails **Ruby on Rails** is an open source framework that provides technologies for developing object-oriented, database-driven Web sites. Ruby on Rails is designed to make Web developers more productive by providing them an easy-to-use environment and eliminating time-consuming steps in the Web development process.

As previously discussed, Web 2.0 refers to Web sites that provide a means for users to share personal information, allow users to modify Web site content, and have application software built into the site for visitors to use. Web 2.0 sites include social networking sites, wikis, blogs, online auctions, and Web applications such as Google Docs.

Web 2.0 Program Development Web 2.0 sites often use RSS, previously discussed, and Ajax. **Ajax**, which stands for Asynchronous JavaScript and XML, is a method of creating interactive Web applications designed to provide immediate response to user requests. Instead of refreshing entire Web pages, Ajax works with the Web browser to update only changes to the Web page. This technique saves time because the Web application does not spend time repeatedly sending unchanged information across the network.

Ajax combines several programming tools: JavaScript or other scripting language, HTML or XHTML, and XML. Examples of Web sites that use Ajax are Google Maps and Flickr.

Most Web 2.0 sites also use APIs so that Web developers can create their own Web applications. An **API** (application programming interface) is a collection of tools that programmers use to interact with an environment such as a Web site or operating system. Mapping Web sites, for example, include APIs that enable programmers to integrate maps into their Web sites (Figure 11-26).

Figure 11-26 Google Maps provides tools for programmers to integrate APIs into their Web sites.

? FAQ 11-5

What are the popular Web programming languages?

The chart to the right shows the popularity of selected Web programming languages when compared to all programming languages.

For more information, visit the Computer Concepts CourseMate Web site at www.cengagebrain.com, navigate to the Chapter 11 FAQ resource for this book, and then click Web Programming Languages.

Web Programming Language Popularity

Source: TIOBE Programming Community Index

Web Page Authoring Software   As discussed in Chapter 3, you do not need to learn HTML to develop a Web page. You can use **Web page authoring software** to create sophisticated Web pages that include graphical images, video, audio, animation, and other special effects. Web page authoring software generates HTML and XHTML tags from your Web page design.

Four popular Web page authoring programs are Dreamweaver, Expression Web, Flash, and SharePoint Designer.

• **Dreamweaver**, by Adobe Systems, is a Web page authoring program that allows Web developers to create, maintain, and manage professional Web sites.

• **Expression Web** is Microsoft's Web page authoring program that enables Web developers to create professional, dynamic, interactive Web sites. Expression Web integrates with Visual Studio.

• **Flash**, by Adobe Systems, is a Web page authoring program that enables Web developers to combine interactive content with text, graphics, audio, and video.

• **SharePoint Designer** is a Web page authoring program that is part of the Microsoft Office and SharePoint families of products.

Multimedia Program Development

Multimedia authoring software allows programmers to combine text, graphics, animation, audio, and video into an interactive presentation. Many developers use multimedia authoring software for computer-based training (CBT) and Web-based training (WBT). Popular multimedia authoring software includes ToolBook and Director. Many businesses and colleges use ToolBook to create content for distance learning courses (Figure 11-27).

Figure 11-27
A sample ToolBook application.

✔ **QUIZ YOURSELF 11-2**

Instructions: Find the true statement below. Then, rewrite the remaining false statements so that they are true.

1. C and COBOL are examples of assembly languages.
2. Delphi is an object-oriented programming language developed by Sun Microsystems.
3. Popular first-generation languages include JavaScript, Perl, PHP, Rexx, Tcl, and VBScript.
4. Four popular markup languages are Dreamweaver, Expression Web, Flash, and SharePoint Designer.
5. Two types of low-level languages are machine languages and source languages.
6. Visual Studio is Microsoft's suite of program development tools that assists programmers in building programs for Windows, Windows Mobile, or any operating system that supports .NET.

💻 **Quiz Yourself Online:** To further check your knowledge of pages 435 through 449, visit the Computer Concepts CourseMate Web site at www.cengagebrain.com, navigate to the Chapter 11 Quiz Yourself resource for this book, and then click Objectives 3 – 6.

Program Development

Program development consists of a series of steps programmers use to build computer programs. As discussed, the system development life cycle guides information technology (IT) professionals through the development of an information system. Likewise, the **program development life cycle** (PDLC) guides computer programmers through the development of a program. The program development life cycle consists of six steps (Figure 11-28):

1. Analyze Requirements
2. Design Solution
3. Validate Design
4. Implement Design
5. Test Solution
6. Document Solution

As shown in Figure 11-28, the steps in the program development life cycle form a loop. Program development is an ongoing process within system development. Each time someone identifies errors in or improvements to a program and requests program modifications, the Analyze Requirements step begins again. When programmers correct errors (called bugs) or add enhancements to an existing program, they are said to be **maintaining** the program. Program maintenance is a ongoing activity that occurs after a program has been delivered to users. Read Ethics & Issues 11-4 for a related discussion.

🜨 **ETHICS & ISSUES 11-4**

Who Is Responsible for Bugs?

The consequences of bugs, or errors, in computer programs can be staggering. A software error in a missile defense system resulted in the deaths of 29 U.S. soldiers. An error in the code controlling a Canadian nuclear facility caused more than 3,000 gallons of radioactive water to be spilled. A bug in long-distance switching software cost AT&T more than $60 million. Sometimes, employees or students who report security-related bugs are disciplined because by finding the bug, they accidently accessed secure information. Experts estimate that there are 20 to 30 bugs per 1,000 lines of code in an average program. Given that many programs contain hundreds of thousands, even millions, of code lines, bugs are not surprising. Most software licenses absolve the software creator of any responsibility for the end user getting the wrong information from a bug-riddled program.

Who should be responsible for mistakes in software? Why? If users find bugs, such as security bugs, should they be disciplined after reporting the bugs? Why? Should those who design a system or write programs for a system be legally responsible if their product results in errors or damages? Why?

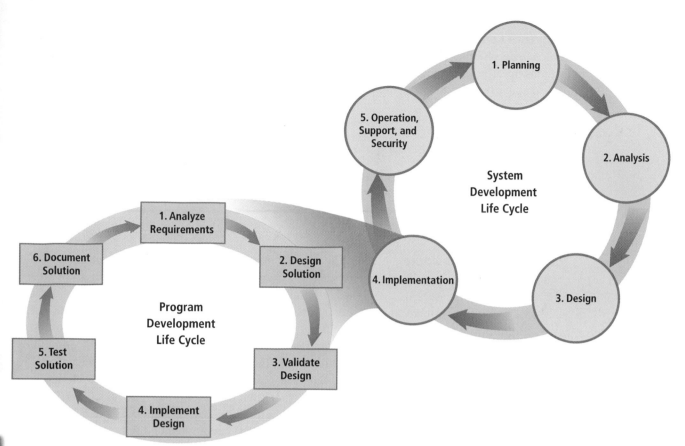

Figure 11-28 The program development life cycle consists of six steps that form a loop. The program development life cycle is part of the implementation phase of the system development life cycle.

What Initiates Program Development?

As discussed, system development consists of five phases: planning; analysis; design; implementation; and operation, support, and security. During the analysis phase, the development team recommends how to handle software needs. Choices include modifying existing programs, purchasing packaged software, building custom software in-house, or outsourcing some or all of the IT operation.

If the organization opts for in-house development, the design and implementation phases of system development become quite extensive. In the design phase, the analyst creates a detailed set of requirements for the programmers. Once the programmers receive the requirements, the implementation phase begins. At this time, the programmer analyzes the requirements of the problem to be solved. Thus, program development begins at the start of the implementation phase in system development.

The scope of the requirements largely determines how many programmers work on the program development. If the scope is large, a **programming team** that consists of a group of programmers may develop the programs. If the specifications are simple, a single programmer might complete all the development tasks. Whether a single programmer or a programming team, all the programmers involved must interact with users and members of the development team throughout program development.

By following the steps in program development, programmers create programs that are correct (produce accurate information) and maintainable (easy to modify).

Control Structures

When programmers are required to design the logic of a program, they typically use control structures to describe the tasks a program is to perform. A **control structure**, also known as a construct, depicts the logical order of program instructions. Three basic control structures are sequence, selection, and repetition.

Sequence Control Structure   A **sequence control structure** shows one or more actions following each other in order (Figure 11-29). Actions include inputs, processes, and outputs. All actions must be executed; that is, none can be skipped. Examples of actions are reading a record, calculating averages or totals, and printing totals.

Sequence Control Structure

Action 1 → Action 2 → Action 3

Figure 11-29   The sequence control structure shows one or more actions followed by another.

Selection Control Structure   A **selection control structure** tells the program which action to take, based on a certain condition. Two common types of selection control structures are the if-then-else and the case.

When a program evaluates the condition in an if-then-else control structure, it yields one of two possibilities: true or false. Figure 11-30 shows the condition as a diamond symbol. If the result of the condition is true, then the program performs one action. If the result is false, the program performs a different action. For example, the if-then-else control structure can determine if an employee should receive overtime pay. A possible condition might be the following: Is Hours Worked greater than 40? If the response is yes (true), then the action would calculate overtime pay. If the response is no (false), then the action would set overtime pay equal to 0.

In some cases, a program should perform no action if the result of a condition is false. This variation of the if-then-else is called the if-then control structure because the program performs an action only if the result of the condition is true.

With the **case control structure,** a condition can yield one of three or more possibilities (Figure 11-31). The size of a beverage, for example, might be one of these options: small, medium, large, or extra large. A case control structure would determine the price of the beverage based on the size purchased.

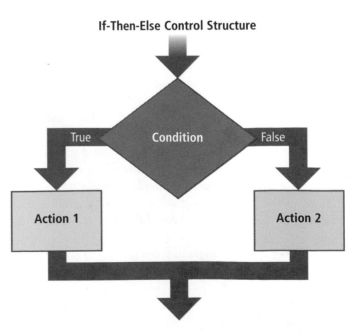

If-Then-Else Control Structure

True — Condition — False

Action 1   Action 2

Figure 11-30   The if-then-else control structure directs the program toward one course of action or another based on the evaluation of a condition.

Case Control Structure

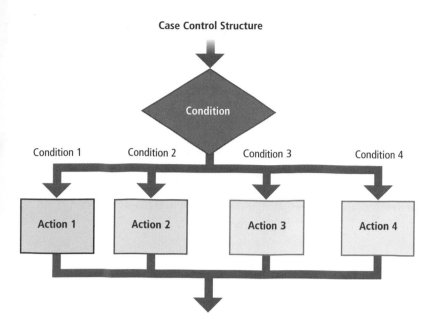

Figure 11-31 The case control structure allows for more than two alternatives when a condition is evaluated.

Repetition Control Structure The **repetition control structure** enables a program to perform one or more actions repeatedly as long as a certain condition is met. Many programmers refer to this construct as a loop. Two forms of the repetition control structure are the do-while and do-until.

A do-while control structure repeats one or more times as long as a specified condition is true (Figure 11-32). This control structure tests a condition at the beginning of the loop. If the result of the condition is true, the program executes the action(s) inside the loop. Then, the program loops back and tests the condition again. If the result of the condition still is true, the program executes the action(s) inside the loop again. This looping process continues until the condition being tested becomes false. At that time, the program stops looping and moves to another set of actions.

The do-while control structure normally is used when the occurrence of an event is not quantifiable or predictable. For example, programmers frequently use the do-while control structure to process all records in a file. A payroll program using a do-while control structure loops once for each employee. This program stops looping after it processes the last employee's record.

The do-until control structure is similar to the do-while but has two major differences: where it tests the condition and when it stops looping. First, the do-until control structure tests the condition at the end of the loop (Figure 11-33).

The action(s) in a do-until control structure thus always will execute at least once. The loop in a do-while control structure, by contrast, might not execute at all. That is, if the condition immediately is false, the action or actions in the do-while loop never execute. Second, a do-until control structure continues looping until the condition is true — and then stops. This is different from the do-while control structure, which continues to loop while the condition is true.

An understanding of these control structures provides an insight into the steps performed by a computer when the computer is used to solve a problem or process data.

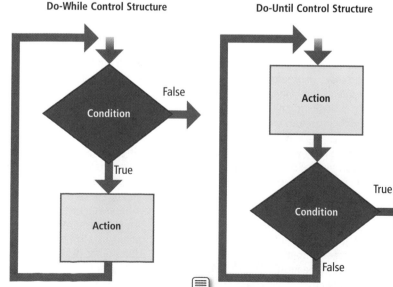

Figure 11-32 The do-while control structure tests the condition at the beginning of the loop. It exits the loop when the result of the condition is false.

Figure 11-33 The do-until control structure tests the condition at the end of the loop. It exits the loop when the result of the condition is true.

✔ **QUIZ YOURSELF 11-3**

Instructions: Find the true statement below. Then, rewrite the remaining false statements so that they are true.

1. Program development is an ongoing activity within system development.
2. The program development life cycle consists of these six steps: analyze requirements, design solution, validate design, implement design, test solution, and hardcode solution.
3. Three basic control structures are sequence, selection, and maintenance.

🖥 **Quiz Yourself Online:** To further check your knowledge of pages 450 through 453, visit the Computer Concepts CourseMate Web site at www.cengagebrain.com, navigate to the Chapter 11 Quiz Yourself resource for this book, and then click Objectives 7 – 8.

Chapter Summary

This chapter discussed the system development phases. The guidelines for system development also were presented. Activities that occur during system development, including project management, feasibility assessment, documentation, and data and information gathering, also were addressed.

This chapter discussed various programming languages and program development tools used to create and modify computer programs. It described a variety of Web development and multimedia development tools. Finally, the chapter discussed program development and the tools used in this process.

Computer Usage @ Work

Manufacturing

Manufacturing plays a crucial role in today's society. To keep up with our growing population's increasing demand for various products, organizations explore ways to streamline manufacturing processes while simultaneously minimizing costs. These organizations often find that using computers in the manufacturing process requires fewer people-hours, and products and parts are manufactured with greater accuracy and less waste.

Automakers, for example, manufacture cars on an assembly line. In the early years of car manufacturing, people were involved at all stages of the manufacturing process, and it was not uncommon to find hundreds or thousands of individuals working along the line. Although the assembly line allowed individuals to manufacture cars as quickly as they could, companies soon realized that computer-aided manufacturing (CAM) would increase output and decrease labor costs. In fact, CAM proved to be most effective when used in conjunction with computer-aided design (CAD). CAD designs an item, such as a car, to manufacture; CAM then manufactures the car according to the original design. Computers also determine the exact amount of material necessary to build the car, as well as the expected output.

Communications during the assembly process is critical. Computers automatically communicate with each other along the assembly line and provide alerts when factors arise that can interrupt the process. For example, running out of hinges that attach the door to the rest of the car's body will halt the line until someone replenishes the hinges. Computers, however, often alert individuals to low supplies before they run out and the assembly halts. Failure to detect the absence of hinges might result in the machinery that is manufacturing the car to think that it is attaching hinges when in fact it is not. This might result in damage to the door and/or the car's body further along the assembly line.

Today, computers assist with manufacturing many types of items. Although some might argue that computers perform jobs that people once held, their introduction has helped to meet our increased demand and desire for low prices.

🖥 For more information, visit the Computer Concepts CourseMate Web site at www.cengagebrain.com, navigate to the Chapter 11 Computer Usage @ Work resource for this book, and then click Manufacturing.

Companies on the Cutting Edge

COMPUTER SCIENCES CORPORATION (CSC) Global IT Services Company

When the space shuttle blasted into space and docked with the International Space Station, Computer Sciences Corporation (CSC) played a major role in the mission. NASA has partnered with CSC to provide support for its Center for Computational Sciences, which contains simulators and supercomputing resources for high-performance aerospace activities.

CSC's three primary lines of services are Business Solutions & Services, Global Outsourcing Services, and the North American Public Sector. Its information technology projects include managing the nation's air traffic control system, providing logistics for the U.S. Army's equipment, stopping security breaches, simplifying the U.S. Patent and Trademark Office's application process, and helping the California Department of Forestry fight wildfires.

The company has grown from a two-person operation in 1959 to an international corporation based in Falls Church, Virginia. Recently, it won the "BEST Award" from the American Society for Training and Development for its global learning and employee talent development programs.

ELECTRONIC ARTS (EA) Entertainment Software Developer

Video gaming is one of the more popular forms of recreation among people of all ages. Game sales are increasing among all age groups, and demand for Wii products is especially high among adult gamers.

Electronic Arts (EA) is an entertainment software publishing company that develops video games for game consoles, computers, mobile devices, and the Internet. The company had thirty-one products that sold more than one million copies in a recent year, three of which sold more than five million copies: FIFA, Madden NFL, and Need for Speed Undercover.

Electronic Arts has been developing video games since 1982. From the beginning, EA has referred to its programmers as software artists who can evoke emotions from game enthusiasts. Its yearly revenues of more than $3 billion are generated from its sales of action, fantasy, sports, and strategy software for the PlayStation, Xbox, Wii, and Game Boy systems.

 For more information, visit the Computer Concepts CourseMate Web site at www.cengagebrain.com and then navigate to the Chapter 11 Companies on the Cutting Edge resource for this book.

Technology Trailblazers

ED YOURDON Project Management Consultant

Much of today's structured system development life cycle is due to the methodologies Ed Yourdon developed more than 40 years ago. Yourdon's work in the computer industry ranges from predicting technology megatrends to recruiting and retaining employees, and much of his current research focuses on developing Web 2.0 and 3.0 strategies, products, and services.

Yourdon is considered one of the ten most influential people in the software field and was inducted into the Computer Hall of Fame. He has written 27 books; the latest, *Outsource: Competing in the Global Productivity Race* and *Death March*, provide guidance to corporate managers facing constrained resources and budgets.

Yourdon began his computer career as a programmer and then founded a consulting firm to provide advice in modern software engineering technology and project management techniques. Today, he maintains his blog, The Yourdon Report, and the Structured Analysis Wiki, and serves as a consultant in his firm, NODRUOY Inc.

JAMES GOSLING Java Engineer and Architect

Songwriter and musician Neil Young has teamed with Sun Microsystems' James Gosling to develop a hybrid 1959 Lincoln Continental that will compete for the Automotive X prize, a contest for vehicles getting at least 100 mpg. The two Canadian-born innovators have named their car the Linc Volt, and its performance system is monitored by Java technology.

Gosling is the mastermind behind Java, and he affectionately is called the "father of Java." He was raised near Calgary, Alberta, and spent much of his free time turning spare machine parts into games. At 15, he wrote software for the University of Calgary's physics department. When he was hired at Sun, he built a multiprocessor version of UNIX, developed compilers to convert program code into machine language, and wrote a UNIX text editor.

He served as Sun's vice president and Oracle's chief technology officer until resigning in 2010. He was named an officer of the Order of Canada for demonstrating an outstanding level of talent and service to Canadians.

 For more information, visit the Computer Concepts CourseMate Web site at www.cengagebrain.com and then navigate to the Chapter 11 Technology Trailblazers resource for this book.

Chapter Review

The Chapter Review reinforces the main concepts presented in this chapter.

To listen to an audio version of this Chapter Review, visit the Computer Concepts CourseMate Web site at www.cengagebrain.com and then navigate to the Chapter 11 Chapter Review resource for this book.

1. **Why Are Project Management, Feasibility Assessment, Documentation, and Data and Information Gathering Techniques Important during System Development?**   **Project management** is the process of planning, scheduling, and then controlling the activities during system development. The goal of project management is to deliver an acceptable system to the user in an agreed-upon time frame. **Feasibility** is a measure of how suitable the development of a system will be to the organization. **Documentaton** is the collection and summarization of data and information. To gather data and information, IT professionals can review documentation, observe, distribute surveys, interview, participate in a **joint-application design** (**JAD**) session, and research.

2. **What Is the Purpose of Each System Development Phase?**   A **system** is a set of components that interact to achieve a common goal. **System development** is a set of activities used to build an **information system**. Most system development cycles contain five **phases**. During the **planning phase**, a **project request** is reviewed and approved, project requests are prioritized, resources are allocated, and a project development team is formed for each approved project. During the **analysis phase**, a **preliminary investigation**, also called the **feasibility study**, is conducted to determine the exact nature of the problem or improvement, and detailed analysis is performed to study how the current system works, determine users' requirements, and recommend a solution. During the **design phase**, any necessary hardware and software are acquired, and the details of the new or modified information system are developed. In the **implementation phase**, the new or modified system is constructed and delivered to the users. During the **operation, support, and security phase**, ongoing assistance is provided for the information system and its users after the system is implemented.

Visit the Computer Concepts CourseMate Web site at www.cengagebrain.com, navigate to the Chapter 11 Quiz Yourself resource for this book, and then click Objectives 1 – 2.

3. **How Are Low-Level Languages Different from Procedural Languages?**   A **programming language** is a set of words, abbreviations, and symbols that enables a **programmer** to communicate instructions to a computer. A low-level language is a programming language that runs on only one type of computer. Each instruction in a low-level language usually equates to a single machine instruction. Procedural languages are high-level languages that can run on many different types of computers and operating systems. In a **procedural language**, often called a **third-generation language** (**3GL**), a programmer writes instructions that tell the computer what to accomplish and how to do it.

4. **What Are the Benefits of Object-Oriented Programming Languages and Program Development Tools?**   Programmers use an **object-oriented programming** (**OOP**) **language** or object-oriented program development tool to implement object-oriented design. A major benefit of OOP is the ability to reuse and modify existing objects, allowing programmers to create applications faster. OOP languages include **Java**, **C#**, **F#**, and **C++**. Often used in conjunction with OOP, **RAD** (rapid application development) is a method of developing software, in which a programmer writes and implements a program in segments instead of waiting until the entire program is completed. **Visual Studio** is Microsoft's suite of program development tools and includes Visual Basic, Visual C++, and Visual C#.

5. **What Are Other Programming Languages and Other Program Development Tools?**   A **4GL** (fourth generation language) is a **nonprocedural language** that users and programmers use to access the data in a database. One popular 4GL is **SQL**. Other program development tools include an **application generator**, which creates source code or machine code from a specification of the required functionality, and a **macro**, which is a series of statements that instructs a program how to complete a task.

6. **How Are Web Pages Developed?**   **Web developers** use a variety of techniques to develop Web pages. **HTML** (Hypertext Markup Language) is a special formatting language used to format documents for display on the Web. **XHTML**, **XML**, and **WML** also are used to develop Web pages. To add interactivity to Web pages, some programmers use a scripting language or **dynamic HTML** (**DHTML**). Other popular languages and tools include **Ruby on Rails**, **Ajax**, and **API**. Web developers also use **Web page authoring software** to create sophisticated Web pages, including **Dreamweaver**, **Expression Web**, **Flash**, and **SharePoint Designer**.

Visit the Computer Concepts CourseMate Web site at www.cengagebrain.com, navigate to the Chapter 11 Quiz Yourself resource for this book, and then click Objectives 3 – 6.

7. **What Are the Six Program Development Steps?** **Program development** is a series of steps programmers use to build computer programs. The **program development life cycle** (PDLC) consists of six steps: (1) analyze requirements, (2) design solution, (3) validate design, (4) implement design, (5) test solution, and (6) document solution. The steps in the program development life cycle form a loop.

8. **What Are the Basic Control Structures Used in Designing Solutions to Programming Problems?** A **control structure** depicts the logical order of program instructions. Three basic control structures are the **sequence control structure**, **selection control structure**, and **repetition control structure**.

Visit the Computer Concepts CourseMate Web site at www.cengagebrain.com, navigate to the Chapter 11 Quiz Yourself resource for this book, and then click Objectives 7 – 8.

Key Terms

You should know each key term. The list below helps focus your study.

To see an example of and a definition for each term, and to access current and additional information from the Web, visit the Computer Concepts CourseMate Web site at www.cengagebrain.com and then navigate to the Chapter 11 Key Terms resource for this book.

4GL (443)
Ajax (448)
analysis phase (425)
API (448)
application generator (444)
assembly language (437)
ATOM (447)
benchmark test (430)
C (439)
C# (441)
C++ (441)
case control structure (452)
change management (420)
chief security officer (434)
COBOL (COmmon Business-Oriented Language) (440)
code snippets (442)
compiler (438)
computer program (435)
computer security plan (434)
computer-aided software engineering (CASE) (432)
control structure (451)
custom software (427)
Delphi (443)
design phase (428)
developer (435)
direct conversion (433)
documentation (422)
Dreamweaver (449)
dynamic HTML (DHTML) (448)
electronic magazine (428)

Expression Web (449)
e-zine (428)
F# (441)
feasibility (421)
feasibility study (425)
Flash (449)
focus groups (423)
HTML (446)
IDE (integrated development environment) (440)
implementation phase (432)
information system (IS) (418)
interpreter (438)
IT consultant (429)
Java (440)
JavaScript (447)
joint-application design (JAD) (423)
machine language (436)
macro (445)
maintaining (450)
multimedia authoring software (449)
.NET (441)
nonprocedural language (443)
object-oriented programming (OOP) language (440)
operation, support, and security phase (434)
outsource (428)
packaged software (427)
parallel conversion (433)
Perl (448)

phased conversion (433)
phases (418)
PHP (448)
pilot conversion (434)
planning phase (425)
PowerBuilder (443)
preliminary investigation (425)
procedural language (438)
program development (450)
program development life cycle (450)
program development tool (436)
programmer (435)
programming language (435)
programming team (451)
project leader (420)
project management (420)
project management software (420)
project manager (420)
project request (423)
project team (420)
prototype (431)
RAD (440)
repetition control structure (453)
Rexx (448)
RSS 2.0 (447)
Ruby on Rails (448)
scope (420)
scripting language (447)
selection control structure (452)

sequence control structure (452)
SharePoint Designer (449)
source program (437)
SQL (443)
standards (419)
steering committee (420)
system (418)
system developer (420)
system development (418)
system development life cycle (SDLC) (418)
system proposal (427)
systems analyst (419)
Tcl (448)
third-generation language (3GL) (438)
training (433)
users (419)
value-added reseller (VAR) (429)
VBScript (448)
visual programming environment (VPE) (443)
visual programming language (443)
Visual Studio (441)
Web developers (446)
Web page authoring software (449)
WML (447)
XHTML (446)
XML (446)

Checkpoint

The Checkpoint exercises test your knowledge of the chapter concepts. The page number containing the answer appears in parentheses after each exercise.

To complete the Checkpoint exercises interactively, visit the Computer Concepts CourseMate Web site at www.cengagebrain.com and then navigate to the Chapter 11 Checkpoint resource for this book.

Multiple Choice   Select the best answer.

1. The _____ manages and controls the budget and schedule of the project. (420)
   a. project team
   b. steering committee
   c. project leader
   d. system developer

2. _____ measures whether the lifetime benefits of the proposed information system will be greater than its lifetime costs. (421)
   a. Operational feasibility
   b. Technical feasibility
   c. Economic feasibility
   d. Schedule feasibility

3. In larger organizations, users write a formal request for a new or modified information system, which is called a _____. (423)
   a. prototype
   b. joint-application design (JAD)
   c. project request
   d. system proposal

4. The purpose of the _____ is to assess the feasibility of each alternative solution and then recommend the most feasible solution for the project. (427)
   a. project plan
   b. system proposal
   c. project request
   d. system review

5. A(n) _____ reads a code statement, converts it to one or more machine language instructions, and then executes those machine language instructions. (438)
   a. compiler
   b. nonprocedural language
   c. source program
   d. interpreter

6. _____ is a subset of the Visual Basic language that allows programmers to add intelligence and interactivity to Web pages. (448)
   a. Ajax
   b. Flash
   c. VBScript
   d. Rexx

7. _____ is an open source framework that provides technologies for developing object-oriented, database-driven Web sites. (448)
   a. PHP
   b. Ruby on Rails
   c. Flash
   d. Ajax

8. _____ is a Web page authoring program that is part of the Microsoft Office and SharePoint families of products. (449)
   a. PHP
   b. Ajax
   c. SharePoint Designer
   d. Flash

Matching   Match the terms with their definitions.

_____ 1. project manager (420)
_____ 2. benchmark test (430)
_____ 3. source program (437)
_____ 4. macro (445)
_____ 5. API (448)

a. set of rules and procedures a company expects employees to follow
b. collection of tools that programmers use to interact with an environment such as a Web site or operating system
c. series of statements that instructs an application how to complete a task
d. the language instructions, or code, to be converted to machine language
e. controls the activities during system development
f. measures the performance of hardware or software

Short Answer   Write a brief answer to each of the following questions.

1. What is system development? _____ Describe the five phases of the system development life cycle (SDLC). _____

2. Why is feasibility evaluated during system development? _____ How are operational feasibility, schedule feasibility, technical feasibility, and economic feasibility different? _____

3. What activities take place during the operations, support, and security phase? _____ How do the roles of the systems analyst and chief security officer differ in this phase? _____

4. How is a compiler different from an interpreter? _____ What is the advantage, and disadvantage, of an interpreter? _____

5. How is XML used? _____ Describe two applications of XML. _____

Problem Solving

The Problem Solving exercises extend your knowledge of the chapter concepts by seeking solutions to practical computer problems that you may encounter at home, school, or work. The Collaboration exercise should be completed with a team.

In the real world, practical problems often can be solved in multiple ways. Provide one solution to each of the following problems using available resources, such as articles on the Web or in print, blogs, podcasts, videos, television, user guides, other individuals, and electronics and computer stores. You may need to use multiple resources to obtain an answer. Present your solutions in the form requested by your instructor (brief report, presentation, discussion, or other means).

@ Home

1. Trial Period Expired While installing a 60-day trial of the latest version of Microsoft Office, your computer displays a message stating that the trial period already has expired. What might be causing this error message to appear?

2. Security Questions Each time you log into your bank's Web site, it asks you to answer a series of security questions you selected when you set up your account. The Web site also asks whether you want it to request the answers to those security questions the next time you log in. You do not want the Web site to ask these questions in the future, so you place a check mark in the appropriate check box. The very next day, however, the Web site asks you the security questions. Why might this be happening?

3. Problem with Macro You created a macro in one document and made it available to other documents on your computer. When you run the macro in another document, however, it does not function properly. What might be wrong?

4. Web Page Syntax Error When you attempt to display a Web page, an error message appears and the Web page does not display properly on your screen. The error message cites a syntax error and asks you if you would like to debug. How will you respond?

@ Work

5. Schedule Delay You are working as a project manager in charge of developing a new information system. Halfway through the project, you realize that you will not meet your deadline. This delay is sure to cost your company additional money. How might you approach your manager about this?

6. Problem Installing Custom Program After using an application generator to create a program, you save it on a USB flash drive and give the USB flash drive to your colleague so that she can install the program on her computer. She claims, however, that the program does not work on her computer. Why might the program work on your computer, but not on her computer?

7. Program Appears Frozen The human resources department has just released a new program used to calculate payroll for each employee. After you enter the payroll data for each employee, you click a button to calculate everyone's pay for that pay period. After clicking the button, the program becomes unresponsive and appears frozen. What might be wrong?

8. Unknown Language Several years ago, a programmer who no longer is with the company wrote a program for your company using an older programming language. Your colleague has discovered a bug in the program, but nobody knows the language to be able to fix the bug. What are your options?

Collaboration

9. Computers in Manufacturing Today, computers are used in the manufacturing of nearly every type of item. Your instructor would like everyone to realize the importance of computers in today's society and requests that each person find an item and determine how computers might have been used to assist in the manufacturing process. Form a team of three people. Each team member should locate one item that he or she believes was manufactured with the help of a computer. Then, team members should research exactly how computers were used and record their findings. Finally, the three team members should compare their research to discover similarities and differences and then compile their findings into a brief report.

Learn How To

The Learn How To activities step you through fundamental technology skills when using a computer. The Learn How To exercises enable you to become more proficient with these skills.

Learn How To 1: Conduct an Effective Interview

As you learned in this chapter, gathering information is a critical element in system development, because without accurate facts, it is unlikely that the finished system will perform in the desired manner. An important means of gathering information is the personal interview. Interviews are used in several stages throughout system development, and they must be thorough and comprehensive.

Prior to conducting an interview, you must determine that an interview is the best means for obtaining the information you seek. You have learned a variety of ways to obtain information, and you should use each of them appropriately. Because an interview interrupts a person's work and takes time, you must be sure the information gained in the interview justifies this interruption. Once you have determined you should conduct an interview to gather information required for system development, a variety of factors become relevant.

Goal: The most important element of a successful interview is for you to determine exactly what knowledge you hope to gain as a result of the interview. If you do not have a goal, you are unlikely to emerge from the interview with much useful information.

Do Your Homework: You should complete a variety of preparatory steps that will help ensure a successful interview. These steps include the following:
1. Gather as much information as you can from the fact-gathering processes that do not require an interview.
2. Be sure you plan to interview the best person to obtain the information you need.
3. Prepare the questions you want to ask prior to setting up the interview.
4. Prior to setting an appointment for an interview, be sure the management personnel of the people you will interview have approved.

Make an Appointment: An appointment almost always is required. By making an appointment, you ensure the person to be interviewed will be available. Normally you should request an appointment in writing, often through the use of e-mail. In this written request, you should set a time and place for the interview, inform the interviewee what you need to know, and establish an agenda with an estimated time. You must recognize that most people do not like to be interviewed, so often you will not be seen as friendly. In addition, it might be possible that the system being developed could eliminate or change the person's job, and clearly this can establish an adversarial relationship. Your task when making an appointment, then, is to establish credibility with the interviewee and set the stage for a successful interview.

Conduct the Interview: When conducting an interview, remember that you are the "intruder." Therefore, you should be polite, prompt, and attentive in the interview. Always understand the perspective of the person being interviewed and understand his or her fears, doubts, and potential hostilities. Sometimes, the interviewee might feel he or she is in conflict with you, so by listening closely and being aware of the body language, you should be able to discern the amount of truth and the amount of hedging that is occurring. Some of the details of the interview of which you should be aware are as follows:
1. If possible, the interview should be conducted in a quiet environment with a minimum of interruptions.
2. The demeanor should be open and friendly, but as noted you should not expect to be welcomed with open arms.
3. Your questions should directly address the goals of the interview.
4. Your questions should be thought-provoking.
5. Listen carefully, with both your ears and your eyes.
6. As you listen, concentrate on the interviewee — when points are being made, do not take notes because that will distract from what the person is saying — stay focused.
7. Throughout the interview, offer reinforcing comments, such as, "The way I understand what you just said is ..." Make sure when you leave the interview there are no misunderstandings between you and the person you interviewed.
8. Before you conclude the interview, be sure all your goals have been met.

Follow-Up: After the interview, it is recommended you send a follow-up letter or e-mail message to the person you interviewed to review the information you learned. This document should invite the interviewee to correct any errors you made in summing up your findings. In addition, for all the people you interview, keep a log of the time and place of the interview. In this way, if any questions arise regarding the interview, you will have a log.

Exercise

1. Using the techniques in this activity, conduct interviews with three students on your campus. Your interview goal is to find out about both the most successful class and the least successful class the student has completed. Why was the class successful or unsuccessful? Discuss the instructor, textbook, subject matter, and other relevant items. After the interviews, write a one-page paper summarizing your findings and identify common elements found in successful classes and in unsuccessful classes. Submit this paper to your instructor.

Learn It Online

The Learn It Online exercises are interactive Web exercises designed to reinforce and expand your understanding of the chapter concepts. The descriptions below briefly summarize each exercise.

To complete the Learn It Online exercises, visit the Computer Concepts CourseMate Web site at www.cengagebrain.com, navigate to the Chapter 11 resources for this book, click the link for the exercise you want to complete, and then read the instructions.

❶ At the Movies — **Electronic Arts Going Mobile**

Watch a movie to learn about how Electronic Arts is tackling the mobile video game market and then answer questions about the movie.

❷ Student Edition Labs — **Project Management and Visual Programming**

Enhance your understanding and knowledge about project management and visual programming by completing the Project Management and Visual Programming Labs.

❸ Practice Test

Take a multiple choice test that checks your knowledge of the chapter concepts and review the resulting study guide.

❹ Who Wants To Be a Computer Genius²?

Play the Shelly Cashman Series version of this popular game by answering questions to find out if you are a computer genius. Panic buttons are available to provide assistance during game play.

❺ Crossword Puzzle Challenge

Complete an interactive crossword puzzle to reinforce concepts presented in this chapter.

❻ Windows Exercises

Step through the Windows 7 exercises to search for executable files, use the Movie Box Office simulation, adjust keyboard speed, and use the Loan Payment Calculator.

❼ Exploring Computer Careers

Read about a career as a programmer, search for related employment advertisements, and then answer related questions.

❽ Web Apps — **Google Earth**

Learn how to download and use Google Earth on your computer, fly to your neighborhood and zoom in, view satellite images of your favorite nearby businesses, and show and hide various layers.

Web Research

The Web Research exercises broaden your understanding of chapter concepts by presenting questions that require you to search the Web for answers.

1 Search Sleuth

Use one of the search engines listed in Figure 2-8 in Chapter 2 on page 65 or your own favorite search engine to find the answers to the following questions. Copy and paste the Web address from the Web page where you found the answer. Some questions may have more than one answer. If required, submit your answers to your instructor. (1) Who are the winners of the most recent Worldwide UML Jokes Contest? What story does the first-place winner tell in UML notation? (2) What is the name of the document Karol Adamiecki developed in 1896? (3) What model was created from the merger of the Objectory Process, the Booch Method, and the Object-Modeling Technique? (4) Which programming language uses a mouse pointer shaped in the form of a turtle? (5) Who gave the keynote address at the latest Microsoft MIX Conference? (6) What is the purpose of a browser sniffer?

2 Green Computing

Corporations are touting their efforts to go green in their computing environments, but a survey of computer professionals found that less than seven percent of companies have implemented their green IT initiatives. One-third still are in the planning stages. Corporations may be choosing to practice green computing, but many times their efforts are driven by a financial goal to save electricity, not an ecological goal to reduce carbon dioxide emissions. Visit the Web sites of several companies profiled in this textbook and locate their environmentally friendly practices. For example, which green practices are featured? What outdated equipment has been replaced with energy-efficient machines? Is virtualization technology implemented? How are they conserving power? Write a report summarizing your findings, and include a table of links to Web sites that provide additional details.

3 Social Networking

Members of online social communities face the responsibility to act civilly and follow proper etiquette rules. *The Ultimate Social Media Etiquette Handbook*, which is posted on the techipedia Web site, states the rules for managing and maintaining online social relationships. In addition, several experts offer advice, including Philipp Lenssen (antispamnews.com), Tim O'Reilly (radar.oreilly.com), and Reihan Salam (slate.com/id/2174439). Read their columns and view the techipedia Web site (techipedia.com/social-media-etiquette-handbook) to learn about the best practices to follow when participating in online social networks. How should a networker create a personalized message giving a compelling reason why someone should join? How can a sender's background information be verified? When is sharing contact lists considered appropriate? Summarize the information you read and viewed.

4 Blogs

Creating a blog and then attracting people to read it requires a keen sense of design, marketing, and editing skills. Blogging services provide assistance in attracting visitors to a Web site and then holding their interest while they are viewing a page. Six Apart owns four blogging services: Blogs.com (blogs.com), Movable Type (movabletype.com), Vox (vox.com), and TypePad (typepad.com). Microsoft Windows Live Spaces (spaces.live.com) and Yahoo 360 (360.yahoo.com) are basic blog editors with a few features. WordPress (wordpress.com) is a blogging service with convenient editing tools. Visit these blog design Web sites and read about the features provided. Which services have blogging tools that seem easy to use? What customization tools are available? What features, such as word counters, are shown? Which Web sites allow users to upload photos?

5 Ethics in Action

Millions of VeriChip microchips have been implanted in pets for identification purposes, but the move to humans has alarmed security experts. VeriChip's Xmark subsidiary distributes the Hugs and the Halo systems of infant protection, the RoamAlert system of wandering protection, the MyCall emergency response system, and the Assetrac asset tracking system. The chips release a code when a scanner is passed over them, and this code is linked to a database that retains the person's information and can be updated. View online sites that discuss using implanted chips in humans. How can they be used to breach the confidentiality of medical records? How are they being used in nonmedical applications? Write a report summarizing your findings, and include a table of links to Web sites that provide additional details about implantable chips.

Chapter Twelve

Enterprise Computing

Objectives

After completing this chapter, you will be able to:

1 Discuss the special information requirements of an enterprise-sized organization

2 Identify information systems and software used in the functional units of an enterprise: accounting and financial systems, human resources information systems, employee relationship management systems, computer-aided design, computer-aided engineering, computer-aided manufacturing, computer-integrated manufacturing, material requirements planning, quality control systems, marketing information systems, sales force automation, distribution systems, and customer interaction management software

3 Describe and list general purpose and integrated information systems used throughout an enterprise: office information systems, transaction processing systems, management information systems, decision support systems, expert systems, enterprise resource planning systems, customer relationship management systems, and content management systems

4 Describe and list types of technologies used throughout an enterprise: portals, communications, data warehouses, extranets, Web services, service-oriented architecture, workflow, and virtual private networks

5 Describe virtualization, cloud computing, and grid computing

6 Discuss the computer hardware needs and solutions for an enterprise: RAID, network attached storage, storage area networks, enterprise storage systems, and blade servers

7 Determine why computer backup is important and how it is accomplished

8 Discuss the steps in a disaster recovery plan

What Is Enterprise Computing?

The term, enterprise, commonly describes a business or venture of any size. In this chapter, the term enterprise refers to large multinational corporations, universities, hospitals, research laboratories, and government organizations. **Enterprise computing** involves the use of computers in networks that encompass a variety of different operating systems, protocols, and network architectures. A typical enterprise consists of corporate headquarters, remote offices, international offices, and hundreds of individual operating entities, called functional units. The types of functional units within a typical manufacturing enterprise are accounting and finance, human resources, engineering, manufacturing, marketing, sales, distribution, customer service, and information technology. Each type of functional unit has specialized requirements for its information systems. These functional units are summarized later in this

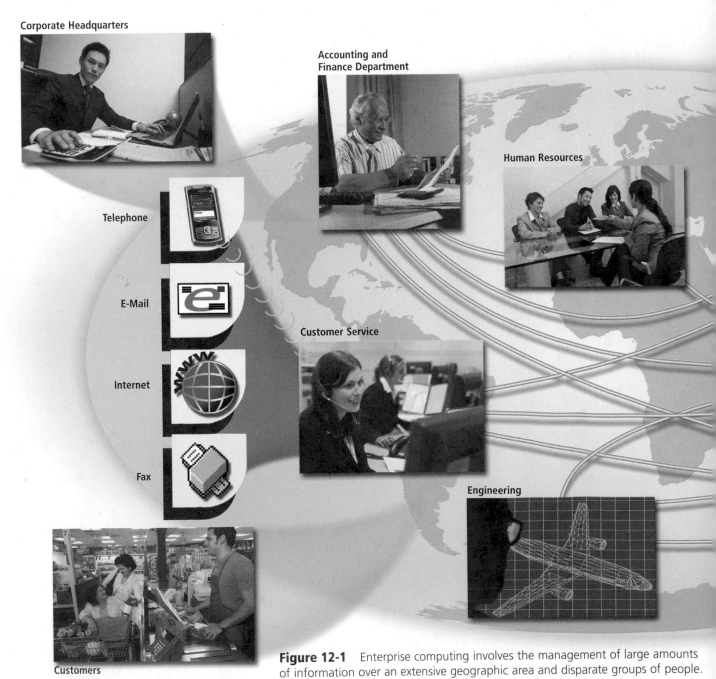

Figure 12-1 Enterprise computing involves the management of large amounts of information over an extensive geographic area and disparate groups of people.

chapter. A **small- and medium-sized business (SMB)** is smaller in size than an enterprise and typically does not have an international presence. Such entities, however, use many of the same technologies and procedures as enterprises, but on a smaller scale.

Enterprises produce and gather enormous volumes of information about customer, supplier, and employee activity. The information flows among an assortment of entities both inside and outside of the enterprise, and users consume the information during a variety of activities (Figure 12-1). Customers, suppliers, and employees interact with the enterprise in a number of ways, and computers track each interaction. Each sale of a product, purchase of a piece of equipment, or paycheck generates activity involving information systems.

Large computers connected by vast networks allow the enterprise to manage and distribute information quickly and efficiently.

Sales Department

Remote Office

IT Department

Marketing Department

Television

Internet

Manufacturing

Distribution

Print

International Office

Types of Enterprises

Figure 12-1 on pages 464 and 465 shows an example of an enterprise whose main focus is in the manufacturing sector. Examples of some types of enterprises are listed below.

- Retail enterprises own a large number of stores in a wide geographical area and use their size to obtain discounts on the goods they purchase; they then seek to sell the goods at a lower price than smaller retailers.
- Manufacturing enterprises create goods on a large scale and then distribute and sell the goods to consumers or other organizations.
- Service enterprises typically do not create or sell goods, but provide services for consumers or other organizations. Examples include companies in the insurance, restaurant, and financial industries.
- Wholesale enterprises seek to purchase and then sell large quantities of goods to other organizations, usually at a lower cost than retail.
- Government enterprises include large city governments, state governments, and the departments and agencies of the federal government.
- Educational enterprises include large universities or school systems that include executives, instructors, and other service personnel and whose reach extends throughout a county, a state, or the entire country.
- Transportation enterprises include airlines, regional transportation authorities, freight and passenger railroads, and trucking firms. The enterprises often include a mix of such types of transportation and have a local or an international reach.

Organizational Structure of an Enterprise

Most traditional enterprises are organized in a hierarchical manner. Figure 12-2 shows an example of an organization chart of a large manufacturing company. Managers at the first two levels at the top of the chart, including the chief executive officer (CEO), mainly concern themselves with strategic decisions and long-term planning.

In Figure 12-2, the chief operating officer (COO) manages the core activities. The supporting activities include financial departments and information technology (IT) departments. The chief

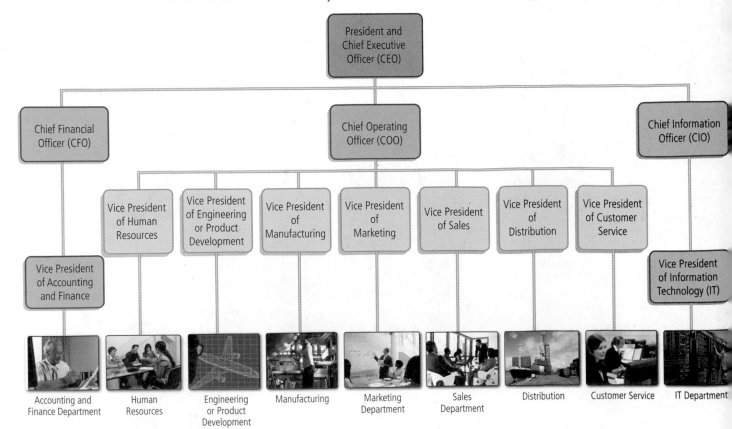

Figure 12-2 Example of an organization chart for a manufacturing enterprise illustrates the hierarchy within an enterprise.

financial officer (CFO) and the chief information officer (CIO) lead these supporting roles. For example, in an airplane manufacturing company, core activity may be the production of wings and cockpits, while a supporting activity may be paying vendors for the parts needed to manufacture those parts.

Each enterprise includes its own special needs and the organizational structure of every enterprise varies. Organizations may include all or some of the managers and departments shown in Figure 12-2.

Levels of Users in the Enterprise

In an enterprise, users of information typically fall into one of four categories: executive management, middle management, operational management, and nonmanagement employees (Figure 12-3). The types of information that users require often depend on their employee level in the organization. Read Ethics & Issues 12-1 for a related discussion.

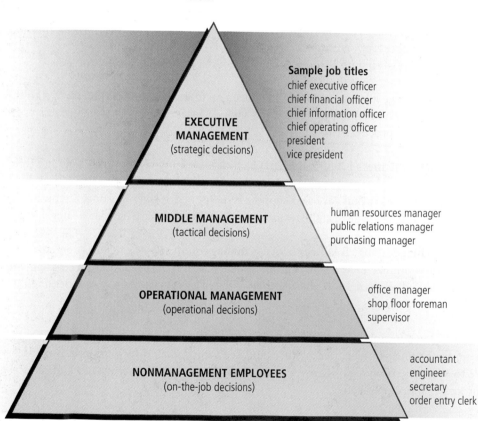

Sample job titles
chief executive officer
chief financial officer
chief information officer
chief operating officer
president
vice president

EXECUTIVE MANAGEMENT
(strategic decisions)

human resources manager
public relations manager
purchasing manager

MIDDLE MANAGEMENT
(tactical decisions)

office manager
shop floor foreman
supervisor

OPERATIONAL MANAGEMENT
(operational decisions)

accountant
engineer
secretary
order entry clerk

NONMANAGEMENT EMPLOYEES
(on-the-job decisions)

Figure 12-3 This pyramid illustrates the levels of users, sample job titles of each level of user, and the types of decisions these users make.

▼ ETHICS & ISSUES 12-1

Should Employees Use Mobile Computers and Devices at Work?

Employers rarely enforce rules prohibiting employees from listening to their portable media players while at work. Other employers do not mind personal phone calls being made at work on employee owned cell phones. A few even allow employees to plug personally owned computers into the company network. Some people argue that some or all of these practices should and could be allowed in most office workplaces if the employer uses proper security measures. They claim that because it is impossible to prevent all employees from bringing in miniature portable media players that the company should plan for all possibilities. Many companies, however, increasingly place these practices under scrutiny. They argue that the devices make data theft unpreventable because the devices can be attached to workplace computers and backups of critical company data made to the devices. Some employers now go so far as to confiscate employees' mobile computers and devices, or to terminate employment for those caught using mobile devices in the workplace. While most employers' policies disallow such devices, the rules sometimes are difficult, if not impossible, to enforce.

Should employees be allowed to use their own mobile computers and devices at work? Why or why not? Is it possible for employers to keep all personal electronics out of the office? Why? If an employer allows employees' mobile computers and devices in the office, what rules should be in effect, how should they be enforced, and what penalties should be assessed for breaking the rules?

How Managers Use Information

Enterprise information is the information gathered in the ongoing operations of an enterprise-sized organization. Enterprise information begins with the day-to-day transactions that occur within a company, such as sales receipts or time cards. The company gathers and stores the information. Over time, employees collect, combine, and analyze the information. Ultimately, the role of information gathered in this way is to allow managers to make better decisions.

All employees, including managers, in a company need accurate information to perform their jobs effectively. **Managers** are responsible for coordinating and controlling an organization's resources. Resources include people, money, materials, and information. Managers coordinate these resources by performing four activities: planning, organizing, leading, and controlling.

- Planning involves establishing goals and objectives.
- Organizing includes identifying and combining resources, such as money and people, so that the company can reach its goals and objectives.
- Leading, sometimes referred to as directing, involves communicating instructions and authorizing others to perform the necessary work.
- Controlling involves measuring performance and, if necessary, taking corrective action.

Managers use a variety of tools and techniques to focus on information that is important to the decision-making process. These tools and techniques include business intelligence, business process management, and business process automation.

Business Process Management
For more information, visit the Computer Concepts CourseMate Web site at www.cengagebrain.com, navigate to the Chapter 12 Web Link resource for this book, and then click Business Process Management.

Business Intelligence   **Business intelligence (BI)** includes several types of applications and technologies for acquiring, storing, analyzing, and providing access to information to help users make more sound business decisions. BI applications include decision support systems, query and reporting, online analytical processing (OLAP), statistical analysis, and data mining. These activities are described later in this chapter.

Business Process Management   **Business process management (BPM)** includes a set of activities that enterprises perform to optimize their business processes, such as accounting and finance, hiring employees, and purchasing goods and services. BPM almost always is aided by specialized software designed to assist in these activities.

Business Process Automation   **Business process automation (BPA)** provides easy exchange of information among business applications, reduces the need for human intervention in processes, and uses software to automate processes wherever possible. BPA offers greater efficiency and reduces risks by making processes more predictable.

Information Systems in the Enterprise

An **information system** is a set of hardware, software, data, people, and procedures that work together to produce information (Figure 12-4). A procedure is an instruction, or set of instructions, a user follows to accomplish an activity.

Information systems can be used in a variety of ways in an enterprise. Some information systems are used exclusively by only one department, or functional unit, within the enterprise. General purpose information systems include categories of information systems that can be used by almost any department within the enterprise. Integrated information systems are used by multiple departments and facilitate collaboration within the enterprise. The following sections discuss each of these three uses of information systems.

Information Systems within Functional Units

Figure 12-5 lists typical functional units, and their purpose within an enterprise, and examples of programs that each might use. The sections that follow discuss the types of information systems and software used within these units. Small- and medium-sized businesses also may use some or many of these products.

hardware

people

procedures

software

data

Figure 12-4 An information system typically contains five components: hardware, software, data, people, and procedures.

Functional Units within an Enterprise

Functional Unit	Description	Program Name
Accounting and Finance	Responsible for managing the business's money. Accounting department tracks every financial transaction that occurs within the company, including billing customers. Finance department manages the business's money as efficiently as possible.	Microsoft Dynamics GP Oracle Financials NetSuite
Human Resources (HR)	Responsible for recruiting and promoting employees, maintaining employee records, evaluating employees, training employees, and managing employee benefits and compensation.	Lawson Human Capital Management Oracle PeopleSoft Enterprise Human Capital Management Sage ABRA HRMS
Engineering or Product Development	Responsible for developing ideas into a product that can be used by customers. Ensures that the product can be manufactured effectively and designs the methods for manufacturing the product.	AutoCAD MicroStation ProductVision
Manufacturing	Responsible for converting raw materials into physical products.	CA-Plus MISys Manufacturing System Horizon Software MRP Plus Plexus Online
Marketing	Responsible for researching the market in which a business operates to determine the products and features that the business should develop. Determines the demographics to target with sales efforts and informs the target market about the company's products through advertising and education.	Aprimo Enterprise Oracle Marketing MarketingPilot
Sales	Responsible for selling the company's products and services.	OpenBOX Sales Force Automation Prophet SalesForce SFA
Distribution	Responsible for delivery of products to customers.	Activant Prophet 21 IBS's Advanced Inventory and Distribution Software Oracle Transportation Management
Customer Service	Responsible for maintaining a relationship with a customer both before and after a sale has been made.	SAP CRM Siebel CRM On Demand Syntellect Customer Interaction Management Suite
Information Technology (IT)	Responsible for designing, purchasing, implementing, testing, securing, and maintaining information systems for the rest of the organization. Sometimes called the information services (IS) department.	Microsoft System Center Configuration Manager VMware vCloud

Figure 12-5 An enterprise is composed of several functional units, each of which may use different programs to fulfill their needs.

Accounting and Finance Figure 12-6 illustrates the separate functions of accounting and financial systems used by accounting and finance departments. Accounting software manages everyday transactions, such as sales and payments to suppliers. Billing software helps the company reconcile purchases with customer payments. Financial software helps managers budget, forecast, and analyze. These types of software include comprehensive and flexible reporting tools to assist managers in making decisions, provide historical documentation, and meet regulatory requirements.

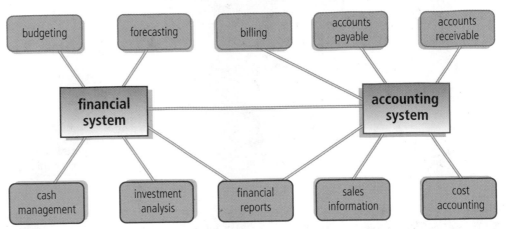

Figure 12-6 Accounting and financial systems perform different tasks but share information and produce financial reports that help management make decisions.

Human Resources A **human resources information system** (**HRIS**) manages one or more human resources functions (Figure 12-7). A human resources information system and its associated software help a company such as Walmart maintain records on its more than 2 million employees. For example, when many retail employees arrive at work, they check in using an electronic clock that automatically allows managers to know who is late, early, or on time. The payroll department then can use this information when determining employee pay.

Figure 12-7 A human resources information system (HRIS) allows human resources personnel to manage employee information, such as benefits, personal information, performance evaluations, training, and vacation time.

An employee relationship management (ERM) system automates and manages much of the communications between employees and the business. For example, an employee may interact with ERM software to gather information about the employee's retirement account. Most ERM software includes a Web interface for the employees and the human resources personnel, allowing both to interact with the system when they are in the office or at home.

Engineering or Product Development   Professional workers, such as engineers, require specialized software and systems to perform their tasks. **Computer-aided design (CAD)** uses a computer and special software to aid in product design.

Computer-aided engineering (CAE) uses computers to test product designs. Using CAE, engineers can test the design of a car or bridge before it is built. These sophisticated programs simulate the effects of wind, temperature, weight, and stress on product shapes and materials. Engineers sometimes use 3-D visualization, which allows them to interact with a product without the need to build a prototype.

Manufacturing   Manufacturing information systems and software not only assist in the actual assembly process, but also assist in scheduling and managing the inventory of parts and products. **Computer-aided manufacturing (CAM)** is the use of computers to control production equipment. CAM production equipment includes software-controlled drilling, lathe, welding, and milling machines.

Computer-integrated manufacturing (CIM) uses computers to integrate the many different operations of the manufacturing process, using technologies such as CAD, CAE, and CAM (Figure 12-8).

Material Requirements Planning (MRP) is an approach to information management in a manufacturing environment that uses software to help monitor and control processes related to production. MRP focuses on issues related to inventory of parts and forecasting future demand so that materials needed for manufacturing can be on hand when they are needed.

Figure 12-8   Computer-integrated manufacturing (CIM) speeds the manufacturing process and reduces product defects.

Quality Control   A quality control system helps an organization maintain or improve the quality of its products or services. A quality control system usually includes quality control software. Quality control software typically requires a great deal of continuous data gathering from the organization's ongoing processes. Using statistical analysis, the software can find and predict product defects and problems with the company's processes. While quality control systems often are costly and disruptive to the organization, the organization typically saves more money by producing a higher quality product or service.

ERM

For more information, visit the Computer Concepts CourseMate Web site at www.cengagebrain.com, navigate to the Chapter 12 Web Link resource for this book, and then click ERM.

Marketing A **marketing information system** serves as a central repository for the tasks of the marketing functional unit. One type of marketing information system is a market research system, which stores and analyzes data gathered from demographics and surveys. Market research software assists in target marketing by allowing marketing personnel to query databases based on criteria such as income, gender, previous purchases, and favorite recreational activities. For example, many companies use market research systems to analyze Web site visitors' use of the company's Web site, such as tracking the users that visit specific Web pages on a site and how long the user views the Web page.

Sales **Sales force automation (SFA)** software equips traveling salespeople with the electronic tools they need to be more productive. Sales force automation software helps salespeople manage customer contacts, schedule customer meetings, log customer interactions, manage product information, and take orders from customers.

Sales force automation software (Figure 12-9) often runs on notebook computers or other mobile devices. The notebook computer or other mobile device may connect wirelessly to the central office, allowing the salesperson to access up-to-date corporate information in real time no matter where he or she is located.

Some sales force automation programs allow the salesperson to upload information to the central office at the end of the day or end of the week. The programs also allow salespeople to download updated product and pricing information.

Figure 12-9
Sales force automation (SFA) software allows the sales force to manage customer and prospective customer relationships more effectively.

Distribution **Distribution systems** provide forecasting for inventory control, manage and track shipping of products, and provide information and analysis on inventory in warehouses. Some distribution systems rely on GPS and other navigation technologies to track shipping in real time. Many companies now employ RFID to track inventory and shipping. Because of the complexity of the tasks of inventory management and shipping, distribution systems often integrate with quality control systems.

Customer Service **Customer interaction management (CIM)** software manages the day-to-day interactions with customers, such as telephone calls, e-mail interactions, Web interactions, and instant messaging sessions. These interactions are logged so that a historical record of interactions with the customer can be viewed or analyzed at any time. A customer interaction management program routes support queries to the most appropriate support person depending on the customer's situation. For example, a call from a pilot with a problem regarding an airplane during a flight requires a different level of service than an airline technician who needs to fix a simple problem with an airplane on the ground. Customer interaction management software also assists support personnel in providing the best solutions for customers.

? FAQ 12-1

When should I supply personal information to a company?

Companies gather personal information about consumers for a variety of reasons. Companies can gather information when you make a purchase, complete a survey, or enter a sweepstakes. Unless you are sure you want the company to communicate with you in some way, few reasons exist to supply personal information to a company. Ask the company why it needs the information and use your judgment. Most companies can supply you with a privacy policy upon request.

For more information, visit the Computer Concepts CourseMate Web site at www.cengagebrain.com, navigate to the Chapter 12 FAQ resource for this book, and then click Sharing Personal Information.

IT Departments

For more information, visit the Computer Concepts CourseMate Web site at www.cengagebrain.com, navigate to the Chapter 12 Web Link resource for this book, and then click IT Departments.

Information Technology   The information technology (IT) department makes technology decisions for the enterprise, such as a decision whether to build or buy new customer interaction management information systems or when a computer or information system has outlived its useful life. Many organizations elevate the importance of information technology by including a **chief information officer (CIO)** executive position that reports to the CEO.

General Purpose Information Systems

Some information systems in an enterprise cross the boundaries of functional units. These general purpose, or enterprise-wide, systems become necessary in an enterprise for two reasons. First, functional units within an enterprise have a significant need to share data among the units. Second, enterprise-wide systems can collect and combine data more quickly and provide executive management access to a more up-to-date and accurate view of what is happening in the organization. Advances in computing speed, storage capacity, security, and networking have made enterprise-wide systems more attractive to organizations in recent years.

General purpose information systems generally fall into one of five categories: office information systems, transaction processing systems, management information systems, decision support systems, and expert systems. The following sections present each type of these general purpose information systems.

Office Information Systems   An **office information system (OIS)** is an information system that enables employees to perform tasks using computers and other electronic devices, instead of manually. An office information system increases employee productivity and assists with communications among employees. Some people describe an office information system as office automation.

An office information system uses many common software products to support its activities. Typical software in an office information system includes word processing, spreadsheet, database, presentation graphics, e-mail, Web browser, Web page authoring, personal information management, and groupware. To send text, graphics, audio, and video to others, an office information system uses communications technology such as voice mail, fax, and video conferencing.

Transaction Processing Systems   A **transaction processing system (TPS)** is an information system that captures and processes data from day-to-day business activities.

Transaction processing systems were among the first computerized systems that processed business data. Many people initially referred to the functions of a transaction processing system as data processing. The first transaction processing systems computerized an existing manual system. The intent of these transaction processing systems was to process transactions faster, reduce clerical costs, and improve customer service.

When you make a purchase with a credit card at a store, you are interacting with a transaction processing system. A transaction is an individual business activity. Examples of transactions are deposits, payments, orders, and reservations. Transactions take place in real time, meaning that as soon as you make a purchase with a credit card, you can visit your credit card company's Web site and view the transaction. In an organization, clerical staff typically uses computers and special software to perform activities associated with a transaction processing system.

Early TPSs mostly used batch processing. With batch processing, the computer collects data over time and processes all transactions later, as a group. As computers became more powerful, system developers created online transaction processing information systems. With online transaction processing (OLTP), the computer processes each transaction as it is entered. Today, most transaction processing systems use OLTP. Figure 12-10 shows an example of the difference between batch processing and OLTP.

For example, when you book a flight using an airline's Web site, the airline probably uses OLTP. You use the airline's Web site to schedule your desired flights. The Web site immediately displays your itinerary and sends you a copy of your itinerary.

Figure 12-10 With batch processing, all airline reservations are processed together at the end of the day. With OLTP, reservations are processed immediately.

Management Information Systems A **management information system (MIS)** is an information system that generates accurate, timely, and organized information, so that managers and other users can make decisions, solve problems, supervise activities, and track progress.

Management information systems often are integrated with transaction processing systems. To process a sales order, the transaction processing system records the sale, updates the customer's account balance, and reduces the inventory count. Using this information, the related management information system produces reports that recap daily sales activities, summarize weekly and monthly sales activities, list customers with past due account balances, chart slow- or fast-selling products, and highlight inventory items that need reordering.

A management information system creates three basic types of reports: detailed, summary, and exception (Figure 12-11). A detailed report usually lists just transactions. For example, a Detailed Flight Report lists the number of passengers booked for a given flight. A summary report consolidates data usually with totals, tables, or graphs, so that managers can review it quickly and easily.

An exception report identifies data outside of a normal condition. These out-of-the-ordinary conditions, called the exception criteria, define the normal activity or status range. For example, a Premier Club Booking Exception Report notifies the airline marketing department that some flights have not met goals for booking Premier Club members.

Exception reports save managers time. Instead of searching through a detailed report, managers simply review the exception report. These reports help managers focus on situations that require immediate decisions or actions. Most information systems support all three types of reports shown in Figure 12-11.

Figure 12-11a   (detailed report)

Detailed Flight Report for March 30

Flight #	Origin/ Destination	Class – Number of Passengers	Premier Club Members
1048	ORD – RSW	A – 5 B – 14 C – 89	A – 1 B – 12 C – 20
543	ORD – BMI	A – 2 B – 7 C – 15	A – 2 B – 5 C – 5
715	ORD – LAX	A – 12 B – 25 C – 123	A – 8 B – 15 C – 39
701	ORD – JFK	A – 9 B – 10 C – 7	A – 7 B – 0 C – 3

Figure 12-11b   (summary report)

Summary Flight Report for March 30

Flight #	Origin/ Destination	Passengers	Premier Club Members
1048	ORD – RSW	108	33
543	ORD – BMI	24	12
715	ORD – LAX	160	62
701	ORD – JFK	26	10

Figure 12-11c   (exception report)

Exception Flight Report for March 30

Flight #	Class	Origin/ Destination	Premier Club Members	Premier Club Member Goal
1048	A	ORD – RSW	1	4
701	C	ORD – JFK	3	5

Figure 12-11   Three basic types of information generated in an MIS are detailed, summary, and exception.

Decision Support Systems   A **decision support system** (**DSS**) helps users analyze information and make decisions. Often, a transaction processing system or management information system does not generate the type of report a manager needs to make a decision.

Programs that analyze data, such as those in a decision support system, sometimes are called online analytical processing (OLAP) programs. A decision support system uses data from internal and external sources. Internal sources of data might include sales orders, Material Requirements Planning results, inventory records, or financial data from accounting and financial analyses. Data from external sources could include interest rates, population trends, costs of new housing construction, or raw material pricing.

Some decision support systems include their own query languages, statistical analyses, spreadsheets, and graphics that help users retrieve data and analyze the results. Some also allow managers to create a model of the factors affecting a decision. A product manager might need to decide on a price for a new product. A simple model for finding the best price would include factors for the expected sales volume at various price levels. The model allows the user to ask what-if questions and view the expected results.

A special type of decision support system, called an executive information system (EIS), supports the strategic information needs of executive management. An EIS presents information as charts and tables that show trends, ratios, and statistics that aid in the decision making process (Figure 12-12).

Figure 12-12   An executive information system (EIS) gathers and presents information to senior management in the form of graphics and reports used to assist in decision making.

Expert Systems An **expert system** is an information system that captures and stores the knowledge of human experts and then imitates human reasoning and decision making. Figure 12-13 shows how one expert system assists with diagnosing a computer problem in Windows 7.

Expert systems consist of two main components: a knowledge base and inference rules. A knowledge base is the combined subject knowledge and experiences of the human experts. The inference rules are a set of logical judgments that are applied to the knowledge base each time a user describes a situation to the expert system.

Expert systems are one aspect of an exciting branch of computer science called artificial intelligence. **Artificial intelligence (AI)** is the application of human intelligence to computers. Artificial intelligence technology senses a person's actions and, based on logical assumptions and prior experience, takes the appropriate action to complete the task. Artificial intelligence has a variety of capabilities, including speech recognition, logical reasoning, and creative responses. New research in the field of artificial intelligence tries to mimic the way that human memory works in order to expedite searches for information.

A Sample Expert System in Windows 7 Help and Support

Step 1
A user enters the nature of the problem.

Step 2
Select a suggested solution from the list presented by the expert system.

Step 3
Expert system displays details about the solution and additional options.

Step 4
Expert system displays detailed steps when requested.

Figure 12-13 This figure shows a sample expert system in Windows 7 Help and Support.

Enterprises employ expert systems in a variety of roles, such as answering customer questions, training new employees, and analyzing data.

Integrated Information Systems

It often is difficult to classify an information system as belonging to only one of the five general types of information systems. Much of today's application software supports transaction processing and creates management information system reports. Other applications provide transaction processing, management information, and decision support.

Enterprise Resource Planning **Enterprise resource planning** (**ERP**) provides centralized, integrated software applications to help manage and coordinate the ongoing activities of the enterprise, including manufacturing and distribution, accounting, finance, sales, product planning, and human resources. Figure 12-14 shows how ERP fits into the operations of an enterprise.

The ERP system installed at each organization must be customized to match the business requirements of the enterprise. At a large company, an ERP system may take four to six years to implement and cost hundreds of millions of dollars. The organization hopes to regain the investment through the advantages offered by ERP.

Figure 12-14   Enterprise resource planning (ERP) encompasses all of the major activities throughout a business.

ERP

For more information, visit the Computer Concepts CourseMate Web site at www.cengagebrain.com, navigate to the Chapter 12 Web Link resource for this book, and then click ERP.

Advantages of enterprise resource planning include complete integration of information systems across departments, better project management, and improved customer service. Enterprise resource planning also helps to manage better the global nature of many enterprises. The reliance on one information system, rather than up to several hundred systems, allows the IT department to focus on one type of technology and simplifies relationships with information technology vendors.

Customer Relationship Management   A **customer relationship management (CRM)** system manages information about customers, interactions with customers, past purchases, and interests. Customer relationship management mainly is used across sales, marketing, and customer service departments. Customer relationship management software tracks leads and inquiries from customers, stores a history of all correspondence and sales to a customer, and allows for tracking of outstanding issues with customers.

Content Management Systems   A **content management system (CMS)** is an information system that is a combination of databases, software, and procedures that organizes and allows access to various forms of documents and other files, including images and multimedia content. The content management system also provides security controls for the content, such as who is allowed to add, view, and modify content and on which content the user is allowed to perform those operations (Figure 12-15). Publishing entities, such as news services, use content management systems to keep Web sites and RSS feeds up-to-date.

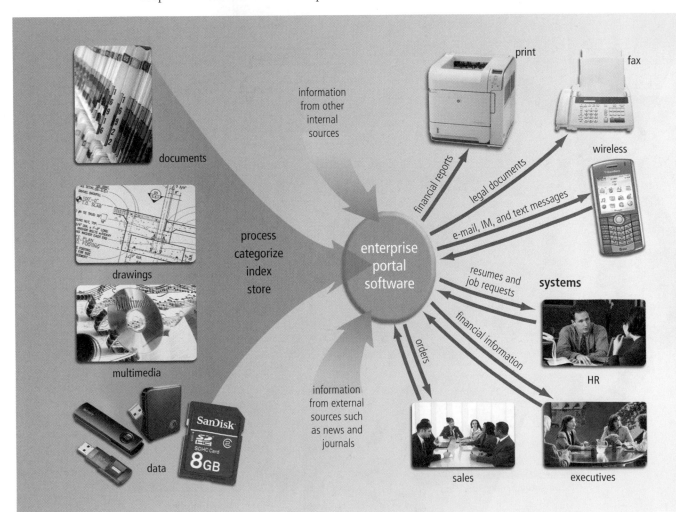

Figure 12-15   A content management system (CMS) helps a company classify and manage volumes of documents and media for future retrieval and use.

✔ QUIZ YOURSELF 12-1

Instructions: Find the true statement below. Then, rewrite the remaining false statements so that they are true.

1. The main task of executive managers is to make tactical decisions.

2. An information system is a set of hardware, software, and people that work together to produce information.

3. A human resources information system serves as a central repository for the tasks of the marketing functional unit.

4. Customer interaction management software manages the day-to-day interactions with customers.

5. Decision support systems capture and store the knowledge of human experts and then imitate human reasoning and decision making.

6. Enterprise resource planning is a combination of databases, software, and procedures that organizes and allows access to various forms of documents and files.

Quiz Yourself Online: To further check your knowledge of pages 464 through 478, visit the Computer Concepts CourseMate Web site at www.cengagebrain.com, navigate to the Chapter 12 Quiz Yourself resource for this book, and then click Objectives 1 – 3.

Enterprise-Wide Technologies and Methodologies

Data Centers

For more information, visit the Computer Concepts CourseMate Web site at www.cengagebrain.com, navigate to the Chapter 12 Web Link resource for this book, and then click Data Centers.

Several technologies adopted by enterprises allow them the flexibility and the ability to move swiftly in a business environment. Some of the common technologies used in enterprises include portals, electronic data interchange, data warehouses, extranets, Web services, workflow, and virtual private networks. Most of the hardware and software that contains these technologies is located in a **data center**, which is a centralized location for managing and housing those items. Read Innovative Computing 12-1 to find out about unique data center solutions. The following sections discuss each of these technologies.

❗ INNOVATIVE COMPUTING 12-1

Unique Data Center Storage Solutions

As data centers' sizes expand, companies are searching for groundbreaking storage solutions that do not necessarily break ground. Google, for example, is considering sea-based centers on barges docked up to seven miles offshore. Energy generated from the waves' motions could help cool and power the supercomputers running the company's search engines.

Sun Microsystems is exploring using space in abandoned coal mines. The cool groundwater would help reduce temperatures and power consumption by 50 percent, resulting in a reduction in electricity costs of at least $9 million.

Another unlikely data center location, Siberia's frozen tundra, looks promising for Microsoft's expansion plans. Currently the company is building centers adjacent to hydroelectric plants, where recycled water will cool the tens of thousands of servers. This water does not need to be drinkable, so no energy is needed to purify it at waste water treatment sites. In another energy-saving measure, Microsoft is using cool outside air instead of air conditioning systems to reduce the computers' operating temperatures.

For more information, visit the Computer Concepts CourseMate Web site at www.cengagebrain.com, navigate to the Chapter 12 Innovative Computing resource for this book, and then click Data Centers.

Portals

A **portal** is a collection of links, content, and services presented on a Web page and designed to guide users to information they likely are to find interesting for their particular job function. A portal often includes searching capabilities or a link to a search engine, such as Google. Organizations often deploy **enterprise search** technology that allows users to perform searches across many enterprise-wide information systems and databases. Users typically can customize the portal Web site to meet their needs.

Information from external sources included on a portal Web page can include weather, news, reference tools, and instant messaging (Figure 12-16).

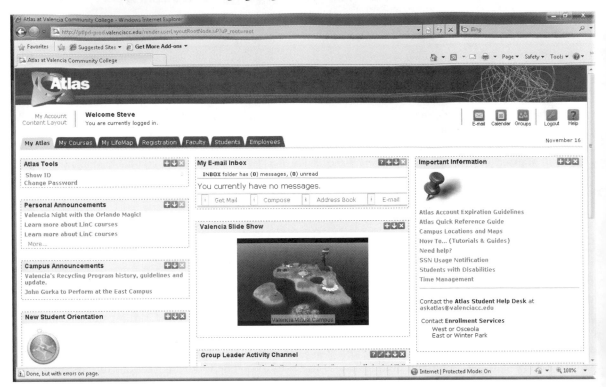

Figure 12-16 Portals allow users quick access to a multitude of information sources that they access on a regular basis.

Communications

The IT department, headed by the CIO, builds and maintains the electronic communications infrastructure of the enterprise. The communications infrastructure consists of hardware, software, and procedures. Examples of hardware include wired network connections, wireless network devices, routers, firewalls, servers, and a variety of long distance communications connections. Software can include e-mail, instant messaging, VoIP, and software applications to manage servers and end users' computers remotely. Procedures include the methods for using and managing the hardware and software. To learn about installing VoIP software on your computer, complete the Learn How To 1 activity on pages 498 and 499.

In addition to the communications software accessed by end users in the enterprise, the IT department manages the software on servers to support the end users' programs. For example, the IT department manages e-mail servers that are accessed by the end users' e-mail programs.

For e-commerce, specialized software often is used to communicate with other computers. **EDI** (**electronic data interchange**) is a set of standards that controls the transfer of business data and information among computers both within and among enterprises. Today, businesses use these standards to communicate with industry partners over the Internet and telephone lines.

Data Warehouses

A **data warehouse** is a huge database that stores and manages the data required to analyze historical and current transactions. Software applications such as ERP programs store and access data in a data warehouse. A data warehouse may be stored in a cloud computing environment. Cloud computing is discussed later in this chapter.

Most data warehouses include one or more databases and one or more information systems storing data in the data warehouse. The data in the databases consists of transaction data required for decision making. This data may come from internal or external sources (Figure 12-17). Some data warehouses use Web farming for their external data. Web farming is the process of collecting data from the Internet as a source for the data warehouse.

Another growing external source of information is a click stream. A click stream is a collection of every action that users make as they move through a Web site. By analyzing visitors' click streams, companies identify consumer preferences and determine which Web pages are most attractive to visitors.

Figure 12-17 A data warehouse can receive data from a variety of sources, including company transactions, the Internet, and Web site visitor click streams.

Extranets

An **extranet** is the portion of a company's network that allows customers or suppliers of a company to access parts of an enterprise's intranet. An extranet provides a secure, physical connection to the company's network. Customers may use the extranet to place and monitor orders electronically or to make payments. Suppliers may check inventory levels of the parts they supply to the company and receive orders and payments from the company. Extranets improve efficiency by replacing the postal service, faxes, or telephone calls as the communications medium of choice.

Web Services

Web services include a relatively new set of software technologies that allows businesses to create products and B2B (business-to-business) interactions over the Internet. Web services do not include traditional user interfaces, such as a Web page. Rather, users build their own interfaces to the Web services when necessary. Two popular platforms for building and running Web services are the Sun Microsystems Java EE platform and the Microsoft .NET Framework.

For example, an airline company may provide up-to-the-minute flight status information as a Web service (Figure 12-18). Travel Web sites, such as Expedia or Orbitz, can query the Web service and then display the information on their own Web pages for their customers. The travel Web site may ask for the status of a particular flight and receive back a scheduled departure or arrival time from the Web service. How the travel Web site then uses that information is of no concern to the Web service. The travel Web site may display the information to a customer who requested the information, or it may send an e-mail notification with the information to the customer. Typically, the customer or consumer of the Web service — the travel Web site in this example — must write a program to use the Web service. Many enterprises now employ a service-oriented architecture because the company requires more communication between diverse information systems. In a service-oriented architecture (SOA), information systems provide services to other information systems in a well-defined manner over a network. One benefit to using an SOA is that services from multiple information systems can be combined to create new services or programs.

Web Services

 For more information, the Computer Concepts CourseMate Web site at www.cengagebrain.com, navigate to the Chapter 12 Web Link resource for this book, and then click Web Services.

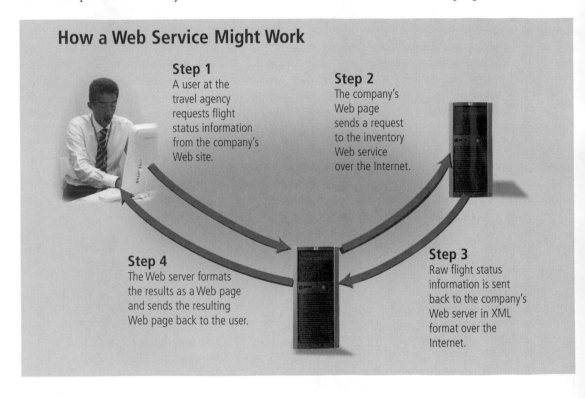

How a Web Service Might Work

Step 1
A user at the travel agency requests flight status information from the company's Web site.

Step 2
The company's Web page sends a request to the inventory Web service over the Internet.

Step 4
The Web server formats the results as a Web page and sends the resulting Web page back to the user.

Step 3
Raw flight status information is sent back to the company's Web server in XML format over the Internet.

Figure 12-18
This figure shows how a Web service might work.

Workflow

A **workflow** is a defined process that identifies the specific set of steps involved in completing a particular project or business process. A workflow may be a written set of rules or a set of rules that exists in an information system.

A **workflow application** is a program that assists in the management and tracking of all the activities in a business process from start to finish. Enterprises use workflow applications to assist in defining complex workflows.

Virtual Private Network

Many companies today allow access to their company networks through a virtual private network. When a mobile user, remote office, vendor, or customer connects to a company's network using the Internet, a **virtual private network** (**VPN**) provides them with a secure connection to the company network server, as if they had a private line. VPNs help to ensure that transmitted data is safe from being intercepted by unauthorized people (Figure 12-19). VPNs securely extend the company's internal network beyond the physical boundaries of the company. The secure connection created over the Internet between the user's computer and the company's network is called a VPN tunnel. Many companies allow external access to their internal networks only via a VPN connection.

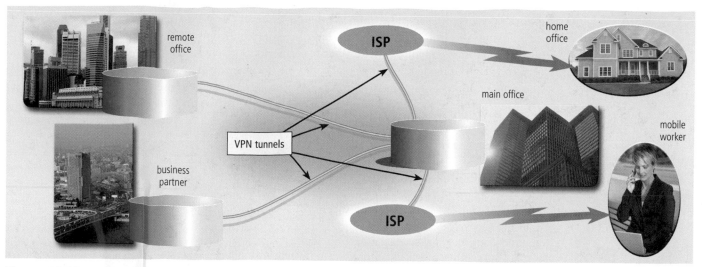

Figure 12-19   A virtual private network (VPN) allows a company to extend its internal network securely.

Virtualization and Cloud Computing

As the cost of hardware and networking services dramatically decreases, the cost of skilled specialists to maintain complex information systems increases. These opposing trends have led to an increase in the use of virtualization and cloud computing. These technologies provide for centralized and/or outsourced management of information system infrastructure, such as servers, security, and networking. The following sections describe virtualization, cloud computing, and grid computing.

Virtualization

Due to the often dynamic nature of enterprise computing needs, IT administrators often use virtualization to adapt quickly to the change. Virtualization is the practice of sharing or pooling computing resources, such as servers and storage devices. Server virtualization provides the capability to divide a physical server logically into many virtual servers. From the end user's point of view, a virtual server behaves just like a physical server. The advantages of server virtualization are that a virtual server can be created and configured quickly, does not require a new physical server, and is easier to manage.

Storage virtualization provides the capability to create a single logical storage device from many physical storage devices. For example, hard disks from many different servers located in geographically disparate areas can be combined to appear as a single hard disk to the users of the storage. The advantages of storage virtualization are that the storage can be configured quickly, may not require the purchase of additional storage devices because the necessary capacity already may exist, and is easier to manage than traditional storage.

Virtualization

For more information, visit the Computer Concepts CourseMate Web site at www.cengagebrain.com, navigate to the Chapter 12 Web Link resource for this book, and then click Virtualization.

Cloud and Grid Computing

As demand for computing resources increases, companies often find that using outside computing resources is more economical than building new computing capacity internally. Cloud and grid computing are two new technologies that provide flexible and massive online computing power. **Cloud computing** is an Internet service that provides computing needs to computer users. When the company uses the computing resources, they pay a fee based on the amount of computing time and other resources that they consume. Cloud computing allows a company to diversify its network and server infrastructure. Some cloud computing services automatically add more network and server capacity to a company's Web site, as demand for services of the Web site increases. The network and server capacity may be duplicated around the world so that, for example, a single outage of a server does not affect the company's operations. Read Looking Ahead 12-1 for a look at the future of cloud computing.

Grid computing combines many servers and/or personal computers on a network, such as the Internet, to act as one large computer. As with cloud computing, a company may pay for the use of a grid based on the amount of processing time that it needs. Grid computing often is used in research environments, such as climate research and life science problems. For example, the SETI@home project uses a grid of millions of personal computers around the world to search radio signals for signs of extraterrestrial life.

↗ LOOKING AHEAD 12-1

Variable Winds Forecasted for Cloud Computing

The forecast for enterprise computing calls for partly cloudy skies. The winds of change in computing are coming to businesses in various degrees, but how and when companies and consumers will adopt the infrastructure is not clear. Most analysts agree that this revolutionary storm is brewing on the horizon and will reach just about everyone before long. Microsoft and Google are predicting cloud computing's future and are developing different business models. Microsoft is focusing on enterprise tools, while Google is working on consumer-based applications.

Small businesses should be the first widespread adopters because of cost-saving measures. Their organizational needs for

occasional computing power, storage, and services make the Web applications ideal. Startup companies increasingly will use pay-as-you-go assistance, such as Amazon's Web Services. Some forecasts predict that the only required hardware will be a monitor, keyboard, and mouse because all computing and storage will be performed offsite.

Large corporations, by contrast, will be slower to adopt cloud computing. Their more specific needs and concerns of security might delay their entry into this newer resource.

 For more information, visit the Computer Concepts CourseMate Web site at www.cengagebrain.com, navigate to the Chapter 12 Looking Ahead resource for this book and then click Cloud Computing.

E-Commerce

Several market sectors have taken advantage of business opportunities on the Web. The more popular market segments include retail, finance, health, entertainment and media, and travel. Figure 12-20 briefly reviews some of the more popular e-commerce market segments.

Examples of E-Commerce

Type	Purpose	Example Web Sites
E-Retail	**E-retail**, also called e-tail, occurs when retailers use the Web to sell their products and services.	amazon.com shopping.yahoo.com shopzilla.com
Finance	**Online banking** allows users to pay bills from their computer or mobile device, that is, transfer money electronically from their account to a payee's account such as the electric company or telephone company. With **online trading**, users invest in stocks, options, bonds, treasuries, certificates of deposit, money markets, annuities, mutual funds, and so on — without using a broker.	vanguard.com fidelity.com e-trade.com
Travel	The Web provides many travel-related services. If you need directions, you simply enter a starting point and destination, and many Web sites provide detailed directions along with a map. Users can make airline reservations and reserve a hotel or car.	orbitz.com priceline.com kayak.com
Entertainment and Media	Music, videos, news, sporting events, and 3-D multiplayer games are a growing part of the Web's future. Newsprint on the Web is not replacing the newspaper, but enhancing it and reaching different populations.	itunes.com youtube.com nytimes.com
Health	Many Web sites provide up-to-date medical, fitness, nutrition, or exercise information. Some Web sites offer the capability to listen in on health-related seminars and discussion.	webmd.com health.gov familydoctor.com drugstore.com

 Figure 12-20 E-commerce allows a variety of industries to extend their relationships to their customers via the Internet.

Enterprises use the Web to provide services to consumers and other businesses. Public relations, online advertising, direct mail, recruiting, credit, sales, market research, technical support, training, software consulting, and Internet access represent a few of the areas of service. Read Ethics & Issues 12-2 for additional information.

ETHICS & ISSUES 12-2

Who Can You Trust When Making Purchases Online?

When you walk into a store, at some point in your shopping experience you almost always interact with a person directly. The online shopping experience, however, distances you from a seller who may be five hundred or five thousand miles away. For many consumers, this type of nonhuman transaction can be a source of stress and concern about the trustworthiness of the merchant. For some merchants, the distance and anonymity of the Internet is an ideal climate for finding unknowing victims for unscrupulous activity, such as fraud. Consumer advocates and government agencies recommend many ways to avoid a bad online shopping experience. When you provide personal information, make sure that you are dealing with a secure Web site whose address begins with https:// rather than http://. Check the site's credentials, which may include seals from TRUSTe, the

Better Business Bureau (BBB), or other certifying organizations. Make sure that the price you pay matches the price listed on the site and that you are not paying too much for shipping your order. When available, check reviews of the merchant offered by other consumers, but be aware that many merchants try to offer phony, positive reviews of themselves. Finally, make it a habit to rate merchants as often as possible so that others can learn from your experience.

When you shop online, how do you go about determining which online merchants are trustworthy? How do the methods that you use differ from merchants you visit when you walk into a store for the first time? Are consumer advocacy groups or the government the better choice for regulating online transactions? Why?

Ethics & Issues

For the complete text of the Ethics & Issues boxes found in this chapter, visit the Computer Concepts CourseMate Web site at www.cengagebrain.com and then navigate to the Chapter 12 Ethics & Issues resource for this book.

✔ QUIZ YOURSELF 12-2

Instructions: Find the true statement below. Then, rewrite the remaining false statements so that they are true.

1. A portal is the portion of a company's network that allows customers or suppliers of a company to access parts of an enterprise's intranet.

2. A data warehouse is a huge database that stores and manages the data required to analyze historical and current transactions.

3. A VPN is a server that is placed on a network with the sole purpose of providing storage to users and information systems attached to the network.

4. A workflow application helps an enterprise collect, archive, index, and retrieve its resources.

Quiz Yourself Online: To further check your knowledge of pages 479 through 485, visit the Computer Concepts CourseMate Web site at www.cengagebrain.com, navigate to the Chapter 12 Quiz Yourself resource for this book, and then click Objectives 4 – 5.

Enterprise Hardware

Enterprise hardware allows large organizations to manage and store information and data using devices geared for heavy use, maximum availability, and maximum efficiency.

Enterprises often rely on legacy systems. A **legacy system** is an information system that has existed within the organization for an extended length of time and is relied upon heavily. Enterprises often struggle with the decision to replace legacy systems with newer technology.

The following sections discuss a variety of enterprise hardware solutions.

FAQ 12-2

Why do enterprises use wikis?

Enterprises are relying more heavily on wikis to create pages that are accessible to employees. These pages might include company information, links to information systems within the enterprise, or serve as a knowledge base for the enterprise's information systems.

For more information, visit the Computer Concepts CourseMate Web site at www.cengagebrain.com, navigate to the Chapter 12 FAQ resource for this book, and then click Enterprise Wikis.

RAID

For applications that depend on reliable data access, users must have the data available when they attempt to access it. Some manufacturers provide a type of hard disk system that connects several smaller disks into a single unit that acts like a single large hard disk. As discussed in Chapter 6, a group of two or more integrated hard disks is called a **RAID (redundant array of independent disks)**. Although quite expensive for large computers, RAID is more reliable than traditional hard disks (Figure 12-21). Networks and Internet servers often use RAID.

A RAID system duplicates data, instructions, and information to improve data reliability. The simplest RAID storage design, called mirroring, writes data on two disks at the same time to duplicate the data. This configuration enhances storage reliability because, if a disk should fail, a duplicate of the requested item is available elsewhere within the array of disks. Some personal computers now include RAID storage.

Figure 12-21 A group of two or more integrated hard disks, called a RAID (redundant array of independent disks), often is used with network servers. Shown here is a rack-mounted RAID chassis including the hard disks.

Network Attached Storage and Storage Area Networks

Network attached storage (NAS) is a server that is placed on a network with the sole purpose of providing storage to users and information systems attached to the network (Figure 12-22a). A network attached storage server often is called a storage appliance because it is a piece of equipment with only one function — to provide additional storage. Administrators quickly add storage to an existing network simply by attaching a new network attached storage server to the network.

A **storage area network (SAN)** is a high-speed network with the sole purpose of providing storage to other servers to which it is attached (Figure 12-22b). A storage area network is a network that includes only storage devices. High-speed fiber-optic cable connects other networks and servers to the storage area network, so the networks and servers have fast access to large storage capacities.

NAS and SAN

For more information, visit the Computer Concepts CourseMate Web site at www.cengagebrain.com, navigate to the Chapter 12 Web Link resource for this book, and then click NAS and SAN.

Figure 12-22a   (network attached storage on a LAN)

Figure 12-22b   (a SAN provides centralized storage for servers and networks)

Figure 12-22   Network attached storage (NAS) and a storage area network (SAN) connect to existing servers and networks in different ways.

Enterprise Storage Systems

Many organizations use networks. Data, information, and instructions stored on the network must be easily accessible to all authorized users. The data, information, and instructions also must be secure, so that unauthorized users cannot access the network. An **enterprise storage system** is a strategy that focuses on the availability, protection, organization, and backup of storage in a company.

The goal of an enterprise storage system is to consolidate storage so that operations run as efficiently as possible. Most enterprise storage systems manage extraordinary amounts of data.

For example, one large retailer manages a several-hundred TB storage system to store sales data. Read Ethics & Issues 12-3 for a related discussion.

To implement an enterprise storage system, an organization uses a combination of techniques. As shown in Figure 12-23, an enterprise storage system may use servers, RAID, a tape library, optical disc jukeboxes, Internet backup, network attached storage devices, and/or a storage area network. Enterprises often use **Fibre Channel** technology to connect to storage systems at data rates up to 4 Gbps.

Some organizations manage an enterprise storage system in-house. Other enterprises elect to offload all (or at least the backup) storage management to an outside organization or online Web service. This practice is known as outsourcing. Some vendors focus on providing enterprise storage systems to clients. A data warehouse might seek this type of outside service.

Figure 12-23 An enterprise storage system uses many types of storage.

ETHICS & ISSUES 12-3

How Much Data Should Companies Be Required to Keep?

After a string of corporate scandals, the Sarbanes-Oxley Act was signed into law in 2002, providing a myriad of financial reporting requirements and guidelines for public companies. A main focus of the law is the retention of business records. As provisions of the law slowly have come into effect, companies have been faced with massive new data storage requirements for these records. For example, all e-mail messages within a company are considered to be business records and must be retained. Deleting stored e-mail messages constitutes a destruction of evidence infraction. Penalties include 20 years in prison for any employee who alters or destroys records or documents. IT departments are faced not only with understanding this complex law, but also with ensuring accuracy of financial data, determining policies for record retention, and building storage capacity to hold all of the data. Supporters of the law cite its need due to the recent wave of corporate scandals. Opponents say that the law is over-reaching and costs too much for the added benefits.

Is the Sarbanes-Oxley Act an unfair burden on companies? Why or why not? Should companies be able to engage in internal communications without the fear that those communications could be used as evidence against them later? Why or why not? Should employees or employers be held accountable if laws are violated? Why? Are such laws necessary in order to protect the public? Why or why not?

Blade Servers

A **blade server**, sometimes called an ultradense server, packs a complete computer server, such as a Web server or network server, on a single card, or blade, rather than a system unit. Each blade server includes a processor, memory, hard disk, network card, and ports on the card. The individual blades insert in a blade server chassis that can hold many blades. Using blade servers allows an organization to fit 16 or more blades in the physical space occupied by a typical, single server. Figure 12-24 shows a blade and a chassis that holds many blades.

Besides the savings in space offered by blade servers, blade servers require less maintenance, use less energy, generate less heat, and easily are replaced or upgraded.

Blade Servers

For more information, visit the Computer Concepts CourseMate Web site at www.cengagebrain.com, navigate to the Chapter 12 Web Link resource for this book, and then click Blade Servers.

Figure 12-24   A blade server contains several very small servers, each on its own blade within the server.

High Availability, Scalability, and Interoperability

Enterprises measure the quality of their operations in a numbers of ways. Often systems have specific requirements for availability, the ability to grow (scalability), and interoperability with other systems. One of the goals of an enterprise's hardware is to maintain a high level of availability to end users. The availability of hardware to users is a measure of how often it is online. The following sections discuss these needs in an enterprise.

High-Availability Systems

A **high-availability system** continues running and performing tasks for at least 99 percent of the time. Some users demand that high-availability systems be available for 99.99 percent of the time. A system that has uptime of 99.99 percent is nonfunctional for less than one hour per year. That one hour, called downtime, includes any time that the computer crashes, needs repairs, or requires installation of replacement or upgrade parts. A system with 99.9 percent availability is said to have three nines of availability, and a system with 99.99 percent availability is said to have four nines of availability.

Telecommunications companies, such as local telephone companies, rely on high-availability systems to deliver telephone service. Emergency 911 communications centers require almost 100 percent uptime for their hardware and software applications as mandated by law. Centralized accounting or financial systems must be available to gather sales and other accounting information from locations scattered around the globe.

High-availability systems often include a feature called hot-swapping. Hot-swapping allows components, such as a RAID hard disk or power supplies, to be replaced while the rest of the system continues to perform its tasks. A high-availability system also may include redundant components. **Redundant components**, such as redundant power supplies (Figure 12-25), allow for a functioning component to take over automatically the tasks of a similar component that fails. When a component fails, the system administrator is notified, but the computer continues to perform its tasks because a redundant component has taken its place automatically in the system.

Scalability

As an enterprise grows, its information systems either must grow with it or must be replaced. **Scalability** is a measure of how well a computer hardware system, software application, or information system can grow to meet increasing performance demands. A system that is designed, built, or purchased when the company is small may be inadequate when the company doubles in size. When making decisions for computing solutions, managers must be careful to consider the growth plans of the company.

A company may find that its Web site is becoming overwhelmed by customers and prospective customers. If the Web site is scalable, then the Web administrator can add more Web servers to handle the additional visitors to the Web site. Similarly, an enterprise's storage needs usually grow daily, meaning that storage systems should be scalable to store the ever-growing data generated by users.

Adding more hardware often is the easiest method to grow, or scale, an information system. Often, at some point, a system no longer scales and must be replaced with a new system.

Interoperability

Enterprises typically build and buy a diverse set of information systems. An information system often must share information, or have **interoperability**, with other information systems within the enterprise. Information systems that more easily share information with other information systems are said to be open. Information systems that are more difficult to interoperate with other information systems are said to be closed, or proprietary. Recent open systems employ XML and Web services to allow a greater level of interoperability.

Figure 12-25
This heavy duty battery rack provides reliable backup power for enterprise hardware.

Backup Procedures

Business and home users can perform four types of backup: full, differential, incremental, or selective. A fifth type, continuous data protection, typically is used only by large enterprises. A full backup, sometimes called an archival backup, copies all of the files in the computer. A full backup provides the best protection against data loss because it copies all program and data files. Performing a full backup can be time-consuming. A differential backup copies only the files that have changed since the last full backup. An incremental backup copies only the files that have changed since the last full or last incremental backup. A selective backup, sometimes called a partial backup, allows the user to choose specific files to back up, regardless of whether or not the files have changed since the last incremental backup. Continuous data protection (CDP), or continuous backup, is a system in which all data is backed up whenever a change is made. A continuous data protection plan keeps a journal of every transaction — reads, writes, and deletes — made to a server or servers.

Whatever backup procedures a company adopts, they should be stated clearly, documented in writing, and followed consistently.

? FAQ 12-3

Can I use CDP at home?

Yes. The price of storage devices is decreasing, and companies that provide continuous data protection are able to offer their services at rates much lower than what once were offered. For instance, one company allows you to back up 2 GB of data continuously for less than $60 per year.

For more information, visit the Computer Concepts CourseMate Web site at www.cengagebrain.com, navigate to the Chapter 12 FAQ resource for this book, and then click CDP.

Disaster Recovery Plan

A **disaster recovery plan** is a written plan describing the steps a company would take to restore computer operations in the event of a disaster. A disaster recovery plan contains four major components: the emergency plan, the backup plan, the recovery plan, and the test plan.

The Emergency Plan   An emergency plan specifies the steps to be taken immediately after a disaster strikes. All emergency plans should contain the following information:

1. Names and telephone numbers of people and organizations to notify (e.g., management, fire department, police department)
2. Procedures to follow with the computer equipment (e.g., equipment shutdown, power shutoff, file removal)
3. Employee evacuation procedures
4. Return procedures; that is, who can reenter the facility and what actions they are to perform

The Backup Plan   Once the procedures in the emergency plan have been executed, the next step is to follow the backup plan. The backup plan specifies how an organization uses backup files and equipment to resume information processing. The backup plan should specify the location of an alternate computer facility in the event the organization's normal location is destroyed or unusable.

When operations are so important that an organization cannot afford to lose the operations to a disaster, the organization often maintains a hot site, which is a separate facility that mirrors the systems and operations of the critical site. The hot site always operates concurrently with the main site, so that if either site becomes unavailable, the other site continues to meet the organization's needs. The process of one system automatically taking the place of a failed system is called **failover**.

The backup plan identifies these items:

1. The location of backup data, supplies, and equipment
2. The personnel responsible for gathering backup resources and transporting them to the alternate computer facility
3. A schedule indicating the order in which, and approximate time by which, each application should be up and running

For a backup plan to be successful, the organization must back up all critical resources. Also, additional people, including possibly nonemployees, must be trained in the backup and recovery procedures because the organization's personnel could be injured in a disaster.

The Recovery Plan   The recovery plan specifies the actions to be taken to restore full information processing operations. To prepare for disaster recovery, an organization should establish planning committees, with each one responsible for different forms of recovery. For example, one committee is in charge of hardware replacement. Another is responsible for software replacement.

The Test Plan   To provide assurance that the disaster plan is complete, it should be tested. A disaster recovery test plan contains information for simulating various levels of disasters and recording an organization's ability to recover. In a simulation, all personnel follow the steps in the disaster recovery plan.

Disaster Recovery Plan

For more information, visit the Computer Concepts CourseMate Web site at www.cengagebrain.com, navigate to the Chapter 12 Web Link resource for this book, and then click Disaster Recovery Plan.

✔ **QUIZ YOURSELF 12-3**

Instructions: Find the true statement below. Then, rewrite the remaining false statements so that they are true.

1. Network attached storage is a high-speed network with the sole purpose of providing storage to other servers to which it is attached.
2. Scalability refers to the ability of an information system to share information with other information systems.
3. A differential backup copies only the files that have changed since the last full or last incremental backup.
4. An emergency plan specifies how a company uses backup files and equipment to resume information processing.
5. The recovery plan specifies the actions to be taken to restore full information processing operations.

Quiz Yourself Online: To further check your knowledge of pages 485 through 491, visit the Computer Concepts CourseMate Web site at www.cengagebrain.com, navigate to the Chapter 12 Quiz Yourself resource for this book, and then click Objectives 6 – 8.

Chapter Summary

This chapter reviewed the special computing requirements present in an enterprise-sized organization. Various types of users within an organization require different types of information systems. Large information systems become more valuable when they communicate with each other and offer users a great deal of flexibility in interacting with the information system and other users. The chapter discussed the benefits of virtualization, cloud computing, and grid computing.

Enterprises manage complex hardware, including storage area networks, RAID, and blade servers. Requirements for this enterprise hardware often include high-availability, scalability, and interoperability. The chapter also discussed the backup procedures present in a large organization.

Computer Usage @ Work

Municipal Services

You stayed up late last night and woke up late this morning. Because you take the bus to work, you hurry to get ready and arrive at the bus stop at 7:45 a.m., the exact time that the bus is scheduled to arrive. Ten minutes elapse and you are unsure whether you missed the bus or if the bus merely is running late. You call the city's transportation department to inquire about the bus, but they are unable to provide you with any information. Fortunately, the person with whom you are speaking informs you that the city currently is investing in a system that will provide exact bus arrival times at bus stops; it also will allow management to track the location of buses on their route. This technology uses a global positioning system to determine each bus's exact location and transmits that information back to a server. The server then can transmit relevant information to displays located at various bus stops throughout the city. Management also can use this information to dispatch additional buses if traffic conditions are poor, determine whether bus drivers are staying on their assigned routes, and discover whether they are obeying speed limits and other traffic laws.

After work, you arrive home to find an electrician installing a new electrical meter on your house. Your curiosity prompts you to approach the electrician to find out about the new meter, because you have had no problems with the old one. The electrician explains that in an effort to increase efficiency and save money, the power companies in the area are installing new meters that record power usage data electronically and then transmit the data wirelessly to the billing office. This new technology eliminates the need for employees to visit each house individually and reduces the possibility of human error in calculating your power consumption.

As the day ends, you watch a news story about how your city is installing sirens in strategic areas that will sound when dangerous weather approaches. These sirens either can be activated manually, or they can sound automatically when the National Weather Service issues a severe weather warning for your immediate area.

Computers have enhanced municipal services greatly during the past several years. Not only do computers provide increased opportunities for efficiency, they also provide a wealth of information to which one might not have access otherwise.

For more information, visit the Computer Concepts CourseMate Web site at www.cengagebrain.com, navigate to the Chapter 12 Computer Usage @ Work resource for this book, and then click Municipal Services.

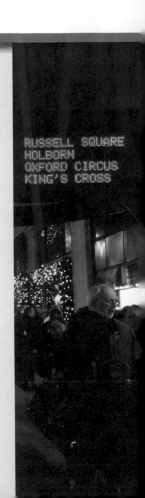

RUSSELL SQUARE
HOLBORN
OXFORD CIRCUS
KING'S CROSS

Companies on the Cutting Edge

EMC Information Management and Storage Provider

Data protection and storage are keys to running a successful business and preserving family memories. EMC specializes in producing innovative solutions for storing, safeguarding, and managing information so that it readily is available, searchable, and sharable.

EMC is the world leader in external storage and storage management systems. It is best known for its large-scale enterprise storage systems, and customers include financial services firms, health-care organizations,

transportation companies, educational institutions, and manufacturers. Its RAID systems, networked storage systems, and storage management software are ranked at the top of the industry revenue shares.

EMC's Proven Professional certification program, aimed at validating knowledge about various IT topics, recently granted more than 45,000 certifications. EMC also has received numerous top awards for its network storage, software, and environmental practices.

IBM World's Largest Information Technology Company

Data centers consume tremendous amounts of electricity, but IBM is working to reduce energy consumption in these centralized locations. Its energy-efficient Active Energy Manager (AEM) tracks electricity usage and allows businesses to set a cap on total energy use for storing, networking, serving, and cooling operations.

IBM's services, consulting, and infrastructure components have helped companies develop new business ventures. Its systems supply nearly one-half of the world's supercomputing processing power, and the company is

noted for its enterprise business focus in financial services, public, industrial, distribution, communications, and small- and medium-sized businesses.

The corporation was founded in 1911 when three companies merged to sell business-related gadgets, including a machine that used punched cards to catalog data. Nine years later, the company changed its name to International Business Machines (IBM). The company recently announced that more than 200 customers switched to IBM servers from Sun and HP servers.

For more information, visit the Computer Concepts CourseMate Web site at www.cengagebrain.com and then navigate to the Chapter 12 Companies on the Cutting Edge resource for this book.

Technology Trailblazers

CHAD HURLEY YouTube Cofounder and CEO

Twenty hours of video are uploaded every minute to YouTube, and much of this Web site's popularity is due to the efforts of Chad Hurley. He and two work colleagues at PayPal cofounded YouTube in 2005, and it grew quickly to become one of the larger Web sites. One year later they sold YouTube to Google for $1.65 billion.

Hurley says he is a user interface expert and that his interests in fine arts and business have been evident since childhood. In first grade he painted photos on plywood and attempted to sell them on his front lawn.

He graduated from Indiana University of Pennsylvania with a degree in fine art, and he used his design skills in one of his first jobs after graduation to create eBay's PayPal logo.

At eBay, he envisioned the concept of adding video to the online auctions. He abandoned that idea when sellers seemed disinterested and then turned his attention to developing the YouTube concept. His goal is to allow every person worldwide to upload video content to YouTube easily and view content on any device that has a screen.

ANITA BORG Champion for Women in Technology

Women from across the globe have been inspired and encouraged to pursue a career in technology with the help of Anita Borg. The Anita Borg Institute for Women and Technology and the Google Anita Borg Scholarship provide programs and resources to help women develop technological innovations.

Borg died in 2003, but her accomplishments throughout her career laid the foundation for advancing women in computer science today. In 1987, she went to a technology conference that had only a few women in

attendance, and shortly thereafter she formed Systers, an electronic mailing list for female engineers to exchange technology ideas. Today, the Systers list has grown to more than 3,000 members in 54 countries.

Borg's computer science research in college focused on operating systems principles, and she earned her Ph.D. degree from New York University in 1981. She then held top research positions at Nixdorf, Digital Equipment Corporation, and Xerox until her death.

For more information, visit the Computer Concepts CourseMate Web site at www.cengagebrain.com and then navigate to the Chapter 12 Technology Trailblazers resource for this book.

Chapter Review

The Chapter Review reinforces the main concepts presented in this chapter.

To listen to an audio version of this Chapter Review, visit the Computer Concepts CourseMate Web site at www.cengagebrain.com and then navigate to the Chapter 12 Chapter Review resource for this book.

1. **What Are the Special Information Requirements of an Enterprise-Sized Corporation?** A large organization, or enterprise, requires special computing solutions because of its size and geographical extent. **Enterprise computing** uses computers in networks or a series of interconnected networks to satisfy the information needs of an enterprise. The types of information employees require depend on their level in the company. **Managers** utilize tools and techniques such as **business intelligence (BI)**, **business process management (BPM)**, and **business process automation (BPA)** to focus on information that is important to the decision-making process.

2. **What Information Systems and Software Are Used in the Functional Units of an Enterprise?** An **information system** is a set of hardware, software, data, people, and procedures that work together to produce information. In an enterprise, each type of functional unit has specialized requirements for their information systems. Accounting and financial systems manage everyday transactions and help budget, forecast, and analyze. A **human resources information system (HRIS)** manages one or more human resources functions. An **employee relationship management (ERM)** system automates and manages much of the communications between employees and the business. Engineers use **computer-aided design (CAD)** and **computer-aided engineering (CAE)**. **Computer-aided manufacturing (CAM)** and **computer-integrated manufacturing (CIM)** speed manufacturing. **Material Requirements Planning (MRP)** is an information management approach that uses software to help monitor and control processes related to production. A quality control system helps an organization maintain or improve the quality of its products or services. A **marketing information system** serves as a central repository for marketing tasks. **Sales force automation (SFA)** software equips traveling salespeople with the tools they need. **Distribution systems** control inventory and manage shipping. **Customer interaction management (CIM)** software manages interactions with customers.

3. **What Information Systems Are Used throughout an Enterprise?** Some general purpose information systems, or enterprise-wide systems, are used throughout an enterprise. An **office information system (OIS)** enables employees to perform tasks using computers and other electronic devices, instead of manually. A **transaction processing system (TPS)** captures and processes data from day-to-day business activities. A **management information system (MIS)** generates accurate, timely, and organized information, so users can make decisions, solve problems, and track progress. A **decision support system (DSS)** helps users analyze data and make decisions. An **expert system** captures and stores the knowledge of human experts and then imitates human reasoning and decision making. **Enterprise resource planning (ERP)** provides applications to help manage and coordinate ongoing activities. **Customer relationship management (CRM)** systems manage information about customers. A **content management system (CMS)** organizes and allows access to various forms of documents and files.

Visit the Computer Concepts CourseMate Web site at www.cengagebrain.com, navigate to the Chapter 12 Quiz Yourself resource for this book, and then click Objectives 1 – 3.

4. **What Are Types of Technologies Used throughout an Enterprise?** Technologies used throughout an enterprise include portals, communications, data warehouses, extranets, Web services, service-oriented architectures, workflow, and virtual private networks. A **portal** is a collection of links, content, and services on a Web page designed to guide users to information related to their jobs. An enterprise's communications infrastructures consists of hardware (such as wired and wireless connections and devices, routers, firewalls, and servers), software (such as e-mail, instant messaging, VoIP, and server management), and procedures for using and managing hardware and software. A **data warehouse** stores and manages the data required to analyze transactions. An **extranet** allows customers or suppliers to access part of an enterprise's intranet. **Web services** allow businesses to create products and B2B interactions. Many enterprises employ a service-oriented architecture, which helps increase communications between diverse information systems. A **workflow application** assists in the management and tracking of the activities in a business process. A **virtual private network (VPN)** provides users with a secure connection to a company's network server.

5. **What Are Virtualization, Cloud Computing, and Grid Computing?** Virtualization is the practice of sharing or pooling computing resources, such as servers and storage devices. Server virtualization provides the capability to divide a physical server logically into many virtual servers; storage virtualization provides the capability to create a single logical storage device from many physical storage devices. **Cloud computing** is an Internet service that provides computing needs to computer users. **Grid computing**, which often is used in research environments, combines many servers and/or personal

computers on a network to act as one large computer. Both cloud and grid computing usually require a company to pay a fee based on usage or processing time.

Visit the Computer Concepts CourseMate Web site at www.cengagebrain.com, navigate to the Chapter 12 Quiz Yourself resource for this book, and then click Objectives 4 – 5.

6. **What Are the Computer Hardware Needs and Solutions for an Enterprise?**   **Enterprise hardware** allows large organizations to manage and share information and data using devices geared for maximum availability and efficiency. A **RAID (redundant array of independent disks)** is a group of integrated disks that duplicates data, instructions, and information to improve data reliability. **Network attached storage** (**NAS**) is a server that provides storage for users and information systems. A **storage area network** (**SAN**) provides storage to other servers. An **enterprise storage system** consolidates storage so that operations run efficiently. **Blade servers** pack a complete computer server on a single card, or blade, rather than a system unit.

7. **Why Is Computer Backup Important, and How Is It Accomplished?**   A backup duplicates a file or program to protect an enterprise if the original is lost or damaged. A full backup copies all of the files in a computer. A differential backup copies only files that have changed since the last full backup. An incremental backup copies only files that have changed since the last full or incremental backup. A selective backup, sometimes called a partial backup, allows users to back up specific files. With continuous data protection (CDP), all data is backed up whenever a change is made.

8. **What Are the Steps in a Disaster Recovery Plan?**   A **disaster recovery plan** describes the steps a company would take to restore computer operations in the event of a disaster. A disaster recovery plan contains four components. The emergency plan specifies the steps to be taken immediately after a disaster strikes. The backup plan specifies how a company uses backup files and equipment to resume information processing. The recovery plan identifies the actions to be taken to restore full information processing operations. The test plan contains information for simulating disasters and recording an organization's ability to recover.

Visit the Computer Concepts CourseMate Web site at www.cengagebrain.com, navigate to the Chapter 12 Quiz Yourself resource for this book, and then click Objectives 6 – 8.

Key Terms

You should know the Key Terms. The list below helps focus your study.

To see an example of and a definition for each term, and access current and additional information from the Web, visit the Computer Concepts CourseMate Web site at www.cengagebrain.com and then navigate to the Chapter 12 Key Terms resource for this book.

artificial intelligence (AI) (476)
blade server (489)
business intelligence (BI) (468)
business process automation (BPA) (468)
business process management (BPM) (468)
chief information officer (CIO) (473)
cloud computing (483)
computer-aided design (CAD) (471)
computer-aided engineering (CAE) (471)
computer-aided manufacturing (CAM) (471)
computer-integrated manufacturing (CIM) (471)

content management system (CMS) (478)
customer interaction management (CIM) (472)
customer relationship management (CRM) (478)
data center (479)
data warehouse (480)
decision support system (DSS) (475)
disaster recovery plan (491)
distribution systems (472)
EDI (electronic data interchange) (480)
enterprise computing (464)
enterprise hardware (485)
enterprise information (468)
enterprise resource planning (ERP) (477)
enterprise search (479)
enterprise storage system (487)

e-retail (484)
expert system (476)
extranet (481)
failover (491)
Fibre Channel (488)
grid computing (484)
high-availability system (489)
human resources information system (HRIS) (470)
information system (468)
interoperability (490)
legacy system (485)
management information system (MIS) (474)
managers (468)
marketing information system (472)
Material Requirements Planning (MRP) (471)
network attached storage (NAS) (486)

office information system (OIS) (473)
online banking (484)
online trading (484)
portal (479)
RAID (redundant array of independent disks) (486)
redundant components (490)
sales force automation (SFA) (472)
scalability (490)
small- and medium-sized business (SMB) (465)
storage area network (SAN) (486)
transaction processing system (TPS) (473)
virtual private network (VPN) (482)
Web services (481)
workflow (482)
workflow application (482)

Checkpoint

The Checkpoint exercises test your knowledge of the chapter concepts. The page number containing the answer appears in parentheses after each exercise.

To complete the Checkpoint exercises interactively, visit the Computer Concepts CourseMate Web site at www.cengagebrain.com and then navigate to the Chapter 12 Checkpoint resource for this book.

Multiple Choice Select the best answer.

1. _____ are smaller in size than enterprises and typically do not have an international presence. (465)
   a. Data centers
   b. Portals
   c. SMBs
   d. Web services

2. _____ includes several types of applications and technologies for acquiring, storing, analyzing, and providing access to information to help users make more sound business decisions. (468)
   a. Business process management
   b. Business intelligence
   c. Business process automation
   d. None of the above

3. Many companies elevate the importance of information technology by including a _____ executive position that reports to the CEO. (473)
   a. chief operations officer (COO)
   b. chief information officer (CIO)
   c. chief security officer (CSO)
   d. chief financial officer (CFO)

4. An advantage of ERP is _____. (478)
   a. complete integration of information systems across departments
   b. better project management
   c. better customer service
   d. all of the above

5. A(n) _____ is an information system that has existed within the organization for an extended length of time and is relied upon heavily. (485)
   a. expert system
   b. high-availability system
   c. office information system
   d. legacy system

6. The _____ of hardware to users is a measure of how often it is online. (489)
   a. redundancy
   b. availability
   c. scalability
   d. interoperability

7. _____ continue running and performing tasks for at least 99 percent of the time. (489)
   a. Distribution systems
   b. High-availability systems
   c. Blade servers
   d. Virtual private networks

8. A(n) _____ can be time-consuming but provides the best protection against data loss. (490)
   a. full backup
   b. incremental backup
   c. differential backup
   d. selective backup

Matching Match the terms with their definitions.

_____ 1. computer-aided engineering (471)

_____ 2. decision support system (DSS) (475)

_____ 3. EDI (electronic data interchange) (480)

_____ 4. extranet (481)

_____ 5. RAID (486)

a. portion of a company's network that allows customers or suppliers of a company to access parts of an enterprise's intranet

b. helps users analyze data and make decisions

c. a group of two or more integrated hard disks

d. allows a business to create products and B2B interactions

e. uses computers to test product designs

f. set of standards that controls the transfer of business data and information among computers both within and among enterprises

Short Answer Write a brief answer to each of the following questions.

1. What are managers? _____ What four activities do managers perform to coordinate resources? _____

2. What is a content management system (CMS)? _____ What type of content may be processed by a content management system? _____

3. Describe two types of virtualization. _____ What are cloud and grid computing, and why do companies use them? _____

4. What are five types of e-commerce? _____ Describe three of the five types that you listed. _____

5. What does a backup plan identify? _____ What factors contribute to the success of a backup plan? _____

Problem Solving

The Problem Solving exercises extend your knowledge of the chapter concepts by seeking solutions to practical computer problems that you may encounter at home, school, or work. The Collaboration exercise should be completed with a team.

In the real world, practical problems often can be solved in multiple ways. Provide one solution to each of the following problems using available resources, such as articles on the Web or in print, blogs, podcasts, videos, television, user guides, other individuals, and electronics and computer stores. You may need to use multiple resources to obtain an answer. Present your solutions in the form requested by your instructor (brief report, presentation, discussion, or other means).

@ Home

1. **Invalid Password**   After typing your user name and password to log onto your school's portal, an error message displays stating that the password is incorrect. What are your next steps?

2. **Suspicious Account Transactions**   After successfully signing up for PayPal's online payment service, you verify the balance in your checking account and notice that two suspicious transactions were conducted, each crediting your account a few pennies. Unsure of whether you now are vulnerable to identity theft, how will you proceed?

3. **Invalid Credit Card Information**   Near the conclusion of an e-commerce transaction, you enter your credit card information, and the Web site reports that your credit card information is invalid. After double-checking your credit card number, expiration date, and security code, it appears that you have entered everything properly. What are your next steps?

4. **Late Fees Assessed**   Your bank recently set up an online bill payment service. You begin paying your bills online and set up each bill's payment information. One credit card company has been applying late fees to your account, although you configured the online bill payment service to pay the balances on time. What might be causing this?

@ Work

5. **Unable to Update**   Your company hosts a portal that enables you to perform tasks such as checking the information stored by the human resources department and viewing electronic paychecks. Having recently married, you access the portal to change your marital status, but the option buttons allowing you to select marital status are disabled. What might be wrong?

6. **Compromised Credit Card**   An e-mail message arrives in your e-mail account stating that a Web site with which you perform a significant amount of business has been compromised. You regularly use a corporate credit card to purchase supplies from this Web site, and you are concerned that someone might have obtained your credit card information. What are your next steps?

7. **Incorrect Pay Rate**   Recently, you received a promotion that included a pay raise. You log into your company portal and verify that your rate of pay has increased. After receiving your next paycheck, however, you realize that you were paid at the previous rate of pay. Why might you not be receiving the new rate of pay?

8. **Missing CRM Entry**   As a customer service representative for a well-known computer manufacturer, you receive a telephone call from an irritated customer who states that he has called five times about the same problem. In an effort to resolve his problem, you search for his call history using your company's CRM program. Much to your surprise, you are unable to locate any information about this customer's previous telephone calls. What might be wrong?

Collaboration

9. **Computers in Municipal Services**   Municipalities are incorporating technology into most, if not all, of their services. As a student in a computer technology class, your instructor provides you with a document that lists various municipal services available in the area. Your instructor requests that teams of three people determine how computers have enhanced various services. One team member should research how computers have enhanced cable television services. Another team member should research how power and water companies benefit from computer technology, and the third team member should identify ways that municipalities can save money by using computer technology.

STUDENT ASSIGNMENTS

Learn How To

The Learn How To activities step you through fundamental technology skills when using a computer. The Learn How To exercises enable you to become more proficient with these skills.

> Premium Activity: To relate this Learn How To activity to your everyday life, see a visual demonstration of the activity, and complete a short assessment, visit the Computer Concepts CourseMate Web site at www.cengagebrain.com and then navigate to the Chapter 12 Learn How To resource for this book.

Learn How To 1: Use VoIP (Voice over Internet Protocol)

Every enterprise and organization depends on reliable communications. An important means of communication is voice, or telephone, communications. In most organizations today, a telephone company is the primary vendor for providing telephone communications. In the near future, however, the Internet might be the largest provider of telephone communications.

You learned in a previous chapter about VoIP, which provides for voice communications using the Internet instead of standard telephone connections. Two advantages claimed for VoIP are improved reliability and much lower costs. Both of these advantages are attractive to businesses, and VoIP is forecasted to become the standard voice communications method within the next 5 – 10 years.

VoIP also is available to individual users. One primary means to use VoIP is through the service offered by Skype, a company that offers free, unlimited calls through an Internet connection. The Skype software also is free. Using Skype, you can talk to another Skype user via the Internet anywhere in the world for no cost whatsoever. If the person you call is not a Skype user, you can use Skype to call their ordinary landline or mobile telephone quite inexpensively. For example, to call someone on a landline telephone in the United Kingdom from anywhere in the world, the cost is approximately 2 cents per minute.

To download Skype, complete the following steps:
1. Start your Internet browser, type skype.com in the Address bar and then press the ENTER key.
2. When the Skype home page is displayed, explore the Web site for information about using Skype. When you are ready, click the Get Skype now button.
3. When the File Download - Security Warning dialog box is displayed, click the Save button.
4. In the Save As dialog box, select the Desktop for the location of the saved file. Then, click the Save button. The Skype Setup file will download. This may take a few minutes, depending on the speed of your Internet connection, because of the large file size.
5. If the Download complete window opens click the Close button. The SkypeSetup icon is displayed on the desktop.
6. Double-click the SkypeSetup icon on the desktop. If the User Account Control dialog box appears, click the Yes button.
7. In the Skype - Install window, select the language you would like to use, and then click the 'I agree - install' button.
8. If you do not wish to install the Google Toolbar, remove the check mark from the appropriate check box. Click the Continue installing Skype button.
9. When the installation is completed, click the Finish button.

Skype now is installed on your computer. The Skype icon should appear on your desktop. To start and use Skype, complete the following steps:
1. Drag the SkypeSetup icon on the desktop to the Recycle Bin.
2. Double-click the Skype icon on your desktop. The first time you start Skype, the Skype - Create account dialog box is displayed (Figure 12-26). In this dialog box, you enter your full name, Skype name, and password. The Skype name is the name you will use to start Skype each time, together with the password. You can use any name and password that has not already been used on Skype. Also, be sure to check the Skype End User License Agreement check box, and then click the Next button to display the next dialog box requesting your E-mail address, Country/Region, and City.
3. Enter your E-mail address, Country/Region, and City, and then click the Sign in button.

Figure 12-26

4. If your Skype name and password have not been used, Skype automatically will sign into your account and open the Skype window (Figure 12-27). If your Skype name or password already have been used by another user, you must select another Skype name or password.

5. After installing Skype, you can make calls to other Skype users anywhere in the world for no cost.

6. To learn the techniques for calling another Skype user, click Help on the menu bar in the Skype window, click Get Help: Answers and Support on the Help menu, and then select the subject about which you want to learn.

Figure 12-27

Exercise

1. Visit the Skype Web site. Examine the various screens and examples shown on the Web site. Do you think this type of service can be useful to you? Why? What are the advantages and disadvantages of using Skype? If you were calling a friend in Australia on a regular telephone, how much per minute would you have to pay? Submit your answers to your instructor.

Learn It Online

The Learn It Online exercises are interactive Web exercises designed to reinforce and expand your understanding of the chapter concepts. The descriptions below briefly summarize each exercise.

To complete the Learn It Online exercises, visit the Computer Concepts CourseMate Web site at www.cengagebrain.com, navigate to the Chapter 12 resources for this book, click the link for the exercise you want to complete, and then read the instructions.

1 At the Movies — **A Tour of Lucasfilm Data Center**

Watch a movie to take a tour of the Lucasfilm Data Center, the high-tech center of IT operations for a movie production company, and then answer questions about the movie.

2 Student Edition Labs — **Project Management and Web Design Principles**

Enhance your understanding and knowledge about project management and Web design principles by completing the Project Management and Web Design Principles Labs.

3 Practice Test

Take a multiple choice test that checks your knowledge of the chapter concepts and review the resulting study guide.

4 Who Wants To Be a Computer Genius[2]?

Play the Shelly Cashman Series version of this popular game by answering questions to find out if you are a computer genius. Panic buttons are available to provide assistance during game play.

5 Crossword Puzzle Challenge

Complete an interactive crossword puzzle to reinforce concepts presented in this chapter.

6 Windows Exercises

Step through the Windows 7 exercises to learn about changing views in Windows 7, using Windows Update, creating a desktop shortcut to the printer, and determining the brand and model of sound cards or audio devices in your computer.

7 Exploring Computer Careers

Read about a career as a CIO, search for related employment advertisements, and then answer related questions.

8 Web Apps — **Microsoft Office Web Apps**

Learn how to create, edit, and share documents, workbooks, presentations, and notes using Microsoft Office Web Apps.

Web Research

The Web Research exercises broaden your understanding of chapter concepts by presenting questions that require you to search the Web for answers.

1 Search Sleuth

Use one of the search engines listed in Figure 2-8 in Chapter 2 on page 65 or your own favorite search engine to find the answers to the following questions. Copy and paste the Web address from the Web page where you found the answer. Some questions may have more than one answer. If required, submit your answers to your instructor. (1) What was the location of the latest International Supercomputing Conference? Who gave the opening keynote address, and what was the topic of this speech? (2) Where is the TSUBAME supercomputer installed? Why is it called "everybody's supercomputer"? (3) What are the primary purposes of the Virtual Private Network Consortium? (4) Which organization sponsors the Envirofacts data warehouse? (5) How many RAID levels exist?

2 Green Computing

The carbon footprint of computers running the Internet is expected to exceed that of air travel by 2020. The world's data centers emit more gas than do people living in Argentina and the Netherlands, which have a combined population of 57.2 million. As you learned in Innovative Computing 12-1 on page 479, companies are developing unique data center solutions to cope with the massive electricity demands. View online Web sites that provide information about green data centers. Which countries can profit from IBM's Liebert SiteScan? How can companies benefit by adopting the Corporate Average Data Efficiency (CADE) metric? Which countries have the world's lowest and the highest electricity rates? How are companies adopting solar power? Write a report summarizing your findings, and include a table of links to Web sites that provide additional details.

3 Social Networking

People who are at least 45 years old comprise approximately 34 percent of Internet users and quickly are becoming the largest demographic age group online. These "silver surfers" are online more than six hours per week and are making their presence known on online social networks. Monster's founder Jeff Taylor created Eons (eons.com), which is promoted as an "online gathering place for people lovin' life on the flip side of 50!" BoomerGirl Diary (boomergirl.com) and Not Over The Hill (notoverthehill.com) feature entertainment, health, financial, and travel information. Visit these Web sites and other online social networks aimed exclusively at a mature audience. Compare the content. Which groups and forums are present? What are the members' interests? Which topics are targeted toward this age group? Summarize the information you read and viewed.

4 Blogs

The brain's 100 billion cells work best when both halves of the brain work together. The left half, often called the judicial mind, controls logical and reasoning tasks, and the right half, referred to as the creative mind, interprets and gives meaning to stimuli. Building right-brain skills is the key to achieving professional and personal success. Many blogs contain exercises and research on developing the right brain. They include The Thinking Blog (www.thethinkingblog.com), Creative Generalist (creativegeneralist.blogspot.com), Creative Think (blog.creativethink.com), and InnovationTools (innovationtools.com). Which creativity tools and strategies are suggested on these blogs? How are enterprises incorporating creative thinking? Which mind mapping and brainstorming resources are listed? Which creativity software and books are promoted? Summarize the information you read and viewed.

5 Ethics in Action

Using grid computing, researchers at the University of Chicago, Northern Illinois University, Argonne National Laboratory, and the Max Planck Institute for Gravitational Physics in Germany simulated how black hole collisions affect gravity. Personal computers also can join millions of other computers throughout the world when they are connected to the Internet and have idle processing time. While grid computing turns inactive computer time into computational power, some critics believe some grid projects are immoral, may compromise intellectual property, and may undertake work that for-profit companies should perform. Visit Grid.org, the Open Grid Forum (ogf.org), the Globus Alliance (globus.org), and other Web sites to learn about current grid computing projects. Should for-profit companies pay grid participants for their computer time? Is data security compromised? Who sets standardization guidelines? How will companies track network resources? Write a report summarizing your findings, and include a table of links to Web sites that provide additional details.

Living Digitally

OUR DIGITAL LIVES are filled with a variety of products. We listen on portable media players to audio files we create or download. We record and view video content that matches our viewing interests. We play recorded files wherever and whenever we desire. We play games solo or with multiple friends across the globe. Our home networks link security, energy monitoring, and leisure activities throughout the house. Wherever we go in our lives, technology is a pervasive part of our daily existence.

igital products
our lives often
clude features that
verlap in various
ntertainment and
ome automation
tegories.

- Audio
- Video
- Recording
- Gaming
- Digital Home

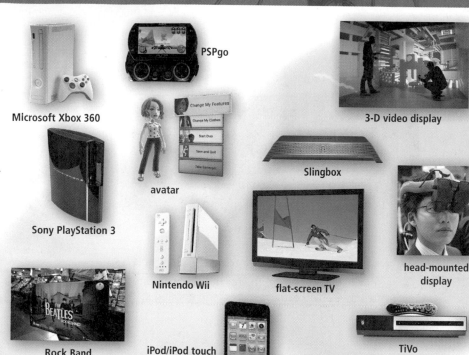

Microsoft Xbox 360

PSPgo

3-D video display

avatar

Slingbox

Sony PlayStation 3

Nintendo Wii

flat-screen TV

head-mounted display

Rock Band

iPod/iPod touch

TiVo

Nintendo DSi

video camera

speakers

chumby

smart phone

Studio Instruments software

Dolby logo

digital frames

Netflix

Nero optical disc burning software

combination drive

home automation dashboard

multi-room audio system

docking station

Audio

THE MUSIC INDUSTRY is a major part of our everyday lives, and digital music sales generate more than $10 billion each year. Audio files can be played on iPods and other portable media players and mobile devices. Musicians of all skill levels can create their own music with Rock Band and Guitar Hero handheld instruments.

Figure 1 Apple has sold hundreds of millions of iPods. The iPod accessory market has grown to a billion-dollar industry, with inventors developing earbuds, cases, and docking stations.

Figure 3 Rock the night away playing set lists from some of the biggest artists and bands of all times. Customize the concert experience by selecting venues and original band members or your own personalized superstars.

Figure 2 Music downloading services allow you to purchase individual tracks or entire albums and then download the music to a computer or portable media player. More than 500 downloading services are available; Apple iTunes and Amazon MP3 are the sales leaders.

Figure 4 Ray Dolby founded Dolby Laboratories in 1965. His company has become the world leader in defining high-quality products, including audio and surround sound in theaters, home entertainment systems, and broadcasting.

Video

WHETHER IN A COMFY CHAIR or on the go, watching television and movies has changed dramatically. Viewers download content and then watch the programs when and where they desire on devices ranging from large flat-screen display devices to compact smart phones. Glasses and 3-D displays add a new dimension to the viewing experience.

Figure 5 A multitude of video streaming devices is infiltrating the marketplace as companies expand their services to add subscribers and bring movies and television programs to homes via a broadband Internet connection. Apple TV takes control of your home theater system by streaming HD movies, television programs, iTunes music, podcasts, and photos to display devices.

Figure 6 Experience a private video viewing with a personal head-mounted display (HMD). Video glasses can be connected to a DVD player, iPod, or game console.

Figure 8 True 3-D video images can be seen on cell phones and video displays without special glasses or goggles. Applications include medical imaging, CAD drawings, mapping, and entertainment.

Figure 7 View your favorite television programs anywhere in the world as long as you have a broadband connection and a Slingbox. This device streams video and audio from your home to any Internet-connected device.

Figure 9 High-definition (HD) digital video recorders (DVRs), such as the TiVo, let you locate and record current and off-air digital broadcasts, pause and rewind live television programs, and create your own instant replays with slow motion.

SPECIAL FEATURE

Recording

WHETHER YOU ARE WORKING OUT at the gym or driving to Grandma's house for dinner, you might want to download or record your favorite audio, video, and photos to transport them from one location to another or upload them to share with friends and family. You also can record movies or television programs when you are not at home and then play them at your convenience on a home entertainment system or portable media player.

Figure 10
Use optical disc burning software to create optical discs quickly and easily with multiformat burners and rewritable drives to store your movies, photos, music, and digital data.

Figure 12 Turn your computer into a virtual bass guitar, drum set, electric piano, or string section with Cakewalk's Studio Instruments software. Then, record, edit, and mix your songs created with these virtual and real instruments and create streaming music players and playlists on your Web site.

Figure 11
Capture video using your video camera and then, with the press of a button, upload recorded clips to social networking Web sites. Each minute, more than 20 hours of video are uploaded to YouTube.

Figure 13 Capture video of friends and family, upload the clips to your computer, and use video editing software to rearrange the sequence of events, add music and titles, and record narration.

Gaming

REVENUE GENERATED BY THE VIDEO GAMING INDUSTRY quickly is approaching $100 billion. The areas experiencing the fastest growth are online and mobile gaming as new game consoles and advanced networking become mainstream.

Figure 14 The three gaming consoles — Nintendo Wii, Sony PlayStation 3, and Microsoft Xbox 360 — offer a variety of game titles.

Figure 16 In a computer role-playing game (CRPG), players interact with one another and generally attempt to accomplish a quest. Massively multiplayer online games (MMOGs) unite millions of gamers worldwide.

Figure 15 Gaming reaches all generations. The Wii game console's interactive quality appeals to players of all ages. The iPod touch's accelerometer, which detects movement and changes the display accordingly, and 3-D graphics immerse players in the action.

Figure 17 Handheld game consoles have large, high-resolution screens and incredible sound to play audio and video files and can display photos. Bluetooth and Wi-Fi technology allows networked gaming and synchronizing with other handheld units or personal computers.

Figure 18 Outdoor treasure hunters use their GPS receivers and navigational skills to create and locate hidden caches throughout the world.

Digital Home

THE AVERAGE HOUSEHOLD has 21 consumer electronics devices, and many of them are linked via home networks and broadband connections that simplify our lives and provide entertainment in innovative ways. Digital music and video are recorded and streamed to multiple devices. Meanwhile, automation systems monitor security, energy usage, and room temperatures to provide optimal conditions.

Figure 19 Set-top boxes stream movies from the Web to your televisions, computers, and mobile devices. On average, Netflix ships approximately two million DVDs each day.

Figure 21 LED screens provide information about home electricity, gas, and water use, and they compare the rates with previous consumption.

Figure 22 Digital picture frames, some as large as 40 inches wide, are among the more popular consumer electronic devices; more than 3 million are sold each year. They provide a convenient method of displaying the billions of digital photos taken each day and may play songs and Web broadcasts.

Figure 20 Program an entire home to fit your lifestyle and needs. A home automation system can set room temperatures, open and close window shades, water the grass, watch for intruders, and play music to wake you or relax you to sleep.

Figure 23 The wireless chumby connects to the Internet and streams news, entertainment, sports scores, video clips, interactive games, photos, and hundreds of favorite widgets.

Computer technology impacts virtually every facet of our lives. From the largest media rooms to the smallest portable media players, we can watch our favorite television programs and movies any place at any time. We can browse the Web, play games with partners on the other side of the world, listen to music we created with handheld instruments, and have fun wherever life takes us. No matter where we are, our digital lives are filled with information and entertainment.

Quiz Yourself Answers

Following are possible answers to the Quiz Yourself boxes throughout the book.

Quiz Yourself 1-1

1. A computer is ~~a motorized~~an electronic device that processes ~~output~~input into ~~input~~output.
2. A storage device records (~~reads~~writes) and/or retrieves (~~writes~~reads) items to and from storage media.
3. An ~~output~~input device is any hardware component that allows you to enter data and instructions in a computer.
4. True Statement
5. Three commonly used ~~input~~output devices are a printer, a monitor, and speakers.

Quiz Yourself 1-2

1. A ~~resource~~network is a collection of computers and devices connected together via communications devices and transmission media.
2. True Statement
3. Popular ~~system~~application software includes Web browsers, word processing software, spreadsheet software, database software, and presentation software.
4. The ~~Internet~~Web is one of the more popular services on the ~~Web~~Internet.
5. Two types of ~~application~~system software are the operating system and utility programs.

Quiz Yourself 1-3

1. A ~~desktop computer~~notebook computer (or laptop computer) is a portable, personal computer designed to fit on your lap.
2. True Statement
3. Each ~~enterprise~~home user spends time on the computer for different reasons that include personal financial management, Web access, communications, and entertainment.
4. A ~~home~~power user requires the capabilities of a workstation or other powerful computer.
5. ~~Mainframes~~Supercomputers are the fastest, most powerful computers — and the most expensive.
6. With ~~embedded computers~~online banking, users access account balances, pay bills, and copy monthly transactions from the bank's computer right into their personal computers.

Quiz Yourself 2-1

1. True Statement
2. ~~A wireless Internet service provider~~An IP address (or Internet Protocol address) is a number that uniquely identifies each computer or device connected to the Internet.
3. ~~An IP address~~A domain name, such as www.google.com, is the text version of ~~a domain name~~an IP address.
4. ~~Satellite~~Cable Internet service provides high-speed Internet access through the cable television network via a cable modem.

Quiz Yourself 2-2

1. True Statement
2. A ~~Web browser~~subject directory classifies Web pages in an organized set of categories and related subcategories.
3. ~~Business~~Consumer-to-consumer e-commerce occurs when one consumer sells directly to another, such as in an online auction.
4. The more widely used ~~search engines~~Web browsers for personal computers are Internet Explorer, Firefox, Opera, Safari, and Google Chrome.
5. To develop a Web page, you do not have to be a computer programmer.

Quiz Yourself 2-3

1. True Statement
2. An e-mail address is a combination of a user name and ~~an e-mail program~~a domain name that identifies a user so that he or she can receive Internet e-mail.
3. ~~FTP~~Internet telephony uses the Internet (instead of the public switched telephone network) to connect a calling party to one or more called parties.
4. Netiquette is the code of ~~un~~acceptable behaviors while on the Internet.
5. VoIP enables users to ~~subscribe~~speak to other users over the Internet.

Quiz Yourself 3-1

1. True Statement
2. ~~Public-domain~~Packaged software is mass produced, copyrighted retail software that meets the needs of a wide variety of users, not just a single user or company.
3. To use ~~system~~application software, your computer must be running ~~application~~system software.
4. When a program is started, its instructions load from ~~memory~~a storage medium into ~~a storage medium~~memory.

Quiz Yourself 3-2

1. ~~Enterprise computing~~Image editing software provides the capabilities of paint software and also includes the ability to modify existing images.
2. Millions of people use ~~spreadsheet~~word processing software every day to develop documents such as letters, memos, reports, mailing labels, newsletters, and Web pages.
3. Professional ~~accounting~~DTP (or desktop publishing) software is ideal for the production of high-quality color documents such as textbooks, corporate newsletters, marketing literature, product catalogs, and annual reports.
4. ~~Database~~Presentation software is application software that allows users to create visual aids for presentations to communicate ideas, messages, and other information to a group.
5. Popular ~~CAD programs~~software suites include Microsoft Office, Apple iWork, Corel WordPerfect Office, and Google Docs.
6. True Statement

Quiz Yourself 3-3

1. ~~All~~Some Web application hosts provide free access to their software.
2. ~~Computer~~Web-based training is a type of ~~Web~~computer-based training that uses Internet technology and consists of application software on the Web.
3. True Statement
4. ~~Legal~~Personal finance software is a simplified accounting program that helps home users and small office/home office users balance their checkbooks, pay bills, track investments, and evaluate financial plans.
5. ~~Personal DTP~~Photo editing software is a popular type of image editing software that allows users to edit digital photos.

Quiz Yourself 4-1

1. True Statement
2. Four basic operations in a machine cycle are: (1) ~~comparing~~fetching, (2) decoding, (3) executing, and, if necessary, (4) ~~pipelining~~storing.
3. Processors contain a ~~motherboard~~control unit and an arithmetic logic unit (ALU).
4. The ~~central processing unit~~motherboard, sometimes called a system board, is the main circuit board of the system unit.
5. The leading processor chip manufacturers for personal computers are ~~Microsoft~~Intel and AMD.

6. The system unit is a case that contains ~~mechanical~~electronic components of the computer used to process data.

Quiz Yourself 4-2

1. True Statement
2. A gigabyte (GB) equals approximately 1 ~~trillion~~billion bytes.
3. Memory cache helps speed the processes of the computer because it stores ~~seldom~~frequently used instructions and data.
4. Most computers are ~~analog~~digital, which means they recognize only two discrete states: on and off.
5. Most RAM ~~retains~~loses its contents when the power is removed from the computer.
6. Read-only memory (ROM) refers to memory chips storing ~~temporary~~permanent data and instructions.

Quiz Yourself 4-3

1. A ~~bus~~port is the point at which a peripheral attaches to or communicates with a system unit so that the peripheral can send data to or receive information from the computer.
2. An ~~AC adapter~~expansion slot is a socket on the motherboard that can hold an adapter card.
3. ~~eSATA~~USB ports can connect up to 127 different peripherals together with a single connector type.
4. The higher the bus clock speed, the ~~slower~~faster the transmission of data.
5. True Statement

Quiz Yourself 5-1

1. A keyboard is an ~~output~~input device that contains keys users press to enter data into a computer.
2. A ~~trackball~~touchpad is a small, flat, rectangular pointing device commonly found on notebook computers, including netbooks and many Tablet PCs.
3. True Statement
4. An optical mouse has <u>no</u> moving mechanical parts inside.
5. A ~~stylus~~graphics tablet is a flat, rectangular, electronic plastic board.

Quiz Yourself 5-2

1. True Statement
2. A fingerprint reader captures curves and indentations of a ~~signature~~fingerprint.
3. After swiping a credit card through ~~an MICR~~a magnetic stripe card reader, it reads the information stored on the magnetic stripe on the card.
4. Video games and computer games use a ~~Web cam~~game controller as the input device that directs movements and actions of on-screen objects.
5. Many smart phones today have ~~POS~~PDA capabilities.
6. RFID is a technology that uses ~~laser~~radio signals to communicate with a tag placed in an object, an animal, or a person.

Quiz Yourself 5-3

1. A ~~lower~~higher resolution uses a greater number of pixels and thus provides a smoother image.
2. An output device is any type of ~~software~~hardware component that conveys information to one or more people.
3. Types of ~~pixels~~display devices include LCD monitors, LCD screens, plasma monitors, and CRT monitors.
4. True Statement

Quiz Yourself 5-4

1. A ~~laser~~thermal printer generates images by pushing electrically heated pins against heat-sensitive paper.
2. A ~~photo~~laser printer creates images using a laser beam and powdered ink, called toner.
3. An ink-jet printer is a type of nonimpact printer that forms characters and graphics by spraying tiny drops of liquid ~~nitrogen~~ink onto a piece of paper.
4. Many personal computer users add surround sound ~~printer systems~~speakers to their computers to generate a higher-quality sound.
5. Multifunction peripherals require ~~more~~less space than having a separate printer, scanner, copy machine, and fax machine.
6. True Statement

Quiz Yourself 6-1

1. True Statement
2. SATA is a hard disk interface that uses ~~parallel~~serial signals to transfer data, instructions, and information.
3. ~~Storage media~~A storage device is the computer hardware that records and/or retrieves items to and from a storage ~~device~~media.
4. Users can move an ~~internal~~external hard disk from computer to computer as needed by connecting the disk to a USB port or FireWire port on the system unit.

Quiz Yourself 6-2

1. A USB flash drive is a flash memory storage device that plugs in a ~~parallel~~USB port on a computer or mobile device.
2. True Statement
3. ~~Cloud storage~~A solid state drive (SSD) is a storage device that typically uses flash memory to store data, instructions, and information.
4. An ExpressCard module is a removable ~~RAID~~ device that fits in an ExpressCard slot.

Quiz Yourself 6-3

1. A ~~CD-RW~~CD-ROM is a type of optical disc on which users can read but not write (record) or erase.
2. A ~~DVD-RAM~~Picture CD is a single-session disc that stores digital versions of film using a jpg file format.
3. DVDs have ~~the same~~much greater storage capacities ~~as~~than CDs.
4. Optical discs are written and read by ~~mirrors~~laser light.
5. True Statement

Quiz Yourself 7-1

1. A ~~buffer~~driver is a small program that tells the operating system how to communicate with a specific device.
2. True Statement
3. A password is a ~~public~~private combination of characters associated with the user name that allows access to certain computer resources.
4. The program you currently are using is in the ~~background~~foreground, and the other programs running but not in use are in the ~~foreground~~background.
5. Two types of system software are operating systems and ~~application~~utility programs.

Quiz Yourself 7-2

1. ~~BlackBerry~~Palm OS devices use Palm OS as their operating system.
2. Examples of ~~embedded~~server operating systems include Windows Server 2008, UNIX, Linux, Solaris, and NetWare.
3. Windows 7 Starter uses Windows ~~Aero~~Vista Basic.

4. True Statement
5. ~~Aero Flip 3D~~Linux is a UNIX-type operating system that is open source software.

Quiz Yourself 7-3

1. A ~~pop-up blocker~~file compression utility shrinks the size of a file(s).
2. An ~~anti-spam~~antivirus program protects a computer against viruses.
3. True Statement
4. You should ~~uninstall~~back up files and disks regularly in the event your originals are lost, damaged, or destroyed.
5. ~~Web filtering~~CD/DVD burning software writes text, graphics, audio, and video files to a recordable or rewritable disc.

Quiz Yourself 8-1

1. A ~~cybercafé~~hot spot is a wireless network that provides Internet connections to mobile computers and devices.
2. True Statement
3. ~~Receiving~~Sending devices initiate an instruction to transmit data, instructions, or information.
4. Users can send pictures and sound files, as well as short text messages, with ~~text~~picture messaging.

Quiz Yourself 8-2

1. A wireless LAN is a LAN that uses no physical wires.
2. An intranet is an internal network that uses ~~video conferencing~~Internet technologies.
3. Five types of digital ~~dial-up~~dedicated lines are ISDN lines, DSL, FTTP, T-carrier lines, and ATM.
4. In a client/server network, ~~servers~~clients on the network access resources on the ~~client~~server.
5. True Statement

Quiz Yourself 8-3

1. A ~~cable~~dial-up modem converts a computer's digital signals to analog signals before they are transmitted over standard telephone lines.
2. True Statement
3. ~~Analog~~Digital signals consist of individual electrical pulses that represent bits grouped together into bytes.
4. ~~Physical~~Wireless transmission media send communications signals through the air or space using radio, microwave, and infrared signals.
5. Most wireless home networks use ~~powerline cables~~Wi-Fi.

Quiz Yourself 9-1

1. A ~~database~~field is a combination of one or more related characters or bytes and is the smallest unit of data a user accesses.
2. A ~~record~~database is a collection of data organized in a manner that allows access, retrieval, and use of that data.
3. ~~Data~~Information is processed ~~information~~data.
4. ~~Hierarchy of data~~File maintenance procedures include adding records to, modifying records in, and deleting records from a file.
5. True Statement

Quiz Yourself 9-2

1. A DBMS is ~~hardware~~software that allows you to create, access, and manage ~~an operating system~~a database.
2. A ~~query~~data dictionary contains data about each file in the database and each field in those files.
3. True Statement
4. Strengths of the database approach include ~~increased~~reduced data redundancy, ~~reduced~~improved data integrity, shared data, easier access, and ~~increased~~reduced development time.

Quiz Yourself 9-3

1. ~~Object-oriented~~Relational databases store data in tables.
2. True Statement
3. SQL is a ~~data modeling~~query language that allows users to manage, update, and retrieve data.
4. The database ~~analyst~~administrator requires a more technical inside view of the data than does the ~~database administrator~~data analyst.

Quiz Yourself 10-1

1. A ~~back door~~denial of service attack is an assault whose purpose is to disrupt computer access to an Internet service such as the Web or e-mail.
2. True Statement
3. Computer viruses, worms, Trojan horses, and rootkits are malware that acts with~~out~~ a user's knowledge.
4. ~~Shorter~~Longer passwords provide greater security than ~~longer~~shorter ones.
5. Updating an antivirus program's ~~quarantine~~signature file protects a computer against viruses written since the antivirus program was released.

Quiz Yourself 10-2

1. An end-user license agreement (EULA) ~~permits~~does not permit users to give copies to friends and colleagues, while continuing to use the software.
2. Encryption is a process of converting ~~ciphertext~~plaintext into ~~plaintext~~ciphertext to prevent unauthorized access.
3. Mobile users are ~~not~~ susceptible to hardware theft.
4. True Statement
5. To prevent against data loss caused by a system failure, computer users should ~~restore~~back up files regularly.

Quiz Yourself 10-3

1. Factors that cause ~~CVS~~tendonitis and CTS (carpal tunnel syndrome) include prolonged typing, prolonged mouse usage, or continual shifting between the mouse and the keyboard.
2. ~~Phishing~~Digital forensics is the discovery, collection, and analysis of evidence found on computers and networks.
3. True Statement
4. You can~~not~~ assume that information on the Web is correct.

Quiz Yourself 11-1

1. True Statement
2. ~~Feasibility~~Project management is the process of planning, scheduling, and then controlling the activities during system development.
3. The five phases in most SDLCs are ~~programming~~planning; analysis; design; ~~sampling~~implementation; and ~~recording~~operation, support, and security.
4. The purpose of the ~~design~~operation, support, and security phase is to provide ongoing assistance for an information system and its users after the system is implemented.
5. Upon completion of the preliminary investigation, the systems analyst writes the ~~system proposal~~feasibility report.
6. Users should ~~not~~ be involved throughout system development.

Quiz Yourself 11-2

1. C and COBOL are examples of ~~assembly~~procedural languages.
2. ~~Delphi~~Java is an object-oriented programming language developed by Sun Microsystems.
3. Popular ~~first generation~~scripting languages include JavaScript, Perl, PHP, Rexx, Tcl, and VBScript.

4. Four popular ~~markup languages~~Web page authoring programs are Dreamweaver, Expression Web, Flash, and SharePoint Designer.
5. Two types of low-level languages are machine languages and ~~source~~assembly languages.
6. True Statement

Quiz Yourself 11-3

1. True Statement
2. The program development life cycle consists of these six steps: analyze requirements, design solution, validate design, implement design, test solution, and ~~hardcode~~document solution.
3. Three basic control structures are sequence, selection, and ~~maintenance~~repetition.

Quiz Yourself 12-1

1. The main task of executive managers is to make ~~tactical~~strategic decisions.
2. An information system is a set of hardware, software, data, procedures, and people that work together to produce information.
3. A ~~human resources~~marketing information system serves as a central repository for the tasks of the marketing functional unit.
4. True Statement
5. ~~Decision support~~Expert systems capture and store the knowledge of human experts and then imitate human reasoning and decision making.
6. ~~Enterprise resource planning~~A content management system (CMS) is a combination of databases, software, and procedures that organizes and allows access to various forms of documents and files.

Quiz Yourself 12-2

1. ~~A portal~~An extranet is the portion of a company's network that allows customers or suppliers of a company to access parts of an enterprise's intranet.
2. True Statement
3. A VPN provides mobile users, remote offices, vendors, or customers a secure connection to the company network server, as if they had a private line~~is a server that is placed on a network with the sole purpose of providing storage to users and information systems attached to the network~~.
4. A workflow application is a program that assists in the management and tracking of all the activities in a business process from start to finish~~helps an enterprise collect, archive, index, and retrieve its resources~~.

Quiz Yourself 12-3

1. ~~Network attached storage~~A storage area network is a high-speed network with the sole purpose of providing storage to other servers to which it is attached.
2. ~~Scalability~~Interoperability refers to the capability of an information system to share information with other information systems.
3. A differential backup copies only the files that have changed since the last full ~~or last incremental~~ backup.
4. ~~A full~~An incremental backup is the fastest backup method, requiring only minimal storage.
5. ~~An emergency~~A backup plan specifies how a company uses backup files and equipment to resume information processing.
6. True Statement

Index

Credits

Chapter 2: Opener © John-Francis Bourke/Getty Images; Opening Collage © ST-Images/Alamy; Courtesy of Cisco; 2-1 Courtesy of Microsoft Corporation; 2-2 Step 1 © ngirish/iStockphoto; 2-2 Step 2 © blue_Iq/iStockphoto; 2-2 Step 3 ARRIS C4® CMTS Courtesy of Arris Systems, Inc; 2-2 Step 4 © Stephen Chernin/Getty Images; 2-2 Step 6 Courtesy of Fujitsu Technology Solutions; 2-14 Courtesy of Hewlett-Packard Company; © titi matei/iStockphoto; © Glowimages/Getty Images; Courtesy of Hewlett-Packard Company; 2-16 Step 1, © Colin Young-Wolff/PhotoEdit; 2-16 Step 2, © Mark Evans/iStockphoto; 2-16 Step 3, © Andrew Lewis/iStockphoto; 2-16 Step 4, © Alexander Hafemann/iStockphoto; 2-16 Step 5, Courtesy of Fujitsu Technology Solutions; 2-16 Step 6, © Ed Hidden/iStockphoto; 2-16 Step 7, © Oksana Perkins/iStockphoto; 2-16 Step 8, © Bill Aron/PhotoEdit; 2-18 Step 1 Courtesy of Hewlett-Packard Company; 2-18 Step 2 Courtesy of Hewlett-Packard Company; 2-18 Step 3, Courtesy of Juniper Networks, Inc; 2-18 Step 4 Courtesy of Hewlett-Packard Company; 2-19 Step 2 Courtesy of Fujitsu Technology Solutions; 2-19 Step 3 Courtesy of Microsoft Corporation; 2-19 Step 4 Courtesy of Acer America, Inc; 2-19 Courtesy of Hewlett-Packard Company; 2-19 Step 5 Courtesy of Hewlett-Packard Company; 2-20 Courtesy of Sony Electronics Inc; Courtesy of Hewlett-Packard Company; (center) © Blend Images/Alamy; 2-21 Courtesy of Cisco; Courtesy of Siemens; © Argunova/Shutterstock.com; Courtesy of Logitech; Courtesy of Hewlett-Packard Company; Computer Usage @ Work © Picture Contact/Alamy; Trailblazer 1 © EPA/Landov; Trailblazer 2 AP Photo/Craig Ruttle; Looking Ahead 2-1 Courtesy of W3C; Innovative Computing 2-1 Courtesy of Microsoft Corporation;

Special Feature 2: © Photodisc/Alamy; © iStockphoto; © Digital Vision/Alamy; © Digital Vision/Alamy; © Alex Segre/Alamy

Chapter 3: Opener moodboard/Alamy; Collage © Getty Images; Courtesy of Corel Corporation; Courtesy of Microsoft Corporation; Courtesy of Microsoft Corporation; Courtesy of Microsoft Corporation; Courtesy of Nokia; Pinnacle Systems, Inc., a part of Avid Technology, Inc; Courtesy of Cakewalk Inc; Courtesy of Intuit Inc; 3-1 Courtesy of Microsoft Corporation; Courtesy of Adobe Systems Incorporated; Courtesy of Corel Corporation; 3-2 © Brooke Slezak/Getty Images; Courtesy of Hewlett-Packard Company; Courtesy of Hewlett-Packard Company; 3-11 Courtesy of Microsoft Corporation; 3-12 Courtesy of Computer Systems Odessa Corporation; 3-13 Courtesy of Microsoft Corporation; 3-16 © Artiga Photo/Corbis; 3-17 Courtesy of Quark Inc; 3-18 © Picture Contact/Alamy; 3-19 Courtesy of Cakewalk Inc; 3-20 Courtesy of SumTotal Systems Inc; 3-22 Courtesy of Intuit Inc; © Digital Vision/Getty Images; 3-23 Courtesy of Nolo; 3-24 Courtesy of 2nd Story Software, Inc; 3-26 Courtesy of Corel Corporation; 3-27 Courtesy of Encore, Inc., a Navarre Corporation Company; 3-28 Pinnacle Systems, Inc., a part of Avid Technology, Inc; 3-29 Courtesy of IMSI/Design; 3-30 Courtesy of Microsoft Corporation; 3-31 Courtesy of Encore Software, Inc. a Navarre Corporation Company; 3-32 © Bernhard Classen/Alamy; © Lon C. Dhiel/PhotoEdit; © Fred Prouser/Reuters/Corbis; 3-37 Courtesy of Moodle; Computer Usage @ Work, © iStockphoto; Trailblazer 1 AP Photo/Steven Senne; Trailblazer 2 © Tom Wagner/Corbis; Looking Ahead 3-1 Courtesy of Microsoft Corporation; Innovative Computing 3-1 © Tetra Images/Getty Images; Innovative Computing 3-2 © Wave Royalty Free/Alamy; Web Research © Brian Stablyk/Getty Images.

Special Feature 3: Figure 1 Courtesy of Microsoft Corporation; Courtesy of Verizon Wireless; © Alex Slobodkin/iStockphoto; © Image Source Black/Alamy; © iStockphoto; © David Hancock/Alamy; Courtesy of Skype; © CostinT/iStockphoto; Figure 3 Courtesy of Microsoft Corporation; © Stephen Wilkes/Getty Images; Figure 5 © CAP/Getty Images; Figure 7 © Picturenet/Getty Images; Courtesy of Research In Motion; © Gary Corbett/Alamy; Courtesy of Microsoft Corporation; Figure 9 Courtesy of Jive Software; © Jeff Greenberg/Alamy; Figure 11 © David R. Fraizer/PhotoEdit; © Jochen Tack/Alamy; Courtesy of Parliant Corporation; Figure 13 Courtesy of Cisco Systems, Inc; © Alex Slobodkin/iStockphoto; Courtesy of Zoom Technologies; Figure 15 © Reggie Casagrande/Getty Images; Figure 17 Courtesy of NASA; © PhotoAlto/Alamy; Figure 18 AP Photo/Screenshot, Peter Zschunke; Figure 21 Courtesy of Microsoft Corporation; p206a © John Lund/Drew Kelly/Sam Diephuis/Getty Images; p206b © Photodisc/Alamy; p206c © MIXA/Alamy; p206 © MIXA/Getty Images; p207 © Corbis RF/Alamy; p207 © Tetra Images/Getty Images.

Chapter 4: Opener © Corbis Super RF/Alamy; Collage Courtesy of Advanced Micro Devices; © imagebroker/Alamy; © Lenscap/Alamy; Courtesy of Intel Corporation; Courtesy of Kingston Technology Corporation; Courtesy of Hewlett-Packard Company; Courtesy of Hewlett-Packard Company; © Dino Ablakovic/iStockphoto; Courtesy of Intel Corporation; Courtesy of Creative Technology Ltd; 4-1 Courtesy of Dell, Inc; Courtesy of Apple; PRNewsFoto/Apple; © Mark Ralston/AFP/Getty Images; Courtesy of Palm, Inc; Courtesy of SanDisk Corporation; Courtesy of Microsoft Corporation; Courtesy of FUJIFILM U.S.A; Courtesy of Hewlett-Packard Company; © iStockphoto; Courtesy of Dell, Inc; 4-2 Courtesy of Creative Technology Ltd; Courtesy of Sapphire Technology; Courtesy of Intel Corporation; Courtesy of Kingston Technology Corporation; Courtesy of Hewlett-Packard Company; Courtesy of Hewlett-Packard Company; 4-3 Courtesy of Intel Corporation; 4-5 © Paul Paladin/Shutterstock.com; 4-6 © iStockphoto; 4-9 Courtesy of Logitech; Courtesy of Hewlett-Packard Company; 4-10 © Wayne Eastep/Getty Images; 4-12 Courtesy of Seagate Technology LLC; Courtesy of Kingston Technology Corporation; Courtesy of ViewSonic Corporation; Courtesy of Seagate Technology LLC; Courtesy of Kingston Technology Corporation; 4-13 © Andrew Howe/iStockphoto; © Jaroslaw Wojcik/iStockphoto; 4-14 © Kim Jae-Hwan/Getty Images; Courtesy of Creative Technologies Ltd; 4-16 © Corey Hayes; 4-18 © Andrew Howe/iStockphoto; 4-19 © David Kilpatrick/Alamy; © Sandeep Subba/iStockphoto; Courtesy of USB Implementers Forum; 4-20 Courtesy of Hewlett-Packard Company; 4-21 Courtesy of Hewlett-Packard Company; 4-22 © Alina Solovyova-Vincent/iStockphoto; © Ruslan Kerimov/iStockphoto; © Sascha Burkard/iStockphoto; Courtesy of Hewlett-Packard Company; © Potapova Valeriya/iStockphoto; © iStockphoto; 4-23 Courtesy of Motion Computing, Inc; 4-24 Courtesy of Intel Corporation; Courtesy of Kingston Technology Corporation; 4-25 Courtesy of Hewlett-Packard Company; 4-26 © Kin Images/Getty Images; © Dwayne Newton/PhotoEdit; © Myrleen Ferguson Cate/PhotoEdit; © Darryl Bush/San Francisco Chronicle/Corbis; © Justin Pumfrey/Getty Images; 4-27 © Paul Maguire/Alamy; Courtesy of Merridrew Enterprises; © Lon C. Diehl/PhotoEdit Inc; © Gary Herrington Photography; Courtesy of Belkin International, Inc; © Felicia Martinez/PhotoEdit; Computer Usage @ Work © Gary Dineen/NBAE/Getty Images; Trailblazer 1 © Yoshikazu Tsuno/AFP/Getty Images; Trailblazer 2 © Andy Rain/Bloomberg via Getty Images; Innovative Computing 4-1 © China Photos/Getty Images; Innovative Computing 4-2 AP Photo/iRobot Corp; Looking Ahead 4-1 Felix Schmidberger; Web Research © Mikael Karlsson/Alamy

Chapter 5: Opener © Image Source/Alamy; Collage; Courtesy of Logic3 plc; PRNewsFoto/Metrologic Instruments, Inc; Courtesy of Wacom Technology Corporation; Courtesy of Hewlett-Packard Company; Courtesy of Logitech; PRNewsFoto/SANYO; Courtesy of Hewlett-Packard Company; © image100/Corbis; Courtesy of Palm, Inc; YONHAPNEWS AGENCY/Newscom; Courtesy of FUJIFILM USA 5-1 © Medioimages/Getty Images; © Carmen Martínez Banús/iStockphoto; © Getty Images; © Beaconstox/Alamy; © Tetra Images/Alamy; © Keith Morris/Alamy; © Christopher Dodge/Shutterstock.com; © Denkou Images/Alamy; © BlueSoul/Shutterstock.com; © Daniel Acker/Bloomberg via Getty Images; © iStockphoto; © iStockphoto; © KAKIMAGE/Alamy; © Bonnie Kamin/PhotoEdit; © Stefan Klein/iStockphoto; © Anatoly Vartanov/Alamy; © Phil Degginger/Alamy; © Sandeep Subba/iStockphoto; © Natalie Jezzard/Alamy; © iStockphoto;

Technology Corporation; Courtesy of UMAX; Courtesy of Creative Technology Ltd; Courtesy of Logitech; Courtesy of SanDisk Corporation; Courtesy of Belkin International Inc; Courtesy of Advanced Micro Devices, Inc; Courtesy of Logitech; © Norman Chan/iStockphoto; p 306 Courtesy of Dell, Inc; Courtesy of Hewlett-Packard Company; Courtesy of Hewlett-Packard Company; Figure 5 PRNewsFoto/Mindjet LLC; Figure 6 Courtesy of Fujitsu Technology Solutions; Figure 7 © MadTatyana/Shutterstock.com; Figure 8 Courtesy of Motion Computing; p 309 Courtesy of Nokia; Figure 9 Courtesy of Verizon Wireless; PRNewsFoto/Verizon Wireless; PRNewsFoto/Verizon Wireless; p 310 Courtesy of Microsoft Corporation; Figure10 Courtesy of Apple; p 311Courtesy of FUJIFILM USA; Figure 11 Courtesy of SanDisk Corporation; © Muhammad Khairul Syahir Bin Abd Haki/iStockphoto; © SasPartout/Shutterstock.com

Chapter 8: Opener © Nick Koudis/Getty Images; Collage: Courtesy of Belkin International; © David Anderson/Shutterstock.com; © Natalia Siverina/Shutterstock.com; © Hugh Threlfall/Alamy; PRNewsFoto/RealNetworks; Courtesy of Cisco; Courtesy of NETGEAR; Courtesy of Garmin Ltd; © Nicola Stratford/iStockphoto; Courtesy of Nokia; 8-1 Courtesy of IBM Corporation; © zentilia/iStockphoto; © Simon Smith/iStockphoto; Courtesy of Nokia; Courtesy of Microsoft Corporation; Courtesy of Toyota U.S.A; PRNewsFoto/NAVIGON; © 2009 Jupiter Images Corporation; © 2009 Jupiter Images Corporation; © Mark Evans/iStockphoto; ©Simon Vine/Alamy; © Keith Binns/iStockphoto; © Luca di Filippo/iStockphoto; AP Photo/Koji Sasahara; © Long Ha/iStockphoto; © Alex Slobodkin/iStockphoto; 8-3 © David J. Green - Lifestyle/Alamy; © Tom Grill/Corbis; © Rob Wilkinson/Alamy; 8-4 Courtesy of NETGEAR; Courtesy of Intel Corporation; Courtesy of SMC Networks; © Justin Sullivan/Getty Images; © James Leynse/Corbis; 8-5 Courtesy of Garmin Ltd; © StockShot/Alamy; © Jasper James/Getty Images; Courtesy of Lok8u; © Fredrik Broman/Getty Images; Courtesy of Nokia; 8-6 Courtesy of Citrix Systems, Inc; 8-7 Courtesy of Hewlett-Packard Company; © Jim Goldstein/Alamy; Courtesy of Nokia; ©Natalia Siverina/Shutterstock.com; © terekhov igor/Shutterstock.com; Courtesy of Hewlett-Packard Company; 8-8 Courtesy of Toyota U.S.A; 8-9 Courtesy of Hewlett-Packard Company; 8-10 Courtesy of Hewlett-Packard Company; Courtesy of Fujitsu Technology Solutions; 8-11 Courtesy of Hewlett-Packard Company; Courtesy of Western Digital; Courtesy of Seagate Technology LLC; 8-12 Courtesy of Hewlett-Packard Company; Courtesy of Cisco; © jossnat/Shutterstock.com; 8-13 © Jakub Semeniuk/iStockphoto; 8-14 Courtesy of Hewlett-Packard Company; 8-15 Courtesy of Hewlett-Packard Company; 8-17 © Erik S. Lesser/Landov; ©tiridifilm/iStockphotp; © image100/Alamy; Courtesy of Hewlett-Packard Company; 8-18 © cheyennezj/Shutterstock.com; Courtesy of Cisco; 8-19 Courtesy of Cisco; Courtesy of SMC Networks; 8-20 Courtesy of Cisco; Courtesy of Hewlett-Packard Company; Courtesy of Acer America Inc; Courtesy of Motorola, Inc; Courtesy of Dell, Inc; 8-21 PRNewsFoto/Verizon Wireless; Courtesy of Hewlett-Packard Company; © Natalia Siverina/Shutterstock.com; © Arkadiusz Stachowski/iStockphoto; 8-22 Courtesy of Hewlett-Packard Company; Courtesy of Motorola; Courtesy of Fujitsu Technology Solutions; Courtesy of IBM Corporation; 8-23 Courtesy of Hewlett-Packard Company; 8-24 Courtesy of Hewlett-Packard Company; © Vladislav Ageshin/iStockphoto; Computer Usage @ Work © eliandric/iStockphoto; Trailblazer 1 © Kim Kulish/Corbis; Trailblazer 2 © Wolfgang Von Brauchitsch/Bloomberg News via Getty Images; Innovative Computing 8-1 AP Photo/The Charlotte Observer, Jeff Willhelm; Looking Ahead 8-1 "A wireless body area network of intelligent motion sensors for computer assisted physical rehabilitation" Emil Jovanov, Aleksandar Milenkovic, Chris Otto, and Piet C de Groen, J Neurocngineering Rehabil. 2005. 2: 6. Published online 2005 March 1. doi: 10.1186/1743-0003-2-6.PMCID: PMC552302 reproduced under Creative Commons License 2.0; Web Research © Konstantin Inozemtsev/iStockphoto.

Chapter 9: Opener © Trevor Smith/Alamy; 9-1 Step 1 Courtesy of FujiFilm USA; © Alex Mares-Manton/Getty Images; Step 2 Courtesy of Seagate Technology LLC; Step 3 Courtesy of Hewlett-Packard Company; Steps 5 & 6 © Alex Mares-Manton/Getty Images; Courtesy of Zebra Technologies International, LLC; desktop PC Courtesy of Hewlett-Packard Company; 9-1 background © Don Smetzer/Alamy; 9-7 © zhang bo/iStockphoto; 9-9 © Davis Barber/PhotoEdit; © Davis Barber/PhotoEdit; 9-21 © Bernhard Classen/Alamy; Trailblazer 1 Courtesy of the National Academy of Engineering; Trailblazer 2 © Justin Sullivan/Getty Images; Innovative Computing 9-1 Courtesy of Challenge Online Games, Inc; Looking Ahead 9-1 © SMC Images/Getty Images; Computer Usage @ Work Hans Neleman/Getty Images; Web Research Courtesy of Google.

Chapter 10: Opener © Mark Scott/Getty Images; Collage: © Peter Macdiarmid/Getty Images; © TM_Design/Alamy; Courtesy of Microsoft Corporation; Courtesy of Symantec Corp; Newscom; © Tomasz Piotrowski/Alamy; Courtesy of Tripp Lite; 10-1 Courtesy of Hewlett-Packard Company; © imagebroker/Alamy; © Mustafa Deliormanli/iStockphoto; © PhotoAlto/Alamy; © blickwinkel/Alamy; © avatra images/Alamy; © Ingvald Kaldhussæter/iStockphoto; © Jupiterimages/BrandX/Alamy; 10-2 Step 3a © Christoph Weihs/iStockphoto; Step 3b © Ruslan Dashinsky/Shutterstock.com; 10-3 Courtesy of McAfee, Inc; 10-5 Courtesy of SonicWALL, Inc; Courtesy of Check Point Software Technologies Ltd; Courtesy of Fujitsu Technology Solutions; Courtesy of Hewlett-Packard Company; 10-8 © Paulo Whitaker/Reuters/Landov; 10-9 Courtesy of Kensington Computer Products Group; 10-13 © David Young-Wolff/PhotoEdit; 10-14 Courtesy of APC by Schneider Electric; 10-15 © Marcela Barsse/iStockphoto; © Krystian Nawrocki/iStockphoto; 10-16 Courtesy of Hewlett-Packard Company; © Daniel Laflor/iStockphoto; 10-17 © C Squared Studios/Getty Images; 10-19 ©Paramount/Courtesy Everett Collection; 10-22 Courtesy of Hewlett-Packard Company; 10-26 Courtesy of ContentWatch Inc; Innovative Computing 10-1 © Andrew Olney/Getty Images; Looking Ahead 10-1 © Ann Cutting/Getty Images; Computer Usage @ Work © Ben Edwards/Getty Images; Trailblazer 1 Courtesy of Dr. Eugene Spafford/Purdue University; Trailblazer 2 REUTERS/Simon Kwong; Web Research © Trevor Fisher/iStockphoto.

Chapter 11: Opener © Jupiterimages; Collage: © Branislav Senic/Alamy; Courtesy of Computer Systems Odessa Corporation; Courtesy of Nokia;© Eimantas Buzas/Shutterstock.com; Courtesy of Adobe Systems Incorporated; Courtesy of Microsoft Corporation; © Ermin Gutenberger/iStockphoto; Courtesy of SmartDraw 11-1 © Purestock/Getty Images; 11-3 a&b Courtesy of SERENA Software, Inc.|www.serena.com; 11-4 © Digital Vision/Getty Images; 11-5 Courtesy of Dell, Inc; 11-10 Courtesy of Visible Systems Corporation; 11-11 © Ciaran Griffin/Getty Images; 11-12 © JUPITERIMAGES/BananaStock; 11-23b PhotosIndia.com/Getty Images; 11-27 Courtesy of SumTotal Systems, Inc; Trailblazer 1 Courtesy of Ed Yourdon; Trailblazer 2 Charlotte Fiorito/Bloomberg via Getty Images; Looking Ahead 11-1 Michael Mullen Design, LSST Corporation; Computer Usage @ Work AP Photo/Abdeljalil Bounhar; WebResearch AP Photo/David Kohl; Innovative Computing 11-1 © Rafal Zdeb/iStockphoto;

Chapter 12: Opener © Flying Colours Ltd/Getty Images; Collage: © Joris van Caspel/iStockphoto; Courtesy of Hewlett-Packard Company; Courtesy of Computer Systems Odessa Corporation; Courtesy of Information Builders; PRIME NEWSWIRE; © imagebroker/Alamy; Courtesy of Promise Technology, Inc; 12-1 © Dean Sanderson/iStockphoto; © Dennis Hallinan/Alamy; © Colin Gray/Getty Images; © Jack Hollingsworth/Getty Images; © imagewerks/Getty Images; © blue jean images/Getty Images; © Dan Moore/iStockphoto; © Jon Feingersh/Getty Images; © Norman Chan/iStockphoto; © iStockphoto; © MAURICIO LIMA/AFP/Getty Images; © Lester Lefkowitz/Getty Images; © Bambu Productions/Getty Images; 12-2 © blue jean images/Getty Images; © Dean Sanderson/iStockphoto; © Dennis Hallinan/Alamy;

© MAURICIO LIMA/AFP/Getty Images; © Jon Feingersh/Getty Images; © Bambu Productions/Getty Images; © iStockphoto; © Colin Gray/Getty Images; 12-4 Courtesy of Hewlett-Packard Company; © AAGAMIA/Getty Images; © Franziska Richter/iStockphoto; © David Kilpatrick/Alamy; © Bonnie Kamin/PhotoEdit; © David Young-Wolff/PhotoEdit; © shuedan/Shutterstock.com; 12-7 Courtesy of Optimum Solutions, Inc; 12-8 AP Photo/Ted S. Warren; 12-9 LiveCRM Courtesy of Genesis Interactive (www.livecrm.co.nz); 12-12 (top) © Akkul/iStockphoto; (bottom) Tetra Images/Getty Images; 12-14 © Laurence Dutton/Getty Images; Courtesy of Computer Systems Odessa Corporation; © Ryan McVay/Getty Images; © Lisa F. Young/iStockphoto; © White Packert/Getty Images; © LWA/Getty Images; © VEER/Getty Images; © Paul Mckeown/iStockphoto;© Andy Sacks/Getty Images; © Inti St Clair/Getty Images; © Diane Diederich/iStockphoto; © blue jean images/Getty Images; © choicegraphx/iStockphoto; 12-15 Courtesy of Hewlett-Packard Company; Slobo Mitic/iStockphoto; Courtesy of Nokia; © LWA/Getty Images; © LWA/Getty Images; © Diane Diederich/iStockphoto; Courtesy of SanDisk Corporation Courtesy of Sony Electronics, Inc; Courtesy of Seagate Technology LLC; © Felix Clouzot/Getty Images; © Chad McDermott/iStockphoto; © Stefan Klein/iStockphoto; 12-17 PRNewsFoto/Verizon Wireless; Courtesy of Hewlett-Packard Company; © Vlad Kochelaevskiy/iStockphoto; 12-18 Step 1 © Studio Paggy/Getty Images; Steps 2 & 3 Courtesy of Hewlett-Packard Company; 12-19 © Ariel Skelley/Getty Images; © Tom Grill/Corbis; © Charles C. Place/Getty Images; © Hisham F Ibrahim/Getty Images; © image100/Corbis; 12-21 Courtesy of Avid Technology Inc; 12-22a Courtesy of Promise Technology, Inc; Courtesy of Hewlett-Packard Company; © Vlad Kochelaevskiy/iStockphoto; 12-22b Courtesy of Hewlett-Packard Company; Courtesy of Avid Technology Inc; © Vlad Kochelaevskiy/iStockphoto; 12-23 Courtesy of Alliance Storage Technologies; Courtesy of Fujitsu Technology Solutions; Courtesy of Hewlett-Packard Company; Courtesy of EMC Corporation; 12-24 Courtesy of Hewlett-Packard Company; 12-25 Courtesy of Telect, Inc; Innovative Computing 14-1 © Eric Foltz/iStockphoto; Looking Ahead 12-1 © Nadezda Firsova/iStockphoto; Computer Usage @ Work © Justin Kase zsixz/Alamy; Trailblazer 1 Reuters/Landov; Trailblazer 2 Courtesy of Anita Borg Institute for Women and Technology-www.anitaborg.org; Web Research © Vasiliy Yakobchuk/iStockphoto.

Special Feature 12: page 501 © Synthetic Alan King/Alamy; © Kevork Djansezian/Getty Images; Courtesy of Microsoft Corporation; AP Photo/Mark Lennihan; Tomohiro Ohsumi/Bloomberg via Getty Images; © Lightly Saled/Alamy; PRNewsFoto/JVC Company of America; PRNewsFoto/Verizon Wireless; Courtesy of Cakewalk; Courtesy of Nero AG; Courtesy of Iomega; Courtesy of Barco; © Roca/Shutterstock.com; © N_design/iStockphoto; Courtesy of Sling Media, Inc; AP Photo/Shizuo Kambayashi; AP Photo/Akira Suemori; Courtesy of Apple; PRNewsFoto/TiVo Inc; © Markos Dolopikos/Alamy; PRNewsFoto/Logitech; PRNewsFoto/Sony Electronics, Inc; AP Photo/Paul Sakuma; Courtesy of Chumby Industries; Exceptional Innovation, maker of Life|ware™; PRNewsFoto/Memorex; AP Photo/Joerg Sarbach; Figure 1 PRNewsFoto/Cambridge SoundWorks; Figure 3 © Chris Polk/FilmMagic/Getty Images; Courtesy of Activision Publishing, Inc; Figure 4 © Judith Collins/Alamy; Figure 5 Courtesy of Apple; Figure 6 PRNewsFoto/Myvu Corporation; Figure 7 Courtesy of Sling Media, Inc; Figure 8 (top) Yoshikazu Tsuno/AFP/Getty Images; Figure 8 (bottom); Courtesy of Physical Optics Corporation; Figure 9 PRNewsFoto/TiVo Inc; Figure 10 (left) Courtesy of LaCie; Figure 10 (right) Courtesy of Nero AG; Figure 11 Courtesy of Facebook; © Colin Young-Wolff/PhotoEdit; PRNewsFoto/JVC Company of America; Figure 12 Courtesy of Cakewalk; Figure 13 PRNewsFoto/SANYO Fisher Company Figure 14 (left) © Lightly Salted/Alamy; Figure 14 (middle) Courtesy of Microsoft Corporation; Figure 14 (right); John MacDougall/AFP/Getty Images Figure 15 (top) © Juice Images/Alamy; Figure 15 (bottom) Daniel Acker/Bloomberg via Getty Images; Figure 16 AP Photo/Eckehard Schulz; Figure 17 (left) © jamalludin/Shutterstock.com; Figure 17 (middle) © Kevork Djansezian/Getty Images; Figure 17 (right) © Hugh Threfall/Alamy; Figure 18 AP Photo/The Lawrence Journal-World, Scott McClurg; Figure 19 PRNewsFoto/TiVo Inc; Figure 20 (top & bottom right) Exceptional Innovation, maker of Life|ware™; Figure 20 (bottom left) Courtesy of NuVo Technologies Inc; Figure 21 Copyright © Lucid Design Group www.luciddesigngroup.com; Figure 22 Courtesy of ViewSonic Corporation Figure 23 Courtesy of Chumby Industries.

SAM 2.0: ASSESSMENT, TRAINING & PROJECT

STUDENT GETTING STARTED GUIDE

SAM 2010 v2.0: Assessment, Training & Projects

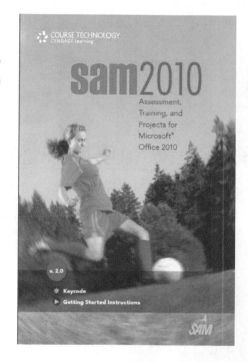

Student Getting Started Guide

Updated June 2011

COURSE TECHNOLOGY
CENGAGE Learning

*Initial Set Up

1. Ensure that you are connected to the Internet.
2. Launch your web browser (Internet Explorer, Firefox, Safari).
3. Enter http://sam2010.course.com to visit the SAM 2010 login page.

*Login Page

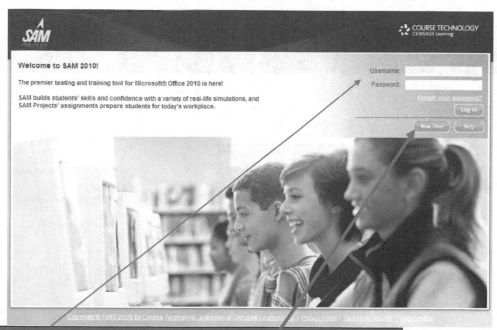

Welcome to SAM 2010!

The premier testing and training tool for Microsoft® Office 2010 is here!

SAM builds students' skills and confidence with a variety of real-life simulations, and SAM Projects' assignments prepare students for today's workplace.

Username:

Password:

Forgot your password?

Log In

New User   Help

Copyright © 1997-2009 by Course Technology, a division of Cengage Learning, Inc. | Privacy Policy | Technical Support | SAM Central

If you have a username/password: Enter your username and password in the appropriate fields, and click the **Login** button.

No username/password: Click the **New User** button; you will follow the on-screen prompts to create your SAM 2010 account.

COURSE TECHNOLOGY
CENGAGE Learning

*Institution Key

SAM

COURSE TECHNOLOGY
CENGAGE Learning

New User

Login Help

How to login to SAM 2010

Technical Support

24/7 Chat Support here

Call (800) 648-7450

Monday - Thursday
8:30am to 9:00pm EST

Friday
8:30am to 6:00pm EST

Submit online request

Your instructor will provide your **Institution Key**. It will contain 8 digits in this format *T2xxxxxx*.

Please enter your 8-digit Institution Key:

Institution Key: T2XXXXXX

Submit   Cancel

Once you have entered the institution key and click Submit, SAM will ask you to verify that you have selected the correct institution key for your institution. Select **"OK"** if this is correct.

COURSE TECHNOLOGY
CENGAGE Learning

*Key Code Entry

Please enter your 18-digit key code:

Key Code:

[ ] [ ] [ ] [ ] [ ] [ ]

Save   Cancel

If your institution is using the **key code** version of SAM 2010, you will enter your key code here. *This will be found inside the flap of the SAM 2010 package (card) you purchased with your textbooks. If you do NOT see this message, please proceed to the next screen.*

Click **Save** to go to the next screen.

NOTE: This 18-digit code is case-sensitive.

COURSE TECHNOLOGY
CENGAGE Learning

*User Profile

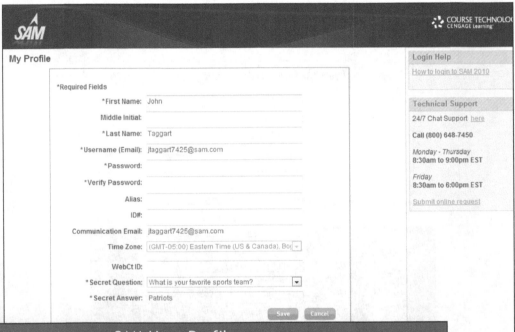

You need to create your SAM User Profile.

Enter your information in all of the required (*) fields, including a secret question and answer that will be used for security purposes should you ever forget your password. *Usernames MUST be an email address*.

Click **Save** when you're done.

COURSE TECHNOLOGY
CENGAGE Learning

*Profile Confirmation

This screen confirms the information entered in the User Profile screen. If all information is accurate, click **Confirm**.

If it's not correct, click **Revise** and go back to the prior screen to edit.

NOTE: If you have tried to enter a username which already exists within Cengage Learning, you will be prompted to confirm your password. (Next screen)

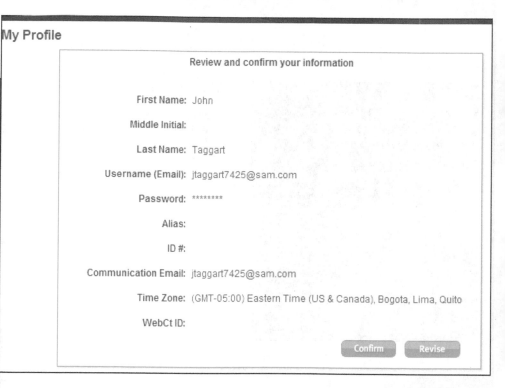

My Profile

Review and confirm your information

First Name: John

Middle Initial:

Last Name: Taggart

Username (Email): jtaggart7425@sam.com

Password: ********

Alias:

ID #:

Communication Email: jtaggart7425@sam.com

Time Zone: (GMT-05:00) Eastern Time (US & Canada), Bogota, Lima, Quito

WebCt ID:

Confirm   Revise

*Username already exists

If you have tried to enter a username which already exists within Cengage Learning, you will be prompted to confirm your password.

If you are unable to retrieve it by using the "Forgot your password?" link, you will need to create a new username to used within SAM 2010.

This Username exists in Cengage Brain

This Username exists in Cengage Brain.

Please enter the Cengage Brain password to log in.
If you have forgotten the password, please click "Forgot your password?" to retrieve it.
If the Cengage Brain account is not yours, please create a new SAM 2010 account with a different Username.

Forgot your password?

Submit   Cancel

COURSE TECHNOLOGY
CENGAGE Learning

*Terms & Conditions

The SAM TERMS and CONDITIONS will display. Read them fully, and then click the **I Agree** button to accept the terms and conditions and continue.

If you click *I Disagree*, SAM automatically exits.

Terms & Conditions

This is a legal document between Course Technology Cengage Learning ("Course Technology") and you. Course Technology is willing to license the Software to you only upon the condition that you accept all of the terms contained in this license agreement. If you agree to all of the terms contained in this license agreement, please so indicate by selecting the "I AGREE" option below. If you do not agree to the terms of this license agreement, please select the "I DISAGREE" option below. If you elect to decline and have purchased your User Manual for the Software (User Manual), you may return it to Course Technology to the address noted below, along with all packaging, proof of purchase and a letter from the institution on whose system the Software is installed certifying that no user profile has been created for you. If Course Technology receives these materials within 30 days of your purchase of the User Manual, Course Technology will issue a refund to you for any fee paid by you for the returned User Manual.

License Agreement

License Grant. Course Technology Cengage Learning ("Course Technology") grants to you, subject to termination as provided in this License Agreement, a nonexclusive, nontransferable license ("License") to use the Skills Assessment Management computer software as accessed through a local area network or single central processing unit ("Workstation"), any accompanying printed information relating to the Software, including the User Manual (collectively, the "Software"). The Software is subject to protection under the copyright, trade secret laws, where applicable, and other intellectual property laws of the United States and other jurisdictions. With this License, you acquire only the right to use the object code version of the Software while the License is in effect and do not acquire any rights of ownership in the Software. You shall not be considered to be an "owner of a copy" and shall not have rights granted under 17 USC Sec. 117 to make adaptations of the Software. You may use the Software on a single microcomputer by accessing the Software through the Workstation.

License Prohibitions. You may not: rent, sell, lease, lend, sublicense, give or permit access to the Software to any third party; remove or obscure Course Technology's proprietary rights notices; alter, decompile or disassemble, nor attempt to alter, decompile or disassemble, nor permit the alteration, decompilation or disassembly of the Software; use the Software on any service bureau, time sharing or any interactive or similar system; develop software derivative of or interfacing with the Software; use the Software to provide training on the Software to third parties; use or copy Software other than as authorized by this Agreement. You may not assign this License Agreement without

I Agree   **I Disagree**

COURSE TECHNOLOGY
CENGAGE Learning

*Home Screen

You should now see the SAM Home screen, where you will begin each SAM session. If the necessary **Flash Player** (v10) is not yet installed on your computer, click the links under Software to install it.

(Check with your instructor first; this may already be done for you.)

*Join a Section

In order to see your SAM Assignments, you need to be enrolled in a Section (class).

From the Home screen, click the **Join a Class** link. You can also click the **Sections** button (left navigation bar), then the **Join a Section** button.

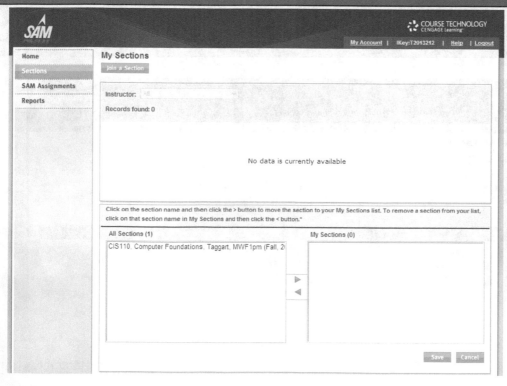

To Join a Section, click the name of the section in the "All Sections" list on the left. Click the right arrow button to move it into "My Sections" and click **Save**.

*SAM Assignments

To begin your SAM Assignments, click My Assignments (from the Home tab) or SAM Assignments (left navigation). You can sort based on Assignment name, type of assignment (Exam, Training, or Project), due date, and more. Simply click on the column heading to re-sort the table.

Click on the name of the assignment (it should be a link) to get started.

*SAM Projects Workflow

| SAM Assignments | Download (or Save) Instructions and Start Files | Complete Project | Submit for grading | Review grades |

*SAM Projects

My SAM Assignments

Print Screen

Chapter 1 (Word) homework

Instructions

Follow the on-screen instructions below to both download your start files and submit your completed files for this class.

⬇ Download File

Start Files

Click on each link to save File(s) to your computer. Note Start Files have been automatically personalized with your first and last name.

⬇ SC_Word2010_C1_L1a_JakeRivello_1.docx
⬇ support_SC_W10_C1_L1a.jpg

Grade Submission

Submit your **Attempt Number 1** for grading using 'Browse...' button. Click 'Browse...' to navigate to the file's location on your computer. The filename(s) should match the filename in italics below

File	File Name	File Location	
1	*SC_Word2010_C1_L1a_JakeRivello_2.docx*		Browse...

Submit   Cancel

After you click the link to the name of the SAM Projects assignment, you will want to download or save the **Instructions** & personalized **Start Files** to your desktop or other location (USB drive, MyDocuments, etc.)

We will get to the submission information later.

* Sample Download #1:

SHELLY CASHMAN WORD 2010
CHAPTER 1: IN THE LAB 1

CREATING A FLYER WITH A PICTURE

SKILLS

- Save a document with a new filename
- Insert text
- Correct a misspelled word
- Center a paragraph
- Change the theme colors
- Change the font size
- Change the font
- Apply a text effect
- Change the color of text
- Bold text
- Create a bulleted list
- Underline text
- Change the zoom level in a document
- Insert a picture
- Apply a style to a picture
- Apply a picture effect
- Resize a graphic
- Add a page border

PROJECT OVERVIEW

As a part-time employee in the Student Services Center at school, you have been asked to prepare a flyer that advertises classes about study habits. First, you prepare the unformatted flyer shown in Figure 1, and then you format it so that it looks like Figure 2.

STUDENT START FILE

SC_Word2010_C1_L1a_FirstLastName_1.docx (*Note*: Download your personalized start file from www.cengage.com/sam2010)

Instructions

1. Open the file **SC_Word2010_C1_L1a_***FirstLastName***_1.docx** and save the file as **SC_Word2010_C1_L1s_***FirstLastName***_1.docx** before you move to the next step. Verify that your name appears in the footer at the bottom of the document. If it does not, please download a new copy of the start file from the SAM Web site. (Note: Do not edit the footer at the bottom of the document.)

2. Type the flyer text, unformatted, as shown in Figure 1. If Word flags any misspelled words as you type, check the spelling of these words and correct them. (*Note*: Figure 1 contains paragraph marks (¶) to show you where to press ENTER while typing the text. If you display formatting marks in the document, you can see these paragraph marks. Do not type these paragraph marks directly into the document.)

FIGURE 1

Studying All Night?¶

LET US HELP YOU! Our expert instructors teach effective study habits, time management skills, and energy-building techniques.¶

Classes are $15.00 per session¶

Sessions last four weeks¶

Classes meet in the Student Services Center twice a week¶

Call 555-2838 or stop by to sign up today!¶

3. Center the headline "Studying All Night?", and center the signature line "Call 555-2838 or stop by to sign up today!"

4. Change the theme colors to **Concourse**. (*Note*: the theme font and theme style should remain Office.)

5. Change the font size of the headline to 48 point and the font to **Comic Sans MS**. Apply the text effect called **Gradient Fill – Dark Red, Accent 6, Inner Shadow**.

6. Change the font size of body copy between the headline and the signature line to 20 point.

7. Change the font of the body copy and the signature line to **Arial**.

8. Change the font size of the signature line to 22 point. Change the font color of the signature line to **Dark Red, Accent 6**. Bold the text in the signature line.

9. Bullet the three lines (paragraphs) of text above the signature line.

10. Bold the text "LET US HELP YOU!", and change its color to **Dark Red, Accent 6**.

11. Underline the text "Student Services Center".

12. Change the zoom to 50 percent so that the entire page is visible in the document window.

13. Insert a picture of your choice below the headline. NOTE: A sleeping student image named "support_SC_W10_C1_L1a.jpg" is available from the SAM Web site, or you can choose to use a different image.

14. Apply the **Soft Edge Oval** picture style to the inserted picture. Apply the glow effect called **Blue, 5 pt glow, Accent color 4** to the picture.

* Sample Download #2:

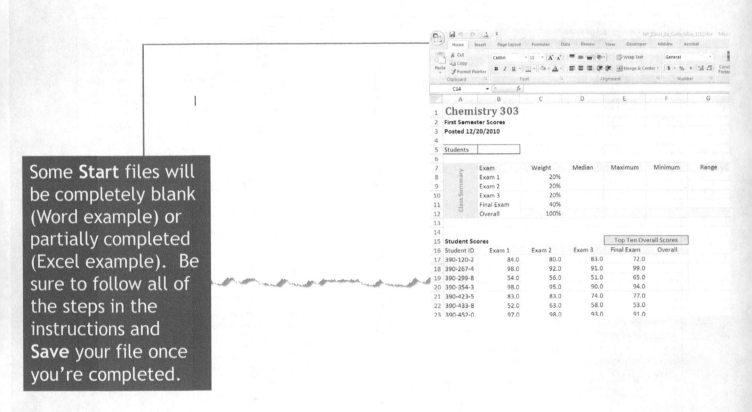

Some **Start** files will be completely blank (Word example) or partially completed (Excel example). Be sure to follow all of the steps in the instructions and **Save** your file once you're completed.

*Submit for grading

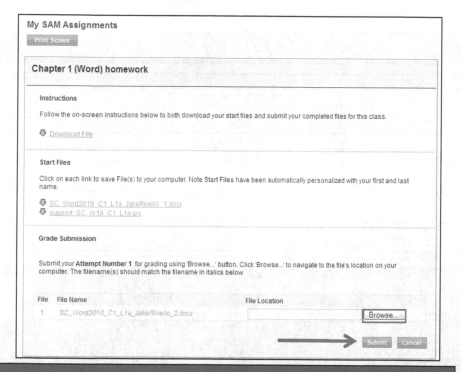

My SAM Assignments

Print Screen

Chapter 1 (Word) homework

Instructions

Follow the on-screen instructions below to both download your start files and submit your completed files for this class.

⬇ Download File

Start Files

Click on each link to save File(s) to your computer. Note Start Files have been automatically personalized with your first and last name.

⬇ SC_Word2010_C1_L1a_JakeRivello_1.docx
⬇ support_SC_W10_C1_L1a.jpg

Grade Submission

Submit your **Attempt Number 1** for grading using 'Browse...' button. Click 'Browse...' to navigate to the file's location on your computer. The filename(s) should match the filename in italics below

File	File Name	File Location	
1	*SC_Word2010_C1_L1a_JakeRivello_2.docx*		Browse...

Submit Cancel

When you've completed your project and saved it one final time, you will revisit the SAM site and Browse for your file, then Submit it for auto-grading.

COURSE TECHNOLOGY
CENGAGE Learning

*Graded file—Summary

This is an example of what the Downloaded File will include, after it's graded.
*Go to Reports, then change the dropdown to Download Submitted Projects and click on the name of the Project to download. <u>Exception:</u> Access results available as Study Guide only.

COURSE TECHNOLOGY
CENGAGE Learning

Graded file—embedded comments
*not applicable for Access

This is an example of the project w/the embedded comments about what was performed incorrectly, with the specific step number to refer back to.

	A	B	C	D	E	F
20	390-354-3	98.0	95.0	90.0	94.0	94.2
21	390-423-5	83.0	83.0	74.0	77.0	78.8
22	390-433-8	52.0	63.0	58.0	53.0	55.8
23	390-452-0	97.0	98.0	93.0	91.0	94.0
24	390-485-7	87.0	77.0	83.0	87.0	84.2

COURSE TECHNOLOGY
CENGAGE Learning

*SAM Exams

To begin a SAM exam, click the link from your SAM Assignments page.

Review your assignment details:
(*which may include*)
•Instructions
•Time limit
•# of chances at each question
•# of retakes of entire exam

When you're ready to begin your Exam, scroll down and click **OK**.

When you do, the exam window will launch.

Assignment Details

Assignment Name: Foundations Pretest
Instructions: Good luck.

Read each task completely before attempting it. Some tasks contain multiple steps.

Exam Details:

Time Limit: **10 min/exam**

Incorrect actions allowed per performance task: 3

SAM exam can be retaken: Yes

SAM exam retakes allowed: 20

SAM exam retakes remaining: 20

You are about to start the exam. Once you start the exam, you **cannot exit** without scoring your exam performance. Do you want to proceed?

COURSE TECHNOLOGY
CENGAGE Learning

*Exam interface

Opened Task List

1. Show Task List, *shown collapsed*, (you can use this list to jump from task to task, in any order)
2. Task ID number
3. Question label with back and forward arrows to jump between tasks
4. Time remaining (if set by instructor)
5. Attempts remaining per question
6. Describes the task that the student must perform.
7. The "simulation" of the application where you will complete the task.

*Student Reports

Students visit **Reports** to see results on all types of assignments.

If you have also purchased SAM Training, you can launch Training activities, right from this Study Guide.

SAM — COURSE TECHNOLOGY CENGAGE Learning

Exam Study Guide

Thursday, July 29, 2010

Student: Rivello, Jake
Assignment: Foundations Pretest

Assignment Date: 7/29/2010
Score(%): 80

Launch All Training

Performance Tasks

Subject	Task ID	Task	Result	Remediation	Training
MS Windows 7	2000	Display the contents of the "PRODUCTS" folder. (DO NOT use ALT-D.)	Correct	<Not Selected>	Display a folder in Expl
MS Windows 7	1883	Use Start Search to open a Word document named "PRINTERS".	Incorrect	<Not Selected>	Open an Office docume Start Search
MS Word 2010	2130	Display the Ruler in the current document.	Correct	Microsoft Office 2010: Introductory [PageNo:] TBD. Chapter 2	Display the ruler
MS Word 2010	2278	Insert a SmartArt graphic of an Inverted Pyramid.	Correct	<Not Selected>	Insert a SmartArt grap
MS Excel 2010	2287	Specify that the cells in the selected range whose cell value is greater than (but NOT equal to) 2000 will be automatically formatted in italics.	Correct	Microsoft Office 2010: Introductory [PageNo:] TBD. Chapter 2	Apply conditional form a range of cells
MS Excel 2010	2035	With a single action, insert a sum formula into each of the selected cells. Press ENTER when done. (Do NOT use ALT-=.)	Correct	Microsoft Office 2010: Introductory [PageNo:] TBD. Chapter 1	Create a formula using the S\ function
MS Access 2010	2337	Create a new blank database named "PRINTERS.ACCDB". (Create the database in the current directory.)	Correct	Microsoft Office 2010: Introductory [PageNo:] TBD. Chapter 1	Create a new blank database
MS ...2010	2020	With a single action, go directly to	Correct	Microsoft Office 2010...	Navigate record a form

COURSE TECHNOLOGY
CENGAGE Learning

*SAM Training

To begin a SAM Training assignment, click the link from your SAM Assignments page.

Review your assignment details: (which may include)
•Instructions
•Due Date

When you're ready to begin your Training, click OK.

When you do, the Training window will launch.

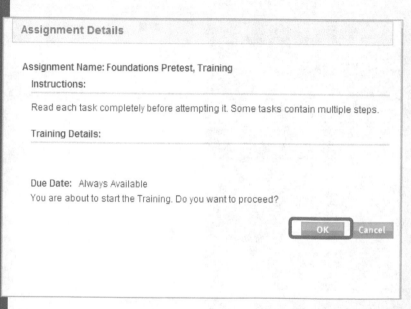

Assignment Details

Assignment Name: Foundations Pretest, Training
Instructions:

Read each task completely before attempting it. Some tasks contain multiple steps.

Training Details:

Due Date: Always Available
You are about to start the Training. Do you want to proceed?

OK   Cancel

*Training interface

The first screen will always provide a written description of the task.

Along the bottom:

Observe- allows students to watch and listen how to perform a task

Practice- allows students to follow along with guided prompts to learn a skill

Apply- students perform actions, unprompted to prove that they know the skill

You MUST complete the Apply and click Task Complete to receive credit for each task.

Just like in exams, you can show/hide the **task list**, move between **questions** w/arrows. Also use **controls** to replay, rewind, forward or pause the movies in progress.

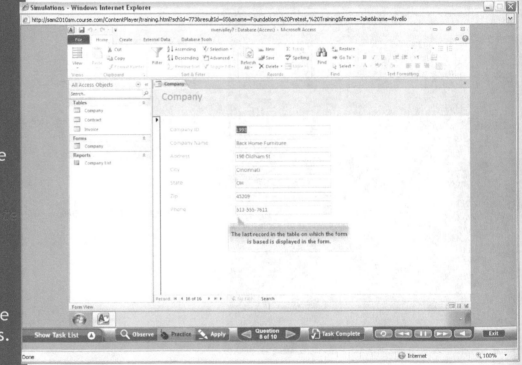

COURSE TECHNOLOGY
CENGAGE Learning